COMMUNITY PSYCHOLOGY

COMMUNITY PSYCHOLOGY
Challenges, Controversies and Emerging Consensus

Jim Orford
School of Psychology
The University of Birmingham, UK

WILEY
John Wiley & Sons, Ltd

Other Wiley Editorial Offices

John Wiley & Sons Inc., 111 River Street, Hoboken, NJ 07030, USA

Jossey-Bass, 989 Market Street, San Francisco, CA 94103-1741, USA

Wiley-VCH Verlag GmbH, Boschstr. 12, D-69469 Weinheim, Germany

John Wiley & Sons Australia Ltd, 42 McDougall Street, Milton, Queensland 4064, Australia

John Wiley & Sons (Asia) Pte Ltd, 2 Clementi Loop #02-01, Jin Xing Distripark, Singapore 129809

John Wiley & Sons Canada Ltd, 6045 Freemont Blvd, Mississauga, ONT, L5R 4J3, Canada

Wiley also publishes its books in a variety of electronic formats. Some content that appears in print may not be available in electronic books.

Library of Congress Cataloging-in-Publication Data

Orford, Jim.
  Community psychology : challenges, controversies, and emerging consensus / Jim Orford.
    p. ; cm.
  Includes bibliographical references and index.
  ISBN 978-0-470-85593-5 (cloth : alk. paper) – ISBN 978-0-470-85594-2 (pbk. : alk. paper)
  1. Community psychology.   I. Title.
  (DNLM: 1. Community Psychiatry.   2. Minority Groups–psychology.   3. Psychology, Social.
  4. Social Environment.   5. Socioeconomic Factors.   WM 30.6 067c 2007)
  RA790.55.0738 2007
  362.196'89 – dc 22   2007039320

British Library Cataloguing in Publication Data

A catalogue record for this book is available from the British Library

ISBN 978-0-470-85593-5 (hbk)   978-0-470-85594-2 (pbk)

Typeset in 10/12pt Palatino by Aptara Inc., New Delhi, India

CONTENTS

ABOUT THE AUTHOR

Jim Orford is Professor Emeritus and Head of the Alcohol, Drugs, Gambling and Addiction Research Group in the School of Psychology at the University of Birmingham, England. He trained in clinical psychology in the 1960s and since then has worked in Manchester, London, Exeter and Birmingham in positions that have always straddled the National Health Service and the university sector. He is committed to public service provision. Through his writings and in other ways he has been an enthusiastic promoter of community psychology in the UK and in the rest of Europe. This is his second book on the subject. The first, *Community Psychology: Theory and Practice*, was published by Wiley in 1992. Other Wiley books include *Psychological Problems: The Social Context* (edited with Philip Feldman in 1980) and *Excessive Appetites: A Psychological View of Addictions* (second edition 2001). Among his other books, the most recent are *Gambling and Problem Gambling in Britain* (with K. Sproston, B. Erens, C. White and L. Mitchell, 2003) and *Coping with Alcohol and Drug Problems: The Experiences of Family Members in Three Contrasting Cultures* (with G. Natera, A. Copello, C. Atkinson, J. Mora, R. Velleman, I. Crundall, M. Tiburcio, L. Templeton and G. Walley, 2005).

PREFACE

COMMUNITY PSYCHOLOGY: EXPANDING, CHANGING, AND ALWAYS CONTROVERSIAL

What is Community Psychology?

As I was putting the finishing touches to this book, a working group of the Community Psychology Network in the UK was planning to submit to the British Psychological Society a proposal for the formation of a Community Psychology Section – Britain has been slow to follow in the footsteps of a number of other countries which have had community psychology divisions or sections of their national psychological associations for some years. As part of the proposal we needed to define 'community psychology' for other members of the Society. Although it may not be the version finally submitted, our draft definition of the subject – shown in Figure P.1 – in my view does a good job of explaining in broad terms what we mean when we talk and write about community psychology.

At the very heart of the subject is the need to see people – their feelings, thoughts, and actions – within a social context. It exhorts us, when thinking of people's health, happiness and well-being, or when thinking about people's distress and disorder, to 'think context'. The context we should be thinking about does not stop at the immediate social environment of family or friendship or work group (the micro-level systems), but should extend to intermediate-level and macro-level contexts. In short, community psychology takes a contextual view of people and their psychology. Take the example of a homeless young person – homelessness will be the subject of part of Chapter 7. Much of the thinking in the rest of psychology about a topic such as homelessness, and much of public opinion, focuses on the person's diagnosis (mental illness or drug dependence for example) or his or her individual personal traits or characteristics (self-esteem or self-efficacy for example). There may be an interest in the stressful nature of the experience of homelessness, but in that case the emphasis is still likely to lie with the individual; for example, how many stressful events the individual experiences, or how they are personally appraised. Community psychology, on the other hand, looks beyond the individual; in this case to the homeless person's family and non-family support networks, and further beyond to the attitudes of local residents towards homeless people, the practices towards homelessness of the local police, local services and whether they include or exclude those who are homeless, the availability of employment of different kinds and conditions in the local area, national attitudes towards homelessness, government policy regarding the availability of social welfare benefits, and global and national trends in the relationship between capital and labour.

Community psychology places people in their social contexts

1. The central idea of community psychology is that *people's functioning, including their health, can only be understood by appreciating the social contexts within which they are placed.* It is 'community' psychology because it emphasises a level of analysis and intervention beyond the individual and his or her immediate interpersonal settings.

2. *Causation is seen as operating through the interaction over time of many factors on a variety of levels, from the micro-level to the macro-level.* Those levels include: family and peer group; organisational, educational and work settings; a geographical community level including neighbourhood; communities of identity based on ethnicity, gender, class or interests; cultural and societal levels; and the multinational and global level.

3. There is awareness in community psychology that there is a bias in psychology, and more generally in the behavioural, health and social sciences, towards looking for causes at individual or micro-social levels when causes are often more appropriately seen as residing at a higher level. It is an important part of community psychology *to bring critical attention to the way in which analyses and interventions may compound distress by blaming individual or family* victims for problems that are the consequence of the way society is arranged.

4. The notion of 'cause' is itself seen as problematic. *People are not merely seen as being at the mercy of constraining social forces, but rather as active 'agents'* who are trying to make real, albeit somewhat constrained, choices, to bear responsibilities, to make sense of what is going on, and to formulate and carry out plans in line with past experiences, present values, and expectations and hopes for the future.

Power, empowerment and disempowerment are central concepts in community psychology

5. Community psychology is concerned with the fact that social and economic arrangements of power and resources generate adversity and distress for communities and individuals. *It recognises that people with psychological difficulties very often have little power over key factors affecting their lives.* When individuals and collectives have relatively little power, health is affected negatively; increasing power and control for individuals and collectives affects it positively. It is recognised that control or power is structured by societal arrangements, including relative wealth, socio-occupational stratification, gender, and dominant – especially ethnic – group membership.

6. Community psychology is 'critical' in the sense that one of its important aims is *to identify and expose the psychologically damaging exercise of power*, particularly

since much of the exercise of power is built into routine and taken-for-granted ways in which social life is conducted, and hence is invisible or easily silenced. A central task is therefore to 'surface', clarify, and raise consciousness about the ways in which power is used and abused in social life, and the ways that may be influencing psychological functioning.

7.   Community psychology aims, not just to analyse power and the way it is exercised, but then *to find ways of helping people combat inequality and injustice,* and to work together with people to help resist oppression and to struggle to create a better world.

8.   *Diversity is a key concept* that can be subsumed under the overarching concepts of power and empowerment. In contrast to prejudice, disrespect and a steep social stratification hierarchy, community psychology seeks to promote respect of diversity and difference and the redistribution of power to achieve greater equality between groups.

9.   The emphasis of community psychology in practice is on *prevention, intervention and policy change at a non-individual level,* rather than on treatment at the personal level. In order to promote individual and collective health and well-being and to reduce distress and difficulties, it is necessary to promote change in the social, economic and environmental arrangements that give rise to such problems.

The practice of community psychology involves working collaboratively with others, usually those who are marginalised and disempowered

10.   Community psychology offers a framework for *working with groups of people who are, or who are at risk of being, excluded or marginalised, hurt or threatened, impoverished or oppressed,* and/or working with others who are trying to help people in such circumstances. The emphasis is upon collaboration and the use of participatory methods and the forging of alliances. There is a very positive orientation within community psychology towards sharing psychology with others.

11.   An objective is to maximise participants' power over key aspects of the joint work, and to minimise practitioners' own control over participants. Community psychology tends to *favour interventions that involve collaborative, multilateral co-research and co-action 'with' participants*, rather than interventions that involve working unilaterally 'for' them. Indeed, there is scepticism about the supposed superior competence of professional 'experts', mindful that expertise is often wielded as power which may serve to help maintain disempowerment rather than to challenge and transform it.

12.   There is an *appreciation of the competence and expertise possessed and exercised by those who have no special training in psychology*, whether they are 'ordinary' members of groups or communities, or non-psychologist professional or non-professional service providers. Those who practice community psychology recognise

that all are 'psychologists' in everyday life, and try to nurture strength, creativity and resilience in themselves and others.

13.   *Transparency is valued*, including: sharing with others rather than doing to others, using ordinary rather than specialist language, accepting unfamiliarity and the need to learn from others, and trying to draw on both everyday and expert forms of psychological knowledge.

Community psychology is committed to using a plurality of research and action methods

14.   It is pragmatic in its choice of methods and is not wedded to any particular methodology. Although it *favours a plurality of methods*, it is very favourably disposed towards qualitative methods such as semi-structured interviewing, ethnographic and other participant methods, and 'case' studies.

15.   Because the particular setting in which research and/or action is carried out is considered to be crucial, community psychology is *not generally looking to establish laws that can transcend the particularities of contexts*. Rather, it aims to achieve empowerment goals with a particular group in a particular setting; whilst also hoping to accumulate knowledge from experience in a variety of settings.

16.   Community psychology is as *committed to the evaluation of its practice* as are other branches of psychology, but leans in the direction of participatory evaluation methods rather than solely expert-led evaluation, and towards forms of quasi-experimental rather than randomised trial designs.

17.   *There is a belief in 'praxis' i.e. the inseparability of knowledge and action*: action builds on knowledge, and knowledge is acquired through action. Action research, especially participatory action research, is therefore prominent amongst the methods used in community psychology.

This figure is taken from a draft prepared by the author on the basis of ideas generated by a working group of the UK Community Psychology Network who were preparing a submission to the British Psychological Society proposing the formation of a Community Psychology Section of the Society. The table includes the ideas of David Fryer, Steph Meadows and Rachel Parcell, Carolyn Kagan, Mark Burton, Annie Mitchell, Jan Bostock, Bob Diamond, the Stirling Community Psychology Group, and the European Community Psychology Association.

Figure P.1   What is community psychology?

Community psychology thinking is therefore recognisably different from that in much of psychology because of the questions it is interested in asking and finding answers to. It is more likely, for example, to be interested in knowing what is the collective experience of homeless people and how that experience is affected by job losses and public attitudes in the vicinity, than in the self-esteem or drug-taking habits of individual homeless people.

Whatever the topic, and whatever the level at which questions are posed, community psychology takes a critical stance towards power, class and inequality. It is interested in where power lies, what form power takes, and how it is exercised in a way that helps maintain dominance, privilege and discrimination, at the expense of those groups who are disempowered and oppressed. In the case of homelessness we would be asking in what ways homeless people are powerless and excluded, by what means attitudes of prejudice towards homelessness and the homeless are perpetuated, and what groups benefit from keeping things the way they are or would be required to sacrifice some resources or power if things were to change. When it comes to action, those who practise community psychology will wish to work in close collaboration with homeless people, will share ideas and findings as much as possible with them, and will consider going further by involving homeless people in prioritising research questions, making decisions about research methods, and contributing to the interpretation and dissemination of findings. They will be attracted to methods of acquiring knowledge that recognise that the real experts are the people who are often seen otherwise as 'subjects' or 'participants'. They value highly the ability to understand in depth what it is that groups of people are experiencing, including how a piece of community psychology action has been experienced, and will place a lower priority on rigorous controlled investigation.

The International Growth of Community Psychology

When I wrote my first book on this subject – *Community Psychology: Theory and Practice* – which was published in 1992, community psychology, as an identified, named branch of psychology, had scarcely got off the ground in Europe or in other parts of the world. The notable exception was the USA where community psychology dates its origins in the 1960s and 1970s – during an era of idealism and social change in that country associated with such movements as those for racial desegregation and community mental health. Since then community psychology has emerged more confidently in a number of other countries, often accompanying social conflict and change. An important element to the present book, compared to my earlier one, is therefore the opportunity that the international development of the subject in the intervening years has given me to draw on ideas and examples of practices from a much broader range of countries. It is also the case that, with the diverse origins and philosophies of community psychology around the world, the contradictions and controversies in the field have become ever more apparent, adding to the richness of the subject. What is evident everywhere is the struggle that is required to maintain the kind of psychology outlined in Figure P.1 in the face of the ubiquitous pressures to persist with or revert to a more conforming, individualistic type of psychology.

The controversies and challenges attending the emergence of community psychology have been evident in every country and region. Latin American community psychology in particular has attracted much comment in English language sources since the early 1990s because of its distinctive origins, the challenge it offers to the previously dominant forms of community psychology, and the attractiveness of its social change orientation (Sánchez *et al.*, 1991; Montero, 1996, 1998, 2004; Leon & Montenegro, 1998; Wiesenfeld, 1998; Freitas, 2000; Krause, 2002; Montenegro, 2002; Burton & Kagan, 2005). Montero (1996), writing from Venezuela, pointed to a number of factors that gave Latin American community psychology its particular strengths. For one thing, the dictatorships and military regimes of the 1960s to 1980s, whilst they had impeded development of academic community psychology in a number of countries, had paradoxically led to a powerful and lasting link between community psychology and political movements, and had given urgency to the development of a psychology responsive to the problems of Latin American societies.

The history of Brazilian community psychology from the 1960s onwards, described by Freitas (1998, 2000), is illustrative of the influence of changing social and political events on the practice of psychology. During periods of military dictatorship, academics involved in work with poor communities were forced to work in secret, to leave the country, or to change their ways of working. The main theories and methods were imported from US and European centres, and practices were often in private psychotherapy, industry, or elite educational institutions. In reaction to political and social conditions, and dissatisfaction on the part of some with existing psychological models, social psychologists joined with others from education, social work and other social sciences to work with community groups in a more overtly political way, assuming the role of leaders, popular educators, or even social activists. From the mid-1980s onwards, with the exit of the military from government, demand for psychological services had increased, psychological posts were formally created within the Brazilian Public Health Service, and work had diversified. Psychological practice had expanded to different settings and there was good work with specific groups – for example work with women, older people, gay communities, black women, and victims of repeated violence. It is interesting, however, to note Freitas' (2000) view that since then much of Brazilian psychology, although it had moved away from being purely office or institution based, had lost much of the political edge that it had had in the 1960s and 1970s, and mostly was not meeting the ideals of community psychology. Often it could be said to be 'psychology in the community' having shifted the location of work without changing the methods or the philosophical basis of the work. It had moved away from concern with macro-social issues and the problems of different sectors of excluded people such as those living in slums, shanty towns or in exile, or those who were unemployed. There was a risk of losing the focus on broad and encompassing social explanations, and hence of diluting the overall approach of community psychology and the original drive that had promoted it:

> Although community social psychology emerged as a response to social problems, it still continues to lie at the crossroads of competing perspectives, and to be entangled in various contradictions that compromise its transforming institutions (Freitas, 2000, p. 321).

Freitas (2000) referred to the danger of reverting to a merely 'assistentialist' mode of practising psychology (i.e. assisting people to adjust rather than challenging social arrangements). The same contrast and change over time in response to political events have been highlighted in accounts of community psychology in Chile (Wiesenfeld, 1998; Krause, 2002).

South Africa is another country that has experienced extreme repression in recent times and where signs of a challenging community psychology have been increasingly seen since the early 1990s (Seedat *et al.*, 2001; Foster, 2004; Hayes, 2000; Hook, 2004; Mkhize, 2004; Ngonyama ka Sigogo & Modipa, 2004). Seedat *et al.* (2001) concluded that community psychology in South Africa still had a way to go in delivering on the promise of 'liberating' South African psychology from Euro-American domination and becoming a force for social change. Ngonyama ka Sigogo and Modipa (2004) also reflected on the difficulty of establishing a critical community psychology in South Africa that would contribute to the transformation of society. Community psychology in South Africa was relatively new and had struggled to create an identity for itself. Training for psychologists had been based on western models and had often ignored indigenous ways of understanding people in context. They discussed the tensions and contradictions experienced by a group at the University of the Witwatersrand struggling to develop a masters programme in community psychology in post-apartheid South Africa. They were a largely white group, with varied backgrounds in clinical, counselling, and community-social psychology. They struggled to reconcile competing models of community psychology theory and practice, to acknowledge indigenous knowledge systems, and to reconcile the promotion of community psychology with the requirements of the higher education system and professional registration. They wrote, too, of the slow diversification of the staff and student groups to better reflect the general population. But there were larger constraints such as dominant psychological epistemologies, the hierarchical power structures of academic institutions and professional registration bodies that sustained rigid notions of expertise, and yet larger issues such as the current government's concessions to the World Bank and the International Monetary Fund resulting in increased privatisation of formerly public resources. Many of these issues will resonate with those who have tried to develop community psychology elsewhere. As Seedat *et al.* (2001, p. 33) put it:

> ...an added challenge for community psychology in South Africa could be to see South Africa as a microcosm of the world and use the opportunities South Africa presents to work towards solving global problems in psychology and other fields.

Australia and Aotearoa/New Zealand are other countries where community psychology has been established since the 1970s, and where a distinctive contribution to the subject internationally has become much clearer, based on the history of colonialism, struggles in the face of oppression of indigenous peoples, and the opportunities that have been taken to understand the operation of prejudice and how it can be combated. A central idea has been the importance of 'world view', the need to gain insight into one's own world view, to appreciate how different can be the world view of others, and to attempt to reconcile world views by adopting a role at the interface and acting as mediator (Veno & Thomas, 1992a,b; Hamerton *et al.*, 1995; Raeburn & Thomas, 2000; Veno, 2000; Bishop & D'Rozario, 2002; Bishop *et al.*, 2002a,b). Bishop *et al.* (2002a, p. 508) hoped that the Australian approach would help to reverse the, "...US hegemony in community psychology theory and practice".

In Europe, Francescato and Tomai (2001) wrote of the development of a form of community psychology that would be less individualistic than had been the case in the USA. Europe's experience with fascism and communism had left Europeans acutely aware that communitarian ideals could be used for both good and ill, and an important part of the European background to community psychology was the history of labour and working class struggles that had given Europeans more social rights such as wide access to free or low-cost health care, higher education, and unemployment protection.

Community psychology has developed at very different rates in different European countries. Italy and Norway are amongst countries where the subject has flourished best. Francescato *et al.* (2006) have written about the development of community psychology in Italy. As in other countries, the development of community psychology there cannot be separated from socio-political conditions and events of the times. The 1970s in Italy was a period of powerful political movements and collective struggles involving students, women, mental health patients, and health professionals. Psichiatrya Democratica, the movement for the closure of mental hospitals, was a notable example. Fascism had been hostile to psychology, and no universities had been offering psychology degrees. Community psychology benefited from the central control of the university curriculum that followed, becoming officially recognised in 1985 as a compulsory subject at all universities offering psychology as a major subject. Francescato *et al.* (2006) saw community psychology in Italy as closer to Latin American community psychology than was the case for other European countries. In some other ways Italian community psychology could be seen, they thought, as appearing quite traditional, compared to countries such as Canada, the USA, Australia, and New Zealand; for example in its lack of debate of post-colonial and feminist theories, and lack of attention to different aspects of diversity, with little focus on minorities, indigenous populations and the heritage of colonisation (likely to change as immigration to Italy increased), and comparatively less work on women and gay communities for example.

Other European countries where community psychology ideas have been developing include those to the south of the continent, such as Portugal and Spain, that have experienced rapid change after the fall of fascist dictatorships and/or new, recent increases in immigration, and those to the east such as Poland and the former East Germany which have even more recently experienced rapid transition and consequent new issues such as high rates of unemployment (Keupp & Stark, 2000; Wingenfeld & Newbrough, 2000; Wosinski, 2006; Zolik, 2000).

Community psychology in North America is longer established, better known, and more easily accessible to English language readers. It is well represented in the present book and I shall not comment on it further here. Progress in North American community psychology has been discussed by, amongst others, Riger (2001) and Toro (2005).

Since my previous book appeared in 1992, community psychology has therefore become much more international. The influence of the USA and Canada remains strong, particularly via the two US journals, the *American Journal of Community Psychology* and the *Journal of Community Psychology*, and the continued appearance of major textbooks. The latter include: the *Handbook of Community Psychology* (Rappaport & Seidman, 2000), *Community Psychology: Linking Individuals and Communities* (Dalton, Elias & Wandersman, 2001), *Principles of Community Psychology: Perspectives and Applications* (third edition, Levine, Perkins & Perkins, 2005), and *Community Psychology: In Pursuit of Liberation and Well-Being* (Nelson & Prilleltensky, 2005). An important alternative English language text is *Community Psychology Theory, Method and Practice: South African and Other Perspectives* (Seedat, Duncan & Lazarus, 2001). Texts in other languages, known of to the present author, include, *Psicologia di Comunità* (Amerio, 2000), *Fondamenti di Psicologia di Comunità* (Francescato, Tomai & Ghirelli, 2002), and *Introducción a la Psicología Comunitaria: Desarrollo, Conceptos y Procesos* (Montero, 2004).

THE PRESENT BOOK

My Own Background and Interest in Community Psychology

The principal topic of my work as a psychologist has been addiction. I shall always be grateful to those who have helped me see that addiction can be understood on many interacting levels, from micro to macro, that are of interest to community psychology. Exaggerated expectancies of the pleasure from drink or drugs, or false beliefs about the probability of winning a bet, may be important, but so too are local norms about substance use, the concentration and type of sales points in the neighbourhood, local gang culture, the regional rate of unemployment, suppliers' profiteering, local authority licensing arrangements, national alcohol and drugs policies, and international control policies and global trade. My interest has focused on two topics in particular. One is the effects of addiction on the family. That interest has involved me, with a large number of colleagues, interviewing at length family members – mostly but not solely women – who have been affected by the excessive drinking or drug use of a close family member – mostly but not solely men. That work has been carried out with poor families in Mexico City, with indigenous families in remote rural and more urban locations in the Northern Territory in Australia, and with majority white and minority Sikh families in England (Orford, Natera, Copello *et al.*, 2005; Ahuja, Orford & Copello, 2003). An important additional component of that work has been study of the effects on children of parental alcohol problems (Velleman & Orford, 1999).

That work has influenced me as a community psychologist in a number of ways. Most importantly, it has allowed me to hear in great detail about how family members are marginalised, misunderstood, and disempowered. There is no room here to enlarge on the nature of that marginalisation and disempowerment, but mention of just one element of it is relevant here because it recurs as a theme so regularly in community psychology work with other disempowered groups. I refer to the tendency for disempowered people to feel a sense of shame and to blame themselves for a state of affairs that is really not their fault. Psychology and allied disciplines and professions have not on the whole served this group well. They have largely confined their analysis to the individual or micro interactional levels, ignoring higher levels of analysis including prevailing norms that govern family and gender relationships in society and the social and material constraints on resources and opportunities for action for wives, mothers, fathers, and others who are abused by excessive substance use. At the same time that work has given me much experience and awareness of the benefits and pitfalls of, and much fondness for, qualitative methods, which figure large in modern community psychology and in the present book. At the same time, because of its cross-cultural aspects, it has raised my awareness of issues around the experiences of minority ethnic groups in my own country and of different cultural groups, including colonised indigenous groups, in other parts of the world. My main personal experience of colonialism is as a beneficiary and descendant of colonists, but my awareness has I hope been broadened to enable me to better appreciate post-colonialism in Europe and elsewhere.

My second focus latterly has been on gambling as an important but relatively neglected potential addiction (Orford *et al.*, 2003). The links with community psychology are two-fold. First, it has thrown me into the intriguing but alarming world of public policy. What I have found is that British government policy on gambling is influenced to a greater extent by commercial, now mostly transnational, interests than it is by those of us concerned with personal, family, and community health. Perhaps that should not surprise me, but the most alarming aspect is the way in which researchers and service providers are encouraged to be complicit with a policy that is increasingly putting people at risk – those on low incomes being most at risk – whilst promoting discourses that exaggerate benefits (e.g. gambling is an innocent form of recreation like any other; gambling is good for urban regeneration), minimising the harms and holding individuals responsible (e.g. gambling problems affect only a small number of vulnerable people). I have found myself doing more media work than ever before, giving evidence to government committees, and penning editorials (Orford, 2003, 2005). Much of that activity has been reactive, but it has set me thinking about a more proactive approach. As a result I find myself in full agreement with those, such as Thomas and Robertson (1990), who have argued for the role of community psychology in social policy analysis and campaigning. One specific aspect concerns public attitudes. One of the things I have noticed about pronouncements from the government–industry gambling coalition is that, while public attitudes are invoked (we are told that the public want as much freedom to gamble as possible), public attitudes have not in fact been assessed. One of my activities as a community psychologist has therefore been to argue – successfully as it turned out – for the inclusion of attitude questions in the latest UK national survey of gambling. This has drawn heavily on some of my basic psychometric knowledge, as well as on a community psychology vision of the purpose of gathering such data, plus large measures of persuasiveness and patience.

The point is often made about community psychology that it occupies a position that overlaps with a wide variety of other disciplines and areas of knowledge (e.g. Maton *et al.*, 2006). One of the areas most often cited in that regard is public health and epidemiology. As I explain shortly, there is a sizeable input from social epidemiology in sections of this book. One recent work activity of mine has been in collaboration with colleagues in public health at my university. We were collaborating on an evaluation of the impact on community health of the British government's urban regeneration scheme known as the New Deal for Communities (NDC). This has been relatively recent work, and was ongoing while I was reading material for this book. It made much of what I was reading all the more salient to me since what I was learning about relatively deprived communities in my region of England in the course of our evaluation resonated with what I was reading of others' experience around the world in a number of respects. Like others we valued using multiple methods for collecting information: we used a mixture of photovoice, focus groups, ethnographic methods leading to interviews with those not involved in focus groups, interviews with NDC staff, analysis of policy documents, and quasi-experimental design in which the health of NDC areas was compared with that of comparison areas (Parry *et al.*, 2003, 2006; Dalton *et al.*, 2007). What we learned from the qualitative work confirmed much of what other qualitative researchers have described of the experiences of living in relatively deprived urban areas (e.g. Popay *et al.*, 2003). In the process, discussions of the nature of 'social capital' and 'sense of community', which can sometimes become rather abstract, have become much more real for me. The concept of 'community participation' has been another point of contact. Participation was a central idea for NDC as it is for most regeneration and development projects, but the literature repeatedly tells us that it is complicated and problematic, and so it proved to be in NDC.

I am grateful for their stimulation and support to many colleagues in those areas of my working life. They include those in the Department of Public Health and Epidemiology at the University of Birmingham and colleagues working on national gambling surveys at the National Centre for Social Research in London. But my greatest thanks must go to my close colleagues in the Alcohol, Drugs, Gambling and Addiction Research Group at the School of Psychology at the University of Birmingham and to those elsewhere, particularly at the University of Bath and at the Institute of Psychiatry in Mexico City, with whom our Birmingham research group has collaborated for a good number of years. In addition to those research colleagues, I have had the pleasure over many years of working with students on their research projects, often in areas outside my own speciality, and I am grateful for the broader perspective that has given me. I might mention in particular doctorate work on unemployment (Ball & Orford, 2002), bullying at work (Lewis & Orford, (2005), and the experiences of transgendered people (Clifford & Orford, 2007).

One of the most stimulating and enjoyable parts of my work since the mid-1990s has been working with colleagues in the UK and other European countries to promote the subject of community psychology at a European level. Since the first European Congress of Community Psychology was held in Rome in 1995, the European Network of Community Psychology (ENCP) has organised biennial conferences, with smaller themed meetings in the intervening years. I had the satisfaction of being the coordinator of the ENCP when it became the European Community Psychology Association (ECPA) in 2005. In 2008 Europe will play host, in Lisbon, to the second international community psychology conference. In Britain the Community Psychology Network has been meeting annually for roughly the same period of time and, as mentioned earlier, is now planning to submit a proposal to the British Psychological Society for the formation of a Community Psychology Section.

Contact with others in Britain and the rest of Europe who have been working to promote the values, theories, and practices of community psychology has been a constant source of encouragement and support.

Features of the Present Book

Writing this book has been immensely stimulating since it has made me read much more of the increasing amount that is being written in community psychology than I would otherwise have done. It is impossible, however, for one person to keep up with the whole field – let alone with what is being written in closely related subjects – and I have often been plagued by the thought that it had been foolish to undertake such a task alone and that I had clearly 'bitten off more than I could chew'. The book is therefore very much a personal take on the subject, reflecting my background and interests, and the journals and books that I happen to read. In any case it could hardly be otherwise since the field is fluid and controversial.

There are one or two features of the book which may be peculiar to it and to which I would like to draw the reader's attention. The first is my preference for exploring an issue, or describing a project, at some length, often in the process quoting liberally from those who have written about community psychology issues in journals or books or from those who have participated in research and action projects. For example, some theoretical issues around the concept of power are discussed in some detail, as are the concepts of social class and social capital. The debates that those and similar notions throw up are, in my view, important and intriguing and deserve extended attention. In later sections of the book, it has been my style to describe each of a number of example projects or pieces of research at some length. I prefer to do that because I believe much of importance lies in the detail of how things are done and what participants say. I often let the projects speak for themselves rather than spend a lot of time telling the reader what conclusions to draw. That probably reflects, in part, my interest in and orientation towards qualitative research. Although I recognise the great value of discourse analysis for understanding how the positions of the relatively powerful are maintained (in the analysis of policy documents for example), when the relatively disempowered are participants in community psychology research, I lean towards the 'realist' end of the realist–constructivist continuum. I believe that good community psychology qualitative research is capturing the collective reality of people's lives. The more we can hear their voices directly, therefore, the better.

A particular feature of the book which might not have been expected in a text on community psychology is the space devoted in Part II to findings and debates in social epidemiology. I provide some explanation for the weight given to those topics at the beginning of that section. Suffice it here to say that social epidemiologists have, in their own way, been grappling with some of the same ideas that are so important in community psychology. The clearest example is the concentration of attention given to social inequality and its relationship with health. In the process it has been necessary to look closely at topics such as social class, area deprivation, and social capital – all of great interest to community psychology but not as thoroughly discussed and debated as they should be. Although as a psychologist I have often found immersion in reports of epidemiological work to be frustrating, I have also found it stimulating and helpful. Collaboration with social epidemiology is one of the forms of inter-disciplinary collaboration in which community psychology should be engaged.

Recognising the international growth of community psychology which was described above, I have tried to include material from as wide a range of countries as possible. This has the effect of stretching the canvass wide, perhaps to the point at which some will question the relevance to their work of examples from very different places. For example, those working with people with disabilities in Birmingham, England, where I work, may wonder at the relevance of a project on forest conservation in India. I hope, however, that it is possible to see how those two areas of work are connected, both in terms of community psychology theory and in terms of practical methods and procedures. At the same time it has to be acknowledged that work from the UK and the USA has the greatest coverage. Included are a number of contributions from Italy and the Scandinavian countries in Europe; Canada, Nicaragua, Venezuela and Brazil in North, Central and South America; and from South Africa, Australia and Aotearoa/New Zealand. Other countries are less well represented or are not represented at all, which no doubt reflects some combination of a relative dearth of community psychology in those countries and my ignorance of what is taking place there.

Community psychology is critical of social arrangements and their impact on health and well-being. To many of those in the field it can only live up to its values and ideals if it acts as an effective site of resistance to those powerful influences that are damaging to human development and collective well-being. Its agenda is therefore a radical one. Those who practise in the name of community psychology position themselves in various places in relation to that agenda, and not all will agree with where this book positions itself. Some will not think it radical enough; others may find it too radical. Yet others may feel that, in its effort to represent a wide range of work on the subject, the book fails to take a clear position.

The Structure of the Book

The book is divided into four parts. Part I deals with three topics of importance for understanding the background to community psychology. In Chapter 1 the critical background to the subject is introduced, contrasting the social orientation of community psychology with neglect of the social in psychology as a whole. Chapter 2 introduces and explores some of the key ideas for community psychology; in particular, empowerment, liberation, and social justice. Chapter 3 addresses the debate about community psychology knowledge and how it is best acquired: the chapter considers how community psychology positions itself in relation to the kind of science favoured in mainstream psychology, and explains why participatory methods are those of choice in community psychology.

It is in Part II that the book draws heavily on social epidemiology. Chapter 4 attempts to summarise a large body of findings on social inequalities and health, in the process considering questions of social status, the social position of women, and the importance of conditions and relationships at work. Chapter 5 introduces the relatively newer epidemiological work on the relationship between health and area deprivation, and some attempts to understand what it is about a place that is good or bad for health and well-being. That exploration is taken further in Chapter 6 where the two concepts of social capital and sense of community are used to try to understand the characteristics of local communities that may be beneficial or harmful.

Part III examines the experience of disempowerment through the findings of community psychology research – much of it qualitative – with people who represent seven different sets of disempowering circumstances. Those affected by war, immigration, homelessness, and unemployment feature in Chapter 7. Women, those experiencing poverty, and lesbian, gay, bisexual and transgendered people are those whose voices are heard in Chapter 8.

Part IV presents a number of examples of community psychology action projects. The examples chosen range from those in Chapter 9 which take the form of peer support programmes, and which result principally in gains in personal empowerment (although they may also have system level effects), to those in Chapter 12 which deal with participation in collective action and projects that aim for collective liberation. In between, Chapter 10 looks at examples of work that involves collective action and the creation of innovative ways of bringing needed services and resources to otherwise disempowered people, and Chapter 11 examines examples explicitly aimed at communities as collective entities.

ACKNOWLEDGEMENTS

I wish to acknowledge the great contribution to this book made by Pat Evans. As Group Secretary to our research group in the School of Psychology at The University of Birmingham she has provided me and our colleagues with unfailing support and dedication. In the preparation of the present book her role has been essential in undertaking the time-consuming and detailed task of preparing the several drafts through which the book has progressed.

PART I

THE BACKGROUND TO COMMUNITY PSYCHOLOGY AND WHAT IT STANDS FOR

Chapter 1

CHALLENGING PSYCHOLOGY OVER ITS NEGLECT OF THE SOCIAL

THE INDIVIDUALISM OF PSYCHOLOGY

Community psychology is about the social context of people's lives. The word 'context' in that statement is used in its broadest possible sense. In the pages of this book we shall touch on topics such as income distribution, social class, work conditions, and people's sense of community. Each of those is deeply psychological. All the time we shall be thinking of people in collectives, and the ways in which those collectives are disempowered and how they can become empowered. That ought, or so it seems to the present author, to be at the very heart of psychology. Yet nothing could in fact be further from the case. Psychology, at least in the form taken in those countries – the richer ones – that have led the discipline, has taken a very individualistic route. Psychology has laid itself open to the challenge that it has neglected whole domains of its legitimate subject matter. There have been many critics of that position from within psychology itself, and their voices have been growing louder and more numerous. Let us hear what some of them have said.

Among the critics is Bruner (1990) who wanted to see the development of a new, "meaning-centered, culturally oriented psychology" (p. 15). He pointed to the disappointing way in which the cognitive revolution in psychology – a reaction to the dominance of purely behavioural explanations grounded in animal models of learning, experimental methods, and a distrust of what people *say* as opposed to what they *do* – had in the event been routed towards an emphasis on individual information processing, with computation as the ruling metaphor. Bruner argued that a human psychology based on the individual alone was impossible, and that studying *shared* meanings and concepts and modes of discourse was essential for understanding our culturally adapted way of life. He accused much of psychology of displaying an anti-historical, anti-cultural, and even anti-intellectual bias. He saw psychology as having remained isolated from recent currents of thought in neighbouring disciplines, attributable in part to psychology's stubborn anti-philosophical position. Glenwick *et al.* (1990) also viewed much academic psychology as being intellectually out of date:

> ...in the academic psychology department, current research practice appears grounded in a way of thinking – logical positivism – that antedates postmodernism. Its dominant attributes are familiar: (a) the experimental method as the only way of knowing; (b) an experimenter who studies 'subjects'; (c) an environment that is typically controlled and artificially manipulated; (d) a process that is 'objective' and seemingly value-free; and (e) a focus that is short-term and interested in a single, or very few, points in time (p. 86).

One effect had been that psychology had not played the role that it might have done in commenting critically on the way society is organised.

> Intellectuals in a democratic society constitute a community of cultural critics. Psychologists, alas, have rarely seen themselves that way, largely because they are so caught up in the self-image generated by positivist science. Psychology, on this view, deals only in objective truths and eschews cultural criticism (Bruner, 1990, p. 32).

Rapley *et al.* (2003) put that point even more pungently:

> ...psychology has largely abandoned any pretence it might once have had to stand for social justice or the rights of the poor, the miserable and the dispossessed (p. 17).

Even social psychology, which might have been expected to have taken a lead in moving beyond an exclusive focus on the personal, has often been surprisingly individual-centered. Hepburn (2003) has described how social psychological studies in the USA in the years after the Second World War, carried out by people such as Allport, Sherif, Asch, and Milgram, who had lived through the depression of the 1930s and the war, and who were often refugees from Nazi persecution, had been motivated by concern with oppression and exploitation (carrying out studies of prejudice, conformity, and obedience, for example), but had later lost track of those big themes, moving away from the 'social' towards the 'individual', and producing what came to be known as the 'crisis in social psychology'. The area of social cognition, for example, has used experimental methods to understand how individuals make social judgements, for example about members of different ethnic groups. The focus has been on establishing general principles about social perception irrespective of the specific context (Marková, 2003).

Himmelweit (1990) and Bar-Tal (2000) are among other European social psychologists who have been critical of the cognitive and individualistic bias of social psychology, particularly in the USA. In Bar-Tal's view, European social psychology, notably Moscovici's (1972, 1984) influential notion of social representations, and Tajfel's (e.g. 1981) social identity theory, had restored to the discipline an interest in macro-social or societal questions that had been promised by the founders of the discipline decades earlier: for example by Wundt (1916), Durkheim (1933) and McDougall (1939), with their notions, respectively, of folksoul, collective representations, and group mind (as Jahoda, 1982, pointed out, psychology was in its earliest days much more closely connected with anthropology that it was later on). Bar-Tal's (2000) interest was in what he called 'societal beliefs', which serve the functions of providing members with knowledge about the society, maintaining social and individual identity, preserving the existing societal system and structure, and motivating and guiding societal action. Consequences might be positive or negative. Among the latter were: the maintenance of a very unequal societal power structure; and the preservation of negative stereotypes about other groups and their members. Himmelweit (1990) proposed a whole new sub-discipline that she referred to as 'societal psychology', which would emphasise the, "... all-embracing force of the social, institutional, and cultural environments, and with it the study of social phenomena in their own right as they affect and are affected by the members of the particular society" (p. 17). Such a psychology would study the socio-cultural context in which people live and act, would draw on a variety of disciplines and theories, would involve taking a historical perspective that is so often lacking in psychology, and would use a multi-level systems approach, combining micro and macro levels of study.

The French psychologist Doise (1986) is among others who have drawn attention to the surprisingly asocial nature of much social psychology. He distinguished the four levels of analysis shown in Figure 1.1: the *intra-personal*; *inter-personal/situational*; *positional*; and *ideological* levels. He believed that Lewin (e.g. 1951) – regarded by some as the originator of community psychology – had been at pains to develop a social psychology that studied the articulation of the individual and the collective, or what Durkheim called the socio-psychical, but that those who followed him had retreated to the first two levels. Much of social psychology had remained at those levels. Another critic, Burkitt (1991), wrote:

> The view of human beings as self-contained unitary individuals who carry their uniqueness deep inside themselves, like pearls hidden in their shells, is one that is ingrained in the Western tradition of thought ... [this] image of humans ... is totally inappropriate for the study of personality. In order to truly understand the human self, [this] vision of humans ... must be dispensed with (pp. 1, 189).

In an attempt to build a better vision of the human self, Burkitt drew heavily upon the writings of George Herbert Mead, whom he described as a philosopher and social psychologist. Mead's theory was that human nature was social, conditioned by the social group from the earliest moments of life and developing in transaction with it throughout life. Individual personality had no meaning taken out of the context of one's social group. It is interesting to note that Mead is often thought of within psychology as a sociologist – a good measure of the extent to which psychology has become over-focused on the decontexualised individual and how social views of human nature have become marginalised within psychology.

Burkitt criticised Mead, however, for saying nothing about society and about social divisions and inequalities within it. As a corrective he drew equally heavily on the writings of the French Marxist psychologist, Lucien Sève. Like Mead, Sève saw personality as constantly shaped by, although never totally constrained by, the present-day system of social relations which have developed in the past up to the present day – a form of historical structuralism. Most of us were unaware, most of the time, how our actions and ways of thinking are shaped by social circumstances: we assume we are free agents – rugged individualists. In particular we are unconscious of the power relations that constrain us and shape our personalities and the ways we interpret and cope with adversity. Some have posited a 'structural

---

The Intra-Personal Level

Theories at this level, "describe how individuals organise their perception, their evaluation of their social milieu and their behaviour within this environment. In such theories, the interaction between individual and social environment is not dealt with directly, and only the mechanisms by which the individual organises her/his experience are analysed" (Doise, 1986, p.11).

The Inter-Personal and Situational Level

This level is, "concerned with inter-personal processes as they occur within a given situation. The different social positions occupied by individuals outside this particular situation are not taken into account... The object of study is the dynamics of the relations established at a given moment by given individuals in a given situation" (p. 12).

The Positional Level

"Differences in social position which exist prior to the interaction between different categories of subject" (p. 13) are brought into the picture at this level. For example pre-existing differences in socioeconomic status, gender differences, or ethnic group membership, might be taken into account in trying to understand people's subjective experience or ways of interacting.

The Ideological Level

At the fourth level, analysis goes further to take into account the "systems of beliefs and representations, values and norms, which validate and maintain the established social order" (p. 15), which are widely shared within a given culture or society, and which powerfully influence a society's institutions.

Figure 1.1 The four levels of analysis in social psychology according to Doise (1986)
Source: Doise W. (1986, originally in French, 1982). *Levels of Explanation in Social Psychology*. Cambridge, UK: Cambridge University Press

unconscious' (Lichtman, 1982, cited by Birkett) paralleling the psychic unconscious. Indeed one might say that psychology as a subject was structurally unconscious, showing little awareness of the, "...social contexts in which people learn and in which they act, nor about the effect that social structure may have on the shaping of predispositions of the personality" (Burkitt, 1991, p. 19). Hence, according to Mead, Sève, Burkitt, and others, "Socio- and psycho-genesis are...two processes which are inextricably linked..." (Burkitt, p. 180). Yet so unconscious are we of the social part of the equation that we are ever ready to individualise or psychologise problems that are, in the true sense of the expression, psychosocial. The theme of consciousness about social conditions that affect us is one that will recur many times later in this book.

A strong voice, raised in support of the same position, has been that of Prilleltensky. In his book, *The Morals and Politics of Psychology* (1994), he had a chapter entitled Abnormal Psychology in which he traced the development of the field over the previous 40 years. He saw a progression having taken place from an *asocial* approach, through an enhanced awareness of *micro-social* elements, to an increased alertness to the *macro-social*. In the asocial approach problems are formulated in terms of individual defects:

> The medical model, in either its organic or psychodynamic version, captures the essence of the asocial stage . . . Environmental factors are not entirely disregarded, but they are given only secondary priority and remain largely in the background . . . the individual is too frequently dissociated from the wider systems of society that shape her or his behaviour extensively, thus creating an ahistorical and asocial image of individuals (pp. 99, 100, 102).

Discussing the micro-social stage in the development of abnormal psychology, Prilleltensky referred to the systemic model of psychological problems as one that had raised expectations that it would address social systems on a number of levels, from the micro-system of family to macro-social and macro-social–political levels. In fact, after radical beginnings in the 1950s and 60s, when it challenged a uniform benign view of the family, it had become entrenched in forms of family therapy that at best were ambiguous about the social structural influences on family life, and at worst perpetuated a psychopathological model, appearing to blame the family unit rather than just individuals. Family therapy, in Prilleltensky's opinion:

> . . . portray[s] the family as the main generator of certain kinds of dysfunctions and omits the fact that the family is very much a product of social forces. Family therapy's analysis is reductionistic . . . By depicting the family as a central perpetrator in the infliction of psychological distress, attention is deflected from macrosocial conflicts that may actively shape and perpetuate the mental health of the population as well as that of the individual and his or her family (Prilleltensky, 1994, p. 112).

Prilleltensky went on to consider whether community psychology had been successful in addressing macro-social and macro-social–political levels, concluding that although steps had been taken in that direction, it was, ". . . still too attached to the comforts of the academic world to venture into the uncertainties of the political arena" (p. 115). In part that was attributable to community psychologists using in their studies variables such as social class or ethnic group, without taking their analyses further. The same criticism was made by Bronfenbrenner (e.g. 1988) who referred to that kind of analysis as using a 'social address model', that is assigning people a social 'address' but without paying attention to what the environment was like at that address – what people's experiences were there and what activities were taking place. Whether community psychology has advanced since then may perhaps be judged by the contents of the remainder of the present book. Certainly Prilleltensky (1994) was of the view that we needed to look to such movements as feminist psychology and the politics of psychiatric consumers and survivors in order to see how the macro-social–political level could be addressed.

Self-Efficacy and Other Individualised Concepts

Nothing illustrates better the individualistic bias of psychology than its preoccupation with individual personalities abstracted from the settings and collectives of which people are a part. From a community psychology viewpoint, the disappointing thing is that concepts are often treated in psychology as if they were solely to do with individual personality, when they might, with a bit of development, serve well as useful concepts for understanding the psychological contexts of people's lives. Examples we shall briefly consider include locus of control, social support, stress, and vulnerability. Paramount in the legion of personalised concepts has, of course, been the 'self', and the many related ideas – self-esteem and self-confidence for example – all treated, in the hands of psychologists, as personal, decontextualised concepts (Bruner, 1990; McKenna, 2002).

A form of the 'self' idea that has been hugely popular in psychology is that of 'self-efficacy' (Bandura, 1977). Franzblau and Moore (2001) analysed the concept from a community psychology perspective. They argued that the concept was derived from a view of the self that stressed autonomy, self-reliance and independence. Change was a question of modifying one's personal beliefs so that one could attain a particular outcome. Both successes and failures were self-made according to that formulation. It derived, according to Franzblau and Moore, from a western view of individual responsibility that supposes that adversities can always be overcome by correcting dysfunctional individual ways of thinking or behaving. That ignores, they argued, the systems of social support that may or may not exist to help an individual action including: economic support for completion of the task; social/emotional and institutional support for engaging in the task and feeling confident about it; whether or not the person has the education and training to do the task; and ideological support embedded in cultural and political expectations of success for someone of his or her sex, ethnic group, or socioeconomic status. It assumes that action is individual in the face of adversity, rather than collective. These social resources remain hidden in self-efficacy studies which only measure the confidence of individuals. When self-efficacy fails, there is every likelihood of 'blaming the victim' (Ryan, 1971). It, "... leaves the ideological, economic, political, institutional, and legal structures of control intact, while the blame for continuing oppression is placed on dysfunctional thinking of the oppressed" (Franzblau & Moore, 2001, p. 94). In later chapters (particularly in Parts III and IV) we shall meet several examples of people blaming themselves for circumstances that are not of their own making (e.g. Bond *et al.*, 2000).

In fact, Bandura (1995) refuted the charge that self-efficacy theory ignored social structural factors, or – another criticism levelled at self-efficacy – that it was of little relevance in less individualistic societies. But, however much he insisted otherwise, the emphasis remained on individual personal beliefs, the exercise of individual agency, personal mastery, and experiences of personal change. Although he introduced the concept of 'collective efficacy', his discussion of that concept actually focused on the many ways in which it could be undermined. He was also suspicious of the idea that how families felt about their communities reflected objective economic conditions rather than their personal sense of efficacy. Nevertheless, the idea of collective efficacy (or what Hobfoll *et al.*, 2002, termed 'collective-mastery') could be considered close to the concept of collective empowerment (to be discussed in Chapter 2), suggesting that efficacy need not remain a purely individualistic concept.

Another popular construct in psychology, also treated as a personal trait, has been 'locus of control' (LOC: Rotter, 1966). It has been treated that way despite its roots in social learning theory, and some developments of the idea that suggest it might have something important to offer community psychology. One of those developments was the recognition that LOC was a multi-dimensional concept and that one dimension was a greater or lesser belief that the world was controlled by 'powerful others'. Some people held views about control suggesting that they were structuralists, believing that societal determinants of behaviour were paramount, while others, who stressed external control, were fatalists, seeing outcomes as dependent mainly on luck, fate or chance (Furnham & Steele, 1993). Another development was the recognition that a person's beliefs in control might depend upon the context, leading to domain-specific measures of LOC (Furnham & Steele, 1993). Others have shown that control beliefs are related to social class and to income (Lachman & Weaver, 1998; Wardle & Steptoe, 2003). Challenging collective beliefs in fate is an important idea in liberation psychology (Martín-Baró, 1994), as we shall see in Chapter 2. Despite those intriguing possibilities, LOC has remained essentially a personal trait concept.

Social support is another such idea. It has been very popular in the field of social psychology and health (Cobb, 1976; Sarason *et al.*, 1990) but, once again, in psychology we have tended to individualise it. We have been inclined to see it in terms of the network of individual supportive people surrounding an individual focal person (Orford, 1992). We have not found it so easy to handle the idea that a person might get support from groups or from settings (Felton & Shinn, 1992), and we have been slow to take advantage of developments in network analysis (Scott, 2000) that treat individuals or groups as parts of interacting networks rather than as foci of individual network diagrams. Arguably the greatest failing of the way in which social support has been used in psychology has been the failure to consider the way in which it relates to questions of influence and power, and empowerment. Social support has been treated as if it were power-neutral. Perhaps because its use has been limited in that way, it can be argued that it has now been somewhat superseded by the more embracing concept of 'social capital'. The latter idea, which will be dealt with at some length in Chapter 6, is better able to deal with the 'vertical' (more powerful–less powerful) as well as the 'horizontal' (between equals) aspects of social relationships.

Another concept that has been ubiquitous in modern psychology is 'stress'. The way in which it has been dealt with has been roundly criticised by Hobfoll (1998). His argument was that we had individualised the idea of stress by the emphasis in stress theory on the way in which an individual appraises his or her circumstances (as in Lazarus & Folkman's, 1984, influential theory). It is as if there is no objective reality out there in the world, only each separate individual's perception, appraisal, or understanding of it. We had lost sight, he argued, of the social context of stress. Particularly if we share a set of social and cultural norms, we know what is stressful and what is not, and we do not need to resort to perception at the individual level in order to know it. He shared the view of Brown and Harris (1989) that, provided enough detail was obtained about stressful events or circumstances and about the context in which they took place, then another person who shared the same culture (a trained research interviewer in the case of Brown and Harris's research on women and depression – see Chapters 4 and 8), could objectively rate the degree of stress, independently of the person's emotional response and the ease and difficulty of coping.

Hobfoll's own theory of stress, which is of considerable relevance to community psychology and bears some similarity to notions of power and empowerment that we shall meet in the next chapter, was that stress occurred when people's resources, necessary for survival and achievement of goals, were lost or threatened. By resources he had in mind a wide range of things, some of them familiar topics of study in psychology, others neglected. As well as *personal resources* such as occupational skills, leadership ability, self-esteem, and self-efficacy, they included what Hobfoll called *object resources*, such as home, household possessions, and transportation; *condition resources*, such as health, employment, seniority, and marriage; and *energy resources* such as money, credit, and knowledge. Hence, unlike much of psychology, Hobfoll's conservation of resources theory gives material resources and social roles a prominent place. The central tenet of the theory is that, "...people work to obtain resources they do not have, retain those resources they possess, protect resources when threatened, and foster resources by positioning themselves so that their resources can be put to best use" (Hobfoll, 1998, p. 55). Because resources are widely valued but often finite, social conflict over resources is a principal source of stress. Individuals and groups with fewer resources are, according to the theory, more vulnerable to further resource loss or threat of loss. Hobfoll emphasised that the notion of possession of resources, motivation to conserve them, and stress occasioned by their loss or threat of loss, could be applied to groups, organisations and communities as well as to individuals. Indeed the need to gain and preserve resources tied individuals into their social groups (although much of the time Hobfoll described the theory as if it were a theory of individual stress).

The tendency to psychologise is not limited to trait terms popular in psychology. Boyle (2003) considered the way in which the term 'vulnerability', popular in political and policy-making circles, was used as an expression, not wholly complimentary, to focus attention on vulnerable individuals, hence diverting attention away from, "...the potentially damaging activities of relatively more powerful social groups" (p. 29). She provided a telling list of pairs of statements, including most of those shown in Table 1.1 (I have added some with which I am familiar from my own work): statements on the left are about the vulnerability of groups of individuals, the paired statements on the right being translations into relational statements focusing on the perpetration of abuse towards those groups.

This proneness to individualise – we might call it psychology's 'default option' – is ever-present and we need to be always on guard against it. Many examples will crop up in later chapters. In the following chapter we shall see that even 'empowerment', which has been a key concept in community psychology, is itself not immune from the individualising tendency.

Table 1.1 How the language of vulnerability diverts attention from oppression

Statements of vulnerability	Statements of oppression
Old people are vulnerable to hypothermia	The government doesn't pay a high enough state pension for old people to pay their heating bills
People from ethnic minorities are vulnerable to racial discrimination	White people discriminate against black people
Lone women drivers are vulnerable at night	Men attack women when they are less likely to be seen
Unassertive people are vulnerable to being bullied at work	Managers in some workplaces pick on weaker employees
School dropouts are vulnerable to developing problem gambling	Gambling operators make money out of the socially excluded

Source: based on Boyle, M. (2003). The dangers of vulnerability. *Clinical Psychology*, **24**, 27–30, Table 1

The Individualism–Collectivism Dimension

Individualised concepts may be the result, as Burkitt (1991) supposed, of the dominance of psychology by western nations, particularly the USA. Hobfoll (1998) made the point that most psychological studies have been carried out in cultures that value individualism, and many with middle-class, youngish adults as participants. Hence the danger is that much of psychology has focused on the very people who might be least dependent on collective resources and action. While concepts such as self-efficacy had been popular, those such as honour and self-sacrifice – more important in collective cultures – had been much less often studied. Indeed a leading idea in cross-cultural psychology has been the concept of *individualism* versus *collectivism* (Hofstede, 1994; Triandis, 1994; Kemmelmeier *et al.*, 2003). Some cultures – the more individualistic ones – are ones in which the self is defined more individually, where personal goals are a priority, where there is a relative emphasis on contractual relationships, and individual attitudes are important. In others – the more collectivistic – the self is defined more collectively, group goals have greater priority, the emphasis is on communal relationships, and social norms are more important (see Table 1.2).

In fact the matter is rather more complicated than that. For one thing it has been a repeated finding that there is a strong association between the relative affluence of a country – as indexed by, for example, GNP, calorie supply per capita, or per capita energy consumption – and the value placed on individualism (Schwartz, 1994; Georgas *et al.*, 2004). Furthermore, different forms of collectivism have been identified, depending on the nature of the collective that is most salient in a particular culture. In some cultures, *mestizo* Mexico for example, the family is all-important and the culture is often said to be one characterised by familial collectivism. In eastern European countries that until 1989 were part of the Soviet bloc, the term 'collective' has a different meaning; for many it has negative associations left over from the era in which individuality is seen as having been subordinated to the goals

Table 1.2   Some of the main distinctions between individualistic and collectivist cultures

Individualistic	Collectivist
Self is defined as an independent entity	Self is defined in terms of in-groups, relationships
Change the situation to fit the self	Change the self to fit the situation
Emotions tend to be self-focused (e.g. anger)	Emotions tend to be other focused (e.g. empathy)
Focus on own needs, rights, capacity (contracts)	Focus on the needs of the in-group (obligations)
Favour beliefs reflecting independence, emotional detachment	Favour beliefs reflecting interdependence
Value pleasure, achievement, competition, freedom, autonomy, fair exchange	Value security, obedience, duty, in-group harmony, personalised relationships
Less willingness to self-sacrifice for the group	Self-sacrifice for the group is natural

Source: adapted from Triandis, H.C. (1994). Theoretical and methodological approaches to the study of collectivism and individualism. In U. Kim *et al.* (eds), *Individualism and Collectivisim: Theory, Method, and Applications* (pp. 41–51). Thousand Oaks, CA: Sage

of a political collective (Marková, 1997; Moodie *et al.*, 1997). Marková contrasted that type of 'collectivism' with a longer central European tradition emphasising a strong historical heritage of democratic communities, a sense of responsibility for self and others, and a stress on the agency and identity of individuals. A special issue of the *Journal of Community and Applied Social Psychology* on 'The Individual and the Community: a Post-Communist Perspective', edited by Marková (1997), focused on the dramatic changes that had occurred in eastern Europe after the break-up of the Soviet bloc. In one contribution, Topalova (1997) reported results from three representative national surveys carried out in Bulgaria in the early 1990s. Results showed that, in that country, traditionally collectivist in its values, values were gradually moving in an individualistic direction. Those who endorsed the more individualistic values tended to be younger, particularly students, more often male, and non-religious. Collectivists tended to identify (referring to 'we' rather than 'they') with social groups with interests in maintaining the status quo and traditional social values (e.g. the Socialist Party, monarchy, religious leaders, and rich people in powerful positions), whereas individualists identified themselves more strongly with social groups who were declaring themselves in support of the new ideology (e.g. opposition political parties, republicans, the non-religious, and individuals whose standing in the social hierarchy was lower).

The Individualism of Psychotherapy

Treatment for an ill-health condition, whether the treatment be medical or psychological, rests on the idea that the individual is suffering from some disorder or defect that lends itself to individual cure or correction. The limitations of that individualistic conception of ill-health have often been pointed out. Porter (1997, reviewed by Mitchell, 1998), for example, developed at length the argument that the technical success of scientific medicine has led to a neglect of the less glamorous preventive health care. He was convinced that the historical evidence showed that the largest improvements in health had been due, not to cures for individuals, but due to the public health movement. He also pointed out that most traditional approaches to life and healing, unlike modern scientific medicine, placed individuals in a wider social context.

Using the often cited analogy of jumping into a river to rescue a succession of people who might otherwise drown, with no time to consider why they are all falling (or being pushed) into the water upstream, Alonzo (1993) was another who eloquently made the point that medicine is largely committed to 'downstream' healthcare while paying only lip service to 'upstream' prevention. He took the reader of his article carefully through the positions for and against different forms of prevention, detection, protection, and health promotion, extending the analogy of drowning in the river to consider the different ways in which people might be deceived into jumping into dangerous waters apparently of their own volition. Much of prevention, he argued, was based on the idea that individuals are responsible for their own ill-health through acts of omission or commission:

> In the Reagan Era of excessive individualism, it was the individual who needed to come into line regarding preservation and promotion of health. This ideological position ... makes it easier for our society, or those charged with providing resources for prevention, to consistently avoid examining the socio-structural impediments to maintaining and protecting one's health (p. 1020).

Psychotherapy is especially vulnerable to the charge that it individualises personal distress, failing to take account of the real world in which people live (Smail, 1987, 1991; Masson, 1989; Pilgrim, 1991). Critics have argued that the promise of psychotherapy, that it would stand for progressive humanism and would therefore be open to consideration of the social determinants of mental distress, has not been fulfilled (e.g. Pilgrim, 1991). It can be said (e.g. Smail, 1987) that psychology and the other 'psy professions' have led us in the direction of strengthening the concentration on the individual in trying to understand the reasons for human difficulty and distress. They have been blinkered when it comes to identifying the social origins of distress, particularly the more 'distal' sources of power or powerlessness in people's lives. For example, Smail (1991) believed that much of his patients' insecurity could be traced to the disruption and confusion caused by mergers and takeovers of international capital. People were often left in despair and their inclination to blame themselves for their circumstances was reinforced, he argued, by the use of concepts such as 'stress management' or 'coping skills'. He particularly noted the neglect of social class:

> While it is considered quite in order to focus on, for example, the 'irrationality' of the patient's 'cognitions' and to imply thereby a voluntaristic psychology of 'change' contingent upon professional criticism, it might seem almost indecent to explicate his or her predicament in terms of class disadvantage ... And yet

> there can be little doubt that, particularly perhaps in English society, occupancy of a negatively valued class position entails much more than mere economic deprivation: it establishes within the individual a (realistic) sense of inferiority which ... colours almost every aspect of his or her social conduct and awareness. How can any psychology purporting to confront personal distress fail to address this issue? (Smail, 1991, p. 63).

Much of the blame is laid at Freud's door for having abandoned his seduction theory, which threatened to expose the prevalence of sexual abuse perpetrated by adult males, in favour of a theory that focused instead on individual mental mechanisms (Masson, 1989; Pilgrim, 1991; Smail, 1991). In fact, the mental health field might have been much more socially oriented if the views of Adler had not been eclipsed relative to those of Freud and other post-Freudian psychoanalysts (Ansbacher, 1979). Adler was much more interested than Freud in the relationship between the individual and the environment, in issues of power and equality, in style of life and positive mental health. In particular he wrote about the values of democracy and cooperation, and about a concept – that has been translated into English as 'social interest' – which he considered to be a fundamental human motive. Some of his writings, however, betray what might be thought of as an over-optimistic, almost metaphysical belief in the human striving for cooperation and perfection, and a corresponding neglect of conflict (Adler, 1933/1979; Ansbacher, 1979).

Later varieties of constructivism and subjectivism, such as Kelly's (1955) personal construct theory, may have compounded the encouragement of therapists in their neglect of the significance of real-world material constraints (we consider the disputed role of social constructionism in community psychology in Chapter 2). The result is what Smail (1987, p. 67) called 'the individualisation of fault':

> ...our beliefs about our reasons for our conduct, and our official psychologies, are above all designed to repress: we come to feel personally to blame for social injustices which are in fact perpetrated far beyond the reach of our awareness (Smail, 1987, p. 69).

Masson's (1989) critique of psychotherapy rested, in addition, on the power differential between therapist and client, and the way in which it served to maintain relationships of power in society, including the powerful position of psychotherapists themselves. As Smail (1987, p. 47) put it:

> ...it [psychology] serves the interest not only of its practitioners, but more importantly of those who have actually achieved power within society and constructed an apparatus to maintain it (... not *necessarily* with any consciously evil intent).

Health psychology – a relatively new branch of psychology, promising a refreshingly new approach – has also been criticised for taking a non-critical and non-reflective stance towards health and illness, failing to address the social causes of distress and focusing all its efforts on individual assessment and individual change (Osterkamp, 1999; Fox, 2003; Fryer *et al.*, 2003; Murray & Campbell, 2003; Prilleltensky & Prilleltensky, 2003a). Murray and Campbell (2003, p. 231) put it thus:

> Through persistently directing attention towards the individual level of analy-
> sis in explaining health-related behaviours, health psychology has contributed
> to masking the role of economic, political and symbolic social inequalities in
> patterns of ill-health, both globally and within particular countries.

Nor has humanistic psychology escaped criticism for its concentration on self-
actualisation, with its assumption that individual emancipation is possible, irrespective of social restraints. In Osterkamp's (1999) view this has turned responsibility on to those suffering misfortunes, hence serving the interests of those with
greater power who need to feel no guilt at others' misfortunes.

How Most Prevention has Remained Person Centred

As a corrective to the dominance of individual therapy, in the early days of community psychology prevention appeared to offer the promising way forward (Bloom,
1968; Heller *et al.*, 1984; Orford, 1992). Blair (1992), for example, writing from Britain
in the early 1990s, was hopeful about the prospects for primary prevention in the
area of mental health, although he recognised that it was, ". . . still in its infancy relative to other levels of prevention and is, as yet, built upon shaky research foundations" (p. 88). Both in Western Europe and North America he saw preventive work
as neglected and marginal within mental health services. Writing from the USA
nearly a decade later, Cowen (2000) similarly concluded that although the evidence
was by then strong for the efficacy of mental health primary prevention (Durlak,
1995, 1997; Durlak & Wells, 1997; Albee & Gullotta, 1997), the mental health system
as a whole remained dominated by an after-the-event, repair-oriented model with
relative neglect of before-the-fact, 'upstream' prevention. Albee (interviewed by
Guernina, 1995) was equally critical. Although individual therapy could do little
to alter the main social sources of people's problems – unemployment for example – the demand for clinical psychology in the USA had greatly expanded from
the time of the Second World War, when large numbers of servicemen and women
developed mental and emotional problems, to the time when he was being interviewed about his career as a psychologist. By then many US clinical psychologists
were in private practice and moves were afoot, encouraged by the pharmaceutical
industry, to obtain drug prescription privileges for clinical psychologists.

Even when prevention rather than treatment has been attempted – such a central theme in the history of community psychology – the form it has taken has
sometimes been criticised as well. An important distinction that is often pointed
out is that between the specific prevention of a particular problem or disease, and
the more general enhancement or promotion of health or well-being. Blair (1992)
referred approvingly to a shift that had occurred in the 1970s away from an exclusive focus on the specific towards considering the general role of stress, differing
ways of managing stress or responding to crises, and the generally protective effects
of social support. He referred, as illustrations, to British work by Brown and Harris
(1978, and see later chapters) on the importance of support from a confiding partner
in protecting against depression, and by Quinton *et al.* (1984) on the prevention of
adult difficulties in women brought up in institutions. Durlak and Wells (1997), in

the USA, also referred to many researchers having widened their goals beyond the prevention of specific disorders, and a trend towards including the enhancement of protective factors (Hawkins *et al.*, 1992), as well as a move towards aiming for the development of positive 'competencies' as well as preventing problems.

Such trends may not have been maintained, however. Rappaport (1992) described what he saw as a dramatic reversion in the USA from 1980 onwards (with a US administration that did not share its predecessor's commitment to community mental health), towards a narrowing of the concept of prevention, now largely being interpreted as the prevention of specific disorders. Writing nearly a decade later, Cowen (2000) was still of the view that the dominant prevention model was that of forestalling serious psychological disorder, requiring that the disorder to be prevented be specified and prevention programmes be designed, tested and evaluated in the light of knowledge about risk and protective factors relating to the specific disorder. Difficulties for that model, according to Cowen, were that paths linking psychosocial risks and a specific disorder were often complex and individual, with both multi-causality and multi-finality being features (i.e. that any particular disorder may come about for very different reasons and via different routes, and that any given risk factor can lead to diverse negative outcomes). Such difficulties had reactivated interest in more general, positive health-building or wellness-enhancing alternatives. Although the two strategies – disorder prevention and wellness enhancement – were not antagonistic, they were distinct conceptually, tactically, and practically, as summarised in Table 1.3.

Wellness enhancement Cowen saw as: more oriented towards whole populations; driven more by protective, health-building factors than by risk factors; aiming to promote wellness from early in life and to maintain and foster it across the lifespan; likely to target broader, ongoing challenges rather than circumscribed, time-limited risks; using tactics maintained over lengthy periods of time, at different levels and in different settings; and calling on the expertise of diverse specialists ranging from teachers to urban planners. Unlike disorder prevention, which has the immediate appeal of promising the prevention of troubling problems – such as substance misuse or major mental disorder, with associated cost savings – wellness enhancement offered fewer immediate, tangible payoffs, was likely to involve long gestation periods and an absence of obvious links to the prevention of specific disorders. It was therefore vulnerable to being seen as dispensable.

Rappaport (1992) suggested that the narrowing down on a disease prevention model in the 1980s was more political than scientific, reflecting a preference for individual over social explanations for deviance during politically conservative times – although he added that in western societies there is a tendency always to blame the individual whatever the government in power. The broader approach to prevention was likely to ally itself with those wishing to redefine social problems and take part in social action research, such as feminists, former patients of mental health services, participants in the self-help and mutual aid movements, and neighbourhood organisation and ethnic minority group leaders. Scientists and practitioners always needed patrons for their research and services, and in modern times the patron was likely to be government in one form or another. Hence the broader view was unlikely ever to be popular with government since it questions the way things are and threatens to undermine those in power.

Table 1.3 Two models for prevention

Model	Risk Detection-Disorder Prevention	Wellness Enhancement
CONCEPTUAL		
Overarching Goal	Prevent serious psychological disorder	Maximise psychological wellness
Guiding Strategy	Identify and neutralise negative effects of specific risk factors for targeted, maladaptive 'end-states'	Identify conditions that promote wellness both as an immediate resource and a protective force that can help to short-circuit major negative outcomes
Proximal and Distal Objectives	*Short-term*: Prevent serious psychological disorder; *Long-term*: Prevent serious psychological disorder	*Short-term*: Enhance wellness and skills; augment life satisfaction; *Long-term*: Build efficacy, and prevent serious disorders
TACTICAL		
Prime Targets	People evidencing risk-signs for specific disorders	All people
Programme Timing	Harness 'windows of opportunity' (i.e. detection of risk-signs) as basis for launching programmes	Utilise diverse levels and types of approaches across the life-span
Programme Scope	Relatively narrow, based on specific steps that seek to neutralise likely negative sequelae of risk factors	Relatively broad, including strengthening: ways of parenting and family operation; influential social settings and institutions; and society's overt (e.g. laws, policies) and hidden 'regularities'
Programme Duration	Relatively brief, to address the perceived needs of a specific disorder-prevention targeted programme	Varies with specific sub-goals and life stages but, in the aggregate, may extend across the entire life span
PRACTICAL		
Hoped for Payoff	Early reduction of frequency of occurrence of targeted psychological disorders, with associated human and financial savings	Relatively long term, with the immediate, way-station goal of promoting wellness indicators (e.g. efficacy, happiness) as well as the ultimate goal of reducing major psychological disorder
Current Interest and Support	Substantial, because of potential for short-term reduction of specific dysfunctions, and financial savings; attracts vocal advocates for preventing particular disorders	Relatively low; has limited constituencies because potential for success in reducing major disorders is non-specific and futuristic

Source: Cowen, E.L. (2000). Now that we all know that primary prevention in mental health is great, what is it? *Journal of Community Psychology*, **28**, 5–16, Table 1

A similar shift in Britain towards a focus on individual responsibility was noted by Blair (1992). The bulk of prevention work, he noted, had been person-centred in orientation. This could be seen as a failure of primary prevention specifically, and in community mental health more generally, to escape a medical model of emotional distress, and a lack of commitment of community mental health towards the more community-oriented, positive health-enhancing concept envisaged by many of its founders. Issues requiring a political frame of reference thereby became depoliticised, and prevention became adaptive rather than transformative. This perpetuated the tendency of the psy professions to focus on adjusting the 'under-privileged' and to avoid attacking the 'over-privileged' (Kolstad, 1987, cited by Blair, 1992), hence helping to maintain those aspects of the existing social order which might be contributing to the distress of individuals.

Levine (1998) gave two specific US examples. One was the lobbying of the US Congress by the National Rifle Association in order to limit research exploring the link between handgun registration and health. The second was the example of sexual abstinence programmes in the USA, such as Best Friends, supported by prominent political figures and rapidly becoming adopted nationally in the USA despite absence of evidence of its effectiveness and some evidence of its *lack* of effectiveness. The need to accept that prevention is political was underlined by Albee (interviewed by Guernina, 1995) when he suggested that, "...prevention efforts almost always mean changes in the social structure, doing something about injustice and about unemployment and poverty" (p. 208).

Much of existing prevention work, despite the enormous gains in the theory and practice made by 'prevention science', had, in Tseng *et al.*'s (2002) view, targeted person-centred deficits among high-risk populations, risking victim blaming and disempowerment through labelling and reduced expectations. Even an emphasis on positive outcomes, as in wellness enhancement and competence promotion, might carry the same risks and serve to maintain the status quo: parenting classes for low-income mothers, for example, were unlikely to alter the dynamics of priv-ilege and oppression and would run the risk of reinforcing assumptions that such mothers are deficient in parenting skills. Despite much of the rhetoric of commu-nity psychology regarding prevention, there had been comparatively little psycho-logical prevention that adopted a social change orientation. They believed there were four ways in which their own conception of the promotion of social change could be distinguished from previous concepts of promotion. First, it aimed to pro-mote positive processes rather than particular end-states or outcomes. Secondly, it targeted social systems rather than individuals, hence allowing for alternative individual pathways for diverse individuals. Third, it showed an appreciation of variations by context, including time, culture, and power structures. Fourth, and most importantly, their framework paid careful attention to values, language, and critical systems analysis. Emphasised was the need to continually examine and re-examine the values of various stakeholders, to generate dialogue, and to ask for whom and in which context a process might be adaptive. Central to their framework was the need to begin with a critical analysis of the system: "...the need to crit-ically view the current, existing system of assumptions and rules in which social *problems* and their *solutions* have been defined and understood " (p. 409). Social change involved more than targeting individuals or small groups for change; it necessitated changing the relationships or rules that operate within the system to maintain the status quo, including existing relationships of power. That is what some systems theorists have called 'second-order change' (Watzlawick *et al.*, 1974) in distinction to 'first-order' individual or small group change. As examples of work that was moving in the right direction Tseng *et al.* cited Fairweather and colleagues' Lodge programme and the work of the Pacific Institute of Community Organizing (PICO) – both described in Part IV.

Also critical of much prevention work was Potts (2003), who focused his critique on prevention programmes in schools (many included in a large meta-analytic review by Durlak & Wells, 1997), from the perspective of emancipatory education in African American communities in the USA. Schools, he argued, were by no means politically neutral, tending to inculcate pupils into the dominant system, and perpetuating oppression and the status quo, "... by marginalizing voices, histories, values, and experiences of oppressed groups; emphasizing the 'classics' and canons of the hegemonic culture; instilling values consistent with the status quo (e.g. individualism, competition, etc.); and ignoring issues such as colonialism and racism" (p. 174). Furthermore, Potts drew attention to inequities in school funding and the fact that African USAmerican students were disproportionately to be found among the expelled, suspended, and those in special programmes for the disturbed, disabled or retarded. In that context, primary prevention programmes that targeted the substance abuse, school maladjustment, teen pregnancy, delinquency and violence of individual students, without paying attention to the historical and socio-political forces that were in operation, ran the risk of protecting and maintaining the status quo, and sending a message that achievement was based strictly upon individual ability and merit and that individuals had only themselves to blame.

Emancipatory models of African USAmerican education, on the other hand, located problems such as substance abuse and violence within a context of the history of violence and abuse experienced by people of African descent. Such African-centred schools in the USA, of which Potts stated there were over 400, were far more than multi-cultural education programmes with additive content. Rather, they aimed at something fundamentally different that 'reclaimed historical memory' (Martín-Baró, 1994 – see Chapter 2), reconnecting students with African and African USAmerican history, traditions, values and principles. The approach to violence, for example, "... is one in which the student is not singled out and castigated as the primary source of violence, yet is challenged to not contribute to a process that continues to harm the community" (p. 181).

Like Tseng *et al.* (2002), Potts (2003) had challenging words for community psychology. The latter was at risk, he thought, of being part of what West (1982, p. 120, cited by Potts, 2003, p. 176) called a "neo-hegemonic... [culture that]... postures as an oppositional force, but, in substance, is a manifestation of people's allegiance and loyalty to the status quo". The kind of interventions that Potts described might not, he thought, be the kinds that many community psychologists would feel comfortable with, but would require a willingness to be involved in 'horizontal' as opposed to 'vertical' collaborations and a commitment to a liberation psychology.

Blair (1992), Albee (1995) and Levine (1998) were among those advocating a broader role for community psychology, involving efforts to change the structures and practices of organisations and institutions, and engaging with public policy, which might include advocating for changes in the law. Objections to moving more into the sphere of political activity, "... ignores the fact that current practice, to the extent that it serves to maintain existing power structures and social inequalities, is also political" (Blair, 1992, p. 87).

THE NEW PUBLIC HEALTH PSYCHOLOGY

In Britain public health psychology is being suggested as a new sub-discipline of psychology, emerging from behavioural medicine, public health, health psychology, and health promotion (Hepworth, 2004). Critical voices are being raised in that context which are encouraging because they hit some of the same notes being struck by critics in community psychology. The idea of a public health psychology has attractions since at least some of the matters that have been of concern to the public health movement are the very ones that are of most interest to community psychology.

The history of public health in Britain (Lewis, 1991), as in the USA (Fee & Porter, 1991), is a long one, certainly going back as far as Chadwick's 1842 report on the health of the working classes that recommended such measures as the provision of clean water supplies, effective sewerage and drainage, and removal of refuse from the streets, as the means of preventing disease, and which established the basis for the sanitary engineering approach to health that, in one form or another, was one of the major approaches to public health in Britain for the following 100 years.

The unequivocally environmental approach of Chadwick and mid-nineteenth-century medical reformers such as Simon in Britain and Virchow in Germany, who believed in medicine as politics (Fee & Porter, 1991), had given way by the time of the First World War to a more personal approach that emphasised what individuals could do to ensure personal hygiene (Lewis, 1991). Maternal and child health, for example, was seen in terms of discrete personal health problems, requiring the attention of health visitors, infant welfare centres, and better maternity services. Mothers were being encouraged, for example, to breast feed and to strive for higher standards of domestic hygiene. Socialist campaigners Sidney and Beatrice Webb were strong supporters of public health, encouraging local authority public health departments to create, "in the recipient an increased feeling of personal obligation and even a new sense of social responsibility ... the very aim of the sanitarians is to train the people to better habits of life" (Webb, Sidney & Beatrice, 1901, p. 206, cited by Lewis, 1991, p. 201). In Lewis's (1991) view the British public health movement had not recovered, by the time she was writing, a thorough-going environmental–political model, and it had certainly not, as some had hoped it would, occupied a central role in medicine. The National Health Service was open to criticism that it was rather more a national sickness service. The following, from a report on training of medical students in preventive medicine in 1930, might well have been true 50 years later and, with a few changes of wording, could be said to be true of psychology still:

> The medical student lives in the atmosphere of the dissecting room, the laboratory, the operating theatre and the hospital ward. His [sic] whole attention is directed to what is abnormal and he is taught to think almost entirely in terms of individual sick persons and never at all to regard himself as a member of a profession with great communal responsibilities (Archives of the Society of Medical Officers of Health, 1930, cited by Lewis, 1991, p. 208).

Hepworth (2004) was positive about the revitalisation of public health in Britain at the turn of the millennium, with increasing recognition of inequalities in health and the need to overcome them (e.g. the British government's policy paper on a new health strategy for England, *Saving Lives: Our Healthier Nation*, Department of Health, 1999), and the development of new infrastructure including the establishment of Public Health Observatories in England and Wales and the Public Health Institute in Scotland. She saw a number of elements as necessary for an adequate public health psychology theory. One was epistemological: a realisation that for a *public* health psychology it was imperative to move away from a view of health as being essentially an individual phenomenon, focused on modifying risk factors such as behaviours related to diet and exercise. A second was a multi-level approach, recognising that improvement in health required strategies at individual, social-relational, and structural levels – all the way from individuals' health knowledge to promoting new legislation such as banning smoking in public places. That would require drawing on other sub-disciplines in psychology, including social and community psychology, and other social sciences such as cultural and communication studies. Third, health behaviour needed to be understood within its social and cultural context. Fourth, public health psychologists should be part of a critical move away from an essentialist, individual focus on health that had dominated health psychology and health education and promotion without much criticism in the 1980s:

> The conceptualization and design of contemporary health interventions need to fully embrace public health practice that eschews individual blame and responsibility as a means to solving problems that are structural, gendered, cultural, social, economic, political and environmental in nature (p. 47).

Hepworth saw psychology, historically practised as a mono-discipline, as lagging behind the more multi-disciplinary and inter-disciplinary field of public health in Britain, and as marginal to public health training programmes. Psychology needed to catch up by focusing on, "... public rather than individual health, inequalities in health, multi-method design and multidisciplinary and interdisciplinary practice" (p. 52), and by sharing with public health increasing recognition of the global nature of public health and the issues it faces. Murray *et al.* (2004) also recommended that, instead of maintaining psychology's carefully nurtured boundaries, community health psychologists should welcome the blurring of traditional boundaries between disciplines, and seek alliances with other health and social sciences that are further ahead in developing a critical perspective and recognising the centrality of power.

There are many indications that writers on health psychology have begun to appreciate the importance of social context. In a review by Taylor and Repetti (1997) that appeared in the *Annual Review of Psychology*, the authors asked a central question for health psychology: What is an unhealthy environment and how does it get under the skin? Among the conclusions of their lengthy review were the following:

> Individual experiences and behaviors predictive of health outcomes are nested within geographic, social, developmental, and economic environments...Psychosocial predictors of health outcomes do not occur and should not be studied in an economic, racial, developmental, and social vacuum... What is an unhealthy environment and how does it get under the skin?...the beginning of an answer is emerging. Consistently across the environments examined – community, family, work, and peers – those that threaten personal safety; that limit the ability to develop social ties; or that are characterized by conflictual, violent, or abusive interpersonal relationships are related to a broad array of adverse health outcomes. These effects appear to occur across the lifespan...(pp. 438–9).

Introducing a special issue of the *Journal of Health Psychology*, Vinck *et al.* (2004) stated their view that mainstream health psychology, traditionally restricted to individual- or group-focused methods, was thereby hindered in making the contribution to public health that it should be making. However uneasy it might make health psychologists feel to work at unaccustomed levels, they needed to work with systems and with those with control over environmental determinants, such as politicians, the food industry, and local communities. The prevention and minimisation of harm associated with alcohol consumption is an example, where interventions can range from: alcohol education/health promotion; to specific environmental initiatives such as advocating for toughened drinking glasses to minimise alcohol-related violent harm, and labelling of drinks containers; to forms of community action and attempts to influence alcohol control policies (Plant & Harrison, 2001). In similar vein, Murphy and Bennett (2004) argued for a psychological approach to public health that encouraged the development of social, organisational, and economic networks, with a long-term goal of increasing social cohesion and social capital (see Chapter 6 for a discussion of social capital). They cited examples of: the influence of gender–power relations on the different positions of men and women in the negotiation of safer sexual practices; and the low power position of young injecting drug users as a factor accounting for the sharing of injecting equipment. More generally they advocated that health psychology might move, "...from a predominantly social regulationist model of prevention to one that is more radical structuralist in nature" (p. 14).

The problem of how to conceptualise the relationship between macro-level, sociopolitical, economic and cultural factors and individual health – a constant theme throughout the present book – was addressed by Cornish (2004). The 'biopsychosocial model', she argued, had failed to challenge the dominance of the biomedical model, and had not proposed theoretical relationships between biological, psychological, and social levels. For example, Bronfenbrenner's (1979) influential ecological model (summarised in Figure 1.2) had the advantage of defining meso- and exo-levels in such a way that it could be seen how they affected concrete experience in a person's micro-systems. The way in which the macro-system affected the micro-system was not clearly specified, however. Without that relationship being satisfactorily theorised, there was the constant danger of slipping back into

Micro-level

> Systems of which the individual person has direct experience on a regular basis, e.g. home, school, work group, club

Meso-level

> System consisting of two or more of a person's micro-level systems and the links between them, e.g. home–school, hospital–patient's family, mother's family–father's family after separation

Exo-level

> Systems that influence the person and the person's micro- and meso-level systems, but which the person has no direct experience of him/herself, e.g. a school governing body, a parent's place of work, the county transport department

Macro-level

> Systems on a larger scale which determine the prevailing ideology and social structure within which the individual person and his/her micro-, meso- and exo-level systems operate, e.g. current rate of unemployment, other conditions of the labour market, gender roles in society

Figure 1.2   Bronfenbrenner's ecological model of systems at four levels
Source: Bronfenbrenner, U. (1979). *The Ecology of Human Development: Experiments by Nature and Design*. London: Harvard University Press

reductive or individualistic language and theorising and person-blaming problem definitions.

The solution to this problem proposed by Cornish was to put at the centre of her approach, "...relationships rather than elements, change processes rather than stable states, and processes of mutual constitution rather than one-way, cause-effect determinism" (p. 284). The basic unit of analysis would be the 'activity system' – a culturally mediated collective activity centred around some particular object or aim – such as the joint activity of a teacher and pupils studying a particular topic. Although such an activity system is concrete and localised, it is at the same time historically and culturally produced, and language and ideology are vital and ever-present (hence going beyond Barker's, 1968, 1978, idea of a 'behaviour setting' – a highly influential idea in an earlier era of community psychology – see Orford, 1992, for a summary, and Chapter 3 of the present book). Within the operation of such activity settings it was possible to identify 'reflected mediating moments' when the influence of macro-level factors could particularly be seen (Seidman's, 1988, 'social regularities' and Tseng *et al.*'s, 2002, 'recurring transactions' are similar ideas). Cornish provided an example from a study, involving semi-structured interviews and group discussions with sex workers and other local people (HIV prevention and community development project staff, clients of sex workers, brothel managers) in the largest red light district in Kolkata, India. In this context a mediating moment that helps show up the link between a sex worker's health risk and her economic and social disadvantage is the moment at which the sex worker feels that she cannot take time to convince a client to use a condom. The 'madam' system, in which a brothel manager employs one or more sex workers, discourages safe sexual practices because the madam's economic interest is tied to the sex worker's earnings, so the latter cannot afford the time to negotiate with a client, or to run the risk of losing the client to another sex worker who may be more accommodating (part of the work of the local prevention project was to disrupt this effect of poverty on health, by encouraging unity among sex workers and commitment to universal condom use, comparing the situation to that of other workers who have trade unions).

Albee and Fryer (2003) have advocated the development of a critical public health psychology, "... which could be as effective in preventing mental ill health and promoting positive mental health in the future as public health medicine has been in preventing physical ill health and promoting positive physical health in the past" (p. 74). Their challenge was a radical one, namely to find ways of preventing and overcoming the noxious effects of racism, sexism and classism, of the stigmatising and disabling stereotypes of mental illness portrayed by the mass media and popular culture, of unemployment and the so-called flexible labour market, of tobacco companies, the pharmaceutical industry that has such a stake in individual treatment, and of corporations generally with their drive for profits and limited capacity for empathy with those harmed in the process, and a patriarchy that all the world's major religions supported. That would require a shift away from the widespread preference that existed for individual treatment, towards prevention at the collective, public level. The latter would not only be difficult to evaluate, less visible, and perhaps conferring lower status to those employed in it, but also, because it would be likely to require organisational, institutional, and social change, and the conceding of power and control, it would be challenging to the status quo and resisted by those who have a stake in it.

Marks (1996, 2002) has provided a useful summary of the options for health psychology. He described the development of health psychology from the 1970s onwards, outlining four alternative approaches to the subject, summarised in Table 1.4. The first and most dominant approach he termed 'clinical health psychology'. Partly overlapping with clinical psychology, that approach was located within the healthcare system and had adopted the, in his view rather nebulous and insubstantial, biopsychosocial model as an attempt to challenge the more limited biomedical model. Although 'public health psychology' – the second approach – placed greater emphasis on health promotion and prevention, on multi-disciplinary activity and on public health interventions and evaluation, it could be criticised for stressing individual responsibility for health and hence risking a victim-blaming stance. Marks' (2002) third approach, 'community health psychology', was situated mainly outside of the healthcare system, in coalition with members of vulnerable groups and communities, targeting conditions such as social exclusion and poverty that render them vulnerable, and aiming for empowerment as a main outcome.

Table 1.4   The characteristics of clinical, public, community and critical health psychology

Characteristic	Clinical health psychology	Public health psychology	Community health psychology	Critical health psychology
Theory/philosophy	Biopsychosocial model: health is the product of a combination of factors including biological, behavioural and social	No single theory and philosophy; supportive role in public health promotion which uses legal and fiscal instruments combined with preventive measures to bring about health improvements	Social and economic model: changes are needed at both individual and systems levels	Critical psychology: analysis of society and the values, assumptions and practices of psychologists, health care professionals, and of all those whom they aim to serve
Values	Increasing or maintaining the autonomy of the individual through ethical intervention	Mapping accurately the health of the public as a basis for policy and health promotion, communication and interventions	Creating or increasing autonomy of disadvantaged and oppressed people through social action	Understanding the political nature of all human existence; freedom of thought; compassion for others
Context	Patients in the health care system, i.e. hospitals, clinics, health centres	Schools, work sites, the media	Families, communities and populations within their social, cultural and historical context	Social structures, economics, government and commerce
Focus	Physical illness and dysfunction	Health promotion and disease prevention	Physical and mental health promotion	Power
Target groups	Patients with specific disorders	Population groups who are most vulnerable to health problems	Healthy but vulnerable or exploited persons and groups	Varies according to the context: from the entire global population to the health of an individual

(cont.)

Table 1.4 *(cont.)*

Characteristic	Clinical health psychology	Public health psychology	Community health psychology	Critical health psychology
Objective	To enhance the effectiveness of treatments	To improve the health of the entire population: reducing morbidity, disability, and avoidable mortality	Empowerment and social change	Equality of opportunities and resources for health
Orientation	Health service delivery	Communication and intervention	Bottom-up, working with or alongside	Analysis, argument, critique
Skills	Assessment, therapy, consultancy and research	Statistical evaluation; knowledge of health policy; epidemiological methods	Participatory and facilitative; working with communities; community development	Theoretical analysis; critical thinking; social and political action; advocacy; leadership
Discourse and buzz words	'Evidence-based practice'; 'Effectiveness'; 'Outcomes'; 'Randomised controlled trials'	'Responsibility'; 'Behaviour change'; 'Risk'; 'Outcomes'; 'Randomised controlled trials'	'Freedom'; 'Empowering'; 'Giving voice to'; 'Diversity'; 'Community development'; 'Capacity building'; 'Sense of community'; 'Inequalities'; 'Coalitions'	'Power'; 'Rights'; 'Exploitation'; 'Oppression'; 'Neo-Liberalsm'; 'Justice'; 'Dignity'; 'Respect'
Research methodology	Efficacy and effectiveness trials; quantitative and quasi-experimental methods	Epidemiological methods; large-scale trials; multivariate statistics; evaluation	Participant action research; coalitions between researchers, practitioners and communities; multiple methodologies	Critical analysis combined with any of the methods used in the other three approaches

Source: reproduced with permission from Marks, D.F. (2002). Editorial essay. Freedom, responsibility and power: contrasting approaches to health psychology. *Journal of Health Psychology*, 7, 5–19, Table 1

Finally, 'critical health psychology' used, ". . . theoretical analysis, critical thinking, social and political action, advocacy, and leadership skills . . . to analyse how power, economics and macro-social processes influence and/or structure health, health care, health psychology, and society at large" (p. 15).

Marks recognised that many health psychologists used more than one of those four approaches, some using three or even all four. He believed them to be complementary and looked forward to greater integration. By the time of his later, 2002, article, he believed things had moved on from 1996 when he had seen health psychology as still heavily dominated by individualistic approaches, concepts, and models such as 'locus of control', self-efficacy, hardiness, Type A behaviour, and the 'theory of reasoned action', derived solely from psychology, lacking in ecological validity and indifferent to culture. There had been neglect of key variables such as social support resources, social class, and material circumstances. Health psychology at that time remained detached from policy matters, and had taking little account of health inequalities (Marks, 1996).

Murray *et al.* (2004) have also contrasted clinical health psychology with community health psychology, the contrasts being summarised in Table 1.5. Their view of community health psychology was that of a psychology which, ". . . emphasizes a critical examination of professional and social power and social change as a necessary strategy for the promotion of health" (p. 328). A similar contrast was drawn by Campbell and Murray (2004) between what they called 'accommodationist' and 'critical' community psychology (terms used by Seedat *et al.*, 2001, cited by Campbell & Murray, 2004). Clinical, accommodationist or mainstream health psychology had focused on individual and micro-social factors, had focused analysis on the impact on health of family, neighbour, peer or sexual relationships, had developed interventions either of a clinical kind in medical settings, or health promotion programmes in the community emphasising lifestyle change, and had followed general psychology's fascination with method. Despite the rapid growth in numbers of health psychologists, their voices had been relatively absent from debates about health inequalities and social injustices, and health psychology had not focused on the larger macro-social determinants of health and illness which lie beyond the boundaries of the families and local communities which had been the focus of most attention. As Campbell and Murray (2004, pp. 191, 192) put it:

> . . . if community psychologists ignore how people are limited by wider structural and institutional structures, they become part of a victim-blaming enterprise. Such analyses implicitly blame local community members for problems whose origins lie outside of their power and control . . . it is vitally important that conceptualizations of participation and community development are located against the backdrop of wider conceptualizations of politics and power.

Critical community health psychology, on the other hand, did not ignore the broader social and political context: it developed a critical consciousness of oppressive relationships and the operation of power, including gross inequalities in material wealth and gender relations. Campbell and Murray (2004) drew here on the work of Freire (1973, and see Chapter 2) including the concept of *conscientisation* and the notion of *praxis* – ". . . action informed by critical social analysis, springing from

Table 1.5 Assumptions and practices of clinical and community health psychology

Assumptions and practices	Clinical health psychology	Community health psychology
Levels of analysis	Intrapersonal or micro-systems	Ecological (micro, meso, macro)
Problem definition	Based on individualistic philosophies that blame the victim	Problems are reframed in terms of social context and cultural diversity
Timing of intervention	Remedial (late)	Prevention (early)
Focus of intervention	Deficits/problems	Competence/strengths
Goals of intervention	Reduction of 'maladaptive' behaviours	Promotion of competence and well-being
Type of intervention	Treatment/rehabilitation	Self-help/community development/social action
Role of 'client'	Compliance with professional treatment regimes	Active participant who exercises choice and self-direction
Role of professional	Expert (scientist-practitioner)	Resource collaborator (scholar-activist)
Type of research	Applied research based on positivistic assumptions	Participatory action research based on critical and constructivist assumptions
Ethics	Emphasis on individual ethics, value neutrality and tacit acceptance of status quo	Emphasis on social ethics, emancipatory values and social change
Interdisciplinary ties	Psychiatry, clinical social work	Critical sociology, health sciences, philosophy, social work, political science, planning and geography

Source: adapted from Prilleltensky, I. & Nelson, G. (1997) and reproduced with permission from Murray, M., Nelson, G., Poland, B., Maticka-Tyndale, E. & Ferris, L. (2004). Assumptions and values of community health psychology. *Journal of Health Psychology*, **9**, 323–33, Table 1

engagement in the real world" (Campbell & Murray, 2004, p. 189). Their concluding recommendation was that,

> . . . as health psychologists we transform ourselves from scientist-practitioners to scholar-activists. Through linking analysis and action our research should not simply be a thing in itself but a means of helping to create health through the broader struggle for social justice (p. 194).

CRITICAL PSYCHOLOGY

Much of this first chapter has taken a critical stance towards the way in which psychology as a discipline has neglected the very aspects of the subject that are of most interest to community psychology. Not only that, but it has also come to be realised that this neglect often has the malign effect of diverting focus from attention on the way in which the status quo may be serving to perpetuate injustice and inequality; hence psychology fails to address major sources of difficulty and distress. Community psychology therefore needs not only to claim part of the discipline of psychology for itself, but also needs to maintain its critical stance towards the parent discipline – and related disciplines too. The rise of a branch of the subject referring to itself as 'critical psychology' has therefore been very welcome.

Critical psychology is important for community psychology because it provides the latter with a core part of its necessary framework of philosophy and values. Critical psychology is about identifying, reflecting critically on, and bringing out into the open the ways in which the dominant, prevailing, or 'ruling' ways of understanding and doing things support the interests of some people and groups and not those of others. It is therefore about ideology and power (Osterkamp, 1999; Fryer *et al.*, 2003). Hepburn (2003, p. 34) suggested that ideology could be treated as a, "... system of concepts or ideas that hides oppression or prevents radical action".

Critical psychology often turns its attention on psychology itself. Indeed the practice of psychology has been a particular object of its critical reflections. Psychology has been criticised for failing to engage with psychological aspects of socially caused problems, and colluding with dominant forces in society, even allying itself frequently with those who favour sexism, racism, and other forms of social oppression, rather than being in the vanguard of promoting social justice and human liberation (Austin & Prilleltensky, 2001; Fryer *et al.*, 2003; Murray & Campbell, 2003). According to Austin and Prilleltensky (2001, p. 1), "Critical psychology focuses on reshaping the discipline of psychology in order to promote emancipation in society". Fryer *et al.* (2003, p. 1) wrote that a critical community psychology should be, "... problem driven, value committed, politically positioned ... [and] ideologically progressive".

Hepburn (2003) suggested that feminism had been the paradigm of how a critical approach can be effective in psychology and more generally. Following Wilkinson (1997, cited by Hepburn, 2003), she summarised the ways in which psychology had tended to work in an opposite direction by asserting women's inferiority, hence supporting the status quo: for example measures had repeatedly taken the male as the norm; the huge body of work on sex differences had uncritically assumed that such differences were 'essential'; and work had focused on internalised attributes such as 'fear of success', thus shifting the focus on to the individual and away from the social origins of inequality. Psychology can be criticised also for its dominant methods of research; for example, its preference for experimental methods that extract people from their social environments and bring them into the laboratory in order to be able to study them more 'objectively', and for its preoccupation with classifying, measuring, regulating and shaping individuals (Osterkamp, 1999; Austin & Prilleltensky, 2001).

The origins of critical psychology are traced by some (e.g. Hepburn, 2003) to the pre-Second World War Frankfurt school in Germany (including Fromm, Adorno and others, most of whom were Jewish Marxist radicals, forced to flee from fascism) and by others (e.g. Austin & Prilleltensky, 2001) to post-war German critical psychology (associated with the Free University of Berlin and particularly associated with the name of Klaus Holzkamp – Tolman, 1994; Osterkamp, 1999). Particularly influential on modern critical psychology have been the writings of the French social theorist Michel Foucault (e.g. 1977, 1979). The importance of Foucault for critical psychology, according to Hepburn (2003), lies in his elaboration of the Marxist notion of power, and the way he saw power, knowledge and subjectivity as linked. Unlike Marx's monolithic concept of the power exerted by one social class upon another, Foucault had seen power relations running through all the social settings and social relations that people are part of, and through all the everyday routines, rituals and disciplines that a person engages in.

A principle in critical psychology is that critical psychologists should be among their own strongest critics, and indeed there are many lively controversies within critical psychology. Among those described by Hepburn (2003) are those surrounding sexuality, feminism, and psychoanalysis. For example, writers such as Kitzinger (1987, cited by Hepburn, 2003) and Butler (1990, cited by Hepburn, 2003) have been critical of the way in which the gay and lesbian and feminist movements, despite their successful social action orientations, had accepted uncritically traditional categories such as 'homosexual' and 'woman', the very categories that have supported oppressive ideologies and practices in the past. What is needed, such writers argued, is a more thorough going post-modernist approach that critically deconstructs those categories and questions whether they are as natural or 'essential' as they have been made out to be.

A different kind of controversy has surrounded the value of the psychoanalytic tradition in critical psychology. Perhaps strangely, a number of prominent critical psychologists have been attracted to psychoanalytic ideas (e.g. Hollway, 2006; Billig, 2006; Parker, 1997). According to Hepburn (2003), the attraction has been that psychoanalysis appears to offer a 'theory of the subject' that fills the gap left by the materialist, anti-individualist orientation of Marxism. Furthermore it offers to correct the assumptions in traditional psychology that we are rational subjects, that cognition can be separated from emotion, and that the individual and the social can be separated. Psychoanalysis may appear attractive because it recognises people's fundamental irrationality, has a life history orientation that challenges the traditional individual/social split, and recognises the inter-dependence of cognition and affect. Others, such as Osterkamp (1999) and Hepburn (2003), have remained sceptical, however, on the grounds that psychoanalysis is basically an individualistic model, that its notions of subjectivity are made to seem fixed and natural, and that, at least in its classic form, it is misogynist and dangerous, as evidenced by Freud's own abandonment of the theory of children's sexual abuse by adults (the seduction theory) in favour of a theory that totally inverted the relationship between victims and perpetrators (children's alleged sexual desires for their parents, as in the Oedipus theory).

Whatever the answers to those and other dilemmas about critical psychology, there is general agreement about the values espoused by critical psychologists and about the need to engage in social action. Exposing and working to eliminate oppression, promoting social justice, freedom and emancipation, and siding clearly with the interests of the poor, oppressed and disenfranchised, are values widely

1. Social interventions and changes in public policy; for example by developing critical work, a contribution can be made to public information campaigns, changes in policy etc.

2. Rhetorical interventions, for example using discursive research to expose the ways in which ideology is used to support current practices, hence encouraging social change.

3. Intervening in psychology, for example by challenging its individualistic and cognitivist bias and identifying the ways in which it is complicit with oppressive values and practices.

4. Practical interventions, for example alongside oppressed and marginalised groups or relatively powerless users of services.

5. Postmodern interventions, examining common sense understandings, how 'truth' is constructed and claims made about 'reality'.

Figure 1.3   Five ways in which critical psychology can address social problems and oppression according to Hepburn
Source: Hepburn, A. (2003) *An Introduction to Critical Social Psychology*. London: Sage

shared (e.g. Austin & Prilleltensky, 2001; Fryer *et al.*, 2003; Murray & Campbell, 2003). An element frequently stressed is the requirement to 'give voice' to those who have been denied a voice either because accounts of their experiences have not been heard and/or because their input to social policies that affect them has not been sought (Sampson, 2000; Ussher, 2000; Austin & Prilleltensky, 2001). Critical psychologists want to enable the voices of the powerless to be heard more and the voices of the hitherto powerful – specifically the interests of large corporations and the voices of noxious consumerism, as represented for example in the media – rather less (Fox, 2003; Lyons, 2000; Murray & Campbell, 2003; Prilleltensky & Prilleltensky, 2003a).

But, as Austin & Prilleltensky (2001, p. 6) put it:

> ... this work needs to be translated into social actions that have a direct impact on the life circumstances of people who suffer because of globalization, unemployment and discrimination. Powerful ideas need to be matched by powerful actions.

Hepburn (2003) saw five major ways, shown in Figure 1.3, in which critical psychologists could go about actively addressing social problems and oppression. Prilleltensky and Prilleltensky (2003a) have also outlined an agenda for a critical health psychology practice. They argued that health psychology has largely adopted practices of reacting to illness rather than proactively promoting wellness, and has largely addressed problems at the individual level, rather than at the level of social systems that maintain power imbalances and therefore the conditions for ill-health. Hence they proposed a set of values for a critical health psychology, with examples of actions that can be undertaken in health settings to promote personal, relational, and collective wellness (see Table 1.6). They recognised the difficulties:

Table 1.6 Ecological levels, values and potential critical psychology interventions in health settings

Timing and population of intervention	Values and ecological levels		
	Values for Personal Wellness *self-determination, protection of health, caring and compassion* Individual Wellness	Values for Relational Wellness *Collaboration, democratic participation and respect for diversity* Group and Organisational Wellness	Values for Collective Wellness *Support for community structures, social justice* Community and Societal Wellness
Reactive to existing illness or disability	• Self-determination in rehabilitation • Power sharing in treatment plans for coping with illness and chronic pain	• Assertiveness training for hospital patients dealing with professionals • Communication training for professionals dealing with vulnerable patients	• Securing access of minorities, refugees and the poor to all health services • Lobbying for funding of health services in deprived areas
Proactive high risk	• Smoking cessation with emphasis on exploitation of community by tobacco companies • Diet and exercise programme for overweight people with emphasis on ill-effects of consumerism	• Exercise programme for disadvantaged populations at high risk for heart disease • Organisational interventions to reduce stress in patients and staff	• Self-help/mutual aid and support groups for people caring for disabled family members • Community-wide programmes to improve diet, lower alcohol consumption and increase exercise
Proactive universal	• Self-instruction guide on breast examination • Self-instruction guide on HIV prevention	• Organisational development to improve working atmosphere • Bill of rights and responsibilities for patients and staff in hospitals	• Critique and boycotts of media and corporations making profits at expense of population health • Promote social cohesion and egalitarian social policies

Source: reproduced with permission from Prilleltensky, I. & Prilleltensky O. (2003a). Towards a critical health psychology practice. *Journal of Health Psychology*, 8, 197–210, Table 2

Re-inventing ourselves as advocates, social critics, community leaders and psychologists at the same time is a necessity that may not sit well with health psychologists. However, to remain at the level of reactive or person-centred interventions is to deny a massive body of evidence linking social and economic structures to physical and psychological health (p. 208).

They also recognised the contrasting sets of values, assumptions, and practices associated with the roles of professional helper on the one hand, trying to bring about amelioration at the individual level, and critical agents of social change, trying to bring about transformation at the systems level. From the perspective of the former, a critical health psychologist should be asking: "How does our special knowledge of wellness inform our social justice work? How does our ameliorative practice inform our transformative practice? How does our insider role of wellness promoter in the health system inform our outsider role as social critic?" (Prilleltensky & Prilleltensky, 2003b, p. 243). From the latter perspective, the questions for the critical health psychologist are: "How does our knowledge of inequality and injustice inform our health psychology work? How does our transformative practice in society inform our ameliorative work in the health system? How does our outsider role as social critic inform or relate to our insider role?" (2003b, p. 243).

Since critical psychologists have been so critical of mainstream or traditional psychology – Sampson (2000) put it pithily when he wrote, "Critical psychology believes that psychology has adopted a paradigm of inquiry that is ill-suited to understanding human behaviour and experience" (p. 1) – it is not surprising that they have often felt uncomfortable working in academic psychology departments where their work may be misunderstood, discouraged, undermined, or openly attacked (Sloan, 2000; Ussher, 2000; Fox, 2003; Fryer et al., 2003). There has been lively disagreement about whether or not to stay in psychology in order to change it from inside and to introduce students to critical psychology ideas. A number of psychologists have found more productive niches, for example in departments of cultural studies, women's studies, social policy and social work, organisational and management theory, or 'third world' development (Hollway, 2000; Ussher, 2000). O'Sullivan (2000) is one who argued that, although it was important to have a critical presence within the discipline of psychology, the primary loyalty of a critical psychologist should be with progressive social movements such as the feminist, gay-lesbian, human rights, anti-racism and equity movements.

One of the implications for community psychology is clearly a need for continual self-criticism since there is always a danger that by, "...collaborating with the establishment in launching and evaluating programs that divert attention from injustice and structural oppression" (Austin & Prilleltensky, 2001, p. 5), community psychology might be practised in a way which goes against the interests of those whose emancipation and health we are trying to promote (Fryer et al., 2003).

In this chapter psychology has been challenged over the way in which it has repeatedly taken individual people out of their social contexts in order to study them more closely, in the process neglecting the very parts of psychology that are of most interest to community psychologists. Even social psychology can be charged with the same crime. Some of psychology's concepts that sound most promising from a community psychology perspective – self-efficacy and social support are examples – have largely remained at an individual level. Individual psychotherapy has been a heavy influence in psychology, with its assumption that the most important site of change is the individual person. Even prevention, which held such promise for community psychology, has not always escaped the individualism which is perhaps the cultural norm in those western nations that have led in psychology. The new public health psychology, and the relatively new critical psychology, are both promising signs that times are changing. The following chapter begins to look at some of the ideas that are near to the heart of community psychology. They include power, empowerment and liberation, and social justice.

Chapter 2
COMMUNITY PSYCHOLOGY'S CORE VALUES: EMPOWERMENT, LIBERATION AND SOCIAL JUSTICE

The principal grounds on which psychology was challenged in Chapter 1 were its continual focus on the individual person and its failure to address the wider context of people's lives, especially the material aspects and the social structures that so powerfully influence people's circumstances. From the criticisms that had been voiced about the dominance of psychotherapy and of the nature of much that comes under the heading of prevention, it is already obvious that it is the neglect of the distribution and exercise of power in its various forms that is seen as central to those critiques. Core ideas in the new public health and critical psychology movements are also about recognising and changing circumstances of disempowerment, inequality and oppression. It is these topics that have emerged as the most important in community psychology, and it is those that the present chapter briefly discusses. They are ideas that we shall meet again, repeatedly, in later chapters – inequality is a major theme of Part II, as is disempowerment in Part III, and ways of empowering groups and communities in Part IV.

EMPOWERMENT

Empowerment has occupied a prominent position in community psychology theory. For many it is the field's central concept. Among definitions of empowerment are those shown in Figure 2.1. Note that while each of those definitions stresses gaining influence, control, mastery or power, the definitions differ in subtle but important ways. Sometimes it is 'people' who are empowered, but sometimes also groups, organisations or communities. Sometimes empowerment is seen as a state, in other cases as a process. Sometimes additional features are emphasised such as critical awareness of the environment and democratic participation. Empowerment may be important but defining is not so straightforward and immediately gets us into deep waters.

Empowerment is a process by which people, organizations, and communities gain mastery over issues of concern to them (Rappaport, 1987).

Empowerment is the aim toward which we strive, a state of affairs in which people have enough power to satisfy their needs and work in concert with others to advance collective goals (Prilleltensky *et al.*, 2001).

Empowerment has been defined as the mechanism through which people gain greater control over their lives, critical awareness of the sociopolitical environment, and democratic participation in communities (Perkins & Zimmerman, 1995).

Figure 2.1   Some definitions of empowerment

Empowerment: Subjective or Material?

One of the keenest debates has been over the question of whether empowerment is viewed as intrapersonal and subjective or material and objective. The former line of thinking has been well spelt out by Zimmerman (e.g. 1995) who has discussed the concept of *psychological empowerment* (PE). Although he stressed that PE was not simply to be equated with personal characteristics such as self-esteem or competence, and that it could not be divorced from the context in which a person felt empowered, it remained for Zimmerman largely an intrapersonal construct. It was to do with people's beliefs about their capability to influence their context, understanding about how things work in that context, and the taking of action to influence the context. It was therefore about personal beliefs, understanding, and behaviour. Zimmerman (1995, p. 592) tried to make the distinction with material power very clear when he stated, "One can be psychologically empowered without having the ultimate authority or power to realize one's objectives". The example he gave, however, immediately muddies the waters. Students and parents may become better informed about how a school works, and may become more involved in decision making, but may not seek to alter the grasp that the school authorities hold on the ultimate power to set school policy. Zimmerman described that as an example of increased PE without actual power or control, but it seems equally appropriate to think of those students and parents as having gained in actual power even if in most respects the greater power remained in the hands of the authorities.

Riger (1993) criticised the way in which the concept of empowerment had been used in community psychology. She criticised it on a number of grounds, although all, she believed, followed from psychology's preference for individualistic explanations. Like others she was critical of the tendency to conflate actual power with a *sense of* empowerment. Since the latter need not necessarily result in more actual influence or control, then there is the danger that the political is made personal and that the status quo is supported rather than challenged. A related criticism was that the way empowerment was being used it seemed to be too much about the individualistic values of agency, mastery, control and status, more highly valued in US society than in others.

Francescato and Tomai (2001) have written, in similar vein, of the need for a European community psychology distinct from that in the USA. The latter, they argued, was too individually centred, with too great an emphasis on individual autonomy and individual empowerment. European community psychology should be built more on the European tradition of political concern to promote social capital (see Chapter 6), reflecting the broad cultural values shared by most Europeans, particularly those from continental Europe. In contrast to US culture, most Europeans did not believe in the myth of the 'self-made man', or that 'men are born free', but that:

> ... each person is born in a social environment embedded in an historically created hierarchical context ... , [that] a disempowered person rarely can empower herself solely by her own efforts, and that the recorded history of mankind shows that individual empowerment has occurred through collective struggles for civil, human and social rights (p. 373).

One the strongest challenges to an intrapersonal view of empowerment has come from Smail (1994, 1995, 2003; Hagan & Smail, 1997a,b), a British community clinical psychologist who has consistently taken a strong line about the dangers of psychologising the effects of structural power relations. He pointed to what he saw as a state of considerable conceptual confusion in the largely US community psychology literature on empowerment. It was not clear he concluded, whether what was being talked about was individuals' *sense of* power, or actual power of real material or political significance (Smail, 1994). The danger he saw was that:

> ... rather than developing a comprehensive theory of the way powerful influences shape individuals' experience and cause their unhappiness, together with an empirical study of how this happens, we shall slide instead into 'psychologizing' power as an internal, personal attribute (Smail, 1995, p. 351).

He believed that it was the readiness of community psychology to face up to the material components of real social power, which inevitably would reflect harmful, real-world economic and environmental factors, that constituted the field's promise of advancing understanding of how emotional distress was generated (Smail, 1994, 1995). He defined power as, "the means of obtaining security or advantage" (1995, p. 348). With the exception of a small number of psychoanalytic psychotherapists who departed from orthodox Freudian views (he cited Adler, Fromm, Horney and Sullivan) and later social theorists outside psychology (he cited Foucault), power had been virtually ignored in psychology and psychotherapy (Smail, 1995). Some of the forms of psychology dominant in the late twentieth century and the beginning of the twenty-first had gone part of the way towards a social materialist understanding but had failed on one count or another. Behavioural psychology, for so long dominant in modern psychology, had recognised the fundamental importance of the material environment, but remained largely focused on the individual. More recent constructionist psychologies (see later in this chapter), such as the discourse and narrative approaches, highlighted the social but focused on the importance of language and ideas and might therefore be thought of as 'interiorist' rather than materialist (Smail, 1995, 2003).

Reviewing papers that appeared in a special issue of the *Journal of Community and Applied Social Psychology* on Power, Control and Health, Smail (2001) took all the authors to task for assuming that material conditions can only affect people if those conditions have, "...somehow worked their way into an internal psychological apparatus" (p. 161). In his view:

> ...psychologists do not *have* endlessly to multiply vague, interior constructs to account for people's experience and conduct. It is perfectly possible to subscribe to a *psychological* theory whose fundamental concepts are material, social and environmental rather than moral, individual and interior (Smail, 2001, p. 164).

Because psychological distress is associated with lower socioeconomic status, poverty and deprivation, the failure of psychology to recognise the importance of material power and the adoption of intrapersonal explanations as the default position leads to a kind of 'internalisation' of deprivation, or what Hagan and Smail (1997a,b) called the 'moralising of power and powerlessness'. The danger is that people are then encouraged to feel a sense of personal responsibility for their social position and a sense of shame for their failure to cope. In their view psychotherapists' task should be to help their clients appreciate the reality of the lack of power, much of it 'distal' to their current lives and hence difficult to appreciate, which constitutes the real cause of current difficulties.

Hagan and Smail (1997a, b) suggested a technique – power-mapping – for describing the powers and resources available to an individual. The 'map' (an example is shown in Figure 2.2) contains sectors relevant to the four principal domains of home and family life, social life, personal resources, and material resources (very reminiscent of the four types of resources that figure in Hobfoll's (1998) conservation of resources theory – discussed in Chapter 1), the last of those being the one which they singled out as being the most important and yet the one to which therapeutic psychology had paid least attention. The map would show both the level of resources available to a person in different domains and sub-domains as well as the control that a person was able to exercise over those resources. In each area there might be assets which a person could make use of, but also liabilities which might significantly impair ability to deal effectively with circumstances.

A less extreme, but no less compelling, position on this question of subjective versus material conceptions of power and empowerment has been taken by Fryer, a British community social psychologist. He agreed with Smail that it was vital not to explain social phenomena overwhelmingly in terms of the make-up of individuals. But, equally, it was important to avoid the tendency to explain individual phenomena overwhelmingly in terms of social structure; lest we, "... render the individual a mere cipher of social forces..." (Fryer, 1998a, p. 81). Fryer has emphasised the importance of *relative* power, as in relative poverty or environmental conditions, and parted company with Smail when the latter would confine the role of psychology to helping people understand the exercise of power on their lives (Fryer, 1994). Fryer placed much more emphasis on promoting people's 'powers to modify' their

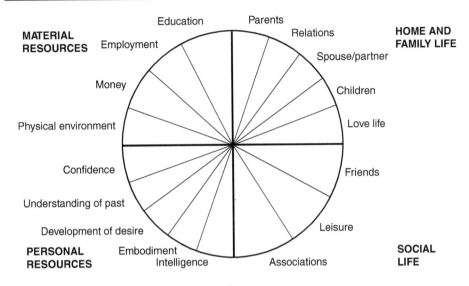

Figure 2.2 Terrain of proximal powers and resources
Source: reproduced with permission from Hagan, T. & Smail, D. (1997a). Power-mapping –
I. Background and basic methodology. *Journal of Community and Applied Social Psychology*, 7,
257–68

disadvantageous circumstances. He used the term 'proactive agency', rather than empowerment. He defined the former as:

> ...the tendency to engage in self-selected goal-directed behaviour wherein the agent chooses to take the lead, initiate and intervene in situations either by actively changing or by creatively re-perceiving and then exploiting revealed opportunities to bring about change in valued directions rather than responding to imposed change passively... (Fryer, 1994, p. 12).

According to his account, circumstances such as unemployment are disempowering, or in his terms they 'restrict agency', by undermining, restricting and frustrating it in various ways (Fryer, 1998a).

Individuals in Modern Society according to Social Theorists

Among influential social theorists of the late twentieth century, Beck and Giddens stand out as two whose thoughts on issues of agency and social structure are of special relevance for community psychology. Both have had important things to say about the relationship between individual and society. Both believed that the world had changed in a way that altered that relationship and that created new tensions and difficulties for individuals in society. Giddens (e.g. 1991) referred to a new era of 'high modernity', and Beck (e.g. 1999) wrote of 'second modernity'. Giddens rejected the idea of social structure as something that was outside of the control of the individual, preferring the conception of individuals using their

personal agency to make and remake social rules and norms. Agency and structure were hence inseparable, and social structures had no determining effects on
individuals that were independent of human agency (Best, 2003, chapter 5). In later
writings he tended to use the word 'self' rather than agency. Not surprisingly he has
been criticised for his over-emphasis on individual freedom of action and his presumption that any structural constraint can be changed by the operation of human
agency.

Beck is famous for his idea that we now live in a *Risk Society* (1986/1992), indeed a
World Risk Society (1999). The threats that face modern man and woman, he argued,
were no longer primarily material wants (both Beck and Giddens are open to the
criticism that their theories are more relevant for those living in richer countries),
but are now *risks*, often on a global scale, and often caused by the very process of
industrialisation that promised to free us from the threats associated with material
wants. Unlike the threats of earlier times, these new risks and hazards are difficult
for people to grasp: it is difficult to detect them, difficult to plan against them, and
understanding of them requires expert knowledge that is beyond most people. It is
difficult to hold any individual or institution accountable for them. The new types
of risk are simultaneously local and global, or what Robertson (1992) called 'glocal'.

Giddens and Beck come together in their portrayal of the new modernity as an
era in which we have lost the comforting securities of traditional communities and
social networks and social class identities. Individuals are cast adrift in a world
that demands of us a continual making of decisions about what we want to do and
who we want to be. Beck (1986/1992) referred to this as 'reflexive modernity', and
Giddens (1991) wrote of self as a 'reflexive project':

> The ethic of individual self-fulfilment and achievement is the most powerful
> current in modern Western society. Choosing, deciding, shaping individuals
> who aspire to be the authors of their lives, the creators of their identities, are the
> central characters of our time (Beck, 1999, p. 9).

> Life politics is a politics, not of life chances, but of life style. It concerns disputes
> and struggles about how (as individuals and as collective humanity) we should
> live in a world where what used to be fixed either by nature or tradition is
> now subject to human decisions (Giddens, 1994, pp. 14–15, cited by Best, 2003,
> p. 187).

Although inequalities persisted, even intensifying, they were no longer distributed, according to Beck and Giddens, in accordance with social class or
gender, at least not in any straightforward way (much of the material to be considered in later chapters of the present book, especially in Chapter 4, argues against
that statement). As Beck (1986/1992) put it, "... class biographies ... become trans-
formed into reflexive biographies ..." (p. 88), or, as Giddens (1994, cited by Best,
2003) had it, emancipatory politics had become life politics. The demand to make
one's own way, to 'do one's own thing', created deep uncertainties and needs
for security, while at the same time offering the promise of liberation. As well as
threatening glocal risks, modern life created many new uncertainties – the need
to create and sustain new social networks, to reconcile mobility and security, to
juggle work and home lives, while at the same time hiding the true cultural–
historical origins of these uncertainties from the people who experience them. The

tendency of psychology to put the onus for understanding and solving human problems upon individuals is therefore magnified under conditions of reflective modernity:

> Psychology has yet to undertake this historization and socio-historical revision of its forms of thinking, necessary if it is not to run aground on the appearance of individuality from which it profits by displacing the causes for problems into the very people who have them (Beck, 1986/1992, p. 119).

The Complex Nature of Empowerment

Community psychologists who have written about empowerment have stressed what a pluralistic, context-specific, and dynamic thing it is. As Foster-Fishman *et al.* (1998, p. 531) put it, "... empowerment's complexity creates a significant challenge for those interested in empowerment research and interventions". Such complexities certainly rule out the idea of any one universally applicable 'measure' of empowerment (Zimmerman, 1995). For one thing what constitutes empowerment is likely to differ for different populations of people – people of different gender, ethnic and social class background for example – depending upon their past histories and present circumstances. Furthermore, what is found to be empowering may be very different in different settings. Empowerment may look very different in different life domains, such as work, family and recreational settings. But it may also take very different forms in different types of setting within the same domain, for example in different work settings that have different norms about how decisions are made and by whom. What is more, empowerment is likely to change, sometimes quite rapidly, over time (Zimmerman, 1995).

Foster-Fishman *et al.* (1998) illustrated this complexity in their qualitative study of employees of a large state-wide organisation in the USA providing a range of services for people with disabilities. They identified six distinct pathways to employee empowerment: "(a) having opportunities for job autonomy; (b) having the freedom to be creative; (c) gaining job relevant knowledge; (d) feeling trusted and respected; (e) experiencing job fulfilment; and (f) participating in decision-making" (p. 521). It had been assumed by those who set up an empowerment intervention in the organisation, that increased empowerment would consist of greater employee participation in organisational decision making. While that was a source of empowerment for some employees, most confined their desires for empowerment to personal control in their own job domain. Their study thus provided a nice example of how definitions of empowerment imposed by leaders or researchers may not synchronise with people's own experiences. Definitions of empowerment were highly personal. For example, some employees experienced job autonomy because they were able to regulate their timetables and 'work at my own pace'. Others felt autonomous when they were able to make independent decisions about the content of their work – 'doing my work anyway I want'. Two levels of context were important to employees. One was the specific site where an employee worked, the other being the larger organisation of which the site was a part. The latter was generally seen as constraining empowerment because of the rules and regulations required of a large organisation. The work sites were where most employees experienced empowerment, although the nature of that empowerment varied from site to site depending on the different norms that currently prevailed at the site. Employee involvement in decision making was encouraged in some sites, but actively discouraged elsewhere.

Peterson and Zimmerman (2004) applied the concept of empowerment at the organisational level as a partial corrective to the way in which most empirical work on empowerment had been limited to the individual level. Even at the organisation level there was a need to make an important conceptual distinction between *empowering* and *empowered* organisations. The former focused on the ways in which organisations could empower its individual members. Peterson and Zimmerman wished to develop a framework for the latter type of organisational empowerment. They discussed a number of desired outcomes, and processes that might facilitate them, at intra-organisational, inter-organisational, and extra-organisational levels. For example, at the first of those levels, the medium or long-term viability of a local neighbourhood association might be facilitated by making sure that incentives for participation outweighed costs, and that the structure of the organisation provided opportunities for members to adopt roles that used and built their skills and abilities. At the inter-organisational level, the empowerment of a community child development organisation for families living in poverty would be facilitated by networking and building alliances with other organisations that enabled it to generate inter-agency agreements and informal arrangements with organisations providing day care, housing, or transportation (Bartle *et al.*, 2002). At the extra-organisational level, a Healthy Start family and child development organisation might use the processes of community actions, in the form of public meetings or other events, and by disseminating information, to create a new housing partnership that helped families find emergency and long-term affordable housing.

Social Psychological Theory of Power

Some of the ways in which social psychologists have theorised about power are undoubtedly relevant here (e.g. French & Raven, 1959; Wrong, 1979; Ng, 1980; Ragan & Wales, 1980; Raven, 1993). Among their insights were that power can be seen as having a number of different dimensions, and that it takes a variety of different forms. The three dimensions of *extensity*, *comprehensiveness*, and *intensity* could be distinguished. Extensity refers to the number of people over whom an individual or group has power: the state has extensive power, a parent has not. Comprehensiveness refers to the variety of other people's actions, sometimes referred to as the number of 'scopes', over which power is exercised: parents have very comprehensive power over young children, whereas health professionals have power of limited scope over their patients. Intensity is the degree of influence of one person or group over another within any one scope or sphere of action.

Variations in the nature of empowerment can also be looked at from the point of view of the different bases of power described some decades ago by social psychologists French and Raven (1959). They described six ways in which authority could be exercised, termed by them: coercive, reward, legitimate, expert, personal,

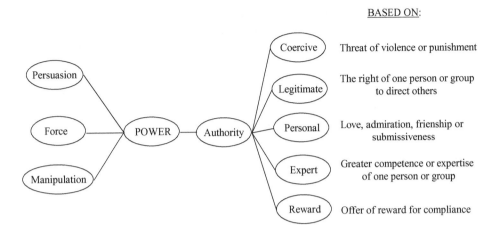

Figure 2.3   The principal forms of power
Source: based on Wrong, D. (1979). *Power: Its Forms, Bases and Uses*. Oxford, UK: Basil Blackwell

and informational power. Wrong (1979) called the last of those persuasion, and added force and manipulation to create the more complete picture of forms of power shown in Figure 2.3. Raven (1993) later elaborated that typology to include: both impersonal and personal forms of coercive and reward power; a number of different ways in which the exercise of power might be seen as legitimate (e.g. not only because the source of power held a position of authority, but also to include the example of obligation or rights on grounds of reciprocity or equity); both positive and possible negative consequences of expert and personal power (being expert or admirable may have the counter-effect of instilling distrust); and both direct and indirect forms of informational power (e.g. direct requests versus hints or suggestions). One of the ways in which such a typology may be useful for understanding empowerment is the way in which it helps understand how opportunities for empowerment are very different depending upon the position of a person, group or community in relation to others. Raven (1993) suggested, for example, that those in less powerful positions might be more likely to resort to indirect forms of informational power, while those in higher power positions may be more likely to use direct informational power.

Many theorists on power have described the ways in which different forms are often exercised in combination, how one form of power can metamorphose into another, and how the exercise of power is often hidden from view. Combined powers are particularly likely to be used by those who are in a position to wield over others power that is intensive but also extensive and/or comprehensive. Different forms of power are likely to be used sequentially, with the forms that are apparently more benign, such as the use of personal authority, used first. The possibility of using more direct forms, such as coercion or force, is always potentially available to the powerful but held in reserve and hidden unless and until necessary. Common transformations in the form of power that is used include: persuasion, repeatedly used effectively, is likely to metamorphose into competent or legitimate authority;

the use of authority, if the relatively powerless become reliant upon it, may become coercion; competent or expert authority, for example of professionals, may drift towards legitimate or even coercive authority, especially when supported by a powerful organisation of experts and when legally recognised by the state.

The often 'hidden' nature of power has been widely recognised. For one thing, power might be exercised, not by openly wielding influence on decision making, but rather by keeping information secret, controlling the agenda, and keeping important decisions from being discussed at all. Hence the status quo is preserved. But power can be even more effectively hidden by a deeper and more subtle process of shaping people's very desires and attitudes and by a general taking for granted that things are as they are. As Ng (1980, p. 14) put it:

> Power derives more from the routine application of effectively unchallenged assumptions than from the manifest dominance of one group over others in open conflict. A major source of power for dominant groups is simply the routine operation of social institutions.

Power, therefore, is depicted by most theorists as being anything other than straightforward. The bases of power are nearly always mixed. Its ground can be shifting, its operation often largely hidden. Furthermore there is usually ambivalence about it. A functional or consensus view of power emphasises the benign role of power that supports order and organisation and the ability to get things done for the general benefit. As well as that side of power, there is nearly always a conflictual side, reflecting the struggle for power between individuals or groups, and the domination of some over others. The latter is the divisive face of power as opposed to its integrating face.

Social Dominance Theory

An interesting theory that has combined individual and societal levels, and which may be of particular interest to community psychology because it addresses issues of unequal social power and oppression, is social dominance theory (Sidanius & Pratto, 1999; Pratto et al., 2000). The theory tries to explain such issues as prejudice, stereotyping, discrimination, and oppression. It draws on a wide variety of psychological, social-psychological, structural-sociological, and evolutionary theories, ranging from the theory of the authoritarian personality to Marxist theory of capitalist society, including social identity theory and ideas of social or collective representations. It draws also on modern theories of racism that suggest that blatant and extreme forms of racism, at least of some kinds, have been replaced with more subtle and indirect forms; and also 'realistic group conflict theory' that asserts, simply, that inter-group discrimination and prejudice result from actual competition between groups over limited resources.

The central idea of social dominance theory is that all societies tend to be stratified in three ways (see Figure 2.4). One is stratification by age, with adults having social power over children and young adults. The second is stratification by gender, with males having disproportionate power (patriarchy) – a dominant theme in

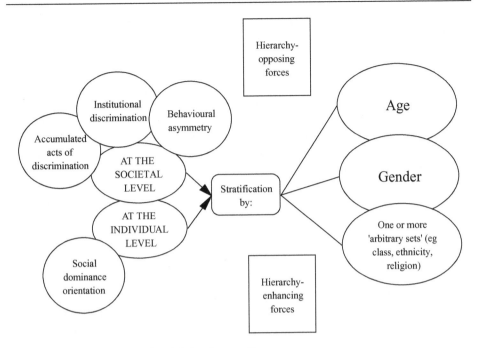

Figure 2.4   An overview of social dominance theory
Source: based on Sidanius, J. & Pratto, F. (1999). *Social Dominance: An Intergroup Theory of Social Hierarchy and Oppression*. Cambridge, UK: Cambridge University Press

community psychology, and one that recurs regularly throughout the present book. The third source of stratification is what is termed an 'arbitrary-set system', with highly salient groups, based on characteristics such as ethnicity, caste, social class, or religion, being hierarchically organised in terms of status and power. It is difficult to find a society, Sidanius and Pratto (1999) pointed out, that does not have an arbitrary-set stratification system.

Group-based social hierarchy is driven at the most individual level by social dominance orientation (SDO), defined as the degree to which an individual supports group-based hierarchy and the domination of 'inferior' by 'superior' groups. At a societal level it is driven by three proximal processes: the accumulation of daily, and often quite inconspicuous, discriminatory acts; the aggregation of discrimination at institutional level, some of which is deliberate and overt and some unintended or covert; and behavioural asymmetry, whereby those in higher status groups defend the hierarchical asymmetry more strongly than those in lower status groups oppose it. Hence those in subordinate positions participate in and contribute to their own continuing subordination: they do that by displaying a lower level of in-group bias, showing deference to those of higher status, higher levels of self-destructive behaviour (self-debilitation), and generally adhering less strongly to social dominance values. Very similar ideas are part of post-colonial theory, as we shall see later in this chapter.

Central to the social dominance model are hierarchy-enhancing forces which include shared or societal beliefs: sexism, racism, nationalism, and certain forms of religious belief are obvious examples, but there are beliefs that operate in a more subtle way, including for example beliefs that attribute responsibility for poverty or ill-health to poor or unhealthy individuals themselves or to the communities in which they live. At the same time, hierarchy-attenuating forces exist in virtually all societies, including feminism, socialism, human rights movements, and movements for the rights of minorities and for social change of many different kinds. The theory sees hierarchy-enhancing and hierarchy-attenuating forces existing in some kind of equilibrium in all societies, with the equilibrium point varying greatly from one society to another. But the general tenor of social dominance theory is that status differences for age, gender, and some arbitrary but highly salient other characteristics, is universal: there is a tendency in the presentation of the theory to be pessimistic about the long-term achievements of social movements for change.

Further examples of hierarchy-enhancing processes were given by Montero (1998c) when she was discussing the empowerment of minority groups, the dynamics of social influence in which both minorities and majorities are influenced, and some of the ways used by a majority to resist the influence of the minority. The latter included psychologisation (explanation of the position of a minority in terms of the psychological characteristics of its members, e.g. caused by bitterness, frustration, envy or resentment) and denial (not accepting and minimising true facts or statements expressed by a minority who are then deprived of their rationality by being accused of being incoherent and illogical).

The relatively powerless position of children, which social dominance theory highlighted, has been taken up by Prilleltensky and Nelson (2000) and by Prilleltensky et al. (2001). They have criticised the empowerment literature not only for showing a psycho-centric bias, concentrating on the cognitive and emotional aspects of personal empowerment to the relative neglect of social, material and political aspects, but also for its adult-centric bias and its relative neglect of empowerment for children. They wrote of the importance of power and control for child 'wellness' (Rappaport, 2000a, is one who has expressed some unhappiness with the concept of 'wellness', arguing that the term invites an individualistic way of looking at things, even akin to medical notions of the prevention of disease). They were attracted to the idea that health involves not only individual well-being but also equality and social justice and that children's wellness is affected by the empowering qualities of social systems at levels from micro to macro. That included investment of societies in public resources that contribute to child health. Policies regarding such investment were likely to differ in societies with an individualistic philosophy of self-care compared to cultures with more collectivist values. The unequal distribution of resources within and between nations was identified by Prilleltensky et al. as a central problem for the promotion of children's health and wellness. The different treatment of male and female children was one of the clearest examples, including practices such as sex-selective abortion and preferential treatment of male children in terms of nutrition and health care (see also Sen, 1999, who wrote about 'missing women'). They were critical also of the proclivity to blame parents for children's problems, since parents themselves have very often experienced abuse and share social circumstances that deprive them of power and control. The material and psychological resources, and opportunities for participation and self-determination, were as important for parents in their roles as carers as they are for children. Prilleltensky and Nelson (2000) cited child maltreatment as an example of a topic where the evidence points to the importance of socioeconomic, cultural, and contextual factors at various levels: the individual (e.g. parenting skills, or whether the person committing abuse was abused himself or herself as a child); the micro-system (e.g. marital cohesion); systems mediating between individual and family and the wider society (e.g. involuntary job loss, work stress, neighbourhood isolation); and the macro-system (e.g. the level of violence in society, social norms sanctioning corporal punishment).

SOCIAL CONSTRUCTIONISM AND ITS CRITICS

In the later decades of the twentieth century European (at least) social psychology, in step with a broad movement in philosophy and much of the human and social sciences (Gergen, 1999; Foster, 2004), turned its focus on language. One of the principal theoretical forms that turn has taken has come to be known as social constructionism (Gergen, 1999). Its influence has been strongly felt in community psychology, as elsewhere in psychology, although not without controversy, as we shall see. The core idea is that language, rather than being a reflection of the 'truth' or the 'reality' of some aspect of the world, is rather an action in itself, a kind of performance that is carried out with others, that helps to create a shared meaning or common understanding of how things are. Language is seen as a set of discourses, and social discourse is seen as creating *a* reality rather than reflecting *the* reality (Hepburn, 2003). There was no ultimate truth to be 'discovered', but rather socially shared traditions of talking about things that are culturally and historically located. As Gergen (1999, p. 49) put it, "... to sustain our traditions – including those of self, truth, morality, education, and so on – depends on a continuous process of generating meaning together".

Social constructionism can be distinguished from theories with which it might be confused, such as Kelly's (1955) theory of personal constructs. Although the latter also was concerned with how people form ideas about the social world, it was largely focused on individuals and conceived of the understanding of the social world being constructed 'in the head' of an individual person rather than in the course of socially shared discourse and action. Gergen (1999) preferred the term 'constructivism' for that type of theory, although that term is often confusingly used to embrace social constructionism as well (e.g. Lykes, 2000). Social constructionists are interested in how discourses are constructed as well as how they are constructive of shared meanings and how they support joint actions. Prominent ideas have been those of metaphor and rhetoric. Not only is it said that we use metaphors explicitly much of the time when talking, but, "... all our understandings can be seen as metaphoric if we but trace them to their origins" (Gergen, 1999, p. 65). Similarly, social constructionists have drawn on the classical Greek discipline of rhetoric to describe how 'claims' are made for particular versions of the truth, including scientific truths. Gergen (1999) wrote of the rhetorical devices that scientists use to support their theories and interpretations, and Potter (1996) reviewed a range of rhetorical procedures, amounting to a 'reality production kit', that we use to establish what we are saying as being credible and not merely our own opinion. In any cultural-historical context certain phrases or sayings are so common and taken for granted that they amount to examples of a 'rhetorical commonplace'. Examples might be, 'You can't turn the clock back', or 'Practice must be evidence-based' (Billig, 1987).

The importance of social constructionism for community psychology lies in the way in which the theory sees discourse and action as intertwined. Ways of understanding things, constructed by shared discourse about them, support or promote certain actions rather than others. In fact talk and action are scarcely separable, since talk is action (Gergen, 1999). The language of emotions is a good example. Rather than thinking of statements about feelings, such as depressed, guilty, ashamed, hopeless, being taken as reflections of an objective psychophysiological state, such statements would be thought of as a kind of active performance, words that are deployed for getting things done (Hepburn, 2003). But the relevance for community psychology becomes clearer still if we accept the social constructionist view, following Foucault, that language is a critical feature of power relations. It then becomes relevant to ask, "What kinds of people, institutions, laws, and so on are favored when we speak in one set of terms as opposed to another; what traditions or ways of life are suppressed or destroyed?" (Gergen, 1999, p. 38). The post-modern view of power, of course, implies that where power lies, and who benefits or suffers from ways of understanding and doing things, are not always starkly obvious but are supported by engaging in everyday, commonplace talk and activities, including what we wear, what we purchase, what is presented for us in the media, our diet, our leisure activities (Gergen, 1999).

An effect of some kinds of discourse is the creation of social categories such as 'man', 'gay' or social class or racial categories. Once people are categorised there is an inevitable tendency to 'essentialise' the category, assuming that it has some essence in terms of intrinsic characteristics or qualities. Since some groups would be talked about as 'not us' but 'other', and since the shared meaning of a category was very likely to include moral or value-relevant components, so "... classes of the undesirable are under construction" (Gergen, 1999, p. 149). Hepburn (2003) made the point that apparently contradictory 'interpretative repertoires', consisting of metaphors and rhetorical devices, were often drawn upon to defend discrimination, but in such a way that the arguments used appeared consistent with liberal values a caring ethos, or common sense. Hence they were subtle and difficult to attack. For example, members of a white majority group might talk in favour of the rights of a minority ethnic group, but at the same time use the notion of culture – for example culture as something that should be protected from impress of the modern world – as an argument for limiting those rights (she cited Wetherell & Potter's, 1992, work on Maori rights in New Zealand).

Social constructionists are concerned not just with explaining how the status quo is maintained but also with how it can be challenged. Since there was more than one way of putting things, and hence no 'last word' on the subject, it was always possible to reflect on the possibility of alternative constructions. Following the ideas of the French theorist Derrida, if shared understandings are socially constructed through language, they could always be 'deconstructed', to understand how they have been constructed, and to think of alternatives. Because constructions were embedded in power relationships, this process of challenging might amount to a critique of dominant ideology, a discovery of whose interests are being served by the status quo and whose voices are absent, an unmasking of concealed interests (Gergen, 1999; Sampson, 2000; O'Sullivan, 2000). Gergen (1999) considered the process of reflexivity about apparent truths – constantly doubting, questioning, listening to alternatives, encouraging multiple voices on the subject – to be crucial for liberation and emancipation.

There have been many criticisms of social constructionism. From traditional social psychology is the criticism that social constructionists have abandoned the rigorous methods required of the discipline such as quantification and experimentation. From within the ranks of social constructionists has come the methodological criticism that discourse has been studied too often in the artificial setting of an interview rather than in real-world settings. But arguably the most telling criticism – and the most salient for community psychology – has been the charge that social constructionism, because it is so focused on language and the challenge to the idea of there being a single reality, neglects the reality of the material world, for example the reality of living in a particular social class position. It is bound to advocate moral relativism, or so it is argued by its critics, leaving it in a weak position in terms of challenging the materiality of economic conditions, or taking a firm position for political action (Hepburn, 2003; Burton, 2004; Foster, 2004; Smail, 2005).

Gergen's (1999) answer was to say that there is nothing in social constructionism that argues against having values. Indeed social constructionism, he claimed, has helped to reintroduce morals and ethics into debates about scientific and other truths after many decades in which scientists had claimed that science was concerned only with facts and that moral questions should not be relevant. Furthermore, Gergen pointed out, it must be recognised that moral positions are situated within culture and history, as expressions of traditions, and that when social constructionists are asked to take a position, they are usually being asked to ally themselves with one particular position. That inevitably implied negating other possible positions, and therefore running the risk of supporting certain powerful interests. The prime interest of the social constructionist is in 'polyvocality' or the existence of multiple and competing realities.

Community psychology is likely to remain ambivalent about social constructionism. On the one hand, it offers us the means whereby we can explore, identify, and begin to challenge the way in which power is distributed and exercised to the benefit of some groups in society but to the detriment of others. It therefore constitutes an essential part of the community psychology toolkit. Its dangers – well recognised and articulated by a number of critics, as we have noted – lie in its tendencies towards relativism. In that respect social constructionism can be used to distance psychology from the very realities of life that the most disempowered are struggling to tell us about. Despite its promise of breaking with much of psychology's past, it can, strangely, fall into the same trap as so much of psychology before it, of not taking seriously enough what people say about their circumstances, and not taking a stand in support of the liberation of people from those conditions. In later chapters, particularly in Part III, we shall give a lot of weight to hearing, and taking at face value, what people say about their circumstances – more weight than would be given by social constructionism.

LIBERATION PSYCHOLOGY

Latin American Liberation Social Psychology

One of the parts of the world where community psychology ideas have been developing most strongly is Latin America. Introducing a special issue of the *Journal of Community Psychology*, Montero (1998b) – a Venezuelan social and political psychologist – described what she saw as the distinctive features of the Latin American approach to community psychology. First and foremost, it was directed towards social change and its character was distinctly political, aiming for the development and empowerment of civil society, and helping construct a 'public space' accessible to all groups including those who were otherwise silent and excluded. There was a commitment to the empowerment of community members. Social change was understood, "... as a consequence of actions by government agencies or by those in positions of power and influence, but also as the outcome of the actions of men and women in daily life" (p. 200).

Community approaches to psychology in Latin American countries began developing in the 1950s, 60s and 70s, particularly influenced by the Colombian sociologist Fals Borda and the Brazilian educator Freire (Wingenfeld & Newbrough, 2000). One of the central ideas is that of liberation psychology, derived from work in central and south America and particularly associated with the name of Martín-Baró. He lived and worked in El Salvador as both Jesuit priest and social psychologist at the University of Central America during the civil war period in the 1980s and was assassinated along with five other priests in November 1989. His extensive writings on liberation psychology are largely in Spanish and have been slow to percolate into English-language psychology (Comas-Díaz et al., 1998; Watts & Serrano-García, 2003; Burton & Kagan, 2005). But a valuable edited collection of his *Writings for a Liberation Psychology* (Martín-Baró, 1994) is available in English. The importance of Martín-Baró's experience in El Salvador lies in the way in which we might understand the realities of the Salvadoran people as paradigmatic, as he himself saw it, of the experiences of oppressed peoples everywhere (Aron & Corne, 1994). The people with whom he was working were living in what he called 'limit situations', that is situations of extreme hardship, oppression, and profound suffering (Lykes, 2000). They would have been subject to the same types of direct and subtle power and control by their oppressors that Foster (2004) wrote about when applying the ideas of liberation psychology to oppression in South Africa – with social domination operating in a variety of ways: through violence of various kinds; via political exclusion; economic exploitation; sexual exploitation; control of culture, including restriction on use of indigenous languages or ways of representing a people's history; and by fragmentation, limiting collective opposition.

Martín-Baró was critical, as many have been, of the weak contribution that psychology had made to the problems of oppression and distress of peoples in Latin America and elsewhere. He blamed the dominance of psychoanalytical, behavioural, cognitive and systems theories, and psychology's preoccupation with the minutia of tests and other methods and procedures, and most particularly its focus on the need for change by individuals, or at most by families or work systems. Those characteristics had led to, for example, forms of educational and organisational psychology that, "...never for a moment put into question the basic schemata by which we live, nor, therefore, how social roles are determined for people" (Martín-Baró, 1994, p. 44). Work in organisational psychology, for example, "...never questions the larger economic setting, the primacy of the profit motive as opposed to service, the division of labour, or the inequality in decision-making power which lies at the foundation of its workplace organization" (p. 95).

Indeed it might be thought that the very term 'liberation psychology' is itself an oxymoron; since psychology, it can be argued, rather than liberating, has often been complicit with racism, patriarchy, class bias and western imperialism (Lykes, 2000; Foster, 2004):

> But the problem is not just that psychology has sometimes behaved badly, collaborating with racism, sexism and exploitation, but also that psychology almost by definition undermines critical social thinking through its idea of the individual who is made the source and focus of all problems, allowing the social world to fade into the background (Foster, 2004, pp. 575–6).

There had, however, been a number of critiques from inside psychology: among them Foster cited efforts to make social psychology more relevant to social issues, feminist psychology, the 'linguistic turn' towards discourse and social constructionism, as well as specific social psychological theories of relevance to the psychology of oppression, such as social identity theory (Tajfel, 1981), and social dominance theory (Sidanius & Pratto, 1999). Other influences, from outside psychology, had included writings of the anti-psychiatry movement of the 1960s, the ideas of certain philosophers and social theorists (e.g. Foucault and Derrida), writings from anti-colonial struggles (e.g. Frantz Fanon) and the emergence of new cross-disciplinary areas such as cultural studies.

Post-Colonial Liberation Psychology in South Africa

Like community psychology in several other parts of the world, in South Africa it grew as part of the response to societal conditions in which certain groups were politically repressed and socially excluded. Among the figures who have inspired South African community psychologists are Frantz Fanon, a psychiatrist, much involved in the liberation struggle in Algeria, an author of the influential book *Black Skin, White Masks* (1952/1986), and Steve Biko, the Black consciousness leader involved in the resistance to apartheid in South Africa (Hook, 2004). Both men wrote of the relationship between politics and psychology and influenced what became the field of post-colonial theory and criticism, aiming to understand relationships of domination and/or resistance when one culture controls another even after the end of the formal colonial period. Fanon's 'psychopolitics' was concerned with both how politics impacts upon the psychological, as well as how personal psychology might serve to entrench political effects at the personal level, 'reinscribing' colonising ways of thinking even in post-colonial contexts. The dominance of white, western ideals, ways of thinking, and assumptions about knowledge and how it was acquired in science generally and in psychology in particular, served to marginalise indigenous experience, making the majority feel inferior and alienated.

Foster (2004) summarised some of the psychological consequences of oppression, variously described by different writers as the 'scars of bondage', the 'mark of oppression', or the 'damage thesis'. Those consequences included 'identification with the aggressors', inhibition of strong emotions such as anger and rage, lateral violence turned against the in-group, including domestic violence, and a heightened prevalence of substance misuse and mental health problems.

Fanon helped explicate how experience was related to social conditions, how the personal-subjective was linked to the socio-historical. Psychology had tended to miss this, depoliticising human experience, reducing social structures to inner feelings and psychological states. Hook (2004) pointed out that in the original Marxist concept, alienation was not an 'experience' but rather a real material process of the separation of the worker from the products of his or her labour. It had not been Fanon's aim to substitute an economic/material analysis with a psychological one, but rather to emphasise the psychological dimension to such events. Alongside the colonisation of a land and its people was also a 'colonising of the mind', hence bringing about a powerful form of psychological damage.

For Biko too, what happened to the mind of the oppressed was one of the most powerful factors maintaining oppression. Political freedom required psychological and cultural liberation of the black mind and a key strategy was *conscientisation*, correcting false images of oneself and one's group. But black consciousness was not to be confused with an exercise in building self-esteem, and Fanon too was often explicitly anti-psychological, believing that most human problems were reality problems, not fantasies, and that psychological treatment often implicitly asked patients to adjust themselves to inequitable social conditions. The primary task of psychology should be, rather, to understand the relationship between the psyche and the social structure and to help transform the latter.

Both Fanon and Biko have been criticised for male-centeredness (indeed overt sexism in places), for use of essentialist categories such as 'black', 'white', 'colonised', and 'coloniser', and for emphasising the effects of colonists and post-colonist oppression to the neglect of the various forms of resistance and opposition that are offered against them. The strongest criticism of Fanon is that he encouraged a kind of victim-blaming by emphasising the pathological effects of oppression, portraying the black subject as damaged and ineffective (Hook, 2004).

Liberation, according to Foster (2004), required a vision or image of what is possible, or of an alternative to the present order. Foster cited The Freedom Charter adopted in South Africa in June 1955 at the Congress of the People, a gathering of 10,000 people held over two days. When it comes to action, Foster highlighted collective action as crucial to resistance. As well as critical reflection and analysis, with new narratives and a new vision and new self-definition, liberatory action required collective organising (as with the numerous organisations that appeared in South Africa from the 1960s onwards, many combining in 1983 to form the United Democratic Front), and collective action with all the dangers and risks that entails (a number of theorists such as Fanon and Foucault have favoured metaphors of war, manoeuvres, strategies and tactics) (Foster, 2004).

An aspect touched on by Foster, reminiscent of the ecological psychology of Barker (1968, 1978, and see Chapter 3), is the spatial dimension, significant in all forms of subjugation. Indeed:

> ... the whole arena of oppression is entirely shot through with spatial metaphors: exclusions, borders, hierarchies, boundaries, dividing lines, buffer zones, safe havens. All forms of subjugation involve spatial remoulding: seizing land, segregating, separating, spatial restrictions, rezoning, apartheid, fencing, walls, enclosures and barriers. Places such as prisons and military barracks, constitute the dividing lines of colonialism (Foster, 2004, p. 595).

Spatial discourses, Foster suggested, revolved around three metaphoric polarities: hierarchy (up and down), distance or centrality (core and periphery, centre and margins), and sphere (public and private).

The Principles of Liberation Psychology

In order to develop a true psychology of emancipation, or liberation psychology, liberating psychology itself in the process, a new form of *praxis* is required. The term praxis indicates the need for two things: (1) reflection, understanding, critical awareness, critical consciousness, or what Freire (1972, 1998) called conscientisation (Martín-Baró, 1994; Watts & Serrano-García, 2003; Foster, 2004); and (2) action to transform the circumstances exposed by the first process of critical reflection. Martín-Baró stressed helping people, "... attain a critical understanding of themselves and their reality" (1994, p. 41):

> Through the gradual decoding of their world, people grasp the mechanisms of oppression and dehumanization. This crumbles the consciousness that mythifies that situation as natural, and opens up the horizon to new possibilities for action (p. 40).

One task, according to Martín-Baró, was the recovery of historical memory, expanding horizons from a limited and fatalistic, exclusive focus on how to survive in the present, towards both contemplating a different future and reconstructing the historical roots of collective identity. A central part of the process was changing the image that people had of themselves – he was concerned to change what he saw as the fatalism, passivity and conformity of the 'popular classes' in Mexico, described for example by Oscar Lewis (e.g. 1961) and Díaz-Guerrero (1990), and Latin American fatalism more generally, characterised by resignation with regard to the demands of one's own fate, passivity towards circumstances in life, and the narrowing of the life horizon to the present. Change required critical analysis that would likely involve re-naming, new narratives, hearing new 'voices', 'coming out'.

Among the principles of liberation social psychology discussed by Burton and Kagan (2005) are those shown in Figure 2.5. Writings in liberation psychology also stress the need to understand the oppressors, and to understand the ways in which power relations of domination are maintained – for example by creating a sense of inevitability, a sense of deference or submission, and a resignation and pessimism about the possibility of alternatives (Martín-Baró, 1994; Watts & Serrano-García, 2003; Foster, 2004). At the same time Martín-Baró (1994) pointed out that alongside a sense of fatalism and resignation there are always indications of rebellion. Similarly,

- Liberation involves a series of processes occurring over time.
- It involves two types of agency or activist: the oppressed groups themselves; and external catalytic agents (which might include community psychologists).
- A central idea is Freire's (e.g. 1972) concept of 'conscientisation', or the acquiring of a critical consciousness as people understand how oppression operates and what its effects are.
- The orientation is social but also historical, aiming for an understanding of how things came to be the way they are and how, "... this history is ever present in the subjectivity of the people" (Burton & Kagan, 2005, p. 69).
- Fundamental is the recognition of conflict in society and the omnipresence of power.
- The primary object of psychologists' attention should be serving the needs of the 'popular' or oppressed majorities.
- LSP is methodologically eclectic, using many different methods. It has included, for example, working with poor communities on a variety of social issues such as health promotion, economic development, housing and community development, as well as community interventions and support in the fields of disability, domestic violence, mental health and drug use.
- Although generally supportive of multiple methods there is an emphasis on the Freirian commitment to reflection–action–reflection, and to action research.

Figure 2.5   The principles of liberation social psychology (LSP)
Source: according to Burton, M. & Kagan, C. (2005). Liberation social psychology: learning from Latin America. *Journal of Community and Applied Social Psychology*, **15**, 63–78

Foster (2004) wrote of efforts to revise and reformulate the 'mark of oppression' claims, restoring a more positive conception of oppressed people, emphasising pride, solidarity and activity, and – evident in the later literature on the subject – resistance, defiance and rebellion.

Prilleltensky (2003) proposed a new form of validity against which to judge psychological practice. He termed it 'psychopolitical validity'. Paralleling the two aspects of praxis – reflection and action – he saw two types of psychopolitical validity, epistemic and transformative. To past the test of *epistemic* validity, knowledge about oppression and power dynamics would need to be incorporated into all activities: for example an understanding of the impact of global, political, and economic forces on the issue at hand and on the individuals, groups, and communities affected by it. Most psychology, notoriously politically illiterate, failed on that score. *Transformative* psychopolitical validity required changes towards liberation at person, interpersonal, and structural levels: do psychological interventions promote psychopolitical literacy, empower participants to take action to address political inequities and social injustice, and promote alliances and coalitions with groups facing similar issues?

As Table 2.1, taken from Prilleltensky's (2003) paper, illustrates, he viewed psychopolitical well-being as operating through the synergy of values, reflections, actions, and outcomes in personal, relational, and collective spheres. This is a theme stressed by others writing in the liberation psychology tradition. For example, Comas-Díaz *et al.* (1998), writing about the effects of traumas and terror associated with civil war in Guatemala, stressed that what was seen was not simply the cumulative effect on individuals of multiple traumatic experiences, but rather something that affected people both individually and collectively, deeply wounding the local culture. There were widespread ramifications, not just in terms of individual symptoms, but also for the, "... possibility of affirming aspects of ... cultural life" (p. 782), currently, and at least for the next generation (see Chapter 7 for more on this). Watts and Serrano-García (2003) also wrote of the need for a liberation psychology that includes, but goes beyond, effects on individuals, to embrace, "... a far reaching conception of healing" (p. 75). Martín-Baró (1994; Mishler, 1994) was critical of an understanding of the effects of war and violence rooted in the individual psyche, such as the medical model of post-traumatic stress disorder (also see Chapter 7). The task for psychologists also required efforts towards:

> ... restoring stable and trusting social relations and the strengthening of the community's capacity for collective action ... [and] the restoration to the community of a "historical memory" as well as the development of popular forms of political organization and action (Mishler, 1994, pp. x–xi).

Martín-Baró asked the question whether individual psychotherapy should therefore be abandoned altogether. His answer implied that it would at the very least need to take a new form:

> Thus, a conscienticizing psychotherapy must construct a process that will enable the individual to assert his or her personal and social identity as part of a movement of collective and national affirmation (p. 43).

It is interesting to note what Martín Baró (1994), as a Jesuit priest, influenced by Latin American liberation theology, had to say about the role of religion in the Salvadoran conflict. Traditionally the church had taught that miserable, oppressed conditions were the will of God and that people should focus their efforts on individual change. Changes in the Catholic church, begun in the Vatican Council II, and taken forward through the experiences of the 'Christian base communities' – the thousands of small lay-led groups working to improve their local communities and establish a more just society – removed the religious justification for passive acceptance of oppression and offered instead a religious basis for social change. The parallel with psychology is clear.

Liberation Psychology and Indigenous Peoples

Among peoples who have suffered from the effects of colonisation, indigenous people in Australasia and North America stand out. The Australian Aboriginal and Torres Strait Islander peoples, for example, have been exposed to wholesale

Table 2.1 Does psychological practice have psychopolitical validity? Understanding, resisting, and overcoming oppression

Psychopolitical well-being: domains and values for liberation	Experiences: voices and expressions of oppression and resistance	Consequences: outcomes of health and social science studies on oppression	Sources: roots of suffering and oppression	Change: actions toward liberation
Collective Social justice Institutions that support emancipation and human development Peace Protection of environment	*Suffering* Insecurity and exploitation Denial of collective rights Depreciation of own culture Disregard for environment *Resistance* Collective action to help community; each community reacts differently to its own oppression	*Suffering* Economic disadvantage and discrimination Vulnerability to disadvantage, illness, and disability Fragmentation within oppressed Reduced opportunities in life *Resistance* Development of activist groups within schools and communities	Economic exploitation Globalisation, colonialism, and power differentials Corrupt government structures Sexism and norms of violence Material and ideological domination, political exclusion	Invest in human and environmental development and health Resist dominant theory that economic growth is main vehicle to well-being Join networks of support that focus on personal, relational, and collective well-being Strive for democracy, peace, and respect for diversity
Relational Social cohesion, respect for diversity Democratic participation	*Suffering* *Exclusion* and intimidations based on class, age, gender, education, race and ability *Resistance* Solidarity and compassion for others who suffer	*Suffering* Lack of support, competition across social groups, isolation and fragmentation Horizontal violence *Resistance* Acts of solidarity with other oppressed groups	In-group domination and discrimination Dehumanising treatment of others in same and different groups Objectification of other Competition for scarce resources	Power equalisation in personal, relational, and collective domains Prevent exclusion and promote liberation through education. Build trust, connections, and participation in groups
Personal Self-determination and human rights Health Personal growth Meaning and spirituality	*Suffering* Multiple restrictions in life Self-deprecation, degradation and shame Powerlessness, hopelessness *Resistance* Strength and resilience	*Suffering* Loss of life opportunities and lack of control Mental health problems, addictions, internalised oppression *Resistance* Resilience and solidarity, development of activism	Insufficient material resources and continued exposure to risk Power inequalities Learned helplessness Acting out own oppression on others	Join social action groups that work to enhance personal empowerment and solidarity at the same time Development of assertiveness and positive self and cultural image Sociopolitical development and leadership training

Source: reproduced with permission from Prilleltensky, I. (2003). Understanding, resisting, and overcoming oppression: toward psychopolitical validity. *American Journal of Community Psychology*, **31**, 195–201, Table 1

subjugation following the British invasion of 1788 (Saggers & Gray, 1998). Even in the twentieth century, policies were pursued in relation to Aboriginal people which met the United Nation's definition of genocide. It is estimated that as many as one-sixth of all Aboriginal children were taken into 'care' under 'protectionist legislation', and that there may be as many as 100,000 Australians of Aboriginal descent who now do not know their ancestors or the communities from whence they came (Bourke, 1998). Land was appropriated to meet the needs of the new settlers, and the freedom of Aboriginal people to pursue their own way of life and their right to self-determination was destroyed. Indigenous people were either forced off their traditional lands and into artificial settlements, missions or reserves, or ended up working on their land that had become the property of others. As Roberts (1998) put it, "Their situation as a colonised people, small in population and widely dispersed across Australia, has forced them into working in and around a complex and foreign system of rules, structures, priorities and controls established by the dominant society" (p. 264). This was exacerbated further by simultaneously being restricted, either in part or in total, from carrying out customary laws and cultural practices. It was only within the last 40 years of the twentieth century that indigenous Australians were also recognised to have voting and citizenship rights.

More recently the culture of indigenous Australians has continued to be under threat, but the threat is in the more subtle forms of lack of employment opportunities, social exclusion, and dependency on welfare. In terms of health, indigenous Australians suffer with unacceptably high rates of child malnutrition, high levels of acute and chronic illness in children and adults, and high mortality rates. As a poor minority in a rich country, Aboriginal people have been said to carry a double health burden, suffering both the typical 'diseases of poverty', as in poorer countries (e.g. acute infectious diseases, malnutrition, and parasitic diseases), and the degenerative 'lifestyle' diseases more characteristic of western countries (cardiovascular disease, chronic lung disease, hypertension, diabetes, and cancer) (Reid & Trompf, 1991; Saggers & Gray, 1991; Burden, 1998). An example is end-stage renal disease (ESRD). The standardised incidence of ESRD is nine times higher than among the majority, non-indigenous Australian population, and a staggering 20 to more than 30 times higher for those living in remote rural communities (Kass et al., 2004). Kass et al. were critical of traditional disease epidemiology that focused on individual risk factors. Relatively ignored were factors such as over-crowding and poor housing conditions, poor access and cultural inappropriateness in the healthcare system, and high levels of stress and loss of control associated with the multiple disadvantages experienced by indigenous Australians consequent upon their long history of being marginalised and discriminated against.

The experiences of USAmerican Indians had much in common with that of indigenous Australians. Whitbeck et al. (2004, p. 121) summarised the experience as follows:

> After military defeat, American Indians experienced one of the most systematic and successful programs of ethnic cleansing the world has seen. They were relocated to what amounted to penal colonies, starved, neglected, and forbidden to practice their religious beliefs. Their children were taken from them and reeducated so that their language, culture, and kinship patterns were lost to them...All were forced to relocate to areas that had no economic value to

> Europeans...Reservations were initially very much like large concentration camps or penal colonies...The residents were dependent on the government representatives for food, shelter, and health care...Traditional means of survival were eradicated and the people were forced to learn new ways of surviving (e.g. farming) that often were culturally distasteful or impossible...

Whitbeck *et al.*, in their research with two reservations in the upper mid-west, USA, used the concepts of 'historical trauma' and 'historical grief', and drew an analogy with the Jewish Holocaust of the Second World War, while pointing out that the forced acculturation of American Indians had continued for more than 400 years through to the present day. The focus of their research was on current daily reminders of the losses that their people had experienced and the feelings of distress occasioned by those reminders. At the first stage, focus groups were held with community elders, with the permission of tribal governments. The losses elders mentioned were numerous, foremost among them being loss of their language, including a sense of guilt that the language was not being passed on and a feeling of hopelessness that it could be regained. Other losses included the erosion of traditional family and community ties, the loss of land and broken treaty promises, and the strong sense of loss and despair regarding alcohol and drug use. At the second stage, a 12-item scale was developed (with the help of comments and suggestions and final approval by community elders and tribal advisory boards) which asked how frequently each of 12 losses were on people's minds. The results are summarised in Table 2.2. Glover *et al.* (2005) wrote of the process of decolonisation, defining it as follows:

> Decolonization is a process that assists indigenous people to identify as members of a racial group that has been systematically oppressed by a dominant culture; it enables them to take action towards social transformation...Members of colonizer groups working on decolonization come to acknowledge their personal participation in the structural and cultural racism that maintains their group's economic and cultural dominance...(pp. 332–3).

The retelling of history in a way that documents the oppression of the colonised by the colonisers – for example the, "relentless array of legislation passed by their settler governments to break down indigenous education, health and community support systems...." (p. 338) – was a fundamental aspect of decolonisation according to Glover *et al.* It made structural and institutional racism, not just personal racism or prejudice, visible, and focused positively on an appreciation of the colonised group rather than just describing the impoverishment and decay of indigenous communities. They cited the example of the course at Curtin University in Perth, Western Australia, that prepares Aboriginal students for tertiary education, and which offers them that kind of view of their history and culture. Some students were said to be hostile to that approach initially, saying they did not want to be 'political', but in the process they often reframed their own life experiences in terms of racism or segregation, understanding why they had been feeling angry, disillusioned, marginalised, or uncomfortable identifying as Aboriginal (Dudgeon, in Glover *et al.*, 2005).

Similar themes could be seen in the case of Maori people. The appropriation of land was again a central issue, Maori people having been deceived by

Table 2.2   How frequently perceived losses were on people's minds

	Never (%)	Yearly or special times (%)	Monthly (%)	Daily (%)
Loss of our land	25	33	25	18
Loss of our language	12	21	31	36
Losing our traditional spiritual ways	11	19	37	33
The loss of our family ties because of boarding schools	44	27	17	13
The loss of families from the reservation to government relocation	52	23	15	9
The loss of self-respect from poor treatment by government officials	29	22	27	22
The loss of trust in whites from broken treaties	29	29	20	23
Losing our culture	11	20	36	34
The losses from the effects of alcoholism on our people	8	13	33	46
Loss of respect by our children and grandchildren for elders	9	10	44	38
Loss of our people through early death	9	16	42	33
Loss of respect by our children for traditional ways	12	18	35	35

Source: reproduced with permission from Whitbeck, L.B., Adams, G.W., Hoyt, D.R. & Chen, X. (2004). Conceptualizing and measuring historical trauma among American Indian people. *American Journal of Community Psychology*, **33**, 119–30.

Pakeha (white) people at the Treaty of Waitangi in 1840, which guaranteed Maori sovereignty and land rights. Contrary to the provisions of the treaty, white settlers established a national government that excluded Maori and used force to support land sales and seizures. Like indigenous Australians, Maori in modern day Aotearoa/New Zealand are over-represented among the unemployed, the poor, the ill, and those in prison (Glover *et al.*, 2005).

A process of decolonisation had been occurring nevertheless, which involved documenting and acknowledging past damage, and reviving Maori knowledge that had been hidden or driven underground. In the 1980s New Zealand recommitted itself to the Treaty of Waitangi and recognised that Maori world views and understandings of knowledge were themselves part of the distinctive culture. A central concept has been *tino rangatiratanga* or the 'unqualified authority' of the indigenous people. An important idea, of general relevance for us, is that of *kaupapa* Maori research. It is based on Maori epistemology and culture, involves an analysis of existing societal power structures and inequalities, and is in the nature of research by, for and with Maori people. Maori exert control over all aspects of the research process including setting the research agenda, and defining outcomes in terms of Maori culture rather than using imported measuring yardsticks which could easily serve as an assimilative device (Glover *et al.*, 2005). Also referred to were Pakeha anti-racism groups launched as part of a national campaign in New Zealand in the 1980s. They presented a more critical view of colonial history, encouraged participants to consider the ways in which their own organisations were complicit in supporting structural and colonial racism, with a national conference organised to consider ways in which the Treaty of Waitangi could be positively supported by people's own organisation (Huygens, in Glover *et al.*, 2005).

A distinctive feature of community psychology in Australia and New Zealand has been the emphasis on diversity and cultural pluralism (Veno & Thomas, 1992a; Wingenfeld & Newbrough, 2000; Bishop *et al.*, 2002b). In Australia, community psychology has been closely allied with the Aboriginal Psychology interest group within the Australian Psychological Society (Bishop & D'Rozario, 2002) and in New Zealand community psychology has been strongly influenced by the promotion of bi- and multi-culturalism and the position of Maori people. That emphasis appears to have been particularly strong in Western Australia (Bishop *et al.*, 2002a) and at Waikato in New Zealand (Hamerton *et al.*, 1995; Raeburn & Thomas, 2000). Bishop and his colleagues have written about the way community psychology in Western Australia (WA) has been influenced by the fact of Australia being the product of colonialism, the scant regard that the dominant white culture has afforded the Aboriginal and Torres Strait peoples, and the continuing deprivation, poor health and high mortality of the latter. Psychologists and other professionals had supported that position, for example by aiding and abetting Australian governments in the forced removal of Aboriginal children from their parents while believing they were acting with the best of intents (Bishop & D'Rozario, 2002; Bishop *et al.*, 2002b). Unlike the more clinical focus of community psychology in other regions in Australia, Western Australian community psychology had developed more out of dissatisfaction with social psychology – its lack of relevance, asocial and ahistorical theory, lack of awareness of values and dominant world views, uncritical empiricism, uncritical acceptance of flawed research methodology, extreme individualism, and dominance of white and US theory.

An Irish View

Writing from an Irish context, and informed by research on colonialism and patriarchy, and post-colonial movements, including Irish women's liberation, Moane (2003) wrote of the need to recognise that challenging oppression involved intervention on three inter-linked levels – the personal, the interpersonal, and the political. She identified the six mechanisms of control, exercised under systems of colonialism and patriarchy, shown in Table 2.3. Each had consequences at the individual level: fear and anxiety, low self-esteem, and social isolation in the face of violence for example; frustration, anger and feelings of powerlessness in the face of political exclusion, as another example. Moane concluded that writings on oppression had recognised effects at the individual psychological level, including tension and ambivalence in areas such as sexuality, spirituality, and creativity; feelings of inferiority, lack of self-worth, and self-doubt; a variety of strong and unpleasant emotions such as fear, hopelessness, anger and shame; and difficulties in relationships

Table 2.3   Six mechanisms of control found in colonialism and patriarchy

Mechanism	Colonialism	Patriarchy
Violence	Military and police violence	Battery Rape Harassment
Political exclusion	No voting rights Restrictions on assembly	Access to voting Attitudes
Economic exploitation	Seizure of land Low paid labour Charges/taxes	Ownership of wealth Low/unpaid labour
Control of sexuality	Control of marriage Enforced motherhood	Marriage laws Birth control
Cultural control	Control of education Stereotypes	Erasure from history Media images
Fragmentation	Enforced migration	Tokenism Competition

Source: Moane, G. (2003). Bridging the personal and the political: practices for a liberation psychology. *American Journal of Community Psychology*, **31**, 91–101, Table 1

arising from misplaced anger, distrust, and competition. Such themes emerged both in personal and autobiographical writings of those who had experienced oppression, and in the writings of those who have worked on their behalf. For some, the ultimate outcome at the personal level was vulnerability to psychological distress and disturbance, and to alcohol and drug misuse. While these negative effects at the personal level had been widely described, there had equally been acknowledgement of the psychological strengths and resources associated with oppression, and the efforts that the oppressed devote to, "... constructing niches, contexts, or ecologies that provide protection again oppression and opportunities for resistance to the forces of oppression, and also for pride, self-expression, and connection with others" (Moane, 2003, p. 96).

Like Freire (1993), Martín Baró (1994), and Holland (1988, 1992 – see Chapter 10), Moane saw the need to address personal oppression as well as social and political oppression, and to help people begin to take action within the confines of their present circumstances, from thence developing a broader analysis and engaging in broader social action.

SOCIAL JUSTICE AS A CORE VALUE

Because psychology can be criticised for trying to maintain an objective, value-free position towards the topics it studies, it is generally taken to be important in community psychology to be explicit about values. Among the values held dear in community psychology, diversity is certainly one (Trickett, 1996; Iijima Hall, 1997; Sue, 1999). Veno and Thomas (1992a) included the promotion of peace and opposing violence in all its forms. But, as the subject has developed and become more confident, it is social justice that has emerged as basic to the philosophy of community psychology. For example, we have already noticed in the previous chapter how some public health and critical psychologists have been writing of the need to engage in a struggle for social justice as a means of promoting health (e.g. Fryer *et al.*, 2003; Campbell & Murray, 2004). The importance of values underlying community psychology, and in particular the pursuit of social justice as a core value, has been considered by community psychologists from Spain (Sánchez-Vidal & Musitu, 1996; Sánchez-Vidal, 2003), Australia (Drew *et al.*, 2002), North America (Prilleltensky, 1994; Fondacaro & Weinberg, 2002), and countries in Latin America (Serrano-García *et al.*, 1987). All have noted that, although it is widely accepted that community psychology activities rely on the notion of social justice (e.g. the evident injustice in analyses of human problems that have the effect of 'blaming the victim': Ryan, 1971), it has been rare for there to have been any critical scrutiny of the concept in community psychology. Fondacaro and Weinberg (2002) pointed out, for example, that despite the roots of community psychology in the USA lying in issues of the 1960s involving social justice, such as the community mental health movement, civil rights, the women's movement, and the War on Poverty, discussion of justice is not to be found in many of the leading US community psychology textbooks.

Other disciplines, such as medicine and economics, have sometimes done better. Among the many medical voices raised in favour of an approach to health that recognises the importance of social justice was that of Donohoe (2003) writing from the Center for Ethics in Health Care, Oregon, USA. He summarised factors bearing on health such as the explosive growth in world population; the huge migrant population, most displaced by war; air pollution, particularly from increased car use in richer areas; environmental destruction including water pollution, toxic pollutants and deforestation, mostly in poorer areas; and maldistribution of the world's resources, resulting in poverty, overcrowding and famine, more than two-thirds of the world's poorer citizens being women. His conclusion was that medicine has to be active in social and political life, and that "Physicians must advocate for the poor, the uninsured, and the disenfranchised, for whom we are 'natural attorneys' ... " (p. 583).

Among others have been Baum (2001) and Labonte (2001) writing in the Debate section of the *Journal of Epidemiology and Community Health* about the dangers of globalisation for world health. They pointed first to the greatly growing economic inequality. They cited figures suggesting that the ratio of the income of the richest fifth of the world's population to that of the poorest fifth had increased from 3:1 in 1830, to 30:1 in 1960, 60:1 in 1990 and 74:1 in 1997. Liberalisation was being unequally practised, with wealthy nations remaining protectionist in areas that benefited their own interests (a good example is the way in which the Mexican government ended its support to corn growers following the formation of the North American free trade area, their market then being flooded with cheaper imports from the USA where production remained heavily subsidised, and Mexican corn production halved, Labonte, 2001). Individuals and countries were being exhorted to accept 'structural adjustment programmes' as if they were part of the natural order, a necessary part of life if the world's economy was to flourish (Baum, 2001). The role of the state in protecting the potentially disadvantaged and countering growing inequality by progressive taxation and public transfer systems, was being marginalised, and the role of the World Health Organization was being questioned.

Both Baum (2001) and Labonte (2001) recommended that all concerned with public health engage in commentary and debate wherever they could; should study the pathways by which economic changes brought on by globalisation might impact on health; encourage social democratic governments to intervene in the interest of public health, and support popular and professional movements opposing the harmful effects of globalisation on health. Baum (2001) wrote of the People's Health Assembly, held in Bangladesh in 2000, attended by 1500 people from 93 countries, involving collaboration between eight non-governmental organisations (NGOs) from rich and poor countries, unanimously adopting the People's Charter for Health demanding transformation of the World Trade Organization, World Bank and International Monetary Fund, the cancellation of third world debt, and effective regulation to ensure that trans-national companies do not have negative effects on people's health, exploit their workforce, degrade the environment or impinge on national sovereignty. She also referred to the World Social Forum, held in Brazil in 2001 as a counterpoint to the simultaneous World Economic Forum held in Switzerland.

Some community psychologists have found the writings of the economist Amartya Sen particularly inspiring regarding freedom and social justice. In fact they provide a good example of how community psychology can draw on work from other traditions and disciplines. Because the values central to community psychology often find themselves in opposition to those of the globalised market place that appear to underlie much of modern economics and politics, it is reassuring and invigorating to know that there is an alternative economics, one with a human face. Sen's book, *Development as Freedom* (Sen, 1999), was based on five lectures Sen gave as Presidential Fellow at the World Bank in 1996. He explained that the World Bank had, "...not invariably been my favourite organization" (p. xiii), acknowledging its power for both good and ill. Much modern economic theory, Sen pointed out, was based on the 'tough' position. That position held that, in the interests of economic development that would benefit everyone in the long run, in the short term universal human services such as education, health, and social security should be resisted. That approach, Sen argued, misunderstood the importance of a number of freedoms that were more fundamental to human life than a nation's gross national product. Those freedoms could be seen as the goals or ends of development, representing things of fundamental value in their own right. At the same time they could be seen as the principal means of development since the different kinds of freedom were related, freedom of one type helping to advance other types of freedom.

Sen was interested in particular in five types of instrumental freedom: economic facilities, political freedom, social opportunities, transparency guarantees, and protective security. The freedom to participate in the labour market, to trade in goods with other people, and to have access to finance (important everywhere, all the way from large enterprises to tiny establishments run on micro credit), had been given pride of place in modern economics, and was, Sen believed, a crucial freedom, as was political freedom. Social opportunities, in the form of arrangements for education, health care, etc., had been relatively neglected, but were equally important not only for the conduct of individual lives, but also for more effective participation in political and economic activities. Transparency guarantees referred to the need for openness and trust in personal dealings. Protective security covered both fixed arrangements of social security as well as ad hoc arrangements to deal with national emergencies. Whereas much of modern economics had focused on incomes and commodities, Sen favoured a broader economics that focused on freedoms, functionings, and capabilities. In fact he argued that his broader conception of economics was much more faithful to the ideas of Aristotle and the much cited Adam Smith, both of whom saw the limitations of a view of quality of life which was focused exclusively on money. Modern economics had lost sight of their broader views, at the cost of neglecting the central value of freedom itself.

Sen considered the connections between his broader view of economics and theories of social justice. The most influential theory of justice had been utilitarianism, initiated in its modern form by Jeremy Bentham and pursued by later nineteenth- and twentieth-century economists and social theorists. A strength in Sen's view was the importance that utilitarianism gave to happiness and quality of life. He identified three major limitations, however. One was its indifference to how a utility such as money or happiness is distributed in the population: only the sum total mattered. Secondly, it neglected many of the rights and freedoms that were central to Sen's broad economics. The third limitation of utilitarianism is perhaps less obvious, and may be particularly pertinent to community psychology. His criticism here was that a focus on psychological characteristics, such as pleasure, happiness or desires, might be easily swayed by what he called "mental conditioning and adaptive attitudes" (p. 62):

> The utility calculus can be deeply unfair to those who are persistently deprived: for example, the usual underdogs in stratified societies, perennially oppressed minorities in intolerant communities, traditionally precarious sharecroppers living in a world of uncertainty, routinely overworked sweatshop employees in exploitative economic arrangements, hopelessly subdued housewives in severely sexist cultures. The deprived people tend to come to terms with their deprivation because of the sheer necessity of survival, and they may, as a result, lack the courage to demand any radical change, and may even adjust their desires and expectations to what they unambitiously see as feasible. The mental metric of pleasure or desire is just too malleable to be a firm guide to deprivation and disadvantage (Sen, 1999, pp. 62–3).

In psychology, one who has consistently addressed social justice is Prilleltensky (1994) who (following Olson, 1978) considered six prerequisites for the 'good society': stability, harmony, social cohesion, material prosperity, social freedom, and social justice. He concluded that the present social order, at least as to be found in the USA and Canada, about which he was writing, was not very satisfactorily meeting those preconditions for the good life. By implication, therefore, psychology, which was largely acting to endorse the present social system, was in those countries not living up to its mandate to promote human welfare. For example, stability, or the maintenance of order and organisation, was continuously affected by economic fluctuations, with downturns in the economy hitting the disadvantaged hardest (see the discussions of unemployment, work conditions, and inequality of income distribution in Chapters 4 and 7). Social harmony continued to be threatened by the survival, despite progress in rights for women and minorities, of social tensions of three prominent kinds: socioeconomic inequality, male dominance, and racism (see the discussion of social dominance theory earlier in this chapter). Material prosperity and social freedom were on average high, but were unequally distributed. Social justice, he suggested, was a candidate for being the principal criterion for a good society. It was notoriously difficult to define, but its distributive character was fundamental. Distribution might be according to rights, deserts or needs, but there was probably agreement that in a good society benefits should be distributed according to need. In contrast, the social philosophy characterising market societies tended to favour distribution by deserts.

Fondacaro and Weinberg (2002) traced the ways in which social justice had appeared in three major domains in community psychology: prevention and health promotion; empowerment; and critical community psychology. Although in the first tradition primary prevention was emphasised, with its focus on whole groups and communities, in practice prevention efforts had been more focused and considerations of social justice had been overwhelmingly about what they called 'just entitlement'. Entitlement had largely been decided by community elites and scientific experts. The empowerment tradition had emerged largely as a reaction to that failure to incorporate the, "... voices, insights, and experiences of people who comprised community psychology's target populations..." (p. 480). It emphasised the importance of voice and participation in decision making, decentralisation and local control by people in their indigenous communities, and of redefining the relationship between professional and client as one of collaboration. It could be criticised, however, for implying that solutions to human problems should take place only at local, grassroots level, hence risking failure to understand the wider context and minimising the importance of actions for social justice at higher levels.

The critical community psychology tradition Fondacaro and Weinberg viewed as the most radical. That was because, first, it placed social justice in the centre of things as both means and ends of community psychology practice (Prilleltensky & Nelson, 1997) and focused attention on the ways in which mainstream psychology had been complicit in supporting forms of social injustice. Further, it took a radical social constructionist approach in challenging the idea that scientific enquiry should be 'value-free', transcending the particularities of cultural and historical contexts. Fondacaro and Weinberg welcomed the way in which critical community psychology moved social justice to the foreground, but, like other commentators on social constructionism (see earlier in the present chapter), considered that the relativistic concept of social justice implied by constructionism might deprive critical community psychology of any claims it might have to objectivity and credibility, or to any claim that community psychologists might be specially fitted to conceptualising or helping to achieve social justice.

Drew et al. (2002) suggested that community psychology might draw on a growing body of research on the concept of justice in social psychology (e.g. Tyler, 1994, cited by Drew et al., 2002). One conclusion that could be drawn confidently was that justice means different things to different people in different circumstances. They pointed to an important distinction between distributive and procedural justice. The former refers to the *distribution* of powers, resources, and outcomes among people in a group, community, or society. Three general rules of distributive fairness are equity, equality, and need. Procedural justice on the other hand is about the *procedures* by which outcomes are allocated. It is at the heart of principles such as empowerment and participation. Research had suggested that people evaluate procedural justice along dimensions including standing, neutrality, and trust. Standing refers to the perception that decision-makers view the person or group as one whose rights, values and opinions are to be respected. Neutrality refers to the perception that there is a 'level playing field' and that decisions are made impartially. Trust is concerned with perceptions of the intentions of the authorities: whether they intend to listen to people and to treat them in a fair and reasonable fashion. More specifically, perceptions of procedural fairness include such things as whether procedures are known about and easy to understand, whether they appear to be consistently applied, whether decisions are perceived as fair and ethical, whether all relevant interests are taken into account, and whether there are procedures such as appeals for trying to correct apparently unfair decisions.

That brief look at the concept of social justice brings this chapter to an end. In the following chapter – the last of the three introductory chapters in Part I – we need to consider another area of debate and controversy in community psychology. If we are to correct psychology's past neglect of the social (as discussed in Chapter 1), and to work to the challenging agenda outlined by those we have heard from in the present chapter, then some hard and creative thinking is called for when it comes to deciding what should be our preferred ways of developing knowledge about the issues that concern us. That is the subject of Chapter 3.

Chapter 3
THE DEBATE OVER KNOWLEDGE IN COMMUNITY PSYCHOLOGY: DISSATISFACTION WITH EXISTING RESEARCH METHODS

Community psychology claims to be a branch of the tree of knowledge. It needs, therefore, to have a suitable epistemology – a position on what constitutes knowledge in the field and how it is acquired. Community psychology also makes claims about being able to change lives for the better. That is a bold claim and it needs to be demonstrated that it is not an empty one. We need in some way to be able to show that our actions help rather than hinder, bring benefits to people's lives rather than harms. The need to have a theory about knowledge acquisition, and to have means to evaluate what we do, has put the field in a quandary. There is general agreement that traditional psychological research methods are not adequate for the task, but, as we shall see in this chapter, there is controversy about what should replace them.

Dissatisfaction with existing methods has been apparent for some time. In her chapter in an important, comparatively early volume, *Researching Community Psychology* (Tolan *et al.*, 1990), Shinn (1990) asked why it was that psychologists had been so wedded to using only reports by individuals, even when it came to assessing phenomena at the setting or system level. One reason, she concluded, was the relative poverty of psychological theory at extra-individual levels. It was relatively rare, she thought, for characteristics of settings to be chosen for study on the basis of good theorising about the likely impact on individuals.

As a notable exception she cited the work of Barker and colleagues who saw that the otherwise atheoretical variable of organisational size, such as the size of a school, might be linked to the activities of individuals via the number of social roles available – for example a small school provided greater opportunity than a large one for students to take on positions of responsibility (Barker & Gump, 1964; Barker and Associates, 1978). The work of Barker and his group (1968, 1978) was highly original and an important part of the background to community psychology. Barker was critical of the way in which psychology had become, "a science of the laboratory and the clinic...more and more removed from settings that are not arranged by scientists" (1978, p. 39). He and his group set up a psychological 'field station' in a small town in the mid-west of the USA. There they studied in minute detail all the public places (ranging from offices to sidewalks, from sports grounds to drug stores) in which any of the town's inhabitants partook. That group established the important concept of a *behaviour setting*, demonstrating the ways in which behaviour and milieu were in synchrony, and the "great coercive power" (Barker, 1968, p. 17) that settings exerted over the behaviour of individuals who occupied them. The emphasis of that work was therefore on the physical environment and the behaviour of individuals: pioneering though it was and very relevant though it remains, it had little to say about structures of social power, subjective meanings, or social change – some of the things that have been of most interest in community psychology since then.

Nearly a decade after Shinn wrote her chapter, Banyard and Miller (1998) suggested that there had still been surprisingly little development of alternative research methods, even in community psychology, despite much talk of a paradigm shift from logical positivism and the latter's reification of quantifiable data, use of reductionist methods, and neglect of context. The field had remained quite traditional in that respect. Several years further on, Luke (2005) argued that community psychology was continuing to use a narrow range of research methods that did not do justice to contextualism – a core value in 'community science'. His review of the contents of the *American Journal of Community Psychology* from 2001 to 2003 compared to 1981 to 1983 showed that there were four times as many articles in the later period that included qualitative content (17% versus 4%) and that statistical methods had moved from reliance on correlations and analyses of variance towards greater use of multivariate methods such as structural equation modelling and path analysis. The latter, however, were not in his view appropriate for understanding human behaviour and health within their physical, social, organisational, cultural, economic, and political contexts. His solution was to advocate greater use of four other statistical methods which were currently very little represented: multilevel modelling (see Chapter 5); use of geographic information systems (GIS) which allow visual and quantitative assessment of geographic information, which has an important role to play in public health for example (see Buckridge *et al.*, 2002, for a Canadian example of a GIS providing analyses of relevant health information and Pearce *et al.*, 2006, for an example from New Zealand); network analysis (see Scott, 2000, for network theory, and Foster-Fishman *et al.*, 2001b, for an example); and cluster analysis (he provided an example by Zapert *et al.*, 2002 that used cluster analysis to identify sub-groups of teenagers on the basis of their trajectories of drug use from early to late adolescence).

Kelly (2003) shared with Luke (2005) the view that community psychology research need not be dominated by statistical techniques such as logistic regression and structural equation modelling, but his solution was more radical. There needed to be a break away from traditional ties to the laboratory, to biomedical science, and to limited concepts of what constitutes 'good science' which most psychologists were taught early on in their careers and which still constitute the standards by which research is likely to be judged in departments of psychology. In fact he could not conceive of a viable community psychology without there being tensions and controversies about how science should be conducted in communities, where complexity is the norm and use of participative methods may be as important as controlled research designs. His inclination was to favour pluralistic methods including qualitative methods, investigative reporting, ethnography, and the construction of oral histories.

Barker and Pistrang (2005) also advocated methodological pluralism, arguing that knowledge accumulates from a variety of sources and in diverse ways: contrary to the belief that some methods were inherently more valid or rigorous than others, no single research method was inherently superior. All methods have their pluses and their minuses. In their paper they outlined what they believed to be central values and principles for community psychology research, as well as criteria by which such research might be judged (summarised in Figure 3.1). Recognising the growth of use of qualitative research methods, Barker and Pistrang divided their suggested criteria into those applicable to all research and those specifically relevant either to quantitative research alone or specifically to qualitative research. In practice, qualitative and quantitative research could be combined in a variety of ways. Either could be primary in time, or the two might be conducted in parallel; and, whatever their order, either one might be primary in size or importance or the two might be seen as equally significant. Qualitative research as a preliminary to a more important quantitative phase – the only role of qualitative research acknowledged by some who are critical of or cautious about it – is only one of the ways in which the two can be combined.

SUPPORT FOR QUALITATIVE RESEARCH

The later chapters of this book (especially those in Part III) draw heavily on the results of pieces of qualitative research. That choice is based on the belief, shared by many in community psychology, that the kind of knowledge needed for practice in the field is likely to come, in large part, from hearing directly from people about the reality of their lives. No one should embark on qualitative research lightly, or in the mistaken belief that it is an easy option. There is a considerable variety of named qualitative research methods to choose from (the grounded theory method, and interpretative phenomenological analysis, to name but two) but few precise prescriptions about how to do it. But that may make it all the more suitable for community psychology: it is an adventurous and creative means of producing knowledge and in no way a mechanical one (Willig, 2001; Marks, 2002).

Wertz (2001) wrote about qualitative research from a humanistic psychology perspective. Although work in the latter tradition is much more focused, than is community psychology, on the inner experience of individuals, those two areas of psychology share much in the way of dissatisfaction with reliance on traditional psychological methods of research and the struggle to find methods that are more suited to the topics that concern them. Wertz made interesting references to comparatively early use of what we would now recognise as qualitative methods by some of the well-known figures in the history of psychology in the USA. He included James's (1902/1982) investigation of the nature of religious experience, Allport's (1942) case for the use of personal documents such as autobiographies,

---

Criteria applicable to all research

       Explication of context and purpose

       Use of appropriate methods

       Transparency of procedures

       Ethical treatment of participants

       Importance of findings

Research-relevant community psychology values and principles

       Sensitivity to people's contexts

       Respect for diversity among people and settings

       Addressing competencies

       Promoting empowerment

       Giving voice to traditionally under-represented populations

       Promoting social justice

       Research using multiple methodologies

Criteria specifically applicable to quantitative research

       Reliability and validity of measurement

       Internal validity

       External validity

       Statistical conclusion validity

Criteria specifically applicable to qualitative research

       Disclosure of perspective

       Grounding interpretations in the data

       Coherence of interpretive framework

       Credibility checks (e.g. consensus; auditing; respondent validation;

       triangulation)

Figure 3.1   Summary of criteria and values applicable to pluralistic community research
Source: reproduced with permission from Barker, C. & Pistrang, N. (2005). Quality criteria under methodological pluralism: implications for conducting and evaluating research. *American Journal of Community Psychology*, **35**, 201–12, Table 1

diaries, letters, and varieties of expressive and projective creations, and Maslow's (1954/1987) study of self-actualisation. Allport's case is interesting because he anticipated later criticisms of qualitative research. For example he recognised that there were those, "... who damn the personal document with faint praise, saying that its sole merit lies in its capacity to yield hunches or to suggest hypotheses ... " (Allport, 1942, p. 191, cited by Wertz, 2001, p. 237). The interesting thing about Maslow's study of self-actualisation, which was to become so influential in western psychology, was the apologetic way in which, according to Wertz, he presented it, assuring the reader that the study was not planned as ordinary research, and that it departed from normal science which insisted on the conventions of such things as reliability, validity, and sampling. More recent forces for qualitative research in humanistic psychology have come, according to Wertz, from a variety of directions. One was from philosophical criticisms of the positivistic model of science, including ideas from feminism that questioned 'essentialism' and the search for universal laws, and which emphasised that research involves a human relationship. Another was via the growth of multi-culturalism that challenged the hegemony of Anglo-Saxon science, leading to an explosion of alternative methods including narrative methods, grounded theory, feminist research, and case study approaches.

In the quite recent past, many writers on community psychology have expressed regret that qualitative research methods were not better represented in research reports than in fact was the case (e.g. Newbrough, 1995; Sue, 1999). Trickett (1996) thought the neglect of qualitative methods, including studies that mixed qualitative and quantitative work, had resulted in, "... an enormous loss in our understanding of context ... [qualitative] work is more likely to illuminate how lives are led locally and in context" (p. 216). Those who have championed community health psychology, or a public health psychology, have also been among the keen advocates of qualitative research methods, arguing that qualitative research is necessary in order to move beyond purely individual psychological models of health, mechanical knowledge production, and putting research participants into the straight-jacket of researchers' preconceptions (Marks, 1996, 2002; Hepworth, 2004).

Qualitative Research Supports Community Psychology's Core Values

Banyard and Miller's (1998) argument was that qualitative research methods could support three core values of community psychology, namely diversity, the importance of context, and the notion of empowerment (Trickett *et al.*, 1993; Rappaport, 1990). Qualitative methods, they thought, were ideally suited to valuing diversity since the 'thick' description such methods offer helps capture the details of multiple perspectives and viewpoints, and gets closer to the *emic*[1] or insider's view than is possible with forced-choice questionnaires developed from general theory. Banyard's (1995) own research on homeless mothers is a good example (see Chapter 7). In Banyard's view qualitative methods – such as focus groups, observations of settings, semi-structured and unstructured interviews, participation in the daily life of community residents, ethnographic methods, and document analysis – were also ideally suited to countering neglect of context. Some of those methods involved researchers actually interacting with the participants in the latter's natural settings, while others at least enquired about the settings for people's experiences. The third core community psychology value, empowerment, could also be served by qualitative research. It might, for example, provide a way for

---

[1]The term 'emic', and its contrast 'etic', are derived from linguistics. Whereas the latter implies comparison between communities or cultures and the use of measures and methods that can be applied across communities, the former suggests in-depth, local study of an individual community or culture in its own right, with no assumption that different communities can be readily compared.

participants to tell their stories in their own words, which itself could be empowering. Some of Banyard's (1995) participants had commented that they felt they had been 'heard', and had been asked some questions not often asked of them, such as about their strengths, that helped them understand their experiences differently. In general they commented that open-ended discussion had helped them step back from their experiences and see them differently. At the community level, the ethnographer might be seen as a kind of historian, documenting communal stories of struggle and oppression, affirming the reality of a community's experience, documenting it in written form, and facilitating its dissemination. The process could be taken a step further by enabling participants to share their stories with one another or by having participants conduct interviews with one another. Support from other group members could enable expression of critical views, raise group consciousness, reduce self-blame, and help generate a shared understanding of the social and political contexts of their circumstances (Rappaport, 1990).

Stein and Mankowski (2004), writing a few years later, thought that there were still few published studies in the field using qualitative research methods, that there was a sense of marginalisation among those in the field who used such methods, an absence of formal training courses, and "a maze of contradictory choices" (p. 22) about how to do it. They shared the view that qualitative research enabled better understanding of diversity, the nuances of social context, development of more ecologically sensitive constructs and measures, and the potential to empower typically marginalised groups. As Mishler (1994) wrote in the foreword to *Writings for a Liberation Psychology*:

> Typically, the motives, behaviours, and personal characteristics of oppressed and marginalized people are studied, analyzed, and interpreted from the position of a presumably neutral, external observer. Their own voices are rarely heard, the particularities of their lives and circumstances are not examined, and they are pathologized and objectified (p. ix).

Stein and Mankowski agreed that the metaphor of 'giving voice' was a powerful one in relation to qualitative research, but they wished to raise a number of issues about it. Might it be the case, they asked, that qualitative research, "... serves to reveal or amplify the voices of participants, but does not transform those voices" (p. 22). Secondly, they wished to make explicit what it was about the qualitative research process that might facilitate social action. They outlined a framework of four inter-related acts – asking, witnessing, interpreting, and knowing – to help understand the qualitative research process and how it might contribute to transformation and change (see Table 3.1). 'Giving voice' involved researchers placing themselves side by side with participants and putting themselves in the role of advocates. As witness, the researcher, "... listens to and affirms the experiences of a narrator giving a testimonial" (p. 24). Indeed qualitative researchers might be among the few to witness participants as, "... valued informants and teachers" (p. 24). That role implies that the researcher is not a dispassionate scientist but is an emotionally involved "impassioned listener" (p. 24). The act of interpreting, in light of the notion of giving voice to participants, involved a tension between participant voice and what Stein and Mankowski called 'researcher authority'. Some qualitative researchers, they suggested, attempted to avoid that tension by quoting

Table 3.1 Qualitative research: a process in four acts

Name of act	Process
Act I: The Act of Asking	Identifying and enlisting the people who will be the focus of qualitative inquiry. Requires reflection about assumptions and goals that motivate selection of qualitative methods. Can choose to enlist disenfranchised groups in qualitative research to support empowerment aims or enlist dominant groups to support power sharing or other transformations designed to end oppression.
Act II: The Act of Witnessing	Listening to and affirming the experiences of research participants. A witness is an open, totally present, passionate listener, who is affected and responsible for what is heard. Focus of witnessing is on acceptance of what is heard and accountability for acting upon it, not on the personal needs of the researcher or a desire of mutuality between researcher and participant.
Act III: The Act of Interpreting	Making sense of the collective experience of participants by transforming 'participant stories' into 'research stories' based on the experiences and knowledge of the researcher. Researcher recognises his or her interpretive authority in working with qualitative material. A critical point of departure in the experience of researcher and participant.
Act IV: The Act of Knowing	Creating publicly accessible representations of knowledge gained by conducting qualitative research. Embodies the reflections and understandings of the researcher about the social context and lives of research participants. Knowing can be represented through variety of activities such as writing, teaching, speaking, organising, depending on research and action goals.

Source: reproduced with permission from Stein, C.H. & Mankowski, E.S. (2004). Asking, witnessing, interpreting, knowing: conducting qualitative research in community psychology. *American Journal of Community Psychology*, **33**, 21–35, Table 1

extensively, directly from participants, and failing to acknowledge their own strong and personal influence in interpreting the data. In their view:

> it was necessary to reflect upon and write about the process of qualitative data analysis, explaining how the researcher's own position influenced the selection and interpretation of material (Stein & Mankowski, 2004, p. 31).

Feminist scholars have been particularly clear that researchers should lay out their own values and personal agendas, but Stein and Mankowski suggested going beyond the brief paragraph or two that was often all that was possible in a research publication or report. Finally, the act of knowing was in their view much more than simply writing up results, but included activities such as teaching, using popular culture to disseminate findings, and creating alternative settings. The giving voice analogy implied that the process needed to 'amplify' such voices. Researchers should respond to Rappaport's (1990) challenge to ask for whose benefit the research was being conducted, who would hear the voices of the participants, what good the outcome would do for them, who might be harmed, and what the long-term contribution to knowledge might be. They referred to a form of validity which Denzin (1989) called 'verisimilitude', or the recreation in the reader of an experience similar to that of the participant's through the use of vivid, thick description and 'experience-near language'.

Stein and Mankowski provided several examples of going beyond academic reports when it comes to the fourth act, the act of knowing. On the basis of Stein's research, adults with diagnoses of 'schizophrenia' who were clients of the local community mental health centre volunteered as 'community teachers' to graduate students. Students were required to complete the project by writing a short paper in the form of a personal narrative about their community teacher, who read drafts, supplied comments, and received a final copy. Several community teachers gave a copy of their student's final paper to family members, friends and case workers. Collaboration on the final paper was one of the most transformative aspects of the project. From Mankowski's work on domestic violence came a joint paper with a graduate student on the subject of men's self-help groups, accompanied by an autobiographical essay from a men's group organiser; a men's group as an extension course at the local YMCA set up with a colleague; a series of local Man-to-Man conferences offering small group discussions on issues which men often find difficult to discuss, such as sexual abuse and victimization, domestic violence, and homophobia; and a weekly call-in radio programme, 'Man to Man: Can We Talk?'

Narrative Research

Narrative research has been championed by a number of writers such as Rappaport (2000) in community psychology generally, Mulvey *et al.* (2000) writing from a feminist community psychology viewpoint, and Josselson and Lieblich (2001) from a humanistic perspective. The latter authors referred to the influence of the so-called 'narrative turn' that has taken place in all of the social sciences. Narrative research they saw as an example of one of the new paradigms in psychology, with their aims of:

> ...understanding and describing rather than measuring and predicting, focusing on meaning rather than on causation and frequency, interpretation rather than statistical analysis, and recognizing the importance of language and discourse rather than reducing to numerical representation. These approaches are holistic rather than atomistic, concern themselves with particularity rather than with universals, are interested in the cultural context rather than trying to be context free, and give over-arching significance to subjectivity rather than questing for some type of objectivity (Josselson & Lieblich, 2001, p. 276).

Mulvey *et al.* (2000) saw narrative research as giving voice to non-dominant, marginalised groups, by allowing their stories to be told, rather than the normally widely distributed stories of those with greater economic, political and cultural power and privilege. According to Josselson and Lieblich (2001), stories can range from complete autobiographies, or long monologues given in response to an interviewer prompt, to a much shorter descriptive statement provided in answer to a single interview open-ended question. Methods could include interviews, diaries, art works, and other forms of testimony.

A good example was provided by Harper *et al.* (2004) who described the use of 'narrative ethnography' in a study of the sexual health of Mexican USAmerican female adolescents in a Chicago community. Their method was based on the theory of narratives. Narratives, or shared or common stories, they explained, were often negative in the case of people with few material resources, and were frequently appropriated into individuals' personal stories. Common stories, or narratives, indicate a psychological sense of community, meaning and identity, explaining to people themselves, and to others, who they are and what they are doing and why. But narratives need not be accessed only via individual stories told during individual in-depth interviews, although that was a method used in this project. They can also be communicated via community rituals, performances, artistic displays, local or culture-specific newspapers and popular magazines, archival data, and academic and other literature written about the culture, in this case about Mexican Americans. That suggested that adding ethnographic data could strengthen the findings. The project was a partnership between a university group and a local HIV prevention programme. Narratives and stories were used throughout to describe both the programme and its clients and staff and the neighbourhood within which it was set. The evaluators spent time observing in the project and in the surrounding neighbourhood, whenever possible using public transport, eating and buying food locally, and holding meetings at the agency. They joined fundraising and local cultural events. Much was learned about 'old stories' that disempowered young women in that community when it came to risks and opportunities in the area of sexual health. They included narratives supporting silence about sexual matters, traditional gender roles that limited women's expression of sexuality, that did not promote knowledge about use of condoms, but perpetuated negative stereotypes about those living with HIV, and even supported attachment to neighbourhood gangs. The project therefore promoted 'new stories', which in some ways could be viewed as 'subverting culture'. In conclusion, Harper *et al.* recommended narrative ethnography as a flexible, context-specific method of research that accessed narratives using a variety of methods and multiple sources, involving continued participation in a variety of community organisations and activities over a longer period of time than is traditional in research.

Issues of Reality and Interpretation

Qualitative methods in psychology have developed very rapidly in the last few years. Watts and Serrano-García (2003), over-viewing articles in a special issue of the *American Journal of Community Psychology* on the psychology of liberation, were able to point to the fact that all had emphasised qualitative methods and that a range of very different such methods were now in existence, from conversation analysis to ethnography, with their very different epistemologies and methodological traditions. One of the liveliest debates is the issue of realism versus relativism (already considered in Chapter 2 when discussing social constructionism). For example, Hepburn (2003), whose sympathies clearly lie with relativism, equated realism with an old-fashioned empiricist–positivist philosophy of science that pretends to display objectively 'things as they really are', and dismisses subjectivity as a set of biases that simply stand in the way of discovering the 'truth'. That position stands opposed to a constructionist perspective which presumes that there is not one truth but many, that truths are socially constructed, and that all descriptions involve interpretation. The criticism of that position is that it denies the 'realities' of people's lives, especially the lives of those who are poor, oppressed or victimised. Hence it is bound, some say, to take a politically neutral position and hence to prevent rather than to promote social and political commitment (e.g. Parker, 1997). The relativist's riposte is to say that, even in the case of extreme adversity, there are different ways of talking about people's circumstances; that in practice relativists are just as socially and politically committed as realists; and that to defend one way of describing things as reality is to hide one's own rhetorically constructed arguments from examination or criticism, and is, therefore, paradoxically, against 'truth'. After all, the most oppressive political regimes have tried to convince their citizens of the truth of a simplified, single version of reality (Hepburn, 2003).

It may be that Hepburn is not being entirely fair to the way in which some community psychologists using qualitative methods have used the term 'reality'. Consider, for example, the 'reality' of the lives of people living in poverty. Reid (1993) was one who recommended the use of qualitative methods for studying the experiences of poor women, and Narayan et al.'s (2000) summary of participatory poverty assessments (PPAs) from around the world (dealt with in more detail in Chapter 8) argued that such open-ended methods – including unstructured interviews, discussion groups, and a variety of participatory visual methods – unlike large-scale surveys consisting of closed-ended questions, were much better able to provide:

> ...rich descriptions of poor people's *realities*, drawing on their experiences of poverty and the quality of their interactions with a range of institutions, from the state to the household. This book is about their voices. Voices of the poor send powerful messages that point the way toward policy change (from the Introduction to *Voices of the Poor*, p. 3, my emphasis).

Among other highly pertinent issues that Narayan et al. touched on were: the dangers in generalising, since experiences of poverty were very heterogeneous and no generalisations applied to every location or every poor person (the idea of 'local' or 'situated' knowledge); the power of direct quotations from individual people in communicating with others about the experiences of poor people; and the responsibility of those carrying out PPAs to follow up with action to empower poor people (or else to be clear that the researchers came 'empty-handed' so that poor people could participate on the clear understanding that researchers were powerless to help them directly, but could enable poor people's voices to be heard and carried to those who might be in a position to help).

Another, rather fundamental, question about qualitative research is to what extent the researcher is allowed to make interpretations of what participants say. For example, that gave rise to a contradiction in Josselson and Lieblich's (2001) chapter which they never resolved. On the one hand they stated that a narrative research interviewer is a listener who, "...accepts the story with complete respect and refrains from judging or evaluating it" (p. 281). The focus was on, "...what the individual thinks he or she is doing and why the individual thinks he or she is doing so" (p. 282) – the position that corresponds more closely to the present author's. But people are not, "...fully the authors of their lives..." (p. 282), because of the difficulty of recognising social processes that affect one's position in life. Hence a narrative researcher will present, "...both what the person studied says about his or her experience (the phenomenology) and the researcher's own interpretation of it" (p. 281).

Stein and Mankowski (2004) argued that it should not only be marginalised groups who were the focus of qualitative research, but also members of privileged or majority groups, since the latter might illuminate dominant cultural narratives and help the dismantling of oppressive systems, even raising critical consciousness among members of dominant groups in the process (the experiences of gay and lesbian groups, discussed in Chapter 8, provide a good example of the importance of majority group attitudes). That inevitably gives rise to a dilemma for the researcher. It was an issue in Mankowski's research with male perpetrators of domestic violence. Giving voice to the latter group was particularly challenging since, although the men participants reported many experiences, including experiences of abuse, in which they had little power or control, Mankowski also saw the group as one that had relative power and control in relation to women, including the women who had been the victims of their own violence. He wished to witness what they had to say in an open, non-judgemental way, but also not to collude with or rationalise oppression. Group members commented that the process had helped them reflect on their lives and discover new potentials. When it came to the act of interpreting, despite the awkwardness that Mankowski felt in bringing a more critical perspective, and his worry that this shift in perspective was contrary to the implicit grounds of the researcher–participant relationship,

> It was necessary to shift my view of the interpretive process from one of 'giving voice' to the 'correct' story from the participants' perspectives, to 'critically appreciating' their experiences within the context of feminist theories of men's gender role socialization and system of masculine power... While this approach to interpretation does not purely 'give voice' to the men's experiences, it does represent their voices within the broader social context in which they are created (p. 31).

PARTICIPATORY AND ACTION RESEARCH

The traditional way of judging whether we are doing good and not harm (the critical perspective demands that we always remain open to the possibility that the latter is the case despite our best intentions) has been to use one of the recognised scientific methods of evaluation. The randomised controlled trial has been the gold standard for many, but non-randomised quasi-experimental evaluation designs have been widely promoted and made use of (Cook & Campbell, 1979; Shadish *et al.*, 2002; and see Humphreys *et al.*, 2004 for an interesting example to do with the promotion of mutual help resources). Evaluation has traditionally been considered an essential element of community psychology for several reasons: because it is a means of identifying positive and negative effects of actions for social change; because it is recognised that resources are usually limited and need to be used as effectively as possible; and because those who seek to promote social change need to be accountable to those who may be affected by it (Veno & Thomas, 1992a). Those who have reviewed preventive work, for example in the area of the prevention of depression (Blair, 1992) or prevention programmes aimed at children and adolescents (Durlak & Wells, 1997, 1998), have often drawn attention to the considerable room for improvement in evaluation research designs. A model of research and action that has been popular in community psychology in the USA is Experimental Social Innovation and Dissemination (ESID) (Fairweather *et al.*, 1969; Seidman, 2003). That model, which will be considered in more detail in Part IV, requires an innovative programme – for example for mental health service users, homeless people, or recipients of domestic violence – to be subject to controlled evaluation, further replication, and then wider dissemination.

ESID and other controlled approaches to evaluation are in keeping with the model of the community activist as a 'scientist practitioner'. That model remains a strong one in community psychology. Alongside it has risen an alternative epistemology, and it is one that has been growing in strength. It embraces action research and participatory ways of doing research, often combined under the rubric of participatory action research.

In their introduction to the *Handbook of Action Research*, Reason and Bradbury (2001) included the following statement about action research:

> It seeks to bring together action and reflection, theory and practice, in participation with others, in the pursuit of practical solutions to issues of pressing concern to people, and more generally the flourishing of individual persons and their communities (p. 1).

Among the origins of action research they included: the experiments of Kurt Lewin in the 1940s (Lewin, K., 1951; Lewin, M., 1992), critiques of positivist science, recognition of the importance of indigenous traditions, Marxist ideas and the educational work of Freire (see Chapter 2), more recent practices of participative research by governments, non-government organisations (NGOs) and supranational bodies such as the World Bank (e.g. Narayan *et al.*, 2000, referred to above), liberating perspectives on gender and race, the self-help and co-counselling movements, and organisational development. While being part of the shift brought about by postmodernity, action research in their view pursued a third way, neither wholly embracing the positivism of modernity nor the constructionist postmodern alternative. The latter they found unsatisfactory because, with its concern for discourse, text, and narrative, there was a comparative neglect of its relationship with action. It was actions in the world that interested Reason and Bradbury. In a world in which production and use of knowledge tends to be monopolised by the powerful, the worldview that appealed to them was a participatory, action-oriented one.

Table 3.2 Principles of appreciative forms of action research

Methods	Results
Zero in on moments of excellence and the factors and forces that make them possible	A release of new constructive conversations, refocusing an organisation's attention away from problems and towards positive possibilities
Dream about what could be, design the future through dialogue, and attempt to construct the future by innovation and action	
Use participants' (e.g. teachers') capacities for reflection, respect their voices and knowledge, take participant-generated knowledge as seriously as other forms of knowledge	A heightened sensitivity to an array of diverse experiences and multiple ways of acquiring knowledge
Invest in the intellectual capital of participants, resulting in them having control over most aspects of the research process	Positive social bonding A creation of self-reinforcing learning communities
Foster intellectual challenge and stimulation in the work, encouraging deep thinking about practice, rather than given 'solutions'	The promotion of egalitarian ways of interacting A creation of a positive orientation towards change
Research takes place over a substantial period of time (at least a year), in a safe and supportive environment, and participation is voluntary	

Source: based on Ludema, J.D., Cooperrider, D.L. & Barrett, F.J. (2001). Appreciative inquiry: the power of the unconditional positive question. In P. Reason & H. Bradbury (eds), *Handbook of Action Research: Participative Inquiry and Practice* (pp. 189–99). London: Sage; and Zeichner, K. (2001). Educational action research. In P. Reason & H. Bradbury (eds), *Handbook of Action Research: Participative Inquiry and Practice* (pp. 273–83). London: Sage

In practice action research has been used in a very wide variety of settings, ranging from a group of health visitors forming a cooperative inquiry group to explore sources of stress in their work (Traylen, 1994), to an attempt to maximise the effectiveness of an NGO – for example the Global Relief and Development Organization, working with over 100 partner organisations around the world (Ludema *et al.*, 2001). Action research has tended towards the use of methods such as 'appreciative inquiry', which aims to counteract the generally critical approach in scholarship and the dominance of vocabularies of deficit. For instance, traditions of action research in education in English-speaking countries, described by Zeichner (2001), contain good examples of methods that aim to respect the voices and knowledge of teachers, and take teacher-generated knowledge as seriously as other forms of knowledge (see Table 3.2).

Both Hall (2001) and Swantz *et al.* (2001) referred to the history of participatory action research in Tanzania going back to the early days of independence in that country when the political programme, under the influence of the then President Nyerere, himself a former teacher, emphasised people's participation in their development and the capacity of education for people's empowerment. Hall (2001) was in favour of a type of participatory action research biased in favour of the least powerful, the goal being the radical transformation of social reality and the improvement of the lives of people themselves. That kind of practice had probably always existed wherever there was collective struggle: the actions of women in the early days of the Women's Movement and the struggle of Aboriginal peoples to recover their own traditions and make land claims, were particular examples of participatory research. If those involved invited a university-based group to become involved, they needed to set up conditions at the start to maintain control of the process. Outside researchers needed to do their best to validate the participatory processes that were already underway, and could help by strengthening the documentational aspects. Particular inspiration had come from the world of the arts – of song and dance and poetry and discussion. Popular theatre was another method that has been widely used. There was danger in the use of concepts like 'participatory research', and even the term 'community', which could serve to help mask relations of power, and render class and ethnic differences invisible. Much of the best participatory research, particularly the early examples, had been done outside the confines of the university. In general, universities, with their tendency to monopolise knowledge production and to privilege academic forms of dissemination, were not, in Hall's view, the best places from which to carry out participatory research (Hall admitted that that put researchers like himself – who acknowledged the importance of a period at the Institute for Development Studies at the University of Sussex, and who at the time of writing held a Chair at the University of Toronto – in an uncertain position).

Writing about 'action science', Friedman (2001) contrasted remaining 'on the high ground' of rigorous research with 'descending to the swamp' (Schön, 1987) of the real world of practice where all the variables are changing at once and where a greater variety of research methods must be entertained. What is then of interest to action science is research *in* practice, uncovering tacit theories of action, and hence building 'theories in practice'.

Balancing Research Rigour with Community Relevance

In a chapter in a volume on *Participatory Community Research* (Jason *et al.*, 2004), Boothroyd *et al.* (2004) also tackled the difficult question of how a functional evidence base for improving practice can be developed in the complex and dynamic context of a real community. Such settings do not easily lend themselves to experimental methods, such as the randomised controlled trial, based on a positivist science-based view of knowledge creation. In order to balance scientific rigour with community relevance, and to resolve the tension between internal and external validity, they recommended a more complete framework for enhancing the knowledge base. It combines scientific assessment with what Boothroyd *et al.* called 'significance assessment' (Figure 3.2). Evidence should be sought, not solely about the outcomes of a project, but also about processes, such as how community members are involved in defining problems and taking action, and about intermediate outcomes, such as whether an intervention makes a change to policies, programmes, and practices. Evidence needs to be based on both research and practice. That meant going beyond the 'proof game', with its requirement for greater

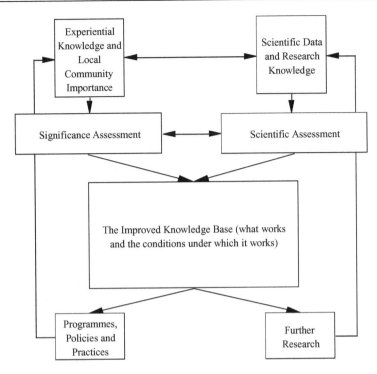

Figure 3.2 A framework for enhancing the knowledge base in community development
Source: adapted from Boothroyd, R.I., Fawcett, S.B. & Foster-Fishman, P.G. (2004). Community development: enhancing the knowledge base through participatory action research. In L.A. Jason *et al.* (eds), *Participatory Community Research: Theories and Methods in Action* (pp. 37–52). Washington, DC: American Psychological Association

experimental control, to include a 'plausibility game', recognising the value of knowledge derived from experience, and being open to a more judicial review of evidence.

That broader view of what constitutes evidence included scientific assessment that may use any one or more method – experimental, quasi-experimental, case study and other methods that may involve randomisation, matched communities, repeated or triangulated measures, and use of extensive study periods – chosen as the most appropriate and feasible with the aim of providing more or less convincing evidence of causality (Boothroyd *et al.*, 2004). Longer term engagement with communities could build capacity for using a wide range of such methods. But in practice failure to demonstrate a causal association between an intervention and outcomes could be related to all manner of factors, including insufficient study periods, lack of statistical power, measurement problems, limited strength of the intervention, and exposure to the same or similar interventions in comparison groups. Scientific assessments needed to be integrated with significance assessments in which community residents, as the primary stakeholders, could contribute, for example by prioritising issues and concerns, framing shared goals, designing and implementing intervention strategies, and contributing to stakeholder interviews and community surveys.

As an example, Boothroyd *et al.* (2004) described a study designed to reduce risks for adolescent pregnancy in three communities in Kansas, USA. It involved various sets of community partners working together to bring about a variety of relevant changes in the way of education, support, public awareness, provision of contraceptives, and access to health services. A scientific assessment, in the form of a multiple time series design with three intervention communities and three matched comparison communities, provided only limited evidence of effectiveness in the form of changes in birth rates for teenage girls in the intervention areas, with slight changes overall and some evidence of a greater effect in target neighbourhoods that had had enhanced exposure to the intervention. Significance assessment came in the form of information from focus groups, surveys, and dialogue among the local action teams and community leaders. Thereby a great deal was learned about what were believed to be critical aspects (e.g. school curricula enhancement and teacher training, enhanced health department clinic hours, access to contraceptives), about satisfaction with leadership and other aspects of the intervention, about the way in which the programme could be adapted to particular communities while at the same time maintaining core components of the intervention, and about the need to make documentation systems fit busy schedules and the needs of community members for useable data reports. Boothroyd *et al.* made the observation that scientific assessments were much more likely to be published and that the published literature therefore under-represented the all-important significance assessment component. Another suggestion was that community collaborators should more often be involved as paid documenters and co-authors of reports. In summary:

> Through collaboration in fact-finding, action, and reflection, local people and outside researchers can contribute to and strengthen the coproduction of information for a knowledge base for community development. By giving voice to the experience of community members and researchers, an inclusive assessment of evidence in community development can help develop a more complete and evolving knowledge base about community-determined change efforts (Boothroyd *et al.*, 2004, pp. 48–9).

Porkorny *et al.* (2004), writing in the same volume, also addressed what they saw as the difficulty of integrating community and academic responses to problems, and hence the limited impact on community efforts of what they termed 'prevention science'. They presented a framework for integration illustrated with two case studies from a programme of youth tobacco use prevention conducted by a university community research centre. The first, a relatively small-scale project in one community, was undertaken on the initiative of an officer of the local police department concerned about the sale of tobacco to minors. It resulted in the passing of a local ordinance that required retailers to obtain a licence to sell tobacco, with a system of warnings, fines and licence suspensions for violations (continuously monitored by compliance checks). These developments were highly effective in reducing sales to young people and, over a follow-up period of several years, in reducing the rate of tobacco use by young people. The project influenced national policy, and the police officer involved was active in persuading other communities to follow the

- Building collaboration on time-honoured management principles, including involving all partners early on, bringing the whole coalition together on a regular basis, defining roles and responsibilities clearly, and addressing conflicts openly and honestly

- Maintaining openness and transparency at every level, for example openly and regularly discussing external constraints

- Attending to leadership and organisational structure and being prepared to adapt (e.g. in their community trial one school system preferred to take the lead in completing the student survey, whereas another preferred the research team to take the lead)

- Acknowledging and managing different agendas, developing mechanisms for balancing different interests, and being committed to continual negotiation

- Preparing for inevitable changes (e.g. in one community that took part in their trial the entire school district was reorganised including the appointment of new senior school personnel)

- Planning for dissemination and the different ideas that different groups may have (e.g. some schools did not want school-specific information disseminated outside the school, whereas others were willing to share that information)

- Attending to small details of collaboration such as locations and times of meetings, openness of language, and equal access to information

- Promoting mutual respect and transfer of knowledge and skills (e.g. grant obtaining skills)

- Addressing barriers to sustainability after academic partners move on (e.g. by building networks of concerned community members and raising community awareness).

Figure 3.3   Guidelines for collaborative prevention work
Source: according to Porkorny, S.B., Baptiste, D.R., Tolan, P., Hirsch, B.J., Talbot, B.J.P., Paikoff, R.L. & Madison-Boyd, S. (2004). Prevention science: participatory approaches and community case studies. In L.A. Jason *et al.* (eds), *Participatory Community Research: Theories and Methods in Action* (pp. 87–104). Washington, DC: American Psychological Association

lead set by the project. This led to the second case example discussed by Porkorny *et al.*, which was a randomised community trial involving young people and their schools in eight towns in northern and central Illinois which were matched and randomly assigned. Porkorny *et al.*'s guidelines for collaborative prevention work are listed in Figure 3.3.

Balcazar *et al.* (2004a) outlined what they believed to be the characteristic features of PAR and its importance for community psychology. For them the defining factor was the degree of control that participants of a study had over the process, related factors being the amount of collaboration between researchers and

Table 3.3 The continuum of participant involvement in participatory action research (PAR)

Level of PAR	Degree of control	Amount of collaboration	Degree of commitment
No PAR	Research participants with no control	Minimal	None
Low	One consumer adviser or a group of consumer advisers	Advisory board members	Minimal
Medium	Responsibility for oversight and representation in research meetings	On-going advisers Reviewers Consultants Possible contractual agreement	Multiple commitments Increased ownership of the research process
High	Equal partners Leading partners with capacity to hire the researchers	Active researchers Research leaders	Full commitment Full ownership of the research process

Source: Balcazar, F.E. *et al.* (2004a). Participatory action research: general principles and a study with a chronic health condition. In L.A. Jason *et al.* (eds), *Participatory Community Research: Theories and Methods in Action* (pp. 17–36). Washington, DC: American Psychological Association, Table 1.1

participants and the degree of the latter's commitment to the process. Each varied along continua, as shown in Table 3.3. The purpose of PAR varied from, at one extreme, participation in the interests of obtaining maximum information and ideas in order to improve efficiency, quality or effectiveness, or to develop new products, to, at the other extreme, PAR as an instrument for social change in the struggle against oppression. Forms of PAR that perhaps fitted best with community psychology, they suggested, lay between those two positions with a focus on empowerment in order to increase people's control over aspects of their lives. In the process participants moved, "… from a passive victim's stance to a proactive citizen-with-rights stance" (pp. 24–5). Balcazar *et al.* saw, as an important and innovative component, the capacity of PAR to empower participants with learning, involving discovering new understandings and new possibilities. It involved learning how to learn, since people with a history of marginalisation or neglect often feel insecure about themselves and their knowledge. Finally, knowledge became social 'praxis' (the uniting of theory and practice) when participants learn how to transform their social reality. New learning was 'co-created' by insiders and outsiders working together. Another strand to PAR, identified by Balcazar *et al.*, was the integration of thinking, feeling, and action in the process of creating knowledge, hence restoring the feeling and acting dimensions, alongside the cognitive dimension that is privileged by traditional scientific methods.

PAR, Balcazar *et al.* argued, was consistent with community psychology aims and values, including the centrality of citizen participation, the desirability of social change as a goal, the need for appropriate methods of research and action, and

---

> ➢ Consider participants as social actors, with a voice, ability to decide, reflect, and capacity to participate fully in the research process
>
> ➢ The ultimate goal of PAR is the transformation of the social reality of the participants by increasing the degree of control they have over relevant aspects of their community or organisation
>
> ➢ The problem originates in the community/organisation itself and is defined, analysed and solved by the participants
>
> ➢ Active participation leads to a better understanding of the history and culture of the community/organisation and a more authentic analysis of the social reality
>
> ➢ Engaging in a dialogical approach also leads to critical awareness
>
> ➢ Recognising people's strengths also increases their awareness about their existing resources and mobilises them to help themselves
>
> ➢ The research process also promotes personal change both for participants and researchers

---

Figure 3.4   General principles for implementing participatory action research
Source: reproduced with permission from Balcazar, F.E. *et al.* (2004b). Participatory action research: general principles and a study with a chronic health condition. In L.A. Jason *et al.* (eds), *Participatory Community Research: Theories and Methods in Action* (pp. 22–3). Washington, DC: American Psychological Association

the possibility of increasing community psychologists' own critical awareness – and potentially their radicalisation and awareness of their own positions of privilege in society. Their general principles for implementing PAR are summarised in Figure 3.4. To illustrate those principles they referred to: work designed to use peer mentors to help recent victims of gun violence who had been paralysed; an advocacy training programme for a small group of people with physical disabilities; a series of qualitative interviews with people with developmental disabilities, family members and service providers, to document the development of a support and advocacy group for individuals with such disabilities; work with a group of immigrant Latin USAmerican parents of deaf children; documentation of the actions and outcomes for advocacy organisations of people with disabilities; and a train-the-trainer approach to increase parent and consumer involvement in a coalition of people with chronic mental illnesses and their family members.

Hoshmand and O'Byrne (1996) considered action research as a guiding metaphor for professional psychology generally. They also drew on the idea of praxis, with its notion of the unity and reciprocity of thought and action, thinking and doing. Much of the early action research had involved research in organisations, aimed at problems of human productivity and organisational health. A distinct conception of action research, favoured by Hoshmand and O'Byrne, highlighted its democratic ideals and emancipatory potential, and its aim of transforming the social order through conscientisation and empowerment. A philosophical assumption was that the kind of gaining of knowledge useful for generating solutions to problems and taking action corresponded to what Gibbons *et al.* (1994) referred to as

---

❖ Be a pragmatic, reflective learner, requiring skills of consultation and understanding of human systems

❖ Draw on multiple conceptual frameworks and methods to study events and systems in their natural ecological settings

❖ Form new relationships and new social structures

❖ Help to generate a culture of enquiry

❖ Show a commitment to disseminating knowledge to policy makers, practitioners and other consumers of the research, as well as attempting to integrate new knowledge with the formal knowledge of the profession

❖ Substitute a cooperative spirit in place of mere competitive careerism

---

Figure 3.5 Requirements for the action researcher
Source: according to Hoshmand, L.T. & O'Byrne, K. (1996). Reconsidering action research as a guiding metaphor for professional psychology. *Journal of Community Psychology*, **24**, 185–20

Mode 2 knowledge production, or the development of local knowledge based on a substantive domain of practice. It would mean the creation of a type of knowledge about the local social and economic context that is not confined to that recognised by one discipline alone. The contrasting Mode 1 type of knowledge production, more familiar in applied psychological research, originated from theory, aiming to produce knowledge recognised in a particular discipline, valid across diverse settings, and often involving the testing of narrow-gauge hypotheses. In fact the detached, objectivist stance in their view had reinforced a non-consultative approach and could create boundaries between professional psychologists and the communities they served. A sea change in methods was required, they argued, requiring the researcher to use the methods shown in Figure 3.5. This was likely to be severely testing, and new forms of training were required. Included should be student access to reflective accounts of carrying out research (see below), rare in traditional published reports. Teaching of research needed to be less abstract and decontextualised, including more detailed case examples and case studies of action research.

NEGOTIATING THE COMMUNITY PSYCHOLOGY RESEARCHER'S ROLE

Participatory forms of research require, as discussed above, a relationship between researcher and participant that is far more engaged and open to negotiation and change than is the case with the more traditional, controlled forms of knowledge acquisition. It may require researchers to make it clear where they stand on issues of concern to the participants. It certainly requires that they be open, at the very least, to modifying methods and procedures in accordance with participants' wishes. In any case it opens up to scrutiny the researchers' values and positions, their practices, and their relationships with those they are working with, in a way that is not the case with other kinds of research. The following are illustrations of that opening up process.

Women Students Researching in a Centre for Women Experiencing Poverty

For example, Brodsky *et al.* (2004) aimed to correct the presumed objectivity and invisibility of the researchers in 'hard' scientific psychology, by reflecting, not merely on the participants and their community, but also on the research community and its relationship with the participant community. The setting was a centre in Baltimore, USA, run by an order of Catholic Sisters, whose purpose was to help women, who were leaving welfare or working in jobs that paid less than a living wage, to get and retain jobs that did provide a living wage. The research group, based at a university, consisted of a faculty member and a group of her undergraduate and postgraduate students. Like the centre's staff and users, all the university students were women, motivated to work on the project for personal reasons or after having taken the faculty member's class in either community psychology or the psychology of women, and selected for their sensitivity to diversity and commitment to the qualitative research to be undertaken. The latter involved a number of focus groups with centre user participants, individual interviews with staff, and individual interviews with former users of the centre who were gainfully employed and others who had left without completing the programme. A few months after data were collected, and while data analysis was ongoing, the research team took part in their own focus group.

Women centre users talked of their appreciation of the cooperative spirit fostered in the programme, and the sharing of current and past struggles and future goals – very different from what many women had experienced in their home community. Staff were described as caring and loving, but the programme was also described as stressful, and at times women were uncertain whether the staff understood that, and some felt they were judged or treated like children. But what was refreshingly original about Brodsky *et al.*'s paper was the discussion of relationships within the research team and between researchers, the centre and centre user participants. The research team met for two hours weekly and intended that they should be meetings of equals. For example coding qualitative data was carried out by consensus, "... to gain from the synergy of our unique perspectives and to equalise power and voice" (p. 326). In practice Brodsky *et al.* admitted that conflict over coding was not always comfortable, and in the event some members had more power than others over final decisions – the faculty member was one, but certain students who were more vocal than others on particular issues were others. Stronger relationships were built by common attendance at leisure activities and conferences, but the reality of the faculty member's senior relationship within the university system meant that the aim of comfortable, egalitarian interactions was not always achieved.

A number of issues regarding the research team's relationships with the centre and women participants were discussed. Because the team did not want to be seen as too closely affiliated with the centre, they compromised on the issue of location for interviews, by holding them at the centre 'after hours'. One thing that had not been anticipated was that the word 'interview' would have troublesome connotations of evaluation and formality. For example:

Participant: When I first found out about the interview it was on my mind every day. *Researcher*: The interview was? *Participant*: Uh-huh. 'Cause I didn't know whether I was gonna be on TV or whatever. I'm getting interviewed. Every time I tell somebody else they was like, "you gonna get another job" and I was like "no, it's not that kind of interview". And I don't even do interviews well. So how did I do? (p. 238).

Brodsky *et al.* also noted that race and ethnicity were among potentially problematic issues that were not raised during interviews, perhaps because the majority of researchers, and centre staff, were European USAmerican, whereas the majority of centre users were African USAmerican. The fact that all involved were women was considered by Brodsky *et al.* to be an important and positive aspect to the work. Despite the differences in backgrounds between researchers and centre users, "Both communities were in women settings in which members . . . . strove to grow professionally and personally" (p. 240).

Dilemmas for a Researcher in a Randomised Controlled Trial

Nama and Swartz (2002) provided a personal account of some of the ethical and social dilemmas they faced in carrying out a randomised controlled trial in a part of the world characterised by poverty and deprivation. Issues of research ethics, with the power imbalance between researchers and participants at the core of such issues, become, they argued, even more problematic in such areas of the world where community psychologists might increasingly find themselves working. The Thula Sana Project – literally meaning 'Hush little baby' in Xhosa – was such a trial, in which one group received an extra home visiting programme within an existing community health project. The location was a large peri-urban settlement in Cape Town, South Africa, characterised by mostly shack dwellings, very high unemployment and poverty, a shifting population, and poor or insecure provision of services such as electricity, running water and rubbish removal. The rate of post-partum depression had been found to be very high, and the intervention was designed to improve maternal mood and mother–child interaction.

The account focused on the role of the first author, a Xhosa-speaking African resident of Cape Town. As one of the first employees of the project it had been her role to introduce the project and establish its credibility; no easy task since local communities were very aware of past researchers, mainly white, collecting data without making any contribution to improving their lives. Later on she took the role of one of the assessors (assessments were made at two, six, and 18 months after the birth). As part of her role she was required to remain blind to whether a mother and her child were in the intervention or control group. Several examples were given of situations in which a mother and children had to be referred for additional services because of what was seen as a health crisis, thus breaking the trial protocol, or in which the protocol was preserved with some unease on the assessor's part. Nama's role clearly was a stressful one, exacerbated by the change of role in the project that she underwent. Resources for the project made that inevitable, and the authors concluded with the observation that using the money spent on the project in another way would have made little impact on local people's lives, other than in the very short term, whereas if the intervention could be shown to be effective an affordable model would have been developed which had potential to impact on the lives of very much larger numbers of people.

Doubts for those Researching with Sex Workers

Boynton (2002) described the experiences of three female researchers in a community study of prostitution in a West Midlands English town. A number of issues were touched on in her report, including the need for strict confidentiality, the difficulty of including under-age sex workers, the need to ensure the safety of researchers, conflicting expectations of researchers and funding body regarding quoting directly from interviews, scepticism on the part of prostitutes about the value of research rather than helpful action, and negative responses from male academic colleagues and fellow students. The researchers, "... negotiated listening to working women and recording their views, whilst living with conflicting ideas about prostitution" (p. 8). For example, the researchers had embarked on the project believing that it was the right of women to choose to engage in sex work, but this position was difficult to maintain in the face of interview material suggesting the limited choices that many participants had, and the abuse to which they were frequently subjected by pimps and punters. The researchers sometimes felt that they were condoning violence that was occurring. In general their position was informed by feminism, a position that was mostly rejected by their participants who perceived feminism as being anti-prostitutes. At the end of the study the researchers felt depressed, deflated and lethargic, concerned about the safety of the women they had interviewed, and wanting to know that their research had made some positive difference to the women's lives rather than contributing to maintaining the negative image of sex workers about which their participants had complained.

Moving from Expert to Collaborator in Research with Mental Health Service Users

Carrick et al. (2001) discussed different models of participant involvement in the research process in the context of their research concerning mental health service users' views about taking anti-psychotic medication. In the context of their own research they distinguished different levels of mental health service user participant involvement: varying from consultation, where researchers choose to ask users for their views (not then acting on those views may be particularly disempowering); collaboration, which entails a greater degree of partnership where the researcher has chosen to give up some control; and user control, where research only involves professionals if invited by users. Level of involvement might vary from one research stage to another. In their own research, although there was commitment to the idea that people taking anti-psychotic medication could give valid accounts of their experiences, the approach early on was very much that of the 'expert researcher', with the assumption that knowledge comes exclusively through an objective, scientific process. As the research progressed, participants' views about how the research should be conducted began to modify the procedure, in keeping with the growing recognition that personal experience of mental health difficulties and of using services provides an alternative source of knowledge and expertise. For example, planned focus groups were abandoned in favour of individual interviews at the request of the participants.

Taking a Stand in Working with Young People with Disabilities

The theme of taking a stand in community psychology research and action was addressed by Balcazar *et al.* (2004a). They described examples of their work in an intervention and research project conducted with 15–20 year olds with disabilities who were in the process of making the transition from school to employment, post-secondary education, and/or independent living. The project took place in two urban high schools in the USA, one a large school with mostly Latin USAmerican students, the other a smaller special school for students with severe disabilities, most students being African USAmerican. The project required the research/intervention team to adopt the roles of instigators of change (e.g. by making students and family members more aware about opportunities and resources in the school and community), as mediators in resolving conflicts between students, teachers, family members and/or administrators, and as advocates for the students and/or their families in making requests to school administrators.

As instigators of change, they gave the example of responding to one school's decision, one year, not to put any special education students in for the test required by colleges that was necessary in order to pursue post-secondary education. The team knew that this deprived some students of their rights and would be against their interests, but rather than fight teachers and administrators over the decision, the team offered to undertake themselves the complicated steps and lengthy paperwork necessary to put students in for the test. The result was success for a number of students and an enhanced reputation for the team with the school (the team member was offered office space and an ID card, sure signs of being admitted to 'insider status'). An example of acting in the role of mediators involved a 16-year-old female student with a mild cognitive disability, described as 'struggling' by the school and as rebellious and challenging by her family. The team provided mentoring support and obtained agreement from her family to involve a social service agency who would provide counselling and support the family members. Communication between school and family improved and the outcome for the student was good: she went on to pursue post-secondary education and to obtain employment.

In their role as advocates, the team found themselves in conflict with a school principal over the exclusion from school of a 17-year-old young man with quadriplegia, suffered as a result of gun violence. The school wished to exclude him after his involvement in an incident in which a high power firecracker had been detonated and a teacher injured. Although in agreement that some severe punishment was indicated, the team knew that immediate expulsion, with no option to return, and no plan to address the student's educational needs, violated his rights, and they also knew that the correct expulsion procedures had not been followed.

The student and his mother requested the team's assistance, and on the grounds of fairness and justice it was agreed to support them. In the end the principal's wish to exclude the student was upheld, but the team was successful in negotiating an improved offer of home-based education. Although intervention with other students was not stopped, relationships with the school principal were undoubtedly negatively affected, and the team thought it likely that there was less chance of future involvement in other projects at that school. Balcazar *et al.* concluded:

> ...power redistribution involves a complex process of making requests for change, advocating, taking actions, and resolving conflicts through negotiation and compromise that is often not reported in the research literature. We also realized that in order to implement an effective program in a dynamic system, we must be prepared to engage the system in unanticipated ways...as community psychologists we must be fully aware of our own position of power and our potential to contribute to preserving the status quo and/or to challenge it (pp. 250, 251).

Commitment in Working with Refugee and Oppressed Communities

Miller (2004) wrote about the neglect in psychology journals of the relationship between the researcher and participants, and particularly the question of trust. That was even the case in his own area – research with members of refugee communities – where the need to develop a relationship in which the researcher was trusted might be thought to be basic. He was inclined to attribute that neglect to the restrictive demands of the methods that have dominated psychology (criticised by so many others), particularly psychology's historical adherence to positivism, according to which the ideal research relationship is an impersonal, objective and unbiased one, using so-called 'objective' methods – conveniently allowing the researcher to *not* examine critically what he or she brings to the relationship personally or in terms of biases of theory and methods. A second possible factor was the perception among researchers who are addressing such issues that journal editors are unlikely to give room to discussion of such issues. Psychological research with refugee communities had tended to be dominated by the medical/psychiatric model of clinical psychology and psychiatry (see Chapter 1), the vast majority of published studies providing little or no information about the nature of the research relationship, the findings being presented as factual and objective. His experience carrying out research with Guatemalan refugees in southern Mexico, and later with Afghan refugees in the Bay area of California suggested that establishing relations of trust was difficult but crucial. Adopting a neutral position would, for a start, have been counterproductive:

> My research in the refugee camps would not have been possible without my having been willing to make explicit, time and time again, my opposition to the policies and practices of the Guatemalan government and military...To have insisted on a stance of political neutrality in the face of the extraordinary repression the refugees have endured, would have been regarded as both insulting and threatening...(p. 218).

Writing about work in Ireland (introduced in Chapter 2) Moane (2003) referred to the arguments of such as Freire (1993) and Comas-Díaz *et al.* (1998) that psychologists should 'accompany' those living in conditions of oppression, standing with them and developing collaborative working relationships with them, and should be critical of working with professionals and experts in position of power. Fals Borda (2001) has also written of dissatisfaction with the academy, and the benefits of forging collaborative links through direct involvement, for example with non-governmental organisations (NGOs), involving convergence between popular thought and academic science, forming new reference groups with grassroots leaders rather than with university colleagues, and breaking down the distinction between expert researchers and 'clients' or 'targets'. Moane herself referred to the neutral and impartial role of facilitator, favoured in the model of community development in the Irish republic, which had been questioned in the Northern Irish context, where facilitators were challenged to situate themselves politically and socially.

Research with Indigenous Groups

The need for non-indigenous researchers to be especially sensitive in carrying out research with indigenous populations has often been noted. As well as the danger that researching and writing about indigenous problems may appear to be 'blaming the victim' (Saggers & Gray, 1998), there is also the need to be aware of the history of negative representations of indigenous people produced and controlled by colonists and other outsiders in a way that has been biased and culturally prescriptive (Bourke, 1998). Those issues have been discussed in the context of research and indigenous peoples worldwide by Tuhiwai-Smith (1999) who was writing from a Maori perspective. She proposed four models of culturally appropriate research by non-indigenous researchers. The first was a mentoring model in which indigenous people guide and sponsor the research. The second was an adoption model in which researchers are incorporated into the daily life of people and sustain a life-long relationship that extends beyond the research. The third was a power-sharing model in which researchers seriously seek the assistance of the community to support the development of research. The fourth was an empowering outcomes model that addresses the sorts of questions indigenous people ask and that has beneficial outcomes. Researchers are expected to have some form of historical and critical analysis of the role of research in the indigenous world. Key questions are "Whose research is it? Who owns it? Whose interests does it serve? Who will benefit from it? Who has designed its questions and framed its scope? Who will carry it out? Who will write it up? How will its results be disseminated?" (p. 10). Otherwise it could feel as if knowledge was being stolen and exported, like cultural artefacts, to the supposed centre of the academic world in western Europe or North America. Texts might use words such as 'we', 'us' and 'our', which appeared to exclude indigenous people:

> When undertaking research, either across cultures or within a minority culture, it is critical that researchers recognise the power dynamic which is embedded in the relationship with their subjects. Researchers are in receipt of privileged

information. They may interpret it within an overt theoretical framework, but also in terms of a covert ideological framework. They have the power to distort, to make invisible, to overlook, to exaggerate and to draw conclusions, based not on factual data, but on assumptions, hidden value judgements, and often downright misunderstandings (p. 176).

WHAT KIND OF SCIENCE IS COMMUNITY PSYCHOLOGY?

The tension created by the parallel existence of two very different ways of accumulating knowledge in community psychology has given rise to a lot of soul searching. Many, the present author among them, brought up to be a scientist practitioner and familiar with the controlled methods that are part of that tradition, are reluctant to part company with traditional scientific ways altogether. At the same time they are challenged and excited by the idea and examples of participatory methods. This tension has naturally led to efforts to reconcile the more controlled and the more participatory strands.

Criticism of Technology Transfer

The struggle to locate community psychology in relation to science is illustrated by papers that appeared in a special section of an issue of the *American Journal of Community Psychology* in 2003 (Wandersman, 2003) and a special issue of the same journal in 2005 (Wandersman *et al.*, 2005). Although the position adopted by different contributors varied considerably, all were critical of the idea that the philosophy and methods of science that had been dominant in the twentieth century, and which continued to be followed in much of mainstream psychology, could be the sole, or even main, basis for community psychology in the twenty-first century. Wandersman (2003) focused his critique on the assumptions in 'prevention science' that the link between research and practice ran exclusively from the former to the latter, the aim being that interventions that had been tested in research trials would either be perfectly replicated in practice settings, or at least would undergo 'technology transfer' with relatively minor adjustments to the 'product' (this issue is taken up again in the discussion of dissemination in Chapter 10). That paradigm, based on the dominant biomedical model, under-estimated the gap that in fact exists between research and practice and failed to capitalise on the possibility of bidirectional influence between research and practice. Hence the process of improving practice had been misunderstood as one of delivering packaged interventions rather than as a process; had failed to give sufficient emphasis to control by practitioners, patients, clients or communities, and had given insufficient emphasis to local evaluation and self-monitoring. Surprisingly little attention had been devoted to understanding the organisations that carry out the interventions (Wandersman was writing about prevention, but much the same could be said about interventions in treatment and education). Price and Behrens (2003) made a similar point, questioning the assumption that the pursuit of knowledge and of more effective practice were separate activities, with the former proceeding to the latter in a linear fashion.

Against Logical Empiricism

Tebes' (2005) critique was more fundamental. He argued that the philosophy of science had moved on, leaving psychology adhering to logical empiricism which was no longer an appropriate framework for science. Logical empiricism had developed from positivism with its assumptions that all human and social events could be studied using basically one scientific method; that good science should be 'value free'; had established statistics as a major tool; and required that all phenomena to be studied needed to be operationalised in a way that allows for measurement, hence, "...relegat[ing] human 'meaning' – historical, linguistic, psychological, cultural – outside the bounds of scientific inquiry unless it is translated into an observational operation" (Tebes, 2005, p. 215). Among the growing criticism of logical empiricism, highlights included Popper's (1935/1959) *The Logic of Scientific Discovery*, that argued that theories could never be proven – the most they can do is survive repeated attempts at falsification; Kuhn's (1962) *The Structure of Scientific Revolutions*, which argued that scientific progress often involves paradigm shifts that are shaped by many factors besides empirical tests of theory; and Feyerabend's (1975) *Against Method*, that went still further by arguing that science is as much shaped by personal and social factors as by rigorous empirical tests, and that when it comes to choosing appropriate scientific methods, 'anything goes'.

Science and Social Criticism

Rappaport's (2005) critique was based on the thought that science itself interferes with pursuing some of the things, particularly social criticism, that are dear to the hearts of community psychologists (see Chapter 1 re critical psychology). It was too easy to assume that the best way to knowledge was to do science; that the only things worth doing were those that had been scientifically demonstrated; and that it was always necessary to claim a scientific basis for things that were worth doing. In his view community psychology was:

> ...a unique blend of science and social criticism. It is a field of practice with explicit goals that might be thought of... as critical consciousness. Combining the goals of fostering critical consciousness with the methods of science makes for an unusual combination, especially in psychology (p. 233).

That combination was much to be welcomed, since in the hands of agents of the state, represented by such bodies as the Institute of Medicine and the National Institute of Mental Health in the USA, science had acquired the status of a quasi religious belief system, and it was not to be expected that such bodies would fund work that was critical of the powers that be. Community psychology added the critical component.

In order to better bridge the gap between science and practice, Wandersman (2003) proposed a form of 'community science' that would start with the community and its values and perspectives, into which models based upon scientific methods would be integrated. It would have a clear value orientation; would place emphasis on the participation of individuals, organisations and communities, rather than seeing them as passive recipients; it would be systems-oriented, viewing individuals as embedded within social relationships at family, friendship network, organisation, neighbourhood and cultural and societal levels; and it would be contextual, by attending to the historical, legal, political, economic, social-organisational, and cultural features of a community. He clearly saw it as remaining theoretically and empirically grounded, and therefore scientific in the traditional sense. But the science he had in mind would be better adapted to the kinds of issues of interest in community psychology. Community science would be:

> ...multidisciplinary, interdisciplinary, and transdisciplinary – drawing upon anthropology, biomedical sciences, education, political science, psychology, prevention science, public health, social work, sociology, and related fields...[it] attempts to bridge the gaps by developing and researching community-centered models geared to the complexities and realities of communities...(p. 236).

Idealised Design

Commenting on a special issue of the *Journal of Community and Applied Social Psychology* on Action Research and Emancipation, Romme (2004) made the observation that action research, increasingly prominent in the social sciences as a response to the relevance gap between academia and practice, in fact had tended to be confined to the interpretation of existing situations rather than the design and creation of actual change. Romme traced that state of affairs to reliance on two of the three archetypical modes of engaging in research: *science*, which tries to understand phenomena on the basis of consensual objectivity, drawing on a representational view of knowledge; and the *humanities*, with its predominantly constructionist and narrative notion of knowledge, and its assumption that all knowledge arises from what people think and say about their worlds. With the science mode continuing to dominate in the social sciences, the humanities mode served as its emerging antithesis. Preoccupied with debate about the relative values of those two modes, action research had neglected the third mode, that of *design*. Design thinking had moved to other sites in society such as consultancy and governmental agencies, and action researchers did not see themselves as design professionals. Romme recommended, "...a pragmatic design orientation focusing on creative and disciplined inquiry into new systems and practices" (2004, p. 496). A key component of that orientation, according to Romme, is 'idealised design' involving a vision of what a group or organisation's stakeholders wanted the group or organisation to be. As practised currently, action research remained situated in the social context as it currently is, hence leaving the status quo relatively intact.

Uncovering Theories that are being Practised

Hess (2005) argued for 'hermeneutics' as a valuable supplement to traditional science, as a way of dealing with the complexity, the 'messiness' of community phenomena, at the same time avoiding strong-form constructionism that rejects any consistent way of choosing between different knowledge claims. Hermeneutics – with its origins in the critical reading and debating of religious texts – would not displace science but would focus more on concrete examples, local settings, providing much fuller accounts than are normally available in research reports of what actually happened. It would not assume that the aim was to produce an abstract, context-less theory that would be generalisable to all contexts. It would pay more attention to 'tacit' knowledge (Polanyi, 1964), often implicit and unarticulated knowledge, including the experience of practitioners. It assumes that knowledge is inseparable from or 'fused' with the world as it is experienced, and that, as with notions of praxis, practice and theory are united. To put it another way, theories are "already housed in practice" (p. 244), and an aim is to uncover or disclose the theory or theories that are in use locally by practitioners or other participants. Like constructionism, it would recognise the importance of personal background, or what Gadamer (1989) called the 'horizon of experience'. In place of a technology metaphor that uses terms such as 'instruments' and 'tools', hermeneutics would emphasise human *dialogue*, stressing the importance of engagement with multiple horizons of experience, learning from fresh interpretations gained by observing contrasting horizons, and the importance of bilateral exchanges. Work would be recentred on human relationships rather than instruments.

Perspectivism

Tebes (2005) went considerably further in suggesting that 'contextualism' was the 'world view' or 'root metaphor' (Pepper, 1942) most appropriate for community psychology, as a replacement for outdated logical empiricism. Human actions were embedded in a particular context – a particular time, place, and culture. Knowledge was 'situated', in the sense that knowledge about the world was dependent on one's point of view or position in the world. It was not the task of science to establish laws that were true in all contexts, but rather to find out which propositions were true in which contexts. An implication for scientific inquiry was that a pluralism of theories and methods was necessary. A danger of radical contextualism, on the other hand, was that it could easily devolve into the kind of relativism favoured by some varieties of postmodernism and social constructionism which deny the existence of a 'truth' or a 'reality', and reject all traditional scientific methods derived from logical empiricism (see Chapter 2 for a discussion of social constructionsim). Tebes' (2005) solution to that dilemma was to advocate a modified version of contextualism, known as 'perspectivism'. The latter assumes that there is a mind-independent reality, "... that can be known, albeit imperfectly" (p. 225), and that it is the task of science to pursue 'truth' by examining the validity of knowledge claims that derive from different methods in different contexts. Knowledge about that reality, however, depends on the perspective from which it is viewed – as has long been argued by feminist philosophers and critical theorists, as well as by those who point to the discrepancy that is frequently found in judgements on outcomes following interventions (positive reports of satisfaction and testimonies of positive change are often at odds with lack of significant effects in terms of 'objective' outcome measures). Perspectivism supports hypothesis testing but would redress the imbalance found in psychology between hypothesis testing and hypothesis generation (an imbalance that could be attributed to the Fisherian legacy in social science that privileges experimental design) by emphasising the process of creative discovery and the importance of additional hypothesis generation at each phase of the research process.

Tebes (2005) thought that advocacy of perspectivism would fall on sympathetic ears in community psychology. It was in line, he thought, with the field's concerns about narrow adherence to experimental and other traditional methods, concern that too few studies examined phenomena at multiple levels of analysis, that the relevance of the researchers' personal knowledge of the subject matter was almost never included in research reports, that the points of view of participants or other stakeholders were rarely taken into account (indeed reports often provided very little information about participants and settings), and that stakeholder perspectives involving experiences of oppression or liberation were often ignored. Perspectivism offered to correct those deficiencies. There were hopeful signs that such a position was becoming more widely accepted in psychology: Tebes (2005) pointed, for example, to the update of Cook and Campbell's (1979) book on quasi-experimental design, by Shadish, Cook and Campbell (2002), that acknowledges that all research methods have biases, and encourages researchers to use multiple methods. The same volume shares Tebes' view that there should also be a shift away from over-valuing internal validity towards a greater emphasis on external validity. Nevertheless, researchers who were moving in the direction that he advocated, "... are challenged at every opportunity – in the competition for funding, in efforts to have their work published, and in the value ascribed to their research by the larger scientific community" (p. 227).

On that note we conclude Part I. My aim in these three chapters has been to represent some of the challenging and often controversial ideas in community psychology. It is a youthful and rapidly changing branch of psychology which promises much. In later chapters a number of actual examples will be given of how community psychology is trying to understand the realities faced by groups and communities who are in different ways disempowered (Part III), and how actions to empower them are being attempted (Part IV). Before that, in Part II, we shall look at some of the evidence that bears on questions of inequality in society. Much of that evidence is epidemiological in kind, of great importance for community psychology but largely neglected in psychology. We shall, among other things, have reason to consider the fashionable concept of 'social capital', and the related idea of 'sense of community' which has a longer history in community psychology.

PART II

UNDERSTANDING INEQUALITY AND ITS EFFECTS ON HEALTH

Chapter 4
SOCIAL POSITION AND INEQUALITIES IN HEALTH

This chapter attempts to summarise what has become a very large body of work on the social epidemiology of health. Although it relates closely to the interests of community psychology, it is not work that is well known in psychology. That is likely to be because it is work carried out with very little influence from psychology and psychologists, and mostly uses methods that are little used in psychology. Those methods are principally large-scale surveys. The main advantage of such methods is the large numbers of people who answer survey questions (in thousands, rather than in the tens or at most hundreds that psychology usually deals with) and the consequent great capacity for carrying out statistical analyses. The obvious disadvantage – and the reason psychology is often disdainful of such methods – is the apparent superficiality that comes with asking a comparatively small number of very standard questions on complex and personal topics.

There are two reasons for giving such weight to social epidemiology in a book on community psychology. The first is the impressive body of knowledge that has been built up about the link between people's health and well-being and their socioeconomic and social class positions, and, in a relatively newer body of work, about the relevance for health of the neighbourhoods where people live. This is all of such significance for community psychology that it is important that it be more widely known. There is a second reason for dipping into this literature. That has to do with the fact that social epidemiologists have had to give much thought to concepts such as social class, work conditions, and lifecourse advantage, in order to operationalise such ideas for inclusion as standard questions in their surveys. In the course of so doing, they have given rather more thought to a topic such as social class, which ought to be central to community psychology, than has psychology itself. In that respect there is much to get intrigued about and much to learn.

There is another reason why I have given considerable space to these matters. It so happens that British social epidemiologists have taken a lead in this area of work. There has been a tradition in British public health and epidemiology of work that has exposed social inequalities and their association with health. In the later part of the twentieth century much of this work has been highly critical of 'modernising' governments. It has drawn attention to the likely relationship between the health of a nation's people and features of the social structure and political actions that affect them – of no little interest to community psychology. At the same time it needs to be acknowledged that most of the work to be reviewed in this chapter comes from western countries, particularly the UK, and also from the Nordic countries and the USA. That is simply because it is in those countries that the research has been concentrated. Needless to say, questions of inequality of social position and place and their influence on health and well-being are of the utmost importance everywhere.

THE ACCUMULATION OF EVIDENCE THAT HEALTH IS RELATED TO SOCIAL POSITION

Health and the Social Gradient

There has now accumulated a large body of evidence demonstrating that inequalities in health are related to social position even within comparatively wealthy countries such as those in western Europe. Social inequalities and health has become a large and prominent subject in professional and academic literatures. Modern interest in the subject in the UK was stimulated by *The Black Report*, the report of a government working party under the chairmanship of Sir Douglas Black, which reported in 1980 (published in 1982 by Townsend and Davidson). It was updated a few years later as *The Health Divide* (Whitehead, 1988), and the two reports were brought together under the title *Inequalities in Health* (Townsend et al., 1992).

Figure 4.1 shows some of the central results from *The Health Divide* in the form of 'social gradients' that have now become very familiar in this field. Each gradient shows the relationship between premature mortality in a particular age group of the population, and socioeconomic status based on occupation. The social gradient was found to exist for mortality from all causes (standardised mortality ratio or SMR) and, with only a few exceptions, for rates of death from each particular illness that was examined.

Another set of British studies that has become a classic in this field is the Whitehall studies of London-based government department workers divided into four grades or levels of occupation (Davey Smith et al., 1990). As Figure 4.2 shows, those in the highest grade (known as the 'administrative' grade in the British civil service) suffered the fewest deaths in the 10-year follow-up period, and those at the other end of the gradient ('other' grades) the most. Car ownership, independently of occupational grade, also predicted survival during the follow-up period. The social gradient still existed when results were confined to non-smokers, providing support for one of the main conclusions of *The Black Report*: differences in rates of unhealthy behaviours such as smoking, heavy drinking, eating a poor diet, and taking little exercise, while they might explain some of the relationship between social inequalities and health, could not explain most of this recurring finding.

Evidence of this kind has continued to accumulate. Among other things this large body of literature shows that the same kind of social gradient appears, not

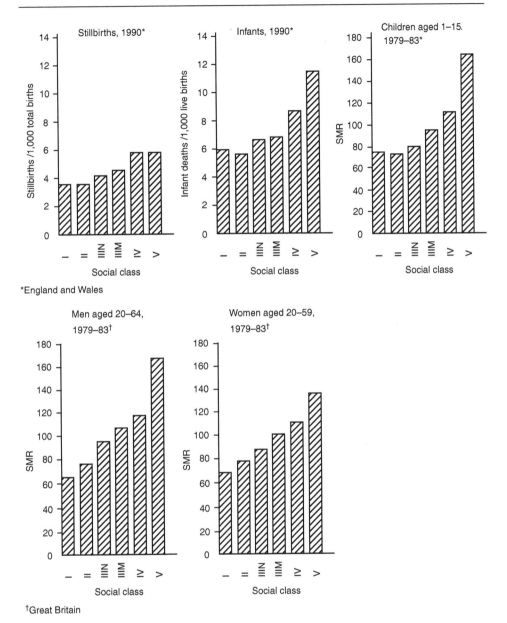

Figure 4.1 Occupational class and mortality in infants, children and adults
Source: Whitehead, M. (1988). *The Health Divide*. London: Penguin

just for premature death, but also for measures of ill-health, both physical and mental; that the gradient appears when social inequality is indexed in a variety of different ways; that social inequalities in health exist across the life-span from birth to older age; and that they are to be found in all European countries. Among British studies, the second study of London civil servants (the Whitehall II study)

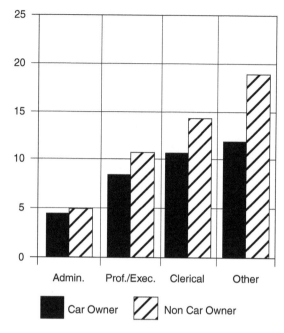

Figure 4.2 All-cause mortality (per 1000 person years) by occupational grade and car ownership in the Whitehall I Study
Source: reproduced with permission from Carroll, D., Davey Smith, G. & Bennett, P. (1996). Some observations on health and socio-economic status. *Journal of Health Psychology*, **1**, 23–39

has been particularly important. That sample has been followed up over a number of years and has generated a large volume of published work on the existence of social inequalities in health and their possible causes. Other large-scale British studies that have produced evidence of social inequalities in health include the biennial random sample General Household Survey (GHS) and the large random population adult sample survey carried out in eight local authority areas in the west of Scotland in 1997 (Macintyre *et al.*, 2001). Other important European studies include Valkonen's (1993) Finnish study (see below) and a study that found higher male mortality among manual than non-manual workers in each of the 11 different European countries examined (Kunst *et al.*, 1998). Other notable studies include Stronks *et al.* (1998) and Van Oort (2005) from the Netherlands, Leclerc *et al.* (2006) from France, Nicholson *et al.* (2005) who analysed data from Russia, Subramanian *et al.* (2003) who analysed data from Chile, and Frank (2003) from the USA.

A large number of studies have shown a link between socioeconomic position and health and development in childhood (e.g. McMunn *et al.*, 2001; Najman *et al.*, 2004). One demonstration that such a link already exists early in life was Baker *et al.*'s (1998) study of wheezing and diarrhoea in the first six months of life, reported by mothers who took part in a longitudinal study of 7000 infants born in Bristol, England in the early 1990s. Those two symptoms are of significance because they are two of the most common reasons for mothers consulting health services in the early months of a child's life, and both are associated with infant mortality in parts of the world where conditions are much poorer, and have been associated with infant mortality in Britain historically. In the Bristol study both were associated with living in rented accommodation, and wheezing was also associated with living in crowded housing conditions.

At the other end of life there have been comparatively fewer studies of socioeconomic differences and health compared to the number focused on younger adults and on children. That may partly be because of the extra difficulty of assessing socioeconomic status among older age groups, but it is probably in large part due to the assumption that the relatively high incidence and prevalence of ill-health in older age render social inequalities less relevant (Breeze *et al.*, 1999). The evidence that has accumulated so far, however, suggests that they remain highly relevant. A number of studies have examined mortality differences in groups of older people, often linking census data with registrations of deaths (e.g. Melzer *et al.*, 2000, Breeze *et al.*, 2004, in the UK, and Huisman *et al.*, 2004, in 11 western European countries). Others have studied the link between social position and disease severity, disability or quality of life in older age. For example, Eachus *et al.* (1999) studied the severity of hip disease, among patients, mostly older people, of general medical practices in England. The poorer members of the sample appeared to be in double jeopardy, not only experiencing greater pain, disability, and interference with independence associated with their hip disease, but also having a greater frequency of concurrent conditions such as respiratory, cardiovascular or eye disease, depression or cancer.

Of all life stages, adolescence, it had been suggested (notably by West, 1997), is unique because, unlike the social inequalities in health that are evident at all other life stages, health *equalisation* occurs in adolescence, due to the increasing autonomy of young people from their families of origin and the homogenising effects of experiences with peer group and youth culture. Evidence produced since West's review has tended to question that conclusion. For example, writing from the USA, Starfield *et al.* (2002) reviewed existing results, concluding that socioeconomic gradients existed for many (but not all) indicators of adolescent health. Data came from The Netherlands, Britain, the USA, and from the World Health Organisation Study of Health Behavior in School-Aged Children (Mullan & Currie, 2000). Health indicators significantly related to socioeconomic measures included lower height, obesity, activity-limiting longstanding illness, depression and suicide attempts, and well-being and health behaviour indices such as smoking, sedentary lifestyle, inadequate consumption of fruit and vegetables, episodic heavy drinking, and lower happiness and confidence. The authors also commented that consideration of the social and material *context* of adolescent health – examples would be access for the family to food markets with affordable nutritious foods and access to safe facilities for physical exercise – was conspicuously missing from all the studies they considered.

Although individual ill-health conditions may not be of such relevance for understanding the effects of social inequalities at the crucial life stage of adolescence as they are at other stages, accidents and injuries may be. They are a major cause of adolescent hospitalisation and mortality and there is evidence that they are related to social position (Bagley, 1992). Blame for accidents can easily be apportioned to the accident victim or to parents, thus avoiding blame attaching to those with powerful vested interests associated with private motor transport (see Roberts &

Coggan, 1994, for an illustrative case study). The relationship is likely to be complex, however, reflecting differences in social and material context, as the results of a questionnaire survey of a national sample of teenagers attending schools in Scotland illustrated (Williams et al., 1997). For example, whereas socioeconomic status indices were inversely related to injuries occurring on the roads – specifically being knocked down by a car or being injured on a bicycle – the relationship was reversed for injuries at school, sports injuries, and being injured while in a car (reflecting, presumably, the greater access to sport and private transport facilities enjoyed by those from better-off families).

Much of the epidemiological work that has established the ubiquity of the social gradient has been about physical illness and mortality. But a number of large national survey data sets in Britain have been used to examine the relationship between socioeconomic indices and rates of the commonest forms of psychological disorder, such as anxiety and depression. The latter are extremely common, with a 12-month prevalence of around 14–15% in the UK; they are associated with a high percentage of all work absence due to sickness (perhaps 15–30%); and account for around one-fifth of consultations in general medical practice in the UK (Lewis et al., 1998; Weich & Lewis, 1998). One such data set was obtained from over 10,000 adults resident in private households in the UK as part of the Office of Population Censuses and Surveys (OPCS, now the Office for National Statistics) national survey of psychiatric morbidity undertaken in 1993 (Meltzer et al., 1995). Lewis et al. (1998) analysed those data, finding a significant relationship between prevalence and both car access and housing tenure. They estimated that about 10% of common mental disorder in the UK could be attributed to the increased prevalence among those without car access who rented their homes. Those relationships were stronger than the relationships of prevalence with either occupational class or educational level, and Lewis et al. concluded that standard of living, as indicated by owning one's home and having car access, was more important for mental health than either educational attainment or occupational status. Other relevant studies include Marmot et al. (1997), Wiggins et al. (2004), and Lorant et al. (2005). Notable is the study by Evans et al. (2000), who took a different angle from most on the subject of social inequalities and mental health, confirming a link between housing quality and mental health in two separate studies of mothers in the USA – one a rural sample, the other urban. They prefaced their results by noting the sub-standard nature of much housing throughout the world, including upward of 10% of housing in the USA. A feature of their work was the objective rating of housing quality made by raters who were trained to rate a home on the six sub-scales shown in Figure 4.4.

Are the Gradients of Health by Socioeconomic Position Steepening over Time?

That is a question that has been asked in a number of papers and the answer appears not to be straightforward. In 1990, Davey Smith et al., reviewing evidence on socioeconomic inequalities in health since The Black Report of 10 years earlier, concluded that inequalities in mortality had continued to widen from the 1950s to at least the early 1980s. Marang-van de Mheen et al. (1998) analysed death certificates to classify occupation (restricted to men aged 15 to 64 because of the difficulties of classifying occupational status for women and older men – discussed later in this chapter) and calculated mortality rates for different class groups based on census data. They confirmed that mortality differences between social classes had increased from 1951 to 1981. The relative index of inequality (RII or the relative rate of mortality for the hypothetically lowest in status compared with the hypothetically highest status person) increased from 1.40 to 2.43 between 1971 and 1981 in England and Wales, and from 1.22 to 2.57 in Scotland. Davey Smith *et al.*'s (1990) predication was that, with a general tendency in the 1980s towards wider material inequality, further widening of social class differences in mortality was to be expected.

Ferrie *et al.* (2002) looked at this issue in the Whitehall II study sample of London civil servants, screened in the late 1980s. At a second follow-up of the sample 11 years later, employment gradients were still in evidence for both women and men – for health self-rated as fair or poor, General Health Questionnaire scores (the GHQ, a much used measure of common symptoms of psychological distress), blood pressure and smoking, as well as for body mass index for women and longstanding illness and cholesterol level for men. On the whole gradients had remained similar over the 11-year period, except for marked changes in GHQ findings where gradients had steepened very significantly. Ferrie *et al.* speculated that the latter changes might be due to a variety of reasons: growing insecurity and deterioration in employment conditions and income as lower grade civil servants were hived off to the private sector or were shed from the workforce, being one of the possible reasons. Sacker and Wiggins (2002) came to a different conclusion, using data up to the year 2000. They combined data from two British cohort studies, one of people born during one week in March 1958, followed-up at ages 7, 11, 16, 23, 33 and 42 years (the National Child Development Study) and those born in one week in April 1970 and followed-up at ages 5, 10, 16, 26 and 30 years (the 1970 British Birth Cohort), both samples later augmented with immigrants to Britain who had been born in the same study week. Their report concerned psychological distress measured by the 24-item Malaise Inventory, which includes statements about anxiety, depression, and associated psychosomatic distress. Their conclusion was that non-manual versus manual occupational class differences had in fact narrowed in the last two decades of the century. Incidentally, their results showed a strong sex effect, with women more than two and a half times as likely as men to experience psychological distress (a sex difference on scales of that sort is a regular finding, but this one was particularly large).

Bartley *et al.* (1999) analysed data from 20–59-year-old women, living in England, who either took part in the 1984 Health and Lifestyle Survey or the 1993 Health Survey for England. Occupational position was significantly related to self-rated health, in both surveys, after controlling for age, own and partner's working status, marital status, and presence of children in the home. Effects were stronger in the results from the later survey, suggesting that women with lower social and material advantage had become more marginalised in the intervening years, during which time there had been a number of significant social changes: for example the proportion of mothers of children under five who were in paid employment had risen from 28% to 42%.

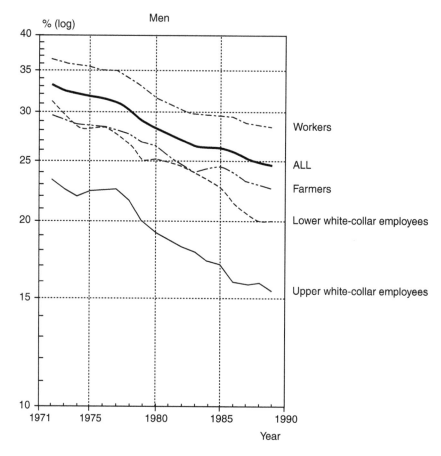

Figure 4.3 Finnish men aged 35–55 during the 1970s and 80s: the probability of dying within 10 years
Source: Valkonen *et al.*, 1993; reproduced with permission from Mackenbach, J.P. & Kunst, A.E. (1997). Measuring the magnitude of socio-economic inequalities in health: an overview of available measures illustrated with two examples from Europe. *Social Science and Medicine*, **44**, 757–71

Research bearing on this question has also come from the Nordic countries and from The Netherlands, with some mixed results, but generally supporting the picture of stable or even increasingly steep social gradients (Otten & Bosma, 1997; Martikainen *et al.*, 2001). For example, Figure 4.3 shows data from a Finnish study reported by Valkonen *et al.* (1993). The figure shows not only the probability of death occurring during the next 10 years for men aged between 35 and 55, but also shows how variation in death rates by occupational class (highest rates for 'workers' and lowest for upper white-collar employees) remained in place between the early 1970s and the early 1990s despite an improvement in expectation of life for middle-aged men in all occupational groups during that era.

Another study used data from comparable surveys carried out in the four Nordic countries in 1986/87 and in 1994/95, to explore whether the serious economic recession that had occurred in the early 1990s, particularly in Finland and Sweden, had had an effect on health inequalities (Lahelma *et al.*, 2002). The finding was that neither self-rated health nor limiting longstanding illness showed significant change in the degree of inequality by employment status or education. They suggested that, unlike in other countries lacking institutional welfare state arrangements, post-communist Russia being a striking example, the arrangements for social benefits and services, cut during the recession but remaining broadly in place, were likely to have buffered against pressures towards widening health inequalities. A Swedish study compared the health of 21-year-old men and women at a time of economic boom in 1986 and in a period of recession in 1994 (Novo *et al.*, 2001). It found that men and women who were aged 21 at the time of recession had more somatic symptoms of ill-health than those who were 21 eight years earlier, and for women the same was true also for psychological symptoms. Youth unemployment was much higher at the later time (17% compared to 5% at the earlier time) and in Novo *et al.*'s samples significantly more participants at the later time had experienced some unemployment (70% men, 78% women compared to 38% men, 43% women at the earlier time) and ratings of high job demands had also risen significantly. Overall women scored higher than men on both symptom checklists, and the analysis showed an apparently greater effect of recession on young women's health than on men's. Dalstra *et al.* (2002), reviewing evidence from The Netherlands between 1981 and 1999, also found a more pronounced increase in the social gradient for women compared to men.

Changes in patterns of smoking provide a good illustration of the way in which links between socioeconomic status and health may not remain invariant for very long. In many western countries rates of tobacco smoking were falling in the last decades of the twentieth century, and a steep class gradient had emerged (Jarvis, 1991), thereby constituting an important contribution to the overall relationship between socioeconomic status and health (the same is true in many countries – see, as an example, Cho *et al.*, 2004, on smoking in South Korea). Sex differences can also change markedly over time. In Europe, the large-scale adoption of smoking by women, and later cessation in large numbers, has tended to follow the earlier pattern for men (Graham, 1996). Within western Europe there have also been differences between countries to the north, such as Denmark, The Netherlands, the UK and Ireland, where large numbers of women took up smoking earlier and where social class gradients emerged sooner, and countries to the south, such as Greece, Italy, Spain and Portugal, where smoking inequalities by socioeconomic status remained small or even reversed for some groups of women and older people (Graham, 1996; Huisman *et al.*, 2004).

'SOCIAL CLASS': COMPLEXITIES AND CONTROVERSIES

It has often been pointed out that social class – particularly, but not only, in psychology – has mostly been relegated to the status of a control variable rather than something that has been systematically studied in its own right (Bronfenbrenner, 1988; Adler *et al.*, 1994; Macintyre, 1997). Adler *et al.*'s (1994) view was that, "Social class is amongst the strongest known predictors of illness and health and yet is, paradoxically, a variable about which very little is known. Psychologists have an important role to play in unravelling the mystery of the SES-health gradient" (p. 22).

In the health inequalities field there has long been constant confusion of terms and concepts. Even in the 1940s Titmuss (1943) was expressing regret over the interchangeable and confusing use of the terms 'social status' and 'economic status'. In practice a wide variety of different measures of social position have been used in epidemiological studies over the years – occupationally based classifications, income, educational qualifications, housing tenure and car access, and other measures of household standard of living included (Lahelma *et al.*, 2004). A selection of them is shown in Figure 4.4. They are based on somewhat different assumptions, each has its own limitations, and the different indices are likely to be associated with different types and degrees of health inequality. Writing from the USA, Oakes and Rossi (2003) have argued that more attention should be paid to the conceptualisation and the measurement of socioeconomic status. Their search of the literature of the second half of the twentieth century showed that the dramatic increase in the amount being written about socioeconomic status and health had not been matched by an increase in the number of articles being written about measurement issues. There had been much disagreement about definitions and little use of explicit theory, particularly in the USA where – unlike in Britain where researchers had built on classical sociological theory and remained committed to operationalising class through employment relations (only true of some UK researchers in fact) – the emphasis had been on educational level and income.

Occupational Status: Prestige, Control, Material Resources or Cultural Capital?

Occupational class alone is a highly problematic and controversial concept. It is interesting to note, for example, how very difficult Kunst *et al.* (1998) found it to achieve comparability between the classifications of occupations in the different European countries included in their study, a division between manual and non-manual occupations being the only element that was common to the different systems of classification. Wohlfarth (1997) argued that conventional scales of occupational class were based on the idea of social stratification according to *prestige*. Self-esteem might therefore be supposed to be a crucial mediator between social position and psychological health. That view was consistent with a functionalist view of society which supposes that there are different positions that need to be filled for the good of the society as a whole. By contrast, conflict, coercion and Marxist theories viewed people as occupying different positions of economic and political power; they tended to focus on *control* as the essence of socioeconomic inequality rather than prestige. In a study of the mental health of people born in Israel between 1949 and 1958 to parents of either European or North African origin, aged at the time of the study between 24 and 33, and interviewed using a standard psychiatric interview, Wohlfarth examined the relationship between a categorisation of occupation based on the Marxist control model of Wright *et al.* (1982 – see Figure 4.5 for details) and the more conventional measures of occupational prestige

Based on occupation

Own occupation graded according to a nationally recognised scale such as the Registrar General's classification in the UK (e.g. Arber, 1997) or the German Labour Authority scale in Germany (Geyer & Peter, 2000); or according to similar scales based more explicitly upon employer—employee relations (e.g. Wright *et al.*, 1982; Erikson & Goldthorpe, 1992), work conditions (e.g. the British National Statistics Socioeconomic Classification scale: Office for National Statistics, 2002) or on social prestige and advantage (e.g. the Cambridge scale: Prandy, 1990).

Sometimes, particularly for women, occupation is categorised according to household, based on the 'chief breadwinner' or the person whose occupation is of highest standing (e.g. Bartley, 1999). Sometimes, especially for children or young people, or when assessing early life experience, a classification based on father's occupation is used (e.g. Pensola & Martikainen, 2004).

An occupation-specific scale may be used for individual studies, as in the British Whitehall II study which used four civil service grades (e.g. Davey-Smith *et al.*, 1990).

Employment status (employed full time or part time, unemployed, economically inactive) or job security are alternatives (Lahelma *et al.*, 2004; Matthews *et al.*, 1999).

Based on education

Usually educational qualifications or years of education (e.g. Manor *et al.*, 1997; Grundy & Holt, 2001).

Sometimes a scale that combines occupation and education (e.g. Borg & Kristensen, 2000).

Based on financial circumstances

Personal income (e.g. Wiggins *et al.*, 2004).

Household income (e.g. Ostrove *et al.*, 1999)

Household accumulated wealth (Martikainen *et al.*, 2003).

Feeling of financial security: 'thinking of the next 10 years, how financially secure do you feel?', rated on a four-point scale from insecure to secure (Singh-Manoux *et al.*, 2003).

Figure 4.4   Illustrations of the variety of measures of social position used in epidemiological studies

A scale of sense of economic hardship, including: insufficient money for necessities (e.g. housing, clothing, home furnishings, car), inability to make ends meet (difficulty paying bills, having money left over at the end of the month), financial strain (anticipation of future hardships and reductions in family standard of living) and economic adjustment and cut-backs (e.g. added another job, received government assistance, sold possessions because money was needed) (Barrera *et al.*, 2001).

Based on standard of living
Access to use of a car, and household tenure (home owning, local authority renting, private renting) are very commonly used indices (e.g. Lewis *et al.*, 1998).

An index of standard of living based on a combination of household income, car ownership and ownership of household durables (Williams *et al.*, 1998).

An index of household resources based on possession of nine household durables and amenities such as a washing machine, video recorder, and central heating (Grundy & Holt, 2001).

The Townsend indicator of household deprivation, based on items such as: meat or fish every other day, a warm winter coat, presents for friends or family once a year, a holiday away from home each year (used by Grundy & Holt, 2001).

The World Health Organization family affluence scale, based on whether the family has a car, whether an adolescent child has his or her own bedroom, and the frequency of family holidays (Mullan & Currie, 2000).

Housing quality rated by trained observers on six sub-scales: structural quality (e.g. ceiling or wall surface loose or missing in places), privacy (e.g. need to walk through the bedroom to get to another room), indoor climatic conditions (e.g. heating breaks down), hazards (e.g. stairs dangerous), cleanliness/clutter (e.g. clutter in the kitchen) and child resources (e.g. accessible toys) (Evans *et al.*, 2000).

A measure of socioeconomic disadvantage that combines living standards with other indices including occupation, education and income (Fergusson *et al.*, 2007).

Figure 4.4 (*cont.*)

and years of education. Wohlfarth's (1997) finding was that there was only very modest overlap between the methods based on control and prestige and that each contributed a significant amount of variance, independently of the other, in the association with mental health.

Manor *et al.* (1997) compared the extent of health inequalities among participants in the 1958 National Child Development cohort at ages 23 and 33. They found

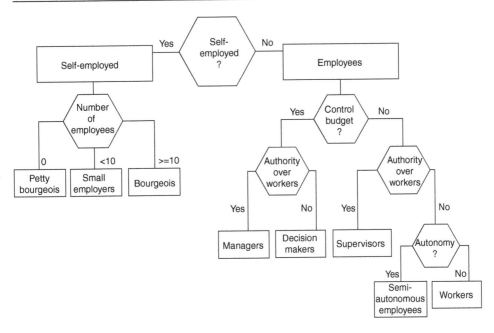

Figure 4.5 Flowchart describing the construction of eight class categories based on four types of control over production
Source: reproduced with permission from Wohlfarth, T. (1997). Socioeconomic inequality and psychopathology: are socioeconomic status and social class interchangeable? *Social Science and Medicine*, **45**, 399–410

educational qualifications, which they suggested were linked to 'cultural capital' – associated with differences in lifestyles, health related behaviours, and illness behaviour – to be consistently more strongly related to health than was social class at the time of birth, based on father's occupation (coded according to the Registrar General's classification). Own occupational status at age 23 was associated with greater inequality than class of birth, but still less than was the case for education (five categories, based on qualifications). Davey Smith *et al.* (1998) also compared occupational class and education – age leaving full-time education in this case – in a study of men aged between 25 and 64 years when they were recruited from 27 work places in Glasgow and west central Scotland in the early 1970s. Each index showed similar gradients, of the familiar kind, with such health indicators as blood pressure, shorter height, poor lung function, and smoking prevalence. Linking with registrations of deaths over the following 21 years also showed mortality to be related to both occupational class and education (but more strongly for occupational class than for education). Those authors concluded, therefore, that both education and occupational class were acting as indicators of life course material conditions. Their results, they believed, favoured an explanation of social inequalities in health in terms of material resources rather than a 'cultural capital' explanation – such as education having specific effects on such things as preferences favourable to long-term investment in one's future or improved health-related knowledge allowing choice of healthy lifestyles.

Income and Wealth

Occupational class is not the same as income or wealth of course. At the fifth wave of data collection for the Whitehall II study in 1997–99, 11–12 years after the sample was first studied, questions were added about income and wealth – factors that had been comparatively little studied up to then compared to factors such as occupational class and amount of education. Martikainen *et al.* (2003) reported strong negative relationships between two measures of poorer health – depression (measured by four items of the GHQ) and poor self-rated health – and each of three indices of income/wealth: *personal income*, total *household income*, and a measure of *household wealth*. The two household measures (it is interesting to note that they were distributed much less equitably than personal income) were the more strongly related to the two health measures. Martikainen *et al.* concluded from their analysis that the relationship between personal income and health, and to a lesser extent household income and health, was to a large extent accounted for by selection on health grounds during the course of the study – for example selection out of the labour force or to lower paid employment. Household wealth, on the other hand, was likely to be a measure of income accumulated over a lifetime, plus inherited wealth, much of it tied up in the ownership of property, and its relationship with health could not be understood simply in terms of baseline ill-health. Indeed it remained significant (just short of significance in the case of GHQ depression for women) after controlling for a variety of other social factors such as number of economically active adults in the household, number of children, marital status, education, and employment status.

Ostrove *et al.* (1999) argued that accumulated wealth – relatively rarely employed as a social indicator – might be a more comprehensive measure of 'command over resources' than either income or education. Analysing results from two US surveys – one a national adult sample first recruited in 1986, the second a pre-retirement national study of 51–61 year olds in 1992 – they found that wealth was only moderately correlated with household income and with education, and that wealth made an independent and significant contribution to explaining differences in physical and mental health.

Two studies that considered the relative utility of different indices of socioeconomic status, including income, were Grundy and Holt's (2001) analysis of data from older British adults, aged 55 to 69 years, who were participants in the Retirement and Retirement Plans Survey in 1988/9 and who took part in a second survey in 1994, and Geyer and Peter's (2000) study of west German adults, aged 25 to 65 years, who had statutory health insurance records. The latter found educational qualifications and official occupational position (according to the German Labour Authority, using a scheme very similar to the British Registrar General's) to be moderately well correlated (0.58), but each was correlated only weakly with income (0.13 and 0.11, respectively). All three indicators were related to mortality between 1987 and 1995, but only income remained significant after controlling for the other two indices. The British survey data included a larger number of variables. Self-rated health (a five-point rating scale) was the health variable of interest. It is a simple measure of health, much used in this kind of epidemiology and not without its critics (Macintyre, 1997), but it has been found to be a good predictor

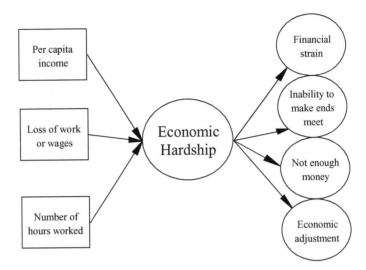

Figure 4.6 Barrera *et al.*'s (2001) model of economic hardship for parents
Source: reproduced with permission from Barrera, M., Caples, H. & Tein, J.Y. (2001). The psychological sense of economic hardship: measurement models, validity, and cross-ethnic equivalence for urban families. *American Journal of Community Psychology*, **29**, 493–517

of mortality. As well as occupational class, educational qualifications, and income, also included were a number of measures of household resources and household deprivation (see Figure 4.4). They found that the variable most associated with self-rated health varied between men and women and between the earlier and later surveys: education was good for men in 1988, but occupational class was best in 1994, whereas income was a strong correlate for women on both occasions. Each of the deprivation indices was also significantly associated with health; the best pair of variables was generally one of education, occupational class or income, combined with one of the household deprivation indices, most often the Townsend score, with household tenure often adding significantly.

Barrera *et al.*'s (2001) structural equation model (SEM[1]) of economic hardship (see Figure 4.6) using data from parents of 11–15-year-old pupils in schools in an area of south-western USA is another example based on the idea of deprivation of resources. They viewed sense of economic hardship as a perception of disparity between needs and resources which, like other forms of stress, would have cognitive, behavioural, and emotional components. They based their model on the work of Conger and Elder (1994) on the economic pressures affecting farm families in rural USA (see later in this chapter for more details of their studies).

---

[1]Structural equation modelling (SEM) is a statistical technique which, among other things, like factor analysis, identifies the common, underlying (*latent*) constructs measured by a number of interrelated indices or scales (the *manifest* variables), and also allows models of how the latent constructs are related to be tested.

The Personal Assessment and Meaning of Social Class

The question has been raised of whether the relatively objective measures of socio-economic position such as occupation, education, and income are missing out on some more subjective, but possibly equally or more important, aspects of social status. This debate reflects two alternative explanations for inequalities in health. One, the *material*, supposes that it is the accumulation of adverse material conditions over the life course that is important for health, and that, "... the ability of people to make healthy choices is substantially constrained by the contingencies of their lives" (Macleod *et al.*, 2005, p. 1917). The second explanation, the *psychosocial*, fuelled by research linking ill-health with inequality in the distribution of incomes (for a discussion of income inequality, see later in this chapter), sees factors such as perception of relative disadvantage or sense of economic hardship as being more important (Barrera *et al.*, 2001; Singh-Manoux *et al.*, 2003).

The fifth wave of the Whitehall II study included a '10-rung ladder' self-rating scale of subjective social status. Participants were given a drawing of a ladder along with the instructions shown in Figure 4.7. It was found that this subjective measure was significantly related to each of five measures of ill-health – angina, diabetes, respiratory illness, perceived general health, and GHQ depression – for both men and women (the only exception being respiratory illness for women). The usual objective measures – civil service grade, education, and income – explained all of the relationship between subjective social status and angina, and the relationship with diabetes for women, but in the case of other health measures they could not explain all of the relationship. In particular they went only a little way towards explaining the link with depression and, particularly for women, the link with self-rated health. Subjective social status itself could be predicted from the three objective indices, particularly employment grade, but was additionally predicted from ratings people made of their satisfaction with their standard of living and of their feelings of financial security (see Figure 4.4 above). Singh-Manoux *et al.* were of the view that subjective social status reflected not only current social circumstances but also an assessment of past socioeconomic, educational and economic

---

Think of this ladder as representing where people stand in society. At the top of the ladder are the people who are best off – those who have the most money, most education and the best jobs. At the bottom are the people who are worst off – who have the least money, least education and the worst jobs or no job. The higher up you are on this ladder, the closer you are to people at the very top and the lower you are, the closer you are to the bottom. Where would you put yourself on the ladder? Please place a large 'X' on the rung where you think you stand.

Figure 4.7 Instructions to accompany the self-rating 10-rung 'ladder' of subjective social status

Source: reproduced with permission from Singh-Manoux, A., Adler, N.E. & Marmot, M.G. (2003). Subjective social status: its determinants and its association with measures of ill-health in the Whitehall II study. *Social Science and Medicine*, **56**, 1321–33

background, plus future prospects. It, "... encompass[ed] the individual's family resources, opportunities and life chances" (p. 1322).

Bolam et al. (2004) were particularly critical of prevailing methods of assessing social position for failing to keep up with wider public and social science debate about the meaning and relevance of social class in contemporary society, for remaining attached to a positivist methodology, and ignoring the subjective and reflexive significance of class as an element of social identity: "People can be both described in objective terms of, and critically aware or reflexive about, their social class" (p. 1357). Epidemiological work on social inequalities and health had failed to acknowledge the reorientation of class analysis that had been taking place, particularly influenced by the work of social theorists Beck and Giddens (see Chapter 2) on individualisation – the process whereby individuals had become disconnected from previous social relations and traditional sources of social identity, such as social class, without becoming re-embedded in new social groupings.

Bolam et al.'s own qualitative analysis of interviews with 16 women and 14 men, diverse in terms of occupation and ethnicity, from one town in the south of England, suggested the existence of two contrasting ways of talking about class. One acknowledged class as a recognisable concept, but resisted it on moral grounds – it was a prejudicial construct contrary to liberal, individualistic norms – but also because it was felt to be of little use in explaining one's own, individual experience. For example: "... those categories, I don't know if they mean so much any more ..."/"... I don't like to differentiate people like that"/"... I don't see myself as any class really. I just see myself as just being me" (p. 1359). This way of talking about class was frequently associated with what Bolam et al. termed "heroic and stoic narratives" (p. 1359). People talked in terms of pride and determination to succeed in the face of adversity, fulfilling responsibilities as a wife and mother, maintaining healthy practices, overcoming injuries. Presenting such experiences in terms of class:

> ... would serve to depersonalise and displace control for events beyond the individual and thereby abdicate personal responsibility for health and illness ... By presenting experiences of this kind as barriers to be overcome by individual strength of character, as opposed to illustrations of class inequalities, class experience, or victimhood, participants could present a morally favourable image of the self ... (p. 1360).

The contrasting way of talking about class was to accept it and its context of power, privilege, and politics. The link between class and health was recognised. For example: "I'd say sometimes health is beyond your control, sometimes we're just destined for ill health. Some people that are living in poverty like pensioners ..."/"... there are a whole group of people who can't get off the bottom rung who have not got the opportunity" (pp. 1361–2). It is very noticeable that all the examples Bolam et al. gave of the narratives of resistance to class involved stories of personal, individual heroism and stoicism, whereas those narratives accepting class were much more likely to talk about health, not just in individual or private terms, but as general social or political phenomena. Bolam et al. also concluded that the acceptance of class in the latter way was more likely to occur for those who were themselves relatively advantaged in educational and occupational terms. That is consistent with Blaxter's (1997) conclusion that social inequalities in health was not a prominent topic in lay discussions of health, and particularly not so among those exposed to disadvantage themselves (although later studies using focus groups have found members of disadvantaged groups well able to talk about structural and material factors affecting their health – see Davidson *et al.*, 2006; Hodgins *et al.*, 2006).

Sex Differences, Women, and Social Class

Neglect of other sources of social stratification, notably gender and ethnicity, is one of the criticisms that has been levelled at the dominant epidemiological approach to assessing class. Systems of classification such as the Registrar General's have particularly been criticised for being insensitive to the social positions of women (Bolam *et al.*, 2004). There has been a tendency in social epidemiology to ignore sex differences either by combining women and men (for example standardising mortality rates for sex and age) or by confining research to men. One justification for the latter approach has been the difficulty of applying occupational class categories to women because the coding schemes, such as that of the Registrar General in Britain, are not well suited to occupations more frequently held by women than by men and because women have been more likely to spend periods out of the labour force or in part-time employment.

One report that did focus on sex differences was that of Matthews *et al.* (1999) who analysed the British 1958 birth cohort data. Looking at seven measures representing a spectrum of physical and psychological health, they found no support for the suggestion that had been made that social health gradients were less steep for women or were less regularly linear. The sample was aged 23 and 33 years at the two time points when the data for those analyses were collected, however, and the authors acknowledged that sex differences in health inequalities might emerge in middle age. They also discussed the possibility that their decision to base women's occupational classification on their own current or most recent occupation, and not that of a partner when married or cohabiting, might also have influenced the results in an unknown way. They did find some gender differences when using educational qualifications as an alternative social indicator; although even then the extent of inequalities was similar for the two sexes, women showing greater inequality in terms of some health indicators, men in terms of others.

Wohlfarth (1997) also discussed the controversy about whether the unit of stratification should be the individual or the family. Classifying women according to their husbands' work corresponded, Wohlfarth argued, to the functionalist approach which considered the family as the unit. Class theorists were divided. Some argued that the economic system required women to take major responsibility for children and household; therefore a measure of social position based on the household or the main breadwinner was the more appropriate. Others argued that such restrictions were themselves an expression of the class system, and that women should be classified according to their own class position. If women were in work, Wohlfarth classified all women according to their own jobs.

A second aim of Matthews *et al.*'s (1999) analysis of the British 1958 birth cohort data was to explore the possibility that explanations for social inequalities in health might be different for the two sexes. They considered a large number of hypothesised explanatory variables – to do with family structure, material circumstances, education, work, and health behaviours. The general conclusion was that explanations were remarkably similar for women and men. The cumulative effect of those variables in explaining the occupational class and poor self-rated health gradient at age 33 was similar for the two sexes, as was the rank order of explanatory variables in terms of their ability to explain the association. For example, qualifications at the end of schooling was ranked highest for both sexes, with housing tenure at age 33 also important for both. There were some notable exceptions, however: job security at age 33 had a greater impact for men than women, and income at age 23 was more important for women. Marital status at the earlier age, and particularly age at first child, were significant for women but had a negligible impact on inequalities for men.

Arber (1997) considered a number of the difficulties of relying solely on a categorisation of a woman's current or most recent occupation as an adequate measure of her socioeconomic position. As well as those already discussed, these include the possibility that the most recent occupation may not be a good indicator for a woman returning to the labour market after a break and taking a lower status job than previously or than she would have attained if she had been promoted in the meantime. Arber also showed, using data from the 1991–2 British General Household Survey, that the distribution of women's occupations across the six Registrar General's categories was very different to the distribution for men's occupations: both within the non-manual categories and the manual, women were much more likely to fall into the lower categories (routine non-manual, or semi-skilled and unskilled manual occupations) whereas men's occupations were much more frequently to be found in the higher categories (professional or managerial, or skilled manual). The Whitehall II study is another illustration of the same thing: the distribution across the three grades of civil service employment was very different for the two sexes: 37.8% of men but only 9.4% of women being in the higher, administrative grade, and 8.3% of men but 48.9% of women being in the lower, clerical/support grade (Fuhrer *et al.*, 1999).

Another illustration of the occupational disadvantage of women, reflected in work status data, comes from the 2000 Barcelona Health Interview Survey, a representative sample survey of the city's adults carried out every five years, analysed to examine the relationship between self-rated health and factors to do with both work organisation and material standards and work in the home (Borrell *et al.*, 2004). Wright's (2000) revised, 12-category system for categorising occupations, now including three categories of 'experts', was used. The position of women and men was very different, as were the factors associated with health for the two sexes. Women were outnumbered at least two to one in all the self-employed, manager, and supervisor occupational categories and were only in the majority among unskilled workers. Within all occupational categories they were more likely to have only a temporary contract or none at all. In nearly all categories they worked somewhat fewer hours but the differences were small and were more than made up for by the greater number of hours spent by women than men on household labour (an

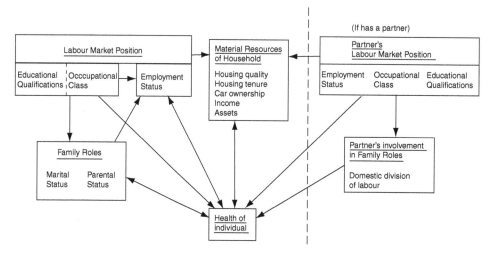

Figure 4.8 Arber's model of women's health, own and partner's labour market position, material resources and family roles
Source: reproduced with permission from Arber, S. (1997). Comparing inequalities in women's and men's health: Britain in the 1990s. *Social Science and Medicine*, **44**, 773–87

average of 15 versus 6 hours). The authors commented that working class women suffered from the double jeopardy of hazardous work and patriarchal relations of unequal power in the household – "...the most hidden and unregulated setting where power, authority and control over the extraction of labour effort are exercised..." (p. 1884).

Arber's (1997) conceptual framework for trying to explain the influence on a woman's health of her own and her partner's labour market positions and their material resources and family roles is shown in Figure 4.8. Her analysis of data from the 1991–2 British General Household Survey supported that complex picture. Own occupational class and employment status were strongly related with both limiting longstanding illness and poor self-rated health, for both women and men. In the case of self-rated health, educational qualifications were also good predictors for both sexes. For women with spouses or partners, longstanding illness could be explained largely in terms of their own labour market position (class and employment status), but self-rated health could better be explained using a range of variables including her partner's occupational class and employment status, household material resources such as housing tenure and car ownership, and her own educational qualifications.

Bartley (1999) raised a number of relevant issues. One was the evidence of a recent polarisation of occupational structure for women, with an increase in both well-paid professional jobs as well as in the numbers of poorly paid low status occupations such as catering and cleaning – she pointed out that there were no similar well-established social roles for men providing sexual or domestic services. Another was the influence on health of the pattern of power and subordination in the home – she remarked that women had not yet the power to require men to undertake equal shares of childcare and domestic labour. She also noted how health gradients for women appeared to be steeper when occupational class was assessed according to the male partner's occupation. That hypothesis was examined in a US sample of women who participated in a twin study in 1989–90 in California (Krieger et al., 1999). A modification of the Wright et al. (1982) occupational classification was used to categorise women as working or non-working class, either according to their own usual occupation (the individual method) or that of the spouse or partner (the conventional method) or that of self or spouse/partner or other head of household if any, whichever was of higher status (the gender neutral method). Those three methods produced very different proportions in the class categories: 45%, 30%, and 21%, respectively (for those women for whom all three methods were relevant) were classified as working class for example. Of 10 measures of health, seven showed the strongest relationship with the gender neutral classification.

Chandola et al. (2004) looked at the incidence of heart disease between phase three of the Whitehall II study (1991–3) and phase five (1997–9). They were interested in extending the work that had suggested the importance for health of control at work (see below) to the issue of control at home, and whether that might be particularly important for women's health. They focused on questions of possible role or demand overload for working women as well as the degree of power or control over decision making at home (previously studied by Rosenfeld, 1989). Control at home was assessed with a single question: 'At home, I feel I have control over what happens in most situations', rated on a six-point, strongly disagree to strongly agree, scale (since most agreed with the statement, answers were dichotomised – those who strongly or moderately agreed versus the rest). Control at home at phase three was significantly predictive of the incidence of heart disease in the intervening six years, after controlling for a number of risk factors such as blood pressure, diabetes, smoking, exercise, and obesity, but only for women. Overall their results suggested that control at home may indeed be important for women's health. There was also evidence that factors such as poorer physical health, caring for an older relative, and household financial problems (a measure based on a rating of how frequently there was insufficient money for the kind of food or clothing the family should have, or difficulty in meeting bills) were factors resulting in lower feelings of control.

Ethnicity and Social Class

Ethnicity is the other major source of social stratification that has been largely neglected (Bolam et al., 2004). One relevant study is that of Geroninus et al. (1999) who used census and death certificate data to examine mortality rates for people living in some of the poorest areas in the USA. Their results suggested the existence of important interactions between poverty, ethnic group, and area of residence. The highest mortality rates were found among African USAmericans living in poor urban areas such as the Harlem area of New York, south-side Chicago and central city Detroit. In 1990 the probability of black men in those three areas, respectively, living to age 65 was found to be 0.37, 0.37 and 0.50, compared to 0.62 and 0.77 for the total black and white male populations of the USA. Equivalent figures for women were 0.65, 0.63 and 0.71 in Harlem, south-side Chicago and central city Detroit, compared to 0.77 and 0.87 for all black and white women in the US population. These figures for black USAmericans in poor urban areas were worse than those for African USAmericans in equally poor rural areas such as Delta Louisiana, Black Belt Alabama and east-north Carolina; and were much worse than figures for white USAmericans living in equally poor urban and rural areas such as Cleveland and Detroit and the poor mountain area of Appalachian Kentucky. In the case of black men and women in Harlem and south-side Chicago, the mortality figures had worsened since 1980, whereas mortality rates had nearly all lessened over that period for the total US population and in the other poor areas that were the focus of the study. Survival of white men and women living in Detroit was an exception, possibly due to the declining population of Detroit during that decade and the possible selective out-migration of economically better-off residents. Circulatory disease was the single most important contributor to premature mortality in these poor populations, although homicide was an important factor in the black urban areas, and HIV and AIDS in Harlem in particular. The authors concluded that their findings indicated:

> ...a poignant dimension of social disparities in health – that young people in some US communities cannot expect to survive through middle adulthood. While highly publicised causes of premature death such as AIDS and homicide do contribute to this, they do so by adding to social disparities in mortality experience that are already substantial and result primarily from chronic disease in young and middle adulthood (p. 333).

Williams *et al.* (1998) used data from the West of Scotland Twenty-07 Study in 1987 to try to explain the apparent absence of the usual social class gradient in the mortality of British South Asians during the 1970s (Marmot *et al.*, 1984). They compared South Asians living in areas in Glasgow with the general survey population. Participants were interviewed in their own homes in the language of their choice, and a number of measures of health were obtained. An index of standard of living was constructed from household income band, car ownership, and ownership of eight household durables (preferred to income alone which was thought to be less sensitive to customs within the South Asian group, such as sharing beyond the immediate families of earners, domestic use of goods owned by small businesses, extended family households, and remittances to wider family). Williams *et al.* were interested in whether the absence of the usual gradient was due to a break in the relationship of class to standard of living, or by a break in the relationship of standard of living to patterns of health behaviour and health risk. Their conclusion was that the former explanation was the right one; there had been, within the South Asian group, "...a wholesale redistribution of class chances...disrupting inter- and intra-generational continuities in the relation between class and standard of living" (p. 1277).

The idea that South Asians were mostly confined within an underclass was not the whole story, although there was considerable evidence of a poor standard of living, lower than that for social classes IV and V in the general population, particularly for Muslims and for non-Muslims below classes I and II. In terms of education, although having obtaining UK 'O' level exams ('ordinary' school exams, normally taken at age 15/16) was related to standard of living for South Asian men, the 'matriculation' qualification (equivalent to 'O' level) from the South Asian subcontinent was not related to standard of living, and women's level of education, whatever the qualification, was unrelated to standard of living. What had improved economic chances for many South Asians was ownership of small businesses, an arena offering control over the means of production and distribution difficult to achieve in the mainstream labour market. The small business economy, however, included a very wide range of prosperity, from those struggling alone and with a low standard of living, through those relying on use of family labour, to employment of outside labour and achievement of a higher standard of living. Whereas in the general population standard of living was unrelated to being employed versus self-employed, in the South Asian group standard of living was significantly higher among the self-employed. Among the latter group living standard was significantly higher for those who employed others, which was not the case in the general population. Standard of living was a better correlate of health indices than occupational class, and was related to health in very much the same way in the South Asian and general populations (an interesting exception was the reverse gradient of accidents among South Asian women, perhaps because most accidents were at work or in the street, reflecting the greater likelihood of better-off South Asian women working and driving cars).

The first British survey of the health of ethnic minority people that had a nationally representative sample and sufficiently detailed questions in order to examine some of the relevant issues, was the Fourth National Survey of Ethnic Minorities carried out by the Policy Studies Institute in England and Wales in 1993–4. Results on health were reported by Nazroo (2001). As well as asking respondents to which ethnic group they belonged, they were also asked about their families' origins, and most of the analyses were based on the latter question, using four groups: Indian or African Asian, Pakistani or Bangladeshi, Caribbean, and White (the study included a white comparison group).

Compared to the White comparison group, both the Pakistani/Bangladeshi and Caribbean groups were significantly more likely to report their general health as fair, poor or very poor. That and other findings well demonstrated the importance of going beyond a crude characterisation of ethnic status, for example simply as 'South Asian', since rates were not significantly higher for the Indian or African Asian group. Longstanding illness that limited ability to work, and activities being limited by health, were also significantly higher, particularly in the Pakistani/Bangladeshi group. A number of differences found in earlier research were also found, for example a significantly higher rate of heart disease in the Pakistani/Bangladeshi group and a higher rate of diabetes in all three ethnic minority groups. One of the few findings in the opposite direction was the significantly lower rate of respiratory symptoms in the Indian or African Asian and Pakistani/Bangladeshi groups, almost certainly attributable to the significantly lower rates of smoking in those groups. Caribbean men had a significantly higher rate of depression compared to the White group, with the other two groups tending to have lower rates than Whites, but Nazroo concluded that the questions asked about depression, even the very concept of 'depression', might not be valid enough for the Asian groups, a conclusion supported by the finding that those who had lived longest in Britain and

Table 4.1 Variations in socioeconomic position within socioeconomic bands for ethnic groups in England and Wales

	White	Indian or African Asian	Pakistani or Bangladeshi	Caribbean
Mean income by Registrar General's class (£)				
I/II	250	210	125	210
IIIn	185	135	95	145
IIIm	160	120	70	145
IV/V	130	110	65	120
% lacking one or more basic housing amenities[1]				
Owner-occupiers	11	14	38	12
Renters	27	28	37	23

[1]This includes exclusive use of bath or shower; bathroom; inside toilet; kitchen; hot water from a tap; and central heating.
Source: Nazroo, J.Y. (2001). *Ethnicity, Class and Health*. London: Policy Studies Institute, Table 6.11

those who were most fluent in English had the higher rates of depression (great care was taken to translate all materials into several languages, with back-translation, and interviews were conducted in the preferred language).

One of the most interesting aspects of Nazroo's analysis was directed at the question of whether health differences by ethnic group could be attributed to structural-material differences, for example differences in socioeconomic status. That had been a controversial issue in the field. Unlike in the USA, where it had been assumed that health differences could at least in part be explained that way, at least one influential early study in Britain (Marmot *et al.*, 1984), carried out as part of the influential *Black Report* analysis of health inequalities, had found that controlling for social class differences made little difference to health inequalities by ethnic group. As a result, structural-material explanations for ethnic group health differences had tended to disappear from view in Britain in favour of explanations in terms of cultural differences. Nazroo showed that there were highly significant differences between the social positions of the different ethnic groups: the Pakistani/Bangladeshi group, and to a lesser extent the Caribbean group, were particularly disadvantaged in terms of socioeconomic status and rate of unemployment. The familiar gradients of health by social position pertained in all the ethnic groups, including the White group.

Nazroo was also able to show, however, that the normal measures of social position – such as occupational status and housing tenure – by no means controlled fully for differences in material circumstances. As Table 4.1 shows, the Pakistani/Bangladeshi group were less well off in terms of income even within socioeconomic status groups, and even owner-occupiers were much more likely than others to lack at least one basic housing amenity. In an attempt to develop a more useful measure of material circumstances, Nazroo developed a standard of living index, which showed clearly the relative disadvantage of ethnic minority groups, again particularly the Pakistani/Bangladeshi group. Controlling statistically for either socioeconomic status, housing tenure, or the standard of living index, considerably reduced, but did not completely eliminate, the differences in health between groups. Nazroo therefore concluded that although there was considerable support here for a structural-material explanation of ethnic group differences in health, 'cultural' differences might remain. He cautioned, though, that it was impossible to completely control for differences in social and material circumstances. Other differences not assessed in the survey included differences between the areas in which people lived (since ethnic minority groups tend to be concentrated in certain areas in Britain, and research has suggested area differences in health – see the following chapter), and the experiences of discrimination and harassment which other research has shown are reported by large proportions of ethnic minority group members (23% of people from ethnic minority groups reported being worried about being racially harassed: Karlsen & Nazroo, 2004).

Explanations of health differences in terms of 'culture' have been criticised for implying an essentialist view of ethnic and racial categories. It has sometimes been supposed that differences are attributable to genetic variations, but even when differences have been attributed to culture in the sense of variations in ethnic group norms, beliefs, and practices, it has often been assumed that 'culture' is fixed and unvarying, applying equally to all members of a defined category, hence appearing to provide the 'explanation' for a difference in health without the mechanism for that explanation being spelt out in any detail. Nazroo (2001, p. 4) joined others who have proposed a more dynamic view of culture. For example:

> While ethnicity is considered to reflect identification with sets of shared values, beliefs, customs and lifestyles, it has to be understood dynamically, as an active social process. In particular, the influence of the culture of individuals and groups on their health has to be properly contextualised. The emphasis is on agency and the construction of identity, but . . . it acknowledges power relations and social structure as well.

Work Conditions and Health

Much attention has been given in the epidemiological studies to the possibility that conditions at work might be responsible for some part of the variation in people's health. Two models of stressful conditions at work have dominated the literature on work and health. One is the Job Demand-Control (JDC) model (Karasek, 1979; Marmot et al., 1997). The other is the Effort-Reward Imbalance (ERI) model (Siegrist et al., 2004; Niedhammer et al., 2004). The former supposes that stress will be at its highest when hard work-task demands – including features such as time pressure and role conflict – are combined with low job control. The latter includes the worker's autonomy in making decisions on the job, and the variety of skills that are used and the discretion employed in their use. In a later version of the model a social support element was added; the most stressful set of work conditions was suggested to be a combination of high demands, low control and low social support (the JDCS model: Johnson, 1989). The ERI model, although in some ways very similar – particularly in the overlap between demand and effort – purports to go beyond the characteristics of the work task per se, and to link more clearly to macro-economic labour market conditions, dealing with factors such as salaries, career opportunities, and job security. Hence it claims to address questions of distributive justice and fairness as well as issues of power and division of labour in the workplace (Siegrist *et al.*, 2004). What is important in the ERI model is the balance, or imbalance, between effort and reward:

> This model assumes that effort at work is spent as part of a contract based on the norm of social reciprocity where rewards are provided in terms of money, esteem, and career opportunities including job security. Furthermore, the model assumes that work contracts often fail to be fully specified and to provide a symmetric exchange where complete equivalence exists between requested efforts and given rewards. In particular, this is the case when there is little choice on the part of employees, such as a lack of alternatives in the labour market (e.g. low level of skill) or restricted mobility . . . Non-symmetric contracts are expected to be frequent in a global economy that is characterized by job insecurity, forced occupational mobility, short-term contracts and increased wage competition (Siegrist *et al.*, 2004, pp. 1484–5).

An addition to the model has been a personal variable termed 'over-commitment', which is described as a motivational pattern of excessive commitment to work that risks exposing a person to very high demands or exaggerated effort (Siegrist *et al.*, 2004). The kinds of questions that have been used to assess the key variables in the JDC and ERI models are shown in Figure 4.9. Other studies that have found support for the working conditions–health link include the Canadian National Population Health Survey (Mustard *et al.*, 2003), the GAZEL study of French workers in the electricity and gas supply industries (Goldberg *et al.*, 2001), and a study of employees in one major city in each of Russia, Poland and the Czech Republic (Pikhart *et al.*, 2004).

The JDC model was used in the Whitehall II study. Job control and civil service grade were highly correlated: 78% of men in lower grades reported low job control compared to 27% in intermediate grades and 9% in the highest grades, corresponding figures for women being 76%, 35%, and 10% (Marmot *et al.*, 1997). Job demands were also found to be correlated in the same direction, although to a slightly lesser degree, with greater demands in the higher grades. High control and high demands were themselves significantly positively associated. Another European study that has used the JDCS model is the EUROTEACH study of secondary school teachers in urban areas in 13 countries. Conditions of work for secondary school teachers were found to be very different in the three European regions, with low control and social support in the East and high demands in the West (Verhoeven *et al.*, 2003).

The Belgian study reported by Godin and Kittle (2004), one of the few to have tested both the JDCS and ERI models, is of additional interest because of its assumption that, quite apart from conditions of work and personal characteristics, macro-economic factors such as working in an unstable work sector, would be important to understand work stress and therefore consequences for health and well-being. As part of the SOMSTRESS project, data were therefore collected from workers in four firms selected according to sector stability (checked by conducting a number of semi-structured interviews with key informants in the selected workplaces). A hospital was chosen as representative of a stable sector; two insurance companies, one in a more stable environment than the other, representing intermediate

THE JOB DEMAND-CONTROL MODEL

Job demands

Do you have to work very fast?

Do you have to work very intensively?

Do you have enough time to do everything? (reverse scored)

Do different groups at work demand things from you that you think are hard to combine?

Job control

Do you have the possibility of learning new things through your work?

Does your work demand a high level of skill or expertise?

Does your job require you to take the initiative?

Do you have to do the same thing over and over again? (reverse scored)

THE EFFORT-REWARD IMBALANCE MODEL

Effort scale

Do you have to work very intensively?

Do you have enough time to do everything? (reverse scored)

Does your work demand a high level of skill and expertise?

Does your job require you to take initiative?

Reward scale

Do you ever get praised for your work?

Does your job provide you with a variety of interesting things?

Do you consider your job very important?

When you are having difficulties at work, how often do you get help and support from your colleagues?

Figure 4.9 Sample questions for assessing variables in the Job Demand-Control (JDC) and Effort-Reward Imbalance (ERI) models of stressful work conditions
Source: Kivimäki, M., Ferrie, J.E., Head, J., Shipley, M.J., Vahtera, J. & Marmot, M.G. (2005). Organisational justice and change in justice as predictors of employee health: the Whitehall II study. *Journal of Epidemiology and Community Health*, **58**, 931–7

stability; and a telecommunications company representing a more unstable environment. There were sizeable differences between the four firms, with job conditions being best in the hospital – higher control, better social support, and less over-commitment. Even allowing for those differences, however, self-rated health was best in the hospital and rates of sickness absence were fewer, with the opposite pertaining in the telecommunications firm.

There is overwhelming evidence that unemployment is associated with poorer health, and that this represents a true cause and effect relationship (Fryer, 1990;

Warr *et al.*, 1988; see Chapter 7). Since labour conditions have changed markedly in recent decades, with an increase in many European and other countries of part-time work, and work on fixed-term contracts or without a contract at all, it is reasonable to ask whether being in employment, but with relatively little security, might also be bad for health. There is some support for that in the results of studies such as the Whitehall II study (phases 4 to 5: Ferrie *et al.*, 2002a), the Household Panel Comparability Project which provided data from large samples of the general populations of Britain and Germany in the early 1990s (Rodriguez, 2002), and the Barcelona Health Interview Study (Borrell *et al.*, 2004).

Others have looked in more detail at conditions at work (e.g. Matthews *et al.*, 1998; Emslie *et al.*, 1999). One question is whether the familiar occupational class gradient in health might be explained by the different work conditions of people in different occupational groups. For example, in the Barcelona Health Interview Study there were systematic relationships between occupational category and nearly all the work variables examined: for example unskilled workers were more likely to have temporary contracts or none, to experience noise or air pollution, and to lack variety and autonomy in their work. Borg and Kristensen (2000) also looked at this question in the data from a Danish population sample of 5000 employees, interviewed in 1990 and again in 1995. They found, as expected, that occupational class in 1990 was significantly related to self-rated health (as was age and gender, with middle-aged people and women also being more likely to rate their health as poor), and also to a deterioration in self-rated health over the five-year period. Occupational class was strongly related to all but one of 11 work environment factors about which respondents answered questions in 1990. Five of those factors, in particular, explained more than half of the relationship between occupational status and five-year decline in self-related health: 'ergonomic exposures', repetitive work, lack of skill discretion, climatic exposures, and job insecurity.

The authors of the EUROTEACH study criticised the JDCS model for being over-simplified, leaving out of consideration most of the important factors about work conditions, and hence explaining only a small amount of the variation in health and other outcome variables (Verhoeven *et al.*, 2003). In the EUROTEACH study, three other work variables were included – environmental risks, physical exertion, and meaningfulness of work – and all were found to be important. There was also some support for that element of Warr's (1987) theory of job conditions which suggests that some features of work may show a curvilinear rather than linear relationship with a health or wellness variable.

The Lifecourse Approach to Social Inequalities

There is now much evidence to support the view that health is related, not simply to contemporaneous social position, but also to positions of social advantage or disadvantage throughout life (including experiences of work). This body of research and theory has come to be known as the lifecourse approach to social inequalities and health (Wadsworth, 1997; Graham, 2002). Three lifecourse models can be distinguished (Graham, 2002). The *critical period model* suggests that social conditions at an earlier period in life are particularly influential in determining health at later stages of the lifecourse. Barker's (e.g. 1991) work on the influence of maternal nutrition during pregnancy, and other adverse influences such as mothers' smoking, and their importance for infant respiratory development, and thereby for risk of chronic obstructive airways disease in adulthood, is an often cited example.

The second model, often referred to as the *pathway model*, suggests that disadvantage earlier in life is harmful for later health via such pathways as restricted educational and employment opportunities. The third, the *accumulation model*, suggests that the greatest risk to health arises from an accumulation of disadvantageous conditions at different lifecourse stages. Graham's (2002) view was that the three models represented complementary and interlocking, rather than exclusive, processes, all in their different ways drawing attention to "biographies of disadvantage" (p. 2008):

> Low parental social class brings with it exposure to the health effects of disadvantage, transmitted in utero and in the early years of life. In addition, low parental social class and poor childhood circumstances set children on educational pathways which direct them onto (un)employment trajectories in adulthood, which bring further exposure to disadvantage in later life (p. 2009).

A good example of evidence for the pathways model in early to mid-adulthood is the study by Pensola and Martikainen (2004) of Finnish men who were aged 30–34 years at the time of the 1990 census. Premature death during the following decade was, as expected, strongly related to a man's adult occupational class. Using earlier census data from 1970 (when cohort members would have been aged 10 to 14 years) onwards, they showed that parental home conditions, especially father's occupational class, was also predictive of premature mortality, reducing the effect of adulthood occupational class considerably. All of the effect of parental class could be accounted for, however, by variables related to educational, marital and employment pathways during the period of transition from adolescence to young adulthood – years of education; whether the man settled with a partner or got married and if so at what age; and whether employment was steady or was interrupted by short periods of unemployment or long or repeated unemployment. Each of those variables was strongly related to premature mortality, substantially reducing the effects of adulthood occupational class once they were taken into account.

Most studies that have taken a lifecourse approach to social inequalities in health have focused on quality of life, illness, and mortality in older people (e.g. Grundy & Holt, 2000; Grundy & Sloggett, 2003; Næss et al., 2004a,b; Adams et al., 2004; Lawlor et al., 2005; Nicholson et al., 2005). Most find support for the accumulation model, although Hallqvist et al. (2004) made the point that these kinds of data are unlikely to provide a critical test of these alternative lifecourse explanations. They found evidence in their data for the accumulation hypothesis in the form of significantly higher rates of myocardial infarction (MI) for those with more periods of adulthood employed in manual occupations. They also found evidence, however, for the idea of a critical period, with a significantly raised probability of MI for those who had been in the manual class at age 25 to 29. Furthermore, there was evidence that could be interpreted as being in favour of a third hypothesis – that social mobility is a key factor – in the form of a significantly raised probability of

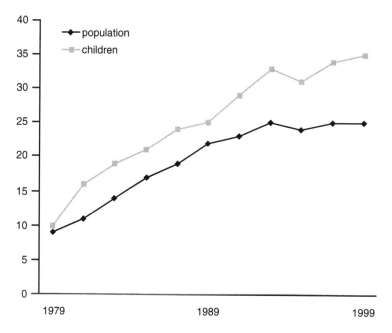

Figure 4.10 Percentage of the general population and the child population in poverty (below 50% of mean equivalent income, after housing costs) Britain, 1979–99
Source: reproduced with permission from Graham, H. (2002). Building an inter-disciplinary science of health inequalities: the example of lifecourse research. *Social Science and Medicine*, **55**, 2005–16

MI for those whose fathers had a non-manual occupation but who had been in a manual occupation themselves in at least one of the two adulthood stages; and significantly reduced MI for those with manual fathers but who had non-manual occupations during one or both adulthood stages themselves.

The Importance for Health of Labour Market and Welfare Changes

Graham (2002) was anxious that the influence of the wider social and political contexts should be recognised, and hence the way in which critical period, pathway or cumulative effects on health might vary over time as social conditions changed (this was part of her broader wish to see the largely atheoretical field of social epidemiology combined with social science – although she had in mind sociology and social policy, and psychology was not mentioned, as it rarely is, directly, in this literature). Wadsworth (1997) and Graham (2002) both pointed to changes that had taken place in the labour market in the UK in the two decades before they were writing: a shift from manufacturing to service industries (hence a growth in skilled non-manual jobs, not easily accessible to those displaced from manual work), economic policy that brought rising unemployment, a break up of established, predictable work lifecourse trajectories, and a steep rise in relative poverty. Figure 4.10 shows the way in which relative poverty, particularly for households with children, rose dramatically in Britain in the last two decades of the twentieth century.

In terms of social policy, Graham (2002) pointed to the importance of the tax system, social security payments, and provision of public services such as education and health, in redistributing wealth, equalising living standards, and protecting households from the harmful effects of disadvantage on health. Cash benefits, which played the largest part, were effective in reducing the percentage of households living in relative poverty (i.e. those with incomes below 50% of national average income), but to a far lesser extent than in countries such as Sweden and Finland where benefits had been maintained at a level that was much more effective in virtually eliminating poverty for households with children (Bradshaw & Chen, 1997). Another difference is the significant link in Britain, but not, for example, in Finland, between health indicators and housing tenure, with home owners having significantly lower frequencies of poor health at most ages – a finding based on analysis by Rahkonen et al. (1995) of British General Household Survey data for 1988 and 1989, and the Finnish Level of Living Survey for 1986. Rahkonen et al. attributed this difference to British government policy since the late 1970s, which had encouraged the sale of public housing, and the intensified labour market divisions between the unemployed and employed, and between skilled and unskilled workers, meaning that lack of home ownership was now more likely to be associated in Britain with poverty, especially for households without earners, including lone parents and disabled people.

Labour market changes in Britain in the 1980s and 1990s had a special impact on the critical life stage of transition to adulthood, with previous opportunities for entering straight into employment after leaving school at the minimum school leaving age of 16 being closed off, and staying on in education and going into government training schemes becoming much more common (Graham, 2002). Parental socioeconomic position continued to predict children's educational pathways during this era. In the 1970 British birth cohort, for example, the proportions of children staying on in school beyond the age of 16 varied from a high of 90% for those with fathers in professional occupations to less than half whose fathers had unskilled manual jobs; and the proportions in those two groups going on to obtain a degree by their mid-twenties were two-thirds compared to only 4% (Bynner & Parsons, 1997).

Summary

What have we learnt from social epidemiology about 'social class' that might be of relevance to community psychology? As might be expected of such a complex and controversial subject, there are more questions than answers. Some of the questions that have arisen in the course of this discussion are summarised in Figure 4.11. These are of vital importance for us because as we shall see in later chapters (particularly in Part III), people's socioeconomic positions – individually, or in terms of their households, neighbourhoods, and collective groups of identity or common interest – are central to understanding their positions of empowerment or disempowerment.

> ➤ Why has psychology neglected 'class'?
> ➤ Are conventional scales of occupational class to be understood as measures of prestige, conditions at work, material conditions more generally, or 'cultural capital'?
> ➤ If occupational class is to be assessed at all, is it better to use a conventional scale of occupational status or a categorisation based on employment relationships?
> ➤ Are scales of occupational status, education, housing tenure, and car ownership tapping different facets of the same idea?
> ➤ Can a single scale be used to indicate the position of all groups in a society, including both women and men and members of all ethnic groups?
> ➤ Why has wealth been even less studied? Are income and wealth quite different from occupational status or education?
> ➤ Is it more relevant to assess class at the level of household or family than at the individual level?
> ➤ Should indices of class take into consideration the whole of a person's life course, and not just current circumstances?
> ➤ How can class measures take into account macro-economic factors such as changes in labour market conditions or changes in welfare provisions?
> ➤ Is it more important how people reflect on their class positions, and how they perceive themselves in terms of advantage and disadvantage, rather than attempting to obtain an objective assessment?
> ➤ Should we resist talking of 'class' altogether? Is it any longer relevant for those who are fortunate enough to be able to choose their position (or positions in the plural) in life? For those who have less choice, is it victimising, neglectful of agency, resilience, and rebellion?

Figure 4.11   'Social class': some outstanding questions

INEQUALITY OF INCOME DISTRIBUTION

The discussion turns now to another area in the social epidemiology of health. It is closely related to the foregoing but is distinct. It is more recent and more controversial. What is important here is not where an individual stands in the hierarchy of social positions (considered up to now in this chapter), nor how the area in which one lives stands in terms of deprivation in relation to other areas (considered in the next chapter), but rather the *degree of inequality* that pertains within one's country, region, area, or neighbourhood. It is to do with the way resources are distributed and how even or uneven, equitable or inequitable the distribution is. The suggestion is that the health of people living within an area is worse, the greater the degree of social inequality that exists among all the folk living in that area.

This suggestion is particularly associated with the writings of Wilkinson, notably in his book *Unhealthy Societies* (1996). Fryer (1998), who edited a special edition of the *Journal of Community and Applied Social Psychology* on the Mental Health Consequences of Economic Insecurity, Relative Poverty and Social Exclusion, obtained no less than nine separate reviews of that important book, and Wilkinson (1998) replied in the subsequent issue. In his book and his reply to the reviews of his book, Wilkinson cited a total of 18 studies showing significant relationships between inequality of income distribution in a country or state and mortality rate (the level of infant mortality or premature adult mortality). These relationships were independent of the absolute level of income in the countries or states concerned, or the percentage of people living in poverty. This further suggestion about social inequality and health (which is not simply about the relative social standing of an individual or household) is intriguing and important and has aroused much interest and debate. The implications are notable: if the average level of income of the population of a country or area remains constant, an increase in the relative incomes of the most affluent (and hence an increase in the relative poverty of the poorest) should lead to an *increase* in the overall level of mortality in that country or area.

To cite one of the most important studies, Kennedy *et al.* (1996) showed an inverse relationship between the degree of income inequality and life expectancy across the different states of the USA: expectation of years of life was highest where incomes were more equitably distributed. Of particular interest in that study was the use of an index of income inequality referred to as the Robin Hood index. As the allusion to the well-known medieval English bandit implies, this index is a measure of the proportion of total income that would need to be taken from the relatively wealthy and given to the relatively poor in order to create complete income equality. There are a number of alternative indices of income inequality, a popular alternative being the Gini coefficient, although Kennedy *et al.* suggested that Gini correlates better with the proportion of total income received by the poorest, say, 20%, while Robin Hood correlates better with proportion of total income received by the poorest 50%. The latter, they argued, is therefore a better measure of income inequality across the whole of a society rather than just the relative deprivation of the poorest. Although, in terms of the general argument of this chapter, the differences between these indices is a detail, it may be important conceptually since a central argument of those who have drawn attention to social inequalities and health, from *The Black Report* onwards, is that there exists a social gradient to health, with differences at all levels not just between the poorest or most deprived and all the rest of society (it is certainly a weakness of this field that a number of different indices of income inequality have been used which can produce very different results; for example, Kennedy *et al.*, 1996, reported a correlation of only 0.29 between the Robin Hood and Gini coefficients).

Wilkinson's thesis has not been without its critics. Both Catalano (1998), who provided one of the nine book reviews referred to earlier, and Judge *et al.* (1998a, b), concluded that the case had not convincingly been made that the extent of social inequality in an area is itself an important determinant of health, independently of the absolute social position of an area and the social standing of individual people or households within it (although there was more support in the case of infant mortality). It should also be pointed out that the 'areas' that have provided the units for analysis in this area of work on social inequalities and health (usually whole countries or states) have been very different in scale from the areas involved in the body of epidemiological work on community or place effects to be considered in the next chapter (postcode areas, enumeration districts, etc.), or the neighbourhoods or communities of most interest to community psychologists (see Chapter 6). One weakness of this line of research is the small numbers of countries involved in the cross-countries analyses, and therefore the poor statistical power to detect an effect. Small numbers also mean that relationships are very sensitive to extreme values: exclusion of the USA, with its high income inequality and infant mortality, reduces correlations considerably.

A number of analyses have cast doubt on the relationship between income inequalities and poorer health across regions, states or provinces within countries (after adjusting for a number of possible confounding variables including individual income, socioeconomic status, employment status, housing tenure, education, and ethnicity). For example, Weich et al. (2002) found a significant relationship between self-rated poor health and the Gini coefficient of income inequality across 18 British regions. Weich et al. nevertheless concluded negatively about the association by the fact that the positive result using the Gini coefficient might be explained on the grounds that the 'high Gini' (i.e. high inequality) regions – inner and outer London, the West Midlands, Greater Manchester, and Merseyside – were also the most urban and that the results might therefore be due to characteristics of cities such as overcrowding, poor schools, traffic, or high crime rates. They also found that the relationship was not significant when a number of alternative indices of income inequality were used.

Table 4.2 summarises a number of later studies, some positively supporting the unequal income distribution and ill-health thesis, some negative, and some mixed. Regidor et al.'s (2003) study of the 17 Spanish regions is of particular interest because the results suggested some support for the hypothesis that in richer countries, as prosperity increased (as it did markedly in Spain in the 1980s), life expectancy would become progressively more dissociated from absolute income and more and more associated with inequality in the distribution of income, as Wilkinson (1996) predicted (the theory is that it is only once a nation's prosperity exceeds a certain level that the way in which income is distributed becomes more important than the country's overall or average level of income).

This important debate goes on. Wilkinson and Pickett (2006) reported a thorough review of all the findings to date. They concluded that the hypothesis linking greater inequality with poorer health (and with homicide rate) was overwhelmingly supported provided the areas that were compared were large enough – whole nations, states or large regions – to include the full variation of existing income levels.

PSYCHOSOCIAL VERSUS MATERIAL EXPLANATIONS

A large part of community psychology's interest in the subject of inequality of income distribution lies in the debate that has arisen regarding the reasons why it might be related to health. There have been two leading ways of understanding

Table 4.2   A sample of studies examining the relationship between income distribution and adult health: illustrating mixed results

Reference	Study area	Result
Blakely *et al.*, 2003	35 regions of New Zealand	No relationship found between the Gini coefficient and mortality in the following three years once ethnicity was controlled
Regidor *et al.*, 2003	17 regions of Spain in 1980 and 1990	Correlations between life expectancy and absolute income were reduced in 1990 compared to 1980, whereas correlations with income inequality (controlling for absolute income) became more positive, although they remained largely non-significant
Sanmartin *et al.*, 2003	Nearly 300 US metropolitan areas, and more than 50 Canadian metropolitan areas	A significant relationship found in the US sample, but not the Canadian one, between premature mortality and each of several measures of income inequality, controlling for employment status
Carlson, 2005	38 Russian regions	A curvilinear relationship found between income inequality and men's self-rated health (but not women's), suggesting that inequality might only have a negative impact at higher inequality levels
De Vogli, 2005	20 Italian regions, and 21 richest countries	A highly significant correlation found between life expectancy and the Gini coefficient of income inequality across countries; and also across Italian regions after controlling for regional average educational level and per capita income

the possible relationship between unequal income distribution and measures of health: the psychosocial and the neo-material (Lynch, 2000; Lynch *et al.*, 2000). The psychosocial versus material debate of course extends far beyond the income distribution question. Indeed, from Chapter 1 onwards it has been a theme that runs throughout the present book. The neglect of the material conditions of life was at the heart of the criticisms of psychology voiced in Chapter 1. It will be a theme again in discussion of the concept of social capital in Chapter 6, and will be a constant presence in the later chapters. When it comes to income distribution and health, Wilkinson (1996, 1998) has been a leading advocate of the psychosocial view, arguing that greater inequality in incomes in a country or region leads to a reduction in *social cohesion*. The latter concept embraces features external to the individual such as increased anti-social behaviour in the community and reduced civic participation as well as features internal to the individual. The latter are said by Wilkinson to be the result of perception of one's position in a social hierarchy, such as feelings of shame and distrust of others that negatively affect health via psycho–neuro–endocrine mechanisms and ways of coping, such as smoking, that are harmful to health.

That kind of psychosocial understanding has been strongly criticised on a number of grounds. Some of the main points of criticism are summarised in Figure 4.12. For example, Muntaner and Lynch (1999), while acknowledging that Wilkinson's model draws attention to income inequality as an emergent social property of populations, not merely attributable to individuals and their lifestyle behaviours (similar, in that sense, to Durkheim's concept of anomie), disliked the way it reintroduces subjectively perceived status, control or prestige, rather than maintaining attention on objective inequalities and their causes and consequences. This, "...conveys the notion that social inequalities are not real, or blurs the distinction between objective and subjective inequalities" (p. 62).

The alternative, neo-material, interpretation suggests that income inequality is simply one among a number of indicators of material conditions that affect population health. They do so through a combination of affecting the degree of exposure to unhealthy conditions, the resources available to individuals and communities to change their conditions, and the degree of government investment in the physical and social infrastructure bearing on health. The latter factor – public infrastructure – includes, "education, health services, transportation, environmental controls, availability of food, quality of housing, occupational health regulations" (Lynch et al., 2000, p. 1202). As Coburn (2000) put it:

> There has been an overwhelming tendency to focus on the possible social/ psycho-biological mechanisms through which social factors might be tied to health rather than on examination of the basic social causes of inequality and health. With only a few exceptions...there has been a startling lack of attention to the social/political/economic context of SES or income inequality – health status relationships (p. 136).

Lynch et al. (2000) stated, "...interpretation of links between income inequality and health must begin with the structural causes of inequalities, and not just focus on perceptions of that inequality" (p. 1202). Elsewhere, Lynch (2000) quoted the economist Sen as saying, "Mental reactions...can be a very defective basis for the analysis of deprivation. Thus, in understanding poverty and inequality, there is a strong case for looking at real deprivation and not merely at mental reactions to that deprivation" (Sen, 1999, p. 363, cited by Lynch, 2000, p. 1003). Using survey data uncritically to support a psychosocial theory such as Wilkinson's theory of social cohesion, may, according to Forbes and Wainwright (2001), "...lead to the stereotyping and psycho-pathologising of people who are at the negative end of the health inequalities spectrum" (p. 802), and, "...can result in victim or community blaming – i.e. all that is needed is to improve the self-esteem and cohesiveness of a community and it will flourish" (p. 807).

Muntaner and Lynch (1999) pointed to various economic, political, and demographic factors that might be held to account for the extent of, and increases in, income inequality. Coburn (2000, 2004) has embraced such factors in a model,

- Although social cohesion should deal with social relations, in fact much of Wilkinson's discussion of social cohesion is about individual psychological attributes such as emotions, stress, self-perception, disrespect.
- The model does not consider possible relationships between class and social cohesion, for example that members of the middle-class may have more time and resources to devote to civic participation, and that the capitalist class has often shown particularly high cohesion.
- It ignores other class-related factors including changes in the labour market such as a shift towards the service sector and polarisation of jobs into high wage and low wage, technological change, and an increase in demand for skilled workers relative to unskilled; and political factors such as decline in union membership, changes in employment practices, cutbacks in social security payments, and changes in personal, family and corporate taxation.
- A psychosocial explanation is over-played in comparison with the importance of differential access to resources such as education, housing, transport, and public safety which may be important in themselves rather than simply as markers for psychological characteristics.
- The survey methods employed did not allow sufficient attention to cultural factors, including sub-cultures, where, despite exclusion from mainstream society, cohesion, and individual self-esteem might be high.
- The mechanisms linking social status with distress were likely to be varied and complex – not necessarily all to do with shame (highlighted in Wilkinson's theory), but sometimes more to do with fear in the face of hostility and contempt from those in more privileged positions.
- It assumes that social cohesion is always good for a population whereas in fact some of the most unhealthy societies in the twentieth century were highly cohesive.
- There is no place in the model for important considerations such as sex discrimination in wages or political under-representation of minorities.
- It displays a middle-class bias, for example by excluding labour unions in the measurement of social cohesion.
- A major flaw is the failure to resolve the question of geographical scale. Do people psychologically compare themselves with others in an immediate locality, or in a larger area, even nationally or internationally?
- Such explanations can easily be used by governments who like to emphasise the need for increasing community social cohesion as an alternative to policies for reducing income inequality, with a tendency then to make communities responsible for their health and to blame the community for not being healthier.

Figure 4.12 Some criticisms of psychosocial explanations of social inequalities, such as Wilkinson's social cohesion theory of the relationship between income distribution and health

Source: Muntaner, C. & Lynch, J. (1999). Income inequality, social cohesion, and class relations: a critique of Wilkinson's neo-Durkheimian research program. *International Journal of Health Services*, **29**, 59–81 and Forbes, A. & Wainwright, S.P. (2001). On the methodological, theoretical and philosophical context of health inequalities research: a critique. *Social Science and Medicine*, **53**, 801–16

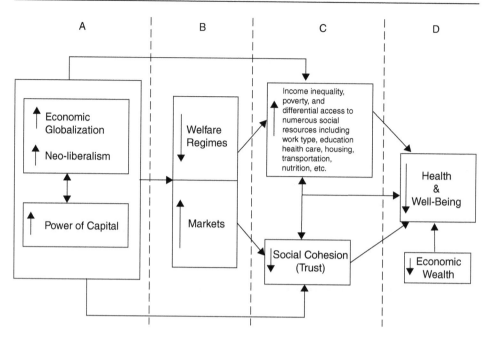

Figure 4.13 Coburn's model of health and features of the macro-social and economic environment

Source: reproduced with permission from Coburn, D. (2004). Beyond the income inequality hypothesis: class, neo-liberalism, and health inequalities. *Social Science and Medicine*, **58**, 41–56

summarised in Figure 4.13, which gives central place to the effects of neo-liberalism. His argument has been that income inequality, although it may be correlated with health, probably reflects a variety of social conditions and is unlikely to be in itself the most important of them. Among the most important pre-conditions of recent years had, in his view, been the rise of neo-liberalism, or market dominance, that had led to both higher income inequality and reduced social cohesion. Behind his model lies a firm belief in the importance of class relations. Coburn's view was that global neo-liberalism has reinforced business class power and reduced that of classes whose interests lie in opposing it. Although not central to his model, social cohesion – the core of Wilkinson's theory – was seen as changing in response to political and market conditions:

> The political rise of neo-liberalism is freighted with a more individualistic view of society and, perhaps, itself reflects a decline in the notion of 'we are all in the same boat' ... Thus the proposition: *The more market-oriented the society, the higher the social fragmentation and the lower the social cohesion and trust* (Coburn, 2000, p. 142).

Coburn (2004) considered his model to be broadly in line with a critical realist perspective, seeing the enactment of neo-liberal policies as exacerbating differences between rich and poor within the market, and at the same time undermining policies and institutions designed to reduce inequalities or buffer their effects on health. Crucial to the latter is the type of welfare state in existence in a particular jurisdiction at a particular point in time. There have been a number of attempts to typologise welfare regimes depending on whether benefits are universal for all citizens or dependent on need, contributions or occupational category, the extent to which benefits make up for reduced income, and the forms of governing social insurance programmes – some regimes being more social democratic in nature, others more neo-liberal. Coburn (2004) used a continuous index of 'decommodification' to assess the degree to which citizens of a particular country could achieve an adequate standard of living irrespective of whether they were employed or not. Much neo-liberal policy involves 'recommodifying' aspects that had, during the rise of welfare states, being 'decommodified', or taken out of the realm of the market. Recommodifying was associated with increased means testing, reduced entitlements, and an undermining of the power of trade unions or other organisations that opposed the strict application of market forces (Coburn, 2000). The index considered pension, sickness and unemployment benefits in terms of ease of eligibility rules, level of income replacement, and range of entitlements provided. Across 14 richer nations Coburn (2004) found a highly significant negative correlation between his index and infant mortality, only slightly reduced by controlling for the Gini index of income inequality (the correlation of infant mortality with Gini was considerably lower and reduced to zero by partialling out the decommodification index).

Post-Transition Experience in Eastern Europe

An important general criticism is that the whole analysis of income inequalities and health (and the theory linking income distribution and health) has been restricted to the richer countries of the world where only a minority of the world's population lives. A telling piece of evidence, presented by Sen (1999), is the imperfect relationship between per capita income (after correcting for the cost of living) and life expectancy in different parts of the world or in different social groups. For example he presented data showing how GNP per head of population in the mid-1990s was considerably lower, but life expectancy considerably higher, in China, Sri Lanka and the Indian state of Kerala, than in Brazil, South Africa, Gabon and Namibia. Kerala state in India, where, despite low average income, infant and childhood, maternal and overall mortality are better than in other Indian states and approaching those found in richer countries, is an often cited example of how government action can buck the trend (Lynch *et al.*, 2000). African Americans in the USA, Sen pointed out, while much richer in purely monetary terms than people in most of the third world, had a lower life expectancy than people in many third world countries such as China, Sri Lanka, or Kerala.

Considerable attention has focused on the countries of central and eastern Europe because of the dramatic changes that occurred in the political regimes of those countries at the end of the 1980s and early 1990s, and the possibility that these macro-level changes had a highly significant effect on people's health. Indeed the political and subsequent economic changes that occurred in those countries have been described as, "... the most comprehensive natural experiment in population-wide stress imaginable, short of war and mass starvation" (Hertzman & Siddiqi, 2000, p. 816). Although, as Carlson (2000) pointed out, views differ about whether the transformation to a market economy has been a success overall, the extent of the economic changes and the almost immediate effects of that 'shock therapy' on the economics of everyday life seem to be undeniable. A reversal of the trend of previous decades which had been towards increasing per capita GDP in nearly all the countries in that region (Hertzman & Siddiqi, 2000), an increase in inequality of income distribution (Hungary is a good example: Kopp *et al.*, 2004), and an increase in the price of food and other basic items along with a reduction of food subsidies and other economic transfers (Russia is an example here: Carlson, 2000), all resulted in an increase in the prevalence of poverty and increasing demands on the ability of households to cope. Although there are some differences of opinion about when deterioration in health was first apparent – Kopp *et al.* (2004) were of the view that deterioration in population health in Hungary was taking place before those economic changes occurred – and about how long such changes in health have lasted, there seems little disputing the fact that the earlier trend towards increasing life expectancy was reversed in nearly all central and eastern European countries, and particularly dramatically for men, at the end of the 1980s and in the early 1990s (Hertzman & Siddiqi, 2000). Among 30 to 49 year olds the rise in mortality was particularly extreme in Russia – an increase of as much as 70 to 80% in men and 30 to 60% in women – and in Ukraine – 30 to 50% in men and 20 to 30% in women – and less extreme in countries such as Hungary, Bulgaria and Romania.

Hertzman and Siddiqi (2000) were of the view that these changes were attributable to socioeconomic and psychosocial factors operating at macro, inter-mediate, and micro levels. Some support for that view comes from Kopp *et al.*'s (2000, 2004) comparison of data from two Hungarian population surveys, the first carried out in 1988, the second in 1995. Compared to results from the earlier survey, in 1995 depression inventory scores were markedly higher (except for those in their 20s and early 30s). Scores on a questionnaire assessing perceived control at work were lower for all age groups but particularly for those over 40, and perceived social support was reduced – particularly from co-workers or school mates, but also from neighbours, friends, relatives, and parents (but not from spouse or children).

Writing about Russia, Carlson's (2000, p. 1364) view was that:

> ... economic reforms were not matched by equally forceful reforms in the area of law, law enforcement, legal institutions, taxation, tax collection, training of civil servants, social legislation and other elements necessary in the building of a democratic structure which protects all citizens and has authority over the unleashed market forces, embodied in a new class of the very rich (Carlson, 2000, p. 1364).

Put another way:

> ... the twin ideologies of individualism and free market gave license to those who had influence at the highest levels of society to abandon their responsibilities (Hertzman & Siddiqi, 2000, p. 817).

Rose (1995) described post-communist Russia as an 'hourglass' society – an elite at the top which controls economic and political structures, a reduced civil society in the middle which is unable to buffer the stresses of daily living (the narrowing in the middle of the hourglass), and those at the bottom who need to rely on family and informal social supports to compensate for lack of supportive structures at higher levels.

Bobak *et al.* (1998) are others who have emphasised the rapid deterioration in social and economic circumstances that occurred since the transition – for example a rapid drop in real income and a corresponding sharp rise in share of expenditures spent on food. Results of a national survey carried out in Russia in 1996 revealed a very high rate of material deprivation – 44% scoring six or more on a nine-point scale asking participants if they went without food, heating or necessary clothes/shoes – and a rate of less than good self-rated health much higher than that found in typical western studies (62% and 79% for Russian men and women, respectively, compared to below 40% for both sexes in western studies). Material deprivation was significantly associated with poor self-rated health and poor physical functioning independently of other variables.

In a later report of results from that survey and parallel surveys in six other post-communist countries between 1996 and 1998, Bobak *et al.* (2000) showed how very different were the post-transition circumstances in the different countries. Income inequality (the Gini coefficient) was the lowest in the Czech Republic and Poland, and highest in Russia. Those living in serious deprivation were least in the Czech Republic, Poland and Hungary (3–4%), intermediate in Estonia, Latvia and Lithuania (8–10%), and much the highest in Russia (25%). The prevalence of poor self-rated health varied from a low of 8% in the Czech Republic to highs of 15–20% in Russia, Latvia and Hungary. Material deprivation was significantly related to poor self-rated health in each country independently of other factors, an effect that the authors attributed to the consequences of the economic reforms after the collapse of communism.

Piko (2004) was among those who, while acknowledging the challenges faced in central and eastern European countries after the transition due to the development of a market economy, have emphasised what they saw as the disastrous health consequences of Soviet occupation for a country such as Hungary with its historic ties to the west. The figures she presented suggest that life expectancy in those countries was static in the two decades prior to transition, unlike in western countries where life expectancy was rising. Authors such as Bobak *et al.* (1998), too, do not deny that life expectancy in Russia had been declining compared to the rest of the industrialised world since the 1960s, nor the legacy of distrust in the state left by the communist regime.

How the Material and the Psychosocial might be Linked: Some Illustrations

There is evidence from many different kinds of research that can be read – depending on one's point of view – as illustrating the false antithesis that has been drawn between psychosocial and material explanations for social inequalities in health

(Macintyre, 1997; Popay *et al.*, 1998), or as illustrating the ways in which macro-level material factors can influence health and well-being via their effects at the psychosocial level. There is room here just to give a small number of examples.

For instance, studies from the USA have produced evidence to support a link between material hardship, parental depression, parents' feelings about their ability as parents, and children's problems (e.g. Barrera *et al.*, 2002). Some of the best evidence of that kind comes from a programme of research conducted by Elder and colleagues. Some of their earlier work traced the effects upon offspring of family economic hardship during the 'great depression' years of the late 1920s and early 1930s, linking macro-economic conditions with the micro-social world of the family and the health and well-being of individual family members, over time, in a way that very few studies have been able to do. Their results suggested that the adverse consequences of stressful economic conditions more often produced effects indirectly via their disorganising effects on family life, for example by increasing negative interactions within the family. Effects on children's health and well-being depended on the child's sex and how old the child was at the time when financial loss for the family occurred, and also upon factors such as the father's personal stability and the strength of the mother–father marital bond (Liker & Elder, 1983; Elder & Caspi, 1988).

Later work, for example with families in a number of inner-city areas of Philadelphia, showed that family economic pressure (lower total household income and unstable work/income, because of having had to change job for a worse one, having been demoted, laid off, fired, stopped working for a time or experienced a cut in salary or wages) was significantly associated with parental feelings of depression which were themselves associated with a lower level of parental beliefs about their effectiveness as parents (e.g. getting a child to study, to stay away from danger, or to make the child's school a better place for the child to learn). Parental efficacy was associated with parental reports of using strategies to promote children's well-being both in the home (encouraging the child to do better, to get ahead, and supervising the child's work and engaging in joint activities) and outside the home (e.g. providing opportunities to get involved in such activities as sports or a choir, and preventive strategies such as pointing out dangers and helping the child get involved in positive neighbourhood activities) (Elder *et al.*, 1995).

A British example comes from the long-running programme of research conducted by Brown and his colleagues which has examined the role of stressful life events and difficulties, and vulnerability factors, in the onset of depression in women. His early work with Harris took place in an area of south London – Camberwell – containing a largely working-class, inner city area, and an adjacent inner suburban area (Brown & Harris, 1978). Later work was carried out on islands in the outer Hebrides – north Uist and Lewis – off the north-west coast of Scotland: a rural area where some residents were still involved in a traditional way of life including working smallholdings known as crofts, and where the influence of the Presbyterian church remained strong (Brown & Prudo, 1981). Later still the work was concentrated in a predominantly working-class area of north London – Islington (Brown & Moran, 1997; Brown, 1998). Their work has consistently shown that the onset of depression in women mostly follows shortly upon the occurrence of a severely stressful life event, thus explaining the greater incidence of depression among women in certain social groups, such as those in lower socioeconomic status groups in south London and non-traditional women in the outer Hebrides (not involving crofting, living in council housing, and non-church attending), who were significantly more likely to experience such life events than other women. Life events alone were generally insufficient to provoke depression, which usually required, in addition, background 'vulnerability' factors, such as having several young children at home to look after or having a low sense of self-esteem. The vulnerability factor that has consistently emerged as important in this line of research is the lack of a confiding, intimate relationship, either because a woman was single and lacking a confidante or because her relationship with husband or partner was a conflictual one or was not a close and confiding one. We shall have reason to consider this important work again in Chapter 8, along with a parallel study among Zimbabwean women.

A principle that Brown and his group have maintained throughout their work, is the importance of knowing about the context in which events occur in women's lives. Procedurally, each life event is rated according to the likely response of an individual to a particular event once her biography and immediate circumstances are taken into account. It is that contextually-understood threat that a life event poses that is considered of significance, rather than the individual woman's stated emotional response to the event. What Brown and colleagues' work on women and depression has always done is to weave together the personal and the social in the understanding of the origins of one of the most common forms of distress. Elsewhere, Brown (1988) has written of the two ever inter-connecting strands to a human life – one personal, which we may think of in terms of constructs such as personal identity and styles of attachment, the other social, composed of a life career of accumulating social assets, resources and status (or their lack). Commenting on Brown's model, Pilgrim (1997) criticised Brown's continued adherence to a positivistic psychiatric diagnostic approach ('depression', 'onset', 'case'), but applauded his and his colleagues' work for exposing, "...the role of material adversity, a lack of direct economic power and social class effects" (p. 89). It is the fact that Brown is equally comfortable writing about the world of personal meanings and the world of material deprivation that makes the contribution of his group an important one for community psychology.

A good example of the interweaving of the personal and the social across the life course was provided by Maughan and Lindelow's (1997) analysis of the antecedents and consequences of teenage motherhood among women who were included in two British birth cohort studies, the National Survey of Health and Development and the National Child Development Study, which followed up samples of children born in 1946 and 1958, respectively. Confirming other research on the subject, analysis of these two data sets each showed that young women who became mothers in their teens were disproportionately disadvantaged in background, being significantly more likely to come from families in manual occupational groups, and to have left school without qualifications (over three-quarters of teenage mothers versus under half of those who became mothers at an older age). Again confirming other research, follow-up of women in both groups into their 30s showed that teenage mothers were significantly more at risk of experiencing subsequent adversities such as a marital breakdown, having had four or more children and not being owner-occupiers of their own housing. Each of those adversity factors (with the exception of large family size for the 1946 cohort) was significantly associated with above threshold scores on standard scales of psychiatric symptoms in the women's mid-30s.

Although the rates of teenage motherhood were virtually identical in the two samples, early motherhood took place in two very different eras. Some of the results were different and may have reflected that differing context. In the earlier cohort (when rates of teenage motherhood were rising), teenage motherhood itself was not significantly associated with mental health. In the later cohort, however (when rates of teenage motherhood were falling sharply), those who had been teenage mothers were significantly more likely to show psychiatric symptoms even after adversities were controlled for. Further analysis found that teenage motherhood in this later cohort was associated with a range of more severe adult adversities which partly accounted for the increased risk of psychiatric problems. Those further adversities included experiencing some level of domestic violence associated with marriage or cohabitation breakdown, as well as the need for financial support, in the form of receiving income support, unemployment benefit, or supplementary benefit.

The inseparability of the material and the psychosocial, illustrated by the studies just described, is in line with the view of Macintyre (1997). She pointed out that the Black Report was in fact part of a lengthy tradition of British study of health inequalities, and that competing explanations – environmentalist, behavioural, and hereditarian – were clearly to be seen in debates on the subject in the early part of the twentieth century. Macintyre believed that debate had been bedevilled by confusion between the 'hard' versions of the different explanations – which supposed that either selection, material conditions or cultural/behavioural factors constituted complete explanations in themselves, explaining away social class gradients – and the 'soft' versions which saw any one set of factors as contributing to, but not totally explaining, the observed class gradient. The Black Report working group had seen the materialist/structuralist explanation as being the principal one, but had not excluded a role for selection or health-relevant behaviour. Non-British observers had often been puzzled by the polarisation of both academic and policy responses since the Black Report in Britain, where reference is often made to the inequalities 'debate'. The debate between Macleod and Davey Smith (2003), favouring a materialist explanation, and Singh-Manoux (2003), arguing for the importance of psychosocial factors, in the pages of the *Journal of Epidemiology and Community Health*, is a good illustration. Even Wilkinson (2000) has on occasion written about the two kinds of explanation – psychosocial and social resources – as not necessarily mutually exclusive, but as part of the same process.

Popay *et al.* (1998) are also among those who have been critical of social epidemiology for failing to see the likely complexity of explanations for social inequalities in health. They were particularly critical of the neglect of individual agency in health inequalities research. The predominant model was essentially a medical model, excluding personal accounts of experiences of individuals or households, and failing to see people as creative agents able to shape the world around them. Much greater respect should be given to lay knowledge and personal narratives and the meanings people give to the relationships between significant events in their lives. Part of the problem was a neglect of place and how neighbourhoods and communities are experienced. It is to a consideration of place and its influence on health and well-being that we now turn our attention.

Chapter 5

PLACE AND ITS INFLUENCE ON HEALTH AND WELL-BEING

The move in social epidemiology towards recognising the importance of place has been welcomed by many (e.g. Macintyre *et al.*, 2002) as part of the move away from the conceptual and political individualism of earlier years, with its emphasis on the role of individual lifestyle choices. It needs to be borne in mind, however, that the evidence to be discussed has all the advantages and disadvantages for community psychology, already mentioned, that derive from the epidemiological methods used. Once again, one disadvantage is the fact that the work is confined to a few western countries. But, yet again, the issues raised have relevance far beyond those countries.

EVIDENCE FOR THE INFLUENCE OF AREA ON HEALTH AND WELL-BEING

There is no dispute over the existence of variations in health and well-being from place to place. It has repeatedly been found that a variety of psychological problems, including treated mental illness, are more prevalent in poorer rather than better-off areas of cities in the western world. One of the earliest such findings was the classic work of Faris and Dunham (1939) on rates of treated schizophrenia in different districts in Chicago. Among more recent studies in Britain are those that have confirmed strong associations between the level of 'deprivation' of place of residence (using standard deprivation indices such as the Townsend index – see Figure 5.1 – the Jarman and Carstairs indices are others) and both admission to specialist psychiatric treatment for any one of a range of diagnoses (Boardman *et al.*, 1997) and the likelihood of being diagnosed with depression in primary care (Ostler *et al.*, 2001). Figure 5.2 shows the relationship between a similar measure of area deprivation and mortality rate in the subsequent decade across the neighbourhoods of Turin, Italy (Marinacci *et al.*, 2004).

The sum of:

% economically active residents aged 16 to 64 years (59 for women) in the area who are unemployed

% private households without a car

% private households NOT owner-occupied

% private households with more than one person per room

Figure 5.1   The Townsend index of an area's socioeconomic deprivation

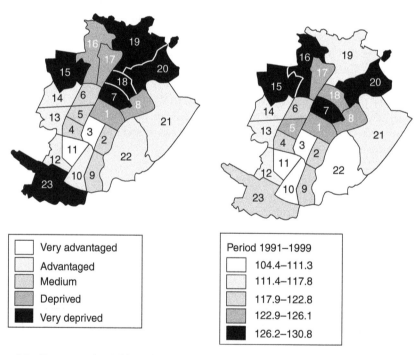

Figure 5.2   Patterns of neighbourhood disadvantage in Turin, Italy, in 1991 (shown on the left) and death from all causes in the subsequent decade (standardised mortality ratio, shown on the right)
Source: reproduced with permission from Marinacci, C., Spadea, T., Biggeria, A., Demaria, M., Caiazzo, A. & Costa, G. (2004). The role of individual and contextual socioeconomic circumstances on mortality: analysis of time variations in a city of north west Italy. *Journal of Epidemiology and Community Health*, **58**, 199–207

British studies of 'parasuicide' (sometimes referred to as deliberate self-harm, sometimes as self-poisoning) in the cities of Bristol (Morgan *et al.*, 1975) and Edinburgh (Holding *et al.*, 1977) found that those attending accident and emergency departments following deliberate self-harm (in Bristol) or admitted to hospital following self-poisoning (in Edinburgh) came disproportionately from certain wards of the city. In Bristol, wards with the highest incidence exceeded those with the lowest by a factor of six (men) or nine (women). The three wards with the highest rates were inner-city wards, two of them areas of sub-standard housing, overcrowding and poor amenities, the third part of the city's bedsitter land with a high proportion of rented accommodation. In Edinburgh there was a six-fold difference, one of three wards with the highest rates being an inner-city area with much hostel and night shelter accommodation, the other two located on the edge of the city, containing large inter-war housing estates noted for social problems. Two decades later, Gunnell *et al.* (1995, 2000) repeated these findings for the city of Bristol, finding that the relative standing of city wards in terms of deprivation had remained much the same over 20 years (the correlation between the Townsend index in 1971 and 1991 was 0.90) and that the relationship between ward deprivation and parasuicide admission rate remained much as it was (the correlation between parasuicide and Townsend score was 0.86). A similar pattern was found for suicide mortality.

Drug addiction is another example of extreme variation from place to place. For example, Brugal *et al.* (1999) used data from a number of different sources to estimate the prevalence of opioid addiction in the 30 or so areas within the city of Barcelona. Rates varied by a factor of more than 10, most of the areas with high rates being city centre areas. A high correlation (0.80) was found between area unemployment rate and addiction prevalence. Reviewing evidence on the importance of neighbourhood generally, Ellen and Turner (1997) concluded that what evidence there was relating to adolescents – they were reviewing evidence mainly from the USA – suggested that adolescent educational attainment, labour market outcomes, early sexual activity and pregnancy, drug use and crime, were all area related.

A feature of area inequalities in health in England and Wales has been a persisting regional difference, usually referred to as the 'north–south divide', with higher mortality and rates of chronic illness in the old industrial heartland regions towards the north that contain more areas of relative deprivation (Law & Morris, 1998; Woods *et al.*, 2005). Rates of limiting long-term illness have been found to be lower in the relatively well-off regions of south-east and central England, and higher in Wales and parts of northern England where traditional manufacturing industry and coal mining have declined (Boyle *et al.*, 1999, 2001). Raleigh and Kiri (1997) concluded that mortality differences by health authority had widened in the decade between the mid-1980s and mid-1990s, with life expectancy increasing only in those areas that already had the greatest longevity of life. A similar geographical gradient exists in Spain, with both mortality and deprivation levels higher in the south-west of the country and lowest in the north-east (Benach & Yasui, 1999).

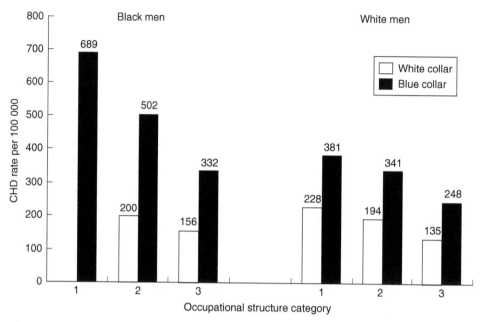

Figure 5.3 Age-adjusted coronary heart disease mortality among men aged 35–64 in upstate New York, USA, in 1988–92 by own occupational status and ethnicity and the county occupational structure

Source: reproduced with permission from Armstrong, D.L., Strogatz, D., Barnett, E. & Wang, R. (2003). Joint effects of social class and community occupational structure on coronary mortality among black men and white men, upstate New York, 1988–92. *Journal of Epidemiology and Community Health*, **57**, 373–8

Multi-Level Analyses

To be convinced that place matters it is necessary to contend with the argument that such apparent area effects are really individual effects due to the presence in certain areas of relatively many vulnerable individuals or families who are at risk of ill-health for individual reasons. In the case of the early studies of schizophrenia, for example, the social causation hypothesis was pitted against the 'social drift' hypothesis which supposed that movement of already ill or at risk individuals into poorer inner-city areas could explain the difference in prevalence in different areas (Cochrane, 1983). In view of all the evidence, discussed in Chapter 4, that socioeconomic status (SES), poverty and a family's living conditions are important determinants of health, in more recent epidemiological work on place it is those individual and family variables that have needed to be controlled. The following is a small sample of studies that, in different places and in different ways, have tried to tease out effects on physical health or in one case on a health behaviour (smoking) which affects health.

Armstrong *et al.* (2003) showed the combined effects, illustrated in Figure 5.3, of individual ethnicity and occupational status, and the occupational structure of the county of residence, among middle-aged men living in upstate New York, on age-adjusted coronary heart disease mortality rates, between 1988 and 1992, using census and death certificate information. The county occupational structure variable was created by categorising the 62 counties of upstate New York into three groups based on the percentage of the total labour force in 'white collar' occupations (20–29%, 30–39%, and 40–50%). The figure clearly shows the additive effects of the two individual level variables and area occupational structure. Note the absence of a figure for chronic heart disease mortality among white collar black men in those counties with the lowest percent of the labour force in higher status occupations, since numbers were too small in that group.

A study showing how smoking rates can vary from area to area independently of occupational status and educational level was Shohaimi et al.'s (2003) study of over 30,000 men and women aged 39–79 living in the English county of Norfolk, recruited through general medical practices between 1993 and 1997. Each person was assigned a Townsend deprivation score calculated on the basis of 1991 census data for the enumeration district in which they lived (an enumeration district has an average of about 150 households). Townsend scores were divided into quintiles. Logistic regression analysis showed current smoking rate to be significantly higher and never smoker rates significantly lower for those who lived in districts with higher deprivation scores, independently of individual occupational status and educational level.

Another study that looked at prediction of mortality was carried out by Martikainen et al. (2003) in the Helsinki metropolitan area in Finland. Information was based on the 1990 census records of all men over 25 years of age and that information was linked to death records for 1991 to 1995. The area was divided into 55 small areas and one of the chosen area variables was a social cohesion measure that combined the following: the proportion of over-15-year-old men living with a partner, the percentage of the population who had voted in the previous municipal elections in 1988, and the proportion of over-15-year-old men living in the same area in 1990 as they had lived in 1985. These three components, measuring adherence to traditional forms of living arrangements, participation in politics, and residential stability, were found in an exploratory analysis to combine into one factor. The analysis found a significant area effect on mortality. Although the area effect was considerably attenuated when individual level variables were added to the model (educational level, occupational status, housing tenure, housing density, and partner status), a moderate but significant effect remained. Figure 5.4 showed the added effect of individual occupational status and area cohesion on mortality for 25–64-year-old men. When data were re-analysed looking at specific causes of death, the most significant area effects were found for accidents and violence and alcohol-related causes for men aged 25–64 and for diseases of the circulatory system for both age groups.

Ever more sophisticated multi-level statistical analyses have been used to try to control for individual sources of variation and hence to find out whether an area effect remained once individual factors had been controlled for. Very often a form of hierarchical multiple regression has been employed which analyses the data in a step-wise fashion, putting into the analysis individual-level variables first, adding area-level variables only at a later step. Pickett and Pearl (2001) reviewed studies carried out in developed countries and published in English language

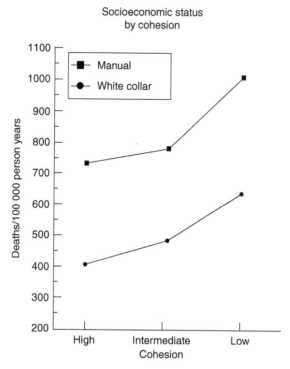

Figure 5.4 Age-adjusted mortality among men aged 25–64 in Helsinki, Finland, in 1991–5, by own occupational status and area cohesion
Source: Martikainen, P. Kauppinen, T.M. & Valkonen, T. (2003). Effects of the characteristics of neighbourhoods and the characteristics of people on cause specific mortality: a register based follow up study of 252,000 men. *Journal of Epidemiology and Community Health*, **57**, 210–17

peer-reviewed journals up to 1998, which had carried out that kind of analysis or similar. They found 25 such studies, 13 conducted in the USA, nine in the UK, two in the Netherlands and one in Finland. As their 'place' measure of the area, each study, in one way or another, had used some index of neighbourhood SES, varying from a single variable index such as median family income to multi-variable indices such as the Townsend, Jarman or Carstairs indices of deprivation (mostly used in British studies) or a combination of average education, occupation and housing type (more often used in the USA).

The results of their review were fairly consistent in finding at least modest effects of area once individual SES had been controlled (risk ratios significantly greater than one but generally less than two, indicating that those living in riskier areas were up to twice as likely to be recorded as unhealthy by some criterion, once individual factors were allowed for). The work they reviewed included studies of adult mortality, others of adult sickness, three of infant birth weight, and several of health behaviours or attitudes, mostly smoking. Among the negative studies was a large cohort study in England and Wales with a nine-year follow-up, which found no area level effect on mortality before age 70 among men and a significant relative risk for women of only 1.02. A follow-up of the same sample after 13 years did find significant area effects, albeit modest in size (men 1.02, women 1.04) (Sloggett & Joshi, 1994, 1998). The largest relative risks in all the studies reviewed concerned rates of male partner violence towards women during the child-bearing years: 3.4 for those living in areas of high unemployment, and 4.4 for those in areas of low income (O'Campo et al., 1995, cited by Pickett & Pearl, 2001).

There has continued to be a, "... growing stream of current multilevel analysis in modern health epidemiology" (Merlo, 2003, p. 550). Studies from a number of countries show that, independently of individual level factors such as socioeconomic status and education or income, indices of the general poverty level or relative deprivation of area of residence are associated with – and in longitudinal studies, predictive of – mortality from all causes, and specifically from heart disease. Samples have sometimes been of middle-aged and older adults, and sometimes of all adults 20 years and over (often with an upper age of 65, sometimes 55, and in other cases 75). For example, a study of residents of two towns in the west of Scotland, itself a relatively deprived area, was one example. Postcode sector deprivation index (the Carstairs and Morris index) was predictive of mortality from all causes and specifically from cardiovascular disease, over the following 15 years (the latter result was independent of baseline risk factors for men). The authors concluded that, "Policies aimed at reducing socioeconomic differentials in health should pay attention to the characteristics of the areas in which people live as well as the characteristics of the people who live in these areas" (Davey Smith et al., 1998, p. 399).

Each of those studies has found an area effect independently of a number of individual-level variables. But not all have been convinced that there is a real area health effect, and there have continued to be some reports of negative findings. For example one analysis of data from Turin, Italy, found that area deprivation played a marginal role besides individual factors such as educational level and occupational status (Petrelli et al., 2006). A similar conclusion was drawn from the findings of a study carried out in rural districts in the Republic of Ireland (Tay et al., 2004).

Some studies have a longitudinal element, following-up or tracing participants over several years. The study reported by Curtis et al. (2004) involved a rather longer time interval, no less than 52 years in fact. The study was based on data from the Office for National Statistics Longitudinal Study for England and Wales, using data from the national censuses of 1971, 1981 and 1991. For over 60,000 individuals tracked anonymously in that study, it was possible, via wartime registration numbers (used at that time to manage food rationing), to determine the place of residence in 1939, when members of the sample would have been children (aged 0 to 16 years). Using 1931 census data it was possible to classify areas of childhood residence by population density, percentage of families in occupational classes IV and V, area housing density, and rate of area unemployment. A minority of areas were designated at that time as 'special' or 'depressed' areas (although it is possible that some individuals were wrongly classified by area because of wartime evacuation to areas very different from those where they had spent most of their childhood).

Independently of individual and area characteristics in 1981, characteristics of the areas in which people had lived in 1939, as children, were predictive of premature death in middle age. An independent effect of area of childhood residence was also apparent for later long-term illness. For example, for those men living in the most deprived areas in the north of England in 1981, those who had lived in depressed areas of high population and housing density in 1939 were almost twice as likely as the average person in the study to report long-term illness in 1991 (a standardised morbidity ratio (SMR) of 186 – the average SMR is 100). By contrast those living in similarly poor areas in 1981 but in relatively advantaged areas as children were actually slightly less likely to report a later long-term illness than the average (SMR 90). Men with the highest rate of illness later in life (SMR 249) were those living in the most deprived Welsh districts in 1981 and in 'depressed' areas of high housing density in 1939. For women there was an effect of residing in childhood areas with high unemployment, higher population density, and in areas classified as 'depressed', although the effects were weaker than for men. As Curtis *et al.* pointed out, it is of course still possible that variables describing area of residence in the 1930s might have been acting as surrogate indicators of individual-level differences in early life, rather than reflecting attributes of places in which people grew up.

Criticisms of Multi-Level Analyses

Attention has been drawn to a number of shortcomings of this kind of multi-level research – see Figure 5.5. For one thing, if one is sceptical about neighbourhood or area effects, you can never be certain that all sources of individual variation have been accounted for. Some studies had only used a single variable, usually SES, to control for individual or family variation. Where does one stop in trying to account for place effects in individual terms? On the other hand, those inclined to believe in place effects may reasonably argue that such factors as individual education, occupation or income are themselves partly determined by where one lives: controlling for them may therefore remove part of the area effect that is being looked for. In an effort to control for the confounding effect of the 'selection' of individuals with different characteristics to different areas, there is a tendency to make adjustments, "until there is nothing for the neighborhood-level variables to explain" (Oakes, 2004a, pp. 1938–9).

The definition of 'neighbourhood' has also been problematic. It has been unusual to do what was done in one study of health in Amsterdam, the Netherlands, which analysed results three ways: by neighbourhoods (i.e. areas with a similar type of building, often delineated by natural boundaries), by postcode sectors, and by boroughs. Poor health was found to cluster most strongly in neighbourhoods, and least in postcode sectors, but there was little difference in terms of the amount of health variance that could be attributed to area deprivation (Reijneveld *et al.*, 2000). A novel approach was taken in a study of healthcare utilisation in France. Instead of dividing a space up into arbitrary areas, space was treated as a continuum, and the degree of correlation between individuals was examined as a function of the distance between their homes (Chaix *et al.*, 2005). The authors claimed that this method used more information about the spatial distribution of the health variable of interest, and was able to provide information not only about the magnitude of o   Studies have used geographical boundaries developed for census or other political purposes, which often fail to correspond to natural communities or areas that might share factors linked to health.

o   It ignores the interesting question of the possible importance of the relative homogeneity or mix of people in an area (e.g. is it better to be poor in an area where most other people are poor or in an area where most people are better off?).

o   The choice of area-level social variables is rarely based on something integral to the neighbourhood such as number of recreational facilities, level of service provision or number of community groups; most area variables are simply aggregates of individual variables (e.g. the Townsend index shown in Figure 5.1).

o   There is a tendency to artificially contrast area explanations with explanations based on individual compositional factors (i.e. the individuals an area is composed of); there is potentially no limit to the number of individual variables that could be controlled, and in practice it becomes impossible to separate the influences of neighbourhoods and information about the individuals who reside there; it may be better to think of neighbourhood effects as emergent properties of the social interactions of the people who live there, and it would therefore be inappropriate to consider the influence of place as somehow 'exogenous', or as something to which people are passively exposed.

o   There is a problem in extrapolating results from areas of one kind to those of a very different kind; multi-level analysis makes the unreasonable assumption that it is possible to imagine what a person with one kind of background would be like in terms of health in a quite different environment; moving people from one area to a very different one would completely alter the social structure.

o   Multi-level modelling has often simplified things by not going beyond a two-level conceptualisation of influences on health and well-being; there is a need to identify other levels such as households or larger macro-levels within which neighbourhoods operate.

o   Migration between areas is usually not considered.

o   This type of analysis can be accused of 'statisticism', unthinkingly using statistical methods without considering the causal theories behind them; methods should be used that require greater immersion in neighbourhood contexts, perhaps through ethnographic methods and making better use of social theory.

Figure 5.5   Shortcomings of multi-level statistical research on place and health
Source: Pickett, K.E. & Pearl, M. (2001). Multilevel analyses of neighbourhood socioeconomic context and health outcomes: a critical review. *Journal of Epidemiology and Community Health*, **55**, 111–22; Macintyre, S., Ellaway, A. & Cummins, S. (2002). Place effects on health: how can we conceptualise, operationalise and measure them? *Social Science and Medicine*, **55**, 125–39; Merlo, J. (2003). Multilevel analytical approaches in social epidemiology: measures of health variation compared with traditional measures of association. *Journal of Epidemiology and Community Health*, **57**, 550–2; Oakes, J.M. (2004a). The (mis)estimation of neighborhood effects: causal inference for a practicable social epidemiology. *Social Science and Medicine*, **58**, 1929–52; Weich, S. (2005). Absence of spatial variation in rates of the common mental disorders. *Journal of Epidemiology and Community Health*, **59**, 254–7

spatial variation, but also on the shape of such variation (i.e. how correlations vary with distance between people).

The choice of area-level social variables has also been criticised. Some studies have tried to overcome that problem by correlating individual health with individual perceptions of the area. For example, Molinari *et al.* (1998) found women's perceived health to be related to their perceptions of the social quality of their communities (the sum of 18 questions about social problems in the area), and men's perceived health to be related to their perceptions of their physical environment (the sum of six questions about the quality of outdoor air, indoor air, drinking water, solid waste or trash disposal, hazardous materials handling, and pesticide use and control), in a cross-sectional study in a rural county in a north-western state of the USA. Wilson *et al.* (2004) found significant differences in self-rated health and emotional distress across four neighbourhoods in the city of Hamilton, Ontario, Canada, corresponding with individuals' reports of disliked aspects of their neighbourhoods' physical environments such as noise and pollution (see Chapter 6 for a discussion of 'sense of community').

The problem of different measures and indices of area quality or deprivation was addressed in a study comparing mortality across the parliamentary constituencies of the UK, which used two area scores – the often-used Townsend deprivation score based on census data about an area's levels of unemployment, car ownership, overcrowded housing, and housing tenure; and a lesser known 'social fragmentation' index, based on Durkheim's theoretical concept of social integration, using census data about amount of private renting, single-person households, unmarried people, and mobility in the previous year. Although the two indices were correlated (0.7), the Townsend index was more strongly associated with all-cause mortality and specifically with mortality from coronary heart disease, stroke, and stomach cancer. On the other hand, the social fragmentation index was more strongly associated with suicide, and the two indices were equally strongly related to cirrhosis mortality (Davey Smith *et al.*, 2001).

Using 1991 census data from Northern Ireland, O'Reilly and Stevenson (2003) drew attention to yet another complication – the possibility that apparently growing inequality in health between different areas might be attributed to migration between areas. The census asked whether people had changed address in the previous 12 months. Just over 7% of the population had done so. Overall there was more movement from more deprived to more affluent areas, and migration was selective, with more affluent people tending to leave poorer areas and move to more affluent areas, and, to a lesser extent, poorer people leaving the more affluent areas to live in a poorer one. Although the amount of migration in a 12-month period was small, the authors calculated that such population flows, occurring year by year, can build up to a sizeable change over time, and that the effect they observed in that 12-month period would be such as to render deprived areas more sparsely populated and the whole socioeconomic landscape more polarised. That mechanism of selective geographical migration, they pointed out, should be contrasted with a different form of social selection whereby social position is determined by health status, rather than the other way round – a kind of social selection which at most makes a very minor contribution to socioeconomic differentials in health.

How Area and Individual Variables Might Interact: Some Examples

We should not expect area effects to be straightforward and invariant. As Pickett and Pearl (2001, p. 111) put it, "... it is probable that neighbourhood or contextual effects will themselves be contextual, and that both the factors themselves and the magnitude of their effects will be context dependent". For example, three of the studies reviewed by them found the effect of neighbourhood on mortality to be modified by age, with neighbourhood apparently having less effect in older age groups.

Several other studies have, intriguingly, found interactions between variables at individual and area levels. For example, analysis of mortality in the UK Health and Lifestyle Survey found evidence that area deprivation interacted with social class, such that in areas of relatively low deprivation there were no SES differences, but in areas of above-average deprivation the experience of those of different social class diverged, with increased mortality for those of lower SES (specifically groups III non-manual, IV and V), and no relative increase in mortality for others (Jones et al., 2000). A study in two Canadian provinces also found interactions, but apparently operating in a different direction. There were significant interaction effects on mortality in both provinces studied – Manitoba and Nova Scotia – with those on lowest incomes who lived in the more advantaged neighbourhoods being the group with the highest mortality rate. Both provinces showed steeper mortality gradients by class in advantaged than in disadvantaged neighbourhoods (Roos et al., 2004).

In their review of place effects on health, Macintyre et al. (2002) cited the following examples of interactions between area and individual characteristics: studies finding that the poverty of an area was related to mortality among under 55 year olds, but not among older people (Waitzman & Smith, 1998); a finding of low social class being associated with high cholesterol in African USAmerican men living in 'richer' neighbourhoods, but low social class being associated with low cholesterol in 'poorer' ones (Diez Roux et al., 1997); and studies in the UK finding steeper health gradients, by individual deprivation, in more affluent districts or regions (Shouls et al., 1996).

Using data from the first wave of the British Household Panel Survey carried out in 1991, Weich et al. (2003) found that ward-level socioeconomic deprivation (using the four-item Carstairs index) only remained statistically significantly related to depression, once individual and household level factors had been controlled, for those individuals who were currently economically inactive (i.e. not currently available for employment and therefore not classified as unemployed). That group, which would have included those with long-term sickness, house people, students and the retired, constituted nearly a third of the whole sample (considerably larger than the unemployed group), and would presumably have spent more time at home and therefore be more vulnerable to the effects of their local areas, compared to the majority employed group. Note that this study was comparatively more sophisticated than most, statistically, not only testing for area effects specific to particular groups of people, but also using multi-level analysis methods which were based on three, rather than the conventional two, levels: individuals were nested within households and households within areas. The method corrected for the clustering of persons in households, and clustering of households within wards.

In a report based on data from a telephone survey of over 2000 adults (aged 18–92) in the state of Illinois, USA, which constituted a survey of Community, Crime and Health carried out in 1995, Ross et al. (2000) looked at the factor of residential stability, which has been recognised by O'Reilly and Stevenson (2003, see above) and by a number of other researchers in the field to be a complicating but important factor. According to some, the more the population of an area remained stable over a period of years, the more will be the positive social ties that develop between neighbours, and the more healthy residents will be (Ross et al. referred to this as the cohesiveness perspective). An alternative, that Ross et al. referred to as the social isolation perspective, is that residential stability may be bad for those living in disadvantaged neighbourhoods because long-term residence implies an inability to escape to safer, less disadvantaged areas. It may not be healthy to live in stable areas characterised by delinquent gang membership, drug dealing, or norms that encourage unhealthy behaviours.

Ross et al.'s (2000) analysis supported the latter hypothesis. Psychological distress (anxiety and/or depression) was not associated, overall, with residential stability, measured by the percentage of people in a census tract who lived in the same home from 1985 to 1990 (which varied from 3% to 78% with an average of 50%). The main finding was a significant interaction between stability and area poverty. In those areas with the lowest levels of poverty, stability was negatively associated with depression and anxiety as the cohesiveness theory would predict. But for most areas there was no relationship with stability, and for those with the very highest levels of poverty (at least two standard deviations above the mean) stability and psychological distress were positively correlated, as the social isolation theory would have it. Further statistical analysis showed that a 14-item measure of neighbourhood disorder, as well as measures of powerlessness (an eight-item measure of general sense of personal powerlessness) and fear (three items: number of days in the last week feared being robbed, attacked or physically injured; worried home would be broken into to; felt afraid to leave the house) explained the interaction of stability and poverty in the prediction of depression and anxiety. Ross et al.'s (2000) conclusion was, therefore, that:

> Living in a poor, stable neighbourhood is associated with distress partly because such neighbourhoods have the high levels of disorder associated with poverty but lack the advantages that stability provides in affluent neighbourhoods for reducing disorder. In these neighbourhoods, residents live daily with the strains associated with drug and alcohol use on the streets, teenagers hanging out, abandoned and rundown buildings, crime, graffiti, and vandalism. Even though most residents do not directly experience victimization, they experience it indirectly through visible signs and cues that social control is absent. The stress of living in a place where the streets are dirty, noisy, and dangerous takes its toll in feelings of depression and anxiety. Beyond that, disorder raises levels of fear at the same time that it reduces the perception that one is in control of one's life, creating a sense that one is powerless to escape a bad situation, which is distressing (p. 594).

HOW NEIGHBOURHOODS MAY (FAIL TO) MEET LOCAL HEALTH NEEDS

Health workers are often left in no doubt about the pervasive effect on health of living in a deprived neighbourhood. Widgery's (1993) account of his experiences as a general medical practitioner in the East End of London is a particularly good example. A small number of social epidemiologists have also carried out more detailed studies of areas than is usually the case in their field. For example, Sooman and Macintyre (1995) found that scores on a scale of anxiety, independently of individual social class, were correlated with an overall assessment of the quality of the local area as perceived by residents of four areas within the city of Glasgow, Scotland. The same was true for two self-ratings of general health: health in the last year and health compared to others of the same age. The study lacked some of the later sophistications of multi-level modelling, but is of particular interest because of the detail it provides about residents' perceptions of the four very different areas of the city. Area 1, in the north-west of the city, containing some of the most desirable addresses, consisted of nineteenth-century villas and tenements built for the Victorian middle classes. Area 2, also in the north-west, was built as a high status public housing extension to the city between the two world wars, with comparatively high rents and purpose-built community facilities, many of the houses now having been bought by their tenants. Area 3, in the south-west of the city, was also an area of high status inter-war development but including some low rent council flats more typical of the city, and situated further from the city centre than Area 2 and adjacent to a more deprived area. Area 4, the poorest and most remote from the city centre, was one of Glasgow's post-war peripheral public housing schemes, built to a low standard because of acute post-war housing shortage, and for many years lacking basic amenities.

Significant differences between the four areas were found in terms of composite indices of local amenities, local problems, area reputation, fear of crime, and general satisfaction with the area. In each case Area 4 was perceived most negatively and in almost every instance Area 1 most positively (Area 2 had a slightly higher score for amenities). A number of the specific perceptions are of interest. For example it was very exceptional for residents of Area 1 to report the lack of a bank within walking distance or half a mile of where they lived, but that was commonly reported in the other areas. A launderette similarly close by was reported by around 70% of those in Areas 1 and 2 but by only 30% and 10% respectively in Areas 3 and 4. The opposite was the case for public houses which were reported to be within easy access for 91% of those in Areas 3 and 4 but only 79% and 85% respectively in Areas 1 and 2. In terms of problems that residents thought existed in their neighbourhoods, vandalism and litter and rubbish were reported by at least half of the residents in all areas but most of all by those in Area 4. Assaults and muggings and also disturbances by youths were reported by around a quarter of those in Area 1 and around a half for those in Area 4, and the problem of discarded needles was reported by increasing proportions across the areas (from 4% in Area 1 to 18% in Area 4). Area 4 had the highest combined score for what Sooman and MacIntyre and others have called 'incivilities', which included problems of litter and rubbish, vandalism, and

1.	*Physical features of the environment shared by all residents in a locality.* These include the quality of air and water, latitude, climate, etc. and are likely to be shared by neighbourhoods across a wide area.
2.	*Availability of healthy environments at home, work and play.* Areas vary in their provision of decent housing, secure and non-hazardous employment, safe play areas for children, etc. These environments may not affect everyone living in an area in the same way that air and water quality do; they may affect the employed more than the unemployed, families with children more than elderly people, and so on.
3.	*Services provided publicly or privately to support people in their daily lives.* These include education, transport, street cleaning and lighting, policing, health and welfare services. Again, how these affect people may depend on personal circumstances. Public transport may matter more if you do not have a car.
4.	*Socio-cultural features of a neighbourhood.* These include the political, economic, ethnic and religious history of a community, norms and values, the degree of community integration, levels of crime, incivilities and other threats to personal safety, and networks of community support.
5.	*The reputation of an area.* How areas are perceived, by their residents, by service or amenity planners and providers, by banks and investors, may influence the infrastructure of the area, the self-esteem and morale of the residents, and who moves in and out of the area.

Figure 5.6   Features of local areas which can influence health
Source: reproduced with permission from Macintyre, S., Ellaway, A. & Cummins, S. (2002). Place effects on health: how can we conceptualise, operationalise and measure them? *Social Science and Medicine*, **55**, 125–39

disturbances by youths. Residents of Area 1 reported the highest average number of neighbours with whom they exchanged favours, and Area 4 the least (2.1 and 1.5, respectively), and a smaller proportion of those residing in Area 4 said they wanted to stay in the area (14% compared to 27–36% in other areas).

Macintyre *et al.* (2002) later attempted to spell out the human needs that might be served by the areas in which people lived, and the five types of local area features which they thought might influence health (see Figure 5.6). The first three of those sets of features could be thought of as material resources or 'opportunity structures', whilst categories four and five relate to collective social functioning and practices (Kelly & Steed, 2004, produced a similar breakdown of community resources based on conservation of resources theory – Hobfoll, 1998; Hobfoll *et al.*, 1995 and see Chapter 1). Macintyre *et al.* were critical of the tendency to see the material and social as either/or categories, seeing no reason why poor health could not be the result both of levels of collective social functioning and of material infrastructure. An exclusive focus on one or the other might be counter-productive. Health might be a function of individual compositional, collective social, and material opportunity structures. For example, children in deprived areas being kept indoors rather than playing outside more might be because families lack gardens or resources to take children to parks, because too few parks are provided and transport links are poor, or because play is not emphasised in the local culture, and/or because it is not considered desirable or safe to children for play with strangers in public areas. Areas might exhibit high rates of poor health because they contain many individuals with personal characteristics predisposing to smoking, because there are many cigarette outlets and low priced cigarettes and cigarette advertisements, and/or because of local pro-smoking norms and traditions.

Drawing on their study of four areas in north-west England, Popay *et al.* (2003) argued for a view of the link between place and health that drew on the normative, material and social aspects of place, giving a central role to people's ability to construct or reconstruct for themselves a positive identity despite the drawbacks of the environments in which they were living. They were at pains to point out that this was not to deny the importance of material circumstances or to suggest that the pathway between place and ill-health was primarily psychosocial. Two of the areas studied were chosen as relatively advantaged areas, and two as relatively disadvantaged – one in each of two towns. The study used both survey methods and in-depth interviews with sub-samples of lone parents, young adults, older people, and parents in two-parent families. In response to survey questions, those in the two relatively advantaged areas were much more likely to disagree with statements that vandalism, burglaries, assaults and muggings, and litter and rubbish were a problem in the area, that there was a lack of safe places for children to play, that they felt dissatisfied, unhappy or terrible about living in the area, and that they would like to move out; and were much less likely to disagree with statements such as, 'I feel that living in this neighbourhood gives me a sense of community', 'I like to think of myself as similar to the people who live in this neighbourhood', and, 'Overall I think this is a good place to bring up children'.

The much more detailed interviews were interpreted as evidence for the idea that there was a normative set of values or guidelines about what constituted a 'proper place' to live, that had a community spirit, where neighbours were mutually supportive, where there was a good level of trust and respect for one another and for property, and where the environment was clean and safe and convenient. The following two quotes are from women who had moved to new areas:

> Here I know more of my neighbours, so the children can play out, where-as in...there was a lot of joy riding and I just wouldn't let [daughter] play out ...but this is more of an old-fashioned community here, like we all know each other, all look after each others' kids, we sit out ...like when I was a kid and we'll have a drink and we've had street parties before, there's a really good community spirit ...I love it here, I really do love it (p. 59).

> Now I have neighbours who are always willing to make themselves known to each other and to help each other. I mean you have your own life, your own friends, your own family, but it's like an extension of that when you feel comfortable with the people around you and that's what I feel here (p. 60).

A common view, particularly among older residents and those who had lived in the same area for a long time, was that trust and respect had declined. Popay *et al.* used the expression 'the privatisation of everyday life' to describe what they were repeatedly told about the process of withdrawal into the security of personal or domestic space, for example by keeping doors locked, not putting washing on the line in case it was stolen, being afraid to go out – leading to what Popay *et al.* saw as a widespread state of alienation, lack of knowledge about other people's lives, an absence of regular social relationships involving acknowledgement and support, and a sheer lack of conversation, leading in turn to an absence of shared narratives and meanings. As one person put it, "I just lock my door when I come [home] and get on with my own little life" (p. 66). Another explained that he and his family had no problem with the neighbours because the neighbours, " ...just tend to look after themselves ... " (p. 66).

It was not always easy to simply 'read off' the links between the experience of an area and people's health from what was said during the interviews. In some cases, however, the link was spelt out more clearly. One mother, for example, who had moved to one of the relatively disadvantaged areas shortly after her child was born, without positive relationships locally with family members or friends, and living on social security benefits, felt overwhelmed by dislike and fear of the area to which she was tied by low income and rent arrears. She described putting on several stones in weight and said:

> The doctor put me on Prozac a few months back for living here. Because it's depressing. You get up, you look around and all you see is junkies ...I know one day I will come off, I will get off here. I mean I started drinking a hell of a lot more since I've been on here. I drink every night. I have a drink every night just to get to sleep. I smoke more as well. There's a lot of things (p. 68).

Another example was that of an older woman and her husband who described living in fear of burglaries and how they were terrorised by young people congregating outside the house at night. They avoided confronting them and had severely restricted their lives, leading to greater social isolation, greater difficulty in managing her disability, increased strain on her husband, and finally a decision to leave their home and to move into sheltered accommodation.

Those more detailed studies and comments on the link between place and psychological distress provide a bridge between the present chapter and the next. In Chapter 6 we shall look in some detail at two leading ideas about the nature of people's social networks, neighbourhoods and communities. One of them – sense of community – has a comparatively long history in community psychology (needless to say, the history of community psychology is remarkably short in the general scheme of things). The other – social capital – comes from more general lines of thought outside community psychology. Its importation is controversial, although the present author believes that the idea has much to offer community psychology if used with care.

Chapter 6

TWO CONCEPTS FOR UNDERSTANDING INEQUALITIES BY POSITION AND PLACE

SOCIAL CAPITAL

One of the biggest ideas in the field of social policy at the beginning of the twenty-first century has been the concept of 'social capital' – thought by some, indeed, to be, "... the most important and exciting concept to emerge out of the social sciences in fifty years" (Halpern, 2005, p. 1). Does that idea resonate with any of the notions, such as empowerment, close to the heart of community psychology? Might it, for example, offer us a route for understanding the psychological effects of area of residence, discussed in the previous chapter? We shall look at a sample of work on the topic to see if we can answer that question. But the idea of social capital has been controversial and contested, and we shall also need to critically examine how the concept has been defined and measured, and what commentators have considered to be its merits and demerits.

Definitions and Indices of Social Capital

Some definitions of social capital are shown in Figure 6.1 and a number of the features of neighbourhoods and areas that have been considered indicative of social capital are shown in Figure 6.2. Let us look at some illustrative examples of the way social epidemiologists have used the idea in their work. Take, as an example, Skrabski *et al.*'s (2003) survey of variation in mortality among several thousand 45–64 year olds interviewed in their homes across the 20 counties of Hungary in 1995. They used three survey measures of social capital: *trust* (agreement or disagreement with the statement, 'People are generally dishonest and selfish and they want to take advantage of others'); *reciprocity* ('If I do nice things for someone, I can anticipate that they will respect me and treat me just as well as I treat them'); and *perceived support from civic and religious organisations* – non-profit, voluntary

❖ The sum of resources, actual or virtual, that accrue to a group by virtue of possessing a durable network of more or less institutionalized relationships of mutual acquaintance and recognition (Bourdieu & Wacquant, 1992).

❖ Features of social organisation such as networks, norms, and social trust that facilitate coordination and cooperation for mutual benefit (Putnam, 1995).

❖ A culture of trust and tolerance, in which extensive networks of voluntary associations emerge (Inglehart, 1997).

❖ The capacity of individuals to command scarce resources by virtue of their membership in networks or broader social structures (Portes, 1998).

❖ The stock of networks that are used to produce goods and services in society, of which health is one example (Rose, 2000).

Figure 6.1   Some definitions of social capital

❑ General trust in others

❑ Feeling of belonging to the area

❑ Relations with neighbours: know them/visit them/can rely on them

❑ Feeling safe/trust in the police/low crime rate

❑ Civic associations: existence of them/participation in them/support from them

❑ Low migrating-out rates

❑ High voting rates/political participation

❑ Social pro-activity, e.g. helping others, picking up litter

Figure 6.2   Indicators of social capital

organisations, societies, self-help groups and clubs (in each case a rating of how much help one could count on in a difficult situation). Results showed the measures of social capital to be significantly associated with county premature mortality rates independently of other county-level variables such as per capita gross domestic product and unemployment rate, and individual level factors such as income, education, and smoking and spirit consumption.

A report on data collected at the eighth wave (in 1998) of the annual British Household Panel Study – an annual survey of a representative sample of adults living in households in England, Wales and most of Scotland – provides another example (McCulloch, 2001a). Eight questions were asked which were summed to yield an index of social capital. They were questions such as: 'I feel like I belong to this neighbourhood', 'The friendships and associations I have with other people in my neighbourhood mean a lot to me', 'I would be willing to work together on something to improve my neighbourhood', 'I like to think of myself as similar to the people who live in the neighbourhood'. Independently of individual age, education, smoking, material deprivation, marital status, social support and economic activity, low social capital was significantly related to mental health problems for both men and women (the 12-item GHQ – General Health Questionnaire) and to certain aspects of reported physical ill-health (problems with chest or breathing).

A survey of 3000–4000 people representative of the population of Malmö in southern Sweden is an example of the common use of *indirect indices* of social capital (Lindström *et al.*, 2003a,b). One analysis of the data used, as an indirect measure of the social capital of different neighbourhoods, the proportion of the population within each of the neighbourhoods into which the city could be divided who had migrated from the neighbourhood during 1993. A second analysis, which was concerned to explain why some people felt a sense of insecurity in the neighbourhood (a single question asking people to rate how secure they felt in the neighbourhood after dark), used the percentage of the population of each neighbourhood taking part in the 1994 municipal elections (which ranged from 55% to 98%) as the indirect measure of social capital. When significant individual variables were controlled statistically (older people and women expressed more insecurity), the effect of the indirect measure of social capital remained significant (Lindström *et al.*, 2003b) – people felt more secure in those neighbourhoods where more people voted.

One apparently simple question that has become popular for insertion into large surveys is one that aims to assess the 'thin trust' aspect of social capital: that aspect of social capital which has to do with perceived level of general trust existing in an area. It is distinguished from 'thick trust', which concerns trusting relationships with small groups of known people such as family members and neighbours (Granovetter, 1973). The usual question is: 'Generally speaking, would you say that most people can be trusted or you cannot be too careful in dealing with people'. Aggregated to the level of whole countries this kind of trust is at a much higher level in some countries – principally the Scandinavian countries, followed by other western European ones – than in others (Poortinga, 2006b). Using data from the World Values Survey, based on information from national surveys conducted in more than 50 countries worldwide in 1995–7, Carlson (2004) examined self-rated health and social capital across 18 European countries. National differences in self-rated health were substantial, with less than good health reported by percentages of national samples varying from a low of 15% in Switzerland to more than 70% in Russia and Ukraine. There were similarly wide divergences in trust in other people, which averaged 48% in western European countries but 23% in central/eastern Europe and the former Soviet Union.

Another popular index of social capital is participation in community activities, referred to as 'civic participation' or 'social participation'. For example an index used in the Swedish study, referred to above, consisted of 13 types of formal and informal group activity such as a study circle or course, union meeting, theatre or cinema, church, sports events, and writing a letter to the editor of a newspaper or journal. Participation in four or more of those activities was taken as 'high' participation and three or fewer as 'less' (Lindström *et al.*, 2003b). Halpern (2005) noted the criticism of measures of social capital based on membership of civic associations which might not do justice to newer forms of association, those preferred by women, and those joined by people of different cultural and ethnic groups.

Different Forms of Social Capital

It can seen from Figure 6.2 how wide is the concept of social capital, covering things as varied as trust in the police, mutual help among neighbours and engagement in local politics. Harpham *et al.* (2004), in the course of their study in the city of Cali, Colombia, distinguished two varieties of social capital: *structural* (e.g. networks, connectedness, associational life, and civic participation) and *cognitive* (e.g. perceived support, trust, social cohesion, and perceived civic engagement). Some had preferred to confine measurement to the structural aspects, while others had maintained that both need to be included. McKenzie *et al.* (2002) pointed out that structural social capital includes both horizontal bonds that occur among family, friends and neighbours, and vertical bonds between groups with different levels of power and influence in society, leading to social inclusion. Studies had tended to concentrate on the former, neglecting the all-important vertical aspects.

Szreter and Woolcock (2004) distinguished three forms of social capital. *Bonding* and *bridging* social capital, respectively, were defined by them as follows:

> Bonding social capital . . . trusting and co-operative relations between members of a network who see themselves as being similar in terms of their shared social identity.
> Bridging social capital . . . relations of respect and mutuality between people who know they are not alike in some socio-demographic (or social identity) sense (differing by age, ethnic group, class, etc).

A third type of social capital identified by Szreter and Woolcock, which picks up the 'vertical' element, was *linking* social capital, defined by them as:

> Linking social capital . . . norms and respect and networks of trusting relationships between people who are interacting across explicit, formal or institutionalised power or authority gradients in society (Szreter & Woolcock, 2004, pp. 654–55, cited by Sundquist *et al.*, 2006, p. 955).

Halpern (2005), in his book, *Social Capital* (described by Putnam on the book cover as, ". . . the best overall introduction so far to the rapidly increasing literature on social capital") concluded that, for health and development, a combination or balance of different types of social capital was best – bonding (sometimes referred to as 'localised' social capital) and bridging, perhaps particularly the type of bridging that enabled 'linking' across groups with different power. The two were distinguishable: for example bridging social capital was correlated with socioeconomic status; and compared to bonding the bridging form tended to decay faster. He used the analogy of vitamins – a healthy social capital 'diet' involved a balance of different types (similar to Warr's, 1987, vitamin model of the functions of employment). Halpern referred to the value of high levels of bonding within groups of recent immigrants, but the need for increasing bridging social capital if such groups were not to be held back later on. School performance provided another example. Coleman's (1988) classic paper on social capital noted the much lower rate of school drop-out in Catholic high schools in the USA, tracing this to the higher level of parent–student–school connectivity in Catholic schools. Subsequent work had confirmed that finding, but had also found evidence for circumstances under which high bonding capital of that kind might instead serve to hold children back. Something very similar had been found by those researching earlier in the social support tradition, before the idea of social capital had come on the scene. For example, Hirsch (1981) found that less dense, less interconnected social networks across the family–friendship boundary were associated with more positive well-being for two groups of women facing life transitions – a group of recently widowed younger women and a group of mature women who had recently returned to studying full time. Hammer's (1983) theory was that dense, tightly interconnected social networks might be better under some circumstances – for dealing with crises for example – but that more defuse networks would be preferable for coping with transitions.

Social Capital Theory

The big names associated with the theoretical idea of social capital are Putnam, Bourdieu, and Coleman. According to Schuller *et al.* (2000), in the introductory chapter to their edited volume *Social Capital: Critical Perspectives*, Bourdieu (e.g. 1985, 1986) could be credited with introducing the term into the social sciences but his concept of social capital was elusive and he initially wrote about 'cultural capital'. Putnam (e.g. 1995, 2000), on the other hand, could be credited with popularising the concept through his work on regional government in different parts of Italy (Putnam, 1993) and the argument he marshalled that social capital had markedly declined in his native USA in the later decades of the twentieth century (*Bowling Alone*, the title of an article and later a book, refers to the idea that US citizens were spending much of their leisure time watching TV, and much less time than earlier generations going bowling together and joining clubs and associations).

A clear distinction is drawn by a number of commentators between the increasingly popular conceptualisation of social capital of Putnam, which focuses on trust, reciprocity, and social participation (and which is often seen as leading to support for narrow communitarian policies that serve parochial interests), and Bourdieu's more sociological theory, which emphasises collective resources that members of groups can draw on for obtaining benefits and services in conjunction with their economic capital or lack of it. Coleman's development of the more specific idea of family social capital – often criticised for over-emphasising close ties to the micro-systems of family and school – is seen as much closer to Bourdieu's ideas (Almedom, 2005; Carpiano, 2006). Bourdieu developed his theory through considering how class and other forms of inequality were socially reproduced; in his view social capital depended, not only on the network connections that a person can mobilise, but also on the capital possessed by those in the network; it recognises the potentially negative, exclusionary, aspects of social capital; and it is less geographically rooted than Putnam's concept (Carpiano, 2006).

Much of what is considered social capital in Putnam's view was considered by Carpiano (2006) to be better thought of as social cohesion. Social cohesion constituted the necessary foundation for social capital rather than being social capital itself. The latter term Carpiano reserved for the actual or potential resources that could be accessed through the social network. His complete model of

Neighborhood-Level

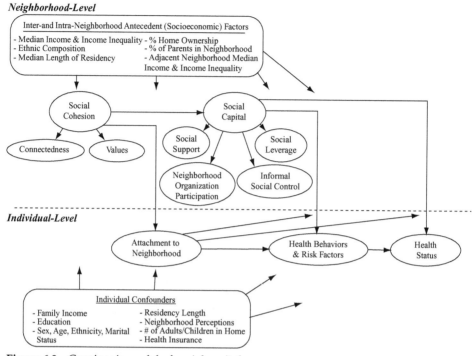

Figure 6.3 Carpiano's model of social capital
Source: reproduced with permission from Carpiano, R.M. (2006). Toward a neighborhood resource-based theory of social capital for health: can Bourdieu and sociology help? *Social Science and Medicine*, **62**, 165–75

neighbourhood social capital is shown in Figure 6.3. It included, in addition, structural antecedents to social cohesion and social capital, reflecting neighbourhood structural characteristics and socioeconomic conditions, as well as the outcomes of social capital, not all of which might be positive. In his model the social capital component embraced four forms: social support that individuals could draw on in coping with daily problems; social leverage that helped residents obtain information and advance socioeconomically; informal social control – the ability of residents to collectively maintain order and safety; and community participation, or organised collective action for addressing local issues.

Other writers on the subject of social capital have made further useful theoretical points. Grootaert (2001), at the time lead economist in the Social Development Department of the World Bank, considered Putnam's concept of social capital to be a comparatively narrow one, consisting of social networks of 'horizontal associations' between people and associated norms that had an effect on the productivity of a community. A more encompassing view would include the social and political environment in which norms develop and which shape the social structure. Furthermore, it would embrace more formalised institutional relationships and structures as well as the largely informal and often local relationships. As an example of the importance of macro-level social capital, Grootaert cited the withdrawal of people from the 'official' economy in the transition economies of eastern Europe and the former Soviet Union (see Chapter 4 for Rose's, 2000, idea of the 'hourglass society' in Russia). Political scientists, such as Ostrom and Ahn (2003), are naturally interested in the more formalised institutional structures of society such as government, the law and civil and political liberties, and the balance between formal, legal rules as a way of creating the order necessary for collective action, and informal rules and norms. The concept of social capital can be seen as drawing attention to that balance, leading to a presumption that power and responsibility should be devolved downwards within the state, a need to foster linkages between different sectors such as health and education, and the need to disperse decision making from state to community and voluntary bodies (Schuller *et al.*, 2000). Halpern's (2005) preference was to embrace factors at all levels – macro, intermediate, and micro. Part of his argument for that was that components of social capital at different levels could, to an extent, substitute or compensate for one another.

Baum and Ziersch (2003) viewed trust as central to the idea of social capital. But they wished to distinguish three broad types: trust within established relationships and social networks; generalised trust (or 'social trust') which extends to strangers; and trust in the formal institutions of governance. Concepts closely related to social capital included civil society (referring to groups of people contributing to change through activities that are not part of the formal political system, commerce, or government), social networks, participation, social exclusion/inclusion, and local opportunity structures. An important debate has been between a communitarian vision of a strong civil society in which the state plays little part (to which Putnam appeared to subscribe) and an alternative vision (following Bourdieu) that sees the state as a necessary support to civil society, in order, apart from anything else, to avoid the possible negative exclusionary consequences of strongly bonded civil society groups. Either way, participation in civil society was usually seen as a crucial element of social capital.

Yet another useful source of theoretical ideas on social capital is Ziersch (2005). She referred to the debate about whether social capital was viewed as a *source*, in which case factors such as general trust and availability of networks would be emphasised, or as an *outcome*, focusing more on factors such as information flow, social support, influence and control, social cohesion and sense of community, and civic engagement and voluntary work. In her own study of social capital in two suburbs in Adelaide, South Australia she referred to the former as social capital infrastructure, and the latter as social capital resources (see Figure 6.4).

Criticisms of the Social Capital Idea

There have been many criticisms of social capital as an idea; for example, that there is no agreed definition of it or that claims for its explanatory value are too wide to be credible (Schuller *et al.*, 2000; Macinko & Starfield, 2001). Most commentators draw attention to problems of measurement, especially the reliance on a few survey questions or on census information about voting or the number of associations of various kinds that exist in an area. The authors of the Swedish report, referred to earlier, acknowledged that, "Social capital is a multifaceted and at present ill-defined concept with a number of competing definitions . . . It is thus, at present, almost impossible to construct a complete empirical measure of social capital that completely covers the concept" (Lindström *et al.*, 2003b, p. 1113).

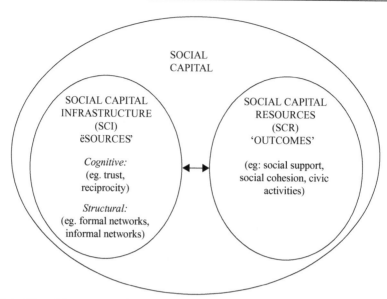

Figure 6.4 Ziersch's conceptualisation of social capital
Source: reproduced with permission from Ziersch, A.M. (2005). Health implications of access to social capital: findings from an Australian study. *Social Science and Medicine*, 61, 2119–31

Another frequent criticism (e.g. Schuller *et al.*, 2000) is that such concepts as trust and networks had been studied, often more deeply and satisfactorily, before being taken up by writers on social capital. For example, they contrasted the restricted use of 'trust' in the writings of the historian Fukuyama (1995), who saw it as a necessary ingredient for the smooth functioning of a modern, 'wealth-creating' economy, and the detailed treatment of trust in the work of the British industrial sociologist Fox (1974). Fox distinguished long-term and short-term, specific and defuse trust, the reciprocal nature of trust (trust tends to evoke trust, distrust to evoke distrust), the distinction between vertical and lateral trust and the possible tensions between them (e.g. worker solidarity may be in opposition to management), and the different ideologies that may be associated with different forms of trust (e.g. high vertical and low lateral trust, and highly differentiated levels of individual reward, may be associated with an ideology of competitive individualism). Fox's ideas lead to a challenging of analyses that rely solely on individual level data. Schuller *et al.* (2000) also reminded readers of the classic work of Bott (1957) – on families and social networks, showing how husbands' and wives' family roles were related to the density of their local networks outside the family – as well as the flourishing field of social network analysis (Scott, 2000; Granovetter, 1973) which exists independently of work on social capital.

A further criticism is the frequent assumption, particularly in the simpler depictions of social capital, that it is, almost by definition, a good thing. It is mostly acknowledged now, however, that there can be a 'dark side' to social capital. High levels of social capital may serve to maintain the relative power or privilege of certain groups, or maintain exclusivity to the detriment of other groups (Grootaert, 2001; Schuller *et al.*, 2000; Ostrom & Ahn, 2003). Homogeneous communities can be comparatively intolerant of diversity and may, for example, successfully lobby against the provision of community mental health facilities, using their resources of both horizontal and vertical structural social capital (McKenzie *et al.*, 2002). It has been pointed out that warlords, terrorists, and the mafia rely for their support on social capital.

Onyx and Bullen (2001), who carried out a study of 1200 adults in five different communities in New South Wales, Australia, conceived of social capital as being both personal and social, potentially both a public and a private good. Two of their community samples were largely rural (and less well-off economically), two outer metropolitan, and one inner city. General factor social capital was highest in the two rural communities, and specifically higher in terms of trust, value of life, community connections, and neighbourhood connections. The urban communities, on the other hand, and particularly the inner city area, were higher in terms of social agency and tolerance of diversity, supporting the view that some communities, such as the rural communities in their study, have the capacity to generate social capital to meet the common good of a relatively homogeneous group, but not necessarily for the common good of other groups or the nation as a whole.

Muntaner *et al.* (2001) were also critical of the way in which discussions about social capital and health had tended to focus on its 'upside'. Examples of the possible downsides to social capital would include: strong friendship networks that increased the risk of smoking, drinking, or use of illicit drugs; non-elected, unaccountable international financial institutions such as the World Bank; anti-immigrant parties, for example in some European countries; and networks of the military, clergy, industrialists and bankers under Francoism in Spain.

Social Capital: A Useful Concept?

Is the rise of the idea of social capital to be seen, then, as a positive development? Ostrom and Ahn (2003) certainly thought so. They saw the literature on social capital as an attempt to integrate important social science concepts into what was otherwise a fundamentally economic approach to community development, even though there might be strains in applying the 'capital' metaphor to the social sphere. For example it was not so comfortable to think of friendship networks as being deliberately developed as assets accumulated for future use, or to accept the idea of being able to sell social capital assets.

Schuller *et al.* (2000) also concluded positively about the social capital idea, while recognising that as a field it was in its early stages, and that it could be abused both analytically and politically. They saw, in the writings of Coleman and Putnam and others, dangers of a nostalgic longing for an earlier, simpler society, a more modern danger of advocacy of a narrow, exclusive communitarianism (such as that espoused by Etzioni, 1997), and a neo-functionalism that assumes a commonality of interests and fails to address conflicts of interest. As we shall see shortly, a number of others have had similar concerns about social capital, as indeed do a number of social and political scientists writing about 'community' in general (e.g. Little, 2002; Delanty, 2003). Schuller *et al.*'s concluding list of the potential merits of the concept of social capital should help to endear it to community psychologists. One was the way it "... shifts the focus of analysis from the behaviour of individual agents to the pattern of relations between agents, social units and institutions" (p. 35). Another was the way it could act as "a link between micro, intermediate and macro-levels of analysis" (p. 35). They also merited its "... multidisciplinarity and inter-disciplinarity", and the way it "... reinserts issues of value into the heart of social scientific discourse" (p. 36). They thought the rise of social capital might partly be generated by widespread concern about the excesses of modern individualism, and thought we might be witnessing a "... revalorization of social relationships in political discourse, after a period of harsh dismissal of them in the face of globalized market relationships" (p. 13).

Muntaner *et al.* (2001) recognised that the concept of social capital implied that there was something inherently social about improving public health which could not be reduced to studying and changing individuals. The idea might therefore offer a new and exciting way of invigorating the public health field by providing for a non-individualised approach. At the same time they were critical that the term had been applied to all types and levels of connections between individuals, families, friendship networks, associations, businesses, and communities. They also criticised the "laundry list" (p. 217) approach to the measurement of social capital:

> There are multiple indicators of social, collective, economic, and cultural resources across the levels of families, neighbourhoods, and communities, but are they all markers of social capital?... We believe that social capital has been under-theorized in its public health usage and that it is time to engage in serious debate about its definition, measurement, and application in public health research and practice (pp. 215, 219).

They were also critical of the way in which social capital appeared to present a model of the social determinants of health that excludes analysis of structural inequalities by, for example, social class, gender or ethnic group. More generally they saw a danger of rejecting materialist explanations of health inequalities in favour of psychosocial constructs such as social capital or social cohesion. They saw a risk of placing responsibility for poor health on to communities themselves, and hence of appearing to blame them (an example of 'blaming the victim') in much the same way as the once popular 'culture of poverty' view appeared to blame poor communities for not being able to lift themselves out of poverty. For Moore *et al.* (2006) it was a case of needing to rehabilitate an idea of social capital that emphasised social networks and the access to resources that such ties afforded. They traced the way in which that notion had been subordinated in the social science literature to one that focused instead on trust and cohesion.

Looking at the larger picture, Muntaner *et al.* asked whether social capital might serve to support the communitarian view that favoured self-reliance and minimal government, emphasising civic organisations, hence helping to undermine the function of state governments in redistributing resources through universal public services and welfare provision. It would thereby support a US-style approach to welfare and public services as opposed to a European-style social democratic approach, would be consistent with 'third way' social policies in the USA and the EU, and, with its emphasis on civic life and reduced state intervention, would explain the attraction of the concept of social capital to the World Bank. Halpern

(2005) also noted the argument that social capital was a 'neo-liberal Trojan horse', complicit with mainstream economics, ignoring the role of inequality and the potential role for the state. Such matters were more difficult to raise in the USA, given the political climate there, but were vital parts of a European perspective. Those areas of neglect were reflected in Putnam's favoured explanations for the decline in social capital in the USA – electronic entertainment, particularly television, a growing intensity of US working life, and urban sprawl and suburbanisation and the long commuting times that came with it. The conclusions of the Saguaro Seminars that discussed practical ways of rebuilding social capital in the USA, emphasising such factors as citizenship education, volunteering, flexible work schedules, reducing urban sprawl, encouraging faith groups, new forms of technology, and participation in the arts, tended to reinforce that non-political picture.

Hawe and Shiell (2000) could see the undoubted attraction of the capital metaphor, unashamedly borrowed from economics, for those in a number of disciplines, such as psychology, facing more mainstream colleagues who were sceptical of our interest in social factors. But, for Hawe and Shiell, it remained the case that the science of social capital was weak relative to that of other constructs with a longer history of detailed work – social support, empowerment, and 'sense of community' were examples. As well as being too broad a concept to be helpful in detailed analysis of an understanding of how social life and health were linked, much of the research that had been done under the social capital heading, including the standard indicators (e.g. of trust and participation) that were being used by the World Bank and others, were focused on the relational aspects of the concept, neglecting the material and political aspects. There was therefore a danger that ways of promoting community health might be advanced that might do more harm than good by diluting or replacing more radical initiatives. Their view was that Bourdieu's concept of social capital was more useful than Putnam's because it dealt better with the complexity of communities, and was more attractive to health promotion practitioners who were aware of the realities of structural power and discourses that defined what was a problem and who was at risk. Putnam's view of social capital they described as, "...romantic, essentially middleclass..." (p. 879).

Among the harshest judgements on social capital was that of Muntaner *et al.* (2000). They were critical of the way the term 'social capital' had, "...slipped effortlessly into the public health lexicon as if there was a clear, shared understanding of its meaning and its relevance for improving public health" (p. 108), as an appealing, commonsense social psychology idea to which everyone could easily relate. It told us little more than that good community relationships were good for health. It seemed to have become a multi-purpose term covering all types and levels of social connections between people, seemingly embracing all that was good in a community. The social capital construct taken up by public health researchers had most often been the more psychological, communitarian one, conveniently fitting 'third way' policies favouring minimal government and self-reliance. It was necessary to get behind the proximal realm of social psychology to include an analysis of structural inequalities based for example on class, gender, or ethnicity. The complexities addressed, for example, by network analysis and sociological approaches that emphasised the roles of institutions and their links, were being ignored. This shallow approach to social capital might wane, they suggested, if third-way

Table 6.1 Social capital: types, components and levels

Type (direction)	Component	Level
Bonding (horizontal)	*Structural* (social networks); *Cognitive* (social control/efficacy; shared values; mutual trust and norms of reciprocity)	*Micro* (individual, family/household)
Bridging (horizontal: between different community and/or voluntary groups; and/or vertical: between such groups and statutory as well as non-statutory organisations with power to make decisions on the distribution and/or allocation of public goods and services) [see Szreter & Woolcock's, 2004, distinction between bridging and linking social capital, referred to earlier]	*Structural* (access to public goods and services, amenities); *Cognitive* (participation; sense of belonging; decision-making capacity)	*Macro* (statutory and/or voluntary organisations – local, national, international)

Source: reproduced with permission from Almedom, A.M. (2005). Social capital and mental health: an interdisciplinary review of primary evidence. *Social Science and Medicine*, **61**, 943–64.

policies begin to lose support in Europe, but might survive longer in the USA with its strong inter-dependence with the World Bank and the relative absence of working class influence on policy in that country.

Qualitative Studies of Social Capital

Almedom (2005) was critical of the simplistic nature of much social capital research. The different types, components and levels of social capital (see Table 6.1), particularly when combined with complexities of gender, class, and ethnicity which were often neglected, meant that participatory and qualitative research evidence was necessary. Those forms of research had not featured prominently in work on social capital. Almedom cited rotating credit and saving associations as an example of local, informal institutions that existed throughout the world, providing support – of emotional, cognitive, and material kinds – directly to women, and hence to their families, in ways that formal institutions could not. Site-specific ethnographic work, with an analysis that focused on gender, was necessary in order to understand how they worked and their effects. Measures of social capital isolated from an understanding of the historical, economic, and political contexts could only be very partial.

Studies of social capital have largely been epidemiological in kind. They have usually involved large numbers and often sophisticated, multi-level statistical techniques. They suggest that social capital may be vitally important for health and well-being (e.g. Lochner *et al.*, 2003; Lindström, 2004; Skrabski *et al.*, 2003; Kim *et al.*, 2005; Poortinga, 2006a,b). But because they are usually partly or wholly dependent on census data or official records, and because measures of place are often simply aggregates of official data about individuals or households, they are often frustrating from a psychological viewpoint. Theories about the ways in which place might affect health and well-being abound, but such studies are rarely able to get to grips with the detail of how people's lives are affected by neighbourhood. It has often been suggested that more fully understanding the origins and influence of social capital will require carrying out and integrating both neighbourhood-level quantitative study and the use of qualitative methods (McCulloch, 2003; Baum & Ziersch, 2003). In contrast to the majority of studies of social capital, studies by Campbell and Gillies (2001), Altschuler *et al.* (2004) and Cattell (2001) are examples of research that has used qualitative methods, focusing in on a small number of communities.

Campbell and Gillies argued for their 'micro-qualitative' approach on the grounds that the large-scale statistical survey type of research was able to make little reference to, "... the daily realities of life in the local communities and neighbourhoods that researchers and politicians speak of" (p. 331). They carried out lengthy individual interviews, averaging three hours each, with 19 men and 18 women living in one or other of two wards in a single town in south-east England. A number of contrasts were revealed. A dominant one was a contrast between perceptions of how things now were – a low level of neighbourliness and 'sense of community' – compared to how things could be ideally and how it was often thought that they had once been. In the two wards, both of which were in the more deprived half of the wards that made up the town, there was perceived to have been a decline in trust, neighbourliness, and reciprocal help and support. For example:

> You don't have neighbours any more in the sense that we used to understand it. No one will pop around and say: 'I have just nipped in for a cup of tea and see how you are'. There's no neighbourhood. Nowadays you see people walk by, you know if you say 'Hello' to them they look at you as if 'What does he want?' (Ward 1, man, aged 50, pp. 334–5).

> These days I would only smile at someone in the street if I knew them, smiling at a stranger might earn you a mouthful of abuse (Ward 2, woman, aged 35, p. 335).

Participants gave examples such as the unwillingness of adults to look out for other people's children or teenagers, through fear of abuse or retaliation by the children themselves or fear that parents would see them as interfering. Offers to help neighbours in small ways, for example with loans of money, borrowing clothing, or looking after a neighbour's children during a family crisis, were no longer made. There was thought to have been a decline in common social identity, with community members now having far less in common with their neighbours; consensus about appropriate behaviour for young people was thought to have broken down; and it was recognised that many people were no longer so dependent on their immediate communities as they had once been.

Campbell and Gillies also reported a contrast by housing type. Those living in tower blocks spoke in particularly stark terms about the obstacles to a feeling of community. Social stigma, lack of communal spaces, and the anonymity and rapid turnover of inhabitants were among the factors that contributed. The following are two quotations from men living in tower blocks:

> Help my neighbours? I can't see any basis that would arise for helping each other. That's just accepted here, everyone keeps himself to himself. I don't think people should get involved. If I hear people screaming, I certainly don't run and find out what is going on…People here don't speak. I have not been in anyone's flat (Ward 2, man, aged 30, p. 338).

> I worry about my child growing up in these flats. Here we are very isolated. There's no communal areas here, no place or reason to interact with anyone. You can't have community in a tower block (Ward 2, man, aged 42, p. 338).

There was also a contrast between Ward 1, the more deprived of the two wards, and Ward 2. Campbell and Gillies found little evidence for a culture of voluntary participation in community activities in either ward. People referred to fear of going out at night, the changed nature of pubs, in one case the closure of a factory social club ("…a terrible crime…it broke all our hearts up here", according to one man in Ward 2), and even an attitude of suspicion towards people who devoted time and energy to community affairs. The attitude towards politicians was mainly a cynical one, and the position taken towards local government was largely a passive one (typical was a woman in Ward 2 who said, "I don't have a lot to do with the council. They take our tax, and come and collect the bins on a Friday, it's not something I think about much") and one of frustration when things went wrong and complaints appeared not to be heard. Where the two wards differed was in mentions of successful attempts at mobilisation or lobbying. Unlike Ward 1 informants, those from Ward 2 made a number of references to their local Tenants and Residents' Association and to several examples of successful small-scale community activism. Examples were a campaign against a local factory causing a public nuisance through noise and smell, and a campaign to stop large lorries using a residential street. Campbell and Gillies referred to this as a striking difference in 'perceived citizen power'.

Altschuler et al. (2004) carried out their research in nine neighbourhoods in Oakland, California, in the USA, involving 38 women and 11 men in all. Some were neighbourhood leaders interviewed individually, but most took part in focus group discussions that lasted on average for two and a half hours. The nine neighbourhoods they studied provided an even greater contrast, ranging from low-income, predominantly African USAmerican neighbourhoods with little green space and close proximity to busy roads, to middle or high-income, predominantly white areas situated amidst hills and trees with more of a suburban feel. The contrasts in the way people spoke about their local communities were very evident. For example, in the lower income neighbourhoods, with higher crime rates, physical safety was an ongoing problem, whereas in the higher income neighbourhoods residents were shocked by evidence of crimes that were taken for granted in the poorer communities. Appreciation of open, green spaces was general, but reactions to proposed community developments could be different and surprising. For example, the researchers were told of reactions to the proposal to restore a currently covered-over creek. Whereas this was supported in a higher income neighbourhood on the grounds that it would signify peace and respite, residents in the lower income neighbourhood were opposed on the grounds that it would invite crime and deviant behaviour. While higher income neighbourhoods often lacked shops of any kind since residents could use their cars to shop outside their immediate neighbourhoods, having a supermarket that sold fresh and lower priced food in the immediate vicinity was important to those in lower income neighbourhoods. Pollution was another issue that was more salient to those in the lower income areas. They were concerned, for example, about high lead concentrations in soil, asbestos associated with major building projects, poor water quality, noise pollution from police helicopters, residential street speeding, and pollution from vehicles on freeways and from a medical waste incinerator. Those in higher income neighbourhoods did not see pollution affecting their own areas but were concerned about pollution as a regional issue.

It was widely recognised, not only in the lower income neighbourhoods, that those neighbourhoods received attention and action from municipal agencies much more slowly than did the higher income neighbourhoods. Whereas stress in the better-off communities was described in terms of feeling worry about long-term financial insecurity and constant pressure between demands of work, commuting and childcare, in the less well-off communities chronic stress was related to fear for safety as well as to financial insecurity that was experienced on a daily basis. When it came to mobilising for community action, those in middle and higher income neighbourhoods tended to mobilise in response to discrete threats. For instance, the proposed opening of a Starbucks in the neighbourhood was successfully challenged; a local Crimewatch programme was reinvigorated in response to the rare event of a neighbourhood homicide; and the proposed installation of street lights, thought by city officials to be likely to improve safety, was defeated by local residents who thought they would diminish the natural, forest-like feeling of their neighbourhood. In lower income neighbourhoods, by contrast, residents were organising in response to chronic, ongoing problems such as the presence of drug dealers, excessive numbers of alcohol outlets, speeding, graffiti, vandalism, and crude and disrespectful behaviour. As one activist in a lower income neighbourhood put it: "... what we are dealing with is totally different and life threatening, every single day is life threatening" (p. 1227).

Altschuler et al. were positive about the use of the concept of social capital to make sense of their results, believing it to be at least one among many such concepts that could help to explain health disparities between neighbourhoods. Participants in their research spoke of the importance of trust and feelings of belonging when defining their neighbourhoods, and Altshuler et al. saw that as an example of bonding social capital. The different experiences of municipal services in the different neighbourhoods, they saw as illustrating the importance of bridging social capital.

Campbell and Gillies were more critical of social capital, particularly of Putnam's (1995) concept that stressed voluntary association membership and community activist groups. Neither were prominent in their findings from the English town, besides which informal family and friendship networks appeared to be much more important. They suggested that Putnam's notion of a cohesive local community, "...might be unduly essentialist, and fail[s] to take adequate account of the complex, fragmented and rapidly changing face of contemporary community life – characterised by relatively high levels of mobility, instability and plurality" (p. 344). Like others they argued that gender, age, socioeconomic, and ethnic differences in social capital were given insufficient attention in Putnam's work. In general they expressed sympathy with the criticism of social capital that it has too narrow an emphasis on community-level determinants of health and gives too little attention to the ill-effects of non-local factors such as material inequalities in an era of reduced welfare spending (citing Muntaner *et al.*, 2001). Campbell and Gillies were also critical of the assumption with which they began their own study, that social capital is best examined at the level of a geographical area such as an electoral ward. Not only did many of their participants use a definition of community based on a smaller area such as a single street or the area that was in easy walking distance from home, but it also appeared to be the case that people's stocks of social capital resided in a range of networks and associations that were non-local as well as local. Altschuler *et al.* also found their participants defining their neighbourhoods in two ways: immediate neighbourhoods, often composed of a single block or less; and a much larger area corresponding to larger communal, historical, commercial, or municipal boundaries.

Cattell (2001) reported the results of interviewing around 50 people – about 35 local residents and 15 people whose work took them into the neighbourhood – in each of two neighbourhoods in east London, England. One remained a traditional working class area with a strong sense of place and shared history, despite the loss of semi-skilled and unskilled work opportunities with the decline of docking that had required a large local labour force. The second neighbourhood, similar in terms of poverty, deprivation and unemployment, had a lot of badly designed and poorly maintained housing and suffered from a negative reputation. It was, however, the focus of a great deal of community development work and voluntary sector activity, and was undergoing redevelopment as a Housing Action Trust at the time of the research. Although on neither estate did the majority of people join activities and organisations, Cattell noted a distinct difference in the way people talked about their area, and their sense of pride in it. On the first estate, for example – "If I'm feeling fed up I take myself down to the market, where I see lots of people. You hear some good gossip, you keep in touch with what's going on", "The people here are brilliant. You can have a laugh and a joke with them, they are good to you...". On the second estate, by contrast, there were many examples of the following kind – "There is no community spirit at all... There's a lot of mistrust, you worry who you talk to. You have to be careful the way you look at some of the neighbours", "My mum won't come and visit me here, it's the dark lifts, the horrible corridors, it's so intimidating". At the same time, she noted the plentiful opportunities that existed in the second area for involvement in projects of various kinds, such as self-help groups, tenants' groups, courses, and toy libraries. Residents of these two areas described personal social networks of very different kinds: Cattell's typology is shown in Figure 6.5. Not all

THE SOCIALLY EXCLUDED OR TRUNCATED NETWORK is limited to a small number of membership groups, and a small number of people within those groups. Residents with these networks include newcomers, unemployed people, women with controlling partners, and some isolated elderly people.

THE HOMOGENEOUS NETWORK consists of a relatively small number of membership groups, but there may be extensive contacts within those groups. It is made up predominantly of a local extended family, plus a smaller number of local friends and neighbours. The networks are dense; its members know each other. Examples include single parents.

THE TRADITIONAL NETWORK is made up of family, neighbours, ex-workmates, old school friends, and friends from social clubs and sports clubs. The structure is tight knit. Individuals have spent most of their lives in the immediate area. Examples are predominantly elderly people, and a smaller number of younger people who worked locally, and had attended social clubs.

THE HETEROGENEOUS NETWORK is an open network consisting of a relatively large number of membership groups. It includes dissimilar people in terms of age, ethnicity, interests, employment status or occupation, and place of residence. Generally the networks are loose knit, but in some cases – such as a person involved in interconnected voluntary organisations – are not. Friends and family are less likely to know each other than in the other models. Principal examples are people active in voluntary organisations. Some are different in some way from their neighbours, such as not born locally.

THE NETWORK OF SOLIDARITY consists of a wide range of membership groups, made up of both similar and dissimilar people. Network structure is both dense and loose. Networks share many of the characteristics of both the Traditional and the Heterogeneous models; that is, strong local contacts of family and or local friends and neighbours on the one hand, plus participation in formal and informal organisations on the other. Residents have a wide range of positive reference groups.

Figure 6.5 A typology of social network in two neighbourhoods in east London
Source: adapted with permission from Cattell, V. (2001). Poor people, poor places, and poor health: the mediating role of social networks and social capital. *Social Science and Medicine*, **52**, 1501–16

residents fitted one of those patterns. The exceptions included some with a 'relocating' network – for example dissociating oneself from a neighbourhood that a resident felt no part of and did not enjoy, in some such cases successfully building relationships outside.

Cattell was impressed by the apparently complex way in which material and social factors interacted to influence the ways people were able to cope with such things as conflicts in the family or a house break-in, and how in combination they might influence feelings and attitudes – hope, fatalism, pessimism, self-esteem, feelings of control – that were closely related to health. Those with traditional social networks had longstanding sources of support that helped to buffer stress. Those with homogeneous networks – confined to the first area – were dependent on the quality of relationships within networks that were more restricted and exclusionary than was the case for those with the wider, solidarity, types of network. The negative, combined influence of poverty and lack of social ties was most clearly evident in the cases of the socially excluded. For example, one woman who had recently split up from her partner, said:

> The system is in control of my life. I wait for Tuesdays, then shop, then put so much by for rent, electricity etc. Any little mistake you make, and you don't eat...I go without to make sure they [her children] are OK...When I split up, I didn't eat properly, my hair started falling out and I lost weight with the worry...My daughter is a fussy eater. Maybe it's because she's unhappy, wondering what's going on, or maybe because I'm not eating (p. 1508).

An unemployed man who took an interest in politics but was not himself participating in local activities, said:

> I don't have the power to straighten out my own life so how can I do other things [like joining the Tenants group]. I feel helpless...I want to lead a normal life, and look after my family. But it's not under my control, when you can't do it the depression and the illness creeps in. I feel tired, very lethargic, dizzy, and I have pains. I hate living on benefits, I try to sign on at a time when no-one will see me...I can positively say, if I'd had someone to lean on, someone to talk to, to console me, [my bad health] would not have gone this far...basically, I was totally alone...(pp. 1508–9).

Those who were active locally, with heterogeneous networks, mostly described how becoming involved had changed their lives for the better, increasing their friendship networks, their enjoyment of life, sense of achievement, confidence and feelings of being in control. A minority of those in the solidarity group believed that they sometimes did too much for others, felt overloaded and out of control, and that their health had been negatively affected.

Cattell's overall conclusion was that issues of poverty and class, often neglected in discussions of social capital and social cohesion, were of vital importance, and that factors such as an area's history, work opportunities, local resources, opportunities for participation, reputation, and housing allocation policies, were all important. Regenerated local work opportunities were particularly important. Different network structures were involved in creating social capital and had implications for health, but the concept of social capital was not sufficient for explaining the harmful effects of poverty on health and well-being.

A Tentative Conclusion about Social Capital

The present author's tentative conclusion about social capital is generally a favourable one. Despite the dangers (and there clearly are a number) it could offer

Table 6.2   Social capital – some pros and cons

For	Against
• Interdisciplinary	• Just old wine in a new bottle
• Anti-individualistic; revalues the social	• Too all-embracing
• Focus on relations between social groups and institutions	• Unclear measurement
• Cross-levels (micro to macro)	• Often in practice assessed at an individual level
• Reinserts values into social science discourse	• Danger of nostalgia and communitarianism
	• Use of the 'capital' metaphor

community psychology much. A summary of the pros and cons for social capital, discussed earlier, is shown in Table 6.2. Perhaps its greatest advantage for us is the attention it calls to the capacity of the social group – whether a group of common identity or interest, a group of place or neighbourhood, or a collective of any kind – to be empowered and to empower its members, both through its own cohesion and via its links with other groups. Although the concept is open to a number of misuses, in the ways that were described earlier, it is very unlikely to suffer the same fate as concepts such as control beliefs and social support (or even empowerment), which in practice have so often been treated as characteristics of individual people (see Chapter 1).

We turn now to an idea whose history is very different but which covers some of the same ground as social capital. It was taken up by community psychologists in the 1970s and 1980s and became one of the leading ideas in the field, much worked over since then. In fact it could be counted as one of the already existing areas of study that the exponents of social capital have neglected.

SENSE OF COMMUNITY

Definitions and Dimensions

One of the leading concerns in community psychology has been to capture the feelings that people have about the communities of which they are part. Following Sarason (1974), it is this area of work that has come to be associated with the term 'sense of community' (SOC). The concept of SOC is necessarily a multi-dimensional one, covering various facets of people's opinions about their communities. There are a number of further complexities to the question, not the least of them being the problem of how people define their communities in the first place. For example, in England research has suggested that people often refer to their immediate localities when asked to say where they live and where they feel they belong, while at the same time they think in terms of a series of overlapping maps of different sizes, each significant in different ways (Hedges & Kelly, 1992; Puddifoot, 1995). Furthermore, there is a need to come to terms with the fact that while many people may define their communities in territorial or locality terms, others do so in terms of common identity with a social, religious, or ethnic group (see Dudgeon *et al.*, 2002, for a consideration of the complications of applying the concept of 'community' to indigenous people in Australia).

Having those issues in mind, Puddifoot (1995) proposed the multi-dimensional model of community identity shown in Table 6.3. It consists of six elements (shown as A to F in the table) subsuming 14 dimensions. It begins with a resident's definition of his or her community in terms of its locus and what makes it distinctive (A and B), proceeding to the degree of identification with the community (C), orientation towards the community on a number of more specific dimensions (D), evaluation of community life in terms of a number of dimensions customarily ascribed to healthy communities (E), and finally evaluation of community services and opportunities – mostly provided for the community by other bodies (F). Note that Puddifoot also tried to deal with the criticism that SOC was too individualistic a concept, by suggesting that a complete account of a person's sense of identity with their community should include perceptions of how other residents see things.

SOC as others have defined and/or measured it, overlaps substantially with Puddifoot's model of community identity. For example, McMillan and Chavis (1986, p. 9) defined SOC as, "...a feeling that members have of belonging, a feeling that members matter to one another and to the group, and a shared faith that members' needs will be met through their commitment to be together". They included the four elements shown in Figure 6.6.

There have been a number of standard measures of SOC and closely related concepts – some of which are summarised in Table 6.4. The 12-item Sense of Community Index (SCI, Perkins *et al.*, 1990), based on McMillan and Chavis's (1986) concept, has been the most widely used measure of SOC, but the supposed four-dimensional structure to the SCI has met with very mixed support. In their reanalysis of data from an earlier US study carried out in the mid-1980s (the Block Booster Project), Long and Perkins (2003) tried to confirm that structure using confirmatory factor analysis, finding that neither a four-factor nor a one-factor solution fitted the data well. They proposed the briefer eight-item SCI referred to in Table 6.4.

Chipuer and Pretty (1999) looked at the internal reliability and factor structure of the SCI, using data collected by them in their studies of adolescents and adults responding to the SCI in terms of their neighbourhoods, and adults referring to their workplace 'communities'. Internal reliabilities of the four presumed sub-scales (corresponding to needs, membership, influence, and emotional connection) were generally low. Furthermore, factor structures based on adult and adolescent data were different in a number of respects, just one of which was that the three supposed influence items loaded on three different factors in the adolescent data – perhaps reflecting the lack of salience of influence for adolescents (but see Chipuer *et al.* on this point below). Chipuer and Pretty concluded that the SCI might be a useful starting point for study of the psychology of community, but that it was safest to treat it as a single scale. They recommended more research into the psychology of community, using a variety of research methods including participant observation and qualitative methods, as well as the development of a more robust measure of SOC.

Obst and her colleagues, who have used the SCI in studies in Australia, are among those who have preferred not to reject the original multidimensional

Table 6.3   Elements and dimensions of community identity

	Territorial	Social/cultural relations
A *Locus*	1 Residents' own perception of boundaries, and key topographical/built features of their community.	2 Residents' own perceptions of key social/cultural characteristics of their community.
B *Distinctiveness*	3 Residents' own perceptions of the degree of physical distinctiveness of their community.	4 Residents' own perception of the degree of distinctiveness of key social/cultural characteristics of their community
	5 Residents' own perceptions of the special character of the community.	
C *Identification*	6 Residents' perceptions of their own affiliation/belonging/emotional connectedness to location.	7 Residents' perceptions of their own affiliation/belonging/emotional connectedness to social/cultural groupings/forms
	8 Residents' perceptions of others' affiliation/belonging/emotional connectedness to location	9 Residents' perceptions of others' affiliation/belonging/emotional connectedness to social/cultural groupings/forms
D *Orientation*	10 Residents' own reasons for identification (or not) with the community. 11 Residents' own orientation to their community. Personal investment Attraction to community Future in community Emotional safety Personal involvement Alienation	
E *Evaluation of quality of community life*	13 Residents' perception of others' evaluation of quality of community life. Community spirit Friendliness Sense of mutuality Cooperativeness Extent of social interaction Commitment to community Extent of neighbouring	
12 Residents' own evaluation of quality of community life. Community spirit Friendliness Sense of mutuality Cooperativeness Extent of social interaction Commitment to community Extent of neighbouring		
		F *Evaluation of community functioning* 14 Residents' own evaluation of community functioning. Community services Leisure services Health services Commercial services Opportunities Material quality of life Quality of environment Quality of community decision-making Ability to influence decisions

Source: reproduced with permission from Puddifoot, J. (1995). Dimensions of community identity. *Journal of Community and Applied Social Psychology,* **5**, 1–14

Membership

> Including a sense of belonging and identification, the feeling that one has invested part of oneself to becoming a member, and the partaking of a common symbol system including name, landmark, logo or architectural style.

Influence

> McMillan and Chavis largely discussed this in terms of the influence of members upon one another, implying a tendency towards conformity. Others who have included influence within their definitions of SOC have put as much emphasis on the influence that members can bring to bear on others to get things done that enhance their communities or solve problems.

Integration and Fulfilment of Needs

> A feeling that members' needs would be met by resources received through membership in the group.

Shared Emotional Connection

> The belief that members have shared, and are committed to continue to share, history, common places, time together and similar experiences.

Figure 6.6   The four elements of McMillan and Chavis's concept of sense of community (SOC)

Source: McMillan, D.W. & Chavis, D.M. (1986). Sense of community; a definition and theory. *Journal of Community Psychology*, **14**, 6–23

conceptualisation of SOC, believing that the four supposed underlying dimensions have theoretical validity and have received support, particularly from qualitative studies. The study by Obst *et al.* (2002), of several hundred residents of towns and cities in south-east Queensland, Australia, was particularly helpful because participants were asked to respond, not only to the SCI items, but also to items from several alternative scales including the Multidimensional Measure of Neighboring (MMN; Skjæveland *et al.*, 1996), and scales assessing identification with the local neighbourhood, making a total of nearly 100 items. Their exploratory factor analysis suggested five factors – the highest loading items are shown in Figure 6.7. It is noticeable, however, that those factors were not identical to the ones identified by McMillan and Chavis (1986) and the SCI items did not perform particularly well. With the exception of the Belonging factor, where three SCI items were among the six loading mostly highly, and one high loading SCI item on the Support factor, SCI items loaded modestly compared to items from other scales.

Italian Studies of Sense of Community

An illustration of a study using SOC as a central idea comes from Italy where the concept has been popular with community psychologists. Prezza and Constantini

Table 6.4 Some standard measures of sense of community (SOC) and related concepts

Reference	SOC measures and related concepts
Bachrach & Zautra, 1985	A seven-item measure of *SOC*, covering: feeling at home in the community, satisfaction with the community, agreement with the values and beliefs of the community, feeling of belonging in the community, interest in what goes on in the community, feeling an important part of the community, and attachment to the community
Long & Perkins (2003)	A brief eight-item *SOC Index*, consisting of three factors: social connections (e.g. 'I can recognize most of the people who live on my block'); mutual concerns (e.g. 'My neighbours and I want the same things from the block'); and community values (e.g. 'Would you say that it is very important, somewhat important or not important to you to feel a sense of community with the people in your block?')
Skjæveland et al., 1996	A measure of *Neighbouring*, covering four dimensions: neighbourhood attachment (e.g. 'I feel strongly attached to this residence'; 'I don't feel at home in this neighbourhood'); supportive acts of neighbouring (e.g. 'If I need a little company, I can stop by a neighbour I know'; 'If I have a personal crisis, I have a neighbour I can talk to); weak social ties (e.g. 'How many of your closest neighbours do you typically stop and chat with when you run into them?'; 'How many of your neighbours who live near you do you say hello to when you meet them?'); neighbour annoyance (e.g. 'Noise which my neighbours make could occasionally be a big problem'; 'In this house I never feel quite safe')
Young et al., 2004	A seven-item scale of *Sense of Neighbourhood* e.g. 'I have a lot in common with people in my neighbourhood'; 'I am good friends with many people in this neighbourhood'; 'I generally trust my neighbours to look out for my property'
Martinez et al., 2002	A *Perceived Neighbourhood Scale*, covering four factors: social embeddedness (e.g. 'How likely is it that you could ask a neighbour to loan you a few dollars or some food?', 'How often do you greet your neighbours when you see them?'); sense of community (e.g. 'There are people I can rely on among my neighbours', 'People trust each other in my neighbourhood'); satisfaction with neighbourhood (e.g. 'My neighbourhood is a good place to live', 'I have good access to public transportation in my neighbourhood'); perceived crime (e.g. 'There are troublemakers hanging around in my neighbourhood', 'Some friends and relatives don't visit me at home because they don't feel safe')
Bass & Lambert, 2004	A 10-item *Neighbourhood Environment Scale* e.g. 'There are plenty of safe places to walk or spend time outdoors in my neighbourhood', 'Every few weeks, some kid in my neighbourhood gets beat-up or mugged', 'I have seen people using or selling drugs in my neighbourhood'
Sampson et al., 1997	A measure of *Collective Efficacy*, consisting of two sub-scales: informal social control (questions asking how likely it was that neighbours could be counted on to intervene in a number of circumstances, such as children skipping school and hanging about on a street corner, children showing disrespect to an adult, or the fire station closest to home being threatened with budget cuts), and social cohesion and trust (e.g. 'People around here are willing to help their neighbours', 'This is a close-knit neighbourhood')

Factor 1: Ties and Friendship

'I feel a strong sense of ties with the other people who live in my local neighborhood'

'If I need a little company, I can contact a neighbor I know'

Factor 2: Influence

'The council does very little for my local neighborhood (negative)'

'The local council cares about what happens in our neighborhood'

Factor 3: Support

'If there was a serious problem in my local neighborhood, people who live in it could get together and solve it'

'I have no friends in my local neighborhood on whom I can depend (negative)'

Factor 4: Belonging

'I plan to remain a resident of my local neighborhood for a number of years'

'I think my local neighborhood is a good place for me to live'

Factor 5: Conscious Identification

'I am not usually conscious of the fact that I am a resident of my local neighborhood'

'In general being a resident of my neighborhood is an important part of my self-image'

Figure 6.7 The five sense of community factors identified by Obst *et al.*: highest loading items

Source: Obst, P., Zinkiewicz, L. & Smith, S.G. (2002). An exploration of sense of community, part 3: dimensions and predictors of psychological sense of community in geographical communites. *Journal of Community Psychology*, **30**, 119–33

(1998) argued that the importance of SOC rested on two assumptions. The first – that higher SOC was associated with greater participation in the joint solving of community problems – they believed had been supported by the research they reviewed. The second – that SOC contributes to subjective quality of life, individual well-being, and greater self-confidence – had less often been investigated. They set out to study that second assumption in three contrasting communities in south-central Italy. One was a small hill town with a medieval centre and fewer than 2000 inhabitants; the second a small city of just over 20,000 inhabitants; the third a predominantly residential and commercial neighbourhood of just over 50,000 inhabitants in the city of Naples. Participants were aged between 20 and 60 years and, as is common in Italy, had mostly been permanently resident in the community for a long time (for an average 31, 32, and 24 years respectively, although those living in the community for less than five years had been excluded). They used the 18-item Italian Sense of Community Scale (a modification of Davidson & Cotter's, 1986, scale). In all three communities SOC was significantly correlated with a scale of efficiency of community services. The latter included questions about social and health services, the school system, social, cultural or recreational services, road management, and green areas.

More specifically, the results were very different for the small town compared to the other communities. For one thing SOC was significantly higher in the small town, services were judged more efficient, and life satisfaction and perceived social support were greater (there were no differences in terms of self-esteem). Only in the small town was SOC significantly correlated with social support or self-esteem. Only in the small town was SOC significantly higher for those with children, and only in the small town was SOC associated with participation in meetings and groups. In the two larger communities, on the other hand, SOC was related to working within the community rather than outside it, and in the big city only was SOC associated with educational level – those with lower levels of education having the higher SOC. Women had a higher SOC than men, only in the big city.

That SOC can be simultaneously positive and negative was shown by Arcidiacono and Procentese's (2005) study of the historic city centre area of Naples. As part of a larger action research project, 15 people were interviewed and the results analysed qualitatively. The group of interviewees was a mixed group of people, including those with some power in the area such as local representatives, and others such as shopkeepers and students; both men and women and long-term and recent residents of the area were included. On the positive side, respondents were proud to be associated with an area rich in history, recently upgraded and now a major attraction for tourists, and to be able to identify with the positive aspects of being Neapolitan, such as genuineness, vitality, and a readiness to welcome and host others. It was seen as a place of opportunity. On the negative side, there was reference to pollution, 'micro-delinquency', lack of accommodation, litter, traffic, unemployment, lack of confidence in authorities, and a feeling of having little power to influence the future of the area.

Young People's Sense of Community

There is a real danger in research on the psychology of neighbourhood or community that adolescents' and younger adults' views are neglected (Pretty, 2002). Chipuer et al. (1999) developed a 22-item Neighbourhood Youth Inventory (NYI) on the basis of semi-structured interviews with nearly 100 adolescents from schools in eastern Canada. They later used the NYI with nearly 1000 adolescents in three school grades (grades 7, 9 and 11, overall average age 13.5 years) in urban and rural localities around a major city in eastern Australia. Factor analysis suggested four factors. Three of the factors – support, activity, and friendships – correlated as expected with other measures of sense of community (the SCI; Perkins et al., 1990) and neighbourhood cohesion index (the NCI; Buckner, 1988), but the fourth, safety, appeared to stand out as a separate dimension from the others. Adolescents living in rural areas reported significantly higher support and safety but lower activity. Those in higher grades reported less support, activity, and friendships. Those who had lived at their current addresses for 10 or more years (the average was 6.4 years) reported more support. Those who knew more neighbours by name (on average 29 could be named) reported more support, activity and friendships, but lower levels of safety. Those who indicated that there were more resources in their neighbourhoods (from a list of 20 potential places and facilities for services and social interactions) reported more activity and friendships but less safety.

Zani et al. (2001) specifically focused on feelings of lack of safety among a similar sized sample of 14–19 year olds living in north-central Italy. About a third lived in one or other of two small cities of between 30,000 and 50,000 inhabitants, the remainder living in small towns in the surrounding area, each town consisting of between 2000 and 10,000 inhabitants. They developed a 30-item scale of feelings of unsafety, covering three aspects: cognitive, emotional, and behavioural – the perceived seriousness of a number of problems in their areas, how worried they were about the possibility of being involved in a number of negative events, and how frequently they used each of a number of behaviours to face feelings of unsafety. The items were partly based on preliminary focus group discussions with adolescents. Results showed that cognitive and emotional forms of unsafety were higher among those living in the small cities as opposed to the smaller towns, and all forms of unsafety were reported at a higher level by female adolescents, the difference between female and male being greater for those who lived in the cities. The relationship between Sense of Community (the SCS, Italian version; Prezza et al., 1999) and city versus town was mixed, with the small towns being favoured in terms of the pleasantness of the living area and social climate, but the small cities were favoured in terms of opportunities for participation and fulfilment of needs. Also included was a measure of negative experiences: adolescents were asked how frequently they experienced each of five events (being alone in a dangerous place; realising that a stranger is staring at you; people's indifference; being annoyed by a stranger; being provoked by older adolescents). It was that scale that provided the strongest associations with cognitive and emotional feelings of unsafety in the regression analysis, besides which the SOC measure was relatively unimportant.

Chipuer et al. (1999) reflected on the notions of neighbourhood and community that had emerged from their initial conversations about adolescents which had led to the development of the NYI. They drew attention to two points. The first was the emphasis adolescents had placed upon safety, a factor that is not identified in the adult SCI. They suggested that many young people might feel more vulnerable in their neighbourhoods than most adults. By contrast, the factor of influence, emphasised in the original McMillan and Chavis (1986) model of SOC, appeared not be salient for the adolescents Chipuer et al. had spoken to. They pointed out that the latter were below voting age, but they thought there might be a more fundamental explanation in terms of lack of young people's expectations of influence in their communities. Pretty (2002) opened up further discussion of adolescents' SOC, pointing out, among other things, the need to be clear about distinctions between community identity, attachment to community, and sense of community. Only the latter referred to something collective, involving a sense of 'we'. Identity and attachment were more individual.

Zeldin and Topitzes (2002) were concerned about the possibility that there had been societal trends towards the separation of adolescents from opportunities to participate in local affairs, with reduced opportunities for developing civic competence, and correspondingly reduced expectations on the part of adults and

---

Adolescents as pro-social community members (questions asked of both adolescents and adults)

      Teenagers in this neighborhood are friendly towards their neighbors

      Teenagers in this neighborhood are interested in helping to improve the neighborhood

Confidence in adolescents as community contributors (asked of adults only)

      How confident are you about teenagers:

      ability to speak to groups about the dangers of drugs?

      representing the community in front of the city council?

      organising a volunteer recruitment drive?

      mentoring other adolescents?

      managing a fundraising event?

      serving as a voting member of a neighborhood association/

Figure 6.8   Questions about young people's participation
Source: Zeldin, S. & Topitzes, D. (2002). Neighborhood experiences, community connection, and positive beliefs about adololescents among urban adults and youth. *Journal of Community Psychology*, **30**, 647–69

adolescents themselves about the participation and general behaviour of youth. This had been an under-researched topic and they set out to correct that by carrying out a telephone survey of just over 300 adults in four neighbourhoods in Washington DC, USA, and a similar number of adolescents from across the city. Some of the questions asked are shown in Figure 6.8. Contrary to stereotypes, average beliefs about adolescents were quite positive. For example, 44% of adults and 42% of adolescents agreed that adolescents were interested in helping to improve the neighbourhood, and just over 50% of adults had some or a great deal of confidence (31% a great deal) that adolescents were able to speak to groups about the dangers of drugs and 48% had at least some confidence (25% a great deal) in the ability of adolescents to represent the community in front of the city council. For both adults and adolescents, the perception of adolescents as prosocial community members was significantly correlated with a rating of neighbourhood safety and in the case of the adult sample (adolescents were not asked these questions) with a measure of neighbourhood resources based on ratings of how good parks, public schools, community centres, and recreation facilities were thought to be. They also found support for the further hypothesis that the relationship between perceptions of the neighbourhood (as safe or well resourced) and positive perceptions of adolescents (as prosocial or as community contributors) was mediated by SOC (six items chosen from the SCI).

Related Ideas: Neighbouring and Collective Efficacy

A concept that overlaps with SOC is that of neighbouring or neighbourhood cohesion and there have been a number of measures such as the Neighbourhood

Cohesion Instrument (Buckner, 1988) – an 18-item unidimensional scale tapping neighbourhood psychological sense of community, attraction to neighbourhood, and neighbouring. Another is the multidimensional measure of neighbouring developed by Skjæveland et al. (1996). The latter was based on the responses of over 1500 residents living in different types of public and private housing in Bergen, Norway. Factor analysis suggested the four underlying dimensions summarised in Table 6.4. One, labelled *neighbourhood attachment*, is central also to the concept of sense of community and two of the others – *supportive acts of neighbouring* and *weak social ties* – were thought by Skjæveland et al. to be better recognised in the idea of neighbouring than in SOC because they were about actual community contacts rather than a subjective sense of being part of a positive community. The one factor in Skjæveland et al.'s measure that is generally completely absent from SOC measures was the dimension they termed *neighbour annoyance*. They argued that a definition of neighbouring should include negative as well as positive aspects, and that difficulties with close neighbours could constitute a form of chronic stress and could 'spoil' the experience of neighbouring. Safety is a factor often included in SOC definitions and forms of measurement.

In their sample, Skjæveland et al. found the three positive types of neighbouring to be higher, and annoyance to be lower, among those aged 65 or over and among those who had lived in the neighbourhood for 10 years or more. Supportive neighbouring and weak ties were higher among women than men. Skjæveland et al. had also predicted that having children would involve residents interacting with other parents in the neighbourhood and developing positive neighbouring experiences. In fact the opposite was the case: attachment was lower and annoyance higher among those with children compared to those without.

Those coming from other traditions, such as social epidemiology, have also often used different sets of items to assess concepts that look very similar to SOC. For example, Young et al. (2004) developed a seven-item scale of Sense of Neighbourhood in a longitudinal Australian study of women's health. They reported data from the oldest cohort (women in their seventies), finding scores on the scale to be significantly higher for those living in small or remote rural communities and among those who had lived for longer in their present homes.

In their study of parents of young children – mainly single mothers – in low income neighbourhoods in Baltimore, USA, Martinez et al. (2002) developed a Perceived Neighborhood Scale (PNS) as a measure of perceptions of aspects of neighbourhood of particular relevance to parents. The factor structure, which was found to remain the same across two waves of the study – when children were aged 3 and 5 years, respectively – involved the four factors summarised in Table 6.4.

In a study of injecting drug users in Baltimore, Latkin et al. (2005) used a scale of social disorder in the neighbourhood which asked for perceptions of the extent of seven problems in the neighbourhood: vandalism, vacant housing, litter or trash on the street, loitering teenagers, burglary, drug selling, and robbery or assault, based on Perkins and Taylor's (1996) Block Environmental Inventory. Also in Baltimore, Bass and Lambert (2004) asked adolescents, enrolled in sixth grade at school, the 10 items of the Neighborhood Environment Scale (NES: see Table 6.4). A particular feature of that study was the use of geographical methods, notably the use of a geostatistical tool termed a variogram, based on a geo-coding of an adolescent's home address. The variogram model confirmed a spatial effect such that adolescents who lived in closer proximity to one another were more likely to have similar NES scores. Census-level characteristics explained much of the variation in NES scores, but did not eliminate that spatial similarity effect.

Sampson *et al.* (1997) developed a measure of *collective efficacy* in their survey of several thousand residents of more than 300 neighbourhoods in Chicago, USA. The scale was a combination of two sub-scales that were found to correlate highly: Informal Social Control and Social Cohesion and Trust. Collective efficacy was higher for home owners, those of higher socioeconomic status, and older people; and lower for the more mobile. Seventy per cent of the variance in low collective efficacy was explained by three clusters of factors about the neighbourhoods derived from the 1990 census – 'concentrated disadvantage' (proportion of residents below the poverty line, on public assistance, female-headed families, unemployed, etc.), larger concentration of immigrant groups, and low residential stability (relatively small proportions living in the same house as five years earlier, and owning their own homes). Concentrated disadvantage in particular was strongly related to three measures of neighbourhood violence: perceived violence in the neighbourhood, personal violence victimisation, and a record of homicides. Much of the relationship between concentrated disadvantage and measures of violence was mediated by low collective efficacy.

In a later review (largely of studies from the USA) Sampson *et al.* (2002) concluded that there was considerable evidence for neighbourhood effects on criminality and mental health among adolescents, in particular for the negative effects of increasing concentration of disadvantage in certain neighbourhoods, usually associated in the USA with a high proportion of African USAmerican residents. Collective efficacy, they maintained, was crucial – clear norms, a high level of mutual trust and a low level of fear, and a shared willingness to intervene for the public good. It could not be separated, however, from a neighbourhood's endowment with resources – including childcare, education, recreational, health and employment facilities and opportunities – and the stability of the resident population. The amount of disorder visible on the streets of a neighbourhood was a good indication in Sampson *et al.*'s opinion – including physical disorder (e.g. cigarettes in the street, garbage, empty beer bottles, graffiti, abandoned cars), social disorder (e.g. adults loitering, alcohol being drunk in public, public drunkenness, fighting, prostitution), the physical condition of housing (e.g. vacant houses, burnt out houses or businesses), and alcohol and tobacco influence (e.g. presence of bars and liquor stores). Such disorder on the streets might signal the unwillingness of residents to confront strangers or to intervene in a crime or call the police if necessary, that is a low level of collective efficacy. Such signs of disorder might act as a reminder that the neighbourhood was deteriorating, and among the consequences might be decreased investment in the area and a higher rate of out-migration.

Critiques of Sense of Community

A number of writers have offered critiques of SOC and ideas about how work on the subject might develop. Hill (1996) made the point that the correlates of

SOC varied from community to community (even the frequently found correlation with length of residence is not universal), illustrating the fact that the nature and effects of sense of community are dependent on the context. She also wanted to distinguish between interactions with specific others, which should more properly be thought of as social support, social networks or strong ties, and SOC, which might be thought of as a form of attachment to community, more characterised by weak ties (see earlier in this chapter for a very similar argument about social capital). Hill made the point, that many have made, that people frequently are members of a number of 'communities', some of them based on common interests rather than on the fact of living in proximity in the same area. She was also concerned, as others have been, that research on SOC has often taken a relatively superficial survey or standard questionnaire form, and that measurement has often remained at the individual level despite the collective entity of community being the intended referent of SOC. She advocated greater efforts being made to measure SOC at a level beyond the individual, and the use of a range of methods including qualitative.

Others have criticised what they perceived as an emphasis in the conceptions of SOC of Sarason (1974), McMillan and Chavis (1986) and others, on similarity, consensus, uniformity of attitudes, and a sense of being 'we'. For example, Wiesenfeld (1996), writing from the perspective of community social psychology in Venezuela, argued that such a homogenising view of community fails to recognise the multiple and often conflicting identities that are likely to be held by different members of one community, the existence of diversity, the possibility of there being dissident minorities within communities, and possibilities for transformation and change within communities. Similarly, Colombo et al. (2001), writing from Italy, drew attention to the assumption in many definitions of community that the term refers to an ideal type of cohesive community, often seen in distinction to the more negatively valenced term 'society', and often associated with rural as opposed to urban life, and with traditional community life that has been lost but might be restored. They were more attracted to the idea that modern communities were characterised by multiple, overlapping community identities, and that social action was not just a case of joint participation for collective community action but also for, "...modifying the power relationships between various social groups and to balance the distribution of resources present within the community by means of conflict strategies" (Colombo et al., 2001, p. 462).

In a similar vein, Brodsky et al. (2002) suggested that the conceptualisation of SOC should be expanded in two directions. First, it should be recognised that SOC can be negative and yet productive of positive change, for example for the resilient single mothers bringing up daughters in a risky urban neighbourhood in the USA who took part in Brodsky's (1996) own research. Participants were 10 African USAmerican single mothers raising their children in an inner city neighbourhood in Washington, DC. Over the previous 50 years the African USAmerican population of the neighbourhood had increased from under 50% to nearly 100%. Housing varied, including a number of public housing and low income complexes, which had some of the worst reputations for disrepair and violence in the city. Between 17% and 38% of residents in the seven census tracts in which participants were living had incomes below the official poverty line. Between 13% and 19%

of households were categorised as overcrowded. Between 72% and 91% of births were out of wedlock, 52% to 65% of births were without adequate prenatal care, and 73% to 85% of youths in those neighbourhoods did not live with both parents. The mothers participated in one- or two-hour-long interviews. Each had been recommended as resilient by an elementary school-based informant. In the interviews they were asked for general descriptions of their roles as single mothers, and were then asked three questions: What issues do you have to cope with (stresses)? What and who helps you cope (resources)? and Do you consider yourself successful, how, and why?

Brodsky concluded that these apparently resilient mothers had, by any accepted definition of the term, a low sense of local community. Far from being a negative thing, as most positive depictions of SOC would suggest, this 'negative SOC' might in fact have been serving these mothers and their daughters well. They were concerned about lack of physical and emotional safety in the immediate vicinities of their homes and they were very concerned to protect their children from what they saw as the negative influences of the neighbourhood. Just as others had noted the way in which a 'retreat from the street' may be used as a strategy for responding to urban poverty (Belle, 1983), and even that individuals may perceive themselves to be in a state of almost 'house arrest' (Zeldin & Topitzes, 2002), Brodsky found women separating themselves from the local community and focusing on home-based family life:

> OK, my court is really quiet ... but getting to me is a problem because you gotta come through all this to get to me ... when you drive up in that court you see things. And when you come into my house it's totally different ... It's my world. And ... when you close that door, leave the world out there (p. 351).

> I don't go out here. I don't start things with people. I don't bother people. I go home, I close my door, I lock my door, I stay in my house. Don't bother me and I won't bother you. Don't bother my kids, I won't bother you (p. 357).

Mothers felt they had little in common with others in the community and had low expectations of joint participation. They described a decline in positive SOC:

> Used to be where the neighborhood was kind of stable, where you knew everybody. But now people move in and move out so fast. So you kind of just keep off to yourself ... Um, sometimes you don't want to get involved, you know, with different things that are going on and maybe you shouldn't just turn away but you do. Like the kids, um, hangin' in the hallway and you know they're smoking reefer in the hallway, and you just tell them to get out of the hallway sometimes. And then sometimes you just leave 'em alone cause you don't wanna have a confrontation (p. 353).

The second way in which Brodsky et al. (2002) advocated expanding the idea of SOC was in terms of the several communities to which a person might simultaneously belong and which might overlap, might be nested within one another, and were likely to interact in terms of their influence. For example, a person might live in one area, work in a setting located in another area, attend adult education classes in yet another, and have common interests with any number of relational communities which might or might not share geographical locations. Within an educational setting a person may feel a sense of belonging to the educational community as a whole but is likely also to have feelings of belonging to sub-communities such as students or members of a religious or sports association within the school, college or university ('microbelongings' to use Wiesenfeld's, 1996, term). The way in which two communities to which a person belongs may have interacting influence was illustrated by a study, cited by Brodsky *et al.*, with women from low income communities, attending an educational and job training centre (Marx, 2000). Like the women in Brodsky's (1996) earlier study, they described their neighbourhoods as inhabited by people who often had different values than their own and who, unlike themselves, did not want to 'do something' with their lives. The positive sense of community that women associated with attending the centre was enhanced when neighbourhood SOC was negative, as the following quotation illustrates:

> I don't go outside cause . . . there is so much trouble nowadays, you don't know where to go and be safe. So, I don't have a lot of friends. And when I come here it's like a relief. Like, you know, you know you're safe and no drugs, no nothing. I like it here. I recommend this place . . . I recommend a lot of people to come here (Marx, 2000, cited by Brodsky *et al.*, 2002, p. 329).

Brodsky *et al.* (2002) recommended that future research on SOC should: allow for the possibility that it can be negative as well as positive; assess SOC associated with more than one community; allow research participants to select their communities for assessment; assess the salience and importance of selected communities; attend to the type of communities involved; and investigate both perceived SOC and aspirations for SOC.

Note also that the concept of sense of community has been applied in a number of settings other than that of a local neighbourhood. A number of those uses of the concept are illustrated in the chapters of a book on *Psychological Sense of Community* edited by Fisher, Sonn and Bishop (2002), three Australian community psychologists. For example, the idea of SOC has been applied to learning communities such as schools (Bateman, 2002) and universities (Mahan *et al.*, 2002; Obst & White, 2004), to community organisations such as an inner-city neighbourhood association, a local action group formed in order to focus on the issue of urban violence, and a city-wide group affiliated with a national, faith-based pressure group organisation in the USA (Hughey *et al.*, 1999), to work organisations more generally (Chipuer & Pretty, 1999), and even to virtual, computer-mediated 'communities' (Roberts *et al.*, 2002; Dunham *et al.*, 1998 – see Chapter 9).

Perkins and Long (2002) considered the undoubted overlap that exists between SOC and social capital. In many ways, they thought, SOC and empowerment were to community psychology what social capital is to political science, sociology, applied economics, and community development. Indeed the implication was that SOC might have remained a much more limited concept because it had so often been measured at an individual level. Perkins and Long concluded that SOC might be thought of as constituting just one of four distinct components of social capital, as shown in Figure 6.9. It had generally been confined to the cognitive or subjective level. Also, it usually referred exclusively to informal social relations. The broader concept of social capital embraced, in addition, the informal behavioural level (neighbouring) and more formal aspects of collective community

	Cognition, Trust	Social Behaviour
Informal	SENSE OF COMMUNITY	NEIGHBOURING
Formally organised	COLLECTIVE EFFICACY	CITIZEN PARTICIPATION

Figure 6.9   The relationship between sense of community and four elements of social capital
Source: Perkins, D.D. & Long D.A. (2002). Neighborhood sense of community and social capital: a multi-level analysis. In A.T. Fisher, C.C. Sonn & B.J. Bishop (eds), *Psychological Sense of Community: Research, Applications, and Implications* (pp. 291–318). New York: Kluwer/ Plenum

organisation at both cognitive and behavioural levels (collective feelings of efficacy and citizen participation, respectively). On further re-analysis of data from the earlier Block Booster Project (Chavis *et al.*, 1987), Perkins and Long found evidence for their four-component model of social capital. But they also found SOC, measured with the eight-item Brief Sense of Community Index (BSCI) scale to be the strongest and most consistent predictor, at both individual and block levels, of the other three dimensions of social capital.

Safe and Green: Neighbourhood Physical Environments

Those who have researched sense of community have not on the whole paid much attention to environmental design features. Amongst the exceptions are Prezza *et al.* (2001) who investigated children's neighbourhood mobility. They interviewed 250 mothers of children aged 7–12 years living in five areas of Rome, Italy. The focus was on the children's level of autonomous mobility in the urban context: autonomy in going to and from school, going on errands or making small purchases, going to play areas, whether adults were present during outside play, and children's use of the areas immediately next to their homes. Prezza *et al.* concluded that children in the urban setting had rather limited opportunities for autonomous movement outside the home and urged that something should be done to reverse the trend in that direction. A seven-item measure of Neighbourhood Relations (partly based on Buckner's, 1988, scale), which asked mothers about the quantity and quality of contacts with neighbours, was associated with children's mobility. Another factor associated with children's mobility was the nature of the environment in the immediate vicinity of the home. Living near a park, but even more living in a building with an inner condominium courtyard – a large, traffic-free area, partly paved and partly green, without children's play equipment but with benches or walls for sitting, mostly used by adults – was associated with greater child mobility. The greater autonomy of children living in homes with courtyards extended, beyond use of that space, to the home–school journey and neighbourhood streets. Prezza *et al.* suggested that this effect might be the result of greater self-confidence on the part of children and greater confidence on the part of parents as a result of using the protected space of the condominium courtyard where people are familiar, but which is also external and open to the wider world, permitting a gradual passage towards autonomy in the city. Similar work in Finland and Belarus, carried out by Kyttä (1997) has found that children's autonomy is greatest in rural environments, and has also drawn attention to the positive role played by courtyards that can provide a 'stepping stone' for entering the larger community.

Kuo *et al.* (1998) were specifically interested in common, green spaces in urban areas and the way in which they might encourage neighbourhood social ties. Their previous research had suggested that the simple presence of trees increased the use of common neighbourhood spaces. They then went on to make observations of a large public housing development in Chicago, USA, and to interview 145 residents. Interviews were carried out by three long-term local women residents. The sample consisted of female heads of household, mostly single, nearly all unemployed, about half with children at home. When the development was built in the 1960s, each of its nearly 30 high-rise buildings was surrounded by grass and trees. Over time most of the green spaces had been paved over in an effort to keep dust down and maintenance costs low. Residents had had no significant input into decisions regarding vegetation in common spaces. Indeed, despite the housing authority having a policy of involving residents in major decisions, that had not included outdoor vegetation and Kuo *et al.* reported observing trees being taken down outside apartment buildings without consultation or notification of residents. As well as having largely bleak neighbourhood outdoor spaces, the development was characterised by other features that Kuo *et al.* expected would work against the formation of neighbourhood social ties, namely the architectural design of the development, crowding, noise, and high rates of crime.

The amount of vegetation left surrounding the buildings that made up the development varied considerably and that provided Kuo *et al.* with the opportunity to test their hypothesis of a relationship with social ties. Since residents had been allocated to buildings on a virtually random basis, there was no relationship between living in a particular building and resident characteristics. Greenness was assessed at two levels: at the building level based on ratings of photographs of the area immediately surrounding the building; and at the individual level by asking each participant to rate the level of vegetation visible from the apartment. Apartment and building greenness (the former more strongly) were significantly positively associated with an eight-item scale about extent of Neighbourhood Social Ties (NSTs). Neither measure of greenness was associated with answers to questions about general social ties, not confined to the local neighbourhood, suggesting that the result was specific to the ease of forming ties with immediate neighbours. A further finding was that NSTs were significantly associated with measures of sense of safety and sense of adjustment, suggesting that higher levels of common green space might yield not only the proximal benefit of stronger NSTs but also those more distal benefits.

Perkins and Taylor (1996) recommended that community psychologists should try to use measures other than the survey questions that were so often used. In their study of the fear of crime among several hundred residents of 50 different neighbourhoods in the city of Baltimore, USA, they combined survey data (three-quarters of their sample were interviewed for a second time a year later) with observations of the blocks in which residents lived and a content analysis of two local newspapers. Unlike Kuo et al.'s (1998) study in Chicago, in this study, public housing projects, high-risk apartment complexes, and the central business district were excluded, so the results were most relevant to low-rise urban residential neighbourhoods of moderate density.

Observations were made using the Block Environmental Inventory (Perkins et al., 1992). The first part of the inventory involved accounts and ratings of the following: number of adolescents and young men and women, younger children, and older adults outdoors at a given point in time, and their general activities (walking, 'hanging out', etc.); abandoned cars; damaged or graffiti-painted public property; types and amount of open land use (vacant lots, church or school yards, parking lots, playgrounds, gardens, etc.); and whether the land was poorly maintained. For the second part, raters began again at the beginning of the block, walking down one side of the street at a time, counting the number of occupied residential units, and rating each non-residential (stores, schools, etc.) or mixed-use buildings for litter in front of the building, vandalism (e.g. graffiti, broken windows) and lack of exterior maintenance (peeling paint, broken fixtures). Inter-rater reliability was checked. The local newspapers were analysed by counting the number of articles that reported crimes committed in or near a given neighbourhood. Perkins and Taylor cited previous British research on media crime coverage, for example that carried out in Birmingham, England by Smith (1984), which had shown how disproportionately media attention was concentrated on personal offences involving violence, sex or public disorder, which were particularly likely to be associated with fear of crime.

Their results showed that several observational and media measures, as well as the average amount of physical and social disorder perceived by block residents, were significantly predictive of fear of crime. In a hierarchical linear modelling analysis, one variable from each of those data sets added significantly to individual level prediction of fear of crime: the disordered appearance of non-residential property on the block; the amount of media coverage of 'disorder news' (stories about the physical deterioration of housing or other property, racial unrest, prison escapes or unrest); and the block average for perceived physical disorder. Perkins and Taylor particularly noted the apparent importance of physical disorder, supporting the view that fear of crime is particularly related to what has been referred to by some as 'signs of incivility'. It should be noted that there have been criticisms of observational studies of communities by outsiders, unless such observation is part of a more participatory process that fully involves local residents (Almedom, 2005).

Neighbourhood Redesign and Regeneration

Plas and Lewis (1996) studied SOC in the newly built town of Seaside in Florida, USA. Seaside had been purposely designed to induce a positive sense of community. For example, all homes were situated within walkable distance of the town centre, and streets and walkways had been designed to encourage pedestrians and to discourage through traffic. Plas and Lewis particularly emphasised the design of the fronts of houses in Seaside, all of which had front porches close enough to the street that interaction between residents and passers-by would be encouraged. Content analysis of interviews with residents suggested that the town philosophy, town design, and architectural features, were all considered important as determinants of positive sense of community. References to SOC itself were frequently coded into the categories of membership, needs, and connections, but rarely into the category of influence. It was not that most participants said they felt impotent or uninfluential within the town, but rather that the issue of influence appeared not to be salient for the large majority.

Community psychology is more likely to be concerned with regeneration of less favoured neighbourhoods such as the one studied by Halpern (1995). He reported a case study of the changes that occurred following refurbishment of a housing estate. Before the refurbishment, the estate, which Halpern called Eastlake, had become very unpopular with prospective tenants and had attracted police attention on account of a rate of crime higher than other neighbourhoods in the area. One of Halpern's main interests was in environmental design. When it was built, 20 years earlier, the estate had been designed according to a plan, popular at the time, that was meant to keep traffic away from the centre of the estate where residents would be encouraged to interact in safety. House fronts faced inwards, with the entry road running at the backs of the houses where garages were also situated. In practice the design had not worked out well. The garages were little used and they and the alleyways between the houses had become trouble spots. The children's play area was frequented more by teenagers than families with young children. An atmosphere of suspicion and mistrust had arisen on the estate which had acquired a bad reputation in the area. Otherwise the estate had the advantage of being composed of low-rise two- or three-bedroomed houses and one-bedroom flats, all brick built and generally well maintained. The local pub had acquired a reputation for fighting, and security grilles on local shops were permanently in place.

Halpern was able to take advantage of a natural experiment. Because of limited resources, the local council planned to refurbish part of the estate – Green Close – first, with the rest of the estate to follow two or three years later. Part of the refurbishment was of the houses themselves, including new front porches, refurbished kitchens and bathrooms, double-glazed windows and more secure locks. Other aspects were to do with external features of the estate such as closing of the problematic alleyways, introducing traffic-slowing measures and narrowing the road that children had to cross in order to reach the play area, and providing more suitable parking areas. Residents were consulted and a number of the changes, such as traffic calming and access to the play area, were decided on after hearing residents' views.

Halpern interviewed 55 residents, approximately equally divided between those from Green Close and elsewhere on the estate, at a time when the first phase of the refurbishment had been announced but no changes had yet been made. Three years later 62 residents were interviewed, again split between Green Close and elsewhere, by which time the Green Close refurbishment had taken place and a

Table 6.5   A summary of changes at Green Close from before to after refurbishment of the housing estate

	Before	After
Residents who described the estate as safe or very safe	41%	81%
Residents who described the estate as a good or very good place to bring up children	22%	52%
Residents who described the estate as a bad or very bad place to bring up children	59%	11%
Residents who had received no visits from neighbours in the previous six months	31%	15%
Residents reporting being able to recognise most or all of their neighbours	55%	74%
Residents who had heard of the Residents' Association	72%	96%
Residents who had attended any Residents' Association meetings	3%	19%
Perceived supportiveness of neighbours (average of 7-point ratings of helpfulness in each of seven hypothetical situations)	4.7	5.6
Residents who say the area is very friendly	7%	26%
Residents who believe people outside the estate think of it as 'terrible'	59%	44%
Residents scoring as 'cases' of anxiety state	57%	22%
Residents scoring as 'cases' of depression	25%	4%

Source: Halpern, D. (1995). *Mental Health and the Built Environment: More than Bricks and Mortar?* London: Taylor & Francis

further phase had been announced. About half of those interviewed on the second occasion had also been interviewed three years earlier. The changes appear to have been impressive and are summarised in Table 6.5. Halpern commented that it was difficult to say exactly what aspects of the changes or the consultation process had led to this marked improvement, "...but it seems likely that a combination of factors acted to reverse the vicious cycle of withdrawal and distrust between neighbours" (p. 195). Interestingly, despite these sizeable changes in feelings about the neighbourhood, social support and mental health, most residents did not think that the estate's reputation in the wider area had improved very much.

A similar study was conducted over a period of 10 years in neighbourhoods in Oslo, Norway (Dalgard & Tambs, 1997). An earlier study (Dalgard, 1986) had found the prevalence of psychiatric disorders varying between different neighbourhoods in the city, the highest prevalence being in a new 'satellite town' on the outskirts of the city, characterised by a relative lack of services and recreational facilities, with economic problems and poor social networks. In the intervening 10 years dramatic improvements had been made in one area (referred to by Dalgard & Tambs as Area V) including the opening of a new public school, the extension of children's playgrounds, the establishment of a sports arena and park, the organisation of sporting activities for adolescents, a new shopping centre with restaurant and cinema, and an extension of the city subway line to that neighbourhood. No comparable changes had been made in other areas.

Of around 1000 residents interviewed on the first occasion, half were reinterviewed 10 years later. Many had moved in the meantime, and the main analysis was a comparison of 31 who had remained in Area V and 217 non-movers in comparison areas. What residents said about their neighbourhoods at the two time points reflected the development that had taken place in Area V. In that area residents expressed significantly greater contentment on the second occasion compared to the first, both in general, and specifically in relation to playgrounds, shops, kindergartens, and youth activities. In most of those respects levels of contentment had risen to the levels pertaining in the other areas, which had not changed over time. Again the principal interest here was in the mental health of residents. Using a scale of 50 questions covering anxiety, depression, and physical symptoms, Dalgard and Tambs were able to show a significant difference between Area V and other areas in symptom change: symptoms had decreased from a comparatively high level in Area V, having remained the same in other areas. There was a tendency for those with better mental health to have moved out of Area V, but analysis showed that this could not account for the main result.

Thomson *et al.* (2003) reported a qualitative study based on 14 focus groups in two areas of relatively high deprivation in the south of Glasgow, Scotland. Just over a year earlier a modern swimming pool and leisure complex had opened in one of the areas (referred to as Riverside), while in the other area (Parkview) the swimming pool, built 70 years earlier, had been closed by the local council because the expense of repair and upgrading could not be afforded. In the previous decade Riverside had been prioritised as an area for regeneration while in Parkview there had been no similar investment. Seven groups were held in each area involving a total of 81 residents. The groups focused on different sections of the resident population, such as middle-aged men and women, older women, mothers of pre-school children, and middle-aged parents, but women outnumbered men by about six to one.

The benefits of having a swimming pool in the area including the obvious link with health and physical exercise, but Thomson *et al.* reported that a striking feature of the results was the way in which a swimming pool was also reported to be important for facilitating social contact, reducing isolation, relieving stress, and facilitating good mental health. Lack of a swimming pool appeared to compound other stresses associated with personal and area disadvantage. Particularly important for mothers of young children was use of the pool as a stress reliever to cope with lively children. As one mother in Parkview put it, "... it let you unwind. Whereas now they are totally about your feet, you are hyper and they are hyper and you are [flop sound as if exhausted/exasperated]" (p. 665). Residents in Parkview reported having had little control over the pool closure. It was thought to illustrate the powerlessness of residents regarding decisions that had an impact on the local environment and living conditions, and was generally seen as symbolic of abandonment by the council. The view was expressed that the closure of the swimming pool had had an effect far beyond the loss of the pool facility itself. For example:

> ... it [the pool building] brought life into that bit of the area because it was lit up, the huge big dome the whole place had an aura about it but now you go up there, you've nae light, the building is dim, the weans have smashed whatever lights hanging about, it's dreary, it's frightening, that's how the shops are shutting because naebody is there at night whereas then the baths were opened at night it lit the whole area up (p. 664).

...thanks to the powers that be they made this one of the biggest ghettos on the south side the day they closed the swimming baths, it was the only thing that the kids had to go and do here, there's no other amenities other than the church...it's overnight they made it into a ghetto practically (p. 664).

Those quotations from some of the less well-off parts of Glasgow bring our discussion of sense of community, and this chapter, to an end. Many questions remain about the best ways of understanding, let alone assessing, the nature of people's neighbourhoods and communities and the support they provide and the functions that they serve. In this chapter we have examined the possible value of two leading concepts – social capital and sense of community. We shall have reasons to bring them to mind again when we consider the examples of community research and action that constitute Part IV. Before that, the chapters that constitute Part III allow us to hear in more detail of the experiences of members of a number of the disempowered groups with which community psychology has been most concerned.

PART III
THE EXPERIENCE OF DISEMPOWERMENT: SEVEN EXAMPLES

Chapter 7

DISEMPOWERMENT BY WAR, IMMIGRATION, HOMELESSNESS OR UNEMPLOYMENT

In this chapter and the next we shall examine the experiences of seven groups of people. Each is a group that finds itself in a disempowered position. Each constitutes a very large group. They have been chosen to illustrate many of the general features of disempowerment as well as some of the experiences particular to one or other group. The seven groups have each been treated as if they were distinct, but in the real world there is much overlap – civilians caught up in war often become immigrants for example, and homeless people are very often unemployed.

These two chapters attempt to convey some of the reality of life for people in these so often disempowered groups. Consistent with what was said in Chapter 3 about the need to draw on a variety of research methods, and particularly what was said about the prominence given to qualitative research in community psychology, several of the sections in Chapters 7 and 8 draw on the latter methods, quoting regularly from those who have participated in research. In this way, it is hoped, the voices of the disempowered can be heard more clearly than would normally be the case in an academic text.

COMMUNITIES CAUGHT UP IN WAR AND ITS CONSEQUENCES

The Trauma of War and Oppression in Europe, Central America and Globally

Groups of people who are caught up in hostilities or who are the subjects of persecution, constitute our first example. One of the most obvious instances, and perhaps the best studied, is the Jewish Holocaust. Nazi persecution of the Jews began with enactment of racial laws in the early 1930s and lasted for more than a decade, involving separation of families, the witnessing of atrocities, hunger and other material deprivations, fear for one's own and family members' lives, cultural-religious persecution, and, for those who survived, the post-war experience of being bereaved and sometimes continuing to be socially rejected (Levav, 1998). As well as many uncontrolled clinical studies suggesting a raised prevalence of psychiatric symptoms among Holocaust survivors, Levav found seven epidemiological studies carried out in Israel (four studies), Norway, Denmark and Canada between the early 1970s and the early 1990s, all finding a heightened prevalence. Commonly experienced symptoms were those of what had sometimes been called the 'survivor syndrome' or the 'concentration camp syndrome', including fatigue, sleep disturbances, nervousness, irritability, emotional instability, headaches, vertigo, loss of initiative and depression. More recently this would have been called 'post-traumatic stress disorder' (PTSD), a term referring to a cluster of symptoms, including intrusive thoughts, flashbacks, hyperarousal and numbing, that can occur after exposure to any major traumatic event. Levav (1998) concluded that such symptoms were caused by the "massive and cumulative trauma" (p. 25) to which holocaust survivors had been exposed. Supportive evidence for the importance of the trauma experiences themselves (rather than personal vulnerability or 'premorbid' factors) came from other studies of Norwegian and Danish prisoners of war (POWs) interned in Germany during the Second World War as well as from studies of Australian and US POWs (Levav, 1998), and other studies of military service personnel who had served in wars such as the Vietnam war (Fontana & Rosenheck, 1993) or the 1991 Gulf War (Stimpson et al., 2003), including studies of child combatants (Peters & Richards, 1998). Since the Second World War many people have experienced some of the massive and cumulative trauma that Levav wrote of.

Central American countries were among those which experienced some of the worst traumas of civil war, repression and dislocation in the second half of the twentieth century. In the case of Guatemala, Comas-Díaz et al. (1998) estimated that during more than 35 years of internal conflict from the 1960s to 1990s, between 150,000 and 200,000 civilians were killed, nearly a million were displaced internally, several hundred thousands fled to other countries, and more than 40,000 became 'the disappeared', i.e. they were illegally abducted by government security forces, after which no information was available to the family and no culpability could be attributed to those responsible. Most likely the disappeared were tortured and killed, but the family was rarely able to confirm that and was left in the dark about the fate of their family member (Quirk & Casco, 1994). In neighbouring Honduras, which did not experience the same level of civil war and insurgency, *contra* military operations were allowed on Honduran territory in return for US aid, and in the late 1970s and 1980s the country experienced an oppressive, highly militarised environment in which popular movements were repressed, scores of people disappeared, and many others were jailed, tortured and killed (Munczek & Tuber, 1998).

Again studies have documented the post-traumatic effects on individuals and their families. Two studies were carried out in collaboration with the Committee of Family Members of the Detained and Disappeared of Honduras (COFADEH), a victim support group formed in 1982. In the first of those studies, interviews were held, mostly in the family home, with 25 family members (parents, spouses, siblings, children, grandchildren, nephews, nieces, and in-laws) of disappeared relatives

(Quirk & Casco, 1994). Disappearances had occurred on average six years earlier. Compared to members of two control groups – one of families who had lost a member due to accident or illness, the other of families where no death had occurred within the past 10 years – families of the disappeared reported significantly more stress-related symptoms. The latter included symptoms indicating increased arousal (increased startle response, tremor, chronic headache, insomnia) and physiological reactions (stomach ache, sweating, dry mouth). Two-thirds of the children in those families suffered from one or more of the following stress symptoms: a sudden drop in scholastic performance, bed-wetting, pronounced fear, angry outbursts, and developmental delays (compared to 30% and 40% of the no death and accident/illness death groups).

The second Honduran study focused on the effects on teenage children. Sixteen young people (from nine families) who had experienced the disappearance of their fathers, on average nine years previously, were interviewed. Also interviewed were 11 children (from nine families) who had suffered the loss of a parent (one mother, the rest fathers) due to political assassination, on average four years previously. Most mothers were also interviewed (Munczek & Tuber, 1998). Use was made of a post-traumatic stress reaction checklist (PTSRC) that asks children (and parents about their children) to describe their current reactions in relation to one war-related event that the child selects as being the 'most disturbing'. Of 14 items on the checklist, most were checked by the majority of children in both groups (e.g. often thinks/speaks about what occurred, scared when thinks about what occurred, often remembers what occurred, thoughts about event make child forgetful, since event more alone/not understood, since frightened of loud sounds). On a child behaviour inventory, with subscales for depression, anxiety and aggression, more than half the children in both groups said that they frequently: worried about many things, were afraid of losing family, feared bad things might happen to them, needed to be with an elder to feel safe, and angered easily. Parents were even more likely to describe post-traumatic stress reactions and child behaviour symptoms.

But the results of such interviews go beyond simple counts of responses to checklists and inventories, revealing though the latter are in themselves. They demonstrate, among other things, the economic and social hardships that are so often experienced by families following such traumatic events, as well as the stigma and social isolation which are frequent themes. For example, in the first study, two-thirds of families of the disappeared reported receiving threats after the disappearance and a similar proportion feared that their neighbours were police or police informers (Quirk, 1992, cited by Munczek & Tuber). The theme of economic insecurity, poverty and destitution regularly recurred for most of those interviewed. Families faced great expenses in their unsuccessful search for their disappeared relatives, and families of the assassinated had funeral and burial expenses. Very few received economic assistance or compensation. Most had lost their principal economic provider, and some mothers were sacked from their jobs because of the political nature of the disappearance or assassination. Mothers frequently had to increase the amount of time they worked outside the home, sometimes working double shifts. Some children had stopped attending school due to the loss of the father and his income, and there was a high percentage of learning problems involving poor concentration and application to school tasks.

Almost all the young people interviewed were experiencing a deep and painful sense of loss. Those from the assassinated group were particularly likely to feel embittered, while those in the disappeared group expressed confusion and uncertainty about whether their fathers were alive or not. Many described being shunned, both initially and sometimes for years afterwards, by neighbours, friends and even other family members. Nearly all reported having felt afraid for years, and some had received anonymous threats of death or harm. Children often described their peer relationships as problematic. Most had some good friends, but as a son of one disappeared father said, "There is always a certain degree of fear of everyone. You cannot confide fully" (Munczek & Tuber, 1998, p. 1706). The daughter of an assassinated father said:

> I do not talk to anyone about my sadness, my feelings . . . If they speak to me, I speak back, but otherwise . . . In school I do not have many friends . . . Sometimes I just want to be alone, just be alone . . . I even go hide in the bathroom to be alone.

A boy whose father had disappeared and whose uncle had been assassinated said, "I only speak to one friend about my father and the problems of my family . . . I do not like to talk". Others admitted to difficulties controlling aggressive feelings and blamed themselves for becoming too easily angered. Children of the disappeared reported receiving valued support from COFADEH, but no comparable support was available to those whose parents had been assassinated.

In western Europe, one of the most serious and longstanding conflicts in the late twentieth century was the civil conflict in Northern Ireland. O'Reilly and Stevenson (2003) analysed data from a representative Health and Wellbeing Survey carried out in that country in 1997 to test the hypothesis that the level of psychological distress, measured by the GHQ (General Health Questionnaire), known to be higher in Northern Ireland than in Scotland, England or the Irish Republic, might be due to the effects of the 'Troubles' in that country. Since the late 1960s, more than 3600 people had been killed as a direct result of the civil disturbances, and thousands more injured or exposed to potentially traumatising events. Two key questions were used in the analysis: ". . . thinking about the whole period since 1969, how much violence would you say there has been in this area because of the Troubles?" and "How much have the Troubles affected your own life and the lives of your immediate family?". Twenty-five per cent reported 'quite a bit' or 'a lot' of violence in their areas, and 21% reported 'quite a bit' or 'a lot' of impact on own or family life. Answers to both questions were significantly related to psychological distress, independently of demographic and socioeconomic factors.

Data collected on a global basis by the World Health Organisation (WHO) since 1990 enabled Ghobarah et al. (2004) to calculate the after-effects for countries in the years following civil war. They examined Disability Adjusted Life Years (DALYs) – a measure of the effect of death and disability on population groups – depending upon whether a country had experienced civil war during the period 1991 to 1997. The analysis supported the hypothesis that the extent of DALYs lost in 1999 was related to 1991–97 civil war deaths – true for all disease and for the whole population, but also for most of the age–sex groupings (including younger and older children and older adults) and for most specific disease categories examined

---

Civil wars substantially increase exposure to risks for disease, injury and death

Population displacement, internally or as refugees, often under poor conditions favouring spread of infectious diseases; military and civilian movement encouraging the spread of AIDS for example; continuing violence magnified by the availability of arms following war.

Civil wars reduce available resources for expenditure on health and reduce the efficiency with which resources for public health are used

Damage or destruction of clinics and laboratories, and water treatment systems; pressure for military spending and the need to rebuild army and police forces; and destruction of transportation infrastructure, weakening the distribution of water, food, and medicine.

Figure 7.1 Some reasons for delayed effects of civil conflict
Source: Ghobarah, H.A., Huth, P. & Russett, B. (2004). The post-war public health effects of civil conflict. *Social Science and Medicine*, **59**, 869–84

(especially HIV/AIDS, malaria, tuberculosis, respiratory infections, and other infectious diseases). Transportation accidents were also raised, mostly among young and middle-aged adults; as was the homicide rate, the victims chiefly being women and younger men. Many of the effects were similar when analysed according to whether civil war had occurred in an immediately adjacent country. Overall the most frequent victims of these lingering effects of civil wars were women and children. Their estimate was that around 12 million DALYs were lost worldwide in 1999 due to civil wars in the same country in those seven years, and around another three million in neighbouring countries – a total almost twice WHO's estimate of the immediate loss of DALYs from all the wars fought in 1999 (civil and international). These effects were independent of low national total health spending, low female school enrolment rate, high urban growth rate, and high income inequality (the Gini coefficient – see Chapter 4), each of which was itself related to DALYs lost. The authors' explanations for these delayed effects of civil conflict are summarised in Figure 7.1.

Community-Level Trauma

The concept of PTSD – popular as a diagnostic entity in psychiatry since around 1980 and used to embrace what is thought to be the essential psychological disturbance following many different types of trauma including war combat, concentration camp experience, torture, forced migration, rape, road traffic accidents, and many other experiences besides – has been criticised for its focus on the assessment and treatment of the individual (see Chapter 1 for a critique of individualism in psychology generally). Bracken *et al.* (1995) based their critique on their experience of working with victims of war in a number of parts of the world, notably the Luwero Triangle, an area to the north-west of Kampala, which became known as the 'killing fields of Uganda' in the 1980s, when hundreds of thousands of civilians were killed in government counter-insurgency operations. Bracken *et al.* cited examples of people exposed to shocking events but who appeared not to have responded with distress of the kind encapsulated in PTSD, apparently because community support had been maintained or new sources of support found. For example, a man who had suffered greatly in appalling conditions in prison said he had been saved from despair by developing solidarity among the prisoners, including Christian and Muslim prisoners learning each other's prayers and praying together; and another had been tortured and had both hands cut off, and was now totally dependent on neighbours, but reported no psychiatric symptoms, saying that support and solidarity shown to him by his neighbours had allowed him to return to a fairly normal life. Others, on the other hand, had not been able to benefit in the same way from social support or community cohesiveness. That included women who had been raped and had been socially stigmatised as a consequence, or who had kept the experience secret from others and felt alienated.

Bracken *et al.* recognised that publicity about PTSD and counts of the number of 'cases' might be of value in drawing attention to, and raising awareness about, people's experiences during war and disruptions of various kinds. As they put it, "... medical formulations such as PTSD are of most value in their use as instruments of testimony against torture and violence" (p. 1080). Their view, though, was that reactions to such experiences can only be understood in the wider context, including such aspects as people's political convictions, the type and extent of support available, the extent to which the whole society and not just individuals has been traumatised, and the forms of therapeutic help that are available. In summary of their framework, they wrote:

> In contrast to this [PTSD] we are proposing that issues of context in terms of social, political and cultural realities should be seen as central. By social reality we are referring to such things as family circumstances, available social networks, economic position and employment status. Political reality refers to the individual's engagement, or otherwise, in a political movement, their social position as determined by gender, class and ethnic factors and whether they are the victims of state repression or other forms of organized violence. By the term cultural reality we are referring to such things as linguistic position, spiritual or religious involvement, basic ontological beliefs and concepts of self, community and illness (p. 1077).

Two studies from South Africa are among those that have pointed to the limitations of the 'western trauma discourse' and the diagnostic or biomedical approach to understanding the psychological effects of violent conflict, which focus on individual behaviour, intrapersonal dynamics, cognitive processing and biological changes, and which take relatively little account of the broader social and community context (Sideris, 2003; Kagee, 2004). One was a qualitative interview study of 20 South Africans (13 men and 7 women), living in the Western Cape region of the country, formerly detained under the apartheid regime. They spontaneously described a number of experiences that would meet some of the criteria for PTSD symptoms, such as difficulty concentrating, acting or feeling as if the traumatic event were recurring, feelings of detachment or estrangement from others, and irritability or outbursts of anger. But Kagee (2004) found them to be less salient than three other themes. One was health problems which were attributed to imprisonment and the abuse and torture experienced in prison. A second was current economic concerns. Poverty was a major concern for nearly all and there was considerable distress that their lives had not progressed as a result of their experiences and lack of support since. For example:

> I could have made a lot of progress in my life but since I was ill treated and punished I was not able to make any changes in my life. My soul is not in peace, since I did not see any progress in my life. I suffered a lot in prison but nothing has been done to support me. I am sick and hopeless (p. 628).

That was related to the third theme – dissatisfaction with the present political situation in South Africa, in particular lack of financial reparations from government, seeming neglect of those who had made personal sacrifices for the anti-apartheid movement, and belief that efforts of the state to redress historical injustices – such as the Truth and Reconciliation Commission (TRC) – had not resulted in meaningful life changes for them. For example:

> Other people have received something in return from the TRC which has done nothing for me. At this point in time I feel that I lost the battle because nothing has been done for me. Today we (former detainees) are inferior in the country they were fighting for. People who were detained and abused before are not recognized and no one cares for us (p. 629).

The paper by Sideris (2003) reported the results of unstructured interviews, followed by discussion of results in focus groups, with 30 women who had fled from their homes in the southern part of Mozambique, the area most affected by the civil war of the 1980s and early 1990s in that country, and who settled in border villages in South Africa. This is one of a number of studies of refugees from war and persecution. Others include studies of refugees from persecution in south-east Asian countries – Cambodia and Myanmar – settled in camps in nearby Thailand (Mollica et al., 1998; Lopes Cardozo et al., 2004). The conflict in Mozambique had been particularly vicious and destructive, involving murder, rape and mutilation on a mass scale, with widespread plundering of homes, burning of land and crops, and butchering of livestock. Rape and other forms of sexual violence were used as weapons of terror and intimidation. Sideris was at pains, not only to insert the social into an understanding of the impact on the refugees' lives, but further to explain the role of gender. Individual distress and social destruction were seen as interdependent. Like the former South African detainees that figured in Kagee's (2004) report, Mozambican women described physical dysfunctions and injuries caused by their experiences, but also personal and spiritual injury linked to war-related deprivation of daily practices, kinship relationships, social rules and obligations, as well as the harsh conditions faced in their new surroundings – including extreme poverty, constant threat of deportation, and exploitation of cheap labour. As one woman put it:

> The war has taken our *ixinzuthi* [spirit or life force]. We are not the way we used to be before the war. In our villages we were people with dignity. We farmed the land of our ancestors. We provided for our families. We were respected. But the war has taken it away. The *ixinzuthi* is who you are. It goes together with your spirit. If your dignity is respected your spirit also will be okay (pp. 716–17).

Gender relations were crucial, Sideris argued, for understanding refugee women's experiences. Historically, in southern Mozambique, partly due to the important role of male migrant labour, women had played a pivotal role in subsistence farming, becoming the backbone of agricultural production, and taking pride in maintaining their families and providing for their children. Unlike the situation following some African conflicts, where women's sense of strength and resilience had grown as a result of taking on new roles, for these Mozambican women loss of access to the land and their traditional economic roles had been one of the worst outcomes for almost all of them. For example:

> In Mozambique we were ploughing. Many of the men were away in Joni and we were doing everything for ourselves. We were respected for the work we did. We had a place in the community. Now we are living as if we are lost (p. 719).

Others, too, have recognised the limitations of the concept of PTSD. One of those was McCloskey *et al.* (1995), who interviewed children, and separately their mothers, who had left one of three central American countries (El Salvador, Guatemala and Nicaragua) on average four years previously. They were recruited through a local refugee support organisation in one town in south-west USA where they were now living. The refugee mothers had on average experienced no fewer than seven to eight out of 12 types of violent political incident. For example, more than 80% had seen dead bodies and 50% or more had been threatened by the police, had their home under surveillance, their house sacked by the police, had witnessed police abduction, and had witnessed bombings. Their children were less likely to report such experiences, but more than 30% said they had witnessed bombings and more than 15% police abduction, and stabbing. It was likely that central American refugees in the USA had endured, in addition to trauma associated with war and repression in the country of origin and economic and social adversity in their new country, traumas of various kinds – including the possibility of robbery, rape and beatings – during the journey from one country to the other.

Munczek and Tuber (1998) also commented that the use of the PTSRC symptom checklist in their Honduran study may have been problematic. The concept of post-traumatic stress assumes a time-limited, distinct traumatising event (in their case the murder or disappearance of a parent) and its consequences. Yet, as they said, all studies of the impact of political repression and violence suggest the existence of multiple, ongoing stressors: "While the loss of the parent was undoubtedly traumatising, it occurred within a context of continuing political repression with multiple interconnecting traumatic consequences" (p. 1711). Comas-Díaz *et al.* (1998) went a step further in their criticism in their consideration of the effects on the Guatemalan people of the traumatic events of those years. They pointed out that a fuller understanding needs to take into account the function of repression and the widespread fear that it created among poor people, mostly indigenous Mayans, in subjecting them, maintaining their position as a source of cheap labour, and eradicating core Mayan cultural values and community solidarity. The population was silenced through terror.

...listing symptoms...barely scratches the surface...The Mayan collective body that is constituted in the individual lives of survivors and that is profoundly communal, has been deeply wounded...Terror's destructive forces affect community and culture, not only individual well-being. Furthermore, terror not only destroys the present and forces a rethinking of the past but also deeply threatens the future through it destructive effects on the next generation's capacity to culturally affirm itself (pp. 782, 783).

GROUPS OF PEOPLE ADJUSTING TO A NEW COUNTRY

The Example of Immigrants to Australia from Bosnia and Other Countries

The focus of the study by McCloskey *et al.* (1995), described above, was the traumatic experiences of refugee families in their countries of origin. Other research has focused on the experiences of immigrants to a new country, on the whole leaving aside the war-related and other forms of trauma that immigrants might have experienced in their countries of origin or on route to their new homes. Australia, which has immigrants from more than 150 ethnic backgrounds (Nesdale & Mak, 2000), is one country where such research has been carried out. Refugees from Bosnia-Herzegovina, who constituted the largest single component of the Australian humanitarian immigration programme during the 1990s, were the particular focus of one study (Colic-Peisker & Walker, 2003). Interviews were conducted with 35 Bosnian refugees, 13 bilingual settlement workers (mostly refugees from Bosnia themselves), and 12 Australian professionals such as teachers of English, community nurses, counsellors, advocates and interpreters.

Several interacting themes were identified. One was the 'identity vacuum' that immigrants had often experienced on arrival, having lost everything that previously represented and anchored their social identities; even, in the case of those who had not had time to prepare for emigration, having had to leave behind everything including photographs and identity documents. The ascribed status of 'refugee' was an administrative and largely negative one, inviting a patronising response from Australians. As one immigrant, previously a director of a large bank, put it: "Many Australians regard us, refugees from the Balkans, as if we never saw a computer or dishwasher before we came to Australia" (p. 342). Connected to the feeling of loss of identity was a feeling of loss of control over one's life. One immigrant, a dentist in Bosnia, said:

> My husband stayed in Sarajevo...we were separated and we really did not have a clue what would happen next. And the absolutely worst feeling of all, perhaps the worst feeling one can have in life, is this feeling of being completely out of control...as if you were thrown into the river and now the stream is carrying you...where? You don't know. No plans, no power to influence things... suddenly you're not who you were before...you're just waiting (pp. 342–3).

Australia represented a big 'culture shock' for most immigrants, particularly those coming from rural areas in Bosnia to live in large cities in Australia. The difficulty of obtaining meaningful work, coupled with mastering a new language,

Degree of retention of culture of origin

		High		Low
		INTEGRATION		ASSIMILATION
Degree of adoption of host culture	High			
	Low	SEPARATION		MARGINALISATION

Figure 7.2   Berry's model of acculturation
Source: Berry, J.W. (2001). A psychology of immigration. *Journal of Social Issues*, **57**, 615–32

was one of the strongest themes, and many had to accept jobs of a status below that of the jobs that they held previously. That 'occupational down adjustment' was particularly the case for the middle-aged. Their aspirations for building human capital in the form of language skills and higher educational qualifications, for example, were transferred to their children. A community worker described the situation of professionals who had lost their jobs and status:

> ...very few people, probably under 10%, work in jobs comparable to the jobs they had in Bosnia. Their qualifications are often not recognized, but then not many people feel confident to go and study at Australian colleges...therefore they go for alternative jobs...there's no way they can be satisfied. Women with children usually stay at home, even women with degrees, so what are they now? Just housewives, without the language, no time to learn English...99% of such women worked back in Bosnia because the system was different...there was cheap and available child care. Here in Australia they are very frustrated with the life they have. Some have casual jobs, a couple of hours, but that's nothing much...The father is never home, he works hard, the children are upset because they hardly ever see him, and the mother is depressed...(p. 347).

Colic-Peisker and Walker interpreted their findings in terms of both acculturation theory (Berry, 2001) and social identity theory (Tajfel, 1981). Berry's model is two-dimensional as shown in Figure 7.2. The earlier, dominant model of acculturation had assumed a unidimensional and linear process whereby immigrants would progressively assimilate to their new cultures, letting go in the process of their old ones. In the US context that was captured by the 'melting pot' metaphor (Deaux, 2000). It was assumed that as people assimilated they would share the opportunities for advancement that the country offered and acquire greater personal and social capital. More recent developments in studying the process of immigration, to which psychology had come relatively late, had shown how much more complex the process actually is (Zhou, 1999). Formerly, it had been assumed that the sole important new identification and comparison that members of an immigrant group would make would be with the dominant, majority host group. With increases in immigration to the USA of people from Latin American or Asian backgrounds, and emigration from different parts of the former Yugoslavia, it was evident that social comparison processes were much more complicated, both in terms of which immigrant group a person identifies with and which part of the new society he or she wishes to join and in what way. A further complexity involves 'reactive ethnic consciousness', whereby an initial shift away from identity with the country of origin group, is followed, in the same or the following generation, by a renewed tendency to identify with the culture of the country of origin (Rumbaut, 1999).

Colic-Peisker and Walker described two acculturation strategies employed by Bosnian immigrants in Australia. One, more likely to be adopted by those who had greater human capital for Australian urban living, corresponded to Berry's 'integration' strategy, which combines a relatively high level of both adoption of the host culture and retention of the culture of origin. In social identity theory terms, this mode of adjustment involved 'exiting' the low status 'refugee' group, both in terms of area of residence and type of occupation, and joining the mainstream of Australian society which values individual and family above the collective, ethnic community. Those with a lower level of human capital for advancement in the new environment (e.g. low skills, limited English, rural origin) were more likely, in Berry's terms, to adopt a 'separation' strategy, involving a relatively high level of retention of the home culture and a relatively low level of adoption of the host culture. That was less likely to involve exiting the refugee status and was more likely to involve survival in low-cost, ethnically more homogeneous communities.

Social identity theory has been criticised for overstating the ease with which people can shed old identities and adopt new ones, and Colic-Peisker and Walker were critical of acculturation theory on the same grounds. Immigrants' solutions to the problems of how to re-establish identity and find a mode of acculturation in a new country are not, they argued, as freely 'chosen' as those theories might suggest, but are largely constrained, even imposed, by immigrants' human capital. Furthermore it can be argued that they focus attention on immigrants' ways of coping, diverting attention from the attitudes, expectations and prejudices that may be held by the receiving society.

Colic-Peisker and Walker largely avoided the language of PTSD. They did, however, acknowledge that some immigrants had adopted what Berry terms 'marginalisation' as a mode of acculturation, which involves a relatively low level of both adoption of the host culture and retention of the home culture. Scepticism, anger, depression, and alcohol problems were risks. As one immigrant put it:

> There is a lot of educated people, intellectuals, professors, from Bosnia here in Sydney, but they are on the margin of all things. Without employment people remain isolated and cannot integrate; they do not want to engage in the community . . . These people are really marginalized: they have withdrawn from social life, they are lonely, closed into themselves . . . it is hard to motivate them for any initiative . . . (p. 347).

In the case of Bosnian immigrants to Australia, coming from Europe, and often seeing an advantage in their 'invisibility' compared to Asian or African immigrants, overt discrimination was not thought to be a major factor – although it seems to have been present in less blatant form. In the case of the more mixed group of immigrants to Australia from a number of Asian countries and from New Zealand, studied by Nesdale and Mak (2000), the degree to which immigrants thought they had been accepted by members of the dominant Australian community was a significant correlate of identification with the host country. Acceptance by

Australians was assessed by two ratings (responses to the statement, 'I feel accepted by Australians' rated on a seven-point scale; and answers to the question, 'How many close Australian friends do you have?' on a five-point scale). Acceptance was highest for immigrants from New Zealand and lowest for those from Hong Kong, Taiwan and China (intermediate for those from Vietnam and Sri Lanka).

Those whose immigration status is uncertain face some of the greatest difficulties. An example was that of Mandaean refugees in Sydney, Australia (Steel *et al.*, 2006) (another example is provided by a study of several hundred refugees from Kosovo, living in reception centres in the north of England: Turner *et al.*, 2003). This was a group originating mainly from Iran and Iraq, sufferers of long-term discrimination and escalating violence and persecution in Iraq in the lead up to the 2003 invasion. As in other western countries, increasingly stringent measures had been adopted towards refugees in Australia. Temporary protection visas had been introduced that restricted access to health care, education and work, and prevented overseas travel. Rates of depression and mental health-related disability were found to be particularly high (between 40 and 60%) for those with temporary visas as well as for those who had spent six months or longer in mandatory detention in Australia. Over half of temporary visa holders reported lifetime exposure to traumas such as the murder of a family member or friend or being close to death themselves, as well as serious living difficulties in the previous 12 months, such as being unable to return home in an emergency, fear of repatriation, concern for family in the country of origin, unemployment, insufficient money to buy food or necessary clothing or to pay rent, and loneliness and boredom. Over half of those who had been detained for six months or more reported negative experiences during detention such as fear of being sent home, not being informed about progress of a refugee application, isolation, racist comments and other forms of humiliation by other detainees, seeing people making suicide attempts or engaging in self-harm, and witnessing physical assault.

The Example of Muslim Workers in Japan

The circumstances faced by Muslim foreign workers in Japan was similar in some ways to that of Bosnian immigrants in Australia, and different in other respects, judging by the research carried out by Onishi and Murphy-Shigematsu (2003). They interviewed 24 single, male, foreign workers from Bangladesh, Pakistan and Iran. They had on average been in their early twenties when they came to Japan, had been there for between 5 and 12 years, and were now on average in their early thirties. Like the Bosnian immigrants to Australia they also faced the threat to a continuous sense of valued self-identity. The threat came from the perception that their personal characteristics or personal histories of which they were proud, were not recognised in their new country. Most also had the experience, like many of the Bosnians, of only being able to obtain work which was of a status below their expectations and below the social status position of their families in their home countries.

More like the Asian and Middle Eastern groups in Australia, however, they did perceive themselves to be the objects of considerable prejudice and stereotypes associated with being seen as under-developed, poor, or even criminal. Nor, it seems, did they have available to them the support of a close-knit cultural community in Japan. Of the four modes of acculturation proposed by Berry (2001), integration (high on both adoption of the host culture and retention of the home culture) was not found (Berry & Kim, 1988, reported evidence that integration was the form of acculturation associated with the best mental health). What were found were three types of 'acculturation narrative', corresponding to the assimilation, marginalisation, and separation forms of acculturation.

The first narrative, 'I am almost like Japanese', involved coping by accepting and adapting to Japanese language, diet and other aspects of the culture including even adopting critical attitudes towards the failure of other foreign workers to assimilate. One example was as follows:

> Japanese and Pakistan have different ways of thinking...I have found that if I insist on Pakistani way, I am not able to get along with Japanese...you need to adapt yourself to the Japanese way, then things go easy. Not only Japanese language skill but also understanding the personality of Japanese is necessary to make relationship with Japanese...Living in Japan over 10 years, it is gradually getting hard for me to become 100% Pakistani again...I feel it hard to go back to Pakistan again because my way of thinking has become totally replaced by a Japanese way (pp. 230–1).

The second narrative, 'They do not see who I am', described a failure to assimilate, attributing that to prejudice encouraged by the media or even to personal deficiencies. This narrative was associated with decreased social interaction, and feelings of meaninglessness, loss of control, and helplessness. The third narrative, 'I have become a better Muslim', stressed distinctiveness by focusing on religious belief and associated practices such as praying and abstaining from drinking alcohol. This was an empowering narrative that explained life in Japan as a path chosen by God:

> It is possible to adapt myself to the Japanese way. Maybe 80% of Bangladeshi in Japan are doing so – drinking alcohol and so on. But it is not my way. Adapting to the Japanese way is easier. If I change myself a bit, it is easier to earn more money and enjoy life. But that is not what I want. People look at me and think my life is boring with no enjoyment. But I do not wish anything if I have to give up my identity as Muslim (p. 234).

With this frame of reference, rejection and discrimination were attributed to Japan's status as a non-Muslim society which lacked the concept of universalism or brotherhood. This strategy of 'assertive distinctiveness' helped maintain a sense of control in the face of a socially ascribed inferior social position.

The Example of Immigrants to England from Former-Yugoslavia

The same feelings of loss of control of one's life, the dilemma of what mode of acculturation to adopt, and the threat to the continuity of a distinct identity, were again found in a qualitative study based on interviews with 24 adult immigrants to London or Birmingham, England, from former-Yugoslavia (some from Bosnia, some from Serbia, and others from Croatia) (Timotijevic & Breakwell, 2000). For example:

> It is a very anxious and stressful situation to have someone else always have the last word in relation to your life; you have no control over your life whatsoever; both here and there, and that's hard, I feel helpless (p. 363).

This group of immigrants, in repositioning themselves, or 'remooring' their identities as Deaux (2000) termed it, had to contend, not only with a complete change of social context and the stressors associated with leaving the home country (sometimes with a little warning but sometimes with scarcely time to pack a suitcase) and adjustments to a new country, but also with the break up of the former state in which they had lived. Like groups of immigrants elsewhere, they often felt keenly the negative ways in which they were represented to the British public in the media:

> I am a refugee, and that sounds terrible, really bad...When you say to the people here that you are a refugee, everyone turns their head away from you. But I understand those people. I could never imagine myself as a refugee – this just happened to me. I was at the wrong place, wrong time... (p. 366).

Like many people who have faced adversity in their lives, there was considerable consensus among this group of immigrants that their experiences of war and migration had also led to some positive self-change and increased responsibility and independence. For example, "I think that all the people that are in my position have learned to cope with life better...We are stronger and more prepared to sacrifice and value things in life" (p. 363).

EXPERIENCING HOMELESSNESS

Home is central to most of our lives, and to be without a home is a very basic form of adversity. Indeed, one prominent line of homelessness research has considered homeless people as being subject to more than the average amount of stressful life events and chronic life stressors. Seen in that light, homeless people are particularly vulnerable to experiencing distress and are faced with the task of finding ways of coping in the face of such events and circumstances. Besides the stress created by the sheer fact of homelessness – including the need to search for shelter and more permanent housing, and the stigma associated with homelessness – homeless people have been shown to experience more than their fair share of a variety of other stressful events and conditions. The latter include: unemployment, economic loss, criminal victimisation, marital and family conflict, dealing with organisations such as shelters, problems with the law, accidents, physical and mental illnesses, and drug and alcohol problems (Banyard, 1995; Muñoz et al., 1999; Wong & Piliavin, 2001). Not surprisingly there is evidence that homeless people are more than averagely distressed. In their study of several hundred people who were residing in shelters or were clients of food-providing agencies in one county in north California, USA, Wong and Piliavin (2001) reported that 64% were classified as 'possibly depressed' according to results on a standard scale, a percentage about three times that found in most general population studies in the USA. When most of the sample was successfully followed-up between 3 and 12 months later, distress was found to be significantly lower among those (approximately a third) who were now living in their own homes.

A number of studies have questioned whether homelessness is the cause or a consequence of traumatic events and circumstances and mental health and substance problems. They include a study of between 200 and 300 people recruited at random from two homeless shelters, a soup kitchen, a social services centre, and two of the routes used by a mobile on-the-spot service for homeless people in Madrid, Spain (Muñoz *et al.*, 1999); interviews with over 300 people living in single-room occupancy hotels or attending shelters, soup kitchens or drop-in centres in Chicago, USA (Johnson *et al.*, 1997); and a study in which 35 homeless people, between the ages of 14 and 25, using homeless youth services run by a charitable organisation in New South Wales, Australia, were interviewed at length (approximately three hours) (Martijn & Sharpe, 2006). The findings serve to caution against too ready an assumption that stressors are all a consequence of homelessness. The opposite assumption, which is often made, that problems such as those of mental ill-health or substance misuse, are more likely to be causes than consequences of homelessness, is equally questionable (Shinn, 1992). Martijn and Sharpe's (2006) findings, for example, suggested that nearly all of the young people had deteriorated significantly psychologically once they had become homeless (on average at the age of 16) and that traumatic events continued to be experienced. Their conclusion was that the experience of being homeless compounded pre-existing psychological differences for this group of young homeless people.

Like experiencing immigration, homelessness is another experience that threatens a person's sense of identity. 'Homeless person' is not a positively valenced category in western countries. It therefore gives homeless people the task, Farrington and Robinson (1999) suggested, of remedying the threat that such an identity poses for self-esteem, a task that social identity theory (Tajfel, 1981) suggests is likely to involve either trying to exit the group who are defined in that way, or else making favourable social comparisons with others in the group or with other groups (an alternative strategy, consisting of trying to change the attitudes of society so that the group is more favourably evaluated, they thought was an unlikely strategy for homeless people themselves to adopt – but see Chapter 10 for a different view of the empowerment of homeless people).

How homeless people use social comparison to ward off a negative self-evaluation was the subject of Farrington and Robinson's (1999) participant observation study carried out at a night shelter for homeless people in an English town. Twenty-one people were observed and talked to over a period of three months. All but one were men. The length of time spent homeless, defined not solely by rooflessness but by lack of satisfactory accommodation while living a homeless lifestyle (and ignoring brief periods when individuals had residencies), ranged from a few weeks to 15 years, averaging six years. Strategies for maintaining identity were found to be associated with length of time homeless. The participants could be divided into three groups. Those who had been homeless for 18 months or less did not identify themselves with other homeless people. They either distanced themselves by talking extensively about ceasing to be homeless, making favourable intra-group comparisons – for example by stressing their skills, travel experience, and coping abilities – identifying with shelter volunteers, or denying that they were homeless (e.g. "got my own flat, my own clothes, my own business", p. 184). An intermediate group, homeless for between two and four years, identified themselves with a sub-group of homeless people in a way that enabled a favourable comparison with other homeless people to be made. For example, one identified himself as a beggar and compared his group favourably with New Age Travellers; and two others said they had a squat, and distanced themselves from those who stayed in the shelter.

The largest group, of 12 people, had mostly been homeless for five years or more. In various ways they all identified themselves with homeless people. One sub-group, 'carers and sharers', compared themselves favourably with other homeless people, most noticeably in terms of the caring, protecting role that they played towards others in the homeless community (e.g. "I don't know why I bother sometimes. I spend most of every day seeing to people. I could just sit about like the others", p. 185). Another sub-group saw themselves as members of a family of homeless people, most of whom had street names depicting their areas of origin or physical characteristics, and who shared resources and supported one another. Contrary to the assumption in social identity theory that people in a stigmatised group would make social comparisons, a further sub-group accentuated their in-group similarity, making no comparisons with others. People in this sub-group categorised themselves as a 'typical dosser' or an 'old alcoholic', or made such statements as, "We're all in exactly the same situation" (p. 185). People in this group were acutely aware of their stigmatised position. For example, one did not want his family to see him, saying, "What must they think when they see me on the other side of the road?", and another said, "I'm a person too, I hate the way people look at me" (pp. 185–6).

Women Experiencing Homelessness

The study by Banyard (1995) is of special interest because, unlike most research that has been confined to the study of single homeless people (Shinn, 1992), she interviewed mothers who had at least one child under the age of 12 years living with them in one of three shelters in a small mid-western city in the USA. Understandably some of the stressors that her participants spoke of were related to the care and disciplining of their children in a strange environment that was not a family home. Furthermore, Banyard wrote of the 'web of stress' experienced by mothers since, in the descriptions they provided, women linked stressful situations together, making it difficult to categorise a stressor into one group or another. The interconnected nature of multiple stressors was illustrated by mothers who could not discuss child disciplinary problems without also discussing money problems that prohibited them from buying snacks or treats for the children, or the stress of being reprimanded in front of their children for breaking shelter rules. Banyard (1995) quoted one of the mothers in her study as saying, "I was so upset, I was mad. I mean, it's just like everything piled up on everything and then that smothered me" (pp. 879–80).

Banyard's (1995) interest was in the ways of coping described by women living in shelters for homeless mothers. Contrary to some earlier work on the psychology of coping with stressful circumstances, which has depicted women as often engaging in passive, 'emotional' coping, Banyard reported much 'active' coping, often to do with home search, care and discipline of children, and coping with bureaucracy. They also described a great deal of what Banyard called 'relational' coping. Although over half of the women reported that there were people, often family members, to whom they could no longer turn for help and support, a number described identifying with the group of mothers living in the shelter and the comfort and strength they could draw from that. The following are two examples:

> Most of my support comes from other residents here, you know, because a lot of us are going through the same things, you know, and so, you kind of sit back and talk to someone else that's going through the same thing you're going through and it kind of makes it a little bit, you know, better that you're not the only one in the world that the world is picking on (p. 884).

Patient endurance was another common coping strategy, as was thinking positively:

> My cup is always half full. I try to be optimistic...gotta have happy thoughts and have a lot of hope and faith...Then I just talk to myself, you know, trying to tell myself that I can handle any situation (p. 886).

Zugazaga (2004) interviewed equal numbers of single men, single women, and women with children (54 of each) residing in emergency homeless shelters in the central Florida area in the USA. Interviews lasted on average about 30 minutes with an emphasis on experience of stressful life events. All three groups were very likely to have experienced a range of economic, social, and personal events. In addition, both groups of women were very likely to have experienced physical and/or sexual violence/abuse either as a child or adult; and the two groups of single homeless people were more likely to have experienced incarceration and/or alcohol or drug misuse (particularly for single men) or serious mental illness and psychiatric hospitalisation (particularly for single women). The homeless women with children were significantly younger (average 30 years compared to 40 or more for the single groups) and had an average of nearly two children (average age six years) living with them in the shelter.

Reporting their study of poor New York mothers seeking emergency shelter accommodation for the first time, Toohey et al. (2004) expressed concern about the rise in homelessness among US families and the need to attend to the special needs, experiences, and risk factors applying to homeless women who had children with them. They were interested in the women's social networks, finding that the newly homeless women were in fact more likely than an equally poor comparison group of mothers (the large majority of both groups were from ethnic minority groups, those entering the shelter were mostly African USAmerican, the poor but housed group mostly Latin USAmerican) to report having a mother or grandmother and other close relative living in the city, with whom they were in touch. The homeless women, however, were significantly less likely to report that these relatives (and the same was true for close friends) had room for them and would allow them to stay in their homes. It was therefore not impoverished social networks to which the women's homelessness could be attributed, but rather the fact that they could not stay with family or friends due to family conflict, family or friends being too poor to help, or their homes being too small.

Being Young and Homeless

From studies of young homeless people in Wales in the late 1980s and very early 1990s come the following quotations, illustrating the multiple stresses involving in being homeless:

> On the streets basically . . . I'd nip on the buses and sleep on there, and I'd get kicked off there at four in the morning. I'd just be wandering around. I was in a hell of a state like, rundown (Hutson & Liddiard, 1994, p. 129).

> Not being able to have a wash and clean clothes, going without food, getting attacked and things like that . . . I mean, I got raped (p. 130).

Unlike the staff of homelessness agencies, interviewed as part of the same Welsh studies, who universally saw the experience of homelessness as a negative one, some of the young homeless people interviewed by Hutson and Liddiard viewed the experience in a more positive or at least a mixed light. For example:

> I lived on the streets for four months . . . Well, the way I look at it now it's just part of life. I've learnt to survive (p. 133).

That confirmed the conclusions drawn by Brandon et al. (1980) who had interviewed young people who were using the services of emergency accommodation projects in central London in the 1970s. They had reported that roughly one-third described the experience of being homeless in London in almost entirely negative terms, another third described the experience mostly negatively with some positive elements, and a third described it in largely or mostly positive terms. Nor did all the young people interviewed by Hutson and Liddiard accept the identity 'homeless' person. For example, asked whether she saw herself as homeless, one of their participants replied, "Well, no, because I've got a home to go to, and yes, because I can't go there" (p. 140). On the other hand others did feel 'homeless':

> . . . the main time when I got kicked out. Not the other times because I always went to friends . . . But the main time, when I had to go to the City Council and there was a big sign saying 'Homeless' and an arrow. When I saw that, I knew that I was homeless. It struck home (pp. 138–9).

Some of the 25 16–19 year olds from Drumchapel, a large peripheral public sector housing estate in Glasgow, Scotland, interviewed by Fitzpatrick (2000), gave evidence that they had accepted an identity as homeless. One group of young men were living, not just temporarily, in hostels for homeless adults. This group appeared to Fitzpatrick to have become resigned to hostel living at a young age. Another group, who spent some time sleeping rough in the city centre, and at other times living in hostels, had developed a friendship network consisting largely of other homeless young people. As one young man put it:

> The mates I grew up wi', most of them have got their ain hooses noo and have got their lives sorted oot. I class them as arseholes noo. And the people that I meet up the toon that are homeless, I class them as good mates. Noo I'm homeless I'm a different class fae all the mates I grew up wi' and went tae school wi' (p. 97).

Ways of Understanding Homelessness

Attempts have been made to think about homelessness, not as a condition, but as a process, referring to phases, pathways, careers, and situations (Hutson & Liddiard, 1994; Fitzpatrick, 2000; Clapham, 2003). One influence on that thinking has been evidence that homelessness is for many people a temporary circumstance, and for others a changing one in which periods of greater or lesser homelessness alternate with periods of stable housing (Sosin, 2003; Thompsett et al., 2003). In fact there is no single, agreed definition of homelessness. The term is sometimes confined to those who are 'literally' homeless – sleeping on the street, in vehicles, in abandoned buildings, or in other places not normally thought suitable for human habitation – although most research on the subject has acknowledged a much larger group of homeless people (Shinn, 1992). We might think of a spectrum of homelessness ranging from those who are 'roofless' or 'sleeping rough' to those who are living in conditions in their own homes that are intolerable for reasons such as physical over-crowding or abusive relationships. In between are those living in temporary hostel or night shelter accommodation, living long term in institutions because of lack of alternative accommodation, those in bed and breakfast or similar accommodation that is unsuitable in the long term, and those living in insecure accommodation with friends, under notice to quit, or squatting (Anderson & Christian, 2003).

Hutson and Liddiard described three phases in the homelessness careers of young people in Wales: an early phase in which living with friends was common and periods of sleeping rough infrequent and short-lived; a middle phase in which greater use was made of residential projects for homeless people and periods of sleeping rough lengthened to two weeks or more; and a late phase which involved using traditional homelessness hostels and squats, with periods of sleeping rough lengthening further. The more advanced the phase the more visible was homelessness and the greater difficulty the person appeared to have in obtaining employment and exiting homelessness.

In Glasgow, Fitzpatrick (2000) described six youth homelessness types or 'pathways'. Like Hutson and Liddiard's phases, Fitzpatrick's six pathways or types differed according to the relative amounts of time spent moving around friends' and relatives' houses, returning to the family home, using special residential accommodation for homeless young people, using traditional hostel accommodation, or sleeping rough. An additional factor highlighted by Fitzpatrick was created by the geographical separation of the Drumchapel estate, where the young people came from, and Glasgow city centre several miles away. A number of the young people interviewed were fiercely loyal to their local area, valued the continuation of social contacts in the area, and were fearful of being homeless in the city centre. Others had migrated to the city and some had cut their ties with their local area. Again, the varying visibility of homelessness, a matter stressed by so many writers on the subject, emerged in the context of youth homelessness in Glasgow. The more homelessness was characterised by the use of a mix of forms of accommodation, including friends and returning home, and the more it was confined to the local home area, the more hidden it was. The more it was characterised by use of home-lessness accommodation and sleeping rough in the city centre, the more visible it became.

A feature of the academic and policy literatures on homelessness is the existence, side by side, of some very different models, or ways of seeing, the phenomenon. In that respect homelessness is an excellent example of the existence of the com-peting perspectives that are available for conceptualising the kinds of experiences focused upon in the present chapter and throughout much of the book. Broadly speaking, individual or person-centred explanations for homelessness can be con-trasted with structural explanations (Shinn, 1992; Clapham, 2003). Person-centred accounts sometimes are explicitly blaming; holding, for example, that homeless people choose to be homeless and are unmotivated to work or to acquire settled homes of their own, or that some homeless young women deliberately get preg-nant in order to achieve a higher priority status for public housing. That individual culpability model of homelessness (Hutson & Liddiard, 1994) is more common in political and media discourse.

More common in academic and professional writings is a deficit or pathologi-cal model that highlights possible individual causes of homelessness such as pre-existing mental illness or substance misuse. Such ways of seeing homelessness afford little place to structural factors such as the availability of affordable housing that fits people's needs, to rates of unemployment and poverty, or to the current welfare system that provides greater or lesser access to housing and other benefits for particular groups of people. Those explanations that place emphasis on such structural factors, sometimes termed the 'political' model (Hutson & Liddiard, 1994), have been criticised for viewing homeless people as passive and powerless victims of the structures of society, in the same way that individual models can be accused of explicitly or implicitly blaming homelessness on individuals and ignoring the social and political context in which homelessness occurs.

Some person-centred models acknowledge the fact that structural factors com-pound existing individual pathology or that individual problems confer vulner-ability to homelessness which is partly caused by structural factors (Shinn, 1992; Hutson & Liddiard, 1994). The latter type of explanation views individual factors as determinants of who becomes homeless and does not assume that such factors constitute the sole cause. Factors at the individual level remain, nonetheless, the principal focus of attention.

In the Welsh study, while agencies that dealt with youth homelessness often stressed structural determinants and the lack of choice some young people had in becoming homeless, the accounts given by young homeless people themselves placed a much greater emphasis on their role as active, decision-making individu-als, and on individual explanations for homelessness. As one young man said:

> I'm a fool to myself as well like. I've got to admit that. I have had some problems and some I've brought on myself because I'm stupid (Hutson & Liddiard, 1994, p. 134).

In the Scottish study, which found evidence for much family conflict preceding youth homelessness, young people most often blamed both themselves and their parents or step-parents. Structural or political explanations for their homelessness were rare among participants in both studies. In that study only one young person located any blame for his problems in the political sphere, even then combining it with attributing blame to a parent:

> If it wasnae for him [his father] I wouldnae be here [adult hostel], and if it wasnae for the Government I wouldnae be here. So it's equal parts (Fitzpatrick, 2000, p. 81).

Hutson and Liddiard (1994) also found that when responsibility was ever directed at structural factors such as the economy or government policy, blame was often directed personally at a particular individual such as the prime minister. Young homeless people themselves, it seems, find it as difficult as academics and policy makers to come to a satisfactory, rounded way of seeing homelessness which acknowledges the importance of both kinds of factor (Anderson & Christian, 2003). It was certainly the case that in the 1980s, under the UK Conservative government's New Right Ideology, associated with championing of the free market and minimal intervention by the state, recorded levels of homelessness in Britain escalated (Anderson & Christian, 2003). Youth homelessness, in particular, increased as youth unemployment increased, the number of single-person households rose, the availability of affordable public or private rented accommodation fell, and young people's entitlement to welfare benefits was restricted (Fitzpatrick, 2000).

Between-country differences in welfare provision affecting homelessness, and differences in attitudes towards homelessness, have been of interest to a number of writers on the subject. They include Anderson and Christian (2003), who pointed out the contrast between the European approach to welfare, typified by Britain's welfare state after the Second World War, at least until the 1980s, based on a universalist orientation, and the more selective, lesser state intervention approach favoured in the USA. They include also Thompsett et al. (2003), who compared attitudes to homelessness among general population samples of several hundred residents of the USA and of Germany. They expected differences on the grounds that Germany is a more collectivist culture, placing a higher value on interpersonal harmony and the welfare of others, in contrast to the more individualistic USA. Germany, they pointed out, also had a more comprehensive unemployment benefit system, and there was evidence that the prevalence of homelessness was lower in Germany than in the USA. In their own study they confirmed the latter difference: the lifetime reported prevalence of 'literal' homelessness being 6.2% for the US sample and 2.4% for the German (corresponding figures for any type of homelessness including 'precarious housing', were 12.9% and 5.6%). As predicted, the German respondents demonstrated higher scores on scales assessing general compassion towards homeless people, the trustworthiness of homeless people, and economic factors as causes of homelessness, but *lower* scores on a scale assessing personal failings as causes and *less* of a preference for limiting the rights of homeless peo-ple (e.g. to sleep in public or to beg). In both countries younger people and those with liberal rather than conservative political affiliations achieved higher scores on trustworthiness of the homeless and economic factors as causes, and the same was true of women compared to men in the USA.

THE UNEMPLOYED AND THE UNDER-EMPLOYED

The numbers of people of working age who are unemployed can be counted in a variety of different ways. Indeed the way in which the UK government counted the number of unemployed people in Britain changed more than 30 times between the early 1980s and the late 1990s, mostly in a direction that made it appear that the number of unemployed people was falling to a greater extent than was actu-ally the case (Fryer, 1998). A variety of different estimates for the UK were cited by Fryer. The government figure for those entitled to claim unemployment bene-fits provided one official estimate. The Labour Force Survey definition, based on numbers not currently working but actively seeking paid work and available to start within two weeks, yielded a higher figure. The Broad Labour Force Survey definition, including those who wanted paid work but were not actively seeking it for a variety of reasons, including not believing that a job was available, produced a figure around twice the official government one. Fryer also estimated the num-ber of unemployed people in all OECD countries to be over 30 million and cited an International Labour Organisation estimate of one billion people unemployed world-wide.

In a review paper, Fryer (1990) concluded that, while research of the 1930s and the 1980s converged in their findings of the effects of unemployment upon mental health, the way those effects were explained had been very different. Whereas in the 1930s the explanation was largely provided in terms of the effects on people of increased poverty and material deprivation caused by unemployment, in the 1980s the dominant explanation had been in terms of deprivation of the psychological resources that employment provides or the psychological functions that it serves (interestingly enough, writing from an historical perspective, Burnett, 1994, noted the unparalleled quantity of autobiographical writing by unemployed people in response to the unprecedented levels of unemployment of the 1920s and 1930s, and, by comparison, the relative dearth of such writing associated with the unem-ployment of half a century later). Most influential had been Jahoda's (e.g. 1982, based on work in the Austrian village of Marienthal in the 1930s) concept of the 'latent functions' served by employment, principally time structure, social contact, collective purpose, status, and regular activity. Like other psychological theories of unemployment that came after it (e.g. Warr, 1987), unemployment was seen in that light as a form of psychological deprivation. The 'manifest function' of work – earning a living – received comparatively little attention in such theories, and the likely psychological effects of material difficulties consequent upon unemploy-ment, and in particular of sheer poverty, were minimised. Fryer (1990) pointed out that psychologists had in any case taken little interest in poverty, perhaps deeming it outside the remit of the discipline, perhaps believing that poverty was a thing of the past or that unemployment crossed socioeconomic class boundaries and hence that poverty itself was not the issue. Much of the unemployment research literature, according to Fryer and Fagan (2003), has paid lip service to the role of income-related factors during unemployment and hence has minimised it, partly due to dominant theories such as Jahoda's that emphasised loss of the latent rather than the manifest rewards of employment.

Those academic ways of trying to understand unemployment are mirrored in unemployed people's own ways of talking about their experiences. In his study of male respectability, consumption, and unemployment in the community of Cauldmoss in central Scotland, Wight (1993) explicitly focused on the material aspects of unemployment rather than the latent benefits of employment. He found that very few men, particularly those over about 25 years of age, coped with unemployment by changing their orientation towards paid work. Employment was central to male identity and the unemployed still aspired to fulfil the same fundamental roles as those who were in work. Even in the face of 30% male unemployment, he commented, there was no evidence of the development of an alternative subculture or counter-culture. He cited the example of mothers, worried about being able to afford Christmas presents for their children, never bemoaning the expense of children's wishes, nor criticising the advertising that was stimulating the demand. As Vogel (1999, cited by Wacker, 2001, p. 321) put it, "The unemployed struggle with themselves, but do not fight against society". Burnett (1994), too, in his historical analysis, found less evidence, in accounts of late twentieth-century unemployment, of collective activity in the face of unemployment than was the case in earlier times.

The Unemployment Experience

Much has been written about the effects of unemployment on the individuals who experience it. A focus of the chapter on unemployment in Wight's (1993) book about Cauldmoss in Scotland was the effects on unemployed men's feelings of respectability. Being seen by oneself and others as a 'hard worker', Wight found to be key for reputation and respectability. Middle-aged and older unemployed men in particular spoke of the shame of being idle. Among the things that were most keenly felt were the inability to buy a round of drinks for friends in the pub, the inability to keep one's car running, and the pressure that was felt to take a job of lesser status or pay than a man had been used to. A range of activities to which an unemployed man might have recourse were described, varying in their implications for maintaining respectability. Doing part-time work, but only if it was paid, was respectable, but 'mooching a drink' (asking someone else to buy you a drink without being able to reciprocate) was clearly not. In between were activities such as hitching a free ride from someone else, which was generally to be avoided if at all possible, and 'coal howking' (collecting low-grade coal from abandoned open-cast sites or exposed seams) or collecting other types of free fuel such as wood or peat – more likely to be regarded as an honourable way of coping, being a return to an historical practice in the area and close to 'real work'. It was noted that domestic, gender roles remained entrenched despite a man's lack of employment outside the home. Indeed gender boundaries, rather than being open to change, appeared often to be more strongly defended during a husband's unemployment.

In their study of male unemployment in a white, working-class, urban area in the English West Midlands, Willott and Griffin (1996) concluded that unemployment threatened two key aspects of traditional masculine identity: the man as 'bread-winner' or good domestic provider, and a man's freedom to move and pay his way in the public sphere. Like the men studied by Wight in Scotland, being able to afford to spend time in the pub was important to many of these men's sense of identity. They too felt the pressure to take low paid jobs. The threat that wives would find another man who was not unemployed was also common. Although some men placed themselves in women's positions – recognising through experience that unpaid domestic work could be 'just as hard', or saying such things as, "most blokes nowadays are more domesticated than women ..." (p. 88) – the most common strategy was one that protected the 'man as breadwinner' discourse and in various ways (casual work, 'fiddling', 'thieving') maintained the position of a man in the public realm, and women in the private, domesticated, presumed subordinate, position.

A paper by Drewery (1998) adopted the approach – unusual in the academic/professional literature – of providing the story of just one person, Somya (not her real name), who had been caught up in the economic changes and rising unemployment that occurred in New Zealand, as elsewhere, in the 1980s and into the 1990s. Somya had lost her night-cleaning job when her employer lost his contract, and her husband had been made redundant. At around the same time a number of school and health problems involving her children and other close relatives came to the fore and Somya was a main source of support for several of them, including providing temporary accommodation for a relative and her children (which helped with family expenses). A main theme of this account was that, despite Somya playing a number of responsible roles during that time – concerned neighbour, partner, mother, hub of the family, and community volunteer – the circumstances of unemployment increasingly made her feel that the position of herself and her family as autonomous, responsible citizens was being undermined. The public focus on the availability of jobs – 'if only they would go and look' – and the need for families to learn to budget better, forced her to have to resist the implications of laziness, although she knew how difficult it was in practice to find work. Unsuccessful attempts to phone up about jobs, making an effort to follow up a lead from the employment service only to find that the job had been filled, or queuing for two or three hours at the employment service office only to be told that jobs had gone, were among Somya's and her partner's experiences. There seemed to be an assumption that welfare claimants had little else to do with their time. Somya described how she and her husband now felt themselves to be objects of welfare regulation rather than autonomous actors in their own right:

> It's the most degrading thing to be on this dole. They can cut it off, and stop it when they feel like it. Then you've got to reapply and get it all back, and wait, but in the meantime, you've got to live ... and she had the cheek to tell me when I rung her up ... 'You're not supposed to go on holiday, or if you do, you have to tell them', and all this and that, but you've gotto stop the dole, then you've got to restart it all when you come back, and you've got to wait, and then she

> said, 'Oh, and when you're on the dole...you're not allowed to go overseas, you're just not entitled to it', she said...and if you've got redundancy you're not allowed to get the dole until you've spent that, you know, you can't put that in for when you retire, because you're just not allowed to save money on the dole, you've got to pick it up this week, spend it this week, ready for next week (pp. 110–11).

The autobiographies and other material collected by Burnett (1994) show that many of such trials associated with unemployment are by no means new. Burnett commented that attitudes towards unemployed people have always been a mix of humanity and distrust, the balance between the two changing with ideological values of the time. He pointed, for example, to the close parallel between Victorian anxiety to distinguish between the 'deserving' and the 'undeserving' poor and more recent government campaigns to root out welfare 'scroungers'.

A recurring response to unemployment over the centuries, according to Burnett, has been the tendency to withdraw from social contact. From an Australian study of people attending a Skillshare programme for long-term unemployed people came a similar mention of the theme of social withdrawal, explained by one participant as follows:

> It [the coping process] only breaks down when other people start talking about all the things they're doing... You're not jealous of them but you feel a little bit, 'Oh God, what have we done wrong?' (Patton & Donohue, 1998, p. 337).

The same theme recurred in Wight's (1963) account of male unemployment in central Scotland. Older men in particular felt they had to withdraw from social activities, keep out of public life, and lead a frugal lifestyle.

The material deprivations associated with unemployment are another constant. In his review of his own (McGhee & Fryer, 1989) and others' work on poverty and unemployment, Fryer (1990) wrote of the drastic drop in living standards regularly found to be associated with unemployment, debt as a common feature, poor diet, and a decline in all sorts of activities that would require the outlay of money. In Cauldmoss, Wight (1993) documented the severe reduction in average family spending associated with unemployment, with proportionately more being spent on fuel, food and alcohol, balanced by large savings in clothing, cars and entertainment. Families were very conscious of needing to make choices, and certain commodities, such as a colour television, Christmas presents for children, and regular meat in the diet, were generally considered priorities. Often families felt they had no alternative but to use expensive credit facilities in order, for example, to afford children's Christmas presents.

Ball and Orford (2002) reported the results of interviewing 24 19–34 year olds, unemployed for at least 12 months, recruited from Jobcentres in inner city Birmingham, England. The sample was equally divided between men and women and between those of Anglo-British, African-Caribbean, and South Asian descent. The primary concern of the study was the ways in which unemployed people might have chosen to compensate for unemployment by developing meaningful activities alternative to formal employment. A main conclusion was that it was possible to find a pattern of activity that was 'meaningful' – one that was challenging, required sustained effort and commitment, and was valued by others. Such patterns of activity – whether domestic, work-like, educational or social – were therefore similar in important respects to good quality formal employment. The results were seen as consistent with Fryer's (e.g. 1986, 1990) agency theory. It is a general theory but one that has arisen specifically in the context of the study of unemployment. Fryer (1990, p. 167) viewed an unemployed person, like everyone else, "...as an active, initiating, future oriented agent, striving to make sense of, and influence events". At the same time agency is, "...limited, restricted, frustrated, discouraged and undercut..." (Fryer, 1986, p.15) by the environment and circumstances. Some people's lives are more restrictive of agency than others. Agency theory has also received support from other studies in Britain and Australia showing how active many people are in the face of unemployment in finding meaningful alternatives to paid work while maintaining pro-employment values and aspirations (Fryer & Payne, 1984; Patton & Donohue, 1998).

One of the most striking features of Ball and Orford's analysis was the extent to which, despite the varied ways in which meaningful and occupying activity patterns could be achieved in the absence of formal employment, unemployment was nevertheless associated with a sense of stigma. People felt excluded from things that it was thought others took for granted such as buying a car or obtaining a mortgage, not being able to afford latest fashions and perhaps as a result refusing invitations, having to 'sign on' for unemployment benefit, needing to admit to the status of unemployment when filling in forms, or deliberating avoiding letting other people know you were unemployed – for example, by unnecessarily paying for a bus pass that was free to unemployed people:

> You're worthless, your worth is nothing. If you (referring to the interviewer) go into a shop with your cheque book and I go there with my unemployment card they're gonna send me home and pamper you, because you've got what it takes, you've got that...that trust...It's like when you watch television, everybody's doing something, nobody's unemployed on television. Even to be on Blind Date [a popular TV programme at the time which involved one person choosing, from a number of contestants, a partner for a holiday trip together] you have to be in a job. Even on game shows you don't hear people saying, 'I'm unemployed, I've been unemployed for two years, and I'm here because I need the money'.
>
> I feel as if everybody knows, I feel as if when I go out anywhere you've got this big 'U' on your head. I can't bring myself to tell people I'm unemployed. I'd rather lie to the people I don't know, I can't tell people. I absolutely cringe (pp. 389–90).

It is not surprising to find, therefore, that unemployment is associated with poorer health. Although the existence of such an association raises the question of cause and effect, the evidence is strong for the claim that, in large part, it is unemployment that causes a decline in health. The evidence comes from longitudinal studies, often involving large numbers, carried out in a range of countries including Australia, the USA and a number of European countries, and including measures of both mental and physical health (Dooley & Catalano, 1988; Warr et al., 1988; Fryer, 1990, 1998; Reine et al., 2004). Fryer (1998) has warned against too simple a dichotomising of social causation (unemployment causes ill-health in this case) and individual drift (people with poorer health tend to 'drift' into unemployment). Although the evidence is overwhelming for social causation in the case of unemployment and health, he acknowledged that 'drift' is likely to be a factor in some instances, and that for others, reduced chances of obtaining work is likely to be one effect of poorer health. The two processes can be viewed as intertwined as part of the dynamics of labour market experiences (Fryer, 1998; Fergusson *et al.*, 2001).

Young and Unemployed

In recent decades unemployment has fallen as heavily upon young people as on any age group. In Cauldmoss, for example, the rate of unemployment among young men in the mid-1980s was as high as 53%, compared to 22% among older men (Wight, 1993). The young unemployed were less attached than older men to the idea that working was important, even if it meant working for low pay or under poor conditions, and their elders were sometimes critical of young people's attitudes. For their part young unemployed men were concerned about not being able to afford to dress to the standard of their peer group, being excluded from places for meeting young women, and the likelihood that girls would not find a young man attractive who was unemployed and had no money (Willott & Griffin, 1996, are others who have raised questions about the likely effects of youth unemployment on heterosexual relationships).

Kieselbach (2003) took a European perspective, looking at the effects of youth unemployment (under 25 years of age) on six types of social exclusion (shown in Figure 7.3) in three northern European countries – Sweden, Belgium and Germany – and three southern European countries – Spain, Italy and Greece. He pointed out that the rate of youth unemployment (1997 figures) was higher than the overall unemployment rate in all six countries. In five of those countries (Germany being the exception), the youth rate was nearly two or more times the overall rate. Fifty interviews were carried out in each country with young adults aged 20 to 24 years, unemployed for at least 12 months. Kieselbach distinguished three groups varying in the extent of their social exclusion – low, intermediate, and high risk. The conclusion was that among the most important vulnerability factors for social exclusion were low qualifications, a precarious financial situation, poor social support, and poor institutional support. Social support was the most important protective factor, with the family being a more important source of support in the southern European countries, and institutional and social network support of greater importance in northern Europe. Kieselbach also highlighted personal factors such as proactivity and self-esteem and mental health. Those in the highest risk group often exhibited 'passivity' towards the labour market, seeing few or no chances of finding regular work, and often stopping seeking work or making efforts to enhance qualifications.

Kieselbach provided a case example to illustrate each of the three risk groups: the 21-year-old Spanish woman used to illustrate the intermediate group provides a good example of the precarious nature of much employment. After leaving school at the age of 15 she had worked intermittently at several jobs, but always without a formal contract; her mother is also described as working in precarious jobs, and the area in which she lived contained many people dependent on irregular work, with petty crime common. She is said to have been protected by emotional and

Labour market exclusion

Economic forces create barriers to employment for those with relatively few skills. Failure to enter, or re-entering, the workforce induces feelings of marginality and of being of little value to society.

Economic exclusion

Poverty induced or sustained by labour market exclusion leads to financial dependency on the welfare state and the loss of ability to financially support oneself or one's family at the norm for society.

Institutional exclusion

The poor and unemployed do not have access to private institutions (e.g. banks, insurance companies) that others can turn to for help in reducing the uncertainties of life. Instead, the unemployed must turn to state institutions that serve marginalised persons. This can induce feelings of dependency that lead to shame and passivity.

Social isolation

These circumstances lead to loss of, or retreat from, one's social network and the reduction of social contacts.

Cultural exclusion

The inability to live according to the socially accepted norms and values leads to stigma and sanctions from the social surroundings.

Spatial exclusion

All the above circumstances lead to geographic concentration and segregation of persons with limited financial possibilities. They often live in areas with missing infrastructure (e.g. lack of transportation, shops, cultural events).

Figure 7.3   Six forms of social exclusion associated with youth unemployment
Source: reproduced with permission from Kieselbach, T. (2003). Long-term unemployment among young people: the risk of social exclusion. *American Journal of Community Psychology*, **32**, 69–76

economic support, especially from her mother, and she herself thought that she would always be able to find 'submerged' jobs and be able to survive.

Bolam and Sixsmith (2002) interviewed 18–25-year-old unemployed people in an English West Midlands market town, regarding their experiences of further education (FE). Among the factors that had previously been found to act as barriers to participation in FE among long-term unemployed people were: financial concerns, travel distance, lack of clear information regarding courses, low educational achievement, negative education experiences, negative perceptions of the college environment, lack of confidence, and sceptical attitudes towards the advantages of educational qualifications in the marketplace. Many of these same factors were confirmed in their own study. People were concerned, for example, about how they would survive financially, and people might find themselves in the bind of starting to study in order to secure long-term occupational goals but having to drop out if a job became available. Bolam and Sixsmith wrote in their conclusions about the fortitude and determination shown by those who had overcome material and psychological barriers in the way of participating in FE. They made an important statement, of very general applicability to the people who feature in the present chapter, when they stated that the young long-term unemployed people who took part in their study were neither passive victims of circumstances nor simply people who could pull themselves up by their own efforts: "Instead, what we see in these accounts is a complex intermingling of structure and agency within which these young people are reflexive social actors responding to the constraints and consequences of their lived circumstances..." (p. 349).

Forms of Under-Employment

Until the late 1980s and 1990s research focused almost exclusively on the dichotomous variable of employment versus unemployment. Since then there has been increased interest in recognising hidden forms of unemployment or the idea that employment and unemployment might lie on a continuum or that there might be, in addition to unemployment, forms of 'under-employment' which might be equally if not more stressful (Dooley, 2003). Fryer (1998) cited a figure for the so-called Slack Labour Force, which included those on employment and training schemes and under-employed part-time workers – in excess of five million in the UK at the time. In a dissertation based on interviews with nearly 100 unemployed men and women in one area near Berlin, Vogel (1999, see Wacker, 2001) referred to the unemployment in the former East German Democratic Republic after German reunification as a historically new type, the so-called *Umbruchsarbeitslosigkeit* or unemployment in the context of radical social change. The rate of unemployment in the area at the time was 15% but only 40% were in regular jobs, 33% were precariously employed and others held jobs in public job-creation companies.

Concern about under-employment arose in the USA in the 1990s, at a time of decreasing unemployment, because of the fear that the globalisation of the world economy and associated labour restructuring, and stricter limits on welfare assistance, had given rise to a polarisation of jobs into those that were stable, full-time, well paying and offering benefits and prospects, and those, on the other hand, that were unstable, poorly paid, often part-time and lacking in those respects (Jensen & Slack, 2003). A number of forms of under-employment have been recognised, as shown in Figure 7.4, based on the idea that people may be formally employed but under-employed in a number of ways: because they are working part-time but would prefer to work more hours, because their earnings scarcely lift them above the official poverty line, or because they are working well below the kind of occupation suggested by their educational level. A further type is the 'discouraged worker' or 'passive unemployed' or 'sub-unemployed', who is not currently seeking work and who is therefore often omitted from the group recognised to be unemployed. Even this categorisation system leaves a lot to be desired. For example: there is always criticism of the current official figures; additional benefits that some receive over and above basic wage or salary, and the lack of such benefits for many, are not taken into account; it is not easy to define under-employment for those who

---

Unemployed

> Those not working but who have been looking for work or are currently laid off.

Under-employed by low hours

> Those who are involuntarily working less than 35 hours a week because they cannot find full-time employment.

Under-employed by low income

> Those whose labour market earnings in the previous year, adjusted for weeks and hours worked, put them below the poverty threshold for a single individual living alone.

Under-employed by occupational mismatch

> Those whose educational level is significantly greater than the average educational level for those working in the same occupation.

Discouraged worker

> Those not currently working and who are not looking for work because they feel no jobs are available.

Figure 7.4   Forms of under-employment
Source: Jensen, L. & Slack, T. (2003). Underemployment in America: measurement and evidence. *American Journal of Community Psychology*, **32**, 21–31

benefit from a family business or from the income of another family breadwinner; and agricultural workers are an example of a group who are often self-employed and for whom under-employment is therefore not easily estimated. In fact early dissatisfaction with the simple employment–unemployment dichotomy arose in the developing world where a high proportion of all adults are engaged in small-scale agriculture or other forms of self- or semi-employment (Jensen & Slack, 2003).

Using data from US Current Population Surveys for the period 1990 to 2000, Jensen and Slack (2003) showed how under-employment (including unemployment) peaked in the USA at just over 20% in the early 1990s, with low income under-employment the largest category. Using data from 2000, they also showed the higher rate for women (15% versus 12% for men) and for black, Latin USAmerican and native USAmerican groups (between 20 and 23% compared with 11% for Whites), for young adults (29% for 18–24 year olds compared to 10–12% for older groups) and an uneven distribution across types of industry (highs of 23% and 19% in extractive and wholesale and retail sectors and a low of 7% in finance, insurance and real estate). The strongest relationship was with educational level, varying from a high of 29% for those with less than high school completion to a low of 7% for those with college degrees or higher. Surveys in the USA (Friedland & Price, 2003) and in the UK (Bardasi & Francesconi, 2004) have found some confirmation for the expectation that under-employment would be associated with ill-health. Evidence from longitudinal studies of youth and young adults in the USA showed that low self-esteem, alcohol misuse, and depression were each affected by becoming or remaining under-employed in much the same way as was true for unemployment (Dooley, 2003).

Thus the experiences of the unemployed and under-employed illustrate themes we have met several times in the present chapter. They include multiple stresses, uncertainty and a precarious existence, meeting with prejudice, and the need to maintain individual and collective respect and identity. Women and young people have their particular experiences of the forms of disempowerment we have considered. A number of the same themes will appear again in the next chapter where we look at three further types of disempowering experience.

Chapter 8

DISEMPOWERED BECAUSE OF INCOME, GENDER, OR SEXUAL ORIENTATION

THE POOR AND SOCIALLY EXCLUDED

This first section of Chapter 8 draws exclusively on two important reports. We shall shortly consider a report on social exclusion in a number of western European countries. That report provides a great deal of insight into the circumstances in which live some of the groups most likely to be excluded from the general wealth and lifestyle enjoyed by most people in the European Union. But first, this section on poverty summarises some of the information to be found in the highly influential *Voices of the Poor* report, which documents in great detail the circumstances faced by poor people in many of the poorer parts of the world. As much space has been given to summarising that report than has been given in the present book to any one source. There are a number of reasons for that. One is on account of the methods used to obtain information, using participatory research of the kind advocated in Chapter 3. As the title of the report suggests, it tries – and in the present author's view succeeds admirably – to give a real feel of the experience of poverty. At the same time it places the local, micro-level, everyday experience of poor people in a wider framework of local, area, national, and even international relationships of power and influence. A further interest in the report for us is its frequent use of the idea of social capital which was studied in some detail in Chapter 6 – indeed the report provides many examples of what it means in practice to be lacking in forms of social capital. A note of caution should be entered, however. The studies that constitute the *Voices of the Poor* report were conducted under the auspices of the World Bank – itself a centre of immense power. As Gaventa and Cornwall (2001) pointed out, there is a danger that participatory methods can be co-opted by the powerful.

Voices of the Poor

Voices of the Poor (Narayan *et al.*, 2000) is a review of 81 Participatory Poverty Assessment (PPAs) reports of studies conducted in 50 countries in the 1990s. The PPAs used qualitative methods and endeavoured to capture what poor people themselves say about the realities of their lives. In total the review drew on discussions with over 40,000 poor women and men. As stated in Chapter 1 of the report, "Despite an age of unprecedented global prosperity and the existence of a worldwide network of poverty-reduction institutions, poverty persists and is intensifying among certain groups and in certain regions around the world" (p. 11). The PPAs sought to understand poverty in its local social, institutional and political context.

Poverty is shown to be a multidimensional phenomenon. Figure 8.1 shows a summary of one aspect of poverty as described by the poor in Vietnam. But poverty was rarely defined solely in terms of income; in fact it was more usually spoken of in terms of managing physical, human, social and environmental assets as ways of coping with vulnerability. Definitions varied by gender, age and culture. For example in Ghana, younger men stressed ability to generate income, older men cited status connected to a traditional agricultural lifestyle as most important, and women defined poverty in terms of food insecurity. The PPA reports were full of accounts of households coping by reducing the quality, quantity or frequency of meals. Poverty was often defined in terms of violation of social norms, not being able to keep up with local customs and norms. In several instances the poor in urban areas, although worse off materially than those in comparable rural areas, were viewed as less poor because of their access to infrastructure and basic services. Entire communities might be considered poor because they lacked such basic amenities as water, sanitation, electricity, roads, school teachers, and much more.

One of the report's conclusions was that, "The poor rarely speak about income, but they do speak extensively about assets that are important to them" (p. 49), which Narayan *et al.* summarised in terms of what they called physical, human, and social capital. The ownership of or access to land was often identified as a key asset under the heading of physical capital, and access to land and land rights, especially in rural areas, was at the centre of much talk about poverty. Sub-standard housing was often a fact that distinguished the poor from others. Personal household property was an important asset, the sale of which constituted one of the few safety nets for poor families. Human capital comprised health, education, and labour. Particularly for those lacking other assets, labour power or a healthy body was the key to most survival strategies. Indeed lack of access to dependable wage labour was a major factor in many people's definition of poverty. More than anything else poor people dreaded serious family illness and the loss of income and increased health care costs which could push a household into destitution. Literacy was valued everywhere, although education received mixed evaluation and growing scepticism in some parts of the world: it was not always perceived as leading to jobs and was not always seen as the best route to exiting poverty.

Many poor people in different parts of the world were especially vulnerable in what are seen as increasingly unpredictable and insecure environments. Many

Relatively Well-Off Households

> Possess solid and stable houses that are usually renovated every 15 years
>
> Have transportation, either a motorbike, or a bicycle, or both
>
> Own a television or a radio, or both
>
> Can send their children to school
>
> Never lack money, even after the harvest has been eaten or sold
>
> Are able to save money
>
> Have a garden with useful plants and trees

Average Households

> Have a stable house that usually does not need renovating for 10 years
>
> Own a television or a radio, or both
>
> Have enough food all year
>
> Can send their children to school
>
> Have a well, or easy access to water

Poor Households

> Live in unstable houses, often made with mud
>
> Have no television or radio
>
> Are not able to save money
>
> May have children who cannot go to school, or have to leave school prematurely
>
> Usually have enough food until the next harvest, although sometimes lack food for one to two months per year
>
> Are unable to utilise surrounding natural resources to their benefit

Very Poor Households

> Live in very unstable houses that often need to be rebuilt every two to three years
>
> Have no wells or easy access to fresh water

Figure 8.1   Summary of household wealth indicators as described by the poor in Vietnam *Source*: reproduced with permission from Narayan, D. R., Patel, K., Schafft, A. & Koch-Schulte, S. (2000). *Voices of the Poor: Can Anyone Hear Us?* New York: Oxford University Press

were prone to seasonal calamities, for example due to floods and famine, and large numbers of the poorest lived in fragile areas with limited soil fertility. Natural resources were said to be disappearing, reducing the extent to which the poor could rely on traditional coping strategies such as gathering wood, hunting 'bush meat', fishing, or harvesting herbs, fruits or nuts. Because of scarce affordable housing, the urban poor often lived in risky locations such as on steep hillsides or marshes that are susceptible to mud slides and floods. Poor families often felt defenceless in the face of the insecurities and risks that they face.

The psychological dimensions to poverty identified by Narayan *et al.* include powerlessness, voicelessness, dependency, shame, and humiliation. This included distress at being unable to feed one's children, not knowing where the next meal will come from, shame at having to go without food; fear of the landlord, the police, or exploitation by the rich; the pain of helplessness; cynicism about politicians who promise action and use bribes or intimidation to secure allegiance; being forced to ask help from the same people who exploit them, such as landlords, pawnbrokers and money lenders; and being unable to reciprocate with gifts or participate in community events, with consequences ranging from humiliation, loss of honour and psychological distress to social marginalisation and exclusion.

In summary, Narayan *et al.* (2000, p. 64) stated:

> What is striking . . . is the extent to which dependency, lack of power, and lack of voice emerge as core elements of poor people's definitions of poverty. Powerlessness and voicelessness also underlie discussions of a heightened sense of vulnerability and the inability of poor people to protect themselves from shocks.

What Narayan *et al.* called social fragmentation was widely reported in the PPA reports in the form of accounts of, ". . . weakened bonds of kinship and community, as well as direct experience of increased corruption, crime, and lawlessness" (p. 219). There were reports of decreasing trust and an increasing inability of families to cooperate with one another, or a strengthening of bonds within social groups that could aggravate existing divisions and further marginalise those already excluded. From many of the countries there were reports of increased domestic violence, crime and violence in the community, and corruption and civil conflict at the state level, often resulting in displacement of large numbers of people. Social cohesion, which both affirmed the humanity of poor people whatever their circumstances and increased access to resources through social connections, was said to have been declining in a number of ways and for various reasons. In Ukraine for example, shrinking incomes combined with rising costs of transportation and telephone services, among other things, had diminished the ability to maintain contact, care for older relatives, or to assist children. In Ecuador, for example, some were no longer participating in celebrations, and fiestas and other community events had been cut back. As an older poor man in Uganda said:

> Poverty has always been with us in our communities . . . But it was a different type of poverty. People were not helpless. They acted together and never allowed it to squeeze any member of the community. They shared a lot of things together: hunting, grazing animals, harvesting, etc. There was enough for basic survival. But now things have changed. Each person is on their own . . . So we are left to fight this poverty ourselves. And yet we only understand a little of it. It is only its effects that we can see. The causes we cannot grasp (Uganda PPA report, 1998, cited by Narayan *et al.*, 2000, pp. 221–2).

There was a widespread perception that new economic opportunities were limited to the rich, the powerful, or the criminal. The perceived unfairness of unequal access to opportunities produced further frustration and disorder. Among the consequences were stress, arguments and violence within families, suspicion of and animosity towards others, and fear of those in authority. Increased community violence was explicitly linked to economic need in reports from countries such as Jamaica, Kenya and South Africa. The pressure on individual family members to migrate to other parts of the country, or to other countries, where there were better opportunities for work, disturbed the social cohesion of families and communities. The PPA from South Africa referred to the severe erosion of the traditional strategy, known as *ubuntu*, of sharing whatever one has. Norms of reciprocity were seen as giving way to norms of opportunism. Crime was perceived to have increased, including theft from neighbours, and aggressive and intoxicated youth in the street were creating fear of going out. Lack of respect of younger for older people was reported, and disciplining or calling attention to the behaviour of a neighbour's child was no longer a good idea. In Thailand poor people reported feeling unsafe and some children had been kept from school by their parents in order to guard the home from break-ins. In Cambodia outbreaks of violence were reported, associated with the heightened availability of weapons such as grenades, light rifles, or land mines.

Narayan *et al.* (p. 229) defined social exclusion as, "... the norms and processes that prevent certain groups from equal and effective participation in the social, economic, cultural, and political life of societies". Although social exclusion and poverty are deeply interconnected, in their view they were not the same thing. They used Bradley's (1994) framework of five mechanisms of exclusion: geography, entry barriers, corruption, intimidation, and physical violence (see Figure 8.2). Some of the most frequently excluded groups, according to PPA reports, were: women, children, the elderly, ethnic groups, people with HIV/AIDS, the disabled, and widows, as well as those who are simply poor.

Narayan *et al.* suggested that poverty could not be understood without understanding the relationship between institutions and those they serve: "Rights, opportunities, and power – all of which institutions can sanction or restrict – play an important role in the extent to which people can successfully use institutions for accessing resources" (p. 11). Later they stated, "Power differences among individuals and groups shape how such assets are controlled and used. The extent to which different resources can be mobilized depends directly on how power is shared within households, communities, and other social institutions" (p. 49). *Voices of the Poor* gave special attention to the institutions of civil society, by which they meant institutions that are not state-affiliated and which occupy a space between the state and the household. At a macro level they included non-government organisations (NGOs), religious and ethnic associations, trade unions, and caste associations. At a more micro level they included community-based organisations, neighbourhoods, kinship networks, traditional leaders, sacred sites, as well as NGOs operating at a local level. Poor people invested heavily in social relationships for psychological, cultural and economic well-being, but there was usually no direct connection between informal networks or organisations of poor people and formal institutions. Unlike the rich who are relatively well connected and have access to more resources, the poor relied on informal and local networks and organisations, but generally did not organise beyond their own communities without long-term external support (poor people's movements may be seen as a threat by the authorities,

---

Geography

> Poor people often live in marginal or outlying areas that are at risk or on unproductive land, in areas that are stigmatised and disrespected by outsiders and authorities, or where travel to schools, hospitals or other institutions is time consuming or costly.

Barriers to entry

> For example to healthcare or to active political participation, including documentation and bureaucracy, compounded by illiteracy, and 'transaction costs', which are costs involved in acquiring a good or service beyond its actual price, such as payments to officials that are seen as necessary to ensure adequate service.

Corruption

> Corruption among local officials was noted as a common problem in all parts of the world, making access harder for the poor, reducing the chances of equal access and fair treatment, and eroding trust.

Intimidation

> Intimidation in the form of threats of violence was reported in half of the Participatory Poverty Assessments in *Voices of the Poor*.

Violence

> Violence itself, whether in the form of domestic abuse of women and children, attacks by loan sharks because of inability to pay back loans, interpersonal and gang-based violence involving guns, or violence perpetuated by the state, were greater risks for the socially excluded and perpetuates social exclusion, and is a subject that it is difficult to speak about openly.

Figure 8.2 Mechanisms of social exclusion
Source: Bradley, C. (1994). Why male violence against women is a development issue: reflections from Papua New Guinea. In M. Davies (ed.), *Women and Violence: Realities and Responses, Worldwide*. London: Zed Books and Narayan, D. R., Patel, K., Schafft, A. & Koch-Schulte, S. (2000). *Voices of the Poor: Can Anyone Hear Us?* New York: Oxford University Press

and if successful are at risk of being taken over by political parties or other elites). Although they may help the poor to survive, they mostly did little to move the poor out of poverty.

Community-based organisations (CBOs – grassroots organisations managed by members on behalf of members) were a key resource, but were often merely substituting for state services. Because they often lacked bridging connections across groups within and beyond the community, their capacity to provide resources and opportunities was limited. For example, parent–teacher associations, women's associations, or seed-buying groups in rural areas, were usually disconnected from other similar groups; although they might improve life for the poor, in the absence of bridging social capital they did not facilitate new partnerships or social movements that sustain improvements or challenge inequalities. Hence CBOs acting alone had not generally been a force for change. Many countries have traditions for collective community work – such as *gotong royong* in Indonesia and *harambee* in Kenya and village associations in Mali – with purposes of keeping cultural traditions alive, strengthening community ties and, especially, sharing labour. Narayan *et al.* mentioned specifically two types of CBO: *tontines* (revolving savings and credit groups) and burial societies – the concern about being able to afford proper funerals and burials is widespread among the poor throughout the world. Poor people usually had no financial savings of their own and rarely had access to formal credit systems. They may be dependent on moneylenders, some of whom are also landlords. This leaves the poor open to indebtedness and exploitation. Even in the case of micro-credit schemes that have become well known for their work with poor people, such as the Grameen Bank in Bangladesh, zealous debt collection could degenerate into intimidation.

NGOs have become an important element of civil society in poor countries, and were often spoken of in more positive terms than were states and government officials. At the same time the limitations of NGOs were apparent in PPA reports. Sometimes funds were inadequate, misdirected or badly managed. They were often unable to reach many of the poor who lived at some distance from passable roads. There were some reports of insulting behaviour, corruption, and nepotism. But the main limitation was that they generally were unable to support the long-term capacity for self-governance, making little difference to local power relations or the inclusion of poor people in local councils or other decision-making bodies.

Poverty in the Midst of Riches

Poverty persists and is constantly recreated also in the richer countries of the world. In Britain in 2003, for example, a quarter of the population lived in homes with less than half the average disposable income and approximately 30% of the population were receiving an income-related benefit. Households with children made up about half of households with the lowest 10% of incomes, and a high proportion of families relying on income support were headed by single mothers. Not surprisingly the credit industry was continuing to thrive: while those on higher incomes (£50,000 a year or more) owed approximately 100% of annual income on average, those on lowest incomes (£11,500 or less) owed on average over 400% of annual income (Bostock, 2003). The psychological effects of debt, described by Bostock (2003), were considerable, with debt often cited as a cause of mental health problems, and people with mental health problems more often being in debt than others.

At the beginning of the twenty-first century there were estimated to be almost 60 million people living in poverty in the European Union (Millar & Middleton, 2002). The European Community Household Panel (ECHP) study was the first to examine poverty and social exclusion across a number of European countries (in the second half of the 1990s), and to examine changes for individual families over time. Its focus was 'social exclusion', hence taking a broad and multi-dimensional view of economic and social disadvantage rather than one based solely on income. It focused also on four groups thought to be at particular risk of poverty and social exclusion: *young adults, lone parents, those with long-term sickness or disability,* and *people in retirement* (Barnes et al., 2002; Apospori & Millar, 2003). The countries studied were chosen to reflect different welfare systems: Austria and Germany, with long-established and well-developed systems of family-oriented social insurance; Norway, typical of the Nordic countries with high levels of universal, individual-oriented benefits and services; the UK, with comparatively low, and increasingly means-tested benefits; and Greece and Portugal, with comparatively rudimentary welfare systems, with minimal welfare and reliance on family solidarity and the informal sector.

'Social exclusion' remains a contested term and is defined differently by different people. All definitions, however, define it not only in terms of income poverty and lack of material resources, but also, "...in terms of the processes by which some individuals and groups become marginalized in society. They are excluded not simply from the goods and standards of living available to the majority but also from their opportunities, choices and life chances" (Middleton et al., 2003, p. 5). In the ECHP study, data were obtained on income poverty, household amenities (e.g. having a separate kitchen, hot running water, central heating), possession of household durables (e.g. a television, telephone, access to a car or van), and household necessities (e.g. affording a holiday once a year, new rather than second-hand clothes, replacing worn out furniture). For each of those criteria a 'deprivation line' was drawn at 60% of the population median (80% in the case of household amenities and durables). In addition three indicators of social relationships were used: not being a member of a club or organisation; talking to neighbours only once or twice a week or less; meeting friends or relatives (outside the household) only once or twice a week or less. Evidence was also collected about social transfers and their effect on poverty alleviation.

Two of the four risk groups were found to have a higher rate of poverty, as well as non-monetary material deprivation, compared to the general population, in all of the six countries. They were lone parents and people who were sick or disabled. In all of the groups there were factors that were consistently related to poverty: employment and higher levels of education were associated with reduced rates of poverty; living alone and living with dependent children were both positively associated with poverty. There were some broad differences between the countries, with Austria having relatively low poverty rates for all risk groups, and risk groups in Greece and Portugal generally being among those with the higher poverty rates.

Lone parenthood, much increased in European countries in recent decades, and in 80 to 90% of families involving mothers, is an increasingly common experience, and one associated with a high risk of income poverty and social exclusion. Whereas in Portugal and Greece lone parents were more likely to be older, widowed women with adult children, in the UK and Norway lone parents were mainly ex-married women with dependent children, and some never-married women. In the UK lone parents included more younger families, without employment and with high rates of both income poverty and deprivation. Norway was a contrast, with similar types of families, but higher levels of employment, more state support to assist working parents, and lower rates of deprivation and poverty (Millar, 2002). In the UK lone parents not only had an increased rate of poverty, but also experienced longer periods in poverty. ECHP data from 1995 and 1996 showed that two-thirds of lone mothers in the UK experienced income poverty in both years, and were over five times as likely as partnered mothers to be continuously deprived of household durables (16% compared to 3%) (Adelman & Cebulla, 2003).

The sick and disabled were more often poor and deprived than others, even in Norway, which had been the most successful in narrowing the gap in poverty between the sick and the disabled and the rest of the population. The main reasons for poverty appear to have been lower rates of employment, greater financial needs associated with sickness and disability, lower educational qualifications, and in some countries a greater chance of living alone (Heady, 2002). In the UK 8% of the working age population were sick or disabled at some point during 1995 and 1996, and over two-fifths of them experienced income poverty at some point in those two years. They were also of higher risk for deprivation in terms of lack of household durables and necessities, and at risk of social isolation in terms of club or association membership and contact with friends or relatives (although not with neighbours) (Adelman & Cebulla, 2003).

As Middleton (2002, p. 77) put it, "The transition to adulthood is a much more complex experience for European young people today than it was for their parents. *Young people* are spending longer in education and entering the labour market later". Governments are containing costs by restricting financial support for students in further education, and relying on families to continue to support their children into young adulthood. Hence, although in general young adults (defined in the ECHP study as aged 16–29 years) were no more often poor or materially deprived than the rest of the population in any of the countries studied, poverty and deprivation were higher in those who were unemployed or living alone. In the UK there was a particularly high risk of material deprivation for poor young people, and poverty in one year markedly increased the risk of becoming materially deprived in the following year (Adelman & Cebulla, 2003).

The position of *retired people* (defined as any aged 45 or over who considered themselves to be retired) was different in different countries, with rates and severity of poverty only higher than for the general population in Greece and Portugal and to a lesser degree in the UK. But in all countries those aged 75 years and over and those living alone were more likely to be poor than the general population (Middleton, 2002). In the UK, where the basic state retirement pension was scarcely above the poverty line, the retired were more likely than others to be poor, more likely to remain poor from one year to the next, and more likely to suffer material deprivation (Adelman & Cebulla, 2003). Except in Greece, women were over-represented among the oldest groups of retired people, and were more likely to be living alone. The part-time, intermittent nature of much women's work, combined with incomplete pension contribution records, meant that women's incomes in retirement were likely to be lower than men's, and in the UK women were also less likely than men to be members of a private or occupational pension scheme (Middleton, 2002).

WOMEN

Albee and Perry (1998) provided a bird's eye view of the broad vista of women and disempowerment, reminding their readers of a number of the more notorious ways in which women around the world have been positioned as subordinate and often cruelly victimised. In the economic sphere they pointed out that women receive a small fraction of the world's income and own an even smaller fraction of the world's property, while putting in more than their fair share of all working hours. Women are more lowly paid (even in comparatively egalitarian countries such as New Zealand, as Drewery, 1998, pointed out) and have often constituted a 'reserve army' of workers, welcomed into the world of work when needed, but more vulnerable to being laid off later (Albee and Perry gave the example of women's experience of employment during the Second World War and subsequent return to domestic work, but numerous such examples could be cited). They pointed also to the way women have been victims of sexual abuse, including widespread rape during wars, have been exploited for purposes of sex work, and in many parts of the world have been – and in many cases still are – submitted to genital mutilation using procedures such as clitorectomy and infibulation that makes sexual pleasure less likely and often makes sex painful. Recall that stratification by gender is one of the three forms of stratification considered in social dominance theory to be universal (Sidanius & Pratto, 1999, and see Chapter 2).

Domestic Violence

Gracia (2004) has drawn attention to the 'hidden iceberg' of domestic violence against women, only a small proportion of which is reported to the authorities. According to Gracia a Eurobarometer survey carried out by the European Commission suggested that instances of domestic violence were often known to friends and wider family. The same survey found 46% of EU citizens believing that the provocative behaviour of women was one of the causes of domestic violence, indicating a high prevalence of victim-blaming attitudes and suggesting that the climate of acceptance of violence was among societal factors responsible for high rates of domestic violence. A report of the United Nations Population Fund (UNFPA, 2005) also showed that high proportions of women in samples in some countries believed that wife beating was justified for at least one of a number of reasons, which included: neglecting the children; going out without telling the partner; arguing with partner; refusing to have sex; not preparing food properly or on time; and talking to other men.

Perilla (1999) discussed domestic violence in the case of Latin American immigrants in the USA. Early theories of domestic violence had either been individualistic, focusing exclusively on the abused woman or on the male perpetrator, or were family systems theories which tended to allocate responsibility for battering to both partners and failed to extend their analyses to include the wider social, economic, political, and cultural environment. Instead, Perilla favoured an understanding of domestic violence that saw it as a form of oppression, even as a variety of terrorism, to be viewed as a community issue, and more specifically a human rights issue. Despite the heterogeneity of the immigrant Latin American group, she believed there were certain basic cultural values held in common – she discussed *machismo* and *respeto* (respect) – which might be relevant to understanding domestic violence in the Latin American culture. The question, often asked, Why do abused women stay in battering relationships?, neglected the many ways in which a Latin USAmerican woman might be asserting herself and coping by actively working on her own and her children's behalf. It also neglected the effects of trauma which may leave her unable to make a decision; the lack of sympathy extended towards her by others, and even implications that she may have provoked attacks; the tendency to blame herself and to carry shame and guilt about speaking to others about the abuse; and considerations such as her resources for subsisting financially and surviving on her own.

Hamby (2000) considered domestic violence among USAmerican Indians. She emphasised the extremely diverse and heterogeneous nature of native USAmerican communities and the over-simplification of including all in one category, as is the case with other categories such as 'Latino' and 'Asian'. She was critical, not only of generalised negative stereotypes of USAmerican Indians, but also of blanket idealisations such as the assumption that all Indian communities were matriarchal or egalitarian. Although it was probably true that European American influence had imposed a number of patriarchal ways, great variety had existed prior to conquest and in the present day. Hamby's was a feminist perspective, emphasising the gendered nature of power and control in intimate relationships as a primary cause of domestic violence. She considered the relevance of three types of dominance that the existing literature had suggested were most closely associated with domestic violence: authority, closely related to decision-making power; restrictiveness, referring to the extent to which one partner feels the right to control and limit the other's behaviour; and disparagement, which occurs when one partner fails to equally value the other and has an overall negative appraisal of the other's worth.

More recently, according to Hamby, feminist accounts of domestic violence had paid more attention to class, acknowledging that although domestic violence crosses all class boundaries, economic stresses increase the likelihood of the occurrence of violence and also curtail the abilities of the abused to respond effectively. USAmerican Indians, as well as other ethnic minorities in the USA, continued to be disadvantaged in terms of wealth, income, education and employment, and in her view no account of domestic violence and native USAmericans could be complete without acknowledging their socioeconomic situation. That situation had changed dramatically in the last 150 years, involving forced transition from hunting, gathering and farming to a cash-based economy, throwing most native groups into a cycle of poverty and indebtedness which it was difficult to break. The ability to develop economically strong communities had been hampered by forms of social and economic marginalisation, including removal of people from their ancestral lands, prohibitions on traditional religious practices, removal of Indian children into foster homes and boarding schools, and a drastic reduction in the native population from the time of western contact until reservations were created (see also Chapter 2 on the oppression of indigenous peoples).

James *et al.* (2003) are others who have tried to put the disempowerment and oppression of women into a wider perspective, in this case around a broad concept of violence towards women. They located interpersonal violence (women as victims of domestic violence for example) and intrapersonal violence (in which they included forms of self-harm including alcohol and drug misuse – themselves associated with the experience of interpersonal violence) within a broader context of 'structural violence'. The latter, which they stated had received little attention in psychology, differed from the other types of violence in that power relations were subtle and submerged. As defined by James *et al.*, it consists of a set of relations, processes, and social conditions that embody and produce other forms of violence. It enjoys the sanction of the ruling authorities and is reflected in the law, media, education, religion, and work relations. It is built into the fabric of society and operates automatically, particularly bearing on the poor and other marginalised groups.

Women and Poverty

Gender relations was also a theme that ran throughout the *Voices of the Poor* report (Narayan *et al.*, 2000), discussed in the earlier section on poverty and social exclusion. A chapter of the report was devoted to gender. Participatory Poverty Assessment (PPA) reports from around the world testified to traditional, unequal gender power relations. Women were identified, and identified themselves, as those responsible for the health, education and well-being of their children, husbands and the family and home as a whole. Women were very often unable to own land or property, lacked inheritance rights, were particularly at risk of exploitation and violence if they had been unable to bring a good dowry, and were often viewed as men's property in themselves. In many parts of the world girls were discriminated against in obtaining education on the grounds that they could not be spared from domestic labour or because education for boys was a better family investment or because of fear of sexual contact or harassment away from home. Lower rates of literacy left women disadvantaged, for example in awareness of government programmes or other services or of their legal rights. Women tended to be the financial losers from marital divorce, tended to avoid legal action, and as female heads of households with children were particularly vulnerable to poverty. In marriage men dominated decision making, and women were dependent on men, had less choice, and were often the subject of domestic violence. Even when community partnership projects required women to be represented on the decision-making body, as described in the PPA from India, it was sometimes the woman representative's husband who was addressed by villagers and congratulated on election victory.

What struck Narayan *et al.* was that, despite widespread changes in gender roles, traditional gender norms had shown greater tenacity, which left families struggling to meet new demands. Men had often lost their traditional roles, and women had taken on new ones. The psychological effects had been profound:

> These changes touch core values about gender identity, gender power, and gender relations within poor households, and create anxiety about what is a 'good woman' or a 'good man'. Values and relations are being broken, tested, contested and renegotiated in silence, pain, and violence (Narayan *et al.*, p. 175).

A strong theme in *Voices of the Poor* was that, in the face of widespread economic disruption, men often responded to displacement from the traditional sole earner role, their actual and felt redundancy, with a lack of adaptability, collapse and defeat, and high rates of alcohol and drug misuse and violence. Many women respondents felt that, because of their responsibility towards children and family, and greater adaptability, they had had to show greater resilience, and had often taken on new roles as earners.

Although this had brought some women greater independence and empowerment, and there were signs in some parts of the world that women were effectively entering the world of trade and migrant work, the changes had mostly had limited impact on women's empowerment. Many of the jobs they were willing to take on were in the informal sector, were those that were too demeaning for men, were low paid, were unsafe or risky in a variety of ways, and had to be combined with continuing traditional work in the home. Women continued to invest heavily in informal social support with other women, whereas poor men were more likely to be involved in vertical patron–client relationships with landlords, employers, or traders, access to which was largely denied to poor women. Even in parts of the world where women's groups were plentiful, as for example in Kenya and Tanzania, groups in rural areas tended to be disconnected from sources of know-how and resources. These differences carried costs for both sexes. While poor women tended to be isolated from vertical sources of social capital, men were relatively isolated from informal, horizontal, bonds that could provide for emotional well-being.

Women's empowerment in their relationships with men was the theme of an interesting report of a qualitative study with three groups of Kenyan women (Friedman & Todd, 1994). Kenya, the authors described as a country undergoing at the time a rapid transition from a rural traditional way of life to a modern urbanised one, with still one of the highest birth rates in the world (there are a number of references to poverty in Kenya in the *Voices of the Poor* report). One group of women participants (the lower class city group) were working as cleaners at the university or in hotels in Nairobi. All had been born and grew up in rural areas but had moved to the city to find a job to support their families, and were on low incomes. The second group (the middle class city group) were working in Nairobi as secretaries, librarians, teachers and travel agents, earning salaries 10–20 times higher than those in the first group. The third group (a rural group) lived in one remote village on the shore of a lake in a semi-desert area, reliant primarily on goat herding and fishing, leading a traditional life. Partly because it was considered intrusive to ask people directly about their personal lives, the indirect technique was used of asking each women to tell a story about a picture (taken from the TAT, the projective Thematic Apperception Test) depicting two African figures, a man looking forward and away, with a woman behind him holding his arms and looking at him, a picture that generally elicits stories of interpersonal conflicts in the relationship between a man and a woman.

Whether one believes that the resulting stories represent people's wishes, stereotypes, projections of their own beliefs and views, or something about the reality of their own lives, it was the case that the stories told by women in the three groups tended to be very different. Over two-thirds of the stories from the lower class city group were about separation in which the man wanted to get away and the woman was the one trying to solve the problem, reach a compromise, apologise, generally showing persistence, submission and obedience. Compared to the other two groups, that group of women was seen by the authors as showing characteristics of strength and resilience in the face of poverty and loss of traditional life, but without having the legitimate, socially granted power to determine one's own fate economically, socially, or politically. As Miller (1988) said of another group of poor women.

> They impressed us greatly with their strength for these women were doing almost the impossible, nurturing and educating their children despite poverty, and doing it with dignity, gentleness, and often elegance. At the same time they had little power to change things, to see that their own needs were met, to have someone listen to them in a respectful way (J.B. Miller, 1988, cited by Friedman & Todd, 1994, p. 543).

In contrast women in the middle classes told stories in which the heroine was usually portrayed as strong and in control of a situation, frequently one in which the man had some problem (sickness, criminality) towards which the woman was supportive, helping or comforting. Only one in five of their stories was of the kind dominant in the lower class city group. Stories told by women in the rural group were mainly short, simple, optimistic, and focused on children – the desire for a child, sorrow over the loss of a child, or unhappiness about barrenness. Almost all described love and togetherness between the couple. None of them ended with the break up of the relationship and most had a happy ending, usually referring to happiness over a child. From their more general observations of the rural women and their village, the authors suggested that rural women, although they were as poor as the lower class city women, or more so, and although their husbands were often absent, they appeared happier and more secure than lower class city women, spending much of their time in the company of other women, enjoying each other's company, exhibiting confidence, and taking care of each other's children with warmth and pride. The picture they painted was of traditional women empowered in certain domains of their lives even though in their roles as wives they might lack autonomy.

Women, Stress and Illness

Grant et al. (2003) wrote of the need to integrate psychological research on girls and women with feminist activism by adopting a unifying theory to guide research, placing individual level findings in social context, and linking research findings and action. They found scarcely any research that tested hypotheses specifically drawn from a theory of sexism, or that set findings within a feminist theory. Their own suggestion was to modify the stress paradigm. They wished to part company with the influential model of stress (Lazarus & Folkman, 1984) that saw cognitive appraisal processes as an integral part of the definition of stress, hence viewing it as in large part a subjective phenomenon. Like Brown and Harris (1978), whose work on women and depression was introduced in Chapter 4, they were interested in events that would be threatening for most people in a given population, given their shared circumstances – for example for most young people of a certain age in a given society. Their definition of stress, therefore, focused on external, environmental changes or conditions. Stress was, "environmental events or chronic conditions that objectively threaten the physical and/or psychological health and/or well-being of individuals of a particular age in a particular society" (Grant *et al.*, 2003, p. 148). They therefore defined sexism as a chronic stressful experience affecting adolescent girls through a variety of specific acute stressors, in a way analogous to poverty or racial discrimination in its pervasiveness. Individual stressors might be acute or chronic major life events or chronic daily hassles.

It may be recalled that Brown and Harris, in their work with women in London and the Scottish islands, found that stressful life events or chronic life circumstances preceded the onset of depression, hence explaining the higher incidence of depression for women in less favoured socioeconomic positions who lead more stressful lives. Further exploration of what it might be about negative life events that provokes depression led Brown (1998) to the view that such events constitute a severe threat to a woman's goals, plans and concerns in life domains, such as marriage, motherhood, or employment to which she is particularly committed and which involve a core element of her identity. They, "...reflect likelihood of being cut off from a key source of self-value or the development of a grave impediment to carrying out of core activity" (p. 362). Although the occurrence of such a life event often involves the experience of loss, their detailed results suggested to Brown that it was events that involved 'humiliation' or 'entrapment' that were particularly likely to precede depression. Humiliation events were those where the description of the event and its context suggested that it would likely have given rise to a sense of being put down or to a marked devaluation of self. Such events included, for example: separation from a partner, where the latter took the initiative or where the woman was forced to leave or break off a relationship because of violence or discovery of infidelity; finding out that a daughter had been stealing from home and playing truant from school; or being criticised by a judge in public for failing to pay her son's fine and being warned that she could go to prison. Events involving entrapment, but not necessarily humiliation, included, for example, learning that an illness was chronic and incurable. Lack of control over important aspects of one's life was picked out as central (Brown, 1998).

Following Brown's work in Britain, Broadhead and Abas (1998) carried out a similar study in a township in Harare, Zimbabwe, finding very similar results which supported the model of the onset of depression in women being provoked by severe, stressful life events and/or major ongoing life difficulties linked to socioeconomic status and/or material conditions. Significantly more women in Harare experienced one or other of these depression-provoking factors in a one-year period than was the case in the earlier study in the Camberwell area of London (63% versus 48%) and life events were rated as more severe in Harare. In fact the four-point rating scale of the threat involved in an event, used in the earlier studies, had to be extended to create a new category for events that were more highly threatening than any that had been encountered in studies in the UK. Cases 1 and 2 in Figure 8.3 are examples.

Case 1: Subject is aged 43, married with nine children. She works informally roasting maize cobs to sell at beerhalls. The family just afford basic food and government schooling costs. The event is her husband's death. His company refuse her access to his pension unless she can persuade a male elder from his family to claim it. His family live 200 miles away and she has no money for the bus fare. The children are subsequently dismissed from school for non-payment of fees. They are living on one small meal a day.

Case 2: The subject is aged 40, is the second wife in a polygamous marriage. Her nine-month old baby has just died after a long illness and her husband has early AIDS. The event is the husband blaming her for the baby's death. Over the next 10 days, she is beaten by him and given a black eye, obvious at the funeral. She is excluded from traditional healer consultations at which she is blamed for causing the child's death through negligence.

Case 3: The subject is aged 43, happily married for 26 years. She lives between Zambia, with her four children, and Harare, where her husband's business is. The event is returning to Harare to find her husband living with a young woman. She is forbidden entry to her own home and has to return to Zambia.

Case 4: The woman is aged 19, married for 18 months. She lives with her husband in three rooms. Since two brothers-in-law moved in seven months ago there has been tension as one of them bullies her when her husband is out. The event is his threatening to hit her for the first time. Despite her pleading, the husband gives no promise that he will ask his brother to leave.

Figure 8.3   Examples of stressful life events and major ongoing life difficulties in Harare, Zimbabwe
Source: Broadhead, J. & Abas, M.A. (1998). Life events, difficulties and depression among women in an urban setting in Zimbabwe. *Psychological Medicine*, **28**, 29–38

Note that, as in other studies in this programme of research, ratings of the severity of life events were based on consensus ratings of the stressfulness of an event for women living in that culture, and not on subjective ratings by individual women of how personally stressful they had found the event. Some events were therefore given a rating in a Zimbabwean context that was different from the rating that would have been given if the event had occurred in London. For example, rated as less severe in Harare than in London were such factors as overcrowding, having to travel long distances to work, and having many children. As in the earlier study in the Islington area of London (Brown & Moran, 1997) those severe events or sequences of related events that were rated as involving a woman's humiliation or entrapment were most likely to be associated with depression onset. In London humiliating events had included 'put downs' and delinquent behaviour by close family members, and entrapment included being told that a very seriously ill partner would not improve. Cases 3 and 4 in Figure 8.3 illustrate severe examples of humiliation and entrapment, respectively, in Harare.

The way in which the material and social conditions of women's lives, including their class and gender positions, are interwoven with health concerns, emerged in a report of interviews carried out with women in a town in south Wales in 1993 (Walters & Charles, 1997). The town consisted of an old, established working class community, characterised by strong extended family ties, where women had often lived all their lives. At that time opportunities for employment were limited for both women and men. The women had volunteered to be interviewed about women's health concerns and worries: in the interviews they spoke of coping with a range of conditions including headaches and migraines, sleeping problems, bad backs, asthma, arthritis, epilepsy, diabetes, gall stones, thyroid problems, chronic fatigue syndrome, hypertension, allergies, tennis elbow, and kidney problems. A central theme was the difficulty of anticipating how a woman would feel from day to day, and how that unpredictability severely limited her sense of control over her life. One woman, for example, who had been forced to give up her job because of poor health, and whose husband was unemployed, said:

> To be healthy, for me, would be to be able to go day by day and plan what I want to do. 'Let's go away tomorrow for the day'. Not, say, 'let's see how I am tomorrow and then we might go'. That would be, I tell you what, to have a completely relaxed and peaceful mind (p. 1732).

Another was unemployed after the factory in which she had worked for over 20 years had closed down: she was without redundancy pay because she had been 'on the sick' just before the factory closed. Several widows spoke at length about losing their husbands and their own subsequent ill-health. Another theme highlighted by Walters and Charles was women's changing sense of self in the face of chronic illness. A number spoke of losing confidence and restricting their lives, while others expressed determination not to. Walters and Charles were impressed with the way women seemed to work hard to conceal their problems, to protect their families from stress associated with them, and to be seen to 'manage' their family caring tasks and responsibilities, and to all appearances to remain 'normal'.

Women talked much about social support, several mentioning the helpfulness of talking with other widows, the support received from co-workers when they were working, and sometimes the support of a neighbour. But, despite being part of extended family networks, family were not always a source of support, sometimes because they were seen as having their own problems and women wished not to be a burden. For example:

> I'm a bit of a worrier but, I mean, I wouldn't show it to other people ... other people don't want your problems, do they? You know some people moan and groan all the time, don't they? Well, I mean, there's no need for that, I don't think really, because I mean, you're only making other people's lives a misery (p. 1736).

In many cases husbands were viewed as being unsympathetic, or as a source of women's problems, often providing no help with household chores, often being uncommunicative, sometimes stopping women going out by themselves. Pubs were not seen as being available to women in the way that they were for men. Walters and Charles concluded that women in their sample lacked the social and economic supports that would have helped them transcend the health problems that they faced. The following quotation is illustrative:

> The morale of women these days is pretty low anyway because, well, there's not much money about and you can't do much without money anyway. And, you know, they're encouraged to go to college even though ... you can't get the funding and the money to go. You can't get the crèche facilities ... we have to pay ... they're quite expensive and you're told you have to pay for it (p. 1738).

Fear of violence in the community was a further restricting factor.

A different group, but one facing some not dissimilar dilemmas, was a group of mature women in the first two years of undertaking a programme of professional higher education at a British university (Johnson & Robson, 1999). In that study – which involved women keeping diaries of their experiences, individual interviews with women, and participant observation – many women described continuing demands, responsibilities and other issues associated with their lives outside the university: most were married or living with a partner, a substantial number had children, and a large proportion were involved in higher education part time while they continued to work, many of them full time. Many expressed feelings of guilt, especially in relation to believing that they were not spending enough time with their children or family. Other studies of mature women students have reported the same things (e.g. Edwards, 1993). Johnson and Robson drew on Edwards' (1993) concept of a 'greedy institution': family, higher education, and, for some, work as well, each demanded a woman's exclusive and undivided loyalty and sought to weaken a woman's ties with the competing 'institutions'. As well, women often had doubts about whether they fitted into the university, whether they were 'real academics' – particularly, as was often the case, if they were studying part time on professional healthcare courses in a discipline that had not traditionally been associated with higher educational qualifications. Some women from working class backgrounds had also experienced negative reactions from friends and relations because of their involvement in higher education. Women found it valuable to have support within each of the 'greedy institutions' that made demands upon them: support from husband or partner, other immediate family, parents or other relatives; support in various ways at the university; and support and understanding from colleagues at work.

It is worth noting here that in their north London study, Brown and Moran (1997) found that full-time employment for single mothers was a risk factor for depression, whereas part-time work was not. In another study carried out in the Southwark area of south London, Haw (1995) produced the same finding, but only for younger women (aged 20–34) with a youngest child five years old or less. For older women with older aged children, working outside the home was associated with better mental health irrespective of whether the paid work was full or part time. In the case of the younger women it was also possible to examine the effect of type of employment, since some of those employed part time worked in a biscuit factory that was close to where nearly all the women lived, and which offered flexible working arrangements including a 'school shift' and a shorter evening shift. They reported less mental distress than other part-time employed younger women, who mostly worked for longer hours in smaller establishments that were unable to offer such flexible working arrangements. As Haw said, the likely explanation for this pattern of results is the distress caused by potentially conflicting role demands and overload when mothers with pre-school children were required to work for longer hours.

As part of their 'bird's eye view' of women and disempowerment, Albee and Perry (1998) discussed beauty as a 'sexist-economic issue'. In a special issue of the *Journal of Community and Applied Social Psychology* on the subject of (Dis)orders of Eating and Embodiment, Malson and Swann (1999) also argued in a theoretical paper that an attempt should be made to consider eating 'disorders' (sometimes experienced by men, e.g. Wilps, 1990, but much more commonly disorders of women, especially young women), not as individual forms of pathology, but rather as experiences and practices embedded within the cultural and political contexts in which women live. That context includes, they argued, both gender power relationships and modern, capitalist consumer culture in which the body of the female consumer subject is literally "prepared for consumption" (p. 403), not only of food products but also of an array of diet-promoting and body-enhancing products and consumer services. A similar point was made by Marshall and Yazdani (1999), writing in the same issue about south Asian young women who were in touch with mental health or social care services in the borough of Newham in east London, after having 'self-harmed' themselves. The borough was one with high levels of social and economic deprivation and a large black and minority ethnic population. The authors concluded from their interviews with service clients and staff that self-harm needed to be understood within a cultural context, a significant feature of which was the female body as, "a site of cultural contestation over ownership and control; the body as belonging within the family/community or the body as individually 'owned' " (p. 424). Part of 'Asian culture' was concern for the family's reputation within the broader community – the importance of *izzat* and *sharam*, honour and shame – which, for example, makes disclosure of such issues outside the family problematic, and disclosure of abuse, which is known to be associated with such problems, particularly problematic. At the same time Marshall and Yazdani warned against too easily characterising 'the south Asian family' as restrictive, stifling of individuality and hence oppressive and pathogenic, and of assuming that in 'Asian' groups such problems can be attributed to 'culture' whereas similar problems in white groups are not so attributed.

Many women writers have addressed what has been seen as the neglect of the position and experiences of women in psychology generally, and perhaps in community psychology in particular (Mulvey, 1988; Williams & Watson, 1991; Ussher, 1991; Reid, 1993; Angelique & Culley, 2003). Angelique and Culley (2000) content analysed articles appearing in the *American Journal of Community Psychology* (*AJCP*) and the *Journal of Community Psychology* (*JCP*) between 1973 and 1997, looking for articles that were relevant to women, and those that adopted a feminist approach. Of over 2000 articles examined, 9.8% were considered women-relevant, but less than 3% feminist. There was a promising increase in both categories from pre- to post-1990, but the authors of the review were concerned on three grounds. First, the most common topics of women-relevant articles were mental health, often focusing on psychological symptoms, and motherhood, suggesting a continuing stereotyping of women, focusing on maternity and potential for psychological disorder to the relative exclusion of other important issues of relevance to women. The reviewers were also interested in the extent to which articles addressed diversity among women, for example in terms of ethnicity, age, sexual orientation, or socioeconomic status. Less than half addressed such issues. There was also a tendency towards stereotyping pressed and marginalised groups. For example one group of articles dealt with combined issues of motherhood, low socioeconomic status, and 'women of color', and such articles often referred to deficits and dysfunctions but without a cultural analysis. Their third concern was that women were 'invisible' in a quarter of even the women-relevant articles, for example by failing to recognise women's presence in the title or the abstract, or by using gender-neutral terms, such as 'parent', masking the presence of women even when the sample was largely or wholly composed of women.

Writing three years later, Angelique and Culley (2003) were more positive about consciousness of gender in community psychology. Although research on women's issues and feminist scholarship might still be under-represented in community psychology, a good proportion of articles in those two US journals now included a discussion of "intersecting identities, especially race and class" (p. 196). In 1997 a special issue of *AJCP* had been devoted to 'women of color', with a number of articles addressing the challenges of multiple oppressions, and dual or even triple minority status and oppression. Nevertheless women's issues, such as reproduction, childcare, single parenting, rape, incest, sexual harassment, woman battering, and the feminisation of poverty, were still under-represented. Although there was a trend towards more feminist content in the later years, only a minority of articles about women's issues had feminist content. Among their recommendations were: that efforts should be made to increase the number of women leaders in the field of community psychology; barriers to women's career advancement in the field be explored; theories that provide a foundation for discussing diversity and challenging the status quo should be supported; the field should live up to its claims to be committed to marginalised groups; and to avoid victim blaming, there should be a focus on environmental contexts of oppression instead of a focus on psychopathology within oppressed groups.

LESBIAN, GAY, BISEXUAL, AND TRANSGENDERED PEOPLE

This chapter's final example of a group of people who have been marginalised and oppressed, and continue to be at risk of being so, is the group of people now often referred to as lesbian, gay, bisexual or transgendered (LGBT). According to authors such as Coyle and Wilkinson (2002) and Kitzinger and Coyle (2002), that group has been as much marginalised in psychology as it has in society in general. The last years of the twentieth century saw a definite increase in studies of lesbian and gay identity and reports of lesbian and gay-affirmative therapy. Bisexuality and transgender had been added but there continued to be little study of either topic. Much of psychology continued to be based on the assumption that, unless otherwise stated, members of samples in psychological research are all heterosexual. As a result, people with other sexual orientations remain virtually invisible, and psychological theories are based on the assumption of heterosexuality.

The Experience of Oppression

A special issue of the *Journal of Community and Applied Social Psychology* (Coyle & Wilkinson, 2002) and an edited volume (Coyle & Kitzinger, 2002), both on lesbian and gay issues, provided ample evidence of the oppressive circumstances experienced by gay and lesbian people and of the prevalence of homophobic or heterosexist attitudes. For example, Rivers (2002), summarising his own and others' research, documented the adverse experiences at home and in education while growing up, and effects on mental health. Some young lesbians, gays and bisexuals reported having been forced to leave home on account of conflict over their sexual orientation, and sometimes that meant relocating to large urban areas and the possibility of being exploited and, for some, falling into prostitution. Bullying at school on account of sexual orientation was common, including name calling, ridiculing in front of others, teasing, having belongings stolen as a form of harassment, and being hit or kicked. Some of the less direct forms of tormenting, such as having rumours spread about them or being frightened by the way in which a person looked or stared at them, were those found to be related to scores on a measure of PTSD. Many reported losing at least one friend as a result of their actual or perceived sexual orientation, with others fearing that they would lose friends if they came out about their sexual orientation. Others had reported the challenges faced by young lesbians and gay men at the time of entering university, especially when moving into halls of residence with people they had never met before. Deliberate self-harm, including attempts at suicide, and other indications of effects on mental health, had been reported in several studies.

Markowe (2002) reported the results of interviews with 40 lesbians, focusing on how they had come to identify themselves as lesbian and their experiences of coming out, or choosing not to, as the case might be, to family, friends and work colleagues. Many described having felt very isolated, especially those who had come to perceive themselves as lesbian as teenagers. They had found the background of rumour and gossip about people's sexual orientation and joking about homosexuality difficult to deal with. Whatever their age, many had recalled negative or conflicting emotions, isolation and fear, often associated with the attitudes of other people. Coming out to oneself had often been a gradual process, sometimes taking years, and meeting other lesbians for the first time had often been difficult and frightening. There were risks and benefits in coming out to different people, and many had been selective about whom they had told. Reactions from others were reported to range from understanding and support through to negative reactions such as disbelief, disapproval or shock. A fear of losing family or friends had stopped some from coming out, and social relationships had become limited for some as a result. As one women put it, "I was beginning to cut my family out of my life because there was so much I couldn't tell" (pp. 76–7); and as another said, she,

"...never really formed any lasting relationships through work ... [because such friends might] ask about my private life" (p. 77).

The desire for authenticity or integrity was a strong theme in many of the women's accounts. Overall, coming out to oneself and others was viewed as having been very beneficial, the majority seeing the main benefit as being true to one's real self, not having to hide an important part of oneself, not having to pretend. That was as true for those who had identified as lesbian when aged 30 or more, and those who had had previous heterosexual experience, as it was of those who had been aware of lesbian feelings quite early in childhood and who had identified as lesbian in their teens or early 20s.

Russell and Richards (2003) asked a sample of over 300 self-identified lesbian, gay and bisexual people in Colorado, USA, about their responses to Amendment II – an amendment to the Colorado State Constitution which denied legal recourse to LGB people who encountered discrimination based on their sexual orientation, hence, in effect, legalising discrimination against them. Their questions were in the form of statements about being stressed as a result of their experiences, but also positive 'resilience' responses, both based on an earlier study of several hundred Colorado LGBs. Factor analysis produced five stressor factors and five resilience factors, summarised in Table 8.1.

Many of the same stressors as those experienced by gay and lesbian people were found in a study that involved 28 women and men who defined themselves as 'trans' – short for transgendered (Clifford & Orford, 2006). Nineteen of the sample were of male sex, transitioning to female (male-to-female or MtF), and nine were female-to-male (FtM). Participants spoke about being acutely aware as children that they were different from others of their sex, being highly sensitive to gender-related expectations, for example in terms of dress, hairstyle, and activities. They recalled becoming secretive about their feelings, trying to cope by participating enthusiastically in 'appropriate' activities, or by trying to emphasise other characteristics such as their sense of humour or academic achievement. Most hoped that their gender dysphoric feelings would in time go away. A move in the direction of acknowledging their difference was sometimes triggered by something in the media, such as the programme *The Decision* shown on British television in 1996, or by an intensification of feelings of difference at the time of puberty, or by a breakdown in an opposite sex relationship. Most spoke of a crisis or turning point in their lives that had occurred anywhere between as young as 10 years old and beyond retirement age. Finding out that sex reassignment surgery was available was a turning point for a number. Telling someone else, sometimes planned and sometimes impulsively, was a crucial stage, and participants had met with a range of different responses to their disclosures, some surprisingly accepting – for example from parents – others a shocked response at first but with later adaptation and acceptance, yet others negative and resulting in long-term estrangement.

The participants were in varied positions in terms of transitioning to the new gender. Positions ranged from living part of the time in the new gender role and without hormonal treatment or sex reassignment surgery, to those who had been living for some time in the new role (the 'real-life test' as it is known in medical sex reassignment circles) and were considering or waiting for surgery, to those who had undergone one or more reassignment surgical operations. They had many

Table 8.1   Sources of stress and resilience for lesbian, gay and bisexual (LGB) people in the face of Colorado State Amendment II: example items

Stressor factors	Resilience factors
1: *Encounter with homophobia* Felt the heterosexual community failed to understand the impact of Amendment II on LGBs Felt shocked by the hostile nature of the campaign	**1: *Movement perspective*** LGB community better understands impact of homophobia Increased potential for building coalitions with other oppressed groups
2: *Community divisions* Felt sad about divisions in LGB community based on sex, race, etc. Disagreements about best strategies for change	**2: *Confronting internalised homophobia*** Finally grasped how homophobia has impacted me personally Felt less shame as a LGB person
3: *Making sense of danger* Felt lack of connection to heterosexual community Felt anger at heterosexuals who say they support LGBs but don't do anything	**3: *Expression of feelings*** Had opportunity to take a stand again Amendment II and vented anger at Colorado for Family Values (a group advocating for the amendment)
4: *Failed witnessing* [based on the idea of a victim, a perpetrator, and a witness as the three agents involved in trauma] Felt lack of connection to family of origin My family of origin failed to understand the meaning of Amendment II	**4: *Successful witnessing*** Opportunity for my heterosexual family members to act on behalf of LGB rights Heterosexual friends offered understanding and support
5: *Internalised homophobia* Increased my use of alcohol and/or drugs Questioned my own religious values/beliefs	**5: *LGB community*** Learned more about other LGBs because of more contact Increased support from LGB community

Source: Russell, G.M. & Richards, J.A. (2003). Stressor and resilience factors for lesbians, gay men, and bisexuals confronting antigay politics. *American Journal of Community Psychology*, *31*, 313–28

comments to make about their experiences with the health service. Some doctors had been knowledgeable and helpful, others much less so. Some participants had found the 12-to-24 month real-life test burdensome and inappropriate, and some had sought private treatment, not all with good results. Nevertheless, receiving a diagnosis as transsexual or transgendered had often been experienced as empowering. People remained highly sensitive to feedback; for example, worrying about 'passing' and the danger of being 'found out'. One participant (MtF) put it thus:

> Would I ever be accepted truly as a member of the opposite sex? Or would I be regarded as a 'trans-person'? Or even worse a freak? Will surgery give me a female body without medical complications? Will hormones screw up my head? Will I ever be passable? Will I ever be able to earn a penny again? Will I have to spend the rest of my life alone? (p. 207).

When that study was carried out, UK law did not recognise trans people in their chosen gender, a state of affairs that changed with the Gender Recognition Act of 2004. At the time participants had been worried about a number of legal issues, for example to do with birth certificates, the possibility of employment discrimination, the danger of being discovered if one had an accident and had to go to hospital, and the awful possibility of, for example, a male-to-female trans person being committed to a male prison. As one participant (MtF) said, "We just would like to live as people with rights" (p. 210).

Participants for that study were recruited by advertising the project through the trans and LGBT press. Finn and Dell (1999) had recruited seven people who identified as transgendered from a pool of social contacts available to them. Although there was also much diversity within this group – all cross-dressing intermittently or permanently, some living or having lived part or full time in the alternative gender role, some having taken hormone treatment and some not – only one had received reassignment surgery, two had returned to their original gender, and all were reluctant to classify themselves in terms of one or other sex. As a group, therefore, they positioned themselves rather differently than most of Clifford and Orford's (2006) group and, unlike them, they mostly rejected the term 'transexual'. They saw the latter as an example of medical labelling, an assumption that there was a disorder that needed diagnosing and treating in appropriate stages (real-life test, hormones, surgery), and that trans people would only be happy if they made the transition from the 'wrong' sex to the 'right' one. Members of this sample were more inclined to emphasise fluidity, the pleasure of ambiguity, and the possibility of having more than just the two choices.

Focus on the Oppressors

One conclusion that emerges from what has been written about the experiences of LGBT people is that the problem, as in all cases of oppression, lies not with the oppressed, who are frequently labelled, taunted, terrorised, and made to feel confused and ashamed, but rather with the oppressors and their attitudes and actions (social dominance theory is highly relevant again here – see Chapter 2). Historically, hundreds of thousands have been executed for homosexual acts in Britain as elsewhere – and quite recently in Europe under the Nazis – and consensual homosexual acts continue to be illegal in many countries, punishable by physical beatings or even the death penalty in some, with explicit protection against discrimination for LGBT people under the law still a comparative rarity (Taylor, 2002; Ellis, 2002). Homophobia persists and there has been evidence of a homophobic backlash in response to the increasing visibility of lesbian and gay culture. In the UK, Section 28 of the 1988 Local Government Act outlawed the 'promotion' of homosexuality in schools (Gough, 2002), and in the USA an example was the Colorado State Amendment II referred to above (Russell & Richards, 2003).

A number of studies have explored the attitudes of young people, finding that negative attitudes persist, in a direct or blatant form in the case of minorities of young people, but more commonly in a more disguised and less blatant form. For example Anderssen (2002) found between one-third and two-thirds of a representative sample of Norwegian men and women who were 19 years of age in 1996 holding somewhat negative or very negative attitudes towards lesbian women, gay men, and cohabitation by couples of the same sex. They were interested in testing, and found moderate support for, the contact hypothesis, which suggests that positive attitudes towards an otherwise oppressed minority group are correlated with the amount of contact a person has with members of that group: less than half had more than minimal contact with any gay man or lesbian woman, but the amount of such contact increased by the time of the repeat survey two years later, and new contact in that time was associated with attitudes becoming more positive. Gough (2002) held three group discussions with second-year male university psychology students in the north of England. He was interested, not so much in how some people might have more prejudiced attitudes than others at an individual level, but how 'hegemonic masculinities' might be reproduced by individuals and groups at sites – educational sites being of particular importance – where male homophobia might be particularly evident. Although gay-friendly sentiments were expressed, as were some blatant anti-lesbian and anti-gay attitudes, it was common for homosexuality to be described as something alien and/or problematic, but in a way that presented the speaker as liberal, rational and egalitarian, or by making distinctions (e.g. between private and public behaviour, or between gay men and lesbian women). For example:

> If it's, if it's treated like conventional heterosexuality, you've got your partner and you keep it to yourself and it's not flaunted, I've always tolerated it but what annoys me is when you see these gay marches, they're all dressed up ... if they were just dressed fairly conventionally, just say 'Look, I'm homosexual, accept me' I'd have no problem whatsoever – you're not tryin' to rape me, you're not tryin' to force it on me, I accept it, but it's that perversion that they seem to put over, not all of 'em, I mean it's a public minority, but it's that that I don't accept (p. 226).

Chesir-Teran (2003) favoured the term 'heterosexism' – referring to a systematic process of privileging heterosexuality over homosexuality – rather than the more individualistic 'homophobia', because the former was more relevant to considering the ways in which whole settings or systems, such as schools, families, religious organisations or neighbourhoods, might display prejudice and encourage oppression, or discourage it, as the case might be, towards any minority or oppressed group. They used Moos and Lenke's (1983) idea of four overlapping domains of ecological settings that created the climate of a setting and a 'press' towards or against certain groups. The four domains and some of the ways in which they can display an institution's position towards sexual minorities are shown in Figure 8.4. Chesir-Teran made the further point that there may be common factors underlying different forms of oppression – such as institutional cultures of supremacy, authoritarianism, or totalitarianism or that show a press for sameness. Challenging oppression of one form was likely to contribute to addressing others. The social activism of gay and lesbian communities had, he added, been a demonstration

---

The physical-architectural domain

> Heteorsexism might be evident in the form of lack of privacy in changing rooms, wall posters that only showed images of heterosexual couples or families, and anti-gay and lesbian graffiti.

The programme-policy domain

> Relevant features would be the presence or absence of anti-discrimination or anti-harassment policies that included sexual orientation, gay and lesbian-affirmative counselling and support groups, and the accessibility of books about homosexuality or written by LGBT authors.

The supra-personal domain

> Important are the visibility of LGBT people, and the numbers of people with 'out' LGBT family members or friends.

The social domain

> A press towards heterosexuality and against homosexuality would be evident, for example, in assumptions that opposite sex dates would be brought to social events or by an atmosphere of acceptance of the expression of prejudiced attitudes or the use of derogatory slang terms for gays and lesbians.

Figure 8.4   Four domains in which an institution can display its position towards lesbian, gay, bisexual and transgendered (LGBT) people
Source: Chesir-Teran, D. (2003). Conceptualizing and assessing heterosexism in high schools: a setting-level approach. *American Journal of Community Psychology*, **31**, 267–79

to community psychology that informed social collectives can impact on social change (D'Augelli, 1989).

Ellis (2002) pointed out that although there had been study of attitudes towards gay and lesbian people, there had been comparatively little study of the subject from the perspective of human rights. What there had been had focused on specific issues such as parenting, the right to serve in the armed forces, and employment rights. She put a number of questions about gay and lesbian people's human rights to a sample of several hundred psychology and social science students from a number of universities in Britain. Even among a group who might be expected to be more positive than most, substantial minorities expressed attitudes against certain aspects of human rights; for example, that 'lesbians and gay men should be granted asylum in another country when homosexuality is persecuted in their own', the right to serve their country in the armed forces, the right to 'flaunt their sexuality in public at marches and demonstrations', and to 'openly express their affection for their partners in public without fear of harassment or violence'. Only just over half agreed that 'books promoting lesbian and gay male homosexuality as a positive lifestyle should be freely available in school libraries', or that 'university modules . . . should explicitly include lesbian and gay male perspectives'.

Using the published records of British parliamentary debates and press cuttings of the time, Ellis and Kitzinger (2002) examined the rhetorical arguments that were used to oppose the equalising of the age of consent in the UK – at 16 years – for sex between males and that for heterosexual acts. The 1967 Sexual Offences Act, which implemented the 1957 Wolfenden Committee's recommendation to decriminalize consensual male homosexual practices, had set the age of consent at 16 for heterosexual sex and 21 for male homosexual sex. This discrimination, seen as a human rights issue, was challenged in the 1990s in a series of campaigns by, among others, the lesbian and gay rights lobbying organisation, Stonewall. It was successful in getting the homosexual age of consent reduced to 18 years, but the House of Lords remained opposed to further equalisation, and only after a ruling by the European Human Rights Commission was the law finally changed to equalise the age of consent. The argument of the campaigners was, all along, in terms of the right for an equal age of consent and the removal of the discrimination of different ages. An analysis of the arguments against change showed there to be three principal arguments that were used. One was that there could be no equality between something that was normal, good, clean and healthy (and in some forms of the argument, supported by scripture) and something that was abnormal, subversive, and likely to undermine the family and morality generally. A second was the majoritarian argument that it was wrong to make a change that the majority of the population were against. The views of the majority should carry the day rather than those of a 'tiny minority'. The third was that the principle of protecting vulnerable young men should take precedence over equalising the age of consent: to do the latter would be to invite exploitation of the young. Two other arguments that were used were in terms of alleged health risks from HIV/AIDS and other sexually

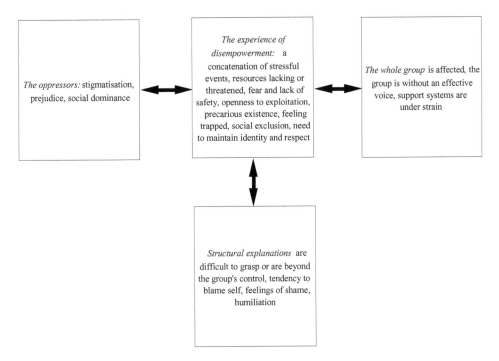

Figure 8.5   The experience of disempowerment: some common elements

transmitted diseases, and the 'slippery slope' argument that equalising the age of consent would encourage demands for further extensions of human rights such as the right to marriage and parenthood.

Ellis and Kitzinger made the additional important point that, when arguing back, those who supported change had often undermined the human rights case by engaging in involved and diversionary debates about whether the 'natural' could always be equated with the morally good, about which sections of the population were in favour or against, about whether the present law failed to protect young men because it made it difficult for them to seek advice and support, and even about whether or not there would be requests for further extension of human rights. In this way the proponents of change allowed the opposition to set the agenda, heterosexism remained largely unchallenged, and the language of human rights was little invoked.

CONCLUDING PART III

It has only been possible to hear of the experiences of members of seven disempowered groups in these two chapters. Although they are large groups, many others of concern to community psychology have not figured at all. Some of those neglected in Part III appear in other chapters, however – users of mental health services, for example, who make an appearance in a number of places in Part IV. It is likely, though, that many of the elements of the experience of being disempowered are very general and are common to a wide variety of particular forms of oppressive conditions. Some of those elements, which have been identified in the course of this chapter and the previous one, are summarised in Figure 8.5. It comes as no surprise that the themes appearing here are in many instances the very ones that were noted in Chapter 1 as those that have been neglected in traditional psychology, and the same ones that are highlighted by empowerment, liberation and post-colonial theories (see Chapter 2).

PART IV

COMMUNITY PSYCHOLOGY ACTION: FROM SUPPORT TO LIBERATION

Chapter 9
STRENGTHENING SOCIAL SUPPORT FOR MEMBERS OF DISEMPOWERED GROUPS

This chapter begins our examination of a representative sample of community psychology action projects by looking at a number which, in one way or another, have tried to help members of disempowered groups by arranging for increased social support. Some of the disempowered groups that figure in this chapter – but not all – are among those that featured in Part III. Much of the social support provided in these action projects is offered by peer supporters who share, or who have shared, the same position of disempowerment as those they are now aiming to support. In other cases support is provided by volunteers.

It has been pointed out that there is some similarity between such ways of enhancing relatively informal social support and, on the other hand, formal, professional psychotherapy (Cowen, 1982; Barker & Pistrang, 2002). In fact there is good evidence, which I reviewed in an earlier work (Orford, 1992), that there is little difference in mental health outcomes between support delivered by professionals and that delivered by 'para-professionals' (Durlak, 1979; Hattie et al., 1984; Faust & Zlotnick, 1995). Although to some, social support interventions may be open to the very same criticisms that were made against psychotherapy in Chapter 1 – that at best they ameliorate and do not transform social structures or power relationships – in fact we shall see several examples in this chapter of the ways in which social support interventions do address broader issues of social structure. In many ways they can be thought of as occupying the large middle ground between professionally delivered help and the more transformative types of community action that will be illustrated in the following chapters.

A helpful systematic review of social support interventions was provided by Hogan et al. (2002). To be included in their review, studies needed to test the efficacy of an intervention and needed to have stated an improvement in social support as a goal of treatment. Nearly 100 studies were included, covering a wide range of interventions. Their review therefore provides a rich and varied picture of the many types of interventions aimed at improving social support. Some were professionally led, others self-help or peer-led; some were delivered in group format, others individually; some aimed to provide social support directly, while others sought to help people enlist their own support or provided training in social skills for improving social support. Their review was therefore unusual because it included forms of help and intervention as widely different as self-help groups, peer-support schemes, professional treatments that included family members or friends, and social skills training. The variation that Hogan *et al.* found in terms of aims, procedures, social support measures (despite the aim of the interventions, the majority used no measure of social support), and research design (small numbers resulting in insufficient statistical power, short or absent follow-up, lack of random assignment, etc., were all common failings), meant that no definite conclusions were possible regarding the relative efficacy of different methods overall or for different people or different problems (a very wide range of problems and concerns were covered, including eating, alcohol or drug problems, smoking, physical conditions including breast and other cancers, rheumatoid arthritis and coronary heart disease, as well as mental health problems; and those involved included young pregnant women, mothers at risk of child maltreatment, and carers, as well as people in different age groups).

SOCIAL SUPPORT FOR YOUNG PEOPLE

Mentors for Young People

One form of social support, originating in the USA, which rapidly became very popular, was that of 'mentoring', particularly mentoring for young people (early examples were Goodman, 1972, and Dicken *et al.*, 1977). Some see its popularity in the context of the increased choices, risks and contradictions facing young people compared to previous generations (the 'risk society' described by Beck, 1992 – see Chapter 2) and in the context of the theory of resilience, that suggests that the long-term presence of one caring adult can help young people overcome adverse circumstances in moving towards adulthood (Philip & Hendry, 2000). Others have suggested that it has been a response to the decline of social capital and the failure of natural forms of social support for young people (Rhodes *et al.*, 2002).

Those who act as mentors for young people may have volunteered to take part in a organised mentoring scheme or may be 'natural mentors'. It was the latter that was examined in a number of papers in a special issue of the *American Journal of Community Psychology* edited by Rhodes *et al.* (2002). Hirsch *et al.* (2002) focused on two kinds of natural mentors: grandparents, because it had been suggested that they have a special role to play in mentoring for their adolescent grandchildren; and non-parental male adult mentors, because of the frequent lack of positive male adult influence in the lives of adolescents. Adolescents, aged between 14 and 19 years, attending the public high school in a suburb of a large mid-western city in the USA, were asked to identify the grandparent, 'who has the most important influence on your life', and to say whether there was an adult male, other than the person's father, 'who you feel has an important influence on your life' (followed if necessary by the probe, 'someone like a relative, a teacher, a neighbour...'). The maternal grandmother was much the most often nominated as the most influential grandparent (60%) and significantly more often so for black than white adolescents (70% versus 52%), reflecting the long documented centrality of maternal grandmothers in African USAmerican social networks. Natural mentors were influential for the young people in three areas: personal growth (e.g. '... is supportive of me when I don't do well at something'); teen–parent relationship (e.g. '... gives me useful advice in dealing with my parents'); and peer relationships (e.g. 'I talk to... about problems I'm having with friends'). Forty-four per cent identified an adult male, other than the father, who had had a significant influence; uncles being most often nominated, followed by adult brothers (typically seven years older than the family adolescent). Hirsch *et al.* suggested that rather than relying on 'the kindness of strangers', as mentoring programmes do, strong kinship ties have the advantage that they do not need to be artificially created from scratch, are unlikely to disappear altogether, and can help an adolescent appreciate the family's history and form an identity that is historically and culturally grounded.

Beam *et al.* (2002) did not confine themselves to particular types of relationship, asking a sample of teenagers (aged on average 16–17 years) at one high school in greater Los Angeles, USA, whether they had in their lives, other than a parent, an 'important adult... someone at least 21 years old who has had a significant influence on you or whom you can count on in times of need' (aunt, teacher, or friend's parent, were given as examples). Eighty-two per cent said they had such a very important person (VIP), almost equally divided between kin (aunts and uncles being most common, followed by siblings, followed by grandparents and cousins) and non-kin (most frequently older friends, followed by teachers). Non-kin VIPs concentrated their support on expressing interest and concern for the adolescent's well-being, letting the adolescent know that he or she had done something well, or indicating that the VIP would always be around if the adolescent needed help. Kin VIPs provided more defuse support, including, in addition, such aspects of support as giving or loaning of money or something else that was needed, or providing a place to stay. Beam *et al.* provided two illustrative examples. The first was a 16-year-old male adolescent whose VIP was a 32-year-old married man with no children of his own, the couple being close friends of the young man. The way the latter described his relationship with his VIP suggested that it combined characteristics of a relationship with a parent and that with an older sibling:

> He's like an older brother to me... I can talk to him about things that I wouldn't talk to my parents about, like relationships or sex. If I did talk to my parents about some stuff, they might set new rules and regulations, and stuff, but if I talk to [VIP], nothing happens – I just get a lot of freebee advice... I can tell him anything that I can tell my friends, but he gives me *correct* advice, as an adult – he wouldn't lead me the wrong way. He knows that I look up to him – he's like a *role model* (p. 318).

The second example was a 17-year-old young woman who described a strong relationship with a sister, six years older, who had become very important to her three or four years previously:

> She [the VIP] started taking me places – to concerts and stuff. That's when I
> started to hang out with her. Nothing [special] was going on my life. That's just
> it. She taught me to get interested in stuff – like music. I really started loving
> music because of her ... She's been there for anything important or exciting that
> has happened in my life. She's either been there or been the one to make it
> happen. I owe a lot of my outlook on life to her (p. 319).

In conclusion Beam *et al.* recommended that greater attention be paid to supporting such natural mentoring rather than putting all the emphasis on arranged
programmes where there was often a waiting list for mentors and where mentor–
youth matches were often less than ideal.

Zimmerman *et al.* (2002) asked several hundred adolescents, in the fourth year
of high school, in a large mid-western city in the USA (they were participating in a
longitudinal study of school drop-out and drug use), about the presence of natural
mentors in their lives. Fifty-four per cent said yes when asked, 'Is there an adult
25 years or older who you consider to be your mentor? That is, someone you can
go to for support and guidance or if you need to make an important decision, or
who inspires you to do your best?' (p. 226), and who was not an immediate family
member. Extended family members such as uncles, aunts, cousins or grandparents were most frequently nominated, but others included professionals such as
teachers, counsellors or ministers, god-parents and god-siblings, friends of family
members, parents and siblings of friends. Results of multiple regression analyses
suggested support for a compensatory model of resiliency: having a mentor was
associated with reduced problem behaviour (less marijuana use and fewer delinquent behaviours) and more positive school attitudes (more likely to like school,
to believe that success at school was important, and to feel capable of succeeding
in school), even after risk factors had been entered into the equation (demographic
variables such as sex, parents' occupational prestige and ethnic group, and problem
behaviours of friends).

Philip and Hendry (2000) have written about the views of mentoring relationships held by adult mentors and young people in one area of Scotland, covering
urban, suburban, and rural neighbourhoods as well as communities of affluence
and others of multiple deprivation. They took a broad view of mentoring, including as mentors professionals whose remit included an element of mentoring, such
as youth and support workers, as well as adults who were identified as mentors by
young people and peer group and friend-to-friend mentoring. Thirty interviews
with mentors were held. Mentors recognised the benefits to themselves as well
as to the young people they were mentoring. Being a mentor sometimes helped
mentors make sense of their own experiences, as in the following case of a young
mother who was working as an unpaid volunteer with young people:

> Well I have been trying to pinpoint what went on in my life and it has helped
> me – seeing what they are going through – I had such a shitty childhood that
> was so full of problems and I think it kicked me into this ... my relationships
> with them has given me more confidence in myself (p. 218).

Mentoring sometimes enabled mentors to gain insight into the realities of youth
experience and to learn from that. Thirdly, it could provide an opportunity to

develop alternative kinds of relationship, such as reciprocal relationships across ages. Fourthly, some said that it enabled them to develop skills in offering support, challenge, and a form of friendship. Although it might pose dilemmas for mentors, an important element in mentoring was the brokering role that was often adopted by mentors in relation to parents or carers, for example a woman mentor helping a young man brake the news of his girlfriend's pregnancy to his mother, or clerical assistants in youth projects helping young people 'try things out' or rehearse issues before raising them with youth workers.

Parra *et al.* (2002) studied intensively, over a period of a year, youth–mentor pairs brought together by an agency in a medium-sized mid-western US city. The agency was affiliated to Big Brothers/Big Sisters of America, one of several thousand organisations in the USA then supporting mentoring activities. Fifty young people, aged 10 years on average (range 7–14), and their mentors, aged on average 27 years (range 18–56), completed separate questionnaires (young people during interviews, mentors by post) at the start of their relationships and at both six-month and one-year points. They were also interviewed by telephone monthly during the year. Parra *et al.* wished to test a number of hypotheses about the circumstances under which mentoring was more or less effective since it had been noted that although mentoring had positive outcomes for young people – in terms of self-esteem and self-confidence, increases in academic achievement, reduced likelihood of initiating drug use, and lower rates of delinquency recidivism – there were substantial variations in outcomes. Their main outcome variables were (1) whether the relationship continued for the full 12 months (the minimum recommended period; 74% did so) and (2) perceived benefits as rated at 12 months separately by young people and their mentors (15 items, each rated on a five-point scale, e.g. 'I have helped my Little Brother form a positive self-concept'; 'My Big Brother has helped me see good things about myself'). The results of a statistical path analysis (summarised in Figure 9.1) showed that the closeness of the relationship that formed between mentor and young person (an average of monthly seven-point ratings made separately by young person and mentor) was the variable most strongly and directly related to outcomes. Perceived quality of training was positively correlated with mentor self-efficacy at the outset. Parra *et al.* had noted that the mentor agency, although it was careful about recruitment and selection of mentors, had only very minimal standards for training. They recommended improved training and supervision standards. Despite the thoroughness of their study, they acknowledged the lack of assessments of more distal outcomes such as improved psychosocial functioning or academic achievement.

Rhodes *et al.* (2002) concluded that the growth in volunteer mentoring programmes was encouraging, but they warned that much more needed to be known about how mentoring schemes work in practice. Not all mentoring relationships lasted for very long and short-lived relationships might do more harm than good. Rhodes *et al.* were also concerned that too much might be expected of mentoring. They noted that US President Bush had referred to mentoring in his 2001 inaugural address. But mentoring would not touch more fundamental issues of, "Family income, systematic school reform, job opportunities, health coverage, child care, affordable housing, neighbourhood revitalization, and public safety all [of which] need to be emphasized" (p. 154).

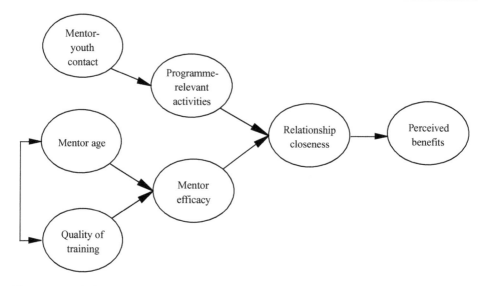

Figure 9.1   Path analysis showing the importance of the mentor–young person relationship for the outcome of mentoring
Source: Parra, G.R., DuBois, D.L., Neville, H.A. & Pugh-Lilly, A.O. (2002). Mentoring relationships for youth: investigation of a process-oriented model. *Journal of Community Psychology,* **30**, 367–88

Grandma Please

Szendre and Jose (1996) reported on a different kind of support programme for young people, operated by a non-profit social agency in Chicago, USA. Called Grandma Please, it was primarily designed for children who might be alone after school, who needed help with homework or for some other reason, or who simply wanted to talk. The programme was available for three hours after every school day and was advertised at all Chicago public schools in the city. Telephone calls from children were received through a central operator and were forwarded to the home phone lines of the elderly volunteers – the 'Grandmas' and 'Grandpas'. A content analysis was carried out of between 4000 to 5000 calls logged during a single year, and just over 100 9–11 year olds were interviewed from one school, half of whom had used the programme during the year. Thirty-seven volunteers participated during the year and were interviewed by telephone. In the event only one was a Grandpa, all the rest Grandmas. They were aged on average 78 years (range 55–93), including some who were home-bound and in one case resident in a nursing home. Unlike some earlier similar programmes, this one involved children at inner-city schools, and approximately half of the volunteers were said to be struggling on low fixed incomes themselves. They varied in educational level, but well over half had worked in teaching and business professions. All but one were white, while the largest number of young people who called were African USAmerican.

The scheme was very well used. The average number of calls made to a volunteer each month was 16 (range 2–48) with a median number of calls per volunteer of 132 during the year. The results of the content analysis of topics discussed during calls

Table 9.1   Percentages of call types, with examples, in the Grandma Please project

Call type	Percent within all calls (categories not mutually exclusive)	Examples
1. Conversation	74%	Events of the school day; things children like to do
2. Positive event	26%	Field trip, birthday, holiday
3. Problem	25%	Hates school, fight with friend, parents getting a divorce
4. Positive support	20%	'Grandma' praises child or sympathises
5. Accomplishment	18%	'A' on a spelling test, winning the science fair
6. Homework	13%	Spelling, math problems
7. Fun conversation	9%	Telling jokes, stories, songs
8. Curiosity	3%	Child wants to know about programme or 'Grandmas'
10. Scared/lonely	1%	Child is afraid of noises, break-ins, states loneliness

Source: Szendre, E.N. & Jose, P.E. (1996). Telephone support by elderly volunteers to inner-city children. *Journal of Community Psychology*, **24**, 87–96

in shown in Table 9.1. Szendre and Jose particularly noted the high proportion of calls that dealt with problems, a departure from findings from previous studies of such programmes. Just over three-quarters of calls were from girls and the median age of callers was 10 years (over two-thirds between 9 and 12 years). Those above the median age, particularly older girls, were more likely to talk about problems and to report that they had received more support from the volunteers. Younger children were much more likely to engage in fun conversations involving jokes and stories. Discussion of accomplishments (ignored in previous research according to Szendrre and Jose) was reported more or less equally by children of all ages. Accounts given by children who had called volunteers were overwhelmingly positive regarding friendliness, liking, positive qualities of the volunteers, and qualities of the programme itself (e.g. "You can pick the Grandma", "It's open every day", "You can call if you need someone to talk to"). The volunteers also indicated that it had been a very satisfying experience for them. They rated the programme highly and indicated that they wanted to continue to participate as long as their health allowed. They were particularly satisfied that they were able to assist parents, indicating that no other schemes existed that provided, "... an instant connection to a safe, available, caring older adult who will listen to both problem and nonproblem calls" (p. 94).

Peer Support at School

Our last example of a social support action project for young people took place in the school setting. It was a bold action research project that took place in 13 secondary schools in one area in South Africa and was reported by Visser (2004). It was a collaboration between the schools, the area Department of Education, and the Department of Psychology at the University of Pretoria. Schools were selected by the Department of Education because it was believed that many of the learners in those schools experienced psychosocial problems, including excessive alcohol and drug use, risky sexual behaviour, aggressiveness, gang-related activities, depression, and suicidal tendencies. The educational system had been undergoing much change; teachers were experiencing high levels of stress, and the focus was on improving academic standards and not on emotional well-being and creating a caring environment. In consultation with guidance teachers in the schools it was agreed to try to develop a system of peer support. In the first year, 10 peer supporters were selected for each school, aged between 14 and 18 years, and chosen from among volunteers for their characteristics of openness, approachability and trustworthiness. In the second year an additional five to 10 peer supporters were recruited, nominated by existing peer supporters and voted for by learners in the schools. Possible roles for the peer supporters were: "To identify and support learners who experienced psycho-social problems and to refer them to appropriate helping facilities"; "To facilitate change in peer group norms from within the peer group, by creating a context for awareness and communication among peers about high-risk behaviour"; and "To mobilize involvement and participation of young people and other stakeholders in addressing the problems experienced by young people in schools" (pp. 444–5).

A great deal of effort was put into training and sustaining the peer supporters and trying to keep everyone informed and committed. Visser used Bronfenbrenner's (1979) concept of nested systems to illustrate the complexity of the systems and subsystems involved in the project. Training of peer supporters, which started with a holiday workshop, continuing with eight, hour-long weekly sessions at the schools, was facilitated by three or four fourth year psychology students who were assigned to each school and who were responsible for the training and implementation of the project. Eight masters psychology students took responsibility for creating a context in the schools for the peer supporters to function in. Principals were kept informed. One teacher in every school was invited to a workshop to discuss the project and in the second year a group of teachers was involved in project implementation. As time went on a management committee was formed consisting of one peer supporter and one teacher from each school, meeting with project co-ordinators from the Department of Education and the University. Some financial support was provided for the peer supporters to create awareness of what they could offer. Facilitators provided weekly reports and had weekly feedback sessions with the project leader. Focus group discussions were held twice a year with peer supporters and were held with the 13 responsible teachers.

Visser's account provides a picture of the difficulties that peer supporters faced and some of the success they achieved. To start with they had to make their services known by introducing themselves at school assembly or by presenting a drama production in different classes or organising events where goals and intentions could be announced. They had to try to build relationships, in order to carry out their work, with their peers, with teachers, and sometimes with organisations to which learners with serious problems could be referred. They had to deal with being made fun of initially, with a prevailing culture of not talking about personal problems, with issues of confidentiality and sometimes with conflicting relationships, with varying support from teachers – some of whom were enthusiastic, others less so – and with the serious lack of mental health resources in local disadvantaged communities.

With perseverance peer supporters made headway. In several of the schools they started an office, with a schedule of supporters available, where learners could come and talk about personal problems or teachers could refer learners. In other schools consultation was carried out more informally on the school grounds. The most important problems discussed were smoking, alcohol and drug misuse, sexual problems such as rape, pregnancy, HIV/AIDS, relationship problems, gambling, and peer pressure. Peer supporters also initiated activities to enhance learners' knowledge and awareness. Activities including inviting guest speakers to talk about topical issues (in nine schools), organising AIDS and drug awareness days with speakers, drama, song and dance (seven schools), establishing feeding schemes for needy children in several schools, and safety, child protection and crime prevention programmes in others. Posters, newsletters, and even painting a graffiti wall were used in some schools to display preventive messages. In a number of the schools peer supporters also presented dramas for other community members and helped children with HIV find orphanages. In some of the schools they were active in trying to make teachers aware of the problems learners experienced or in helping agencies such as police, health clinics and social workers to address problems in their schools.

When a representative sample of nearly 700 learners at the schools were asked about the project, two-thirds overall reported that they knew about peer supporters in their schools (the percentage varied between schools from a low of a quarter to a high of nearly 80%). Twenty per cent reported that they had consulted a peer supporter. Fifty-seven per cent evaluated the service positively, saying that they thought it was useful and served a need in the schools. Negative comments from the remainder included the following comments: it was not well marketed in the school; the teachers did not support it; there were too few peer supporters; the peer supporters should be more available; the peer supporters were too young; the peer supporters could not be trusted. Visser concluded that the peer support system, building on the fact that peer supporters came from the same age and cultural groups as the learners, had the potential to reach the goal of making resources available to young people. In the second year it was mainly driven, she stated, by "... the enthusiasm and energy of the peer supporters, a few committed teachers and groups of student facilitators" (p. 451).

SOCIAL SUPPORT INTERVENTIONS FOR WOMEN

Befrienders Against Depression

As a development of their earlier work on the causes of depression among women (see Chapters 4 and 8), Harris, Brown and Robinson (1999a,b) set up and evaluated a befriending scheme for depressed women in an inner city area of north London.

The service was provided as an extension of a befriending service for ex-mental hospital patients run by the local branch of the Family Welfare Association. Women who were depressed were identified by postal screening of all women registered with certain general practices in the area (using a version of the GHQ, amended to distinguish chronic from shorter episodes: the screening process was partly designed to exclude cases where depression had not lased for 12 months or more). Eighty-six women were entered into the trial, half allocated to befriending.

Volunteer befrienders were recruited through advertisements in the local press, churches, and health centres. All those responding were given several interviews before being accepted for a three-day training course. Current depressive symptoms were not an exclusion criteria. Befriending involved meeting and talking with a depressed woman to whom the befriender was assigned for a minimum of one hour each week, acting as a 'friend', listening, and 'being there' for her. The emphasis was on facilitating and confiding, but befrienders were also encouraged to accompany their befriendees outside on trips, to broaden their range of activities, to offer practical support with ongoing difficulties and to create what Harris *et al.* called 'fresh-start' experiences – events that appeared capable of introducing new hope into a situation of ongoing deprivation, such as re-establishing contact with an old friend, finding a new social activity, or meeting a new partner. Befriending was designed to continue for up to 12 months, and at that time all the depressed women were re-interviewed. A significantly larger percentage of those in the befriending group than in the control group had dropped below GHQ 'definite caseness' level (65% versus 39%), and that was more likely when befriending had lasted a full 12 months. Further analysis suggested that befriending had been most effective for those who were under particular stress (combining severe interpersonal difficulties at first interview and any new severe stress event or difficulty during the year) and who had no fresh-start experiences that year.

Woman-to-Woman Support via Computer

A project that provided mutual social support via computer for single young mothers (aged 15 to 20 years) in Halifax, Nova Scotia, appeared to meet with great success (Dunham *et al.*, 1998). It also provides us with a good example of one form of evaluation. Fifty young women were each provided with a terminal or micro-computer, donated by individuals or organisations – finding sources of second-hand computer equipment was no problem according to the authors. Using an anonymous name and private password, participants could access a bulletin board system, called Staying Connected, which enabled them to use any of three different forms of communication: (1) a public forum, called Moms and Kids, where messages could be posted that could be read by all other participants, remaining accessible for 60 days before deletion; (2) private e-mail messages could be exchanged with one, selected, other participant; and (3) teleconferencing with up to eight participants at a time. In addition, the equipment could be used to access an updated list of community services available to single mothers in the area.

The amount of use of these opportunities was very considerable. Figures are provided for 42 of the women who were followed up after six months. They had

Treating sore breasts associated with nursing, finding a cheaper apartment, dealing with various family court procedures, managing child custody issues, treating persistent ear infections, managing various kinds of allergies, coping with an infant's sleep patterns, worrying about developmental milestones, dealing with teething problems, understanding social service regulations, using community transportation, managing birth control, using hospital emergency services, settling conflicts with parents, using a breast pump, resolving conflicts with male partners, continuing education, finding a cheap source of diapers, and managing infant constipation.

Figure 9.2 Topics discussed on one typical day in the computer support project
Source: reproduced with permission from Dunham, P.J., Hurshman, A., Litwin, E., Gusella, J. & Ellsworth, C. (1998). Computer-mediated social support: single young mothers as a model system. *American Journal of Community Psychology*, **26**, 281–306

accessed the network over 16,000 times in the six months, averaging nearly 400 calls per participant; had spent a total of over 4000 person hours on-line, averaging over 100 hours per person or approximately four hours a week; nearly 1500 messages had been posted in the public forum, and had received a total of nearly 4000 replies. Participant figures were highly skewed, however: a core group of 15 had used the network virtually every day throughout the six months (high participation), eight had participated consistently on a more or less weekly basis (moderate), and 19 had used the network with varying degrees of consistency early on but had stopped using it at some time prior to the end of the six-month period (low). Those with younger infants, and those rated on the basis of initial interviews as being the most isolated, used the network more often. Social isolation was rated on two dimensions: absence of caregiving assistance; and the presence of either an older male partner or a parent who actively restricted, and in extreme cases completely inhibited, the young mother's social contacts with peers.

At the end of the intervention a measure of sense of community (SOC) with the group – assessing feelings of attachment to the group, perceived similarities to other members, and interest in and satisfaction with this group – showed a high level of SOC, with scores correlating significantly with amount of participation. The researchers also analysed the content of messages posted in the public forum and replies received. It was found that three-quarters focused on the mother, half of those on her mental health and social isolation, the remainder focusing on the child, mostly about the child's physical health. Only 2% of replies were coded as being negative in tone, rude or non-supportive, with all the remainder providing support of some kind, over half of these providing emotional support, a third informational support, and a very small number material support. The topics of discussion on just one typical day are shown in Figure 9.2. An instance was cited of very significant emotional, informational, and material support: one mother spoke to another about her past experience of receiving abuse from a partner, leading to the mother she was exchanging with revealing a similar problem in her current relationship. That led to daily exchanges over several weeks, joint planning for the latter's escape, and the offer of practical assistance, and much support from other women when a series of messages about these events were posted on the public forum. Dunham *et al.* attempted further evaluation using a standard 120-item Parenting Stress Index (PSI) at baseline and again six months later. For the 42 followed-up mothers together, there was no significant change. However, a significant relationship was found between participation and PSI change, with most of the high participators showing a decrease, and the majority of others an increase in PSI scores.

The authors admitted to some initial scepticism about the ability of computer-mediated interaction to be more than superficial and unemotional. Their experiences of the project convinced them otherwise. They concluded that the safety of a controlled site that facilitated communication among a relatively homogeneous group of people with common interests and needs, had enabled a number of socially isolated young mothers to engage in meaningful exchange that in many cases had been of benefit to them. A number had decided to stay connected after the project, and at the time of writing 15 of the mothers had attended a party at which they had met face to face, and another social gathering was planned.

Listening Partners for Mothers

Bond *et al.* (2000) described and reported an evaluation of a Listening Partners programme for mothers of pre-school aged children living in a rural, impoverished, sparsely populated part of north-eastern Vermont, USA. Small family farms that had once been the foundation of the area's economy had been largely abandoned and many community residents were now employed in conditions of low pay and little security. The area was characterised by high levels of poverty and unemployment, teenage pregnancy, child abuse and neglect, domestic violence, and drunken driving. The project was designed for women who were living below the poverty line, in conditions of social and rural isolation, at risk for abuse or neglect of the children or under unusual stress, and lacking any history of involvement in self-help/mutual support groups. Potential participants were identified by lay support people, professionals or agencies in the communities, or were suggested by women who had already expressed an interest in taking part. Each Listening Partners group met for weekly three-hour sessions for eight months, meeting in a comfortable neighbourhood setting such as a church basement, school annex, or family centre. Arrangements were made for participants to share transportation to and from meetings and childcare was provided nearby. Each group included about 10 community participants and two group facilitators who were social workers, educators, or health service workers who had lived and worked in the community themselves.

The philosophy of the programme was that isolated, poor, rural mothers of young children often felt, "...an overwhelming sense of living on the margins of the community, feeling inadequate, unconnected to others, and powerless to change their own lives or the lives of others, including their own children" (Bond *et al.*, 2000, p. 700). It was common for women to blame themselves for their isolation and powerlessness, and the programme aimed to empower the women, not just by building individual autonomy, but rather via an empowerment process that involved both individual and community development. Drawing on traditions of study circles, collaborative learning, and participatory democracy, as well as the mutual support, self-help movement, the programme had the objective of encouraging, "... growth of self, voice, and mind among all participants... " (p. 704). Adopting a problem-solving approach was an important principle that involved working from a strengths perspective, identifying problems, helping to find solutions, and often re-framing as examples of resourceful and creative coping experiences, actions that had previously been attributed to personal limitations. But the centrepiece was what Bond *et al.* called 'reflective dialogue', which aimed to give participants the experience, quite unusual for that group, of being encouraged to express oneself, of knowing that one had been heard, and seeing or hearing one's own words reproduced. A number of creative methods, summarised in Figure 9.3, were used to 're-present' the women's words. Those methods varied all the way from practising reflecting and restating what another participant had said in a meeting, to sharing their stories with people of influence in the community.

The evaluation compared outcomes for a total of 60 participants from six Listening Partners groups and a control group of 60 women matched with the participants for age, family configuration/marital status, numbers and ages of children, living conditions, sources and amount of income, ethnicity, religion, employment status, and education. All participants and controls were interviewed extensively at home (or elsewhere if preferred) pre-intervention, post-intervention eight months later, and again at follow-up 10 months further on. On a checklist of changes, a greater proportion of participants indicated that their housing situations had stayed the same or improved as opposed to getting worse, and they were also less likely to smoke at follow-up. But the main assessment was a semi-structured interview to assess Ways of Knowing which categorised women's responses into one of five levels (see Figure 9.4). Women who entered the programme in the categories 'silenced knowing' and 'received knowing', the lowest of the two categories, were more likely to change, and that change was more likely to occur for those who had attended five or more sessions.

Qualitative analysis suggested changes in terms of the following: an increased sense of mind and voice; greater pleasure in learning that they could be helpful to their friends; new abilities to cultivate family environments that promoted more thoughtful dialogue and reflection; increasingly reciprocal and respectful relationships being cultivated with their young children; a changing sense of self-image and personal agency; greater self-confidence; ability to control their lives and to take care of themselves; improved ability to speak up for themselves, while simultaneously considering the needs of others; greater use of problem-solving strategies; greater capacity to make and be a friend; and evidence of providing leadership in more public domains such as becoming active in volunteer community organisations, network, or committees – for example with their children's schools and community education groups and women's shelters. Examples of things some women said before the programme were:

> I usually got nothing to say, I just don't have any opinion. And when I do have something, I can't get it out, or if I say it, nobody listens anyway. So that's it. I'm a dead end. I just shut up, or I get shut up (p. 700).

a)   We practised the art of attempting to re-say the words of another during dialogue, encouraging reflective restatement.

b)   Given constraints on literacy skills, each participant received a tape recorder she could use in the groups and/or at home to capture and replay her thoughts and group discussions.

c)   We transcribed portions of the group's discussion and personal stories and returned the transcriptions at subsequent meetings for reflection and revision.

d)   During group meetings, we created a written record of the dialogue on large pieces of newsprint posted around the room, allowing group members to observe words and ideas emerging and focusing as we proceeded. Subsequently we typed and distributed portions of these conversations that reflected particular themes and movement so that the group could reconsider its creations.

e)   Participants received a folder for storing their transcriptions, journal entries, and other creations; through their periodic review, participants could trace transitions in their thinking and recorded action.

f)   We designed sessions where women took turns telling their life story, portions of which were transcribed.

g)   As women worked on developing good listening and interviewing skills, they collaborated in pairs, or in small or large groups to draw out and record one another's 'growth stories' – stories of personal vision, strength, and accomplishment that had gone unnamed and unrecognised within the narrow definitions of our gender- and class-based value systems. We focused on the women's emerging strengths. Experience and actions that had been attributed to personal limitations were often reframed as examples of resourceful and creative coping. The power and influence of socio-political contexts came more clearly into focus, as did strategies for identifying and reshaping these contexts.

h)   The stories were transcribed and returned to the authors for revision and reflection, with the support of probing from peers, working in small groups. With the author's permission, some of these stories were shared with other Listening Partners groups, schools with adult literacy classes, and community social service agencies. 'Publishing' was a very empowering experience for the women, encouraging the author to see herself from a broadened perspective, constructing and naming the truth of her experiences in a form that is preserved and attended to by others.

i)   We also arranged for some of the women to share their stories with educators, newspaper reporters, legislators, and others who were trying to educate the public on life and childrearing in poverty and rural isolation.

j)   As the peer group sessions neared an end, participants took turns focusing on each group member, describing what each woman had come to appreciate about each other as well as herself. These comments were transcribed onto a diploma for each woman.

Figure 9.3   Methods used to 're-present' women's words in the Listening Partners programme
Source: adapted with permission from Bond, L.A., Belenky, M.F. & Weinstock, J.S. (2000). The listening partners program: an initiative toward feminist community psychology in action. *American Journal of Community Psychology*, **28**, 697–730

> I don't know; sometimes I think I just dream this stuff up. Half the time I couldn't tell you what I feel anyway. I know it doesn't feel good, but nobody else seems to see it like me... so maybe it's just me. I'm probably just weird. I don't know (p. 700).

At follow-up two of the participants said:

> I think a lot more about things and whether or not they can be changed. If they can, then I try to think of [things] I can do to change them. If they can't be changed, then I try to think of ways of dealing with them...I never used

(1)   *Silenced Knowing*

        People think of themselves as generally mindless, voiceless, and unable to learn from others or figure things out for themselves.

(2)   *Received Knowing*

        Learning is equated with passively receiving and storing information, with dualistic notions of truth and knowledge that are to be passed from expert to novice.

(3)   *Subjective Knowing*

        Knowledge and truth are conceived as highly personal, private, and essentially incommunicable, and as such cannot be shared, evaluated, or developed with others.

(4)   *Procedural Knowing*

        People envision that knowledge and truth can be developed, identified, evaluated and communicated using systematic procedures.

(5)   *Constructed Knowing*

        Knowledge and truth are conceived of as constructions of humankind and, as such are dynamic, contextual, and evolving.

Figure 9.4   Five 'Ways of Knowing'
Source: reproduced with permission from Bond, L.A., Belenky, M.F. & Weinstock, J.S. (2000). The listening partners program: an initiative toward feminist community psychology in action. *American Journal of Community Psychology*, **28**, 697–730

to think about anything like that before... Now I care about other people and myself, I have a new self-assuredness – that I can do it right *and* that I have rights (p. 720).

I think I've grown up. I'm just more serious about life. I can handle problems a lot better. Before, anytime a problem came up I just couldn't take it. Now I think about things before I jump into them. Now I learn from my past. I just realized that I've got the power to change whatever I don't like... Before my life ran me; now I'm running my life (p. 720).

Workshops to Formulate Change Plans

The final example in this section was, unlike the other examples, delivered by professionals. It has been included as an intriguing example of work that sits between the clinical domain of professionally delivered personal psychology services and that of social and community projects aimed at natural groups and collectives. It is notable, however, for eschewing a personal, diagnostic approach and for its attempt to go beyond intrapyschic change. Although it lacks the explicit social action orientation of the work of Holland (1988, 1992), which will be discussed in the following chapter, its concern to help women overcome feelings of helplessness about making social changes puts it on the same track as some of the more explicitly liberatory approaches. Like Bond *et al.*, Day *et al.* (2003) aimed to help women living in rural communities, in this case in Western Australia. They had all experienced economic and environmental changes – including technological and business changes and the introduction of government policies – which had left them in less stable employment positions. They were left feeling that they had been the subject of forces over which they had had little control, and which, indeed, were beyond the control of individuals.

Seventy-six women, recruited for a 'personal development course' from five rural towns, were randomly assigned to a standard or an experimental intervention. Each involved three one-day workshops. The standard type was based on cognitive behavioural principles and included material on identifying and challenging irrational negative self-talk, strategies for refuting or replacing unrealistic negative self-talk, information on dealing with external criticism, and assertive communication styles and stress management techniques. In the experimental group workshops, material on negative self-talk was also included, but in addition material included attributional retraining, helping participants identify aspects of their lives that were within their control to change, identifying target areas they would like to change, and helping participants problem-solve and formulate realistic action plans to make those changes, drawing on and contributing to personal resources as well as strategies involving using community resources. The intervention devoted considerable time to considering how to discriminate between levels of controllability and the need to focus efforts on areas that could be controlled. The workshops were facilitated by two psychologists who alternated between standard and experimental workshops across the five towns. Because of the stigma associated with depression, no mention was made of depression at any time during the project, although pre-project assessment suggested that a third of the women were reporting mild to severe depressive symptoms, and the prevention of depression was an aim.

To overcome the ethical problems associated with having a no-treatment control group, Day *et al.* included an additional control group consisting of friends or acquaintances of the main participants (nominated by the main participants themselves). Assessments were filled in pre-project, post-project, and at six-week and six-month follow-ups. Changes in self-rated depression and in negative attributional style (attributing negative outcomes to internal, stable and global causes) occurred for both project groups and not for the control group, but changes were better maintained at follow-up for those who had taken part in the experimental workshops. Asked to rate level of satisfaction with the programme, the large majority in both experimental and standard groups agreed that the workshops had helped them, had meaning for them, had helped them understand why they thought, felt and acted the way they did, were relevant to rural women, and that there was need for such workshops in rural communities. Three-quarters of the experimental group had either carried out plans for action made during the workshops or had pursued other courses of action to improve the quality of their lives. The latter included personal actions, such as teaching their sons to cook and taking

two nights off from cooking or addressing outstanding health problems or starting a business enterprise such as a bed and breakfast or a beautician service, and
community activities, such as serving on the local hospital board or forming a
committee to open a tele-centre or obtaining a grant to run business enterprise
development courses in the town.

Rather like Bond *et al.* (2000), Day *et al.* suggested that the apparent superiority of the experimental group workshop was due to its action-oriented, problem-
solving approach that provided participants with mastery experiences that gave
them opportunities to unlearn some of the helplessness engendered by years of
enduring aversive conditions that seemed to be beyond their control. While many
cognitive interventions might be concerned with helping people adapt to uncon-
trollable circumstances, they suggested that this experimental intervention had
shifted the focus to the control of those aspects of women's lives or communities
where they could make a difference.

SUPPORT FOR THOSE WITH ILLNESS OR DISABILITY OR FOR THEIR FAMILIES

For the next section I have chosen a small number of examples of peer support for
people with an illness condition – breast cancer is the main example here – or for
family members such as parents of ill or disabled children. There is only space here
to provide a very small number of examples. The range of similar conditions that
place people in circumstances where they might benefit from support is almost
endless (Orford, 1987; Hogan *et al.*, 2002). One such group that the present author
and colleagues have worked with over many years, and whose needs for support
are very considerable, are close family members of relatives with alcohol or drug
problems (Orford *et al.*, 2005).

Parents of Children with Illness or Disability

Parents of children with continuing illnesses or disabilities are a group who face
considerable stress (Eiser, 1987) and they have particular needs for support. Among
those who have sought to meet that need were Silver *et al.* (1997), who examined
the effects of a support intervention for mothers of children with ongoing health
conditions. The mothers were recruited at two large urban medical centres in New
York that served a predominantly inner-city, low-income, minority population.
They each had a five-to-eight-year-old child with one or more of a number of
health conditions that included asthma, sickle cell anaemia, epilepsy, congenital
heart disease, cleft lip or palate, cancer, endocrine disorders, and spina bifida and
various other congenital anomalies. They were randomly assigned to a support
intervention called Parent-To-Parent Network, a community-based programme
provided by 'lay intervenors'. The latter were women who had raised children with
ongoing health conditions themselves, recruited through advertisements in neighbourhood newspapers. Of 10 women selected to receive a 40-hour training, three
eventually accepted jobs as lay intervenors and worked approximately 21 hours

a week throughout the project, supervised by a clinical psychologist and a social worker.

The network intervention lasted for 12 months, during which time mother and intervenor were expected to have six face-to-face meetings in the home (or hospital if preferred), lasting about an hour, with telephone calls at least once every two weeks. In practice, meetings were fewer than planned but lasted longer, average face-to-face time working out slightly more than expected, at 6.7 hours. The number of telephone calls averaged 18, lasting for a total average time of four hours. Families were also invited to three group activities such as picnics and holiday parties that brought mothers and children together with others in the programme. The main aim of the intervention was to improve mothers' social support and their access to relevant information, services and knowledgeable advisors, thus increasing mothers' feelings of empowerment and active participation in their children's healthcare. There was emphasis on the fact that parents themselves had a great deal of experience, and that it could be shared to the benefit of other mothers, as well as for enlightening and educating professionals who care for children with chronic health conditions.

This project was unusual in focusing on the health of mothers, as opposed to an exclusive focus on their children's health. The main outcome measure was an index of psychiatric symptoms pre-intervention and at 12 months, which showed reductions for the intervention group of nearly 200 mothers compared to an equally sized control group. Analysis supported the conclusion that the intervention had buffered the effects of stress: the greater reduction in symptoms between the two groups was significant for those with higher numbers of stressful life events during the year, and the correlation of life events and symptoms at 12 months was significantly lower in the intervention group than for controls. Qualitative feedback found many mothers reporting changed perspectives on being parents of children with ongoing health conditions, saying they felt more understood, more hopeful about the future and more empowered.

Another group with needs for support that can easily be overlooked are parents of children with disabilities. Solomon *et al.* (2001) interviewed 56 members of six mutual support groups in the greater London area, and carried out focus group discussions with five of those groups. The average age of children with special needs was nine years. They had specific learning difficulties, dyspraxia, attention deficit disorder or speech delay, a severe or profound mental or physical disability or both, autism or disorders on the autistic continuum, or moderate learning disabilities. Parents, all but four of whom were mothers (four of the groups consisted of mothers only), had been members of their groups for an average of four years.

On a set of standard rating scales, parents described their groups very favourably in terms of helpfulness and satisfaction, and gave particularly high ratings for cohesion and task orientation on the Group Environment Scale (GES: Moos, 1986). Qualitative data from the focus group discussions suggested three higher order themes. One Solomon *et al.* termed 'control/agency in the world'. Parents universally reported that groups provided them with information which helped to reduce their uncertainty and sense of 'not knowing'. Information came from other group members, group resources such as lending libraries and newsletters, and visiting professional speakers. This was especially valued by some with regard to their relationships with professionals. They commonly talked about 'fighting battles' with professionals, for which information was 'ammunition'. They felt stronger in taking up issues, some describing their groups as 'pressure groups', sometimes with representation on local committees, and sometimes with real political power:

> Previously, I'd been fighting on my own for a number of things already. But after joining the group, I felt much stronger about the things I was fighting for because a number of people were fighting for the same thing. For the group to take on issues and work through them is encouraging for individuals in the individual battles (p. 121).

The second category, 'community/belonging', referred to being understood by others in the group, being able to share experiences, feeling 'less alone', developing friendships and valuing social activities together, having a sense of belonging to the group, and being able to share emotions including grief and anger:

> We know we don't have to explain that to each other because we all know we're going through exactly the same grief. If you lose a child, everyone understands your grieving, but if you've got a handicapped child you're treated as a second class citizen, the whole family are. But there's nobody you can turn to. You're lucky if someone in your family understands you, but they never understand like these people here (pp. 122–3).

The third category was 'self-change', which included feeling more confident, more assertive, 'tougher', less easily intimidated, and also more accepting of their child's disability. The three categories together pointed to the role of mutual support groups in creating change both socially and individually, and Solomon *et al.* integrated them in terms of a core category of 'identity change'. In place of a prevailing discourse of disability including notions of victimhood, powerlessness, isolation and being the recipient of help, mutual support groups could provide, "... an alternative discourse, which included agency, control, and empowerment, as well as actively sharing in communities rather than passively suffering as isolated individuals" (p. 127).

Solomon *et al.* also commented on the role of professionals in working in partnership with members of mutual support groups such as the ones they studied. Professionals, they suggested, should take care not to interfere with or reduce the control and autonomy of group members. Hence indirect participation in the form of consultation, or serving as referral agent, or initiator of a group, would seem more appropriate than direct participation as group leader or facilitator. None of the groups they studied had professional leaders or facilitators. Professionals might also see themselves as students in relation to mutual help groups, learning from groups about alternative ways of help, support and coping, and about the deficiencies in services that are highlighted by groups. The variable attitudes of professionals towards self-help/mutual help organisations and the issue of how best professionals can relate to such groups are topics that have been much discussed (see Orford, 1992; Nelson *et al.*, 1998; Salzer *et al.*, 2001; Chinman *et al.*, 2002).

Women with Breast Cancer

Dunn and Steginga and their colleagues have reported on different ways of providing peer support for women with breast cancer. A form of support that had become popular in Queensland, Australia, where they were working, and in other parts of the world, is the provision of a Breast Cancer Support Service (BCSS). Women volunteers, at least one year on from their own breast cancer treatment, and after the completion of a training programme, acted as volunteers to visit women recently diagnosed with breast cancer, a few days after surgery, usually in the hospital or treatment setting, followed by a telephone support call three weeks later, plus providing the patient with an information kit and temporary breast prosthesis or bra filler.

Dunn et al. (1999) reported an evaluation of the BCSS that involved two phases. At the first phase, six focus groups were held with a total of over 50 women who had received the service some time in the previous two years. The conclusion was drawn that two sets of processes were important: receiving helpful social support, and a process of social comparison in which women perceived similarity with the volunteer visitor. A total of 17 questions, based on phase one, were developed for use in the second phase which involved analysis of over 200 postal questionnaires returned by women who had been visited by a BCSS volunteer within the previous 16 weeks. The most positively rated were five of the social support items: 'Made me feel I was not alone'; 'Gave practical advice about bras, etc.'; 'Reassured me that I was reacting normally'; 'Made me feel hopeful about the future'; 'Reassured me that I would look feminine again' – as well as one social comparison item: 'Had an experience with cancer like me'. The best predictors of a global rating of the helpfulness of the service were: 'Visited me at the time I most needed her' (helpful social support), 'Had a similar way of life to me' (social comparison), and, negatively, 'Left me feeling uncertain about the future' (unhelpful support).

In a later report, Steginga and Dunn (2001) reported the development of a Young Women's Network (YWN) for young women with breast cancer, a group believed to be particularly at risk due to the greater likelihood of their cancer being associated with fears about their children, greater disruption to body image, and financial and practical difficulties, plus feelings of social isolation and stigma within their social group. Their report was about a community development process used to build a peer support programme for this group. The impetus arose from feedback from young women whose support needs were not being met, resulting in the holding of group and individual consultations with them. Meetings were facilitated by the authors, with assistance from several young women who acted as key informants. A decision was then made to hold a general public meeting to discuss their needs. Twenty-four young women attended. The group first developed as a professionally supported peer support group, later electing to become a reference group for further research and development. An initial qualitative study was undertaken leading to an action plan, a schedule of monthly meetings (so arranged as to make attendance easy), and the undertaking of a series of media stories to promote a more positive image of young women with breast cancer than the negative image that was often portrayed in the media. A research project was commenced to describe the needs of young women and monitor the effectiveness of the YWN. Twelve months after inception there were already YWN groups in five regional centres and the group was preparing to develop a website chat room and to trial tele-conferencing. Members of the original project reference group were funded by the Queensland Cancer Fund to present about the group's activities at an Australian national breast cancer service consumers' conference, which played a central role in the instigation of a study of the support needs of young women with breast cancer on a national basis.

Ussher *et al.* (2006) reported the results of qualitative analysis of data from group meetings with attenders at nine cancer peer support groups in New South Wales, Australia. Nearly 100 group members participated, over three-quarters women. Data were obtained by participant observation of regular support group meetings, followed by focus groups. The results were interpreted in terms of how the support group experience was positioned in contrast to support outside the group, particularly in terms of four themes. One – community versus isolation – positioned the group as providing a strong sense of family-like community in which emotions, including much humour, could be shared. This was in contrast to the common experience of having no one to talk to openly about the experience of cancer outside the group. A second theme – non-judgemental acceptance versus rejection – was based on a sense of empathy and identification in the group, contrasted with the experience of having their feelings dismissed, or feeling pressured to contain feelings so as not to distress family or friends, or simply to 'be positive'. As one person put it, "everyone [in the group] has walked in our shoes and they know exactly how we're feeling" (p. 2569). The third theme – information versus lack of knowledge – referred to the group as an invaluable source of information, in contrast to lack of knowledge and sometimes serious misunderstanding met with outside the group. The fourth theme – challenging versus normalising experience – referred to the challenge of facing the progressive illness and death of a group member which was described as a difficult but integral part of the group experience, in contrast to the experience outside the group, where illness and death were not the major focus and those with cancer were treated like normal people.

In terms of self-positioning, the main theme was an increase in empowerment and agency. That included an increased feeling of not being alone, being in control and able to cope, feeling empowered in relation to cancer as an illness – now 'living with cancer' – and in relation to interactions with others, particularly health professionals, for example feeling more confident about asking questions and seeking information. The contrast between descriptors of self before and after joining the group are shown in Table 9.2.

> It gives you the control back and some power; that's one thing you lose when you're diagnosed. You try and get back the self confidence you lose, you think 'I'm unhealthy', 'I'm sick' and you lose power because the doctor starts telling you 'you will do this' and then you get into a group like this and you start to gain a bit of self-management back and power and control . . . and end up managing it yourself (p. 2572).

The picture that emerges from that study and the others reviewed in this section confirms the idea that social support can contribute to an improvement in personal health and empowerment for people in such illness or disability-related stressful

Table 9.2 Descriptors of self before and after joining a cancer peer support group

Pre-group	Post-group
Defensive	Open
Sad	Humorous
Pessimistic	Optimistic
Despairing	Hopeful
Sorrowful	Joyful
Angry	Accepting
Vulnerable	Strong
Low morale	High morale
Negative	Cheerful/positive
Hard done by	Feeling fortunate
Impatient	Patient
Timid	Confident
Seen as a 'cancer patient'	Seen as a person with cancer
Afraid	Confident
Intolerant	Tolerant
Ignorant about cancer	Knowledgeable about cancer

Source: reproduced with permission from Ussher, J.M., Kirsten, L., Butown, P. & Sandoval, M. (2006). What do cancer support groups provide which other supportive relationships do not? The experience of peer support groups for people with cancer. *Social Science and Medicine,* **62**, 2565–76

circumstances. Alongside the all-important emotional support, the value of information stands out. Emotional and informational forms of social support (and sometimes practical advice as well) impact on health and empowerment via lessened feelings of isolation, hopelessness and being judged by others, and increased feelings of friendship, knowing and being understood. The greater strength and self-confidence that result may, on the one hand, allow people to accept chronic illness or disability and allow them to live with it with greater acceptance. At the same time, however, there is evidence here that the gains in personal empowerment enable people better to 'fight battles' with those in authority, and to be more active and less intimidated than formerly (recall the discussion of the complexities of power and empowerment in Chapter 2).

RESPONDING TO DOMESTIC VIOLENCE

In Chapter 8 the issue of violence towards women was highlighted – including Gracia's (2004) reference to the 'hidden iceberg' of domestic violence, and James *et al.*'s (2003) advocacy of a wider concept of violence towards women. Deficiencies in the coordination of services for women who have experienced violence, including rape, is another aspect that has received attention in community psychology (Campbell & Ahrens, 1998). In Chapter 11 we shall meet an example of a community-level project that raised local awareness about domestic violence (Romito *et al.*, 2004). Here, just three projects are described, each of which had features that are instructive for us (again limitations of space prevents including more of the many pieces of work that have been reported).

Advocacy for Women

Sullivan and her colleagues reported an advocacy intervention programme for women with physically abusive partners (Sullivan *et al.*, 1994; Bybee & Sullivan, 2002; Sullivan, 2003). It offers us a particularly good example of research and action in combination. Participants were women recruited from a domestic violence shelter in a city in the midwest USA. Violence reported by participating women when they entered the shelter was severe, ranging from being grabbed, pushed and shoved (92%), to being raped (48%), kicked (47%), and/or threatened with a gun or knife (40%). Based on the evidence, referred to earlier, about the effectiveness of paraprofessionals (Durlak, 1979; Hattie *et al.*, 1984; Faust & Zlotnick, 1995), the advocates in this programme were female undergraduate students enrolled in a community psychology course. Advocacy was available for 10 weeks during which time each advocate was required to work between four and six hours a week with and on behalf of a single client. Advocacy consisted of five phases, shown in Figure 9.5, although in practice the phases were not distinct and advocates often engaged in several phases simultaneously. Advocacy efforts could be classified as either individual-based – working with or on behalf of the individual woman to ensure access to resources and opportunities – or systems-based. It was an aim of the programme that the individualised interventions should also create community-level change, and in practice advocacy often involved both types. Just one example was altering local police actions: advocates would often send letters to the local police chief either commending or criticising police action. Along with similar comments from other service providers, these commentaries were influential in leading to police department policy changes. Sometimes advocates' supervisors worked on systems-level changes while the advocates were working with their individual families. For example, it became clear that court workers responsible for handling child visitation and child support issues were unlikely to be taking domestic violence into account. Policy changes resulted from advocacy supervisors documenting a number of cases where that had occurred and discussing the results at senior management level.

A number of features of the programme were highlighted by Sullivan (2003). One was the collaborative relationship between the principal researcher – herself an advocate in the domestic violence area who took an explicitly feminist approach to the project – women survivors of domestic violence and other advocates. For example, collaborative discussion led to detailed protocols for the training and supervision of the student advocates (which involved a whole semester of training and continued weekly supervision during the programme in groups composed of around six students and two supervisors), a protocol designed to maximise

Phase 1 Assessment

Consisted of gathering important information regarding the client's needs and goals. This was accomplished by directly asking women what they needed as well as by observing women's circumstances (e.g. extent of furniture and clothing in the home).

Phase 2 Implementation

In response to each unmet need identified, the advocate actively worked with the woman to generate or mobilise appropriate community resources. This involved exploring who in the community controlled the desired resource, deciding how best to obtain that resource from the resource provider, and actively working to obtain the resource. Although this was sometimes straightforward (e.g. obtaining a rental agreement from a potential landlord or receiving groceries from the local food bank), at other times creative strategies needed to be used (e.g. insisting that a police officer arrest an assailant for violating a personal protection order, or convincing a potential landlord to accept a lease with no security deposit).

Phase 3 Monitoring

Monitoring the effectiveness of the implemented intervention. The advocate and woman with whom she worked assessed whether the resource had successfully been obtained, and whether it was satisfactory to meeting the unmet need.

Phase 4 Secondary implementation (if necessary)

If initial implementation was not meeting the unmet need. For example, if they had obtained after-school child care for the woman's daughter, the advocate would ask how the child care was working and whether both the mother and daughter were pleased with the arrangement. Dissatisfaction would result in either modifying the current child care arrangement, obtaining new child care, or eliminating the need for child care altogether. Specific pros and cons of each scenario would be discussed, and the project participant would ultimately decide how next to proceed.

Phase 5 Termination

Consisted of three components. First, advocates stressed their termination dates from the very beginning of their interventions, to eliminate the possibility that their leaving would come as a surprise to the women with whom they worked. Keeping this date in mind also helped both the woman and advocate focus their energies on the very limited time period they had together. Beginning about week seven of the 10-week intervention, the advocates intensified their efforts to transfer the skills and knowledge they had learned throughout the course. Advocates also left families with written 'termination packets' containing lists of community resources, helpful tips for obtaining difficult-to-access resources, and useful telephone numbers.

Figure 9.5   Five phases of a programme of advocacy for women who have been assaulted by partners or ex-partners

Source: reproduced with permission from Sullivan, C.M. (2003). Using the ESID model to reduce intimate male violence against women. *American Journal of Community Psychology*, **32**, 295–303

the safety of advocates and women clients, and an extensive protocol to max-imise maintaining contact with women participants during the advocacy period and throughout a two-year follow-up period. The latter was highly successful, resulting in retention rates of 94–5% post-advocacy and at 6, 12, 18, and 24 months follow-ups.

A further feature stressed by Sullivan (2003) was the use of an evaluative research design strong enough that conclusions about effectiveness could be drawn. Sullivan considered the project to be in the tradition of the Experimental Social Innovation and Dissemination (ESID) model initiated by Fairweather (Fairweather et al., 1969; Fairweather & Tornatsky, 1977 – and see Chapter 10). After initial resistance by advocates and survivors, lengthy discussion led to adopting a randomised design in which half of the nearly 300 women participants were assigned to the advo-cacy intervention and the others to a services-as-usual control group. That enabled analysis to be carried out that showed a significant multivariate time × condition interaction effect, with women who worked with advocates reporting higher qual-ity of life (nine standard questions), social support (nine items asking about amount, quality, and overall satisfaction with support), and decreased difficulty in obtain-ing community resources (of 11 different kinds, reflecting the multiple needs very often experienced by women who have been physically abused). Perhaps most importantly, because such an outcome could not be assumed, women who had worked with advocates also reported less violence over time (a modified Conflict Tactics Scale including ratings of frequency and severity of violence of different kinds from original assailants as well as any new partner). Because of the success in obtaining information at several follow-up points, it was also possible to test a model of how change for women might be unfolding over time. Using structural equation modelling (SEM), and tests of mediation effects, it was possible to show that reduced risk of reabuse was mediated by improved perceived quality of life, which itself was mediated by the immediate effects of the advocacy intervention on improved access to resources and greater social support (Bybee & Sullivan, 2002).

An important consideration was the sustainability of the programme. Sullivan (2003) therefore worked with the local domestic violence shelter programme to obtain funds to create a new advocacy coordinator position within the shelter programme, providing direct advocacy services to women while resident in the shelter and training volunteers to provide advocacy services.

Studies of Male Perpetrators

The two studies to be described next were targeted, not at those on the receiving end of domestic violence, but rather at the male perpetrators of such violence. The first was reported by Morgan and O'Neill (2001; O'Neill & Morgan, 2001). They provided a discourse analysis of material collected in the course of a 'stop-ping violence' programme run by the Men For Non-Violence (MFNV) network, a nationwide New Zealand collective. The programme started with an all-day session and was followed by one evening meeting a week for several weeks. Fifteen men attended the first session. Roughly half were ordered to attend through the court system and most of the others were there because their partners had given them one last chance. A core group of 11 men remained throughout. The materials analysed were: the social science literature surrounding wife abuse; semi-structured interviews with the men before and after the programme; and notes made by a participant observer who attended the sessions.

Analysis of the relevant literature revealed five distinguishable discourses regarding male violence towards partners. Of these, two predominated in the way men spoke about their violence prior to taking part in the programme. One was what the authors called the Romantic discourse of violence as expressive of inner tension, suggesting that aggression is a response to stress and a 'build up' of tension and frustration. Men would typically account for their violence in terms of 'blowing up', 'losing control', 'snapping' or 'getting wild'. That discourse was, prior to the programme, often found in combination with an account that used the Medical discourse of personal pathology. For example:

> I've got a bad temper. I've always had a bad temper ... I've got a problem ... That's the type of person I am. I'm the one that's dishing out the violence ... I can certainly do without it as part of my character. It's a part of my life that I don't want (p. 281).

Extensions of the pathology discourse included accounting for violence in terms of the temporary pathology induced by the consumption of alcohol or drugs, or by reference to the partner's pathological behaviour that had incited the man to violence.

Analysis of participant observation notes illustrated the way in which the Liberal Humanist discourse of instrumentalism was taken up by the men. That discourse, which corresponded most closely to the programme's philosophy, held a man responsible for his own actions and interpreted violent acts as deliberately undertaken with the aim of the man getting his way with, or controlling, his partner. Following the programme, some men were making statements consistent with that type of discourse. For example:

> I do take full blame for the violence and that, that was my choice if you like ... I mean it was totally wrong of me (p. 283).

Both during the programme and after it, however, the Liberal Humanist and Romantic discourses were very often found side by side or in combination, as in the following example:

> I was feeling hurt, jealous, scared, yeah pretty uptight ... I tried to make her feel worthless so she wouldn't go (p. 283).

The other two discourses identified in the literature were less prominent in Morgan and O'Neill's reports, although both were apparent in the participant observation notes. The Structural discourse of constraining social systems was much used by the programme facilitators when referring to the constraints of gender norms and stereotypes, including male lack of emotional expressiveness, which facilitators were at pains to challenge. The Learning discourse of acquired behaviour was also implicit in the programme since there was much reference to acquiring new ways of recognising and responding to tension or insipient anger.

In summary, the authors were encouraged that the programme had brought about changes in the way participants talked about their aggression; they saw that type of discourse analysis as complementary to more conventional, statistical, outcome evaluation. They were left with doubts, however, about the apparent, and unacknowledged, contradiction between the Liberal Humanist and Romantic discourses, and the way in which the Romantic discourse remained, as a possible excuse for violence, in men's talk after the programme was over.

The second project for men was a preventive programme aimed specifically at male athletes in the USA. It contained some elements that the authors admitted might be found unconventional and controversial (Jackson & Davis, 2000). The Preventing Assault by Young Student Athletes (PAYS) programme was designed to tackle the apparently very high rate of physical and sexual assault of women by young male athletes. The 'culture of athletics', with its emphasis on aggression, dominance, vitality, speed, and hyper-masculinity, was believed to be a large part of the cause. Young athletes were taught 'to score', 'win at all costs', 'don't think, act', 'dominate your opponent', and 'aggression succeeds', and *not* sensitivity to others, communication and dating skills, or the difference between assertion and aggression. The latter skills, along with an overview of evidence on the nature and incidence of sexual and physical assault, and the nature of the short and longer term harm caused to women who were assaulted, constituted the main part of the PAYS presentation, which had been made to over 150 athletic departments involving approximately 5000 athletes. The potentially controversial aspects were:

1. the requirement that the presenter should be male, preferably with some athletic background himself;
2. that he should be comfortable with open discussion of sex, violence and other sensitive topics, often discussed with the audience in terms that some would consider crude; and
3. that the presentation and discussion recognised that young male athletes were often themselves in a vulnerable position because of their training, the high expectations placed on them, the ease with which an athlete could acquire a bad reputation, the possible harmful effects on his career, and the knock-on negative effects for the whole team and athletics department.

Before–after comparisons, carried out for some of the presentations, showed that athletes had particularly retained three messages: imagining the most sensitive woman that the athlete had known and imagining what she would think; always asking first; and accepting that 'no' always means 'no'.

SUPPORT FOR LGBT GROUPS

The stresses faced by members of LGBT groups at different stages of their lives were the subject of part of Chapter 8. Included was a particular consideration of the position of lesbian women (Markowe, 2002). Attitudes of homophobia or heterosexism that impinge on LGBT people were also a focus (e.g. Ellis, 2002; Russell & Richards, 2003). Among the many projects that could be described here, two have been chosen that provided support for lesbian women, and one that entailed contact between students and an LGBT youth centre. In the following chapter two LGBT projects will be described that go beyond the provision of social support.

Support for Younger and Older Lesbian Women

Bridget and Lucille (1996) described the development of a Lesbian Youth Support Information Service (LYSIS) in the north-west of England. The forerunner of LYSIS was a study involving lengthy interviews with 20 lesbians, most aged 25 years or less. Interviews lasted between two and over six hours – that was the limit of tolerance for the interviewers, although many of the participants were willing to continue, nearly all saying that they enjoyed being interviewed and that, although it had been painful to talk about some of their experiences, they were pleased to be talking about them for the first time (a frequent comment heard by those who conduct longish interviews with members of disempowered groups). The results suggested that most were facing serious difficulties. More than three-quarters reported having had long periods of depression or sadness, two-thirds had attempted suicide (totalling more than 40 suicide attempts between them), over half had abused themselves in other ways such as cutting, banging or putting a fist through a window, half had serious alcohol problems, half had used illegal drugs, half had been homeless, half had felt lonely and isolated at school, and half had been sexually abused or raped. A survey of support available to young lesbians in the county found that none of 40 voluntary and statutory agencies contacted offered support specifically for the needs of young lesbians. LYSIS was set up to challenge their isolation, to help them develop self-esteem, to encourage positive ways of dealing with external and internal homophobia, to conduct research into the needs of young lesbians, and to encourage other agencies and parents to develop knowledge and provide appropriate support. At the time of writing, LYSIS was providing: a national helpline, 'correspondence counselling' – since many young lesbians made contact by letter in response to reading about LYSIS on the problem page of a young woman's magazine and most found talking about their sexuality far more difficult than writing about it in a letter – the facilitation of peer support, for example through a national LYSIS Penpals scheme, and the provision of a information pack and a free copy of a booklet adapted from one written by a Young Lesbian Group in the USA. Funding had been received from a national charity for further development of the work, and from a national research council to study the relationship between lesbianism and alcohol misuse.

LYSIS had not been set up without considerable struggle. Bridget and Lucille had to weather considerable negative publicity in the early days. For example a very negative report appeared on the front page of the local newspaper quoting a community group leader who was against the project on the grounds that young girls would be influenced at an impressionable age. Concern was expressed from within the county council, and, after further negative publicity, funds were withdrawn because the conditions being imposed on the project were thought to be unacceptable. The research project went ahead on a voluntary basis.

Aware that many studies and projects had failed to include older lesbians and gay men, particularly the former, Nystrom and Jones (2003) started an Elder Initiative for lesbian women in a major city in the north-west USA. A first meeting was advertised by posters in grocery stores, bookshops, doctors' offices and shopping centres, and notices were placed in local and specialist newspapers. They were surprised that as many as 36 women attended the first meeting, all involved in the general community as volunteers, organisers or activists, and all keen to organise themselves into a group to address their issues and concerns. Sixty-seven women attended a second meeting, and after three months membership had grown to more than 125, and within three years to 550. A particular model of community building, described by Kretzmann and McKnight (1993), was chosen to guide the work. The model had five objectives: (a) to focus on the skills and resources of individuals, which was done by creating an inventory or 'map' of all the skills and resources available to the group; (b) to identify all community associations and groups that might be helpful and to build relationships with them, for example coalitions with police, libraries, churches, colleges, hospitals, and community-based organisations; (c) to 'map' community assets, including developing partnerships with schools, police, park systems and others that might contribute resources such as meeting space, sponsorship or volunteers; (d) to collectively develop a plan of action, giving each member a voice; and (e) to seek outside financial resources and support.

In the early days of the project, the needs of this older group, aged on average 59 years, centred on health and housing, nearly all preferring housing focused on lesbian and gay issues. A major theme was their desire to have help with minor home repairs, and this led to the development of a tool bank, and later to a skills bank that acted as a clearing house for services, including transportation and maintaining contact with the housebound. A newsletter and a website were developed, and several sub-groups were formed, including a health support group, a book club, and a social committee.

A decision was made early on to lower the membership age limit to 40 years in order to attract more new members. That decision in the event lowered the average age of members to 47 years and in the process shifted the focus of activities from such things as creation of the tool bank and a grief and loss support group, to a greater focus on social matters, including information about lesbian-oriented community events. The result was that older women appeared to feel disenfranchised and their attendance declined. It was thought that this reflected one of the limitations of the community building model that was being used: it lacked an internal monitoring and evaluation system which might have alerted the group to what was occurring. The assumption that community businesses and agencies would contribute turned out to be over-optimistic, particularly in the case of groups that did not have a specific neighbourhood boundary, and this was thought to constitute another limitation of the model. Another shortcoming was thought to be the assumption that communities, however favourable their resources, would be able to provide the necessary range of skills and resources, with a subtle implication that communities might be at fault if they were unable to do so. Also, the model made no allowance for the teaching of leadership skills, and did not address questions of how to create new leaders and sustain their interests and energy, nor how to work with a group when its energy flagged.

Students Work with an LGBT Centre

Stanley (2003) described a project carried out by two groups of graduate community psychology students at a US university. Each group of five to seven students chose a semester-long project working with an 'underserved population' in the community, making presentations to their class group during the planning and later stages of the project, and receiving ongoing support from teaching staff. Over two consecutive spring semesters, two groups of students had chosen to work at an urban youth-operated LGBTQ (lesbian, gay, bisexual, transgender, and questioning) centre. The centre was unique in being run by a youth-selected board, who, along with the centre's director, oversaw planning, implementation and direction of the centre. Its goal was the creation of opportunities for youth to meet and exchange support with others, to counteract the prejudice and oppression faced by LGBTQ young people, and to provide an extensive range of activities, which included tutoring, workshops, films, choir, an acting group, and on-site counselling. The chosen project came out of discussion between the students and youth at the centre, and became known as The Café project. It involved creating a social space in the centre by repairing and redecorating a large room that was out of use because of significant physical damage and disrepair. Students, the first year, worked with youth at the centre to raise money for the construction of the café. In the second year, youth and students carried out renovations and redecorating and made the room ready for use, including creating a coffee bar and portable stage.

Interviews with a proportion of students and youth participants after the project was over suggested that both had benefited from contact with each other, had learned a great deal about working together to achieve a realistic objective, and had acquired skills and interests which in some cases had been significant in choice of future careers. Among the things that the students had learned were the need to limit the project to something that was feasible within the limitations of time and resources available, and also the importance of collaborating. Students had often entered the project with their own ideas and agenda, and had learned the lesson of listening to community members and appreciating their needs and wishes. As one former student who had gone on to work in a community-based prevention project, put it:

> So, I learned that now when I go into a certain community I first go to the block and find out what the families think is going on. I don't look first at best practice, I look for what is really going on and have the project be tailored to the individuals' needs and wants, like we did at the [center]. If we had gone in there with our own agenda like, "We are going to paint your building," we would have been like many other prevention programs out there... (p. 263).

Students had also learned a great deal about LGBTQ issues, the fluidity of personal sexuality, and their own latent prejudice.

Concluding Chapter 9

In this chapter the emphasis has been on ways of providing social support. We have seen evidence from a number of the illustrative projects presented that people who are disempowered because of the stress they are under can be enabled, through receiving social support, to believe that they can take social action. Although the resulting empowerment is largely personal, there are hints that this can result in challenges being made to the existing order, certainly by individuals and perhaps by people acting together. In the next chapter we consider examples of work that moves on towards collective social action and the creation of innovative ways of providing otherwise disempowered people with needed services and resources.

Chapter 10

SOCIAL ACTION AND INNOVATION

MOVING TO COLLECTIVE SOCIAL ACTION

Local Action by Women

Particularly inspiring for community psychology, in terms of both its theory and its practice, is the *psychotherapy and social action* model described by Holland (1988, 1992). Her background as both a psychotherapist and someone with experience of community action primed her, when she came to work with women living on a large housing estate in west London, to see women's private troubles in a broader social context. The programme she developed as a result she depicted, theoretically, as shown in Figure 10.1. Depression, which was highly prevalent among women on the estate, was generally viewed in an individualised way and treated with psychoactive medication (bottom right of the figure). In Holland's project, women might start with an initial period of a few months' individual therapy (bottom left), progressing to involvement in groups aiming to locate women's mental health difficulties within the context of family and society (top left). The final move was to a stage of collective social action in the form of Women's Action for Mental Health. At that stage they raised mental health as a social issue on the estate and had some success in improving their environment and facilities (top right). As Holland put it: "This progression within a neighbourhood therapy programme, could be described in terms of trying to move the depressed women through psychic space into social space and so into political space" (1988, p. 134).

There are two features of Figure 10.1 that are particularly important for a theory of community action. They correspond to the vertical and horizontal dimensions of Holland's four-cell framework. The vertical dimension contrasts changing individuals to fit social conditions (the bottom two cells) with changing social conditions to fit people (the top two cells). The bottom half of the diagram corresponds to individualised, therapeutic approaches that have the aim of fixing people rather than helping people to change their social conditions. It has largely been concerned

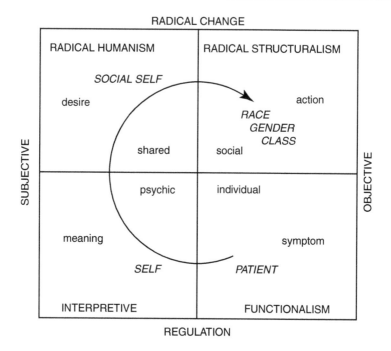

Figure 10.1 The psychotherapy and social action model
Source: Holland, S. (1988). Defining and experimenting with prevention. In S. Ramon &
M. Giannichedda (eds), *Psychiatry in Transition: The British and Italian Experiences* (Chap-
ter 11). London: Pluto

with private distress and difficulty. It is no accident, therefore, that in Holland's
programme women joined together in a collective, whether in the form of group
therapy or social action, in those parts of the programme corresponding to the top
two cells of the figure. Individual psychotherapy, on the other hand, requires giving
people a private space, private time, and the exclusive attention of a therapist.

The horizontal dimension is equally challenging. Psychotherapy, whether individual or group, differs from prescribing drugs because it attends to the subjective meaning of people's troubles. Holland's framework, however, suggests that
when women move to social action (top right) they move back to a focus on the
objective. The objective facts are no longer private, individual matters, but are to
do with shared social, material, and working conditions (the latter including lack
of outside work, insecure work, or too great a demand from work and domestic responsibilities combined). The position adopted is a radical structuralist one.
What is important is that people actually are poor or poorly housed, and that these
material conditions have psychological effects.

In a special issue of the *Journal of Community and Applied Social Psychology*,
edited by Bostock and Smail (1999), on the topic of Power, the Environment
and Community Psychology, appeared two articles on local mental health action
projects which acknowledged their roots in Holland's (1988) pioneering work. Both

were located in the city of Nottingham, England. One was run by local women for women (Women's Action for Mental Health, WAMH; Fenner, 1999), the other by local men for men (Men's Advice Network, MAN; Melluish & Bulmer, 1999).

Fenner (1999) described how, through her own experience of mental health difficulties, she had been one of the early members of WAMH in London and, with support from a community development worker employed by the city council, had taken the initiative to set up a WAMH project in a large council estate after she moved to Nottingham in the early 1990s. Discovering that there were no services specifically for working class women in the area that were active in preventive mental health, she embarked on an intensive period of lobbying, searching for premises, and obtaining funding, leading to successful three-year funding from the Joint Finance Committee of the local health and social services authorities. Funding was given to provide a Community Preventative Mental Health Project for the women of the estate, and for the opening and running of a crèche facility that formed the centre of the project. At the time of writing, the three-year funding period was coming to an end and continued funding had not yet been obtained.

Fenner's article is a moving personal account of the struggle to develop a facility. It begins, unusually for an article in an academic journal, with a summary of the author's own background and credentials for running such a mutual-help project. Among points of particular note are the following. Although some local professionals expressed interest and some gave support, some were notable for their apparent lack of interest. Local GPs (primary care, general medical practitioners), for example, were described as being 'unapproachable', never responding to approaches and invitations. Social services were described as having difficulty in grasping the aims and objectives of WAMH. It had to be made clear, for example, that social workers could not just, "... nip into the Project and talk to their clients, to see who of all the women in the Project needed a social worker" (p. 81). The collaboration with professionals was also reflected in the management arrangements. Management was initially made up of the community development worker, a member of the local community who was a qualified accountant, employed by the city council, the vice-principal of the local college, a member of the community psychology and primary care service, and a worker from the Citizens' Advice Bureau. But from the outset all were informed that they would have to stand down at the first AGM, at which point management was taken over entirely by local women. Of particular interest is the mix of activities that took place, including: the Cookpot, where culinary skills were shared and confidence increased; discussions of everyday stressful situations and how women dealt with them; providing practical support and skills sharing, for example by organising decorating parties for women who had recently moved into the community; and a study group that raised and discussed issues about politics, racism, class, and power. Along the way women had experience of running meetings and effectively making complaints, for example to a local school governor:

> Through WAMH...the women have become aware of collective power. Through belonging to a group they have become stronger, and would be heard. They have become confident in speaking in public and have learned to question calmly at meetings (Fenner, 1999, p. 91).

Another women's collective project, with some very similar aims and outcomes, took the form of participatory research and community organisation around the issue of nutritional inequalities. Travers (1997) conducted participant observation as a volunteer at a community drop-in Parents Center in an urban neighbourhood in Nova Scotia, Canada. All of the women were on low incomes, many living in a public housing project within walking distance of the centre, others in non-subsidised rental units in an area of the city with a high density of apartment buildings. Participant observation was followed by group interviews held with women attending the centre over a 16-month period. A total of 27 one- to two-hour group interviews were held with a regular core group of five or six women, but a total of 33 women actively took part in the group at some point.

Travers described the process of change that occurred during the project, beginning with early meetings at which participants simply talked, often expressing bitterness and anger, about the difficulties of feeding their families, blaming both the 'system' and themselves for their perceived inadequacies in stretching their budgets. Early on, conversations mostly took place between the researcher/facilitator and individual women. As the process progressed, participants more often asked each other questions, challenged others, and supported one another's concerns. In the process they learned coping strategies from each other, and more importantly began to realise that they could not be solely responsible for the difficulties they faced. They experienced a consciousness-raising or 'perspective transformation' whereby they were:

> ...able to name and analyze their experiences that had previously been regarded as trivial, unimportant, and uniquely personal. Their common experiences enabled them to explore the sources of oppression as socially organized ... They came to recognize the common and political roots of their oppression and thus were able to shed their self-blame (Travers, 1997, p. 349).

Later the group moved towards social action. Based on the contents of a standard national 'nutritious food basket', the group carried out a pricing exercise in two stores in low-income inner city areas and two stores in the suburbs, confirming their suspicion that food cost more in the former (a 10% price differential was found between the store most commonly frequented by the women in the group and the store furthest from their neighbourhood). A campaign of writing letters to the stores pointing out the differences and the possibility that the women might withdraw their business, resulted in both stores changing buying practices to decrease price inequalities between the locations – a change that lived on long after the research process had ended. Still being reliant on commercial outlets for most of their food, a sub-group secured funding for a grassroots cooperative grocery enterprise run by an organising committee of women from the community and operating out of the Parents Center. A more political dimension was added by concluding from the pricing survey that welfare food allowances were inadequate to meet the basic nutritional needs of their families. A campaign of writing letters to political leaders, along with the work of a grassroots anti-poverty group in which some of the participants had become active, helped to raise welfare allowances – albeit only marginally and temporarily, since allowances continued to fail to keep pace with cost of living increases. Finally, group members acted collectively when the city proposed closing the Parents Center due to budget restraints. A campaign, including press conferences, and marching to city hall, caught the public's attention and saved the centre from closure.

Travers was aware, nevertheless, of a number of constraints. The women's views were often ignored or misrepresented. For example, at public meetings called by the city encouraging citizens to express ideas about community health, their views about over-reliance on food banks were often 'lost' although as the women explained, they "kept bringing it up ... " (p. 354). There was also a process of becoming 'media literate'. Women were often critical of the small amount of a media interview that was used. On one occasion, following the visit of a politician to the centre, women were angry that the media had admonished them for being too civil, and they started to realise how the media operated to construct stereotypes:

> Melinda: That's when we got in trouble ... snubbed by that [media] lady because we ... gave her the red carpet treatment instead of yelling at her ... We brought her out into the community to meet us. We did not bring her out to hang her, but the media didn't want to hear that ...

> Bessie: They didn't want that because all they were looking for was [imitates a screaming person] ... And we don't have to be that way! (p. 350).

Other constraints included women's feelings of vulnerability and reliance on the government for their sole source of income, and the fear of having welfare benefits withdrawn. Other constraints were practical. Some of those, for example lack of a typewriter or word processor and inexperience of writing formal letters, the researcher/facilitator was able to help with (she also helped with grant preparation, gave some assistance in organising and operating the co-op in the early stages, and acted more generally as an advocate). Lack of childcare arrangements was responsible on one occasion for not going ahead with a planned march on the provincial legislature.

Travers framed this project as an example of emancipatory health education involving a process of conscientisation (Freire, 1970), very different from traditional health education. The latter failed to address the role of the environment and the need for social change, and, by imposing solutions (what Freire called 'cultural invasion'), was likely to perpetuate inequalities. Travers viewed the process as revealing oscillations between various levels of the empowerment continuum described by Labonti (1994). The continuum theorised empowerment as a complex set of intersections and progressions through empowerment at the personal level, small group development, community organisation, coalition advocacy, and political action. Travers saw it as having three implications for the practice of health education: the need for greater sensitivity by understanding the realities of life for those people that health educators hope to reach; a re-orientation in practice away from the dominant individual orientation to a social one; and a role change for the health educator from expert to facilitator and advocate.

Local Men's Action

The Men's Advice Network (MAN), described by Melluish and Bulmer (1999), was set up in an area of Nottingham composed of several housing estates with great social need and high rates of male unemployment. It was aimed at men aged between 35 and 60 who had been unemployed for at least a year and who were experiencing mental ill-health. It began as a support group jointly run by a community clinical psychologist and a community development worker, but that was always seen as a first step towards the development of a local health resource for men. Inspired, like Fenner's (1999) WAMH project, by the White City model of practice that combined individual psychotherapeutic work with social action (Holland, 1988), the project did successfully move from one that focused on individual distress and the difficulty of articulating that personal experience (although such discussion always ran alongside discussions about the men's families, their local community, past experiences of work, and current struggles to survive) towards a reflective process in which participants began to question the origins of their mental health difficulties and to shift from a preoccupation with personal troubles to neighbourhood and society problems. The theme of injustice or unfairness at treatment by the authorities and in their dealings with professionals was a common one. There was frustration at the involvement of professionals in many aspects of their lives and many professionals' apparent lack of trust in the capacity and willingness of local people to run their own affairs – although, due to recognition of the need for help from professional agencies and the influence of a natural leader who emerged in the group, that never developed into an anti-professional stance. Discussion of injustice increasingly was spoken about in terms of social class, and there was an awareness of how, "...class had been edited out as a structural component of society..." (p. 97).

The group took an increasingly action-oriented turn when it made a successful bid for the contract for maintaining the community garden attached to the community centre where the group met. Sense of collective strength was increased further when they made a successful objection to demolishing a repeatedly vandalised shelter in the garden. Group meetings increasingly focused on action and a plan was developed for a resource centre with the components shown in Figure 10.2. At the time of writing, that project had been running for a year and 43 local men had used the resource in one way or another. While the psychologist and community worker had acted as leaders and facilitators in the beginning, their roles changed as the group evolved and the men took more control for themselves, forming their own management committee. The project was largely self-funding through the gardening contract and further contracts that the group took on – for example for delivering and later publishing the local community newspaper.

Melluish and Bulmer commented that this model of work was particularly relevant to addressing the mental health needs of working class men since, "...its orientation emphasizes the role of the group rather than the individual, the social as opposed to the intrapsychic aetiology of distress, and the importance of action rather than introspection" (p. 94). Unlike the concept of support dominant in therapy, 'support' or 'help' was equated for the men who participated in MAN with action, often visiting or joining together to help one another through an immediate crisis, for example 'I'll show you how', 'I'll drive you there', 'I'll come with you' (p. 99).

Another men's collective – the Avalon Gardens Men's Association – was a group that started to meet regularly in the aftermath of the riots that occurred in south

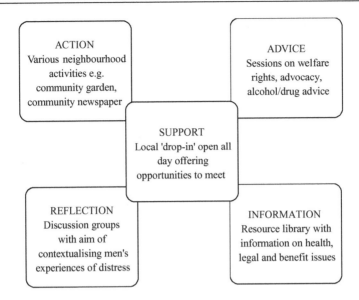

Figure 10.2   Five key components of the Men's Advice Network resource centre
Source: reproduced with permission from Melluish, S. & Bulmer, D. (1999). Rebuilding solidarity: an account of a men's health action project. *Journal of Community and Applied Social Psychology*, **9**, 93–100

central Los Angeles in 1992 (sparked by the verdict in the Rodney King police brutality case), with the support of an intervention team contracted by Los Angeles city officials to implement a community-based empowerment intervention that would address chronic issues affecting the area (Borg, 2002). Those issues included racism, poverty, violence, unemployment, alcohol and drug misuse, epidemic health problems including HIV/AIDS, heart disease, diabetes and hypertension, academic under-achievement, as well as problems related to the recent crisis itself, such as rioting, looting, arson, and inter-racial violence. Avalon Gardens was a government subsidised housing project in the middle of the area, largely African USAmerican in population, with a minority Latin American population, characterised by low income, unemployment, and single-headed households, and crime rates much higher than national averages. In addition to what appeared to be a community-wide sense of powerlessness, hopelessness and apathy, men in particular were stereotyped as irresponsible, apathetic and lazy. Sub-groups in the community were often scapegoated by other groups as the 'cause' of the community's problems. The growing commitment of the Men's Association to empowerment came as a surprise and was initially treated with some scepticism, for example by some women leaders. The origin of the negative stereotype of men in the community was discussed in the Men's Association meetings, and was traced in part to the defensive reaction of keeping one's head down in order to minimise the danger of standing out and being targeted by others in what was a hostile environment with similarities to a 'war zone'. Powerful rival gangs operated in the area, and there was deep suspicion of the city police department who were thought by many men to be playing a significant role in perpetuating community violence.

The empowerment approach involved, among other things, analysing and identifying the root causes of community problems. Professional help that limited itself to experts giving advice about intra-psychic adjustment was antithetical to the approach, which needed to understand the influences of chronic illness, infectious disease, transmission of illness, racism, prejudice and oppression, as well as environmental factors such as exposure to toxic waste and pesticides, and substandard housing. The focus was on enhancing strengths and promoting health, not simply on risk factors. Empowerment was viewed as a multi-level construct involvement empowerment of individuals via opportunities to become active in community decision making, organisations that are empowering because they provide a setting in which individuals can attempt to take control of their own lives, and communities that can be empowered and empowering for their residents.

The Men's Association, as an early activity, developed a partnership with the city police department. Although initially tense, the partnership was considered an essential first step in addressing the possibility of a healthier community. Medical and social service providers were also invited to weekly meetings, outreach programmes from community and local hospitals were sponsored, and networks with local schools, churches and other service agencies were developed. As a result some service agencies began to offer their services within the community. Rather than an externally imposed form of evaluation, empowerment-oriented participatory action research was used that involved a spiral process of planning, fieldwork, analysis, and reflection, followed by a spiralling up to further, better informed planning (Baum, 1998). Processes included 'capacity asset mapping' that required community members to put together a description of their situation as well as an inventory of community strengths and resources. Another technique was the 'physical quality of life plan' that involved assessing the physical environment and recording the state of physical structures including homes, other buildings, playgrounds etc. The final report on the project drew attention to substantial changes that had occurred in terms of a reduced incidence of violence, both publicly and in the home, and reduced crime, unemployment, school truancy and school failure and teen pregnancy, as well as an increased rate of health screenings. The involvement of men through the Men's Association was considered to have been an important ingredient in breaking the cycle of chronic dependency. At follow-up in 2000, alliances had been maintained and a resident-driven comprehensive community revitalisation organisation – the Avalon Gardens Community Service Association – had been formed and had achieved non-profit organisation status.

Action by Mental Health Service Users

One component of care 'in the community' for people with mental health difficulties has been the provision of day care, ranging from more formal, usually larger, services such as day hospitals, to the more informal, usually smaller, units including drop-in centres. Hall and Cheston (2002) reported the results of a qualitative study of one such drop-in centre in the south of England. Run, like most drop-in services in the UK, by a voluntary sector organisation, this informal facility helped provide social contact for people who previously might have maintained contact with services after being discharged from the, now closed, in-patient mental illness unit. The centre was staffed by a rota of volunteers all of whom had themselves at some time used mental health services.

Over the six-month period of the study, the main researcher attended 14 sessions as a participant observer, sat in on relevant meetings, and carried out semi-structured interviews, lasting up to 90 minutes, with 14 users of the centre (chosen to reflect the diversity of centre users). Users repeatedly answered questions about the service, not so much in terms of their mental illnesses, but in terms of coping with the rejecting treatment they felt they had received from society at large, denying them opportunities for establishing social networks and support. It was common for users' social networks to be confined to others who were using statutory or voluntary mental health services, and all described being made to feel 'different' or 'apart' because of their experiences of mental illness when in contact with others outside that group. Only a few centre users were in full-time paid employment which compounded social isolation. The fact that all attenders, and staff, had experience of using mental health services, allowed users to, "... frame their group membership within a more positive context" (p. 35). For example:

> Everyone here knows that you've had psychiatric problems. Me, I've had 13 episodes, but in here I feel totally accepted. We sometimes laugh about our experiences of psychosis. It's amusing. I think if anybody outside here were to ridicule anyone in here ... I probably think that it would upset me (p. 36).

Drop-in centre users often needed to vary their strategies for coping with rejection and stigma depending on circumstances (for example revealing illness to other centre users but concealing it from other friends) or current severity of illness – as one centre user said, "It's nice to have somewhere to go when I'm really ill ... to be with other people who know what it's like" (p. 41). A number of occasional users of the centre explained why they did not attend more frequently. Some were women who found the mostly male mix of users uncomfortable and sometimes threatening. Some others adopted more of an empowerment strategy for coping with rejection and stigma, finding most attenders too passive, and sometimes preferring other groups such as a local Survivors' Network. As one centre user said:

> For me, one of the things is how to change things. It's quite empowering – collectively changing something. I want to organise collectively, and change issues. Also trying to educate some of the users. It's important to make the user movement more representative, such as supporting black users. These issues aren't tackled and looked at. To empower ourselves as users means looking at these issues (pp. 37–8).

Nelson *et al.* (1998) pointed to the diverse range of self-help/mutual aid organisations that existed in the mental health field. Some organisations took a more radical view than others of the need to change oppressive social conditions such as poverty, loss of civil liberties, abuse, poor housing, and stigma (Sagarin, 1969, noted some years earlier that some self-help groups had social action aims while others eschewed such aims). It was that contrast that was of particular interest to

Hatzidimitriadou (2002), who analysed 67 questionnaires returned by members of 14 mental health self-help/mutual aid groups in the London and south-east England area. Identifying such groups was difficult due to the lack of any central clearinghouse information. The 14 participating organisations were classified, on the basis of information they provided, into three types: eight conservative (personal change of members was the sole stated aim); three radical (changing/improving the mental health system was stated as the aim); and three combined (both personal and social change were aimed for). Although the numbers were small, some interesting differences emerged. Most of the members of radical groups who returned questionnaires had been sectioned under the Mental Health Act, whereas almost all conservative group members had been admitted as voluntary patients. In answer to questions about helping processes, conservative group members reported significantly more self-disclosure than members of radical groups, and those in the conservative and combined groups together reported more sharing and catharsis than members of radical groups. The latter, however, reported more establishment of group goals than members of the other two types of group. In radical groups there was a significant positive association between group identification and the establishment of group goals, whereas in the other two types of group, identification was significantly correlated with supportive, helping processes. The 'combined' group constituted an interesting case which appeared able to combine the more 'therapeutic' helping processes with more radical system-change aims.

From the early 1990s onwards the UK government was issuing policy statements requiring mental health services to think of ways of finding out about service users' views of services and involving users in the monitoring and design of services (Williams & Lindley, 1996; Rutter *et al.*, 2004). Williams and Lindley saw the involvement of service users in changing mental health services to be part of a broader move towards a greater understanding of the ways in which experiences of abuse and social inequalities were, "... causally linked to the despair, distress, and confusion that is named mental illness" (p. 359) and towards greater recognition of the power imbalances that exist between mental health patients and staff, and the lack of choice for patients and the abuses to which patients are sometimes exposed in the services. For example, they quoted from a 'psychiatric survivor' speaking at a British Psychological Society, Psychology of Women section conference:

> We are never given real choices, and therefore we are indecisive. Now this submissiveness, lack of initiative, apathy and indecisiveness are all taken to be symptoms of our mental illness. We just can't win against such odds (cited by Williams & Lindley, 1996, p. 4).

Williams and Lindley described their own work in developing a training course, the Consultancy Development Programme (CDP), to provide mental health service users with a safe environment in which to develop the skills necessary for working as consultants, trainers, and advocates in local mental health services. All participants were linked into service user groups. One of the ways in which Williams and Lindley became involved was as members of a support team formed to help the development of a Patients' Council in a secure psychiatric hospital. They did not underestimate the degree of professional resistance there was to a change of that kind:

> Seen from this perspective consultation and collaboration with service users means asking, or hoping that, extremely dis-empowered people will make tangible the processes of oppression within society and specifically the mental health services. It is work that is both risky and difficult. To speak honestly carries the risk of reprisal. To be effective means coping strategically with considerable institutional and individual resistance (p. 6).

In their paper they set out a number of practical suggestions for helping users become involved, based on their own experience. For example, they recommended acknowledging the ambivalence that users may well feel about whether a team such as theirs could be trusted. Among the strategies they suggested were: providing information about themselves and inviting further questions; agreeing ground rules relating to confidentiality; confirming that Patient Council members would chair meetings and set the agenda; and including Patient Council officers in any meeting between management and the support team. Experience also taught them that conflicts could occur between members – as with all groups – as well as between members and those with power. A set of ground rules was therefore developed by service users in training which included: respecting confidentiality; people should feel free to come and go; allow others to speak – try not to interrupt; no sexism or racism; always give positive feedback first. The experience of trying to change services when one is a consumer of those services, and the way power can be used to prevent user consultation being anything other than a token, were both considered, and suggestions were developed for looking after yourself and recognising when users are being kept in their place (shown in Figures 10.3 and 10.4).

Rutter *et al.* (2004) reported a qualitative study of user involvement in the planning and delivery of adult mental health services run by National Health Service Trusts in two areas of London. One area covered a number of boroughs of high deprivation in the inner city, the other covering two boroughs, one inner-city, the other more suburban. A steering group was composed of users, academic researchers, and practitioners. The study involved interviews with nearly 50 stakeholders including users and user groups, voluntary sector representatives, and Trust staff – including chief executives, senior middle managers, consultant psychiatrists, and ward managers.

Considerable variation was found. Most, but not all, boroughs had one or more user groups. Some groups were working closely with professionals to achieve change to services, while others were aiming to maximise their independence from the Trust, for example by attempting to achieve self-funding status. Some had opted out of involvement with services altogether, in order to pursue other activities such as mutual support, national campaigning, or self-expression, sometimes because of dissatisfaction with the outcomes of previous involvement. Where there had been involvement, the process was thought to have been positive, although user involvement had been more effective in the case of concrete, project-managed developments such as health and social service integration and building works. Patients had not been invited to discuss issues of clinical practice or policy, including control and restraint procedures. For example, in one Trust a user group that had

- Find allies and supports – get linked in to a local user group and the United Advocacy Network
- Work in pairs – never work alone or without the support of other like-minded people
- If you are a woman go with another woman and learn the ways in which women get put down so that you can defend yourself against them
- Find a safe place to practise
- Think carefully before you take on work in a place where you receive or have received treatment – it might be better to do it elsewhere
- Be careful about taking on work if your experience doesn't seem relevant
- It usually feels safer when other mental health service users are contributing or are in the audience
- Think about what you might feel afterwards:
  - Who will listen if you want to offload?
  - Who can you trust?
- Remember that there are plenty of other things to do in life as well as try and change services!

Figure 10.3   Advice to members of mental health service users Patients' Councils about 'Looking After Yourself'
Source: Williams, J. & Lindley, P. (1996). Working with mental health service users to change mental health services. *Journal of Community and Applied Social Psychology, 6*, 1–14

worked closely with managers discovered they had not been consulted over new security arrangements for the in-patient unit. In another case a user-led attempt to introduce formal standards of patient–nurse interaction time on the wards was explicitly rejected.

Among specific issues that emerged were representation, payment of users, and the independence of user groups. Some Trust staff were concerned that users who became involved were more representative of those with negative views than of those who were more satisfied. There was specific criticism of inappropriate emotional contributions by users based on their own experiences; users themselves felt that their own experiences were central to their involvement. User representatives were sometimes criticised, not just by Trust staff, but also by other users who felt issues had not been raised or that they were not being well represented. Users were strongly opposed to Trusts selecting representative users, but in general the issue of representativeness had not been solved. Regarding payment, most respondents agreed that some kind of payment was important, but some staff felt payment caused divisions between users, and there was the risk that welfare payments might be reduced. On the issue of independence, members of user groups said that they struggled to maintain their independence from the Trust. New and emergent groups commented on the need to meet separately from Trust staff, and

Making it difficult for service users to attend the meeting by:

 the choice of venue e.g. a psychiatric hospital

 not notifying them of changes in the venue, or time, of the meeting

 not providing the necessary resources e.g. money, information, support, child
 care

Making service users feel marginalised by:

 saying 'I'll chair this meeting'

 ensuring that they are an obvious minority

 only introducing them

 failing to explain the background to the meeting, its purpose and rules

 calling service users by first names and everyone else by their title and
 surnames

 referring to meetings, events when they were not present

 failing to ask the user what he or she thinks

 having a 'service user slot'

 leaving it to the end to ask the service user to speak

 using offensive language such as 'high-grade', 'patient'

Making it difficult for service users to participate by:

 controlling the agenda

 talking in jargon

 talking too fast, with too much information

 by being overly attentive

 asking questions in such a way that the service user can't answer

Undermining the contribution of service users by:

 being patronising

 questioning the representativeness of their experiences, view and opinions

 rushing the user, saying 'we've got 10 minutes left'

 non-verbally communicating that they are e.g. disengaged or angry

 talking in the third person about the service user consultant/trainer

 asking them questions about their mental health

 interrupting and finishing sentences for the service user

 taking over, saying that they know what the service user means

Reducing the influence of service users by:

 having very quick meetings and making decisions elsewhere

 not giving anyone responsibility for taking action

 making unreasonable demands on them

 setting the service user (inappropriately) as an expert

 trying to claim their support e.g. 'you were at the meeting, remember what we
 agreed...'

Figure 10.4 Advice to members of mental health users Patients' Councils about recognising some of the things that managers do to 'keep us down'
Source: reproduced with permission from Williams, J. & Lindley, P. (1996). Working with mental health service users to change mental health services. *Journal of Community and Applied Social Psychology*, **6**, 1–14

all well-established user groups had aspirations to be independent, to raise funds autonomously, and to be capable of financing office accommodation outside the Trust.

Overall Rutter *et al.* detected a fundamental conflict of views about user groups. While users themselves were looking for partnership and wanted to see evidence of positive outcomes in terms of actual influence on decisions about how services ran, managers appeared to believe more in consulting users while retaining the power to make decisions themselves. They appeared to be more interested in the process of user involvement (where, when, how) rather than with outcomes. The views of nursing staff were interesting. They portrayed themselves as a relatively powerless professional group, caught between managers and users, rarely consulted about policy themselves, visible targets for patients' criticisms, of which they had to bear the brunt, and even vulnerable to being suspended if a user complained (although there was little direct criticism of nurses on the wards by users in the study, and most users wanted more communication with nurses). In general Rutter *et al.* appeared to agree with Williams and Lindley about the support that service users need: "... it seems unlikely that these relationships will have the potential for actual *partnership* without heavy investment in the resources and powers of the 'lesser' partner" (Rutter *et al.*, 2004, p. 1981).

EXPERIMENTAL SOCIAL INNOVATION AND DISSEMINATION (ESID)

The Original ESID Work: Community Living for Former Mental Hospital Patients

Experimental Social Innovation and Dissemination (ESID) is a model of research and action that grapples with the issues surrounding changing organisations that provide services to people, and evaluating the results. We have already met one example of ESID in the previous chapter – Sullivan's (2003) advocacy project on violence towards women. ESID was pioneered in the USA by Fairweather and his colleagues in the 1960s and 1970s (Fairweather, 1964; Fairweather *et al.*, 1969, 1974). That work was with the provision of alternative forms of community living for former long-term mental hospital patients. It was a good example of a programme of work in which one component built upon the next. It began with an experiment inside an old-style mental hospital. Patients were randomly assigned to either a traditionally organised ward or to a ward that was in all ways similar except in its social organisation, which was on small group lines. On admission patients joined one of a number of small groups of fellow patients who were jointly involved in helping making decisions and recommendations – even about the progress of fellow patients and their readiness for discharge – that were outside the traditional patient remit. The effects on social interaction and observed behaviour on the ward were dramatic (much more socialising and less inactivity on the small group ward), and some of the positive effects of the small group ward were still apparent at follow-up in the community. Those who had had the small group ward experience were more likely, for example, to be employed and to have interactions with friends.

The differences were weaker than they had been in the hospital setting, however, and there were no differences in symptoms. Community intolerance of psychotic symptoms was thought to be partly to blame, and Fairweather et al. (1969) developed the 'Community Lodge' that built on and developed further the idea of giving people roles and responsibilities in a safe but relatively unsupervised community living environment. Such an environment for discharged mental hospital patients was unusual at that time, and the Lodge became famous within community psychology circles as a prime example of the creation of an 'alternative setting' in contrast to institutionalisation or neglect within the community. Another often cited example is the residential youth centre (RYC) set up by Goldenberg (1971) in New Haven, USA, where young residents took far greater responsibility for making decisions and running activities than would have been the case in mainstream organisations for delinquent and under-privileged youth. Similar residential programmes for people with alcohol or drug problems, as alternatives to custodial or mental health institutions, were also part of that period of innovation in the UK, USA, and elsewhere (Otto & Orford, 1978).

In the Lodge, as in these other alternative settings, a variety of roles, other than that of mental patient, were available to residents. In the process, role expectations were changed. Neighbours, and customers of the small commercial enterprises such as gardening and janitorial services that were set up and operated from the Lodge, came to respect the residents, and residents themselves gained in confidence and self-respect. It was a principle that no one Lodge should exceed a certain size; 33 members was the maximum ever reached. The social and political tolerance of the San Francisco Bay region, where the Lodge was first established, may have been a factor, plus the economic growth of the area at the time (Levine et al., 2005). Over a three-year follow-up period those who had been in the Lodge spent more time out of hospital and more time working than did members of a control group, although in terms of symptoms and psychosocial adjustment differences were not significant.

Fairweather et al. (1974) took their work to the final stage of the ESID model by attempting to disseminate the idea of the Lodge across the whole of the USA. Their insistence on experimental methods was maintained even in that aspect of their programme, with a randomised test of whether it was more effective to approach hospitals via administrators or professionals in direct contact with patients, and whether it was more effective to offer a brief introduction to the idea of the Lodge first, or whether it was more effective to offer a full training package. They were able to show that replication was possible while at the same time acknowledging the effort that was required to interest others in taking up the work.

Introducing a special issue of the American Journal of Community Psychology devoted to ESID, Seidman (2003) pointed to Fairweather's orientation towards providing social resources (e.g. housing instead of interventions targeting symptoms of mental illness) and his insistence that the kind of social innovation he was interested in involved changing the role relationship between service provider and server recipient: "Social innovations, in contrast to technological ones, seem to be much more difficult for a society to adopt, probably because new social innovations typically require radical changes in accepted role behaviours or the social structure of existing societal organization" (Fairweather, 1972, p. 6, cited by

Seidman, 2003, p. 373). Seidman also pointed to the marginal role in which social change agents frequently found themselves, not being fully a part of the service organisation or population with whom they were working, and often marginalised within their parent institutions (like community psychologists in universities – see Chapter 1), and also to the need for perseverance in producing social change: "...social change takes a long, long time, and requires an enormous amount of hard work and tolerance for confusion. Rewards and personal gratifications are slow in coming, if they come at all" (Seidman, 2003, p. 374).

Putting Housing First

Programmes, using ESID principles, have focused more recently on the needs of people who have mental health difficulties and who are also homeless – there is much evidence from a number of countries that mental health problems and homelessness very often occur together (Calsyn, 2003). One such programme, in New York City, USA, for people with problems of mental illness and homelessness was aptly termed Housing First (Tsemberis et al., 2003; Gulcur et al., 2003). The programme's philosophy was that mental health service consumers often place a higher value on meeting basic needs such as housing than on addressing mental health or substance misuse problems, and that, given a choice among housing options, the ability of consumers to function independently is much greater than is often assumed. True to ESID principles, the study of Housing First was preceded by an experiment in which people with severe psychiatric disabilities living on the streets were randomly assigned, either to a traditional outreach and drop-in centre programme that emphasised the predetermined sequence of services to which consumers would have access depending on meeting progress targets, or to a service (based at a centre appropriately called the Choices Center) which gave consumers much more choice over the selection, order and extensity of services (medical, psychiatric, and social). Consumers had an input into decisions affecting the programme generally, for example in developing a system of banking for managing clients' money, determining the centre's hours of operation, and deciding to employ a formerly homeless person as a floor manager rather than hire a security guard. Altogether 168 people were assigned to one or other group. Follow-up at six-month intervals over a 24-month period found that time spent in the street decreased twice as much for those in the Choices group (55% versus 28%), who also found it easier to get food, find a place to sleep, and keep clean, and participated in more services, including day programmes and self-help groups and alcohol and drug programmes, and had less contact with the police. Only a minority of even the Choices participants, however, were able to find stable, independent housing in the community. The barrier in most cases was the inability of many to meet the demands of housing programmes such as medication compliance and abstinence from alcohol and drugs. It was as a result of that experience that the Housing First programme was developed.

It was concluded that a more effective programme needed to provide permanent housing with the minimum of restrictions to access – unlike the prevailing 'continuation of care' model that required evidence of 'housing readiness' before access was given to a more independent stage in a housing continuum. Efforts were therefore made to persuade existing housing providers to implement such a housing programme. The proposal met with considerable resistance, most mental health service and housing providers holding the view that uncoupling mental health and housing needs in that way, allowing clients to choose to move into independent living before they were ready for it, would be counterproductive and even unethical. The programme therefore set up its own supported housing development (Pathways to Housing). Service users were given the option of moving into an independent furnished apartment of their own at the point of admission into the programme. An important requirement was that clients contributed 30% of monthly income towards rent by participating in the money management plan, and another was that they should meet with a staff member at least twice a month. Clinical and support services were provided by an assertive community treatment (ACT) team which, like traditional ACT teams, was on call 24 hours a day, seven days a week, but which, unlike traditional teams, incorporated the user choice elements of the preceding Choices programme.

A total of 225 people were randomly assigned to Housing First or to a control programme based on the continuum of care model. All were adults, all had lived on the streets or in other public places not intended for sleeping for at least 15 of the last 30 days (or the last 30 days prior to hospitalisation for those referred from psychiatric hospitals), all had a history of chronic homelessness for at least six months, and all were diagnosed with serious and persistent mental disorder. Most in addition had substance misuse problems. Follow-up was carried out every six months for 24 months (with at least 90% success at each point) with monthly five-minute telephone calls in between to maintain contact and establish participants' whereabouts. At the first six-month follow-up point those in the experimental programme had spent a significantly greater proportion of the time in stable accommodation (59% versus 15% of the time – which included own apartment or house, group home, boarding house or long-term transitional programme or stay in someone else's apartment or house) and significantly less time homeless (19% versus 48% of the time) or in transitional housing or institutions. The difference was particularly marked for those who at baseline had spent a greater proportion of days homeless. Contrary to pessimistic predictions, these gains in housing stability were not made at the expense of mental health or substance misuse outcomes, for which there were no significant differences (Tsemberis et al., 2003). A report covering the whole 24-month follow-up period showed that the housing differences between the two groups were maintained: the experimental group had spent significantly less time homeless and less time in hospital. Taking the costs of all types of housing provision into account, it was also possible to show that housing costs over the two-year period were significantly less for those in the experimental group (Gulcur et al., 2003).

Tsemberis et al. noted the resistance there appeared to be in the system to adopting new working methods that research had suggested were effective. They suggested that a single, poignant example can be as effective in swaying policy decision-makers as any amount of research evidence (the two in combination they suggested were particularly effective). The example they gave was that of a client – originally thought to be a poor risk for independent living – who greatly impressed a manager who was among people invited to the client's new home and entertained to an excellent meal cooked by the client.

Social Action for Safer Sex in Gay and Bisexual Communities

Other notable examples of the use of ESID principles have involved action in gay and bisexual communities to promote safer sexual practices. One such project, the Mpowerment Project, aiming at the prevention of HIV infection among young gay and bisexual men, was pilot-tested in one area in California, USA, and later implemented in four other communities, one in each of four US states (Hays *et al.*, 2003). Its objectives were based on, "an extensive process of formative research" (p. 302), that included social marketing research, focus groups with young gay and bisexual men, and interviews with key informants. That crucial early work convinced Hays *et al.* that a project directly aiming at increasing safe sexual practices in order to prevent AIDS would not be successful, and that young men would respond better to a project that tied HIV risk reduction to other needs such as the development of one's social network, enjoying social interactions, and enhancing self-esteem. HIV was merely one threat among many faced by gay and bisexual men in a still-homophobic society (see Chapter 8). Furthermore, many perceived AIDS as mainly a problem of older gay men. The primary goal of the project was therefore to create healthy friendship and social support networks. In most communities there were few settings where young and bisexual men could meet and socialise safely in a supportive and health-promoting atmosphere. Bars and other settings where they met were often ones that encouraged excessive alcohol and drug use, were highly sex-charged, and were frequently competitive and critical rather than supportive. The Mpowerment project aimed to create settings where young men could express themselves, form positive links with similar others, gain support, and join together to take action on issues of importance to them (see Crossley's, 2001, evaluation of the Armistead project in Liverpool, England, for a similar conclusion that such projects are better not having an exclusive health focus).

The project was based on the theory of diffusion of innovations (Rogers, 1995), which suggests that people are mostly likely to adopt a new practice, such as safer sex, if a favourable evaluation is conveyed to them by people who they perceive as similar and whom they respect. In practice, therefore, the structure of the project included between two and four young gay or bisexual men employed to coordinate the programme. It was then their task to conduct a community assessment, working like ethnographers, visiting relevant settings and interviewing both young men and key opinion leaders, and then assembling a 'core group' of between five and 20 diverse young men representing various segments of the local young gay and bisexual community. The core group, meeting weekly, made most of the major decisions about the project, including choosing its name and image, and planning and executing project activities. The project relied heavily on volunteers beyond core group members: completion of an 'interest sheet', listing ways in which people could volunteer, contributed to the aim of allowing every young man who wanted to be involved to be so in some way or another. The core group was assisted by a Community Advisory Board of interested people from the LGBT, public health, business and university communities, meeting monthly to give the core group ideas and advice, but in no way to tell them what to do.

The whole programme was designed to combine fun and supportive socialising with information and reminders about safer sexual practices. The programme attempted to strengthen pride and exploration, and focused on a variety of safe sexual activities, with all materials showing positive, diverse images of gay/bisexual men. Activities included: (1) formal outreach, involving groups of men going to settings frequented by young gay/bisexual men, with the aim of promoting safer sex, and using a variety of creative ways of doing so in a light-hearted fashion (e.g. a September Back to School outreach, wearing costumes representing different college stereotypes), as well as the creation of new social events (dances, house parties, community forums, picnics, art or fashion shows, etc.) attracting up to 200 people; (2) M-groups – peer-led, single meetings of 8–10 young gay/bisexual men, lasting two to three hours – which clarified misconceptions about safer sex, built communication skills for negotiating safer sex, addressed interpersonal issues, and provided training on how to talk to others to encourage them to practise safer sex; (3) informal outreach; and (4) publicity campaigns, focusing on articles and advertisements in the gay press, posters in settings frequented by young gay/bisexual men, and a project website (but not advertisements in mainstream media channels, to avoid arousing homophobic individuals or making discomfort for those who might be thinking of becoming involved but who did not wish to be associated with a publicly gay-identified organisation). Building supportive relationships with organisations and service providers in the area was considered very important. Gaining the cooperation of bar owners and managers was found to be particularly challenging but very worthwhile.

Tailoring the project to the community was also important. For example, in one area the project had a more activist tone in the light of a major political issue that was brewing: a change to state law was proposed eliminating formal legislation that forbade discrimination against gay men and lesbians in areas such as housing and jobs. In another area, with a strong family-centred Hispanic culture, the project promoted itself in family terms and used less explicit imagary in its safer sex materials. In a third area, with a vibrant gay scene, the project promoted itself in a more trendy and exciting way, with more explicitly erotic sex materials. Further challenges had been the following: maintaining the balance between a focus on the social aspects of the project and the HIV prevention aspects, the latter sometimes tending to be neglected; keeping on renewing the core group membership and preventing it from being seen as a clique; and criticisms of sexism or ageism because the project provided no services for women or for older men. The latter criticisms were responded to by referring to the evidence that young men were the group at greatest risk and the evidence suggesting that programmes were most effective when designed for a particular risk group.

Another example, concerned with changing social and peer norms about behaviour putting people at risk for HIV, and using some of the same principles as the Mpowerment project, was described by Fernández et al. (2003). Using the relatively inexpensive method of recruiting popular peer group members to change social norms, this programme started with work in three relatively small southern US cities. AIDS had apparently been less prevalent there than in bigger cities, but preliminary discussions and observations suggested a high level of HIV-high-risk sexual behaviour and norms within the gay community. There was understandably initial distrust and suspicion of researchers, in particular of psychologists because of psychology's traditional tendency to psychopathologise gay people. Effort was therefore put into preliminary work – often referred to in community psychology circles as the 'before the beginning' stage of a project – by forming a multidisciplinary research team that included community members, an advisory committee composed of community leaders, owners of gay establishments, and members of the local gay community. The team then spent at least six months in community-involvement activities before beginning the study. The study itself consisted of: training bartenders to conduct careful behavioural observations to identify key opinion leaders (those who greeted others, were greeted most often, and whose advice was sought); inviting those identified to take part in a training programme (four, weekly, 90-minute sessions led by male and female facilitators); after which the opinion leaders were asked to initiate at least 10 safe-sex conversations with peers over the following two weeks.

True to the experimental principle underlying the ESID model, the project was conducted in one of the three cities initially, with the others serving as controls. Before and after surveys, conducted as people entered clubs, showed a significant reduction (25%) in unprotected anal intercourse, and a significant increase (16%) in condom use, with little or no change in the comparison cities. The programme went on to replicate the work in the two other southern cities, and in eight further cities in four other regions of the country (one in each region randomly assigned to intervention, the other serving as comparison), all with similar results. Finally, recognising the change that had taken place in the epidemiology of the HIV epidemic, the same principles were used to conduct a randomised controlled trial in 18 low-income housing developments across five US cities (nine intervention, nine control), with women identified as popular by their peers being trained to plan and run HIV-risk reduction workshops and ongoing community events. Again there were very significant reported reductions in unprotected intercourse (25%) and increased condom use (56%).

The Dissemination Component of ESID

As well as having a commitment to innovation and participation in the delivery of human services, ESID is committed to scientific evaluation. That evaluation ethos should apply, not only to evaluation of the early trials of a new form of service, but also to the dissemination phase. Gray et al. (2003) described the four levels of dissemination shown in Figure 10.5. Levels 1 and 2 referred, respectively, to advocating for dissemination of a model of service delivery that had been found on initial testing to be effective, and an activist approach that tries to disseminate effective social models by word or deed. Only levels 3 and 4 satisfied the requirement that the dissemination phase itself should be scientifically studied. At level 3 the factors that affect adoption of a new style of service are studied. Only at level 4 does the process reach the standard laid down by Fairweather et al. (1974) in their research on the dissemination of the Community Lodge experiment. At that level

Level 1: *Dissemination advocate* is aware of and supportive of the need to disseminate effective social models.

Level 2: *Dissemination activist* actively tries to disseminate effective social models by word or deed.

Level 3: *Dissemination researcher* engages in social science research on factors that affect the adoption and/or implementation of the social models they develop.

Level 4: *Experimental dissemination researcher* uses experimental methods to evaluate the effectiveness of the strategies and tactics they use to disseminate an effective social model.

Figure 10.5   Four levels of dissemination of an innovative and effective social programme
Source: reproduced with permission from Gray, D.I., Jakes, S.S., Emshoff, J. & Blakely, C. (2003). ESID, dissemination, and community psychology: a case of partial implementation. *American Journal of Community Psychology*, **32**, 359–70

the process of dissemination itself becomes the object of study. Gray *et al.* looked for evidence of how seriously dissemination was being taken in community psychology; the picture they found was somewhat disappointing. It seems that the least well-addressed component of ESID is the D element.

One of the issues in the field of dissemination highlighted by both Gray *et al.* (2003) and Emshoff *et al.* (2003) – who described a multiple case study of the dissemination of substance abuse prevention programmes disseminated by the Center for Substance Abuse Prevention (CSAP) in the USA – is the question of fidelity versus adaptation, that is the extent to which benefits are affected by either maintaining a high level of fidelity to the original demonstration model, or alternatively adapting it to suit local circumstances. Adopting organisations in Emshoff *et al.*'s study felt that finding the ideal balance between fidelity and adaptation was a delicate process; some thought it was important to maintain the principles but not necessarily the specific procedures, curriculum, or staffing patterns of the original model. A number of replications took place in settings culturally distinct from the original, and some materials, role-plays, and examples were culturally irrelevant, disrespectful or confusing, and needed to be changed. Some made more substantial changes, although most saw the advantage of, and felt an obligation to, maintaining fidelity. Most had found the technical assistance from the project developers, in the form of a replication manual and direct consultation, to be very helpful.

Both Gray *et al.* (2003) and Emshoff *et al.* (2003) argued that ways should be found to make a greater commitment to dissemination. Both papers considered why it might be that dissemination was being neglected. It might be because project originators provide inadequate or incomprehensible information about an innovation. Or it might be because those who might take up the innovation suffer from 'information fatigue', or are wary of programmes that have been invented elsewhere, or question the appropriateness of a generic method for a specific context, or simply lack trust in scientific findings, or are overwhelmed by daily management and organisational survival (Emshoff *et al.*, 2003). Gray *et al.* (2003) considered the difficulties in the way of disseminating "complex and potentially fragile social technologies" (p. 362) within organisations that are themselves complex. Community psychologists had tended to gravitate towards working with person-centred social problems rather than social change through organisational change. Dissemination research, "... is a complex, messy, multilevel, undertaking with uncertain payoffs" (pp. 367–8). Furthermore, agencies funding original innovations may feel no responsibility for further dissemination, and funding opportunities for the latter are relatively limited. Nor may professional and academic career structures favour following through innovative work with dissemination. Their evidence from publications and training curricula suggested that the interests and skills relevant to dissemination were not being properly developed either. Among the requirements for effective dissemination may be a greater awareness and knowledge of how organisations work than community psychology has demonstrated in the past (Orford, 1992; Boyd & Angelique, 2002).

Miller and Shinn (2005) were critical of the over-simple idea that dissemination of projects and programmes followed a linear movement from basic research through to application. They identified several problems with that idea. First, there was often a mismatch between what the originators had designed and what communities had the capacity to implement. By 'capacity' they had in mind much more than simply budgets, but also numbers and types of personnel, physical plant, equipment, and issues such as leadership, involvement, and sense of community. Capacity they saw as a multi-level and multi-dimensional construct, relevant for considering strengths and assets of individuals, families, organisations, neighbourhoods, and communities – including dimensions such as skills, resources, leadership, social capital, and power. It was rarely examined in the course of intervention and dissemination research, but a gap between programme requirements and organisational capacity often led to failure of dissemination.

A second factor that was often ignored according to Miller and Shinn is the gap that often exists between the values and principles underlying the evidence-based prevention programme and those of the host community or organisation. One example was the clash between the sex-positive and sexually explicit principles and materials underlying some AIDS-related educational programmes and the different values of some organisations providing HIV prevention services to gay men. Differences of view regarding an inclusion philosophy of services for people with disabilities was another example. A third, related factor identified by Miller and Shinn is one they referred to as pro-innovation bias, or the assumption that innovations that appear effective in controlled settings are likely to be more efficacious than methods that already exist in the community. That, seemingly arrogant, position assumes that communities are passively awaiting the evidence of controlled trials, and implies a scepticism about indigenous methods and community capacity. It diverts attention from studying the unintended consequences of adopting innovations, and exploring the reasons for rejecting or discontinuing innovations. In the real-world decisions about adoption are influenced by a wide range of stakeholders and local conditions.

The alternative proposed by Miller and Shinn was to identify already functioning, promising programmes in communities, learning from the 'ordinary' knowledge and skills of service providers. A second suggestion was that researchers should focus less on programmes and more on powerful ideas for improving community quality of life: the emphasis might more usefully be placed on specifying and promoting core elements or active ingredients, such as the idea of training popular members of a network to change norms (central to the HIV-risk work described by Fernández *et al.*, 2003), or the idea of availability of roles espoused by Barker (1968) and used to good effect by Fairweather *et al.* (1969) in the Lodge experiment. Looked at that way:

> ...dissemination becomes not simply the routine application of knowledge developed elsewhere and codified in prevention programs, but the theoretically motivated search for underlying principles of programs or practices that can inform both understanding of change and programs to create it (Miller & Shinn, 2005, p. 177).

In their view, formal evaluation should ideally *follow* a lengthy period of collaboration and learning, rather than the other way round (they cited the Housing First programme of Tsemberis *et al.*, 2003, as a good example – see above).

Concluding Chapter 10

In this chapter we have seen how disempowered groups can be helped to take action that aims, not just to improve the personal empowerment of individual members, but also to begin to transform the social circumstances that give rise to and maintain disempowerment. That always necessitates struggle, creativity and persistence. Sometimes the changes are modest or ephemeral. In other cases they are truly transformative and often an inspiration to others.

Chapter 11
EMPOWERING COMMUNITIES

Attention turns in the present chapter to interventions that are explicitly aimed at communities as collective entities. The chapter begins by considering some general ideas and principles; proceeds by looking at a selection of example projects; focusing towards the end of the chapter on the role of young people in action for community empowerment.

THE THEORY OF COMMUNITY COALITIONS

In the later years of the twentieth century, the development of 'coalitions' became a leading idea in the work of those, including community psychologists, concerned to 'build capacity' for improving the life of communities (Wolff, 2001). Much has been written in community psychology journals about the principles of coalition building and community organising. Among those who have written on the subject are Speer and his colleagues, basing their ideas on experience with the community organising network known as the Pacific Institute for Community Organizations (PICO), and its affiliated organisations in a number of cities across the USA (Speer & Hughey, 1995; Speer et al., 2003). A guiding principle of community organising in their experience was the focus on building relationships. Successful community organising paid as much if not more attention to relationships as it did to focusing on the issue at hand. Only through collective organisation could empowerment be realised. They wrote of a 'cycle of organising practice' consisting of the four phases shown in Figure 11.1: *assessment, research, action,* and *reflection.*

Speer and Hughey (1995) provided several examples of the activities of community organisations that were members of the PICO network. For example, one organisation discovered that absentee landlords were being paid by a local social service agency for housing newly resettled immigrants in badly sub-standard housing. When the organisation asked the agency to use its financial leverage to press landlords into making improvements, the request was rejected. The next step was to find out from what sources the social service agency was funded. That information

---

Assessment

> Consisted largely of one-to-one conversations, often held between community members in their own homes, that served to gather information about community issues and build relationships.

Research

> Conducted through organisational meetings with knowledgeable people and groups, to gather information about the nature of the issue and in particular the ways in which the issue was affected by the allocation of resources and how social power was exercised around the issue.

Action

> Consisting of public events that demonstrated organisational power, brought together large numbers of community members, plus media, public officials and other organisations, and entailing both strategy development and mobilisation for collective action, culminating in a directed target of, "... extract[ing] a tangible and measurable shift in the flow of community resources" (p. 735).

Reflection

> On the effectiveness of strategies implemented, discussion of lessons learned and thoughts about future directions (a dialectic of action and reflection as an important basic principle).

Figure 11.1   The four phases of the cycle of organising practice
Source: Speer, P.W. & Hughey, J. (1995). Community organizing: an ecological route to empowerment and power. *American Journal of Community Psychology*, **23**, 729–48

was made public at a meeting attended by about 500 community members – an 'action' in PICO terms. Those present indicated by a show of hands their willingness to write to the agency's funders requesting termination of funding if landlords were not pressed to make improvements, and the agency capitulated on the spot.

Central to Speer and Hughey's conceptualisation of successful community organising was the multi-dimensional concept of power. They outlined three 'instruments' of social power: bargaining resources, for example in the form of organised money or influence with which to exert power; the ability to control what gets talked about in public debate, by constructing or eliminating barriers to participation, and by setting agendas and defining issues; and the ability to shape how residents and public officials think about a community by influencing shared consciousness through myths, ideology, and controlled information. Social power is manifested, according to Speer and Hughey, at individual, organisational, and community levels. They were critical of the way the term empowerment had often been confined to increases in individual self-efficacy, sense of achievement, or

personal adjustment (see also Riger, 1993, and Chapter 2), often without considering how individual empowerment was linked to social power. The organisational
level was, in their view, the most critical for community organisations, since individuals could only exercise social power through organisations of which they were
a part, and organisations could be both *empowered* or *empowering* (to use the distinction made by Zimmerman, 2000). One of the ways in which organising was
empowering for individuals was through the creation of multiple participatory
'niches' for individuals. Rather than locking people into a few, relatively permanent positions, their experience was that successful community organisations managed to identify multiple and varied roles that were arranged in horizontal rather
than hierarchical fashion, rotated among individuals, and changed with changing
circumstances. Examples included one-to-one conversations, asking questions of
officials during meetings, arranging media coverage, researching and contributing information to public records, leading public events, mobilising organisation
members, time-keeping for events, and arranging venues and transportation.

   Foster-Fishman *et al.* (2001a) contributed to a special issue of the *American Journal of Community Psychology* on coalitions by reporting, on the basis of a review of
the literature, a framework consisting of critical elements of collaborative capacity
and strategies for building those elements (see Figure 11.2). Collaborative capacity, they concluded, was necessary at four levels: within members, relationships,
organisational structure, and sponsored programmes. Their framework contained
a large number of detailed suggestions for building capacity (Figure 11.2 only
shows the outline of the framework). Much of the detail consisted of wise counsel
about methods, although if all the advice were followed the task would certainly
be a demanding one. At the least, it demonstrated well the point that institutional
change requires much effort and time. Specific suggestions ranged from including
as diverse an array of stakeholders as possible, using members' skills to the full and
helping develop other skills, making it as easy as possible for people to contribute
(e.g. by car pooling or using interpreters), and trying to understand individuals'
motivations and being sensitive to signs of member dissatisfaction – all ways of
building member capacity; making sure that all members have a voice in decision making, dealing with conflict as it emerges, and creating opportunities for
informal socialising – ways of building relational capacity; recruiting people who
are good at administration and organisation, developing an active sub-committee
and working group structure, managing time well during meetings and keeping
members on task during meetings, and disseminating information in a variety of
different ways (such as minutes of meetings, e-mail, a phone tree) – all ways of
building organisational capacity; to having explicit objectives, assessing outcomes,
and conducting regular assessments – for building programmatic capacity.

   In a contribution to the same special issue, Himmelman (2001) offered an analysis in terms of social power. He contrasted *collaborative betterment* with *collaborative empowerment* (see Table 11.1). He began by defining collaboration as the most
demanding of four strategies for working in coalitions, starting with networking –
the least demanding – followed by coordinating (involving sharing information
and altering activities for a common purpose), and cooperation (which in addition involves sharing resources), and finally collaboration. The latter went further,
requiring a willingness to enhance the capacity of another for mutual benefit and

Building Member Capacity

    Understand current member capacity

    Value the diversity of member competencies

    Enhance current member capacities

    Engage in incentives management

    Foster positive inter-group understanding

    Build diverse membership

    Support diversity

Building Relational Capacity

    Building positive inter-group interactions

    Create group norms

    Develop superordinate, shared goals

    Create inclusive decision-making processes

    Value member diversity

    Build external relationships

Building Organisational Capacity

    Proactively build leadership

    Develop task focus

    Formalise roles/processes

    Develop quality plans

    Create committee infrastructure

    Promote active communication

    Build financial resources

    Develop skilled staff

    Develop an outcome orientation

    Develop a monitoring system

Building Programmatic Capacity

    Seek community input

    Develop innovative programmes

Figure 11.2   Strategies for building core elements of collaborative capacity
Source: Foster-Fishman, P.G., Berkowitz, S.L., Lonnsbury, D.W., Jacobson, S. & Allen, N.A. (2001a). Building collaborative capacity in community coalitions: a review and integrative framework, *American Journal of Community Psychology*, **29**, 241–61

common purpose. It involved the greatest level of trust, commitment of time and energy, and sharing of risks and rewards. As Speer and Hughey (1995) noted, it is often poor, minority, urban communities that are involved in community better-ment projects, and their issues are frequently the result of deteriorating physical and social infrastructures and the outflow of many kinds of resources.

Table 11.1   The contrast between collaborative betterment and collaborative empowerment coalitions

Collaborative Betterment	Collaborative Empowerment
Usually planned, funded and controlled by large public, private or non-profit institutions, including government agencies and universities	Occurs when communities themselves initiate coalition building by inviting the participation of larger institutions
Likely to use the language, frameworks, assumptions and value systems of the initiating institutions	Identify challenges to be addressed by combining analysis of data with narrative examples from community residents
Likely to rely on staff, primarily responsible to those institutions, with community representatives often in advisory roles only	Agree representation on the coalition's decision-making body and sharing power
Unlikely to transform existing power relationships	An action plan is negotiated based on the coalition's agreed mission
Likely to support the position that increased public sector spending is not the favoured way of solving societal problems	More likely to change power relationships and/or increase public resources
Funding often short-term, and the people and the organisations involved commonly find themselves over-extended, striving to resist decreased resources	New alliances formed which are more likely to be sustainable

Source: Himmelman, A.T. (2001). On coalitions and the transformation of power relations: collaborative betterment and collaborative empowerment. *American Journal of Community Psychology, 29,* 277–84

Community Regeneration

National programmes of urban regeneration – sometimes referred to as 'area based initiatives' (ABIs) – have received massive funding in a number of countries in recent decades. Table 11.2 lists the main programmes conducted in the UK over a period of 30 years or so. Thomson *et al.* (2006) reviewed the evidence for the effect of such programmes on health, finding little concrete evidence of positive impact (although they acknowledged that the difficulties of evaluating the impact of such programmes are formidable). Evaluations had tended to rely on reports of money spent or gross outputs such as numbers of new houses built. Changes in health variables, where they had been assessed, had been small but positive, although in some instances, and in some areas, adverse effects had also occurred. Their conclusion, therefore, was that, despite the large amounts of money spent – an estimated £11 billion in England alone between 1980 and 2002 – "The potential... for this significant public investment to ameliorate deprivation and improve health and reduce inequalities remains unknown" (Thomson *et al.*, 2006, p. 113).

The UK government's New Deal for Communities (NDC) urban regeneration scheme is a good example with which the present author is familiar. It promised to

Table 11.2 Major national UK Urban regeneration programmes 1969–2008

Programme and estimated expenditure	Main focus of programme
Urban Programme 1969–1980s about £274m/year	Grant-based programme to deal with areas of special social need through supplementation of existing programmes covering economic, environmental, employment and social projects
Urban Development Corporations (UDC) 1981–1998 £2120m	Property and economic regeneration to attract inward investment
Estate Action 1985–1995 £1975m	Housing-led regeneration addressing both improvements to physical aspects of housing as well as housing management
New Life for Urban Scotland (New Life) 1988–1998 £485m	Comprehensive multi-agency regeneration programme to improve housing, environment, service provision, training, and employment for local people in four areas
Small Urban Renewal Initiatives (SURI) 1990–2003 £160m+	Housing-led regeneration to widen housing choice, improve housing quality and the local environment, improve economic prospects, and lever public and private funding
City Challenge 1992–1998 £1162.5m	Comprehensive multi-agency regeneration to improve quality of life of residents in run down areas
Single Regeneration Budget (SRB) 1995–2001 £5703m+ £20301m from private sector	Comprehensive multi-agency regeneration through initiatives on employment, training, economic growth, housing, crime, environment, ethnic minorities, and quality of life (including health, sport, and cultural opportunities)
Regeneration Partnerships (now known as Social Inclusion Partnerships) (SIPs) 1996 £52m	Coordinated approach to tackle and prevent social exclusion and demonstrate innovative practices. Main activities focus on education and training, and initiatives to reduce poverty, crime, and promote employment, enterprise, empowerment, and health
New Deal for Communities (NDC) £2000m 1998–2008	Neighbourhood-based programme delivered through multi-agency partnerships. Aims: to reduce inequalities in crime, worklessness, education, housing, and health between the 39 target areas and the rest of England. Key characteristics of this programme are: long-term commitment to deliver real change, communities in partnership with key agencies, community involvement and ownership, joined up thinking and solutions, and action based on evidence about 'what works' and what doesn't

Source: reproduced with permission from Thomson, H., Atkinson, R., Petticrew, M. & Kearns, A. (2006). Do urban regeneration programmes improve public health and reduce health inequalities? A synthesis of the evidence from UK policy and practice (1980–2004). *Journal of Epidemiology and Community Health,* **60**, 108–15

improve on previous such schemes by maintaining financial support over a period of 10 years for innovations decided upon locally in the domains of health, housing, education, employment, and crime. In practice, however, the decision-making structures that were required were largely set by government and constrained local residents' actions (Parry *et al.*, 2005, 2007). Dinham (2005) interviewed 30 local people in one NDC area in East London, concluding, similarly, that such a scheme was predicated on the idea of activating otherwise uninvolved citizens by a process that required, among other things, election of representatives to a decision-making board. In practice meetings were often found to be formal and 'off-putting', and representatives sometimes felt they were not able to 'be themselves', and that the process undervalued what was (and often had already been) going on at a more informal level:

> In conceiving of local people primarily as dormant citizens in need of activation, their diversity and talents are thereby underestimated and undervalued ... NDC processes are too fast, too formal, and fail to take account of local histories and relationships ... local people are asked to come together as though nothing had ever happened to them before and in ways in which they have rarely, if ever, operated (pp. 309–10).

The dangers of cooption and tokenism in regeneration schemes were pointed out by Kagan and Burton (2005), citing the example of one such scheme that took place in the early 1990s in an area of one British city. In competition with other areas, the local council won central government funding for a large rebuilding project. Although the lead redevelopment agency stressed the importance of working closely with the local population, and a number of public meetings were held, in practice there was only token resident participation and real citizen control and power was never attained (see Chapter 12 for a fuller discussion of participation). It seemed that the project could be presented cosmetically as one that really involved local people, but in practice the greatest power to influence the design and execution of the project was in the hands of private development companies who profited from the scheme.

Kagan and Burton (2000) described their own work with a women's group on a council housing estate – much more modest in scale than the large regeneration schemes, but perhaps more empowering for those involved. The work began by helping women identify their vision for change, which resulted in women forming an alternative residents' association and struggling to gain recognition as the legitimate representative association on the estate. The work included helping women write up a survey that they had undertaken themselves, and helping them identify the most useful negotiation strategies to begin trying to improve life on the estate. A specific aim was resisting the transfer of housing stock from the city council to a landlord who was perceived as malevolent. A link was created with a group of students studying community psychology at the local university, who, over a period of several months worked on a number of projects identified by residents, including an adult literacy project, a gardening project for older residents, a project to improve the availability of local transport, and the development of a welfare and resource pack. The students also helped transform the community house from one that was under-used, unattractive and generally padlocked, to one that was newly decorated, lively and accessible, with attractive facilities for children. Placing this work in the context of 'prefigurative action research', Kagan and Burton identified a number of points for learning. They included residents learning about the positive possibilities of linking with the university – some visited a university for the first time when they attended to hear students present their work – and learning about how a component of students' education, unorthodox and radical within the university psychology environment, could be promoted and maintained.

Another project carried out in three electoral wards of a British city, largely consisting of local authority housing, was the project described by Fryer and Fagan (2003). The area was characterised by many houses in poor physical condition, a degraded environment, and absence of facilities. Specific problems included houses with inadequate thermal insulation, dampness, lack of play space, lack of good shopping and banking facilities, disputes between neighbours, rapid turnover of tenants, unrented houses, and dumping of refuse. The population had declined more rapidly in that area than in others in the city, health indices suggested relatively poor health, and drug misuse had become a particular problem in the area. Car ownership and owner occupation of homes were low. Another indication of the level of poverty in the area was that around two-thirds of tenants in the three wards were in rent arrears. Unemployment, at 13%, was nearly double that for the city as a whole, with male unemployment reaching 20% in one of the wards.

The research focused on work with a total of 55 participants in 30 households. It involved multiple interviews, and specifically the use of a portable notebook computer, with software that enabled detailed family financial information to be recorded, welfare benefit entitlements to be calculated, and benefit advice delivered. As a result, one in five families who took part learned about and claimed income to which they had not previously known they were entitled; others reported relief at understanding why they were, or were not, entitled to particular benefits; and some used the intervention to work out the implications of different potential courses of action. Emphasis was placed on using action research methods that were not only sensitive to the details of participants' financial affairs, but were also relevant to family members, sensitive to the needs of those already at risk of depression and anxiety, stigma, low self-confidence, and invasion of privacy, which would be non-threatening, transparent in purpose, and which would facilitate respect and trust. The research interviews were therefore preceded by several months in which the field worker took part in a variety of activities in the community, including backstage work with a community drama group and participation in a women's group, a local activists' group, and an arts organisation, and helping with gala day and a photography exhibition. Towards the end of that period, she began to make contact with those, such as health visitors and members of local organisations, who might help her gain access to specific research participants. Besides the research interviewers, the field worker involved herself with families in such activities as baby sitting and child minding, helping with household chores such as getting clothes in from the washing line and giving lifts, as well as helping fill in forms and write letters. In the course of this "modest but time consuming project" (p. 95), much was learned about the way in which time was structured for women in unemployed families – for example around a partner's non-employment routine, around nursery school and primary school hours, the routines involved in signing on for, receiving and cashing benefits, and family shopping – about the pros and cons of working on the side (the 'black' economy) – including pride at doing a good job with self-taught skills, but also the anti-social and immoral associations and the fear of neighbourhood informers – as well as about the feelings of humiliation, stigma, and passivity associated with being dependent on benefits.

COLLABORATIONS, CONSORTIA AND COALITIONS: EXAMPLES OF PROJECTS

Six example projects have been chosen to illustrate some of the practicalities of developing coalitions for social action. The specific topics they addressed were diverse – some much more focused (e.g. on providing dental care) and others much broader (having a vision for a whole city for example) – as were their methods. All in their different ways, however, entailed collaborating in order to build capacity (or one might say to build social capital – see Chapter 6) to enable action for collective empowerment.

Example 1: Providing Dental Care in an Isolated Area

The first example is provided by Hathaway (2001), who had served as coordinator of a Community Coalition, formed with the aim of improving quality of life for the nearly 50,000 people living in a group of towns at the furthest end of Cape Cod in Massachusetts, USA. Although for part of the year the Cape was an attractive area for seasonal visitors, many of the permanent residents struggled financially and were not well provided with a number of human services. The Coalition had been successful in the development of services, such as an inter-faith homelessness prevention programme, an economic development agency, and a family resource centre. The Coalition saw it as its task to rally the community around significant issues, at times to undertake more formal assessments of needs, resources and community opinions. Task forces on particular issues would undertake a number of steps: identifying others who were involved, interested, or affected by a problem (stakeholders); defining the problem and deciding whether additional data were needed; investigating options, including consulting experts and finding out what others had done in similar circumstances; designing a response; securing resources; implementing a plan; evaluating and adapting; and deciding how the response should be sustained, including options of being managed by an existing agency or organisation, or standing alone.

The particular example described by Hathaway concerned dental care. Community health outreach workers had alerted the community to the lack of accessible dental care. Subsequent surveys, carried out through local elementary schools and the regional technical high school, found that the large majority of Cape households were without dental insurance, and that only four dentists in the whole area accepted work under the state version of Medicaid. They had long waiting lists. The Coalition dental care task force, which included a retired paediatrician and a retired public health physician who provided valuable help and access to others, considered a number of options including a mobile dental van, which would have been ideal but was unaffordable. The solution was found through developing a partnership between the Coalition, a dental service provided at an off-Cape community health centre that was willing to provide its services at a satellite site in the area, the regional technical high school which had a dentistry instructional suite that was enthusiastic about providing the site, and funds provided through the University of Massachusetts Medical School. In the course of their work the task force discovered that rural areas in neighbouring states were experiencing the same problems, and as a result the Coalition also began to address wider issues about the provision of dental care, for example by testifying at public hearings on dental care access, and joining state-wide advocacy campaigns to increase dental care funding.

Example 2: Raising Community Awareness about Domestic Violence

A small town in north-east Italy and its surrounding province is the setting for the second example (Romito et al., 2004). The background was the silence that very often surrounds the issue of violence towards women, neglect of the subject in the public health services, and what they believed to be the lack of serious study of it in Italy and in southern European countries generally. Initiated by the observation of a woman doctor – one of six family doctors practising in the town – that she had never seen a 'battered woman' in her practice, a screening survey was carried out among all women over 17 years of age attending any of the six practices between April and July 2001. The response rate was 79%. Women were asked about their experiences of physical or psychological violence in the last 12 months or earlier in their lives, and were asked whether they thought family doctors should ask all patients about violence.

Five per cent reported recent physical or sexual aggression (pushing, slapping, stabbing, hitting, biting or choking were given as examples of what was meant by physical violence; and sexual violence was defined as being forced to submit to a sexual act), inflicted by a male partner or ex-partner in over 80% of cases. Even larger numbers reported recent psychological violence, nearly half the time from a male partner or ex-partner, but also quite often by other family members, neighbours, co-workers or others. Previous to the past 12 months 25% reported receiving any physical or sexual violence – 38% of that violence from male partners or ex-partners. In general, younger respondents reported more recent violence from male partners, and pregnant women, women with young children, and separated and divorced women were more likely than others to report violence. Eighty-five per cent answered that the family doctor should ask all women about violence, and another 8% were uncertain. Just over half chose the family doctor when asked with whom they would like to talk about the violence, 28% chose a psychologist, 22% other women with the same experience, 9% a social worker, and 7% the police.

The findings were presented at three public meetings. One was held at the local hospital, attended mainly by a psychologist and social workers, the other two open to the community and well attended, one in the town, the other in the main city in the province. The Mayor, the Chief of Police and the President of the judicial system were present and there was good press coverage. Funding for a training course for health professionals and a survey of medical records at the hospital emergency department were among the actions that resulted. The doctor who had initiated the study began to identify women patients who had experienced domestic violence, identifying 20 cases of her own and 10 among patients of other doctors. Dealing with the first case required contacts with the hospital emergency department, social services, police, the prosecutor, and a shelter in another city. That stimulated the creation of the first women's group in the provincial capital. Since then the group had built contacts, gained experience, carried out advocacy work, and prepared a booklet on violence for women, and was lobbying to raise funds to start a telephone helpline. Romito *et al.* were convinced of the importance in this process of the research that was carried out:

> The study's results were crucial in making violence against women visible and in convincing many people, both women and men, that it represents a serious problem ... The study brought together women from various institutions – health and social services, the university, the city hall, from women's groups and from the community, and created an opportunity to work towards a common goal. Moreover, although women are carrying out most of the work, many men from this community have been ready to collaborate and be supportive (p. 262).

Example 3: A Local Consortium for Safer Housing

A community characterised by poverty, a high level of risk, and widespread scepticism among residents about the attitudes of the authorities towards them, was the barrio of Catuche in Caracas, Venezuela, that was the subject of a report by Giuliani and Wiesenfeld (2003). Typical of many such poor neighbourhoods in Caracas, it was of only recent origin, part of the response to rapid and uncontrolled migration to the city, which had been unable to provide enough proper housing to keep pace with the growing population. Families had resorted to self-help in providing their own housing, which usually meant illegally occupying unused land and building their own houses, initially with scrap materials, gradually replaced later with brick. Such squatter settlements are to be found in urban areas throughout the so-called 'third world'. In Caracas they were often built on land subject to landslides or flooding, or were close to fuel storage facilities. Catuche extended from the foot of a mountain at the northern edge of Caracas to an area of old buildings in part of the historical city centre. It was crossed by a stream which was liable to flooding. Giuliani and Wiesenfeld reported a qualitative study, consisting of individual interviews and focus groups, of a housing substitution project in which 33 families were moved from houses built on the stream bank, where there was the greatest risk of flooding, to two new, safer buildings nearby.

With its origins lying in years of pastoral work carried out by Christian-based organisations, composed of community residents supported by Jesuit priests, a process of community urban management was launched in order to clean up the then badly polluted river. It required engineering work to channel the stream in a different direction and an environmental education project accompanied by the installation of garbage dumps. A Social Consortium was formed, composed of the community itself, a group of independent architects and urban planners, a non-government organisation concerned with local development, and a popular education movement. The consortium was answerable to the Community General Assembly. The housing substitution project was then identified as the most important and the research was focused on it. It involved not only the 33 families directly involved but also the wider community. Through construction micro-businesses, work was created for many unemployed local residents who took on the construction of the buildings, and women in the barrio had a source of income through cooking for the workers. The community was committed to the project because of the benefits in terms of everyone's safety: collapse of the buildings next to the river in a flood would have created a dam with serious consequences for the neighbourhood. The families directly involved committed themselves to participate in a condominium board and to be responsible for such things as collective payment of public utilities. They were involved at an early stage in discussion with architects about the design of apartments suited to their needs as well as individual families' preferences for sharing a floor with other families to whom they were related by family, friendship or neighbourhood ties.

The following three quotations from research informants are expressive of, respectively, the threat posed by the danger of flooding, scepticism about the authorities, and the growing sense of community that came with the project:

> ... we didn't sleep when it rained, but kept watching the hillside to see whether the stream was rising. When it rose we had to get out because the water would get into the houses; then we went to Milagro's house, and she gave us sheets and we spent the night there until dawn and we went back. Then came another rainstorm and once again we had to get out on the run. We spent a lot of years living like that (p. 169).

> You get tired of all the baloney, all the promises they make. They remember the barrio when elections are coming. But then you don't see them around here again. Anybody here can tell you that no one believed in it, everyone thought this was just another trick, the same as all the rest. But then we saw the priest, the architect, all the people who were here, who little by little explained it to us (p. 170).

> This is the product of many people, of the institutions that were here, of Father Joseph, of the architects, of the community itself, of everyone ... Now I'm more a part of the community, because as a community we got all this and we are at this point. And now I myself continue supporting all this, and I'm working for all the others, so that they can get ahead too, just as we have (p. 176).

Giuliani and Wiesenfeld presented the Catuche project as an example of the way in which the psychosocial dimension could be incorporated into the idea of sustainable development. They considered three processes to be important: problematisation, participation, and appropriation. Without *problematisation* – agreeing that a problem does exist and identifying what it is – which came about through dialoguing and critical reflection, there would be likely to be continued passivity, continued damaging of the environment, and failure to strengthen group identity. *Participation*, which was very apparent in the project, generated the conditions that people needed in order to be able to visualise a solution to their problem of risk. But they concluded that it was not just a process in which people took part in making decisions, but in addition a process of *appropriation* whereby people identified with a project and made the project and the new places it created their own.

It was not long after the completion of the Catuche housing substitution project that Venezuela was hit by the natural disaster of December 1999 that brought extensive flooding, several thousand deaths, and colossal material damage. In Catuche 14 lives were lost and around 800 houses destroyed. The new buildings were among the few structures that remained standing. Had the original housing on the riverbank not been replaced, the disaster locally might have been far greater. Furthermore, the strengthened community organisation came into its own in organising the necessary evacuation quickly and efficiently, and providing support for shelters where members were temporarily housed.

Example 4: A Community Crime Reduction Campaign

The fourth example is part of the PICO network, described earlier. This was the Camden Community Housing Campaign organised by a coalition of 18 churches in Camden, one of the poorest cities in New Jersey, USA (Camden Churches Organized for People or CCOP, which had two staff organisers and approximately 60 active leaders) (Speer *et al.*, 2003). Based on the PICO model, CCOP was committed to the need for social change brought about through the exercise of power that required citizens to come together collectively. The process began with several hundred one-on-one conversations. What emerged was widespread concern about raised levels of violent crime in the city, its association with drug dealing, and the importance of vacant houses in encouraging drug dealing (18% of the housing stock in Camden was vacant at the time, which was double the national average). Approximately 20 meetings were then held with both public and private sector officials, including the city mayor. It was concluded that no one in the city had knowledge of the extent of vacant housing, and that officials saw no link between vacant housing and drug crime. CCOP then drew upon their relationship with the Centre for Social and Community Development at Rutgers University and a joint project was carried out using a Geographical Information System (GIS) to plot drug crime geographically and to examine the association with vacant housing. Through relationships already developed, CCOP was able to obtain crime data from the police. Drug arrests were found to be three or four times greater in census block groups with greater than the median amount of vacant housing. Where vacant housing was at least twice the median, violent crime was nearly seven times greater than in the below-median areas. Maps showing this relationship provided compelling evidence at an 'action' public meeting attended by about a thousand people. An example was presented of one vacant house that had cost the city over $50,000 in the previous three years on account of receiving over 200 calls to the police, having been boarded up seven separate times, and contributing no local taxes. Personal accounts of the experiences of local residents were also shared.

The result was a series of meetings between CCOP, the city mayor and representatives of a number of city departments (housing and community affairs, fire, police, public works) and other individual organisations, to consider the impact of vacant housing. These meetings led to the development of the Community Housing Campaign. The local newspaper ran a series of stories on the subject, including some GIS maps. The local fire department conducted an inventory of all vacant housing. A new competitive bidding process was put in place to lower demolition costs, more efficient methods were used to board up vacant houses, and CCOP obtained funding to support housing campaigns. An evaluation conducted by the university research centre after one year found that nearly 200 houses with structural damage had been demolished and nearly a thousand others boarded up.

Although Speer *et al.* acknowledged the difficulty of attributing changes to the campaign, drug crime dropped by 30%, and by over 50% in blocks with two or more boarded up or demolished houses. Speer *et al.* believed that CCOP had been able to, "... redefine the public debate ... [as] an important mechanism for exercising power" (p. 404). Fundamental was their understanding of power and how to exercise it to address a community problem, plus their strategy of demanding an open planning process. A spin-off was drawing the attention of researchers to the application of GIS for supporting community action.

Example 5: Street-Based Communities in an Environment of Urban Poverty

From a very different part of the world came Trout *et al.*'s (2003) description of the establishment of Street-Based Communities (SBCs) that were set up under the guidance of a missionary society priest (the first author) in one parish in Lagos, Nigeria. Trout *et al.* observed how people appeared to experience a sense of belonging when attending church on Sunday, but returned home to isolation, loneliness and fear associated with the harsh socioeconomic and environmental conditions of modern urban life – noise throughout the night, irregular electricity supply, overcrowding in hot and poorly ventilated buildings, inadequate transportation with large crowds scrambling for the few public transport vehicles, roads in disrepair and practically unusable in the rainy season, no public hospital and unaffordable for-profit health agencies, poor water quality, high crime rate and the need for bars on windows and doors and security gates at the end of the street. They used the principles of Latin American liberation theology to recruit around 50 young professionals from the parish to become community trainers. Their task was to encourage the formation of area SBCs, of which ultimately there were 40 in the parish. Each elected three leaders, of whom at least one was required to be a woman, in order to make sure that women, who constituted the majority of members, would have leadership roles available to them. Trout *et al.* believed that ethnic/tribal differences, often a source of conflict in the city, were minimised, since faith identity rather than ethnic identity was the motivation for coming together.

A survey of SBC community leaders suggested that weekly meetings were important but that participation was much more than attendance at meetings. The meetings involved sharing and reflecting about common experiences and problems, often leading to actions such as visiting the sick and arranging financial and medical assistance; and in some cases leading to community action, such as agreeing to put disputed land to common use to build a clinic providing basic health services (subsequently receiving a substantial grant from the Irish government). In general it was thought that membership provided people with, "...the opportunity to move from being helpless victims to becoming agents of their own transformation and that of the socioeconomic environment in which they live" (p. 139). SBCs encouraged people to express their thoughts and feelings, to grow in self-confidence, and to take initiative. It was thought that a real 'sense of community' could develop. At the same time the research identified a number of obstacles. One was the overwhelming oppressiveness of the poverty experienced by most members whose circumstances meant a hectic daily struggle for survival often requiring long hours working. Another was the discomfort many felt at attending community activities, due to the siege mentality caused by lack of safety, and sometimes unwillingness to share problems because of fear of gossiping and back-biting. While leaders were mostly middle-aged, middle-income, moderately well-educated women, the majority of members were low-income women with little formal education, reticent about sharing their experiences. They tended to be "willing followers but reluctant leaders" (p. 139). In part Trout *et al.* attributed such reticence to Nigeria's history of British colonisation, and in part to the way in which certain forms of religion failed to focus attention on present political, economic and social realities, therefore tending to, "...enslave[ing] people to their life circumstances rather than mobilize them to address the root causes of poverty" (p. 139).

Example 6: Having a Vision for a City

Imagine Chicago is a good example of projects that aim to produce a citizens' vision of a better city. Browne (2004) described the thinking behind the Chicago project and some of its achievements and difficulties. As a corporate banker, Anglican priest, mother, and civic activist, her vision was of a city to which everyone, especially young people, could contribute, and from which everyone would benefit – unlike the divided city that she believed Chicago had become. Quitting her banking job along the way, she joined with 20 city leaders – educators, corporate and media executives, philanthropists, community organisers, youth developers, economists, religious leaders, social service providers – to form Imagine Chicago in 1992. Two ideas emerged early on: that a pilot should attempt to discover what positively gave life to the city, as opposed to focusing on problems; and that it should provide significant leadership opportunities for young people. The pilot used a process termed 'appreciative inquiry' that involved about 50 young people, in the company of adult mentors, interviewing about 250 Chicago citizens – including artists, media executives, civic and grassroots leaders, politicians, business and professional leaders, and other young people – identified as 'Chicago glue'. The aim was to locate and illuminate the 'life-giving forces' of a community and to help members of the group envisage a collectively designed future, thereby helping to, "...translate images of possibility into reality" (p. 397).

Following the interviews, several groups of young people summarised the data which were shared at three public events, including a city-wide 'imagination celebration' to which all interviewers and interviewees were invited. The room was organised into small inter-generational table groupings, arts-based activities were used to further develop emerging themes, and a Chicago 'dream tree' was used to depict the results: 'leaves' drawn in advance by youth analysts who read the interview transcripts and identified themes, the 'trunk' being used to record emerging common themes. This process of shifting 'civic conversation' away from problem solving and towards collective visions of the future helped participants begin to understand the commonalities in their ideas for the city's future. It also changed the image that many of the adult participants had of 'inner-city kids from tough neighbourhoods'. Browne also referred to the subtle and positive shift for many participants that came about through learning to ask and answer positive questions and to engage in active listening, as part of the appreciative inquiry process.

In the subsequent decade Imagine Chicago had developed over 100 learning partnerships with schools, churches, museums, community groups and businesses. In one programme, Citizen Leaders, participants were invited to articulate a vision for community change, design a project that could be implemented within a relatively short time and at low cost, and to recruit at least six other neighbourhood volunteers to bring the project into being. A step-by-step Community Innovation Guide was used to help participants organise their projects. In the process, leaders learned to recruit volunteers, design and organise a project, prepare a proposal, and implement, evaluate and sustain their work. In the Citizen Leader workshops they were learners, but in their neighbourhoods they became project leaders. Browne gave the example of Tina, an initially shy, recent graduate of an alternative high school, living in public housing. She was concerned that there were many young men in her neighbourhood who were unemployed, in gangs, and needing something worthwhile to do. Knowing that they liked to play basketball but had no league, supposedly because of lack of interest, she put up a notice inviting young men to sign up if they wanted to play basketball, and offered to help organise a team for her project. Over 200 signed up in the first week and Tina got donations for equipment from local businesses. By the end of that summer there were hundreds playing basketball in the local league, rival gangs were playing without fighting, the league led to a leadership development and job-training programme for the young men, and Tina, previously unemployed, got offers of jobs as a community outreach worker.

Another example was the creation of the Urban Imagination Network. This was a collaboration of Imagine Chicago and the Centre for Urban Education at DePaul University, linking seven Chicago public schools in very poor urban communities, with Imagine Chicago and with six city museums. An aim was to build students' reading and thinking skills by encouraging them to research particular topics and develop exhibits displaying what they had found out. An example was children from elementary school working with the city Botanic Garden to create a garden in their school courtyard. In another school each class created an illustrated quilt for the school hallway. A parent element called Reading Chicago and Bringing It Home focused on computer and 'civic literacy' skills to connect families to the life of the larger city, with monthly workshops held in each participating school. Browne believed that, "By learning to read their city, parents re-envision themselves as educators, community leaders, thinkers, parents, citizens, not objects or victims" (p. 403). Also included was a teacher renewal programme structured around quarterly weekend retreats held at the Botanic Garden.

o Different stakeholder groups are brought together around an agreed problem

o New groups and roles are created

o New data about the problem are collected

o Joint commitment to an action plan is agreed

o New resources are obtained, and contacts made, for example with outside experts and
   with the media

o A public event(s) is held, with people in authority invited, at which findings are
   presented, and further action called for

o Commitment is sustained for long enough for change to occur and to be maintained

o Once real progress has been made with the initial problem, new and wider issues may
   start to be addressed

Figure 11.3   Principles for effective collaboration suggested by six example collective action
projects

Among the problems encountered were the sheer weight of bureaucracy in the
school system, scepticism about engaging parents, and the difficulties of securing
ongoing funding.

In Figure 11.3 is to be found a summary of some of the principles for effective
collaboration for collective action suggested by those six example projects. Despite
their diversity, there are a number of general conclusions that can be drawn. Bringing a sizeable group of people together to collaborate around a common issue,
building a sound base of knowledge about the issue, mobilising resources and
expertise, effectively presenting ideas to those in influential positions, and establishing and carrying through a plan of action are all said to be among the key
ingredients for success.

YOUNG PEOPLE AND COLLECTIVE ACTION

It was noted in Chapter 6 that young people tend to have a distinctive view of
their communities, having a 'sense of community' that may not be shared with
older people. Furthermore, there was evidence that older people may under-value
the contribution that young people can make to the community. Young people
themselves may sometimes feel negative and hopeless about influencing things
for the better. The following are examples of projects in which young people were
actively engaged in joint action for community improvements.

Young People's Positive Involvement in Improving Resources

One of Speer and Hughey's (1995) examples from the PICO network involved the
coming together in one city of 14 congregations that had separately been engaged in
action to improve job and recreation opportunities for young people. They identified a problem of lack of access for children after school hours and during summer,

to facilities such as swimming pools, gymnasia, health facilities and computer resources, due to the absence of a working relationship between the public schools, the city government, and recreational institutions. Over 20 public 'research events' were held to discover what resources were available and how they were controlled. A carefully planned joint 'action' meeting was then held attended by about a thousand people, including the city mayor and other public and private officials and journalists. The action included testimony by both children and adults, and the call for specific, measurable steps to be taken by city government, the school district, and the parks commission, was successful.

A similar process of overcoming official resistance to allocating resources for youth in a rural Australian town was described by Bradley *et al.* (2004). There had been general recognition in Australia that rural youth were at special risk, for example for substance misuse and mental illness, and most of the surrounding towns had responded by initiating development projects aimed at increasing teenage participation in local affairs. In the target town, on the other hand, youth were often viewed by citizens, including councillors and service providers, as being *a risk* rather than *at risk*. One night wheelie-bins had been set alight and shop windows smashed in the middle of the town – referred to by the local newspaper as the town's 'night of shame'. A part-time researcher had been employed to assess the needs of youth, but her report was dismissed out of hand and her post terminated. It subsequently emerged that the Council, who employed her, had not wholeheartedly supported her work and a number of councillors had actively undermined what she was trying to do.

A new initiative was then taken by the Centre for Cultural Research into Risk (CCRR) at a local university. The authors described three action research cycles. During the first cycle, minutes of Council meetings held over the previous decade were reviewed and phone interviews were held with seven youth sector service providers, the Council's administrator for youth, and the recently sacked researcher. A 'public conversation' was then staged, prior to the Council's annual budget meeting, bringing together 35 participants from the CCRR, the Council, the police, housing, schools, mental health services, the local technical and further education college, churches, sports organisations, the women's shelter, drug and alcohol services, and youth arts. It began with each participant sharing a brief personal story about an event they had experienced which had given an insight into what it was to be a 'youth at risk', followed by the construction of a 'collective biography' of youth at risk. The event produced much information about how young people were seen in the town and the differences of opinion about what might be done. The attempt to get the Council to allocate specific resources was unsuccessful. There was success, however, in getting the CCRR to fund a half-time youth coordinator/researcher and setting up a youth theatre group, 'Voices'.

At the second cycle, a core group of 10 teenagers met weekly for several months. The group developed a collective identity and openly discussed the risks young people faced in areas such as drug misuse, sexual orientation and sexual abuse, relationships with adults, educational difficulties, and breakdown in close relationships. The group put on a performance attended by over 200 people (mainly aged under 20 but including two local councillors), later putting on a performance at the town's art gallery, producing a Voices videotape and devising and performing a short script about Voices at a youth arts festival in Sydney. The whole process was researched, mainly qualitatively, including analysis of verbatim notes, mini-scripts, tape recordings of group meetings, theatrical exercises and interviews. For example, when asked to say what difference the project had made to their lives, replies from group participants included the following:

> I'd felt like I'd got no direction to my life. Now I feel I am going somewhere.
>
> I'd got talent, I just wanted to show it. Now I can show my talent.
>
> Now I can finally be me.
>
> I can do more stuff. Like being out there and open to people to tell people about stuff that they like didn't know that other people had.
>
> It's helped me to deal with a lot of my problems. I suppose, I have put a lot of things behind me since I joined up here but it's a simple fact that I can come here and say what I want to say and don't have to worry about things (p. 206).

At the third cycle the CCRR returned to the aim of persuading the Council to appoint a more permanent youth worker. As before they attended the regularly held Council open forum. They were informed beforehand that the Council was split seven to five against the proposal but in the event it was swayed by a late intervention by one of the members of the theatre group who told her story, and voted ten to two in favour. The young woman who told her story had dropped out of school, been a drug taker and heavy drinker and had experienced homelessness, but thanks to the Voices group had regained her confidence, stopped taking drugs and was successfully attending the college. One of the councillors described the young woman's intervention as a 'masterstroke'. As Bradley *et al.* (2004, p. 210) put it, "Academic work and second-hand reports no longer have rhetorical force enough to persuade. The voice of experience is what persuades".

Young People and Participatory Forms of Research and Evaluation

Bostock and Freeman (2003) wrote of the benefits and difficulties of using a participatory action research approach to studying the needs of young people in one county, Northumberland, in northern England. The 'No Limits' project was funded by the Northumberland Health Action Zone, which had been set up to improve health by addressing inequalities and involving the public in order to increase service responsibility and accountability. The project focused on 14–18 year olds and the needs of young people generally, rather than on those who fell into specific high risk groups. Young people were contacted through 12 youth projects. Twenty-seven young men and 47 young women took part in a total of 12, mostly single sex, focus groups. Three young people from one youth project helped with the qualitative analysis of transcriptions of tape-recorded group discussions. Some of the main issues discussed were: having nothing to do, peer pressure, drug taking, sexual matters including sexually transmitted diseases, violence and harassment, bereavement, and housing and money issues. Although some had positive experiences of counselling, others had had negative experiences, and some thought of counselling as alien, official and scary, or associated with discipline. The greater emphasis was on informal support, girls generally having larger support networks and being more likely to be open about problems with their friends than boys. Rather than suggesting new service developments, it was the attitudes of professionals towards young people that were stressed, many young people having felt misjudged or stereotyped. Friends and family were seen as sources of support, but the ability to keep matters private and the need for good, clear rules about confidentiality were important. Young people valued youth workers, school nurses, teachers and doctors who were non-judgemental, down-to-earth, experienced and friendly.

Although, due to time limits, young people were not involved in writing the report of the project, three helped by reading drafts and contributing their perspectives on the analysis. Despite the report containing many direct quotes from young people, a written report was not considered sufficient for the needs of feeding back results to young people and making an impact in the county. A conference was planned, preceded by a residential weekend, attended by 12 young people from four of the focus groups. Two drama workers were brought in to facilitate presentation at the conference, where six of the young people performed a piece of theatre that powerfully communicated some of the research findings. Among the recommendations were that: young people needed a place where they would be listened to in a relaxed, friendly environment on a one-to-one basis, open at convenient times; anti-bullying policies should be adhered to in schools; confidentiality policies should be clear; and support should be offered to young people who were living independently, in particular regarding accessing benefits and paying bills.

Bostock and Freeman concluded that the process had been empowering for young people who took part, and had increased their social support and in the process the development of a number of new skills. At the county level the process had contributed to some specific developments such as the setting up of a county-wide group to address lack of support for young people living independently, the development of a school health drop-in/coffee shop in one town, and improvement in the layout of the reception area in one general practice surgery. More generally, young people's views were now routinely being sought in the discussion of a national urban regeneration scheme taking place in the county. Among the difficulties were the problems of maintaining the involvement of young people over a period of several months while results were being analysed and the conference organised. The participating young people were scattered around a large county area and the young people's lives were changing and not all remained engaged. It had been intended, for example, that young people should outnumber professionals at the conference. In fact it was attended by 16 young people and 36 paid staff who commissioned or delivered services for young people in the county.

A good example of participatory evaluation involving young people was provided by a Canadian centre that offered free material services, such as food, showers, laundry, as well as counselling and referral, for 'street-involved youth' (Whitmore & McKee, 2001). There was controversy about the centre, which was open 10 hours a day, every day of the year, was well used by young people facing serious difficulties in their lives, but was staffed by only three front-line workers. While some thought it offered a safe place where young people could 'hang out' and form relatively informal, trusting relationships with staff who could help them, others thought there should be more structured activities and tighter rules. Yet others thought it attracted 'high risk' young people to the area, and that it should be shut down. The evaluation used the Latin American community development concept of *acompañamiento* or 'accompanying the process', implying that outside evaluators do not impose their concepts and methods but 'accompany' the process that is owned and controlled by insiders. The evaluation was conducted by a team consisting of six young people – current or past users of the centre, recruited via advertising, application and interview, and paid for their time with funds from a provincial government foundation – and two staff members and one outside evaluator. The group met two afternoons a week at the centre, devoting considerable time to building the team, with an important role played by joint snacks or meals – themselves exercises in negotiation and compromise – and monthly outings.

The team initially decided to use a conventional questionnaire survey of centre users, young people who did not use the services, the business community, staff at the centre and other youth services, the police, and security staff at the neighbouring shopping mall. Through working together on the development of the questionnaire, new members of the team developed a sense of ownership of the process, but became bored with surveys and felt isolated from their peers. At this point it was decided to use methods that were more participatory, such as semi-structured interviews and exercises such as mapping the local downtown area, specifying locations where drugs were sold and prostitutes were operating (after discussion about how much of this information should be shared with police and other authorities, it was decided to summarise these data, protecting confidentiality). The evaluator conducted individual interviews and focus groups with staff. The team produced a good quality formal evaluation report. Chapters were drafted by the evaluator, fully discussed with the team and revised until all were happy with it. The youth members produced graphs and charts, the cover design and appendices. An unexpected outcome was 'The Kit', a colourful guide for other young evaluators, designed and produced entirely by the youth members. The participatory methods were more youth-friendly, and a combination of conventional and participatory methods was thought to have produced more comprehensive results and a deeper analysis than the surveys alone could have done.

Young People Involved in Promoting Sexual Health

Among the many, diverse programmes for youth are those that aim to contribute to sexual health, often with specific aims of preventing HIV or other sexually transmitted infections or reducing rates of teenage pregnancy (e.g. Guzmán *et al.*, 2003; Træn, 2003). In Peru, Ramella and de la Cruz (2000) reported their early impressions of an adolescent sexual health promotion programme, Salud Reproductiva para Adolescentes – Reproductive Health for Adolescents, or SaRA – which was implemented in 15 communities in very deprived rural or urban-marginal areas in the coastal Andean and jungle regions of Peru. In each area the SaRA team worked with local people – adolescents, their families, and local leaders – to set up networks of adolescents that would organise and carry out a range of social, information-providing (mainly on issues of sexual health) and economic activities – the latter with the goal of becoming self-sustainable. These networks, called Clubs by the adolescents, were successfully set up in all but four of the communities. A fundamental part of SaRA, according to Ramella and de la Cruz, was the access that all Clubs were given to video cameras, photo cameras, tape recorders and paper and pencils, and help and encouragement to generate accounts of their social, informational and economic activities (e.g. a football match, a visit to a health centre, or a Salsa party fundraising event). These textual and audio-visual stories, usually in the form of documentaries or dramas, were shown to other Clubs. As well as being fun, they also acted as catalysts for further social activities and for the articulation and discussion of pressing issues, often directly or indirectly relevant to sexual health.

At the time of writing, the Clubs were fairly new and it was only possible to cite impressionistic evidence that there had been a substantial decrease in the level of unintended pregnancies among adolescent girls partaking in SaRA activities, and that in the communities with Clubs the use of locally available health services and products by adolescents had increased.

Ramella and de la Cruz described SaRA as having been inspired by the liberation psychology ideas of Freire (1970, 1998, and see Chapter 2), including the idea that knowledge, rather than being passed from one person who possesses it to another who receives it, is jointly created during communication (ideas of 'intersubjectivity' and 'intercommunication'), and the associated idea of critical consciousness (Ramella and de la Cruz' translation of the Portuguese word '*conscientização*', referred to elsewhere as 'conscientisation'). Hence the notion of students and teachers with distinct roles would recede and the idea of adolescents as agents in their own development of knowledge would become more important. Ramella and de la Cruz noted the criticisms that had been made of conventional health promotion, including criticism of the idea of participation in health promotion, which might be strong in rhetoric but runs the risk of blaming people for not doing their duty by participating. The aim of the SaRA project was that adolescents themselves would decide on the character and content of activities, with the SaRA team facilitating assistance and collaboration from locally available resources.

The key ingredient identified in each of those projects with young people was the young people's full participation, often necessitating overcoming older people's negativity about young people's capacity for constructive engagement and the young people's own reluctance to participate. In Chapter 12, this central idea of citizen participation is examined further.

Chapter 12
PARTICIPATION AND LIBERATION

PARTICIPATION IN LOCAL ACTION

The Conditions Necessary for Participation

There is a tradition within community psychology in the USA concerned with understanding the conditions under which people participate, and do so effectively, in local action. Pilisuk *et al.* (1996) were concerned with two forms of 'grassroots community organising', namely social action and locality development. The first they described as being oriented more towards conflict than consensus, focusing on direct action, and aiming at organising a disadvantaged or aggrieved group to take action on their own behalf. They cited, as examples, the Civil Rights Movement, community participation programmes, the New Left, and identity-oriented activism by women, gays, lesbians, and the disabled. Ideas of voice, dialogue, social construction, and consensus politics were each important. Locality development on the other hand was about, "... the slower process of creating a web of continuing relationships so that people may indeed come together, share their supportive attentions and resources, and experience a sense of belonging to their community" (p. 17). Examples cited were the development of culturally sensitive services and developing a sense of community for recent immigrants. For both types of action the task of 'capacity building' was crucial, including developing an organisational framework and learning the skills to maintain the group and to take action (see Chapter 11). There are clear links that can be made here with what others have been writing since then about social capital (see Chapter 6).

Pilisuk *et al.* argued that conditions in the post-modern era had made local involvement in decision making more problematic, but at the same time had made organising for local action more necessary and more popular. For one thing, rapid societal change had left individuals less securely embedded in family, workplace, neighbourhood or village – the kind of organic solidarity that Durkheim (1933) had thought so important. Mobility, transportation, information technology, and an emphasis on choice and marketability, had all had an effect. A second factor had been the intrusion of global forces upon domestic settings as a result of modern technology, leaving many people unemployed or else employed in alienating or underpaid forms of work of a non-traditional kind, often involving the production of commodities for export (see Donohoe, 2003, and Smail, 2005, for strong statements of the psychological and health effects of globalisation). Related factors were the remote, centralised control over local resources exercised by transnational companies, the central domination of symbols of legitimacy (e.g. privilege given to experts by government or financial interests), the remoteness of information about power and control, and the message of passive non-participation given by television and other media. Pilisuk *et al.* believed, nevertheless, that examples of local action had multiplied. The numerous local social action groups responding to the threat of exposure to toxic waste constituted one example (see below and later in this chapter). A feature had been the way in which organisations that began in response to a specific local issue had expanded to become organisations with broader goals. For example, local breast cancer support groups had evolved into broader coalitions demanding effective health care and opposing environmental contaminants. A local shelter for women victims of domestic violence had taken on broad feminist aims addressing the social causes of violence against women more generally. A project that began by providing individual support for older and ill residents of a rundown single room occupancy hotel had evolved into a coalition of tenants' organisations covering a number of such hotels. The prominent role of women in many local social action projects had been a feature – a theme taken up later in this chapter. On a broader canvas still, Pilisuk *et al.* saw the prospect of countering a borderless, global world that deprived local people of decision-making power, with another borderless world corresponding to what Falk (1992) has called the 'global civil society'.

Rich *et al.* (1995) considered the structures and processes necessary for effective citizen participation in local action. They identified two broad factors. The first was the community's capacity for responding to an identified problem, determined by a combination of financial, psychological and social resources. The second was the capacity of formal institutions to respond to citizens and to involve them in decision making. As a case study example they cited the action of local residents, many of them small farmers, to the nauseating odour created by a new facility in their area of New York State, USA, that received sewage sludge, stored it in lagoons, and seasonally spread it on the land. Rich *et al.* cited evidence that such local environmental hazards could have serious repercussions for people's social and emotional and even family lives. The case study included an account of the experience of attending and giving testimony at local hearings, as was their right. The daytime scheduling of the hearings, the very legalistic setting, the dominance of lawyers and experts from outside the area, and their failure to be heard, had left local residents feeling powerless, trapped, and facing a crisis that seemed to have no clear end point. Despite the frustrations in that case, after several years the facility had been classified as hazardous and the operators of the facility had been forced to draw up plans for site closure.

Rich *et al.* concluded in favour of a partnership approach, emphasising an open process of sharing and evaluating information, as opposed to an adversarial notion of social action which would likely be beyond the resources of local residents. As a good example they referred to The Good Neighbor Project (Lewis, 1993) which brought together industry, residents, and local governments in voluntary 'good neighbour agreements'. Community advisory panels were set up under such agreements, with resident members selected by community organisations, with access to a facility's data on environmental hazards, safety measures and emergency plans, and given funds to hire outside experts to help evaluate the information (Rich *et al.* acknowledged problems that might arise, e.g. that the residents involved might not be truly representative, might appear to others to become coopted by the 'polluting' industry, and might therefore lose their effectiveness).

Who Participates?

Wandersman and Florin (2000) reviewed evidence on the antecedents, processes, and effects of participation in community organisations, drawing largely on work carried out in the USA in the 1970s and 1980s (see Saegert & Winkel, 1996, 2004, for an example of later US work). Some of the predictors of participation were in the nature of individual or family characteristics such as home ownership, length of residence in the area, having children, or ethnicity (in the USA there was evidence that, controlling for factors such as socioeconomic status, black people participated more than white). Other factors were more to do with attitudes towards the community, such as intention to remain in the area, the feeling of belongingness, and more contact with neighbours – elements of 'sense of community', discussed in Chapter 6. There was broad support for a number of theories, including a social exchange model that proposes that people participate when benefits (material, social, and goal-oriented) outweigh the costs (e.g. time, frustration), and one suggested by Perkins *et al.* (1990) that proposed that for participation to happen both 'catalyst' factors in the local environment (e.g. poorly maintained properties) and 'enabling' factors (e.g. good contact between neighbours) were necessary.

Comparatively little evidence existed about the factors to do with the organisations themselves that were associated with member satisfaction, effectiveness, and longevity. Local organisations can be fragile. Some of the figures that Wandersman and Florin presented suggested that between one-third and one-half of neighbourhood organisations that figured in the studies they reviewed had ceased to exist a year or two later. The evidence they reviewed suggested that participation was greater and organisational continuity more likely when members were more fully involved in clearly defined tasks and democratic decision-making procedures, when the atmosphere in the organisation was positive and cohesive, and when there existed firm, clear leadership and greater structure (including clear rules and procedures, a greater number of officers, and a larger number of committees to carry out specialised work). Furthermore, successful organisations carried out a wider range of activities and were better at establishing ties or linkages with other organisations from which they received help (shades of 'social capital' again).

Wandersman and Florin pointed out that it was often impossible to attribute cause and effect to such factors, many of which were likely to be both antecedents and consequences of successful organising. Perkins *et al.* (1996) presented evidence from a study of participation in grassroots community organisations in three areas in the USA, with follow-up one year later in each case. The study involved community councils in Salt Lake City, neighbourhood associations in Baltimore, and block associations in New York City. A number of the factors that they looked at were non-significant or inconsistently associated with participation cross-sectionally or predictively and comparatively few were significant after controlling for other factors in a multiple regression analysis. For example, fear of crime, which it had been expected would correlate with participation, in practice did not. Another factor, 'incivilities' in the neighbourhood (perceived and objective litter, graffiti, unkempt property), was sometimes negatively and sometimes positively related to participation. Home ownership, minority ethnic status, and residential stability were positively, but inconsistently related to participation. The most consistently positive factors were what Perkins *et al.* referred to as 'community-focused social cognitions and behaviors' – again reminiscent of 'sense of community'. Cognitions included a sense of civic responsibility for what happened in the immediate neighbourhood (the 'block') and the perceived efficacy of block associations. Most consistently associated with participation, at both individual and block levels, and both cross-sectionally and predictively, were community-focused social behaviours such as neighbouring and involvement in religious or other community service organisations.

The Benefits of Participation

When it came to the effects of citizen participation, Wandersman and Florin broke these down into three broad categories: impacts on conditions in the neighbourhood, on relationships between neighbours, and on individual activists themselves. The clearest evidence for impact on the neighbourhood showed that participation in local action could produce improvements in the physical quality of the neighbourhood and greater feelings of confidence in the neighbourhood and commitment to stay there. There was some evidence for effects in terms of reduction in crime but less clear evidence of a reduction in fear of crime. Although an impact on relationships between neighbours was rarely a stated objective, they found evidence that local social action could significantly increase positive neighbouring.

   They also found evidence for impacts of the third kind, in terms of increased skills for those who participated as well as increased feelings of efficacy in joint community action to solve problems. Kieffer (1984), who carried out a qualitative study of individuals who had become empowered through citizen participation, used the term 'participatory competence' to refer to what these activists had acquired as a result of their participation. It encompassed acquiring activist skills, developing a critical understanding of the socio-political environment, and an ability to cultivate individual and collective resources for community action. Themes that were prominent in the accounts given by these activists included: the way in which growth and conflict (e.g. between competing groups or competing commitments) were constantly intertwined; the way in which action and reflection were also inseparable throughout; and the constant interweaving of individual and community. Kieffer concluded that even if participation did not overcome powerful forces, individual activists gained psychologically.

Dalton *et al.* (2001), drawing on the ideas of Rappaport (1987) and of Zimmerman (1995) on empowerment (see Chapter 2), made the point that individuals can be empowered as a result of taking part in collective action, but that empowerment, as they used the term, was essentially a collective, social process, involving engagement with others. Rich *et al.* (1995) also used the idea of empowerment to understand the process of participation. They distinguished between several varieties of empowerment. *Formal empowerment* was created when government, business, or other institutions provide mechanisms for the public to influence decisions. By itself it was neither sufficient nor necessary for effecting change; indeed the trappings of formal empowerment could even be disempowering, as was the case at the public hearing to consider the objections to the sludge facility, referred to earlier. *Intrapersonal empowerment* was a feeling of personal competence in the situation, some degree of which was probably a prerequisite for active participation in decision making. *Instrumental empowerment* referred to an individual's actual capacity for participating and influencing decision making, and *substantive empowerment* to the ability to reach decisions that solve problems or produce desired outcomes. Finally, they used the term *community empowerment* to refer to the capacity of communities to respond effectively to collective problems. It only occurred, they concluded, when both individuals and institutions have been empowered to achieve satisfactory outcomes.

Participation in Black and Minority Ethnic and Immigrant Communities

As part of their study of social capital and social participation in two of the most economically deprived wards of a single town in south-east England (described in Chapter 6), Campbell and McLean (2002a, 2003) made a special study of participation by members of black and minority ethnic groups. In their first paper they reported the results of carrying out detailed, three-hour interviews with 25 African-Caribbean residents, otherwise diverse in terms of sex, age (15 years and over), with or without an employed person in the household, and whether or not they were involved in at least one local community organisation. African-Caribbean people constituted 5% of the population of the two study areas, with 50% South Asian and 45% White. Their report highlighted a number of obstacles in the way of local community participation on the part of African-Caribbean residents, which they believed should be understood if calls for local minority group participation were to be realistic. Despite a strong sense of pride in their African-Caribbean origins and way of life, including family solidarity, an ethic of respect and care for older people, relaxed inter-connectedness and creativity, and relying largely on African-Caribbean networks of support, there was little reference in the interviews to involvement in voluntary associations or interest in local community activism. An exception was young men who spoke positively about local sports and youth clubs. Churches, that had played a large role in creating a sense of community among older people when they had first arrived in England, were thought to have failed to continue to provide a sense of unity. Some spoke of the disappointment and frustration at the difficulty of 'getting people involved', and some attributed the difficulty to apathy, individualism, lack of confidence among African-Caribbean people, or pride that drove them to struggle with problems alone. Experiences of exclusion at school and at work had been common and were unlikely to have encouraged people to think of themselves as welcomed or empowered members of the local community. Young men in particular expressed regret and bitterness at limited employment opportunities. For example:

> [This ward] is one of the most unemployed areas in the town. So that means that our culture, a place where there's predominantly ethnic people just happens to be the most unemployed area. So, as usual, ethnic people ain't getting work, they're not getting no money. And it's a sad situation. You know, I mean, we have to uplift ourselves which we're trying to do, but the powers that be ain't making it easy for us (p. 651).

Young women were more likely to refer to lack of confidence. For example, one successful young woman said:

> We're all feisty, so why can't we say to ourselves and one another – I'm a black man, I'm a black woman, living in this country, living in [this town], living in [this ward], and I'm going to make something of my life. I can do it because I've got the brain. And I've known particularly guys – men who are black who have lived in this town all their lives with the brains on them that they could be such entrepreneurs. They could really make something of their lives, but they say, but I'm not going to because I'm black (p. 651).

A contrast was often drawn with 'the Asian community', which was seen as much stronger, more organised, more assertive, and more successful in getting things done. One informant compared the Asian community's success in forcing the owners of the local bingo hall to change the name 'Mecca', with his failure when trying to mount a campaign against a local shop selling 'gollywogs'. Several people commented on the influence of the history of colonialism and slavery, leaving the African-Caribbean community with less of a sense of entitlement and less assertiveness in making claims:

> The reason why today we see the advancements made in the Asian community and the lack of advancement in the Black community, is the Windrush mentality. Asians are not enslaved. Black people are still very much, whether they accept it or not, enslaved (p. 653).

Another theme was some regret about the way in which African-Caribbean culture and identity, unlike that of the Asian community, had become 'mainstreamed', as evidenced, for example, by the growing mixing of White and Black youth lifestyles and a decline of Black consciousness.

In a later paper, Campbell and McLean (2003) reported on local community participation among members of the Pakistani/Kashmiri community living in the same areas. They noted the relatively poor health of certain minority ethnic groups in England (see Chapter 4) and the particularly high level of material deprivation among British Pakistani people, with particularly high rates of unemployment and low incomes. They interviewed 26 people who identified themselves as Pakistani, evenly divided between men and women, those born in England and those born in Pakistan, and those with and without an employed person in the household, with ages spread across four age groups from 15–20 to 55 plus. Eleven chose to be interviewed in Urdu and 15 in English.

UK government policy statements about health inequalities and community regeneration had emphasised the importance of minority ethnic participation in decisions about health service design and delivery, in community-based public health projects designed to promote healthy behaviours, and grassroots involvement in local community organisations and groupings to build social capital. Campbell and McLean, however, found a low level of involvement in local voluntary organisations linked to leisure, hobbies and personal spiritual development or local community activist groups devoted to promotion of quality of local community life. They were critical of the vague and general way in which the policy documents suggested that participation should occur. What they did find was that their Pakistani participants were far more likely to be engaged in and committed to informal face-to-face networks of extended families, neighbours and friends. Among the factors that were cited as contributing to the exclusion from more formal community participation were the language barrier and the experience of overt racism. Only a few were regular mosque attenders and mosque networks were often seen as dominated by a small group of powerful people, mostly men. Often voiced was the preference for keeping problems within the family, and the fear of gossip was often cited as a factor. Local involvement in community affairs was often seen as a 'white thing', even to the point of being criticised for 'acting white' by involving oneself in a local organisation. Although many experienced inclusion in the wider town community through education or work, most described that as a selective participation in mainstream English life, preferring reliance on the Pakistani community in the private spheres of life.

At the same time Campbell and McLean emphasised the diversity of views resulting from multiple configurations of intersecting dimensions such as age, sex, language, place of birth, and other factors. Some were motivated to protect Pakistani young people from what was seen as the corrupting influence of English morals in areas including smoking, drinking, bad language, dating and sex. Some, especially men, wished to police the boundary between the Pakistani and white English communities. Some women who had come to England to marry and whose lives were centred on the home, had poor English language skills and virtually no contact outside the Pakistani community. Some, particularly but not only those born in England, found an exclusive Pakistani-based informal social life restrictive and regretted that some others were not making more effort to integrate.

The barriers to participating in community affairs in a country of immigration was the focus of another qualitative interview study, in this case of Hmong people from the highlands of Laos, resettled in the USA and now resident in one of three multi-ethnic, low-income, public housing developments in a medium sized city in the mid-west (Goodkind & Foster-Fishman, 2002). As a result of the Vietnam war they had been forced to flee to Thailand, to then be accepted as refugees in the USA, where initially they had been intentionally dispersed, later regrouping somewhat through secondary migration within the USA. In the housing developments where they now lived they constituted 10–15% of the residents. The average age of the 54 people interviewed was now 46 years and they had been in the USA for an average of 12 years. Most Hmong people in the USA were on low incomes and were receiving public assistance. Many of those interviewed in this study were not literate in any language. Overall they valued participation and wanted to be involved in their communities, most feeling that participation was important, both for the broader community of the housing development in which they lived and for personal reasons such as acquiring language skills, useful knowledge and experience, and the liking and respect of others. Some reported formal or informal participation, but many did not, and some had given up participating because of frustrations:

> I went to meetings before, but when you have a question, they [the other residents/resident council leaders] don't let you say. I raise my hand, but others raise their hands and talk first. The meetings don't help me, so it wastes my time (p. 398).

Some felt that it was their own ability or capacity that stood in the way of participation, and some blamed themselves for lack of skills and resources:

> The reason that I don't go to meetings is that I can't speak the language. Even if I have a good idea, I can't tell them so I just stay home and keep it to myself (p. 400).

Some felt they were too new in their particular housing development, and some were not aware of opportunities for participation. For some, lack of time due to work or childcare commitments was a factor. But the adaptation of an immigrant group should be thought of as a bidirectional matter (Deaux, 2000) and organisations and communities that contain immigrant groups can easily be inadvertently ethnocentric. Hmong interviewees pointed out that notices for meetings were posted in English only and that translators were never present. Others said they would participate more if childcare was available. Many identified discrimination by members of other ethnic groups as constituting a major barrier to participation:

> If Hmong people go to the meetings or not, it doesn't matter. Their opinion isn't counted. There is discrimination now, so Hmong opinions don't count (p. 402).

> Very rarely do I go to meetings. We see a lot of papers saying, 'meeting, meeting', but we ignore them because if you don't know the language well, I don't think they will listen to you (p. 403).

The Barriers to Participation

Kagan *et al.* (2005) used two models of the degree of participation in local action in order to understand some of the difficulties in maintaining a continued, high level of participation and commitment, and a real degree of citizen power and control. One was Arnstein's (1969) 'ladder' of increasing citizen participation (see Figure 12.1). The other was Montero's (2004) diagram of concentric circles depicting levels of participation and commitment (see Figure 12.2). A feature of the latter is the idea that individuals and groups move in and out of greater participation. Aims

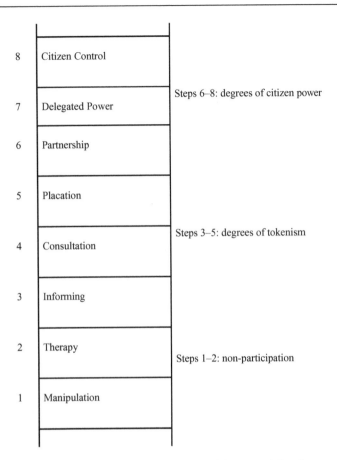

Figure 12.1   Arnstein's, 1969, 'ladder' of increasing citizen participation
Source: Kagan, C., Castile, S. & Stewart, A. (2005). Participation: are some more equal than others? *Clinical Psychology Forum*, **153**, 30–4

therefore include encouraging movement from outer to inner levels and supporting those at inner levels so that commitment can be retained. Kagan *et al*. cited examples from their own work on a housing estate in north Manchester, England, providing evidence of the frustrating and exhausting nature of local activism, which was often being carried out in the face of what was seen as lack of support from the authorities, combined with being coopted and relied upon by them. Others have also written about the difficulties and costs of active local participation in different settings. For example, as part of their study of social capital and health in a socially disadvantaged area in a town in northern England, Boneham and Sixsmith (2006) interviewed 19 women aged 55 years and over, finding that most did not take an active role in community events, often because of declining health and mobility problems. The few who had taken on active community roles spoke of frustration at the slow pace of change, the risk that their own positions were misunderstood and that they might be unfairly personally vilified within their own communities, the difficulty of negotiating their role when trying to represent local residents and

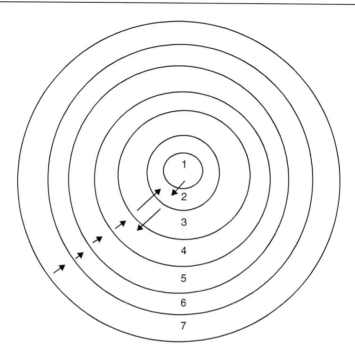

Figure 12.2 Montero's, 2004, model of levels of participation. Key: 1 – Nucleus of maximum participation and commitment; 2 – Frequent participation and high commitment; 3 – Specific participation, medium commitment; 4 – Sporadic participation, low commitment; 5 – New and tentative participation, low commitment (e.g. financial donation, support material); 6 – Tangential participation, unclear (e.g. approval, agreement); 7 – Positive, friendly curiosity, no commitment.
Source: reproduced with permission from Kagan, C., Castile, S. & Stewart, A. (2005). Participation: are some more equal than others? *Clinical Psychology Forum*, **153**, 30–4

work with professionals from public agencies, the high levels of worrying and helplessness associated with their roles, and the wish for a greater understanding and sharing on the part of others.

In 2000, the British General Household Survey included a social capital module on the basis of which they identified a group of people whom they referred to as 'civically disengaged': they had not been involved in a local organisation, had not taken any action to solve a local problem, did not feel well informed, and did not feel that they could influence decisions that affected their neighbourhoods, either alone or working with others. Sixteen per cent fell into that category, varying from 7% in the most affluent areas to 22% in the most deprived. The disengaged were more likely to be younger, women, from ethnic minorities, less highly educated, with dependent children, renting their accommodation, and having moved house recently (Coulthard *et al.*, 2002).

A good illustration of some of the difficulties in the way of participation was the Highfield Community Enrichment Project, part of an initiative operating in several communities across the province of Ontario, Canada – the Better Beginnings, Better

Futures Project (Nelson *et al.*, 2004). This was an example of a programme aiming to work with families with pre-school children, to promote the latter's development and to enhance family and community functioning. Like Head Start (perhaps more widely disseminated in the USA than almost any other social programme), Surestart in the UK, and Early Enrichment in Turkey, such programmes try to be sensitive to local needs and diversity, and a key principle is that of promoting the involvement of local families in design and implementation of services (Kağitçibaşi, 1996; Miller & Shinn, 2005). A valued principle of the Canadian project was resident participation and self-determination, the key being the breaking down of social distance and power differentials between professionals and residents and the building of trust and relationships between them. The Highfield Project took place in a single junior school in a socioeconomically disadvantaged area of Toronto where more than half the population was born outside Canada, the two largest ethno-cultural groups being those from India and the Caribbean. A core group of seven service providers and one community resident came together to make plans to submit a proposal. A needs survey was conducted with the residents and a meeting, with childcare and translation provided (note how important such details can be), was organised to discuss the results in small groups. The meeting was attended by 70–80 parents. An inter-disciplinary research team from several Ontario universities carried out research that involved semi-verbatim recordings of project meetings and activities, analysis of programme documents, and interviews with 50 parents at two points in time. Once the project was funded a group of around 10 residents became very active (all but one women – 'where are the men?' is a question often heard asked in community projects), and resident participation increased over time as parents became more familiar and comfortable with the project. For example:

> …a lot of the parents were hesitant in coming on board because it seemed so big and over-whelming … and 'what are they talking about?' … and they didn't really understand … it had to be explained several times before parents really understood what the project was about and even then they were hesitant on coming on board because of all the agency people. There's a lot of distrust with the CAS [child protection agency] and people were very hesitant … 'we don't know those big words', 'we're not government people', … 'we can't talk with them' … we were also feeling 'what if our personal lives are dug into?'…so there was a lot of fear (community resident) (p. 219).

In terms of Arnstein's (1969) ladder of citizen participation (see Figure 12.1), participation generally moved from minimal levels to more substantial participation, but remained highly diverse in terms of level of responsibility, leadership, and decision making. It included working as unpaid volunteers, engaging in joint planning of events such as celebrating south Asian holidays or black history month, being hired by the project (11 of 17 full-time and part-time paid staff were community residents), doing occasional work for the project for a fee, or joining the Steering Committee or one of the other project committees, and becoming involved in advocacy and lobbying politicians and others. Although some took on leadership roles, there was difficulty recruiting residents for such roles:

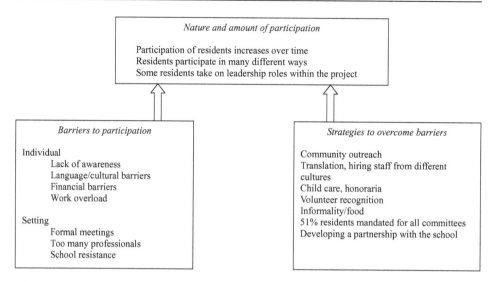

Nature and amount of participation

Participation of residents increases over time
Residents participate in many different ways
Some residents take on leadership roles within the project

Barriers to participation

Individual
　　Lack of awareness
　　Language/cultural barriers
　　Financial barriers
　　Work overload

Setting
　　Formal meetings
　　Too many professionals
　　School resistance

Strategies to overcome barriers

Community outreach
Translation, hiring staff from different
cultures
Child care, honoraria
Volunteer recognition
Informality/food
51% residents mandated for all committees
Developing a partnership with the school

Figure 12.3   Overcoming barriers to participation in the Highfield Community Enrichment Project
Source: reproduced with permission from Nelson, G., Pancer, S.M., Hayward, K. & Kelly, R. (2004). Partnerships and participation of community residents in health promotion and prevention: experiences of the Highfield community enrichment project (better beginnings, better futures). *Journal of Health Psychology*, **9**, 213–27

> It's easier for us to get people to come in and help in the kitchen or help on a trip or help with skating than it is to get people to come and work on committees and do those sorts of things (project staff member) (p. 221).

Some of the barriers to participation and strategies used to overcome them are shown in Figure 12.3. For example, sheer lack of awareness of the project was responded to through advertising and outreach efforts. Tangible, financial barriers that inhibited resident participation in committee work, for example, were responded to by providing childcare and covering travel costs and meals. Various support mechanisms, including training and mentoring, were responses to those who became actively involved becoming vulnerable to being over used and 'burning out'. At the setting level, the formality of meetings with service providers was inhibiting. For example:

> I remember one of the first ones [Steering Committee meetings], two parents came, I won't mention names, and they sat through the Steering Committee and they never said one word and as soon as it was over, they said 'Don't ever ask me to go to that again'. They were really bowled over by how formal it was (community resident) (p. 222).

Making the meetings more informal, avoiding jargon, providing food and creating a family-like atmosphere were responses:

> I am asked for my opinion and feedback ... I found the service-providers went out of their way to make you feel comfortable ... They didn't treat you as if they're above you (community resident) (p. 223).

The aim was to have residents make up at least half of all committees. A further barrier was the discomfort that school staff initially experienced about having a community project operating in the school, and this was overcome only with time.

Nelson *et al.* emphasised the importance of having many different opportunities for participation at different levels. One problem that remained was the relative absence of men participating in the project. In fact only one man played a major volunteer role in the 10-year history of the project. The large majority of volunteers were low-income women to whom the project offered an opportunity to gain skills, to experience support, and to improve their lives – although it was recognised that from another perspective they might be seen as having worked for free to provide human services that society was not willing to pay for.

DRAWING ON A DIVERSITY OF WORLD VIEWS

Mediating Between Indigenous and European World Views

In Australia, according to Bishop *et al.* (2002a), there was vast scope for work as an active mediator between groups with very different world views. Such work was often in the control of public programmes in areas such as waste water treatment, forestry, irrigation, regional planning, and community needs assessment. Bishop *et al.* (2002b) described two projects carried out in Western Australia. One was in association with a firm contracted by government to develop a pilot programme to increase the participation of Aboriginal people in the hospitality industry. This was ground breaking but controversial since it was seen by Aboriginal people as an opportunity for economic development and employment, but seen by some as incompatible with Aboriginal cultural values. Of six five-star hotels in Perth, two agreed to participate. The programme involved tackling entrenched racism by conducting a programme for managers that involved learning about Aboriginal values and culture, first-hand contact with indigenous people, as well as changing recruitment and selection, line management, and supervision practices. Aboriginal recruits could receive up to 400 hours of training, and had mentors in the community and at the workplace. The two pilot programmes were successful, with most trainees graduating and continuing their employment. At the time of writing the programme was then running in five Perth hotels.

The second project involved a collaboration with the Commonwealth Scientific and Industrial Research Organisation (CSIRO), with whom local community psychologists had collaborated on a number of projects. CSIRO were commissioned by the WA Chamber of Mines and Energy to investigate how Aboriginal people wished to be consulted by mining companies wanting to mine on traditional Aboriginal lands. The project involved interviews with a wide variety of stakeholders. This was certainly a project that required tolerance of uncertainty and ambiguity. Mining companies had a poor reputation with Aboriginal communities for trying to negotiate with individuals or families and failing to understand the different Aboriginal conception of 'ownership' vested in both families and communities. It slowly emerged that Aboriginal people were not opposed to mining on land that was traditionally theirs (but not in sacred site areas) provided there was fair and open consultation. There were differences, however, between those who were happy for Land Councils to handle negotiations on their behalf, and others who wanted to deal directly with the miners without intermediaries. The different perspectives of urban Aboriginal people, with greater access to European education, employment, and economic resources generally, and traditional people who were stronger in terms of Aboriginal culture and Aboriginal Law, was also an important factor.

In the Australian context, with its heightened awareness of the existence of different world views, there was continued uncertainty and reflection about the role of European Australian community psychology, and whether work matched up to ethical and value standards. One criticism of the hospitality project, for example, was that it was assimilationist rather than reconciliatory, designed to get Aboriginal people into white employment, and hence contributing to the erosion of their culture (Bishop *et al.*, 2002b).

Education for the Children of a Minority, Excluded Group

Crespo *et al.* (2002) described the process of negotiating with members of a Gypsy community in the Sant Roc area of Barcelona, Spain (the project itself is described in full elsewhere – Lalueza *et al.*, 1999). Because of difficulties connected with schooling for Gypsy children, Crespo and her colleagues, from the Department of the Psychology of Education at Barcelona's Autonomous University, wished to carry out research to understand more about the ecological and social context of the Gypsy community. Part of the legacy of the historical marginalisation of Gypsies in Spain was the deep distrust felt by many Gypsies towards mainstream social institutions, including education. Indeed only in quite recent times, since the end of the Franco era in Spain in the later 1970s, had serious attempts been made to insist that Gypsy children attended school. Low school performance and high truancy rates had then been detected among Gypsy children, leading to interventions implicitly or explicitly based on the idea of 'deficit'. Crespo *et al.* came to understand that schooling changed Gypsy children in the direction of 'modernisation', a process in which priority is given to the rights, progress and future of individuals, and the need to acquire knowledge from outside the Gypsy community – a process that threatened the cohesion of the community, which was based on the more collective values of mutual interdependence and traditions, the sharing of knowledge within the community, and respect for community elders. Schooling could sometimes set young Gypsy people against their families: an example given by Crespo *et al.* was of Gypsy girls in residential care, who, after a number of years of formal education, did not wish to return to their families when the opportunity was offered.

The process of negotiating involvement in the community was a long one, involving many conversations with representatives of the local Gypsy Association, and, only after some time, an introduction to a senior figure in the community. For a long time each party saw the other largely as representing the Gypsy or Payo (the Gypsy word for all non-Gypsies in Spain) world. In time closer friendships developed – which Crespo *et al.* described as having had a challenging transforming effect on their own sense of identity.

One of the projects co-directed by Crespo *et al.* was the creation of a new social setting, *La Casa De Shere Rom*, which organised activities for children that would help develop skills and abilities to help improve performance at school (e.g. activities involving the use of computers), as well as other programmes oriented towards the achievement of equal opportunities in education, access to jobs, and promotion of women. Participation was open to Payo people as well. The institution belonged to and was controlled and managed by the community itself. The paper by Crespo *et al.* did not bear the names of any of the Gypsy participants, they explained, since the latter had no interest in academic papers. When it came to writing related to administration, public opinion and funding organisations, on the other hand, authorship was always shared between the university team and members of the Association. Also, because leaders of the Gypsy Association did not want others to come and solve their problems, but wanted to be active protagonists in their own change, when it came to authorship and citations they preferred to be identified with their real names rather than to hide behind anonymity.

Crespo *et al.* believed that the empowering process of taking responsibility for setting up new projects of that kind was part of a broader empowering process of social change. They saw three options for Gypsy communities in the modern world. One, 'deculturation', involved the abandonment of traditional ways in the face of pressure towards individuation. Combined with poverty, that option might lead to family and community disintegration and exclusion. Resistance to modernisation was another option, reinforcing and re-valorising traditional ways in opposition to the main society towards which there would continue to be attitudes of suspicion and distrust. That option would be likely to lead to further legitimisation of the exclusion of the Gypsy minority. The third option, chosen by the Gypsy Association of Sant Roc, was 'cultural redefinition', incorporating the notion of 'minority' but with acceptance of a degree of openness to progress in mainstream society (there are obvious similarities here to Berry's, 2001, two-dimensional model of acculturation – see Chapter 7). That difficult balancing act of avoiding both assimilation or exclusion, was well put by one of the Association members, Raimundo:

> They let us in, but little by little – especially teachers, psychologists and people like that – but it isn't enough yet. Let's hope the future will be different. They must know that we are people with our own ideas, personality, roots ... that we have an identity as a 'people' ... They must realise that in the near future, if things don't change, we gypsy people will have no way out but beggary. That's not fair. Instead of catching up, we're falling further behind by the moment, and we have to say it. Let's work, gypsies and non-gypsies, to make that distance smaller (Crespo *et al.*, 2002, pp. 59,60).

Crespo *et al.* admitted to a concern that their involvement might in effect be part of a process of subjecting a community, that traditionally had been able to pursue a life of freedom, relatively unhampered by the formal controls of modern society (e.g. undertaking 'marginal' work that required few fixed routines, timetables or controlling procedures), to pressure to become a community that was more 'visible' and subject to controls – including controls on such things as movement, or where things can be sold.

Restorative Conferencing as an Alternative to School Exclusion

Drewery (2004) described a trial of 'restorative conferencing' that took place in five schools in New Zealand, carried out by the University of Waikato, contracted by the Ministry of Education, in response to concern at the growing number of children who were being temporarily or indefinitely suspended from schools. The peak age for suspensions was 14 years, the rate was higher in schools drawing from lower and middle socioeconomic communities, and Maori and boys were over-represented. An interest in restorative conferencing in New Zealand and other countries paralleled growth of interest in restorative justice more generally. In Aotearoa/New Zealand there was also the Maori tradition of restorative justice and the use of *hui* style conflict resolution meetings to draw on.

In contrast to retributive justice in which offences are dealt with as offences against the state and justice is dispensed by dispassionate third parties in accordance with the law, "... restorative justice is focused on the emotional and social disruption that results from offending, and is preoccupied with processes that will not only redress the effect of the offence on the victim, but will also restore the situation, including the damage done to relationships, and even to offenders themselves" (pp. 334–5). The process, very different from a court of law, involved a facilitator, drawing on principles of group process, mediation, and counselling, meeting with those who have a stake in a particular troublesome situation, to discuss what the problem might be, to pool ideas about what might be helpful, and to make a plan for restoration of the situation, especially the relationships that have been affected. Meetings might include the school student(s), 'victims', teachers, parents, extended family, peers, community members, police, community elders, social workers, sports coaches, or any other concerned person. Particular attention was paid to giving victims a voice and meeting their needs, ensuring the community is heard in matters that affect them, and finding an alternative positioning for the 'young offender' by displacing the issue away from the offending person towards the search for the problem. In the school context the process benefited from a commitment on the part of the school to encourage a spirit of restitution throughout the school culture, and a recognition of important linkages between school and community and an openness to the contributions of people who are not usually considered part of the immediate school community.

An aim of restorative conferencing, according to Drewery, is to place young people, their families, schools, and victims of recent events in the centre of a process of deciding what should happen, rather than positioning them as bystanders who have a decision imposed on them. A broader objective was the building of a peaceful community. It corresponded to an ethic of care rather than an ethic of justice. Whereas the latter draws on universal or abstract principles of justice, the former used a more context-specific approach that makes relationships of care a priority. Drewery also argued that the process draws on a constructionist view of knowledge: the aim is not to discover the truth about events that have happened but, by hearing about the different perspectives on events, to come to a common interpretation.

Drewery acknowledged that restorative conferences could take a wide variety of forms, and if unsuccessful could simply, "... provide an audience for public retribution ..." (p. 336), and be seen by a student as simply 'more of the same'.

Some form of punishment might be part of what the conference recommends, but it was just as likely to result in the student writing letters of apology, explaining what changes are intended, how amends will be made, and the capabilities and resources that will be used to achieve successes. A successful conference normally resulted in plenty of offers of help to support the student maintain the different story of who he or she is.

The Maori tradition was drawn on in a number of ways. As in *hui* meetings, hospitality, involving sharing food and drink after the conference, was an important element. But that was part of the more general concept that a person's *mana* – roughly translated as 'agency', including a sense of strength and respect, closely tied to the *mana* of tribe and family – should never be diminished by such a process. That philosophy is very different from the 'possessive individualism' of the euro-western world view. Education was one of the Pakeha (the Maori term for people of, mainly, European origin) imports that Maori people value, but it was also a domain in which there continued to be lively discursive struggle in New Zealand between those different views. Some of the students who were now being suspended from schools were the grandchildren and great grandchildren of those who were caned for talking Maori at school in the early part of the last century.

PROJECTS TO PROTECT AND SUSTAIN NATURAL RESOURCES

Water Projects

Community interventions more often than not involve a large number of individuals representing different groups or 'stakeholder' interests. The different groups involved are likely to occupy different positions in terms of their power to influence decisions. They may also 'frame' problems differently, seeing the nature of a problem and its likely solution from very different perspectives. This complexity is well illustrated by accounts of collaborations between different parties in tackling such issues as water management in 'developing' countries. Outside experts, facilitators, or researchers may come from other countries. A number of reports of such collaborations have come from the Catholic University at Leuven, Belgium. One was a collaboration between the Centre for Comparative, Intercultural and Development Education at the university and the Institute of Ethnology at the National Centre for Social Sciences and Humanities in Vietnam, concerning water management in villages in two provinces in mountainous karst areas of north-west Vietnam (Quaghebeur *et al.*, 2004). Another report involved collaboration between the Centre for Organizational and Personnel Psychology at the university and ACORDES, the Centre for Organisational Consulting for Development at the University of Cuenca, Ecuador, concerned with the sustainability of drinking water in the rural southern Andes of Ecuador (Craps *et al.*, 2004).

Quaghebeur *et al.* (2004) focused on the idea of 'participation', almost all modern development projects claiming to adopt a participatory approach. They discussed some of the difficulties and paradoxes that are often involved. The Vietnamese–Belgian project was no exception. It began with the creation of a local working group designed to function as a means of liaison between local people, local authorities and researchers for the purpose of discussing water problems. A preliminary assessment of the working group, involving interviews and participatory observations, revealed some problems. For a start, the appointment of members of the group was made by local community authorities, with the result that group composition reflected local power relationships and regional or national political and social interests rather than local village or community concerns. Group members appeared to lack a clear idea about their roles, saw their task as a burden, and showed a rather passive attitude towards organising activities or consulting and informing the villagers they were meant to represent. The project team proposed that the working group should conduct surveys of local people in their own homes, and should make 'participatory video recordings' as a participatory rural appraisal tool for encouraging people to record their own knowledge and visions. The former was successful, creating enthusiasm and yielding much information, revealing that what was thought to be a shared, common water problem actually differed between villages and between families. The latter was not so successful: it was not clear to people what should be filmed or why.

The work really only started to move forward when the project team tried to provide new impetus by proposing to finance and construct some small-scale water supply systems which would replace old collective systems that relied on public water taps with private pipes supplying households separately. The first proposal was refused by the working group and villagers after animated discussion, but a second proposal that was accepted provoked much discussion on issues such as the private and/or public ownership of the supply system, regulations regarding its management, and ways of maintaining the systems. Several management boards were set up to deal with different aspects of the running of the systems. Two years later, by which time the project team had withdrawn direct involvement, the water systems as well as the management groups were still operating (unlike a large, partly internationally funded, water supply system for 10 nearby villages which, unknown at first to the project team, was initiated at about the same time, but which ceased to function after one month).

Reviewing their experiences of that project, Quaghebeur et al. (2004) discussed what they called the 'hegemony of participation', whereby those in authority or outsiders are often the ones who decide what the problem is that requires a solution, assume that there is homogeneity of needs and expectations in local communities, give local people a voice but influence what voices will be heard and which not, make assumptions – for example that women will be particularly concerned about water issues – and over-estimate the value of certain kinds of data (e.g. video recordings). There was also often a failure to take into account the way in which local knowledge and expressions of need are themselves shaped by power relations. The fact should be recognised that participation, often conceived from the viewpoint of the western world, also involves a certain imposition of power, requiring people to participate in certain ways and not in others. They quoted Kothari (2001, p. 144):

> Even when individuals think they are most free, they are often in the grip of more insidious forms of power, which operate not solely through direct forms of repression but often through less visible strategies of normalisation (cited by Quaghebeur et al., 2004, p. 162).

Craps *et al.* (2004) also referred to criticisms of participatory approaches that have arisen as awareness has grown of the social inequalities involved and as it has come to be appreciated that certain assumptions – for example, that all actors see the problem in the same way, contribute voluntarily, and have equal power to influence decisions – may not hold. That may particularly be the case, they suggested, in areas such as rural Andian Ecuador where there are deep social inequalities and the ever-present risk that members of local communities will be excluded from participation.

In the area of rural Ecuador that Craps *et al.* were writing about, a rapid rural appraisal in the mid-1990s had found that the majority of communities in the area had a drinking water infrastructure, but that only 15% indicated receiving acceptable water quantity and quality. The rural development project in south Ecuador invited an additional, foreign NGO which specialised in water projects, to convene a new initiative. The Ecuadorian and Belgian universities became involved in evaluation. A 'stakeholder analysis', involving a first round of questionnaires and a second round of more interactive conversations and focus groups, and feedback of results to all participants, revealed the large number of stakeholders, a number of mutual sensitivities and rivalries, and different ways of understanding the problem (stakeholders included: four Ecuadorian and two international NGOs, four local government organisations, four government institutions, a regional development project, three international funding agencies, more than 200 rural communities, eight indigenous umbrella organisations, and seven village councils).

ACORDES designed and facilitated a two-day workshop, taking care to include both homogeneous and heterogeneous sub-groups, small mixed workshops of representatives from different institutes and communities, and exercises such as sharing a reconstruction of common history. The workshop resulted in setting short, mid and long-term goals and the forming of 'commissions', with representatives from different institutions and community organisations, to work on financial, technical and administrative proposals. In practice the commissions turned out to be better adapted to the interests and capacities of the professional experts than to those of the local representatives. The former were focused on water as the central issue and working in the commissions was part of their job. For locals, water was just one important issue among many, and contributing to the commissions had to be done in addition to their own agricultural work. One of the requirements was the setting up of a legal framework. Communities often did not have proprietary titles for their drinking water systems, and Ecuadorian law did not provide a legal structure that allowed for the integration of different types of organisations such as communities or municipalities. It required a lot of creative lobbying by the convening NGO to bring about a legal 'consortium' that satisfied all parties.

All were agreed on the need for maintenance support to sustain rural drinking water provision. It took almost six years to bring about the first 'service centre' supporting a cluster of 25 communities and managed by a consortium. Service centres were real buildings, preferably situated away from the municipality building in order to symbolise their relative autonomy, responsible in the first instance for operational services such as technical support and monitoring of water systems, supply of spare parts, administrative, technical and organisational capacity building. Later they assumed other relevant activities such as planning, environmental and health education, protection of water wells, river catchment management, emergency interventions, and fund-raising. In the past people had needed to go for such services to the region's only large city, a bus drive of at least two hours away where people often felt abused by merchants who were not from their communities. Local service centre personnel, in contrast, were from their own communities.

Opposing the Dumping of Toxic Waste

Santiago-Rivera, Morse, Hunt and Lickers (1998) described the process of building a research partnership between a multidisciplinary university environmental health research group, represented by the first three authors of the paper, and an indigenous environmental task force, represented by the fourth author, in the area of the St Lawrence river on the east coast of North America between Canada and the USA. The subject was the continuing impact of toxic waste, particularly polychlorinated biphenyls (PCBs), on the fishing, hunting and agriculture of the Mohawk Nation of Akwesasne – an example of the contribution of environmental destruction to loss of indigenous tribal identity, erosion of religious values, and reduced quality of life. A turning point in getting an investigation set up was the observations of a prominent community leader, who was also a traditional midwife, regarding exposure of nursing mothers and their infants. The research followed the guiding principles of respect, equity and empowerment, which corresponded to Mohawk beliefs in the need to strive for peace (*Skennen*), a good mind (*Kariwiio*) and strength (*Kasastensera*). These research principles were established by Mohawk community leaders to make sure that local people would benefit from the research and to offer direction about it. Developing a collaborative partnership was mandatory. The university researchers learned to respect the vast amount of valuable information, relevant to a scientifically conducted research project, that the community possessed. In terms of equity, a Mohawk advisory board ensured that funds and resources to allocate to the community were asked for, and that financial support for the community residents was budgeted for: residents were hired as field staff for example. The latter were empowered by receiving training in various aspects of carrying out psychological research, earning college credit in the process.

   Much time was spent early on in discussion about the conduct of the research, educating the university researchers about Mohawk culture and history, reaching a consensus about the roles and responsibilities of the field staff, agreeing that copies of forms and data should be stored on the reservation, that data ultimately belonged to the community, that results should be presented to the advisory committee before publication, and that authorship should include the Akwesasne task force on the environment, or a designated member. The community had legitimate reasons to be suspicious of outside information gathering about their community, and their message was quite clear: " ... scientists working in our community must take direction from us. We respect scientific methodology, but the purposes of all studies must be guided by our own need to know what is happening to us – individually and as a community" (Cook, 1995, p. 64, cited by Santiago-Rivera *et al.*,

1998, p. 171). None of this was easy for the researchers, trained as they were in academic environments that fostered competition and individual achievement in contrast to the indigenous community's value on cooperation for the good of the group. One specific challenge was the Mohawk custom of resolving problems by discussion until consensus was reached, a principle that conflicted with university researchers' wish to make decisions more quickly and to meet deadlines. The value that Mohawk staff placed on direct face-to-face contact created difficulties because the university and the reservation were more than four hours travelling time apart: meeting about once a month at a halfway point was one solution.

A second example of collective opposition to toxic waste comes from the High-lander Research and Education Center in Tennessee in the southern Appalachian mountains in the USA. Influenced by social gospel theology, Christian socialism, and the populist politics of the times, the centre was described by Lewis (2001) as an adult education centre originating in the early 1930s and involved since then in most of the major movements for social justice in the area. The song 'We Shall Overcome' was finally crafted at Highlander in the 1940s. With a philosophy simi-lar to that of Freire in Brazil, the Highlander philosophy was that, for institutional change to be effective, the solutions must come from those who are experiencing the problem and who will be directly affected by any action taken. Its projects had included: literary schools to teach African USAmericans to read and write in order to vote, developing into the 'freedom schools' and voter registration movements; the mobilising and training of grassroots 'researchers' to gather data about land and mineral ownership in the Appalachian coal mining region; the use of mem-bers' own and others' oral histories; and surveys to gather data and mobilise local discussion about problems (Lewis, 2001).

In the 1970s, the centre developed a participatory research approach – supported by their own resource centre which provided research assistance to community groups and training for citizens to do their own research and to participate in public policy decisions. An example was the Bumpass Cove Story. The Cove was a former zinc and manganese mining community in a remote mountainous area. Local res-idents were pleased when a company announced plans to resume mining and to backfill mined areas with household rubbish. It slowly emerged, however, through a number of incidents and particularly through the observations and research of one man who had previously worked in the mines and had spent much of his life in and around the local hills – easily dismissed by opponents as a 'crazy old man' – that what was going into the landfill sites was toxic chemical waste. Most people did not believe this evidence until one day when a flood washed chemicals out into the river, toxic fumes became so strong that some people passed out, and the local Red Cross ordered the community to be evacuated. Action was then taken, including blocking the way of the landfill trucks and using the Highlander Centre resources to become knowledgeable about the chemicals involved. None of those involved were trained health scientists and a number had dropped out of high school. Being able to challenge the local health department when they used tech-nical and scientific terminology to obscure what was really going on, gave local people a growing sense that they had knowledge that the scientists did not have, and that they had a right to speak out about what they knew (Lewis, 2001).

Opposing Forest Destruction

From an area in south-eastern India known as Jharkhand (*Jhar* meaning 'forests' and *khand* meaning 'area') comes an example of successful local activism with some outside support, in this case involving the preservation of rights to use forest resources and a successful campaign to prevent forest destruction (Bhatt & Tandon, 2001). Most tribes in the area were settled agriculturists but historically they had had unlimited rights to use the abundant forests in the area to supplement food resources and for other purposes. Successive policies, which put the 'political economy of profit' above the 'moral economy of provisions', had eroded those rights. In addition, trees that provided local people with leaves, seeds, firewood, and sometimes fodder were replaced by trees with high timber value but of little use to local people. From the early 1970s onwards industries began to exploit the last tract of the former type of forest, and in the early 1980s villagers were surprised to learn that the forest department had ordered the clearing of the forest.

Outside support was provided by a voluntary organisation called *Lok Jagriti Kendra* (LJK) who approached the tribal community in the area and started a process of dialogue on the importance of the forests in people's lives. A series of discussions led to a plan of action that involved blocking roads, hugging trees, and trying to convince the felling workers why the trees should not be cut down. Despite police being sent in (who had to withdraw because of the large crowds), and intimidation of leaders by the local administration, the action was successful and the forest was saved. The participation of hundreds of women in the campaign was central, motivated by the growing realisation that the forests were essential to their livelihoods. All illegal and commercial felling in the area was banned, and regulated use of the forest by villagers was reinstated, management being entrusted to the local Peasants Labour Committee. Each year the victory was celebrated in *Bir Mela* (*Bir* meaning 'forest' in local tribal dialect and *Mela* meaning 'festival').

Opposing the Destruction of Fishing Grounds

Swantz *et al.* (2001) provided a good example of actions by women in Tanzania, a country with a history of several decades of participatory action research and other participatory methods, under the political rhetoric of 'people's participation in their own development'. It illustrated successful resistance, in this case against inappropriate and damaging fishing practices. This emerged during participatory rural appraisal in one fishing village. Using methods such as apportioning seeds to parts of a matrix representing different problems, and drawing a mobility map of fishing grounds, it emerged that the problems were largely due to the practice by fishermen from neighbouring villages and further afield of using dynamite in fishing which exhausted fish stocks, was ecologically damaging, and occasionally had resulted in very serious injuries to local people. Another contributing factor was the increasing tendency of men to fish with small nets in-shore – previously the prerogative of women who fished by wading on foot in waters close into the shore – hence rendering women jobless and robbing them of their main source of cash income and a daily source of food.

A workshop, supported by the Rural Integrated Project Support (RIPS) programme, produced a declaration condemning the illegal practice of dynamiting, and a documentary video was made of all discussions and proceedings and subsequent visits that were made to the scenes of action. Meanwhile women turned to planting and harvesting seaweed for the export trade. Realising that their main efforts had not brought results, a further RIPS-supported workshop was held, with greater representation from other coastal villages, local MPs, marine police, and other authorities. Women shared their views equally with men, and their determination was a surprise and something new to men in the fishing communities. In addition to the previous declaration, a confederation on environmental protection was formed and it was decided to send a delegation to parliament. It was agreed to name individual dynamite fishermen, which took great courage, and a list of over 500 names was presented to the Prime Minister, who later came to the region, read out some of the names, and gave instructions that the practice should stop. Fines and jail sentences were tightened and some changes were made to the Fisheries Act (Masaiganah, in Swantz *et al.*, 2001).

TOWARDS LIBERATION FOR THE POOR AND OPPRESSED

Examples from Latin America and South Africa

Lykes, Blanche and Hamber (2003) described examples of the practice of 'liberatory community psychology' in Guatemala and South Africa following years of conflict and repression in those countries. In Guatemala, after the years of repression in the 1980s which was estimated to have claimed between 150,000 and 200,000 lives and over 40,000 disappearances, many survivors spoke of their experiences as part of the Peace Accords, and some psychologists were involved in designing training programmes to ensure effective, efficient, and psychologically beneficial gathering of testimony. Among those who had not 'testified' were a large number of women in part of the Ixil region which had been deeply affected by the war. The first author of the paper was invited to work with that group.

The work focused on three areas: psychological issues that women encountered as they responded to the multiple effects of violence and repression; the development of a new organisation – the Association of Maya Ixil Women – New Dawn; and concrete work to improve conditions within the local community. Participatory workshops integrated Freirian pedagogical and analytical techniques, creative resources such as storytelling, dramatisation and drawing, and indigenous practices including weaving, religious ceremony and oral history, as well as strategies of participatory action research. Photographic methods were found to be particularly useful. Women recorded their own life stories, sometimes assisted by a facilitator, in dialogue with another participant. They photographed life in their village and travelled to neighbouring villages, photographing other women and their families. The action research team made a selection from the more than 2000 photographs that were taken, and drew on hundreds of interviews, group-based analyses and stories, to develop a shared story of the violence that had occurred, its effects, and ways people had found of remaking individual and collective lives. Participants often spoke of the project as providing them with their first opportunities to talk about events that had occurred. There were some criticisms of the project on the grounds that it introduced 'western' technology into a rural community, and that it was economically non-sustainable. But participants repeatedly described the project's positive impact both on their local community and their own increased self-understanding and self-esteem. Among other things it honed analytical and organisational skills, and for some, computer skills and facility at data recording, financial accounting, and even writing grant proposals. Some had spoken publicly in national forums about the work.

As in Guatemala after the war there, poverty continued to be the experience of many in South Africa after the years of *apartheid* which was thought to have been directly responsible for about 20,000 deaths as well as widespread oppression of the black population. The post-apartheid Trust and Reconciliation Commission (TRC) afforded many victims the chance to tell their stories; unlike in Guatemala, often very publicly via television, radio and newspapers. One of the 17 TRC commissioners was a psychologist, a number of psychologists presented evidence to the Commission about inequities in the apartheid mental health system, and a few provided support and counselling to survivors who were giving evidence before the Commission.

The third author of this paper was involved with a human rights non-government organisation, the Centre for the Study of Violence and Reconciliation (CSVR) which gained particular impetus from collaboration with Khulumani (Zulu for 'speaking out'), a support group for survivors of gross human rights abuses. Local Khulumani self-help groups were initiated by holding workshops with NGOs in an area, followed by educational workshops for survivors, which emphasised story-telling and the importance of dialogue and discussion around the TRC. At times there were as many as 35 such groups running in the greater Johannesburg area and neighbouring provinces, membership consisting mainly of women, many in their late forties and above. Members were typically the relatives of victims of apartheid security forces. Lykes *et al.* wrote about the complex and ever-changing nature of the work. At various times a survivor might tell her story in order to share her pain, to place facts on record, to instigate an investigation, to ensure justice was done, or in the hope of receiving compensation. Restitution, in the form of payment, jobs, or symbolic contributions such as gravestones, became an important theme. Imparting a sense of community was an important aspect throughout. For some women Khulumani was a way of re-establishing contact and allegiance to the struggle after losing touch with the liberation movement. Groups also became informal networks for sharing information about such things as job opportunities and income generation projects. Lykes *et al.* were of the view that Khulumani had helped to shift the TRC's discourse and practices from being principally about granting amnesty to perpetrators, towards becoming a forum where survivors could make themselves heard. Once again there were criticisms. For example, when Khulumani picketed the opening of the TRC to protest about inadequate information about the amnesty process, the third author of this article was held responsible by one of the TRC's most senior figures.

Those two examples that Lykes *et al.* described, of collaboration between community psychologists and local survivors – from Guatemala and South Africa respectively – may, as they suggested, demonstrate:

> the possibilities of 'giving voice' to or empowering the marginalized and the disenfranchised, while at the same time celebrating basic community psychology principles of respectful engagement and participatory action (p. 89).

Community Development in a Brazilian City

Guareschi and Jovchelovitch (2004) described the achievements of the *orçamento participativo* (OP) in Porto Elegre in Brazil. The OP process in Brazil, which had been listed by UNESCO as one of its Best Practices, is a process whereby decision making over public resource allocation is given to forums that are elected at open neighbourhood or thematic meetings. The Porto Elegre OP had been particularly successful, having grown from small beginnings into a dynamic interaction between community members, technical people, and the state, and had managed to mobilise principally poor people, unlike the dominance of participatory forums by middle-class and elite groups that had often been noted in the literature. Over a period of 12 years the face of this part of the periphery of the city – made up of hillside *favelas*, and *vilas* consisting of small groups of people occupying land illegally and gradually constituting themselves as a community requiring resources – had changed dramatically, with the provision of running water and sanitation, public transport, health clinics, schools, paved streets, and waste collection (although continued migration from rural areas continued to produce new squatter communities).

The authors developed a model of community participation in which the notion of conscientisation (Freire, 1973) and sensitivity to local social representations (Moscovici, 1984) were considered to be central. Getting to know a community and its way of life involved overcoming the feeling of strangeness between researchers and local people; in the case of a typical southern Brazilian *vila*, simply crossing the town and entering the community was itself a challenge, demanding training, supervision, and follow-up. Crucial was the long tradition of alliances between members of deprived communities and health workers in Brazil, much facilitated by the OP structure that provided a site for community members, academics and students to meet in a 'productive alliance'. A number of qualitative methods, such as interviews, group work, participant observation, and filming, were used to enable listening, observing and talking to the community, with the aim of uncovering and systematising knowledge about the community, and making it public for reflection and debate. That 'critical reflexivity' lead to conscientisation, whereby people became aware of the socioeconomic, political and cultural contradictions shaping their lives and identities.

Among the challenges were: the assumption by many that meetings were somewhere to go to make demands of politicians, rather than the start of getting involved in a lengthy process; the frustration for many advocates of the OP because informed participation did not occur in the ideal way they had envisaged; the clear preference in the *vilas* for professional handling of healthcare matters and a reluctance to accept the idea of training community members to become local health agents; and the criticisms often directed at some of the most committed community participants for becoming too closely connected with the 'doctors' or for being thought to be seeking personal advantages.

Black Socio-Political Development in the USA

In a series of studies conducted over a number of years, Watts and his colleagues have focused attention on the socio-political development of black men in the USA. In one of these studies, Watts (1993a) had content analysed the answers given to a number of questions about their organisations by leaders of 40 manhood development organizations (MDOs) from around the country. These were organisations serving African USAmerican men, using a comprehensive, human development approach that relied on various methods that reinforced cultural and religious values – in contrast to single-focus programmes on such topics as the prevention of drug misuse or early pregnancy. The results suggested a number of conclusions. One was that, although young men were the focus, respondents viewed parents and family as the most important units of analysis and as the key players in a successful programme. A second theme was the importance of cultural socialisation through emphasis on the history, traditions, values, and greatness of one's people, drawing on contemporary African USAmerican activist scholarship, such as work by Asante (1988). Although it is often rejected in community psychology because of its intrapsychic focus (see Chapter 1), the term 'self-esteem' was often used, indicating that MDO leaders believed that an important outcome of their programmes was the transformation of how people viewed themselves and their world. Intrapsychic and social change were not seen as antithetical but rather as complementary. Words commonly associated with socio-political analysis, such as 'oppression' and 'racism', rarely appeared. Watts speculated that many respondents may have believed that life skills or cultural socialisation were sufficient, and may have been more concerned with transforming African USAmerican communities rather than with changing European USAmerican-dominated institutions. 'Giving back' was a theme: young men were expected to develop themselves as individuals, but complete success depended on using their new skills to benefit the whole community. Another theme was 'holistic change', which was viewed, not just in terms of preventing individual, specified adverse outcomes such as crime, violence or unhealthy behaviours, but rather in terms of a development of a strong character and social support structure that would enable young black men to avoid contributing to the statistics which showed the much greater presence of young black men among those imprisoned, unemployed, leaving education comparatively early, and misusing substances. Finally, although religion was important to some church MDO programmes, spirituality was essential to most.

Ideas on socio-political development (SPD) were developed by Watts *et al.* (1999) in a report of one version of the Young Warriors programme conducted with young African USAmerican high school students in a mid-western city. The programme took the form of eight weekly meetings, varying in attendance from five to 12, with 32 young men attending at least one session. The aim was to promote socio-political

Table 12.1 Stages of socio-political development and associated challenging questions

Stage of sociopolitical development	Key action concepts for enhancing critical consequences
Acritical stage: Resource asymmetry is outside of awareness, or the existing social order is thought to reflect real differences in the capabilities of group members. In essence, it is a 'just world'.	*Challenge internalised oppression*: What contributions have African Americans made to the US and the world? *Critical thinking on class and race inequity*: Why can't kids in this (impoverished, all-Black) school take their books home when kids in other (affluent White) schools can?
Adaptive stage: Asymmetry may be acknowledged, but the system maintaining it is seen as immutable. Predatory, anti-social or accommodation strategies are employed to maintain a positive sense of self and to acquire social and material rewards.	*Encourage critical thinking about socialisation agents and psychic alienation*: What do rap videos tell us about Black men and their lifestyles? *Decision-making and values clarification*: What's the connection between choices of lifestyle and quality of life and neighborhood?
Precritical stage: Complacency gives way to awareness of and concerns about asymmetry and inequality. The value of adaptation is questioned.	*Cognitive reframing*: How many explanations can we come up with for the differences in the quality of high and low income communities?
Critical stage: There is a desire to learn more about asymmetry, injustice, oppression, and liberation. Through this process, some will conclude that the asymmetry is unjust and social change efforts are warranted.	*Critical consciousness*: What events now and in the past maintain the differences in the quality of life in some Black and White communities? *Moral reasoning*: Is the inequity a sign that something is wrong with society? Why? Why not?
Liberation stage: The experience and awareness of oppression is salient. Liberation behaviour (involvement in social action and community development) is tangible and frequent. Adaptive behaviors are eschewed.	*Community activism, solidarity, and liberation behaviour*: What can you do (personally and as a group) to improve the situation?

Source: Watts. R.J., Griffith, D.M. & Abdul-Adil, J. (1999). Sociopolitical development as an antidote for oppression – theory and action. *American Journal of Community Psychology*, **27**, 255–71

development by raising critical consciousness. Believing that the media was often an agent of oppression against young people, the vehicle for this process was the analysis of what the young men could see in rap music videos, television shows, and film, what they thought it meant, why, how it made them feel, and what they thought they could do about it. This corresponded to the five supposed stages of socio-political development (see Table 12.1). Through discussion about images of

African USAmericans in mass culture, and how those images might contribute to conditions in their community, group trainers coached the participants in thinking critically. Content analysis suggested that critically conscious talk increased across the sessions of the programme.

A central aim was the raising of awareness about oppression, defined by Watts *et al.* (1999) as an asymmetric distribution of coveted resources among politically salient populations. As critical consciousness developed, understanding would be gained of the historical, social, racial, political, and cultural concomitants of asymmetry. Outcomes such as poverty, family disruption, drug misuse, anti-social behaviour and violence, which might be seen as signs of psychopathology, would be viewed in this perspective as (mal)adaptive strategies that evolved in response to oppression.

Later, Watts *et al.* (2003) looked at the socio-political development of people of African descent who had become activists in the USA in such movements or settings as black, revolutionary nationalist, progressive, communist, reform, or community or progressive human service organisations. They interviewed 24 activists, covering a range of ideologies and settings, in New York City, Chicago, and the San Francisco Bay area. They concluded that their five-step SPD model neglected much of the complexity of socio-political development, failing to capture the role that settings and specific experiences played in development. SPD, they concluded, was a cumulative and recursive process with development being the cumulative result of many transactions over time. Particularly important were what they called 'experience venues' in three developmental periods: *upbringing* – including family, school, neighbourhood, and community groups (e.g. "My maternal grandmother was more along the lines of your sort of community leader ... she was quite a militant for her time ..."; "I saw the difference between my neighborhood and my high school friend's neighborhood ..."); organisations and institutions of higher *education* in late adolescence and early adulthood (e.g. "We had workshops on different issues that were going on around the world. It was the first time that I really began to realize that oppression was happening everywhere ..."); and *influences later in life*.

Community Empowerment of Women: General Principles

Kar *et al.* (1999) reviewed reports of 40 case studies from across industrialised and 'developing' parts of the world in which women and mothers (WAM) had been empowered in improving the quality of life of the powerless in one of four areas: basic human rights, equal rights for women, economic enhancement, and health promotion. They observed that psychologists and sociologists had tended to be preoccupied with individuals and micro-systems, while social activists and community organisers had not generally produced scholarly reports of their work. As a result it was difficult to find good descriptions of such case studies, even of those that had been successful. They focused on WAM because women and mothers are the primary care givers in their families, and relatively powerless compared with men, and tend to place a high priority on the well-being of their children and family rather than on their own needs. Furthermore:

Table 12.2   The EMPOWER framework: seven empowerment methods used by women and mothers in 40 successful community campaigns

EMPOWER methods	Primary aim	Activities	Total number of cases (and %) per method ($n = 40$)
(1) Empowerment training and leadership development	To educate individuals about rights and opportunities, to develop leadership skills	Leadership training, organisational training, conference/symposium	19 (47.5)
(2) Media use, support and advocacy	To influence public policy through various media venues	Media events/coverage, media campaign, press release/conference	20 (50.0)
(3) Public education and participation	To promote public and leader awareness, support and action	Speakers' bureau, newsletter, community advisory board	23 (57.5)
(4) Organising partnership: associations, cooperatives and coalitions	To enhance negotiating power, self-reliance, resources and facilities within communities and community based organisations	Labour unions, coalition, mothers' clubs	20 (50.0)
(5) Work/job training and micro-enterprise	To promote economic self-reliance and employable skills	Vocational training, income-generating projects, micro-enterprise	8 (20.0)
(6) Enabling Service and Assistance	To provide relief and critical services	Medical/legal/financial assistance, counselling/ support groups, community outreach	31 (77.5)
(7) Rights protection and social action/ reform	To protect from abuse, promote rights, to reform laws, policies and programmes	Lobbying, strikes/ marches/picketing, delegation to see government officials	24 (60.0)

Source: adapted with permission from Kar, S.B., Pascual, C.A. & Chickering, K.L. (1999). Empowerment of women for health promotion: a meta-analysis. *Social Science and Medicine*, **49**, 1431–60

Several innovative and well-regarded community development models...hold that *community empowerment, especially empowerment of women*, is the key to successful programs for social change that affect the quality of life and health of poor and powerless families and communities. Our review of literature and case studies furnished strong evidence in support of this contention (p. 1433, original emphasis).

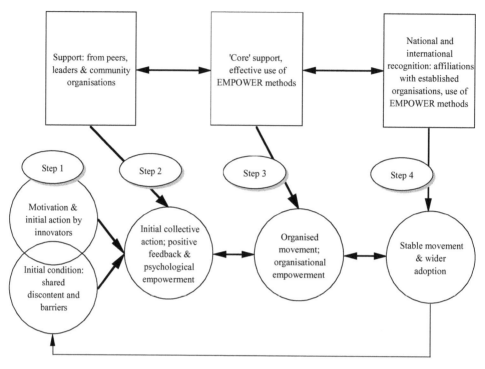

Figure 12.4   A model of the process of empowerment in successful women's and mothers' projects
Source: reproduced with permission from Kar, S.B., Pascual, C.A. & Chickering, K.L. (1999). Empowerment of women for health promotion: a meta-analysis. *Social Science and Medicine*, **49**, 1431–60

The many forms of action covered in their review included such movements as organisations for mothers and other relatives of those who had been kidnapped – the 'disappeared' – under state terrorism in Latin American countries in the 1970s and 1980s, as examples of human rights actions; rural women workers' organisations in countries such as India, the Philippines and Sri Lanka; and Mothers Against Drunk Drivers and Women Against Gun Violence in the USA. Their analysis showed the significant role played by the leadership of one or a small number of people, sometimes from outside but usually from among victims within the community – who were therefore facing great threat on account of their action. Another common finding was the barriers to women's movements that usually existed, with women initially being met with scepticism by established organisations and male members of the community. In fact one of the most common findings was the transformation of the attitudes of men from one of male chauvinism to one of acceptance of women as equal partners. Kar *et al.* identified seven empowerment methods most frequently used, and shown here in Table 12.2 using their acronym EMPOWER. Many incipient movements, they suggested, flounder under the combined pressures of: traditional gender roles that discourage social action by women, inadequate personal efficacy and competency, lack of access to essential resources and organisations to protect and promote their cause, lack of public awareness and support, and strong opposition from the oppressors or abusive systems.

Kar *et al.* concluded with the proposed model shown in Figure 12.4. Action generally began with a state of deep discontent and strong motivation to change the status quo, maternal motivation to prevent harm to children being a common driving force. A positive experience of initial action by innovators was empowering and energising and laid the foundation for an organised movement. CORE support, particularly at the early stage, was essential: Community support from fellow victims and others; Organisational support from community-based organisations; Resource support of various kinds; and Empowerment support. An effective movement and organisation gained recognition, legitimacy and support from the local community, media, general public, and established organisations that shared a similar mission. The support of prominent leaders, government, national and international organisations provided immediate protection against opponents and distracters. Fear of retaliation by abusers often deterred victims from seeking help and/or resisting abuse. Struggles by women for minimal survival needs (e.g. a minimum wage or against human rights violations) or for their children's well-being, safety and prevention of harm, were particularly likely to engender wide social support, even in societies under authoritarian rule. Participation and involvement – including training and leadership developments – had empowering effects on both individuals and organisations independently of tangible programme outcomes. Media use, support and advocacy enhanced effectiveness. Non-violent social action for a just cause was likely to gain social approval and enhance ultimate effectiveness. Kar *et al.*'s most important conclusion was that:

> ... even the most disenfranchised and deprived women and mothers (WAM) can and do lead successful social action movements that are self-empowering and significantly enhance the QOL [quality of life] of their families and communities (p. 1437).

That is an inspiring note on which to end this chapter and the last main section of this book. It remains for the final chapter to bring the book to a conclusion by offering the suggestion that community psychology has now reached a point in its yet short history when agreement is emerging about its central paradigm – a consensus about its core concepts, purposes and methods which can guide the field for at least the next few years.

FINALE: CONSENSUS AND CHALLENGE

Community psychology faces a number of challenges. Some of them are shown in Table F.1. The first is crucial. Is there yet any coherence in the field around a leading model? I believe a consensus is beginning to emerge but others may disagree. It would hardly be surprising if consensus was difficult to achieve since the origins of community psychology lie in sources as diverse as clinical psychology, applied social psychology of European and North American kinds, and liberation and post-colonial theory from South Africa and countries in Latin America. Indeed, many of the field's core ideas come from outside psychology or are shared with other disciplines – theories of 'empowerment' and 'participation' are examples.

The emerging consensus that I discern can be pictured as shown in Figure F.1. It has four inter-dependent elements. The first is *Knowing*. There is a strong emphasis in community psychology on the importance of disempowered people gaining knowledge about the nature and origins of their circumstances, and on the multiple ways in which people are kept in ignorance of the historical and contemporary social arrangements that have resulted in them being in their current positions. Although increased knowledge can not itself be equated with action to transform those circumstances or necessarily with an increase in power or resources, increased knowing is itself empowering. Many of the most useful forms of knowledge are specific and local, but those shown in Figure F.2 are among some of the more general sources of knowledge about empowerment and disempowerment. Figure F.3 gives four more specific examples, based on projects described in earlier chapters, showing the relevance of increased knowledge and the way that may be linked with action.

Some of those forms of knowledge draw on findings in the professional journals – for example the relationship between class and health. But once the participatory principle is accepted, the distinction between 'expert' forms of knowledge and those possessed by groups and communities themselves, begins to break down. As discussed in Chapter 3, consensus has been growing that research and evaluation should be as participatory as possible, and that useful knowledge takes a variety of forms. Some of the ways in which community-relevant knowledge can be enhanced are shown in Figure F.4. The list includes the collection of relevant facts and stories as well as the established psychological methods of qualitative and quantitative research. In sum, "... Knowledge and practice ... [would be] built

Table F.1 Community psychology: challenges and responses

Challenge	Response
1. Community psychology is a fragmented subject with no single, strong model to guide the field	This may have been true in the past, but a consensus is now emerging
2. It is too idealistic and contrary to the way the world is moving	The modern world is full of contrary movements, and community psychology is strong on practical action as well as values and theory
3. This is not psychology, which is about individual thought, feeling and behaviour	That is an arbitrary definition of psychology and reflects quite recent biases which community psychology aims to correct
4. Community psychology theory and practice is difficult to distinguish from those of other subjects and disciplines	There are large areas of overlap, which is why collaboration with others is highly valued in community psychology; but the main issues, such as power, social position, ways of knowing, and collective action, are as much psychological as anything else
5. There is a lack of demand for community psychology	That is hardly surprising in countries such as the UK where community psychology is little known; the experience in countries where it is better established, such as Aotearoa/New Zealand, is that there is demand
6. There is no support amongst students for learning about community psychology: most want to do counselling and psychotherapy	That is more a reflection of the availability of career pathways; experience is that support for community psychology ideas is strong amongst students
7. As a subject community psychology is past its peak	Some have suggested that to be the case for community psychology in the USA where membership of the Community Psychology Division peaked in the late 1970s and early 1980s, but that is not true in other countries where the subject is now developing; meanwhile US community psychology continues to be a vibrant source of creative ideas for theory and practice
8. There is a danger that community psychology might become an orthodoxy	That is a danger, but provided community psychology retains its critical faculties orthodoxy is likely to be strongly challenged
9. As presently practised it is not radical enough: it is not acting as an effective site of resistance to powerful and harmful influences or effectively helping to transform damaging social arrangements	Community psychology is a broad church and responses to that challenge differ: but it is a vital one for the subject and we must go on posing the challenge and debating the answer

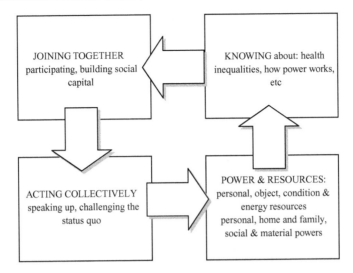

Figure F.1 A four-element model for community psychology

❖ Occupational status and other 'class' indicators and how they are related to health

❖ The greater stress to which disadvantaged groups are exposed

❖ Work conditions and the theories that link them to health

❖ The universal hierarchy by gender and the ways it operates and is manifest

❖ The universal hierarchy by age and the ways it operates and is manifest

❖ What 'arbitrary' hierarchical sets there might be in one's own society (for example by ethnic group or sexual orientation) and the ways they operate and are manifest

❖ Forms and mechanisms of social exclusion

❖ The direct and subtle ways in which power operates, and exploitation and oppression flourish

❖ The blatant and subtle ways in which prejudice is expressed and some people and groups are 'kept down'

❖ The ways in which organisations and institutions support expressions of power and discrimination

---

Figure F.2 Things that people should know about

---

with, and for, the people as well as for the scientific construction of the community psychology field in a dialetic relationship" (Freitas, 1998, p. 267).

There continues to be a role for evaluative research that includes comparisons and controls (as in the Experimental Social Innovation and Dissemination work discussed in Chapter 10), but it is more likely to take a quasi-experimental rather

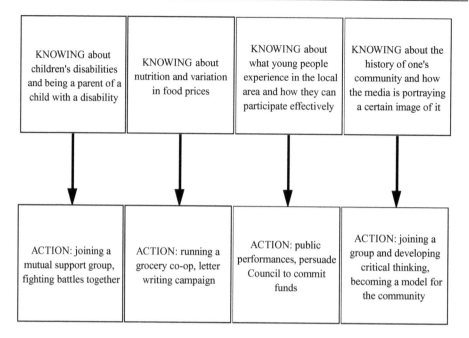

Figure F.3   Four examples of relevant knowledge and its relationship with action

- *Facts*: In the form of statistics or scientific knowledge, e.g. regarding the chemistry and toxicity of waste dumped in people's vicinity; or the geo-statistical clustering of a health problem in certain neighbourhoods; or facts about the activities of a multinational company operating in the area.
- *Public opinion*: Assessed by surveys, e.g. attitudes towards the opening of a casino in a residential area of high deprivation.
- *Local experience*: Using interviews and focus groups to find out in depth about people's experience, e.g. the experience of local services on the part of those of a particular ethnic group or those living in an outlying area.
- *Power discourses*: Analysing public or media statements by those in authority in order to understand how certain interests are supported and others neglected, e.g. how authoritative statements support the adoption of suspicious attitudes towards immigrants.
- *Individual stories*: Telling of the experiences of one or two individuals, families or groups to support the other forms of new knowledge, e.g. the stories of those who have benefited from a service that should be extended to others, or who have experienced discrimination in the area.

Figure F.4   The variety of ways in which collective empowerment can be aided by new knowledge than randomised trial form (see Shadish *et al.*, 2002, for the principles of quasi-experiments and Humphreys *et al.*, 2004, Nelson *et al.*, 2006, and Janzen *et al.*, 2006, for some good examples). But those are specialist ways of enhancing knowledge and there is agreement that when they are used they must be carried out with the closest collaboration with local groups – as was the case in those examples – so that the research questions and results have local significance, and that research and action are part of the same process. Other ways in which groups and communities gather useful knowledge include the many examples described in earlier chapters: holding conversations in people's homes as part of the PICO process (Speer & Hughey, 1995) and developing new ways of knowing in the Listening Partners programme (Bond *et al.*, 2000) are just two of them. These are ways of raising consciousness – conscientisation in the language of the popular education and liberation models coming to us from Latin America – about some of the circumstances shown in Figure F.2.

The second key part of the consensual model is *Joining Together*. The basic idea here – for which there was so much evidence in the examples in Part IV – is that, "... the main hope for ordinary people of exercising power is to do so in cooperation with others (solidarity)" (Smail, 2005, p. 29). This was evident in peer support groups (Chapter 9), Women's Action for Mental Health and Men's Advice Network programmes (Chapter 10), the examples of coalitions described in Chapter 11, and the various forms of participation needed in order for groups to act to protect and sustain natural resources (Chapter 12). This is one of the many points of agreement between feminist psychology and community psychology: central to the feminist approach to social science according to Campbell and Wasco (2000) is connecting women, including bringing women together to collect relevant data. Although there may not be complete consensus about the value of importing into community psychology the concept of social capital, it could be seen as highly relevant at this point. Without the increased social capital that comes with bonding, bridging and linking with other individuals and groups, and the increased capacity to access and utilise resources that is brought about as a result, individuals remain powerless in the face of powerful constraints and pervasive hierarchies that place them in subordinate positions.

Acting Collectively is the third element shown in Figure F.1. This is the, "...mobilizing collective action...to bring about change...", that Hur (2006, p. 529) talks of in the course of his attempt to construct an overarching empowerment framework; and the, "...possibilities for communities to challenge and transform the operation and effects of stigmatizing representations and practices", that Howarth (2006, p. 449) refers to in her paper on positioning stigmatised groups as agents, collectively capable of effecting change, rather than as simply passive victims of stigma and prejudice. We met many examples of the power of collective action in the later chapters, starting with Holland's (1988, 1992) insight that individual psychotherapy clients could come together for effective local action.

The fourth and final component is *Power and Resources*. We can draw here on Hobfoll's (1998) conservation of resources theory, and Hagan and Smail's (1997) concept of power maps (see Chapters 1 and 2) – the latter described in terms of power available to an individual person in a number of domains, including the material, but equally applicable to collectives. Figure F.1 should, more accurately show a reciprocal relationship between this element and the others. In his paper on the social psychology of power, Turner (2005) wished to correct what he saw as the bias in power theory towards seeing cause and effect running from control of resources, via power and influence, to group formation (or what I am calling 'joining together' and social capital). He proposed reversing the order such that group formation and the emergence of shared social identity, via influence and power, led to the control of resources. In my view the relationship between joining and resources is best seen as a reciprocal one: it is easier for those with power and resources to combine to protect their interests, but solidarity and joint action are also potent means for the relatively deprived to improve their position.

Students embarking on a career, and wondering about community psychology, are interested in the practical question of what community psychology looks like in practice (Jozefowicz-Simbeni *et al.*, 2005). The long answer, to which I hope this book has made a contribution, is to be found in the various texts and journals referred to in the Preface. A summary answer, based on the four-element model described above, might take the following form:

> The practice of community psychology requires collaboration with others to identify and use existing strengths and resources available to disempowered groups, in order to facilitate people joining together so that they can develop relevant knowledge about social arrangements and act collectively to change them, with the aim of enhancing their power and resources.

Community psychology, as I hope this book has made clear, is attended by a number of challenges, controversies and contradictions. Hence the field is now a lively and contested one. That is as it should be, perhaps in any branch of human endeavour, but certainly in community psychology which deliberately adopts a constructively critical stance. It aims to be critical both of social arrangements that are found to be harmful to health and well-being and of the practice of psychology itself. A leading characteristic – perhaps even its chief hallmark – is its criticism of psychology's connivance with a widespread bias towards explaining human ills at an individual level and the promotion of individual-level methods of amelioration – a bias that many fear has been intensifying globally. Not only does that place community psychology in opposition to many powerful others both within and outside psychology, but it also creates much debate within community psychology about whether we are succeeding in challenging those powerful sources of bias and about what constitutes an adequate community psychology. Is it critical enough? Is it a force supporting social justice and social change? Does it give sufficient support to other social change movements, for example those in support of the rights of children, indigenous people and ethnic minorities, women, people with disabilities, or sexual minorities. In Table F.1 that is shown as the last (but certainly not the least) in the list of challenges for community psychology. It constitutes the most significant challenge facing the subject in its present state of development.

REFERENCES

Acheson, D., Barker, D., Chambers, J. *et al.* (1998). *Independent Inquiry into Inequalities in Health.* London: The Stationery Office.

Adams, J., White, M., Pearce, M.S. & Parker, L. (2004). Life course measures of socioeconomic position and self reported health at age 50: prospective cohort study. *Journal of Epidemiology and Community Health,* **58**, 1028–9.

Adelman, L. & Cebulla, A. (2003). The dynamics of poverty and deprivation in the UK. In E. Apospori & J. Millar (eds), *The Dynamics of Social Exclusion in Europe: Comparing Austria, Germany, Greece, Portugal and the UK* (pp. 139–63). Cheltenham, UK: Edward Elgar.

Adler, A. (1933/1979). On the origin of the striving for superiority and of social interest, a paper read at the Vienna Medical Society for Individual Psychology. Reprinted in Ansbacher, H.L. & Ansbacher, R.R. (1979). *Alfred Adler: Superiority and Social Interest* (pp. 29–39). New York: Norton.

Adler, N.E., Boyce, T., Chesney, M.A., Cohen, S., Folkman, S., Kahn, R.L. & Syme, S.L. (1994). Socioeconomic status and health. *American Psychologist,* 15–24.

Agger, I. & Jensen, S.B. (1990). Testimony as ritual and evidence in psychotherapy for political refugees. *Journal of Traumatic Stress,* **3**, 115–30 (cited by Sveaass, 2000).

Albee, G.W. & Fryer, D.M. (2003). Praxis: towards a public health psychology. *Journal of Community and Applied Social Psychology,* **13**, 71–5.

Albee, G.W. & Gullotta, T.P. (1997). *Primary Prevention Works.* Thousand Oaks, CA: Sage (cited by Cowen, 2000).

Albee, G.W. & Perry, M. (1998). Economic and social causes of sexism and of the exploitation of women. *Journal of Community and Applied Social Psychology,* **8**, 145–60.

Alcalde, J. & Walsh-Bowers, R. (1996). Community psychology values and the culture of graduate training: a self study. *American Journal of Community Psychology,* **24**, 389–411.

Allamani, A., Forni, E., Ammannati, P., Basetti Sani, I. & Centurioni, A. (2000). Alcohol carousel and children's school drawings as part of a community educational strategy. *Substance Use and Misuse,* **35**, 125–39.

Allik, J. & Realo, A. (2004). Individualism-collectivism and social capital. *Journal of Cross-Cultural Psychology,* **35**, 29–49.

Almedom, A.M. (2005). Social capital and mental health: an interdisciplinary review of primary evidence. *Social Science and Medicine,* **61**, 943–64.

Alonzo, A.A. (1993). Health behaviour: issues, contradictions and dilemmas. *Social Science and Medicine,* **37**, 1019–34.

Altschuler, A., Somkin, C.P. & Adler, N.E. (2004). Local services and amenities, neighborhood social capital, and health. *Social Science and Medicine,* **59**, 1219–29.

Amerio, P. (2000). *Psicologia Di Comunitá.* II Mulino: Bologna (cited by Francescato & Tomai, 2001).

Anderson, I. & Christian, J. (2003). Causes of homelessness in the UK: a dynamic analysis. *Journal of Community and Applied Social Psychology,* **13**, 105–18.

Anderssen, N. (2002). Does contact with lesbians and gays lead to friendlier attitudes? A two-year longitudinal study. *Journal of Community and Applied Social Psychology*, **12**, 124–36.

Aneshensel, C.S. & Sucoff, C.A. (1996). The neighbourhood context of adolescent mental health. *Journal of Health and Social Behavior*, **37**, 293–310.

Angelique, H.L. & Culley, M.R. (2000). Searching for feminism: an analysis of community psychology literature relevant to women's concerns. *American Journal of Community Psychology*, **28**, 793–813.

Angelique, H.L. & Culley, M.R. (2003). Feminism found: an examination of gender consciousness in community psychology. *Journal of Community Psychology*, **31**, 189–209.

Angelique, H.L., Reischl, T.M. & Davidson II, W.S. (2002). Promoting political empowerment: evaluation of an intervention with university students. *American Journal of Community Psychology*, **30**, 815–33.

Ansbacher, H.L. (1979). The recognition of Adler. In H.L. Ansbacher & R.R. Ansbacher (eds), *Alfred Adler: Superiority and Social Interest* (pp. 3–20). New York: Norton.

Apospori, E. & Millar, J. (eds) (2003). *The Dynamics of Social Exclusion in Europe: Comparing Austria, Germany, Greece, Portugal and the UK*. Cheltenham, UK: Edward Elgar.

Arber, S. (1996). Integrating nonemployment into research on health inequalities. *International Journal of Health Services*, **26**, 445–81.

Arber, S. (1997). Comparing inequalities in women's and men's health: Britain in the 1990s. *Social Science and Medicine*, **44**, 773–87.

Archives of the Society of Medical officers of Health (1930). *Minutes of the Society of Medical Officers of Health*. 11 April, A.12. Oxford, UK: Wellcome Historical Unit (cited by Lewis, 1991).

Arcidiacono, C. & Procentese, F. (2005). Distinctiveness and sense of community in the historical center of Naples: a piece of participatory action research. *Journal of Community Psychology*, **33**, 631–8.

Aristotle, (1980). *The Nicomachean Ethics*, translated by D. Ross. Oxford, UK: Oxford University Press, revised edition, book 1 (cited by Sen, 1999).

Armstrong, D.L., Strogatz, D., Barnett, E. & Wang, R. (2003). Joint effects of social class and community occupational structure on coronary mortality among black men and white men, upstate New York, 1988–92. *Journal of Epidemiology and Community Health*, **57**, 373–8.

Arn, D., Stieger, C., Lobnig, H., Guschelbauer, H. & Fryer, D. (1998). European network of community psychology. *Journal of Community and Applied Social Psychology*, **8**, 429–31.

Arnstein, S.R. (1969). A ladder of participation. *Journal of the American Planning Association*, **35**, 216–24 (cited by Kagan *et al.*, 2005).

Aron, A. & Corne, S. (1994). Introduction. In A. Aron & S. Corne (eds), *Writings for a Liberation Psychology* (pp. 1–12). Cambridge: MA: Harvard University Press.

Asante, M.K. (1988). *Afrocentricity*. Trenton: African World Press (cited by Watts, 1993a).

Austin, S. & Prilleltensky, I. (2001). Diverse origins, common aims: the challenge of critical psychology. *Radical Psychology*, **2**, (2).

Bachrach, K.M. & Zautra, A.J. (1985). Coping with a community stressor: the threat of a hazardous waste facility. *Journal of Health and Social Behavior*, **26**, 127–41 (cited by McMillan & Chavis, 1986).

Back, K.W. (1992). This business of topology. *Journal of Social Issues*, **2**, 51–66.

Bagley, C. (1992). The urban environment and child pedestrian and bicycle injuries: interaction of ecological and personality characteristics. *Journal of Community and Applied Social Psychology*, **2**, 281–9.

Baillie, L., Broughton, S., Bassett-Smith, J., Aasen, W., Oostindie, M., Marino, B.A. & Hewitt, K. (2004). Community health, community involvement, and community empowerment: too much to expect? *Journal of Community Psychology*, **32**, 217–28.

Baker, D., Taylor, H., Henderson, J. & the ALSPAC Study Team (1998). Inequality in infant morbidity: causes and consequences in England in the 1990s. *Journal of Epidemiology and Community Health*, **52**, 451–8.

Balcazar, F.E., Garate-Seerafini, T.J. & Keys, C.B. (2004b). The need for action when conducting intervention research: the multiple roles of the community psychologist. *American Journal of Community Psychology*, **33**, 243–52.

Balcazar, F.E., Taylor, R.R., Kielhofner, G.W., Tamley, K., Benziger, T., Carlin, N. & Johnson, S. (2004a). Participatory action research: general principles and a study with a chronic health condition. In L.A. Jason, C.B. Keys, Y. Suarez-Balcazar, R.R. Taylor & M.I. Davis (eds), *Participatory Community Research: Theories and Methods in Action* (pp.17–36). Washington, DC: American Psychological Association.

Ball, M. & Orford, J. (2002). Meaningful patterns of activity amongst the long-term inner city unemployed: a qualitative study. *Journal of Community and Applied Social Psychology*, **12**, 377–96.

Bandura, A. (1977). Self-efficacy: toward a unifying theory of behavioral change. *Psychological Review*, **84**, 191–215.

Bandura, A. (1995). Exercise of personal and collective efficacy in changing societies. In A. Bandura (ed.), *Self-Efficacy in Changing Societies* (pp. 1–45). Cambridge, UK: Cambridge University Press.

Banyard, V.L. (1995). 'Taking another route': daily survival narratives from mothers who are homeless. *American Journal of Community Psychology*, **23**, 871–91 (cited by Banyard & Miller, 1998).

Banyard, V.L. & Miller, K.E. (1998). The powerful potential of qualitative research for community psychology. *American Journal of Community Psychology*, **26**, 485–505.

Bardasi, E. & Francesconi, M. (2004). The impact of atypical employment on individual wellbeing: evidence from a panel of British workers. *Social Science and Medicine*, **58**, 1671–88.

Bargal, D., Gold, M. & Lewin, M. (1992). Introduction: the heritage of Kurt Lewin. *Journal of Social Issues*, **2**, 3–13.

Barker, C. & Pistrang, N. (2002). Psychotherapy and social support: integrating research on psychological helping. *Clinical Psychology Review*, **22**, 361–79.

Barker, C. & Pistrang, N. (2005). Quality criteria under methodological pluralism: implications for conducting and evaluating research. *American Journal of Community Psychology*, **35**, 201–12.

Barker, D.J.P. (1991). The foetal and infant origins of inequalities in health in Britain. *Journal of Public Health Medicine*, **13**, 64–8 (cited by Graham, 2002).

Barker, R. (1968). *Ecological Psychology: Concepts and Methods for Studying the Environment of Human Behaviour*. Stanford, CA: Stanford University Press.

Barker, R. and Associates (1978). *Habitats, Environments, and Human Behavior*. San Francisco: Jossey-Bass.

Barker, R. & Gump, P. (eds). (1974). *Big School, Small School*. Stanford, CA: Stanford University Press.

Barnes, M., Heady, C., Middleton, S., Millar, J., Papadopoulos, F., Room, G. & Tsakloglou, P. (eds) (2002). *Poverty and Social Exclusion in Europe*. Cheltenham, UK: Edward Elgar.

Barrera, M., Caples, H. & Tein, J.Y. (2001). The psychological sense of economic hardship: measurement models, validity, and cross-ethnic equivalence for urban families. *American Journal of Community Psychology*, **29**, 493–517.

Barrera, M., Prelow, H.M., Dumka, L.E., Gonzales, N.A., Knight, G.P., Michaels, M.L., Roosa, M.W. & Tein J. (2002). Pathways from family economic conditions to adolescents' distress: supportive parenting, stressors outside the family, and deviant peers. *Journal of Community Psychology*, **30**, 135–52.

Bar-Tal, D. (2000). *Shared Beliefs in a Society: Social Psychological Analysis*. London: Sage.

Bartle, E.E., Couchonnal, G., Canda, E.R. & Stakere, M.D. (2002). Empowerment as a dynamically developing concept for practice: lessons learned from organizational ethnography. *Social Work*, **47**, 32–43 (cited by Peterson & Zimmerman, 2004).

Bartley, M. (1999). Measuring women's social position: the importance of theory. *Journal of Epidemiology and Community Health*, **53**, 601–2.

Bartley, M., Sacker, A., Firth, D. & Fitzpatrick, R. (1999). Social position, social roles and women's health in England: changing relationships 1984–1993. *Social Science and Medicine*, **48**, 99–115.

Bass, J.K. & Lambert, S.F. (2004). Urban adolescents' perceptions of their neighborhoods: an examination of spatial dependence. *Journal of Community Psychology*, **32**, 277–93.

Bateman, H.V. (2002). Sense of community in the school: listening to students' voices. In A.T. Fisher, C.C. Sonn & B.J. Bishop (eds.), *Psychological Sense of Community* (pp. 161–79). New York: Kluwer/Plenum.

Baum, A., Garofalo, J.P. & Yali, A.M. (1999). Socioeconomic status and chronic stress. Does stress account for SES effects on health? *Annals of the New York Academy Sciences*, **896**, 131–44.

Baum, F. (1998). Measuring effectiveness in community-based health promotion. In J.K. Davies & G. MacDonald (eds), *Quality, Evidence and Effectiveness in Health Promotion* (pp. 68–89). New York: Routledge (cited by Borg, 2002).

Baum, F. (2001). Health, equity, justice and globalisation: some lessons from the People's Health Assembly. *Journal of Epidemiology and Community Health*, **55**, 613–16.

Baum, F. & Ziersch, A.M. (2003). Social capital. *Journal of Epidemiology and Community Health*, **57**, 320–3.

Beale, D. (2001). Monitoring bullying in the workplace. In N. Tehrani (ed.), *Building a Culture of Respect: Managing Bullying at Work* (pp. 77–94). London: Taylor & Francis.

Beam, M.R., Chen, C. & Greenberger, E. (2002). The nature of adolescents' relationships with their 'very important' nonparental adults. *American Journal of Community Psychology*, **30**, 305–25.

Beck, U. (1992). (1986, translated by M. Ritter, 1992). *The Risk Society: Towards a New Modernity*. London: Sage.

Beck, U. (1999). *World Risk Society*. Cambridge, UK: Polity Press.

Belle, D.E. (1983). The impact of poverty and social networks and supports. *Marriage and Family Review*, **5**, 89–103.

Benach, J. & Yasui, Y. (1999). Geographical patterns of excess mortality in Spain explained by two indices of deprivation. *Journal of Epidemiology and Community Health*, **53**, 423–31.

Benne, C.G. & Garrard, W.M. (2003). Collaborative program development and evaluation: a case study in conflict resolution education. In Y. Suarez-Balcazar & G.W. Harper (eds), *Empowerment and Participatory Evaluation of Community Interventions: Multiple Benefits* (pp. 71–88). New York: Haworth Press.

Ben-Shalom, U. & Horenczyk, G. (2003). Acculturation orientations: a facet theory perspective on the bidimensional model. *Journal of Cross-Cultural Psychology*, **34**, 176–88.

Berkman, L.F., Glass, T., Brissette, I. & Seeman, T.E. (2000). From social integration to health: Durkheim in the new millennium. *Social Science and Medicine*, **51**, 843–57.

Berry, J.W. (2001). A psychology of immigration. *Journal of Social Issues*, **57**, 615–32 (cited by Colic-Peisker & Walker, 2003).

Berry, J.W. & Kim, U. (1988). Acculturation and mental health. In P.R. Dasen, J.W. Berry & N. Sartorius (eds), *Health and Cross-Cultural Psychology: Toward Applications* (pp. 207–36). Newbury Park, CA: Sage (cited by Onishi & Murphy-Shigematsu, 2003).

Best, S. (2003). *A Beginner's Guide to Social Theory*. London: Sage.

Bettcher, D. & Lee, K. (2002). Globalisation and public health. *Journal of Epidemiology and Community Health*, **56**, 8–17.

Bettcher, D. & Wipfli, H. (2001). Towards a more sustainable globalisation: the role of the public health community. *Journal of Epidemiology and Community Health*, **55**, 617–18.

Bhatt, Y. & Tandon, R. (2001). Citizen participation in natural resource management. In P. Reason & H. Bradbury (eds), *Handbook of Action Research: Participative Inquiry and Practice* (pp. 301–6). London: Sage.

Billig, M. (1987). *Arguing and Thinking: A Rhetorical Approach to Social Psychology*. Cambridge, UK: Cambridge University Press (cited by Hepburn, 2003).

Billig, M. (2006). The persistence of Freud. *The Psychologist*, **19**, 540–1.

Birman, D. (1994). Acculturation and human diversity in a multicultural society. In E.J. Trickett, R.J. Watts & D. Birman (eds), *Human Diversity: Perspectives on People in Context* (pp. 261–84). San Francisco: Jossey-Bass (cited by Trickett, 1996).

Birman, D., Trickett, E. & Buchanan, M. (2005). A tale of two cities: replication of a study on the acculturation and adaptation of immigrant adolescents from the former Soviet Union in a different community context. *American Journal of Community Psychology*, **35**, 83–101.

Bishop, B.J. & D'Rozario, P. (2002). Reflections on community psychology in Australia: an introduction. *Journal of Community Psychology*, **30**, 591–6.

Bishop, B.J., Higgins, D., Casella, F. & Contos, N. (2002b). Reflections on practice: ethics, race, and worldviews. *Journal of Community Psychology*, **30**, 611–21.

Bishop, B.J., Sonn, C.C., Drew, N.M. & Contos, N.E. (2002a). The evolution of epistemology and concepts in an iterative-generative reflective practice: the importance of small differences. *American Journal of Community Psychology*, **30**, 493–510.

Bishop, B.J., Sonn, C.C., Fisher, A.F. & Drew, N.M. (2001). Community based community psychology: perspectives from Australia. In M. Seedat (ed.), *Community Psychology in Southern Africa*. Cape Town: Oxford University Press.

Blair, A. (1992). The role of primary prevention in mental health services: a review and critique. *Journal of Community and Applied Social Psychology*, **2**, 77–94.

Blakely, T., Atkinson, J. & O'Dea, D. (2003). No association of income inequality with adult mortality within New Zealand: a multi-level study of 1.4 million 25–64 year olds. *Journal of Epidemiology and Community Health*, **57**, 279–84.

Blakely, T., Collings, S.C.D. & Atkinson, J. (2003). Unemployment and suicide: evidence for a causal association. *Journal of Epidemiology and Community Health*, **57**, 594–600 (cited by Preti, 2003).

Blaxter, M. (1993). Why do the victims blame themselves? In A. Radley (ed.), *Worlds of Illness: Biographical and Cultural Perspectives on Health and Disease* (pp. 124–42). London: Routledge (cited by Blaxter, 1997).

Blaxter, M. (1997). Whose fault is it? People's own conceptions of the reasons for health inequalities. *Social Science and Medicine*, **51**, 747–56.

Bloom, B. (1968). The evaluation of primary prevention programs. In L. Roberts, N. Greenfield & M. Miller (eds), *Comprehensive Mental Health: the Challenge of Evaluation*. Madison: University of Wisconsin Press.

Boal, A. (1974). *The Theatre of the Oppressed*. London: Routledge.

Boardman, A.P., Hodgson, R.E., Lewis, M. & Allen, K. (1997). Social indicators and the prediction of psychiatric admission in different diagnostic groups. *British Journal of Psychiatry*, **171**, 457–62.

Boardman, J.D., Finch, B.K., Ellison, C.G., Williams, D.R. & Jackson, J.S. (2001). Neighborhood disadvantage, stress, and drug use among adults. *Journal of Health and Social Behavior*, **42**, 151–65.

Bobak, M., Pikhart, H., Hertzman, C., Rose, R. & Marmot, M. (1998). Socioeconomic factors, perceived control and self-reported health in Russia. A cross-sectional survey. *Social Science and Medicine*, **47**, 269–79.

Bobak, M., Pikhart, H., Rose, R., Hertzman, C. & Marmot, M. (2000). Socioeconomic factors, material inequalities, and perceived control in self rated health: cross-sectional data from seven post-communist countries. *Social Science and Medicine*, **51**, 1343–50.

Bolam, B., Murphy, S. & Gleeson, K. (2004). Individualisation and inequalities in health: a qualitative study of class identity and health. *Social Science and Medicine*, **59**, 1355–65.

Bolam, B. & Sixsmith, J. (2002). An exploratory study of the perceptions and experiences of further education amongst the young long-term unemployed. *Journal of Community and Applied Social Psychology*, **12**, 338–52.

Bond, L.A., Belenky, M.F. & Weinstock, J.S. (2000). The listening partners program: an initiative toward feminist community psychology in action. *American Journal of Community Psychology*, **28**, 697–730.

Bond, M.A. & Mulvey, A. (2000). A history of women and feminist perspectives in community psychology. *American Journal of Community Psychology*, **28**, 599–630.

Boneham, M.A. & Sixsmith, J.A. (2006). The voices of older women in a disadvantaged community: issues of health and social capital. *Social Science and Medicine*, **62**, 269–79.

Boothroyd, R.I., Fawcett, S.B. & Foster-Fishman, P.G. (2004). Community development: enhancing the knowledge base through participatory action research. In L.A. Jason, C.B. Keys, Y. Suarez-Balcazar, R.R. Taylor & M.I. Davis (eds), *Participatory Community Research: Theories and Methods in Action* (pp. 37–52). Washington, DC: American Psychological Association.

Borg, M.B. (2002). The Avalon Gardens Men's Association: a community health psychology case study. *Journal of Health Psychology*, **7**, 345–57.

Borg, V. & Kristensen, T.S. (2000). Social class and self-rated health: can the gradient by explained by differences in life style or work environment? *Social Science and Medicine*, **51**, 1019–30.

Borrell, C., Muntaner, C., Benach, J. & Artazcoz, L. (2004). Social class and self-reported health status among men and women: what is the role of work organisation, household material standards and household labour? *Social Science and Medicine*, **58**, 1869–87.

Bostock, J. (2003). Addressing poverty and exploitation: challenges for psychology. Paper presented at the UK Community and Critical Psychology conference, Birmingham, 11 September.

Bostock, J. & Diamond, B. (2005). The value of community psychology: critical reflections from the NHS. *Clinical Psychology Forum*, **153**, 22–5.

Bostock, J. & Freeman, J. (2003). 'No limits': doing participatory action research with young people in Northumberland. *Journal of Community and Applied Social Psychology*, **13**, 464–74.

Bostock, J. & Smail, D. (1999). Power, the environment and community psychology. *Journal of Community and Applied Social Psychology*, **9**, 75–8.

Bott, E. (1957). *Family and Social Network*. London: Tavistock (cited by Schuller *et al.*, 2000).

Bourdieu, P. (1985). The genesis of the concept of 'habitus' and 'field'. *Sociocriticism*, **2**, 11–24 (cited by Montenegro, 2002).

Bourdieu, P. (1986). The forms of capital. In J.G. Richardson (ed.) *The Handbook of Theory and Research for the Sociology of Education* (pp. 241–58). New York: Greenwood Press (cited by Baum & Ziersch, 2003).

Bourdieu, P. & Wacquant, L. (1992). *Invitation to Reflexive Sociology*. Chicago: University of Chicago Press (cited by Macinko & Starfield, 2001).

Bourke, E. (1998). Australia's first peoples: identity and population. In C. Bourke, E. Bourke & B. Edwards (eds), *Aboriginal Australia* (pp. 38–55). Queensland: University of Queensland Press.

Boyd, N.M. & Angelique, H. (2002). Rekindling the discourse: organization studies in community psychology. *Journal of Community Psychology*, 30, 325–48.

Boyle, M. (2003). The dangers of vulnerability. *Clinical Psychology*, **24**, 27–30.

Boyle, M.H. & Lipman, E.L. (2002). Do places matter: socioeconomic disadvantage and behavioral problems of children in Canada. *Journal of Consulting and Clinical Psychology*, **70**, 378–89.

Boyle, P.J., Gatrell, A.C. & Duke-Williams, O. (1999). The effect on morbidity of variability in deprivation and population stability in England and Wales: an investigation at small-area level. *Social Science and Medicine*, **49**, 791–9.

Boyle, P.J., Gatrell, A.C. & Duke-Williams, O. (2001). Do area-level population change, deprivation and variations in deprivation affect individual-level self-reported limiting long-term illness? *Social Science and Medicine*, **53**, 795–9.

Boynton, P.A. (2002). Life on the streets: the experiences of community researchers in a study of prostitution. *Journal of Community and Applied Social Psychology*, **12**, 1–12.

Bracken, P.J., Giller, J.E. & Summerfield, D. (1995). Psychological responses to war and atrocity: the limitations of current concepts. *Social Science and Medicine*, **40**, 1073–82.

Bradley, B.J., Deighton, J. & Selby, J. (2004). The 'Voices' project: capacity-building in community development for youth at risk. *Journal of Health Psychology*, **9**, 197–212.

Bradley, C. (1994). Why male violence against women is a development issue: reflections from Papua New Guinea. In M. Davies (ed.), *Women and Violence: Realities and Responses, Worldwide*. London: Zed Books (cited by Narayan *et al.*, 2000).

Bradshaw, J. & Chen, J.R. (1997). Poverty in the UK: a comparison with nineteen other countries. *Benefits*, **18**, 13–17 (cited by Graham, 2002).

Brandon, D., Wells, K., Francis, C. & Ramsay, E. (1980). *The Survivors: A Study of Homeless Young Newcomers to London and the Responses made to them*. London: Routledge & Kegan Paul.

Breeze, E., Jones, D.A., Wilkinson, P., Latif, A.M., Bulpitt, C.J. & Fletcher, A.E. (2004). Association of quality of life in old age in Britain with socioeconomic position: baseline data from a randomised controlled trial. *Journal of Epidemiology and Community Health*, **58**, 667–73.

Breeze, E., Sloggett, A. & Fletcher, A. (1999). Socioeconomic and demographic predictors of mortality and institutional residence among middle aged and older people: results from the longitudinal study. *Journal of Epidemiology and Community Health*, **53**, 765–74.

Bridget, J. & Lucille, S. (1996). Lesbian youth support information service (LYSIS): developing a distance support agency for young lesbians. *Journal of Community and Applied Social Psychology*, **6**, 355–64.

Broadhead, J. & Abas, M.A. (1998). Life events, difficulties and depression among women in an urban setting in Zimbabwe. *Psychological Medicine*, **28**, 29–38.

Brodsky, A.E. (1996). Resilient single mothers in risky neighborhoods: negative psychological sense of community. *Journal of Community Psychology*, **24**, 347–63.

Brodsky, A.E., Loomis, C. & Marx, C.M. (2002). Expanding the conceptualization of PSOC. In A.T. Fisher, C.C. Sonn & B.J. Bishop (eds), *Psychological Sense of Community: Research, Applications and Implications* (pp. 319–36). New York: Kluwer Academic/Plenum.

Brodsky, A.E., Senuta, K. R., Weiss, C.L.A., Marx, C.M., Loomis, C., Arteaga, S.S., Moore, H., Benhorin, R. & Castagnera-Fletcher, A. (2004). When one plus one equals three: the role of relationships and context in community psychology. *American Journal of Community Psychology*, **33**, 229–41.

Brody, G.H., Ge, X., Conger, R., Gibbons, F.X., McBride Murry, V., Gerrard, M. & Simons, R.L. (2001). The influence of neighborhood disadvantage, collective socialization, and parenting on African American children's affiliation with deviant peers. *Child Development*, **72**, 1231–46.

Brody, G.H., Ge, X., Kim, S.Y., McBride Murry, V., Simons, R.L., Gibbons, F.X., Garrard, M. & Conger, R.D. (2003). Neighborhood disadvantage moderates associations of parenting and older sibling problem attitudes and behavior with conduct disorders in African American children. *Journal of Consulting and Clinical Psychology*, **71**, 211–22.

Bronfenbrenner, U. (1979). *The Ecology of Human Development: Experiments by Nature and Design*. London: Harvard University Press.

Bronfenbrenner, U. (1988). Interacting systems in human development. Research paradigms: present and future. In N. Bolger, A. Caspi, G. Downey & M. Moorehouse (eds.), *Persons in Context: Developmental Processes* (pp. 25–49). Cambridge, UK: Cambridge University Press.

Brown, G.W. (1988). Casual paths, chains and strands. In M. Rutter (ed.), *Studies of Psychosocial Risk: The Power of Longitudinal Data*. Cambridge, UK: Cambridge University Press.

Brown, G.W. (1998). Loss and depressive disorders. In B.P. Dohrenwend (ed.), *Adversity, Stress, and Psychopathology* (pp. 358–70). Oxford, UK: Oxford University Press.

Brown, G.W. & Harris, T.O. (1978). *The Social Origins of Depression*. London: Tavistock.

Brown, G.W. & Harris, T.O. (1989). *Life Events and Illness*. New York: Guilford (cited by Hobfoll, 1998).

Brown, G.W. & Moran, P. (1997). Single mothers, poverty and depression. *Psychological Medicine*, **27**, 21–33.

Brown, G. W. & Prudo, R. (1981). Psychiatric disorder in a rural and an urban population: 1. Etiology of depression. *Psychological Medicine*, **11**, 581–99.

Browne, B.W. (2004). Imagine Chicago: a methodology for cultivating community. *Journal of Community and Applied Social Psychology*, **14**, 394–405.

Brugal, M.T., Domingo-Salvany, A., Maguire, A., Caylà, J.A., Villalbi, J.R. & Hartnoll, R. (1999). A small area analysis estimating the prevalence of addiction to opioids in Barcelona, 1993. *Journal of Epidemiology and Community Health*, **53**, 488–94.

Brugha, T.S. (2002). The end of the beginning: a requiem for the categorization of mental disorder. *Psychological Medicine*, **32**, 1149–54.

Bruner, J. (1990). *Acts of Meaning*. Cambridge, MA: Harvard University Press.

Brunner, E. & Marmot, M. (1999). Social organization, stress, and health. In M. Marmot & R.G. Wilkinson (eds), *Social Determinants of Health* (pp. 17–43). New York: Oxford University Press.

Buckner, J.C. (1988). The development of an instrument to measure neighborhood cohesion. *American Journal of Community Psychology*, **16**, 771–91 (cited by Chipuer *et al.*, 1999).

Buckridge, D.L., Mason, R., Robertson, A., Frank, J., Glazier, R., Purdon, L., Amrhein, C.G., Chaudhuri, N., Fuller-Thomson, E., Gozdyra, P., Hulchanski,D., Moldofsky, B., Thompson, M. & Wright, R. (2002). Making health data maps: a case study of a community/university research collaboration. *Social Science and Medicine*, **55**, 1189–206.

Bull, P. (2006). Shifting patterns of social identity in Northern Ireland. *The Psychologist*, **19**, 40–3.

Burden, J. (1998). Health: a holistic approach. In C. Bourke, E. Bourke & B. Edwards (eds), *Aboriginal Australia* (pp. 189–218). Queensland: University of Queensland Press.

Burkitt, I. (1991). *Social Selves: Theories of the Social Formation of Personality*. London: Sage.

Burnett, J. (1994). *Idle Hands: The Experiences of Unemployment, 1790–1990*. London: Routledge.

Burrell, G. & Morgan, G. (1979). *Sociological Paradigms and Organisational Analysis*. London: Gower (cited by Holland, 1988).

Burton, M. (1983). Understanding mental health services: theory and practice. *Critical Social Policy*, **7**, 54–74 (cited by Kagan & Burton, 2000).

Burton, M. (2004). Radical psychology networks: a review and guide. *Journal of Community and Applied Social Psychology*, **14**, 119–30.

Burton, M. & Kagan, C. (2005). Liberation social psychology: learning from Latin America. *Journal of Community and Applied Social Psychology*, **15**, 63–78.

Butler, J. (1990). *Gender Trouble: Feminism and the Subversion of Identity*. London: Routledge (cited by Hepburn, 2003).

Bybee, D.I. & Sullivan, C.M. (2002). The process through which an advocacy intervention resulted in positive change for battered women over time. *American Journal of Community Psychology*, **30**, 103–32.

Bynner, J. & Parsons, S. (1997). Getting on with qualifications. In J. Bynner, E. Ferri & P. Shepherd (eds), *Twenty-Something in the 1990s* (pp.11–29). Aldershot: Aldgate (cited by Graham, 2002).

Cable, S. (1988). Attributional processes and alienation: a typology of worker responses to unequal power relationships. *Political Psychology*, **9**, 109–27 (cited by Martín-Baró, 1994).

Calnan, M. (1987). *Health and Illness: The Lay Perspective*. London: Tavistock (cited by Blaxter, 1997).

Calsyn, R.J. (2003). A modified ESID approach to studying mental illness and homelessness. *American Journal of Community Psychology*, **32**, 319–31.

Calvino, M. (1998). Reflections on community studies. *Journal of Community Psychology*, **26**, 253–9.

Campbell, C. (1999). *Social Capital and Health*. London: Health Education Authority.

Campbell, C. & Gillies, P. (2001). Conceptualizing 'social capital' for health promotion in small local communities: a micro-qualitative study. *Journal of Community and Applied Social Psychology*, **11**, 329–46.

Campbell, C. & Jovchelovitch, S. (2000). Health, community and development: towards a social psychology of participation. *Journal of Community and Applied Social Psychology*, **10**, 255–70.

Campbell, C. & McLean, C. (2002a). Ethnic identities, social capital and health inequalities: factors shaping African-Caribbean participation in local community networks in the UK. *Social Science and Medicine*, **55**, 643–57.

Campbell, C. & McLean, C. (2002b). Representations of ethnicity in people's accounts of local community participation in a multi-ethnic community in England. *Journal of Community and Applied Social Psychology*, **12**, 13–29.

Campbell, C. & McLean, C. (2003). Social capital, local community participation and the construction of Pakistani identities in England: implications for health inequalities policies. *Journal of Health Psychology*, **8**, 247–62.

Campbell, C. & Murray, M. (2004). Community health psychology: promoting analysis and action for social change. *Journal of Health Psychology*, **9**, 187–95.

Campbell, R. & Ahrens, C.E. (1998). Innovative community services for rape victims: an application of multiple case study methodology. *American Journal of Community Psychology*, **26**, 537–71.

Campbell, R. & Wasco, S.M. (2000). Feminist approaches to social science: epistemological and methodological tenets. *American Journal of Community Psychology*, **28**, 773–91.

Cardozo, B.L., Talley, L., Burton, A. & Crawford, C. (2004). Karenni refugees living in Thai-Burmese border camps: traumatic experiences, mental health outcomes, and social functioning. *Social Science and Medicine*, **58**, 2637–44.

Carlson, P. (2000). Educational differences in self-rated health during the Russian transition. Evidence from Taganrog 1993–1994. *Social Science and Medicine*, **51**, 1363–74.

Carlson, P. (2005). Relatively poor, absolutely ill? A study of regional income inequality in Russia and its possible health consequences. *Journal of Epidemiology and Community Health*, **59**, 389–94.

Carlson, P. (2004). The European health divide: a matter of financial or social capital? *Social Science and Medicine*, **59**, 1985–92.

Carpiano, R.M. (2006). Toward a neighborhood resource-based theory of social capital for health: can Bourdieu and sociology help? *Social Science and Medicine*, **62**, 165–75.

Carrick, R., Mitchell, A. & Lloyd, K. (2001). User involvement in research: power and compromise. *Journal of Community and Applied Social Psychology*, **11**, 217–25.

Carroll, D., Davey Smith, G. & Bennett, P. (1996). Some observations on health and socio-economic status. *Journal of Health Psychology*, **1**, 23–39.

Cass, A., Cunningham, J., Snelling, P., Wang, Z. & Hoy, W. (2004). Exploring the pathways leading from disadvantage to end-stage renal disease for indigenous Australians. *Social Science and Medicine*, **58**, 767–85.

Catalano, R. (1998). An epidemiological perspective: a review of *Unhealthy Societies* by R.G. Wilkinson. *Journal of Community and Applied Social Psychology*, **8**, 165–8.

Cattell, V. (2001). Poor people, poor places, and poor health: the mediating role of social networks and social capital. *Social Science and Medicine*, **52**, 1501–16.

Catty, J., Burns, T., Knapp, M., Watt, H., Wright, C., Henderson, J. & Healey, A. (2002). Home treatment for mental health problems: a systematic review. *Psychological Medicine*, **32**, 383–401.

Chaix, B., Merlo, J. & Chauvin, P. (2005). Comparison of a spatial approach with the multilevel approach for investigating place effects on health: the example of healthcare utilisation in France. *Journal of Epidemiology and Community Health*, **59**, 517–26.

Chandola, T., Bartley, M., Wiggins, R. & Schofield, P. (2003). Social inequalities in health by individual and household measures of social position in a cohort of healthy people. *Journal of Epidemiology and Community Health*, **57**, 56–62.

Chandola, T., Kupeer, H., Singh-Manoux, A., Bartley, M. & Marmot, M. (2004). The effect of control at home on CHD events in the Whitehall II study: gender differences in psychosocial domestic pathways to social inequalities in CHD. *Social Science and Medicine*, **58**, 1501–9.

Chavis, D.M. (1993). A future for community psychology practice. *American Journal of Community Psychology*, **21**, 171–83.

Chavis, D.M., Florin, P., Rich, R.C., Wandersman, A. & Perkins, D.D. (1987). *The Role of Block Associations in Crime Control and Community Development: The Block Booster Project* (Final report to Ford Foundation). New York: Citizens Committee for New York City (cited by Perkins & Long, 2002).

Chavis, D.M. & Pretty, G.M.H. (1999). Sense of community: advances in measurement and application. *Journal of Community Psychology*, **27**, 635–42.

Chesir-Teran, D. (2003). Conceptualizing and assessing heterosexism in high schools: a setting-level approach. *American Journal of Community Psychology*, **31**, 267–79.

Chinman, M., Kloos, B., O'Connell, M. & Davidson, L. (2002). Service providers' views of psychiatric mutual support groups. *Journal of Community Psychology*, **30**, 349–66.

Chipuer, H.M. & Pretty, G.H. (1999). A review of the sense of community index: current uses, factor structure, reliability and further development. *Journal of Community Psychology*, **27**, 643–58.

Chipuer, H.M., Pretty, G.H., Delorey, E., Miller, M., Powers, T., Rumstein, O., Barnes, A., Cordasic, N. & Laurent, K. (1999). The neighbourhood youth inventory: development and validation. *Journal of Community and Applied Social Psychology*, **9**, 355–68.

Cho, H.J., Song, Y.M., Davey Smith, G. & Ebrahim, S. (2004). Trends in socio-economic differentials in cigarette smoking behaviour between 1990 and 1998: a large prospective study in Korean men. *Public Health*, **118**, 553–8.

Church, K. (1995). *Forbidden Narratives: Critical Autobiography as Social Science*. Amsterdam: Gordon & Breach (cited by Nelson *et al.*, 1998).

Church, K. (1996). Beyond 'bad manners': the power relations of 'consumer participation' in Ontario's community mental health system. *Canadian Journal of Community Mental Health*, **15**, 27–44 (cited by Nelson *et al.*, 1998).

Clapham, D. (2003). Pathways approaches to homelessness research. *Journal of Community and Applied Social Psychology*, **13**, 119–27.

Clifford, C. & Orford, J. (2006). The experience of social power in the lives of trans people. In V. Clarke & E. Peel (eds), *Out in Psychology: Lesbian, Gay, Bisexual and Trans Perspectives* (pp. 195–216). Chichester, UK: John Wiley & Sons, Ltd.

Coakes, S.J. & Bishop, B.J. (2002). Defining the nature of participating in rural Australian communities: a qualitative approach. *Journal of Community Psychology*, **30**, 635–46.

Cobb, S. (1976). Social support as a moderator of life stress. *Psychosomatic Medicine*, **38**, 300–14.

Coburn, D. (2000). Income inequality, social cohesion and the health status of populations: the role of neo-liberalism. *Social Science and Medicine*, **51**, 135–46.

Coburn, D. (2004). Beyond the income inequality hypothesis: class, neo-liberalism, and health inequalities. *Social Science and Medicine*, **58**, 41–56.

Cochrane, R. (1983). *The Social Creation of Mental Illness*. London: Longman.

Cockerham, W.C., Hattori, H. & Yamori, Y. (2000). The social gradient in life expectancy: the contrary case of Okinawa in Japan. *Social Science and Medicine*, **51**, 115–22.

Coleman, J. (1988). Social capital in the creation of human capital. *American Journal of Sociology*, **94** (Suppl. 1), S95–S120 (cited by Kar *et al.*, 1999).

Coleman, J. (1990). *The Foundation of Social Theory*, Cambridge, UK: Belknap (cited by Oakes and Rossi, 2003).

Colic-Peisker, V. & Walker, I. (2003). Human capital, acculturation and social identity: Bosnian refugees in Australia. *Journal of Community and Applied Social Psychology*, **13**, 337–60.

Colombo, M., Mosso, C. & De Piccoli, N. (2001). Sense of community and participation in urban contexts. *Journal of Community and Applied Social Psychology*, **11**, 457–64.

Comas-Díaz, L., Lykes, M.B. & Alarcón, R.D. (1998). Ethnic conflict and the psychology of liberation in Guatemala, Peru, and Puerto Rico. *American Psychologist*, **53**, 778–92.

Condor, S. (2006). Public prejudice as collaborative accomplishment: towards a dialogic social psychology of racism. *Journal of Community and Applied Social Psychology*, **16**, 1–18.

Conger, R.D. & Elder, G.H. (1994). *Families in Troubled Times: Adapting to Change in Rural America*. New York: Aldine de Gruyter (cited by Barrera *et al.*, 2001).

Cook, R., Roehl, J., Oros, C. & Trudeau, J. (1994). Conceptual and methodological issues in the evaluation of community-based substance abuse prevention coalitions: Lessons learned from the national evaluation of the Community Partnership Program. *Journal of Community Psychology*, Special Issue, 155–69.

Cook, T. & Campbell, D. (1979). *Quasi-Experimentation: Design and Analysis Issues for Field Settings*. Chicago: Rand McNally.

Cornish, F. (2004). Making 'context' concrete: a dialogical approach to the society-health relation. *Journal of Health Psychology*, **9**, 281–94.

Coulthard, M., Farrell, M., Singleton, N. & Meltzer (2002). *Tobacco, Alcohol and Drug Use, and Mental Health*. Office for National Statistics, London: The Stationery Office.

Cowen., E.L. (1982). Help is where you find it. *American Psychologist*, **37**, 385–95.

Cowen, E.L. (2000). Now that we all know that primary prevention in mental health is great, what is it? *Journal of Community Psychology*, **28**, 5–16.

Cowen, E.L., Hightower, A.D., Pedro-Carroll, J.L., Work, W.C., Wyman, P.A. & Haffey, W.G. (1996). *School-based Prevention for Children at Risk: The Primary Mental Health Project*. Washington, DC: American Psychological Association (cited by Durlak & Wells, 1998).

Coyle, A. & Kitzinger, C. (eds), *Lesbian and Gay Psychology: New Perspectives*. Oxford, UK: Blackwell.

Coyle, A. & Wilkinson, S. (2002). Social psychological perspectives on lesbian and gay issues in Europe: the state of the art. *Journal of Community and Applied Social Psychology*, **12**, 147–52.

Craps, M., Dewulf, A., Mancero, M., Santos, E. & Bouwen, R. (2004). Constructing common ground and re-creating differences between professional and indigenous communities in the Andes. *Journal of Community and Applied Social Psychology*, **14**, 378–93.

Crespo, I., Pallí, C. & Lalueza, J.L. (2002). Moving communities: a process of negotiation with a Gypsy minority for empowerment. *Community, Work and Family*, **5**, 49–66.

Crossley, M.L. (2001). The 'Armistead' project: an exploration of gay men, sexual practices, community health promotion and issues of empowerment. *Journal of Community and Applied Social Psychology*, **11**, 111–23.

Curtis, L.J., Dooley, M.D. & Phipps, S.A. (2004). Child well-being and neighbourhood quality: evidence from the Canadian National Longitudinal Survey of Children and Youth. *Social Science and Medicine*, **58**, 1917–27.

Curtis, S., Southall, H., Congdon, P. & Dodgeon, B. (2004). Area effects on health variation over the life-course: analysis of the longitudinal study sample in England using new data on areas of residence in childhood. *Social Science and Medicine*, **58**, 57–74.

Dalgard, O.S. (1986). Living conditions, social network and mental health. In S.O. Isacsson & L. Janzon (eds), *Social Support, Health and Disease* (pp. 71–87). Stockholm: Almquist and Wiksell (cited by Dalgard & Tambs, 1997).

Dalgard, O.S. & Tambs, K. (1997). Urban environment and mental health. *British Journal of Psychiatry*, **171**, 530–6.

Dalstra, J.A.A., Kunst, A.E., Geurts, J.J.M., Frenken, F.J.M. & Mackenbach, J.P. (2002). Trends in socioeconomic health inequalities in the Netherlands, 1981–1999. *Journal of Epidemiology and Community Health*, **56**, 927–34.

Dalton, J.H., Elias, M.J. & Wandersman, A. (2001). *Community Psychology: Linking Individuals and Communities*. Belmont, CA: Wadsworth.

D'Augelli, A.R. (1989). The development of a helping community for lesbians and gay men: a case study in community psychology. *Journal of Community Psychology*, **17**, 18–29 (cited by Chesir-Teran, 2003).

D'Augelli, A.R. (2003). Coming out in community psychology: personal narrative and disciplinary change. *American Journal of Community Psychology*, **31**, 343–54.

Davey Smith, G., Bartley, M. & Blane, D. (1990). The Black report on socioeconomic inequalities in health 10 years on. *British Medical Journal*, **301**, 373–7.

Davey Smith, G., Dorling, D., Mitchell, R. & Shaw, M. (2002). Health inequalities in Britain: continuing increases up to the end of the 20th century. *Journal of Epidemiology and Community Health*, **56**, 434–5.

Davey Smith, G., Hart, C., Hole, D., MacKinnon, P., Gillis, C., Watt, G., Blane, D. & Hawthorne, V. (1998). Education and occupational social class: which is the more important indicator of mortality risk? *Journal of Epidemiology and Community Health*, **52**, 153–60.

Davey Smith, G., Hart, C., Blane, D., Gillis, C. & Hawthorne, V. (1997). Lifetime socioeconomic position and mortality: prospective observational study. *British Medical Journal*, **314**, 547–52 (cited by Hallqvist *et al.*, 2004).

Davey Smith G., Hart, C., Watt, G., Hole, D. & Hawthorne, V. (1998). Individual social class, area-based deprivation, cardiovascular disease risk factors, and mortality: the Renfrew and Paisley study. *Journal of Epidemiology and Community Health*, **52**, 399–405.

Davey Smith, G., Shipley, M.J. & Rose, G. (1990). The magnitude and causes of socioeconomic differentials in mortality: further evidence from the Whitehall study. *Journal of Epidemiology and Community Health*, **44**, 265–70.

Davey Smith, G., Whitley, E., Dorling, D. & Gunnell, D. (2001). Area based measures of social and economic circumstances: cause specific mortality patterns depend on the choice of index. *Journal of Epidemiology and Community Health*, **55**, 149–50.

Davidson, L., Shahar, G., Chinman, M.J. & Stayner, D.A. (2004). Supported socialization for people with psychiatric disabilities: lesson from a randomized controlled trial. *Journal of Community Psychology*, **32**, 453–77.

Davidson, R., Kitzinger, J. & Hunt, K. (2006). The wealthy get healthy, the poor get poorly? Lay perceptions of health inequalities. *Social Science and Medicine*, **62**, 2171–82.

Davidson, W.B. & Cotter, P.R. (1986). Measurement of sense of community within the sphere of city. *Journal of Applied Social Psychology*, **16**, 608–19 (cited by Prezza & Costantini, 1998).

Day, C., Kane, R.T. & Roberts, C. (2003). The prevention of depressive symptoms in rural Australian women. *Journal of Community and Applied Social Psychology*, **13**, 1–14.

Day, G. (2001). *Class*. London: Routledge.

Deaux, K. (2000). Surveying the landscape of immigration: social psychological perspectives. *Journal of Community and Applied Social Psychology*, **10**, 421–31.

Delanty, G. (2003). *Community*. London: Routledge.

Denzin, N.K. (1989). *Interpretive Interactionism*. Newbury Park, CA: Sage (cited by Stein & Mankowski, 2004).

Department of Health (1999). *Saving Lives: Our Healthier Nation*. London: HMSO.

Deutsch, M. (1992). Kurt Lewin: the tough-minded and tender-hearted scientist. *Journal of Social Issues*, **2**, 31–43.

De Vogli, R., Mistry, R., Gnesotto, R. & Cornia, G.A. (2005). Has the relation between income inequality and life expectancy disappeared? Evidence from Italy and top industrialised countries. *Journal of Epidemiology and Community Health*, **59**, 158–62.

Dewulf, A., Craps, M. & Dercon, G. (2004). How issues get framed and reframed when different communities meet: a multi-level analysis of a collaborative soil conservation initiative in the Ecuadorian Andes. *Journal of Community and Applied Social Psychology*, **14**, 177–92.

Díaz-Guerrero, R. (1990). *Psicología del Mexicano: Descubrimiento de la Etnopsicología*. Mexico: Editorial Trillas.

Dicken, C., Bryson, R. & Kass, N. (1977). Companionship therapy: a replication in experimental community psychology. *Journal of Consulting and Clinical Psychology*, **4**, 637–46.

Diez Roux, A.V. (2002). A glossary for multilevel analysis. *Journal of Epidemiology and Community Health*, **56**, 588–94.

Diez Roux, A.V. (2004). Estimating neighbourhood health effects: the challenges of causal inference in a complex world. *Social Science and Medicine*, **58**, 1953–60.

Diez-Roux, A.V., Nieto, F.J., Muntaner, C., Tyroler, H.A., Comstock, G.W., Shahar, E., Cooper, L.S., Watson, R.L. & Szklo, M. (1997). Neighborhood environments and coronary heart disease: a multilevel analysis. *American Journal of Epidemiology*, **146**, 48–63 (cited by Macintyre et al., 2002).

Dinham, A. (2005). Empowered or over-powered? The real experiences of local participation in the UK's New Deal for Communities. *Community Development Journal*, **40**, 301–12.

Dohrenwend, B.P., Levav, I., Shrout, P.E. et al. (1992). Socioeconomic status and psychiatric disorders: the causation selection issue. *Science*, **255**, 946–52 (cited by Wohlfarth & van den Brink, 1998).

Doise, W. (1986, originally in French, 1982). *Levels of Explanation in Social Psychology*. Cambridge, UK: Cambridge University Press.

Dokecki, P. (1992). On knowing the community of caring persons: a methodological basis for the reflective generative practice of community psychology. *Journal of Community Psychology*, **20**, 26–35 (cited by Bishop et al., 2002a).

Donohoe, M. (2003). Causes and health consequences of environmental degradation and social injustice. *Social Science and Medicine*, **56**, 573–87.

Dooley, D. (2003). Unemployment, underemployment, and mental health: conceptualizing employment status as a continuum. *American Journal of Community Psychology*, **32**, 9–20.

Dooley, D. & Catalano, R. (1988). Recent research on the psychological effects of unemployment. *Journal of Social Issues*, **44**, 1–12.

Dressler, W.W., Ribeiro, R.P., Balieiro, M.C., Oths, K.S. & Dos Santos, J.E. (2004). Eating, drinking and being depressed: the social, cultural and psychological context of alcohol consumption and nutrition in a Brazilian community. *Social Science and Medicine*, **59**, 709–20.

Drew, N.M., Bishop, B.J. & Syme, G. (2002). Justice and local community change: towards a substantive theory of justice. *Journal of Community Psychology*, **30**, 623–34.

Drewery, W. (1998). Unemployment: what kind of problem is it? *Journal of Community and Applied Social Psychology*, **8**, 101–18.

Drewery, W. (2004). Conferencing in schools: punishment, restorative justice, and the productive importance of the process of conversation. *Journal of Community and Applied Social Psychology*, **14**, 332–44.

Droomers, M., Schrijvers, C.T.M. & Mackenbach, J.P. (2002). Why do lower educated people continue smoking? Explanations from the longitudinal GLOBE study. *Health Psychology*, **21**, 263–72.

Drukker, M., Kaplan, C.D., Feron, F.J.M. *et al.* (2003). Children's health-related quality of life, neighbourhood socio-economic deprivation and social capital: a contextual analysis. *Social Science and Medicine*, **57**, 825–41.

Dudgeon, P., Mallard, J., Oxenham, D. & Fielder, J. (2002). Contemporary Aboriginal perceptions of community. In A.T. Fisher, C.C. Sonn & B.J. Bishop (eds), *Psychological Sense of Community* (pp. 247–67). New York: Kluwer/Plenum.

Duncan, T.E., Duncan, S.C., Okut, H., Strycker, L.A. & Hix-Small, H. (2003). A multilevel contextual model of neighborhood collective efficacy. *American Journal of Community Psychology*, **32**, 245–52.

Dunham, P.J., Hurshman, A., Litwin, E., Gusella, J. & Ellsworth, C. (1998). Computer-mediated social support: single young mothers as a model system. *American Journal of Community Psychology*, **26**, 281–306.

Dunn, J., Steginga, S.K., Occhipinti, S. & Wilson, K. (1999). Evaluation of a peer support program for women with breast cancer – lessons for practitioners. *Journal of Community and Applied Social Psychology*, **9**, 13–22.

Durkheim, E. (1933). *The Division of Labor in Society*. New York: Macmillan (cited by Bar-Tal, 2000).

Durlak, J.A. (1979). Comparative effectiveness of para-professional and professional helpers. *Psychological Bulletin*, **86**, 80–92.

Durlak, J.A. (1995). *School-Based Prevention Programs for Children and Adolescents*. Thousand Oaks, CA: Sage (cited by Cowen, 2000).

Durlak, J.A. (1997). *Successful Prevention Programs for Children and Adolescents*. New York: Plenum (cited by Cowen, 2000).

Durlak, J.A. & Wells, A.M. (1997). Primary prevention mental health programs for children and adolescents: a meta-analytic review. *American Journal of Community Psychology*, **25**, 115–52.

Durlak, J.A. & Wells, A.M. (1998). Evaluation of indicated preventive intervention (secondary prevention) mental health programs for children and adolescents. *American Journal of Community Psychology*, **26**, 775–802.

Eachus, J., Chan, P., Pearson, N., Propper, C. & Davey Smith, G. (1999). An additional dimension to health inequalities: disease severity and socioeconomic position. *Journal of Epidemiology and Community Health*, **53**, 603–11.

Edwards, R. (1993). *Mature Women Students: Separating or Connecting Family and Education*. London: Taylor & Francis (cited by Johnson & Robson, 1999).

Einarsen, S., Raknes, B.I. & Matthiesen, S.B. (1994). Bullying and harassment at work and their relationships to work environment quality: an exploratory study. *European Work and Organizational Psychologist*, **4**, 381–401.

Eiser, C. (1987). Chronic disease in childhood. In J. Orford (ed.), *Coping with Disorder in the Family* (pp. 217–37). London: Croom Helm.

Elder, G.H. & Caspi, A. (1988). Economic stress in lives: developmental perspectives. *Journal of Social Issues*, **44**, 25–45.

Elder, G.H., Eccles, J.S., Ardelt, M. & Lord, S. (1995). Inner-city parents under economic pressure: perspectives on the strategies of parenting. *Journal of Marriage and the Family*, **57**, 771–84.

Elias, M.J. (1994). Capturing excellence in applied settings: a participant conceptualizer and praxis explicator role for community psychologists. *American Journal of Community Psychology*, **22**, 293–318.

Ellen, I.G., Mijanovich, T. & Dillman, K.N. (2001). Neighborhood effects on health: exploring the links and assessing the evidence. *Journal of Urban Affairs*, **23**, 391–408.

Ellen, I.G. & Turner, M.A. (1997). Does neighborhood matter? Assessing recent evidence. *Housing Policy Debate*, **8**, 833–66.

Ellis, S.J. (2002). Student support for lesbian and gay human rights: findings from a large-scale questionnaire study. In A. Coyle & C. Kitzinger (eds), *Lesbian and Gay Psychology: New Perspectives* (pp. 239–54). Oxford: Blackwell.

Ellis, S.J. & Kitzinger, C. (2002). Denying equality: an analysis of arguments against lowering the age of consent for sex between men. *Journal of Community and Applied Social Psychology*, **12**, 167–80.

Ellison, G.T.H. (2002). Letting the Gini out of the bottle? Challenges facing the relative income hypothesis. *Social Science and Medicine*, **54**, 561–76.

Emshoff, J., Blakely, C., Gray, D., Jakes, S., Brounstein, P., Coulter, J. & Gardner, S. (2003). An ESID case study at the federal level. *American Journal of Community Psychology*, **32**, 345–57.

Emslie, C., Hunt, K. & Macintyre, S. (1999). Gender differences in minor morbidity among full time employees of a British university. *Journal of Epidemiology and Community Health*, **53**, 465–75.

Eng, E., Parker, E. & Harlan, C. (1997). Lay health advisor intervention strategies: a continuum from natural helping to paraprofessional helping. *Health Education and Behavior*, **24**, 413–17.

Erikson, R. & Goldthorpe, J.H. (1992). *The Constant Flux*. Oxford, UK: Clarendon (cited by Bartley, 1999).

Etzioni, A. (1997). *The New Golden Rule: Community and Morality in a Democratic Society*. London: Profile Books.

Evans, G.W., Wells, N.M., Chan, H.E. & Saltzman, H. (2000). Housing quality and mental health. *Journal of Consulting and Clinical Psychology*, **68**, 526–30.

Ewart, C.K. & Suchday, S. (2002). Discovering how urban poverty and violence affect health: development and validation of a neighborhood stress index. *Health Psychology*, **21**, 254–62.

Fairweather, G.W., Sanders, D.H., Cressler, D.L. & Maynard, H. (1969). *Community Life for the Mentally Ill: an Alternative to Institutional Care*. Chicago: Aldine.

Fairweather, G.W. (1972). *Social Change: The Challenge to Survival*. New Jersey: General Learning Press (cited by Seidman, 2003).

Fairweather, G.W. & Tornatzky, L.G. (1977). *Experimental Methods of Social Policy Research*. Elsford, NY: Pergamon Press.

Falk, R. (1992). *Explorations at the Edge of Time: The Proposals for World Order*. Philadelphia, PN: Temple University Press (cited by Pilisuk *et al.*, 1996).

Fals Borda (2001). Participatory (action) research in social theory: origins and challenges. In P. Reason & H. Bradbury (eds.), *Handbook of Action Research: Participative Inquiry and Practice* (pp. 27–37). London: Sage.

Fan, A.P. & Eaton, W.W. (2001). Longitudinal study assessing the joint effects of socio-economic status and birth risks on adult emotional and nervous conditions. *British Journal of Psychiatry*, **178**, 78–83.

Fanon, F. (1986). *Los Condenados de la Tierra*. Mexico: Fondo de Cultura Económica (cited by Varas-Díaz & Serrano-García, 2003).

Faris, R. & Dunham, W. (1939). *Mental Disorders in Urban Areas*. Chicago: University of Chicago Press.

Farrell, S.J., Aubry, T. & Coulombe, D. (2004). Neighborhoods and neighbors: do they contribute to personal well-being? *Journal of Community Psychology*, **32**, 9–25.

Farrington, A. & Robinson, W.P. (1999). Homelessness and strategies of identity maintenance: a participant observation study. *Journal of Community and Applied Social Psychology*, **9**, 175–94.

Faust, D. & Zlotnick, C. (1995). Another dodo bird verdict? Revisiting the comparative effectiveness of professional and paraprofessional therapists. *Clinical Psychology and Psychotherapy*, **2**, 157–67.

Fawcett, S.B., Boothroyd, R., Schultz, J.A., Francisco, V.T., Carson, V. & Bremby, R. (2003). Building capacity for participatory evaluation within community initiatives. In Y. Suarez-Balcazar & G.W. Harper (eds), *Empowerment and Participatory Evaluation of Community Interventions: Multiple Benefits* (pp. 21–36). New York: Haworth Press.

Fawcett, S., White, G., Balcazar, F.E., Suarez-Balcazar, Y., Mathews, R.M., Paine-Andrews, A., Seekins, T. & Smith, J.F. (1994). A contextual-behavioral model of empowerment: case studies involving people with physical disabilities. *American Journal of Community Psychology*, **22**, 471–96 (cited by Foster-Fishman *et al.*, 1998).

Fee, E. & Porter, D. (1991). Public health, preventive medicine, and professionalization: Britain and the United States in the nineteenth century. In E. Fee & R.M. Acheson (eds), *A History of Education and Public Health: Health that Mocks the Doctors' Rules* (pp. 15–43). Oxford, UK: Oxford University Press.

Felton, B.J. & Shinn, M. (1992). Social integration and social support: moving 'social support' beyond the individual level. *Journal of Community Psychology*, **20**, 103–15.

Felner, R.D., Brand, S., Adan, A.M., Mulhall, P.F., Flowers, N., Sartan, B. *et al.* (1993). Restructuring the ecology of the school as an approach to prevention during school transitions: longitudinal follow-ups and extensions of the School Transition Environmental Project (STEP). *Prevention in Human Services*, **10**, 103–36 (cited by Tseng *et al.*, 2002).

Fenner, J. (1999). Our way: women's action for mental health (Nottingham). *Journal of Community and Applied Social Psychology*, **9**, 79–91.

Fergusson, D.M., Horwood, L.J. & Woodward, L.J. (2001). Unemployment and psychosocial adjustment in young adults: causation or selection? *Social Science and Medicine*, **53**, 305–20.

Fergusson, D.M., Horwood, L.J., Boden, J.M. & Jenkin, G. (2007). Childhood social disadvantage and smoking in adulthood: results of a 25-year longitudinal study. *Addiction*, **102**, 475–82.

Fernández, M.I., Bowen, G.S., Gay, C.L., Mattson, T.R., Bital, E. & Kelly, J.A. (2003). HIV, sex and social change: applying ESID principles to HIV prevention research. *American Journal of Community Psychology*, **32**, 333–44.

Ferrie, J.E., Shipley, M.J., Stansfeld, S.A. & Marmot, M.G. (2002a). Effects of chronic job insecurity and change in job security on self reported health, minor psychiatric morbidity, physiological measures, and health related behaviours in British civil servants: the Whitehall II study. *Journal of Epidemiology and Community Health*, **56**, 450–4.

Ferrie, J.E., Shipley, M.J., Davey Smith, G., Stansfeld, S.A. & Marmot, M.G. (2002b). Change in health inequalities among British civil servants: the Whitehall II study. *Journal of Epidemiology and Community Health*, **56**, 922–6.

Feyerabend, P. (1975). *Against Method: Outline of an Anarchist Theory of Knowledge*. London: New Left Books (cited by Tebes, 2005).

Finn, M. & Dell, P. (1999). Practices of body management: transgenderism and embodiment. *Journal of Community and Applied Social Psychology*, **9**, 463–76.

Fisher, A.T. & Sonn, C.C. (2002). Psychological sense of community in Australia and the challenges of change. *Journal of Community Psychology*, **30**, 597–609.

Fitzpatrick S. (2000). *Young Homeless People*. London: Macmillan.

Flaspohler, P., Wandersman, A., Keener, D., North Maxwell, K., Ace, A., Andrews, A. & Holmes, B. (2003). Promoting program success and fulfilling accountability requirements in a statewide community-based initiative: challenges, progress, and lessons learned. In Y. Suarez-Balcazar & G.W. Harper (eds), *Empowerment and Participatory Evaluation of Community Interventions: Multiple Benefits* (pp. 37–52). New York: Haworth Press.

Flewelling, R.L., Austin, D., Hale, K., LaPlante, M., Liebig, M., Piasecki, L. & Uerz, L. (2005). Implementing research-based substance abuse prevention in communities: effects of a coalition-based prevention initiative in Vermont. *Journal of Community Psychology*, **33**, 333–53.

Fondacaro, M.R. & Weinberg, D. (2002). Concepts of social justice in community psychology: toward a social ecological epistemology. *American Journal of Community Psychology*, **30**, 473–92.

Fontana, A. & Rosenheck, R. (1993). A causal model of the etiology of war-related PTSD. *Journal of Traumatic Stress*, **6**, 475–500.

Forbes, A. & Wainwright, S.P. (2001). On the methodological, theoretical and philosophical context of health inequalities research: a critique. *Social Science and Medicine*, **53**, 801–16.

Foster, D. (1987). *Detention and Torture in South Africa: Psychological, Legal, and Historical Studies*. Cape Town: David Philip (cited by Hayes, 2000).

Foster, D. (2004). Liberation psychology. In D. Hook (ed.), *Critical Psychology* (pp. 559–602). Cape Town, South Africa: University of Cape Town Press.

Foster-Fishman, P.G., Berkowitz, S.L., Lonnsbury, D.W., Jacobson, S. & Allen, N.A. (2001a). Building collaborative capacity in community coalitions: a review and integrative framework, *American Journal of Community Psychology*, **29**, 241–61.

Foster-Fishman, P.G., Salem, D.A., Chibnall, S., Legler, R. & Yapchai, C. (1998). Empirical support for the critical assumptions of empowerment theory. *American Journal of Community Psychology*, **26**, 507–36.

Foster-Fishman, P.G., Salem, D.A., Allen, N.A. & Fahrbach, K. (2001b). Facilitating interorganizational collaboration: the contributions of interorganizational alliances. *American Journal of Community Psychology*, **29**, 875–905.

Foucault, M. (1977). *Discipline and Punish: The Birth of the Prison*. Sheridan, A. (Trans.). London: Penguin (cited by Hepburn, 2003).

Foucault, M. (1979). *The History of Sexuality, Volume 1: An Introduction*. Harmondsworth, UK: Penguin (cited by Hepburn, 2003).

Fox, A. (1974). *Beyond Contract: Work Power and Trust Relations*. London: Faber (cited by Schuller *et al.*, 2000).

Fox, D. (2003). Expanding critical psychology's challenge for health and justice. *Journal of Health Psychology*, **8**, 219–21.

Francescato, D., Gelli, B.R., Mannarini, T. & Taurino, A. (2004). Community development: action-research through community profiles. In A. Sánchez-Vidal, A. Zambiano Constanzo & M. Palacín (eds), *European Community Psychology: Community, Power, Ethics and Values* (pp. 247–61). Barcelona: Publicacions Universitat de Barcelona.

Francescato, D. & Tomai, M. (2001). Community psychology: should there be a European perspective. *Journal of Community and Applied Social Psychology*, **11**, 371–80.

Francescato, D., Tomai, M. & Ghirelli, G. (2002). *Fondamenti di Psicologia di Comunitá*. Rome: Carocci.

Frank, J.W., Cohen, R., Yen, I., Balfour, J. & Smith, M. (2003). Socioeconomic gradients in health status over 29 years of follow-up after midlife: the Alameda county study. *Social Science and Medicine*, **57**, 2305–23.

Franzblau, S.H. & Moore, M. (2001). Socializing efficacy: a reconstruction of self-efficacy theory within the context of inequality. *Journal of Community and Applied Social Psychology*, **11**, 83–96.

Freire, P. (1970). *Pedagogia del Oprimido*. Ediciones Universitaris: Lima (cited by Ramella & de la Cruz, 2000).

Freire, P. (1972). *Pedagogy of the Oppressed*. Harmondsworth: Penguin (also New York: Continuum, 1993) (cited by Burton & Kagan, 2005 and by Moane, 2003).

Freire, P. (1973). *Education for Critical Consciousness*. New York: Seabury Press (cited by Pilisuk *et al.*, 1996 and Campbell & Murray, 2004).

Freire, P. (1998). *Pedagogy of Freedom: Ethics, Democracy and Civil Courage*. Rowman and Littlefield: Lanham, MD (cited by Ramella & de la Cruz, 2000).

Freitas, M. (1998). Models of practice in community in Brazil: possibilities for the psychology–community relationship. *Journal of Community Psychology*, **26**, 261–8.

Freitas, M. (2000). Voices from the south: the construction of Brazilian community social psychology. *Journal of Community and Applied Social Psychology*, **10**, 315–26.

French, J.R.P. & Raven, B.H. (1959). The bases of social power. In D. Cartwright (ed.), *Studies in Social Power* (pp. 150–67). Ann Arbor, MI: Institute for Social Research.

French, J. & Raven, B. (1960). A model of person-environment. In D. Cartwright & A. Zander (eds), *Society, Stress and Disease*, Vol. 5. *Ageing and Old Age*. Oxford, UK: Oxford University Press.

Friedland, D.S. & Price, R.H. (2003). Underemployment: consequences for the health and well-being of workers. *American Journal of Community Psychology*, **32**, 33–45.

Friedman, A. & Todd, J. (1994). Kenyan women tell a story: interpersonal power of women in three subcultures in Kenya. *Sex Roles*, **31**, 533–46.

Friedman, V.J. (2001). Action science: creating communities of inquiry in communities of practice. In P. Reason & H. Bradbury (eds), *Handbook of Action Research: Participative Inquiry and Practice* (pp. 159–70). London: Sage.

Frohlich, K.L., Corin, E. & Potvin, L. (2001). A theoretical proposal for the relationship between context and disease. *Sociology of Health and Illness*, **23**, 776–97.

Fryer, D. (1986). Employment deprivation and personal agency during unemployment: a critical discussion of Jahoda's explanation of the psychological effects of unemployment. *Social Behavior*, **1**, 3–23.

Fryer, D. (1990). The mental health costs of unemployment: towards a social psychological concept of poverty? *British Journal of Clinical and Social Psychiatry*, **7**, 164–75.

Fryer, D. (1994). Commentary: community psychology and politics. *Journal of Community and Applied Social Psychology*, **4**, 11–14.

Fryer, D. (ed). (1998a). Mental health consequences of economic insecurity, relative poverty and social exclusion: community psychological perspectives on recession. *Journal of Community and Applied Social Psychology*, **8**, 75–180.

Fryer, D. (1998b). Editor's preface, special issue: mental health consequences of economic insecurity, relative poverty and social exclusion: community psychology perspectives on recession. *Journal of Community and Applied Social Psychology*, **8**, 75–88.

Fryer, D., Duckett, P. & Pratt, R. (2003). Critical community psychology: what, why and how? Paper presented at the annual conference of the UK Community Psychology Network, Birmingham, September.

Fryer, D. & Fagan, R. (2003). Toward a critical community psychological perspective on unemployment and mental health research. *American Journal of Community Psychology*, **32**, 89–96.

Fryer, D. & Payne, R. (1984). Proactive behaviour in unemployment: findings and implication. *Leisure Studies*, **3**, 273–95.

Fukuyama, F. (1995). *Trust: The Social Virtues and the Creation of Prosperity*. New York: Free Press (cited by Schuller *et al.*, 2000).

Furnham, A. & Steele, H. (1993). Measuring locus of control: a critique of general, children's health- and work-related locus of control questionnaires. *British Journal of Psychology*, **84**, 443–79.

Gadamer, H.G. (1989). *Truth and Method* (2nd edn), (trans J. Weinsheimer & D. Marshall,). New York: Crossroad (cited by Hess, 2005).

Galea, S., Ahern, J., Rudenstine, S., Wallace, Z. & Vlahov, D. (2005). Urban built environment and depression: a multilevel analysis. *Journal of Epidemiology and Community Health*, **59**, 822–7.

Galobardes, B. & Morabia, A. (2003). Measuring the habitat as an indicator of socioeconomic position: methodology and its association with hypertension. *Journal of Epidemiology and Community Health*, **57**, 248–53.

Gatz, M., Brounstein, P. & Taylor, J. (2005). Serving the needs of women with co-occurring disorders and a history of trauma: special issue introduction. *Journal of Community Psychology*, **33**, 373–8.

Gaventa, J. & Cornwall, A. (2001). Power and knowledge. In P. Reason & H. Bradbury (eds), *A Handbook of Action Research: Participative Inquiry and Practice* (pp. 70–80). London: Sage.

Georgas, J., Van de Vijver, F.J.R. & Berry, J.W. (2004). The ecocultural framework, ecosocial indices, and psychological variables in cross-cultural research. *Journal of Cross-Cultural Psychology*, **35**, 74–96.

Gergen, K.J. (1999). *An Invitation to Social Construction*. London: Sage.

Geronimus, A.T. (1992). The weathering hypothesis and the health of African-American women and infants: evidence and speculations. *Ethnicity and Disease*, **2**, 207–21 (cited by Ellen *et al.*, 2001).

Geronimus, A.T., Bound, J. & Waidman, T.A. (1999). Poverty, time, and place: variation in excess mortality across selected US populations, 1980–1990. *Journal of Epidemiology and Community Health*, **53**, 325–34.

Geyer, S. & Peter, R. (2000). Income, occupational position, qualification and health inequalities – competing risks? (comparing indicators of social status). *Journal of Epidemiology and Community Health*, **54**, 299–305.

Ghobarah, H.A., Huth, P. & Russett, B. (2004). The post-war public health effects of civil conflict. *Social Science and Medicine*, **59**, 869–84.

Gibbons, M., Limoges, C., Nowootny, H., Schwartzman, S., Scott, P. & Trow, M. (1994). *The New Production of Knowledge: The Dynamics of Science and Research in Contemporary Societies*. London: Sage (cited by Hoshmand & O'Byrne, 1996).

Giddens, A. (1991). *Modernity and Self-Identity: Self and Society in the Late Modern Age*. Cambridge, UK: Polity Press.

Giddens, A. (1994). *Beyond Left and Right*. Cambridge, UK: Polity Press (cited by Best, 2003).

Giorgi, A. (1990). Towards an integrated approach to the study of human problems: the parameters of a human science. *Saybrook Review*, **8**, 111–26 (cited by Krippner, 2001).

Giuliani, F. & Wiesenfeld, E. (2003). Promoting sustainable communities: theory, research, and action. *Community, Work and Family*, **6**, 159–81.

Glenwick, D., Heller, K., Linney, J. & Pargament, K. (1990). In P. Tolan, C. Keys, F. Chertok & L. Jason (eds.), *Research in Community Psychology: Issues of Theory and Methods*, Chapter 8. Washington, DC: American Psychological Association.

Glover, M., Dudgeon, P. & Huygens, I. (2005). Colonization and racism. In G. Nelson & I. Prilleltensky (eds.), *Community Psychology: In Pursuit of Liberation and Well-Being* (pp. 330–47). Basingstoke: Palgrave MacMillan.

Glynn, T.J. (1981). Psychological sense of community: measurement and application. *Human Relations*, **34**, 780–818 (cited by McMillan & Chavis, 1986).

Godin, I. & Kittel, F. (2004). Differential economic stability and psychosocial stress at work: associations with psychosomatic complaints and absenteeism. *Social Science and Medicine*, **58**, 1543–53.

Godley, M.D. & Velasquez, R. (1998). Effectiveness of the Logan Square prevention project: interim results. *Drugs & Society*, **12**, 87–103.

Goffman, E. (1959). *The Presentation of Self in Everyday Life*. New York: Doubleday.

Gold, M. (1992). Metatheory and field theory in social psychology: relevance or elegance? *Journal of Social Issues*, **2**, 67–78.

Goldberg, D.P., Gater, R., Sartorius, N. *et al.* (1997). The validity of two versions of the GHQ in the WHO study of mental illness in general health care. *Psychological Medicine*, **27**, 191–7 (cited by Turner *et al.*, 2003).

Goldberg, M., Gueguen, A., Schmaus, A. *et al.* (2001). Longitudinal study of associations between perceived health status and self reported diseases in the French Gazel cohort. *Journal of Epidemiology and Community Health*, **55**, 233–8.

Gonzales, N.A., Cauce, A.M., Friedman, R.J. & Mason, C.A. (1996). Family, peer and neighborhood influences on academic achievement among African-American adolescents: one-year prospective effects. *American Journal of Community Psychology*, **24**, 365–87.

Goodkind, J.R. & Foster-Fishman, P.G. (2002). Integrating diversity and fostering interdependence: ecological lessons learned about refugee participation in multiethnic communities. *Journal of Community Psychology*, **30**, 389–409.

Goodman, G. (1972). *Companionship Therapy: Studies in Structured Intimacy*. San Francisco: Jossey-Bass.

Gordon, G.B. (2001). Transforming lives: towards bicultural competence. In P. Reason & H. Bradbury (eds), *A Handbook of Action Research: Participative Inquiry and Practice* (pp. 314–23). London: Sage.

Gough, B. (2002). 'I've always tolerated it but...': heterosexual masculinity and the discursive reproduction of homophobia. In A. Coyle & C. Kitzinger (eds), *Lesbian and Gay Psychology: New Perspectives* (pp. 219–38). Oxford, UK: Blackwell.

Gracia, E. (2004). Unreported cases of domestic violence against women: towards an epidemiology of social silence, tolerance, and inhibition. *Journal of Epidemiology and Community Health*, **58**, 536–7.

Graham, H. (1996). Smoking prevalence among women in the European community 1950–1990. *Social Science and Medicine*, **43**, 243–54.

Graham, H. (2002). Building an inter-disciplinary science of health inequalities: the example of lifecourse research. *Social Science and Medicine*, **55**, 2005–16.

Granada, H. (1995). Intervenciones de la psicología social comunitaria: El caso Colombia [Interventions in community social psychology: The Columbian case]. In E. Wiesenfeld & E. Sánchez (eds), *Psicología social comunitaria. Contribuciones Latinoamericanas* (pp. 117–49). Caracas, Venezuala: Tropykos-Universidad Central de Venezuela (cited by Wiesenfeld, 1998).

Granovetter, M. (1973). The strength of weak ties. *American Journal of Sociology*, **78**, 580–92.

Grant, K.E., Finkelstein, J.A. & Lyons, A.L. (2003). Integrating psychological research on girls with feminist activism: a model for building a liberation psychology in the United States. *American Journal of Community Psychology*, **31**, 143–55.

Gray, D.I., Jakes, S.S., Emshoff, J. & Blakely, C. (2003). ESID, dissemination, and community psychology: a case of partial implementation. *American Journal of Community Psychology*, **32**, 359–70.

Griffin, C. (2002). Girls' friendships and the formation of sexual identities. In A Coyle & C. Kitzinger (eds), *Lesbian and Gay Psychology: New Perspectives* (pp. 45–62). Oxford, UK: Blackwell.

Grootaert, C. (2001). Social capital: the missing link? In P. Dekker & E.M. Uslaner (eds), *Social Capital and Participation in Everyday Life* (pp. 9–29). London: Routledge.

Grundy, E. & Holt, G. (2000). Adult life experiences and health in early old age in Great Britain. *Social Science and Medicine*, **51**, 1061–74.

Grundy, E. & Holt, G. (2001). The socioeconomic status of older adults: how should we measure it in studies of health inequalities? *Journal of Epidemiology and Community Health*, **55**, 895–904.

Grundy, E. & Sloggett, A. (2003). Health inequalities in the older population: the role of personal capital, social resources and socio-economic circumstances. *Social Science and Medicine*, **56**, 935–47.

Guareschi, P.A. & Jovchelovitch, S. (2004). Participation, health and the development of community resources in southern Brazil. *Journal of Health Psychology*, **9**, 311–22.

Guernina, Z. (1995). Community and health psychology in practice: Professor George Albee interviewed by Dr Guernina. *Journal of Community and Applied Social Psychology*, **5**, 207–14.

Gulcur, L., Stefancic, A., Shinn, M., Tsemberis, S. & Fischer, S.N. (2003). Housing, hospitalization, and cost outcomes for homeless individuals with psychiatric disabilities participating in continuum care and housing first programmes. *Journal of Community and Applied Social Psychology*, **13**, 171–86.

Gulerce, A. (1996). Bridge over troubled waters: a Turkish vision. In K.J. Gergen, A. Gulerce, A. Lock & G. Misra (eds), Psychological Science in Cultural Context, *American Psychologist*, **51**, 500–3.

Gunnell, D.J., Peters, T.J., Kammerling, R.M. & Brooks, J. (1995). Relation between parasuicide, suicide, psychiatric admissions, and socioeconomic deprivation. *British Medical Journal*, **311**, 226–9.

Gunnell, D., Shepherd, M. & Evans, M. (2000). Are recent increases in deliberate self-harm associated with changes in socio-economic conditions? An ecological analysis of patterns of deliberate self-harm in Bristol 1972–3 and 1995–6. *Psychological Medicine*, **30**, 1197–203.

Guzmán, B.L., Casad, B.J., Schlehofer-Sutton, M.M., Villanueva, C.M. & Feria, A. (2003). CAMP: a community-based approach to promoting safe sex behaviour in adolescence. *Journal of Community and Applied Social Psychology*, **13**, 269–83.

Hagan, T. & Smail, D. (1997a). Power-mapping – I. Background and basic methodology. *Journal of Community and Applied Social Psychology*, **7**, 257–68.

Hagan, T. & Smail, D. (1997b). Power-mapping – II. Practical applications: the example of child sexual abuse. *Journal of Community and Applied Social Psychology*, **7**, 269–84.

Hall, B.L. (2001). I wish this were a poem of practices of participatory research. In P. Reason & H. Bradbury (eds), *Handbook of Action Research: Participative Inquiry and Practice* (pp. 171–88). London: Sage.

Hall, S. & Cheston, R. (2002). Mental health and identity: the evaluation of a drop-in centre. *Journal of Community and Applied Social Psychology*, **12**, 30–43.

Hallqvist, J., Lynch, J., Bartley, M., Lang, T. & Blane, D. (2004). Can we disentangle life course processes of accumulation, critical period and social mobility? An analysis of disadvantaged socio-economic positions and myocardial infarction in the Stockholm heart epidemiology program. *Social Science and Medicine*, **58**, 1555–62.

Halpern, D. (1995). *Mental Health and the Built Environment: More than Bricks and Mortar?* London: Taylor & Francis.

Halpern, D. (2005). *Social Capital*. Cambridge, UK: Polity Press.

Halpern, R. (1995). *Rebuilding the Inner City: A History of Neighborhood Initiatives to Address Poverty in the United States*. New York: Columbia University Press (cited by Tseng *et al.*, 2002).

Hamby, S.L. (2000). The importance of community in a feminist analysis of domestic violence among American Indians. *American Journal of Community Psychology*, **28**, 649–69.

Hamerton, H., Nikora, L.W., Robertson, N. & Thomas, D. (1995). Community psychology in Aotearoa/New Zealand. *The Community Psychologist*, **28**, 21–3 (cited by Wingenfeld & Newbrough, 2000).

Hammer, M. (1983). Core and extended social networks in relation to health and illness. *Social Science and Medicine*, **17**, 405–11.

Hanson, B.S., Larsson, S. & Råstam, L. (2000). Time trends in alcohol habits. Results from the Kirseberg project in Malmö, Sweden. *Substance Use and Misuse*, **35**, 171–87.

Harper, G.W., Contreras, R., Bangi, A. & Pedraza, A. (2003). Collaborative process evaluation: enhancing community relevance and cultural appropriateness in HIV prevention. In Y. Suarez-Balcazar & G.W. Harper (eds), *Empowerment and Participatory Evaluation of Community Interventions: Multiple Benefits* (pp. 53–70). New York: Haworth Press.

Harper, G.W., Lardon, C., Rappaport, J., Bangi, A.K., Contreras, R. & Pedraza, A. (2004). Community narratives: the use of narrative ethnography in participatory community research. In L.A. Jason, C.B. Keys, Y. Suarez-Balcazar, R.R. Taylor & M.I. Davis (eds), *Participatory Community Research: Theories and Methods in Action* (pp. 199–217). Washington, DC: American Psychological Association.

Harpham, T., Grant, E. & Rodriguez, C. (2004). Mental health and social capital in Cali, Colombia. *Social Science and Medicine*, **58**, 2267–77.

Harris, T., Brown, G.W. & Robinson, R. (1999a). Befriending as an intervention for chronic depression among women in an inner city. 1: Randomised controlled trial. *British Journal of Psychiatry*, **174**, 219–24.

Harris, T., Brown, G.W. & Robinson, R. (1999b). Befriending as an intervention for chronic depression among women in an inner city. 2: Role of fresh-start experiences and baseline psychosocial factors in remission from depression. *British Journal of Psychiatry*, **174**, 225–32.

Hathaway, B.L. (2001). Case story #2: growing a healthy community: a practical guide. *American Journal of Community Psychology*, **29**, 199–203.

Hattie, J., Sharpley, C. & Rogers, H. (1984). Comparative effectiveness of professional and para-professional helpers. *Psychological Bulletin*, **95**, 534–41.

Hatzidimitriadou, E. (2002). Political ideology, helping mechanisms and empowerment of mental health self-help/mutual aid groups. *Journal of Community and Applied Social Psychology*, **12**, 271–85.

Haw, C. (1995). The family life cycle: a forgotten variable in the study of women's employment and well-being. *Psychological Medicine*, **25**, 727–38.

Hawe, P. & Shiell, A. (2000). Social capital and health promotion: a review. *Social Science and Medicine*, **51**, 871–85.

Hawkins, J.D., Catalano, R.F. & Miller, J.Y. (1992). Risk and protective factors for alcohol and other drug problems in adolescence and early childhood: implications for substance abuse prevention. *Psychological Bulletin*, **112**, 64–105.

Hayes, G. (2000). The struggle for mental health in South Africa: psychologists, apartheid and the story of Durban OASSSA. *Journal of Community and Applied Social Psychology*, **10**, 327–42.

Hays, R.B., Rebchook, G.M. & Kegeles, S.M. (2003). The Mpowerment project: community-building with young gay and bisexual men to prevent HIV. *American Journal of Community Psychology*, **31**, 301–12.

Heady, C. (2002). Sickness and disability. In M. Barnes, C. Heady, C.S. Middleton *et al.* (eds), *Poverty and Social Exclusion in Europe* (pp. 101–22). Cheltenham, UK: Edward Elgar.

Heady, C. & Room, G. (2002). Patterns of social exclusion: implications for policy and research. In M. Barnes, C. Heady, C. S. Middleton, J. Millar, F. Papadopoulos, G. Room, G. & P. Tsakloglou (eds), *Poverty and Social Exclusion in Europe* (pp.146–54). Cheltenham, UK: Edward Elgar.

Hedges, A. & Kelly, J. (1992). *Identification with Local Areas*. Report of a qualitative study. London: HMSO.

Hegarty, P. (2002). 'It's not a choice, it's the way we're built': symbolic beliefs about sexual orientation in the US and Britain. *Journal of Community and Applied Social Psychology*, **12**, 153–66.

Heller, K., Price, R., Reinharz, D., Riger, S., Wandersman, A. & D'Aunno, T. (1984). *Psychology and Community Change: Challenges for the Future*. Homewood, IL: Dorsey.

Henderson, C., Thornicroft, G. & Glover, G. (1998). Inequalities in mental health. *British Journal of Psychiatry*, **173**, 105–9.

Hepburn, A. (2003). *An Introduction to Critical Social Psychology*. London: Sage.

Hepworth, J. (2004). Public health psychology: a conceptual practical framework. *Journal of Health Psychology*, **9**, 41–54.

Herman, J.L. (1992). *Trauma and Recovery: The Aftermath of Violence – from Domestic Abuse to Political Terror*. New York: Basic Books.

Hernandez, E. (1998). Assets and obstacles in community leadership. *Journal of Community Psychology*, **26**, 269–80.

Hertzman, C. & Siddiqi, A. (2000). Health and rapid economic change in the late twentieth century. *Social Science and Medicine*, **51**, 809–19.

Hess, J.Z. (2005). Scientists in the swamp: narrowing the language-practice gap in community psychology. *American Journal of Community Psychology*, **35**, 239–52.

Hill, J.L. (1996). Psychological sense of community: suggestions for future research. *Journal of Community Psychology*, **24**, 431–8.

Hill, M.E. & Augoustinos, M. (2001). Stereotype change and prejudice reduction: short- and long-term evaluation of a cross-cultural awareness programme. *Journal of Community and Applied Social Psychology*, **11**, 243–62.

Himmelman, A.T. (2001). On coalitions and the transformation of power relations: collaborative betterment and collaborative empowerment. *American Journal of Community Psychology*, **29**, 277–84.

Himmelweit, H.T. (1990). Societal psychology: implications and scope. In H.T. Himmelweit & G. Gaskell (eds.), *Societal Psychology* (pp. 17–45). Newbury Park, CA: Sage.

Hingson, R.W. & Howland, J. (2002). Comprehensive community interventions to promote health: Implications for college-age drinking problems. *Journal of Studies on Alcohol*, Suppl. **14**, 226–40.

Hingson, R., McGovern, T., Howland, J., Heeren, T., Winter, M. & Zakocs, R. (1996). Reducing alcohol-impaired driving in Massachusetts: the saving lives program. *American Journal of Public Health*, 86, 791–7 (cited by Levine, 1998).

Hirsch, B. (1981). Social networks and the coping process: creating personal communities. In B. Gottlieb (ed.), *Social Networks and Social Support*. Beverly Hills, CA: Sage.

Hirsch, B., Mickus, M. & Boerger, R. (2002). Ties to influential adults among black and white adolescents: culture, social class, and family networks. *American Journal of Community Psychology*, **30**, 289–303.

Hobfoll, S.E. (1998). *Stress, Culture, and Community: the Psychology and Philosophy of Stress*. New York: Plenum.

Hobfoll, S.E., Briggs, S. & Wells, J. (1995). Community stress and resources: actions and reactions. In S.E. Hobfoll & M.W. de Vries (eds), *Extreme Stress and Communities: Impact and Intervention* (pp. 137–58). Maastricht, The Netherlands: Kluwer Academic (cited by Kelly & Steed, 2004).

Hobfoll, S.E., Jackson, A., Hobfoll, I., Pierce, C.A. & Young, S. (2002). The impact of communal-mastery versus self-mastery on emotional outcomes during stressful conditions: a prospective study of native American women. *American Journal of Community Psychology*, **30**, 853–71.

Hodgins, M., Millar, M. & Barry, M.M. (2006). '. . . it's all the same no matter how much fruit or vegetables or fresh air we get': traveller women's perceptions of illness causation and health inequalities. *Social Science and Medicine*, **62**, 1978–90.

Hoel, H. & Cooper, C.L. (2001). Origins of bullying: theoretical frameworks for explaining workplace bulling. In N. Tehrani (ed.), *Building a Culture of Respect: Managing Bullying at Work*. London: Taylor & Francis.

Hofstede, G.H. (1994). *Uncommon Sense About Organizations: Cases, Studies and Field Observations*. Thousand Oaks, CA: Sage.

Hogan, B.E., Linden, W. & Najarian, B. (2002). Social support interventions: do they work? *Clinical Psychology Review*, **22**, 381–440.

Holder, H.D. & Moore, R.S. (2000). Institutionalization of community action projects to reduce alcohol-use related problems: systematic facilitators. *Substance Use and Misuse*, **35**, 75–86.

Holding, T., Buglass, D., Duffy, J. & Kreitman, N. (1977). Parasuicide in Edinburgh – seven-year review 1968–74., *British Journal of Psychiatry*, **130**, 534–43.

Holland, P., Berney, L., Blane, D., Davey Smith, G., Gunnell, D.J. & Montgomery, S.M. (2000). Life course accumulation of disadvantage: childhood health and hazard exposure during adulthood. *Social Science and Medicine*, **50**, 1285–95.

Holland, S. (1988). Defining and experimenting with prevention. In S. Ramon & M. Giannichedda (eds), *Psychiatry in Transition: The British and Italian Experiences* (Chapter 11). London: Pluto.

Holland, S. (1992). From social abuse to social action: a neighbourhood psychotherapy and social action project for women. In J. Ussher & P. Nicholson (eds), *Gender Issues in Clinical Psychology*. London: Routledge.

Hollway, W. (2000). Practising critical psychology within a British psychology department. In T. Sloan (ed.), *Critical Psychology: Voices for Change* (pp. 34–45). New York: St Martin's Press.

Hollway, W. (2006). Psychoanalysis in social psychological research. *The Psychologist*, **19**, 544–5.

Hook, D. (2004). Frantz Fanon, Steve Biko, 'psychopolitics' and critical psychology. In D. Hook (ed.), *Critical Psychology* (pp. 84–114). Cape Town: University of Cape Town.

Hope, S., Power, C. & Rodger, B. (1999). Does financial hardship account for elevated psychological distress in lone mothers? *Social Science and Medicine*, **49**, 1637–49.

Hopkins, N. (1994). School pupils' perception of the police that visit schools: not all police are 'Pigs'. *Journal of Community and Applied Social Psychology*, **4**, 189–207.

Hopper, K. (1999). John Berger and Erick Holtzman. *Social Policy*, **30**, 13–21 (cited by Watts *et al.*, 2003).

Horelli, L. (2001). Commentary: a comparison of children's autonomous mobility and environmental participation in northern and southern Europe – the cases of Finland and Italy. *Journal of Community and Applied Social Psychology*, **11**, 451–5.

Hoshmand, L.T. & O'Byrne, K. (1996). Reconsidering action research as a guiding metaphor for professional psychology. *Journal of Community Psychology*, **24**, 185–200.

Howarth, C. (2006). Race as stigma: positioning the stigmatized as agents, not objects. *Journal of Community and Applied Social Psychology*, **16**, 442–51.

Hughey, J., Speer, P.W. & Peterson, N.A. (1999). Sense of community in community organizations: structure and evidence of validity. *Journal of Community Psychology*, **27**, 97–113.

Huisman, M., Kunst, A.E., Andersen, O., Bopp, M., Borgan, J.K., Borrell, C., Costa, G., Deboosere, P., Desplanques, G., Donkin, A., Gadeyne, S., Minder, C., Regidor, E., Valkonen, T. & Mackenbach, J.P. (2004). Socioeconomic inequalities in mortality among elderly people in 11 European populations. *Journal of Epidemiology and Community Health*, **58**, 468–75.

Humphreys, K., Macus, S., Stewart, E. & Oliva, E. (2004). Expanding self-help group participation in culturally diverse urban areas: media approaches to leveraging referent power. *Journal of Community Psychology*, **32**, 413–24.

Hunt, H. & Crow, G. (2000). Commentary on Prilleltensky and Nelson. *Journal of Community and Applied Social Psychology*, **10**, 117–22.

Hur, M.H. (2006). Empowerment in terms of theoretical perspectives: exploring a typology of the process and components across disciplines. *Journal of Community Psychology*, **34**, 523–40.

Husain, N., Creed, F. & Tomeson, B. (1997). Adverse social circumstances and depression in people of Pakistani origin in the UK. *British Journal of Psychiatry*, **171**, 434–8.

Hutson, S. & Liddiard, M. (1994). *Youth Homelessness: The Construction of a Social Issue*. London: Macmillan.

Huygens, I. (2000). Feminist power sharing: lessons for community psychology. In A. Mulvey, M. Terenzio, J. Hill, M.A. Bond, I. Huygens, H.R. Hamerton & S. Cahill (eds), Stories of relative privilege: power and social change in feminist community psychology, *American Journal of Community Psychology*, **28**, 887–93.

Iijima Hall, C.C. (1997). Cultural malpractice: the growing obsolescence of psychology with the changing US population. *American Psychologist*, **52**, 642–51.

Inglehart, R. (1997). *Modernization and Postmodernization*. Princeton: Princeton University Press.

Institute of Medicine (1994). *Reducing Risk for Mental Disorders: Frontiers for Preventive Intervention Research*, Washington, DC: National Academy Press (cited by Durlak & Wells, 1998).

Jackson, T.L. & Davis, J.L. (2000). Prevention of sexual and physical assault toward women: a program for male athletes. *Journal of Community Psychology*, **28**, 589–605.

Jahoda, G. (1982). *Psychology and Anthropology: A Psychological Perspective*. London: Academic Press.

James, S.E., Johnson J., Raghavan, C., Lemos, T., Barakett, M. & Woolis, D. (2003). The violent matrix: a study of structural, interpersonal, and intrapersonal violence among a sample of poor women. *American Journal of Community Psychology*, **31**, 129–41.

Janzen, R., Nelson, G., Trainor, J. and Ochocka, J. (2006). A longitudinal study of mental health consumer/survivor initiatives: part 4 – benefits beyond the self? A quantitative and qualitative study of system-level activites and impacts. *Journal of Community Psychology*, **34**, 285–303.

Jarvis, M.J. (1991). A time for conceptual stocktaking. *British Journal of Addiction*, **86**, 643–7.

Jason, L.A., Keys, C.B., Suarez-Balcazar, Y., Taylor, R.R. & Davis, M.I. (eds), *Participatory Community Research: Theories and Methods in Action*. Washington, DC: American Psychological Association.

Jensen, L. & Slack, T. (2003). Underemployment in America: measurement and evidence. *American Journal of Community Psychology*, **32**, 21–31.

Johnson, J.V. (1989). Control, collectivity and the psychosocial work environment. In S.L. Sauter, J.J. Hurrell & C.L. Cooper (eds), *Job Control and Worker Health* (pp. 55–74). Chichester, UK: John Wiley & Sons, Ltd (cited by Verhoeven *et al.*, 2003).

Johnson, T.P., Freels, S.A., Parson, J.A. & Vangeest, J.B. (1997). Substance abuse and homelessness: social selection or social adaptation? *Addiction*, **92**, 437–46.

Johnson, S. & Robson, C. (1999). Threatened identities: the experiences of women in transition to programmes of professional higher education. *Journal of Community and Applied Social Psychology*, **9**, 273–88.

Jones, K., Gould, M.I. & Duncan, C. (2000). Death and deprivation: an exploratory analysis of deaths in the health and lifestyle survey. *Social Science and Medicine*, **50**, 1059–79.

Josselson, R. & Lieblich, A. (2001). *Narrative research and Humanism*. In K.J. Schneider, J.F.T. Bugental & J. Fraser Pierson (eds), *The Handbook of Humanistic Psychology: Leading Edges in Theory, Research and Practice* (pp. 275–88). London: Sage.

Jozefowicz-Simbeni, D.M.H., Israel, N., Braciszewski, J. & Hobden, K. (2005). The 'big tent' of community psychology: reactions to Paul Toro's 2004 presidential address. *American Journal of Community Psychology*, **35**, 17–22.

Judge, K., Mulligan, J.A. & Benzeval, M. (1998a). Income inequality and population health. *Social Science and Medicine*, **46**, 567–79.

Judge, K., Mulligan, J.A. & Benzeval, M. (1998b). Letter to the Editor, reply to Richard Wilkinson. *Social Science and Medicine*, **47**, 983–5.

Kagan, C. & Burton, M. (2000). Prefigurative action research: an alternative basis for critical psychology? *Annual Review of Critical Psychology*, **2**, 1–15.

Kagan, C. & Burton, M. (2005). Marginalization. In G. Nelson & I. Prilleltensky (eds), *Community Psychology: In Pursuit of Liberation and Well-Being* (pp. 293–308). New York: Palgrave Macmillan.

Kagan, C., Castile, S. & Stewart, A. (2005). Participation: are some more equal than others? *Clinical Psychology Forum*, **153**, 30–4.

Kagee, A. (2004). Present concerns of survivors of human rights violations in South Africa. *Social Science and Medicine*, **59**, 625–35.

Kağıtçıbaşi, C. (1996). *Family and Human Development Across Cultures: A View from the Other Side*. Mahwah, NJ: Lawrence Erlbaum.

Kalichman, S.C., Simbayi, L.C., Kagee, A., Toefy, Y., Jooste, S., Cain, D. & Cherry, C. (2006). Associations of poverty, substance use, and HIV transmission risk behaviors in three South African communities. *Social Science and Medicine*, **62**, 1641–9.

Kar, S.B., Pascual, C.A. & Chickering, K.L. (1999). Empowerment of women for health promotion: a meta-analysis. *Social Science and Medicine*, **49**, 1431–60.

Karasek, R.A. (1979). Job demands, job decision latitude, and mental strain: implications for job redesign. *Administrative Science Quarterly*, **24**, 285–308.

Karasek, R.A. & Theorell, T. (1990). *Health Work, Stress, Productivity and the Reconstruction of Working Life*. New York: Basic Books (cited by Verhoeven *et al.*, 2003).

Karlsen, S. & Nazroo, J.Y. (2004). Fear of racism and health. *Journal of Epidemiology and Community Health*, **58**, 1017–18.

Keel, M.R. & Drew, N.M. (2004). The settlement experiences of refugees from the former Yugoslavia. *Community, Work and Family*, **7**, 95–115.

Kelly, G.A. (1955). *The Psychology of Personal Constructs*. New York: Norton.

Kelly, J.G. (2003). Science and community psychology: social norms and pluralistic inquiry. *American Journal of Community Psychology*, **31**, 213–17.

Kelly J.G. & Steed, L.G. (2004). Communities coping with change: a conceptual model. *Journal of Community Psychology*, **32**, 201–16.

Kemmelmeier, M., Burnstein, E., Krumov, K., Genkova, P., Kanagawa, C., Hirshberg, M.S., Erb, H., Wieczorkowska, G. & Noels, K.A. (2003). Individualism, collectivism, and authoritarianism in seven societies. *Journal of Cross-Cultural Psychology*, **34**, 304–22.

Kennedy, B.P., Kawachi, I. & Prothrow-Smith, D. (1996). Income distribution and mortality: cross sectional ecological study of the Robin Hood index in the United States. *British Medical Journal*, **312**, 1004–7.

Keupp, H. & Stark, W. (2000). Germany. In J. Rappaport & E. Seidman (eds), *Handbook of Community Psychology* (p. 798). New York: Kluwer/Plenum.

Keys, C.B. & Frank, S. (1987). Community psychology and the study of organizations: a reciprocal relationship. *American Journal of Community Psychology*, **15**, 239–51 (cited by Boyd & Angelique, 2002).

Kieffer, C.H. (1984). Citizen empowerment: a developmental perspective. In J. Rappaport & R. Hess (eds), *Studies in Empowerment*. New York: Haworth (cited by Wandersman & Florin, 2000).

Kieselbach, T. (2003). Long-term unemployment among young people: the risk of social exclusion. *American Journal of Community Psychology*, **32**, 69–76.

Kim, D., Subramanian, S.V. & Kawachi, I. (2005). Bonding versus bridging social capital and their associations with self rated health: a multilevel analysis of 40 US communities. *Journal of Epidemiology and Community Health*, **60**, 116–22.

Kitzinger, C. (1987). *The Social Construction of Lesbianism*. London: Sage (cited by Hepburn, 2003).

Kitzinger, C. & Coyle, A. (2002). Introducing lesbian and gay psychology. In A. Coyle & C. Kitzinger (eds.), *Lesbian and Gay Psychology: New Perspectives* (pp. 1–29). Oxford, UK: Blackwell.

Kivimäki, M., Ferrie, J.E., Head, J., Shipley, M.J., Vahtera, J. & Marmot, M.G. (2005). Organisational justice and change in justice as predictors of employee health: the Whitehall II study. *Journal of Epidemiology and Community Health*, **58**, 931–7.

Klebanov, P.K., Brooks-Gunn, J. & Duncan, G.J. (1994). Does neighbourhood and family poverty affect mothers' parenting, mental health, and social support? *Journal of Marriage and the Family*, **56**, 441–55.

Kolstad, A. (1987). Comments. *Acta Psychiatrica Scandinavica*, **76**, 15–19 (cited by Blair, 1992).

Kopp, M., Skrabski, A. & Szedmak, S. (2000). Psychosocial risk factors, inequality and self-rated morbidity in a changing society. *Social Science and Medicine*, **51**, 1351–61.

Kopp, M., Csoboth, C. & Réthelyi, J. (2004). Psychosocial determinants of premature health deterioration in a changing society: the case of Hungary. *Journal of Health Psychology*, **9**, 99–109.

Kothari, U. (2001). Power, knowledge and social control in participatory development. In B. Cooke & U. Kothari (eds.), *Participation: The New Tyranny?* New York: Zed-Books (cited by Quaghebeur *et al.*, 2004).

Krause, M. (2002). The institutionalization of community interventions in Chile: characteristics and contradictions. *American Journal of Community Psychology*, **30**, 547–70.

Krawitz, R. & Watson, C. (1997). Gender, race and poverty: bringing the sociopolitical into psychotherapy. *Australian and New Zealand Journal of Psychiatry*, **31**, 474–9.

Kretzmann, J.P. & McKnight, J.L. (1993). *Building Communities from the Inside Out: A Path Toward Finding and Mobilizing a Community's Assets*. Chicago: ACTA Publications (cited by Nystrom & Jones, 2003).

Krieger, N., Chen, J.T. & Selby, J.V. (1999). Comparing individual-based and household-based measures of social class to assess class inequalities in women's health: a methodological study of 684 US women. *Journal of Epidemiology and Community Health*, **53**, 612–23.

Krippner, S. (2001). Research methodology in humanistic psychology in the light of post-modernity. In K.J. Schneider, J.F.T. Bugental & J.F. Pierson (eds), *The Handbook of Humanistic Psychology: Leading Edges in Theory, Research and Practice* (pp. 289–304). London: Sage.

Kristenson, M., Eriksen, H.R., Sluiter, J.K., Starke, D. & Ursin, H. (2004). Psychobiological mechanisms of socioeconomic differences in health. *Social Science and Medicine*, **58**, 1511–22.

Kroeker, C.J. (1995). Individual, organizational, and societal empowerment: a study of the processes in a Nicaraguan agricultural cooperative. *American Journal of Community Psychology*, **23**, 749–64.

Kroeker, C.J. (1996). The cooperative movement in Nicaragua: empowerment and accompaniment of severely disadvantaged peasants. *Journal of Social Issues*, **52**, 123–38.

Kuhn, T.S. (1962). *The Structure of Scientific Revolutions*. Chicago: University of Chicago Press.

Kunst, A.E., Groenhof, F., Mackenbach, J.P. & the EU Working Group. (1998). Mortality by occupational class among men 30–64 years in 11 European countries. *Social Science and Medicine*, **46**, 1459–76.

Kuo, F.E., Sullivan, W.C., Coley, R.L. & Brunson, L. (1998). Fertile ground for community: inner-city neighborhood common spaces. *American Journal of Community Psychology*, **26**, 823–51.

Kyttä, M. (1997). Children's independent mobility in urban, small town and rural environments. In R. Camstra (ed.), *Growing Up in a Changing Urban Landscape*. Van Gorcum: Assen (cited by Horelli, 2001).

Labonte, R. (1997). Health promotion and empowerment: reflections on professional practice. *Health Education Quarterly*, **21**, 253–68 (cited by Travers, 1997).

Labone, R. (2001). Liberalisation, health and the World Trade Organisation. *Journal of Epidemiology and Community Health*, **55**, 620–1.

Lachman, M.E. & Weaver, S.L. (1998). The sense of control as a moderator of social class differences in health and well-being. *Journal of Personality and Social Psychology*, **74**, 763–73.

Lahelma, E., Kivelä, K., Roos, E., Tuominen, T., Dahl, E., Diderichsen, F., Elstad, J.I., Lissau, I., Lundberg, O., Rahkonen, O., Rasmussen, N.K. & Aberg Yngwe, M. (2002). Analysing changes of health inequalities in the Nordic welfare states. *Social Science and Medicine*, **55**, 609–25.

Lahelma, E., Martikainen, P., Laaksonen, M. & Aittomäki, A. (2004). Pathways between socioeconomic determinants of health. *Journal of Epidemiology and Community Health*, **58**, 327–32.

Lahelma, E., Rahkone, O. & Huuhka, M. (1997). Changes in the social patterning of health? The case of Finland 1986–1994. *Social Science and Medicine*, **44**, 789–99.

Lalueza, J.L., Crespo, I., Pallí, C. & Luque, M.J. (1999). Intervención educativa, comunidad y cultura gitana. Una experiencia con nuevas tecnologías: la Casa de Shere Rom. In M.A. Essomba (ed.), *Construir la Escuela Intercultural* (pp. 185–94). Barcelona: Graó (cited by Crespo *et al.*, 2002).

Larkin, M.J. (1995). What's the story? *Bacas (U.W.E. Magazine)*, Spring Term ed. pp. 18–19 (cited by Farrington & Robinson, 1999).

László, J. & Farkas, A. (1997). Central-eastern European collective experiences. *Journal of Community and Applied Social Psychology*, **7**, 77–87.

Latkin, C.A., Williams, C.T., Wang, J. & Curry, A.D. (2005). Neighborhood social disorder as a determinant of drug injection behaviors: a structural equation modeling approach. *Health Psychology*, **24**, 96–100.

Law, M.R. & Morris, J.K. (1998). Why is mortality higher in poorer areas and in more northern areas of England and Wales? *Journal of Epidemiology and Community Health*, **52**, 344–52.

Lawlor, D.A., Ebrahim, S. & Davey Smith, G. (2005). Adverse socioeconomic position across the lifecourse increases coronary heart disease risk cumulatively: findings from the British women's heart and health study. *Journal of Epidemiology and Community Health*, **59**, 785–93.

Lazarus, R.S. & Folkman, S. (1984). *Stress, Appraisal and Coping*. New York: Springer.

Leclerc, A., Chastang, J., Menvielle, G. & Luce, D. (2006). Socioeconomic inequalities in premature mortality in France: have they widened in recent decades? *Social Science and Medicine*, **62**, 2035–45.

Lee, K. (2001). A dialogue of the deaf? The health impacts of globalisation. *Journal of Epidemiology and Community Health*, **55**, 619.

Leon, A. & Montenegro, M. (1998). Return of emotion in psychosocial community research. *Journal of Community Psychology*, **26**, 219–27.

Levav, I. (1998). Individuals under conditions of maximum adversity: the Holocaust. In B.P. Dohrenwend (ed.), *Adversity, Stress, and Psychopathology* (pp. 13–33). Oxford: Oxford University Press.

Levine, M. (1998). Prevention and community. *American Journal of Community Psychology*, **26**, 189–206.

Levine, M., Perkins, D.D. & Perkins, D.V. (2005). *Principles of Community Psychology: Perspectives and Applications* (3rd edition). Oxford: Oxford University Press.

Leviton, L.C. (1996). Integrating psychology and public health: challenges and opportunities. *American Psychologist*, **51**, 42–51.

Lewin, K. (1951). *Field Theory in Social Science*. New York: Harper.

Lewin, M. (1992). The impact of Kurt Lewin's life on the place of social issues in his work. *Journal of Social Issues*, **2**, 15–29.

Lewis, G., Bebbington, P., Brugha, T., Farrell, M., Gill, B., Jenkins, R. & Meltzer, H. (1998). Socioeconomic status, standard of living, and neurotic disorder. *The Lancet*, **352**, 605–9.

Lewis, H. (2001). Participatory research in education for social change: Highlander Research and Education Center. In P. Reason & H. Bradbury (eds), *Handbook of Action Research: Participative Inquiry and Practice* (pp. 356–62). London: Sage.

Lewis, J. (1991). The public's health: philosophy and practice in Britain in the twentieth century. In E. Fee & R.M. Acheson (eds), *A History of Education in Public Health: Health that Mocks the Doctors' Rules* (pp. 195–229). Oxford, UK: Oxford University Press.

Lewis, O. (1961). *The Children of Sánchez: Autobiography of a Mexican Family.* London: Secker and Warburg.

Lewis, S. (1993). *The Good Neighbor Handbook.* Acton, MA: CSPP (cited by Rich *et al.*, 1995).

Lewis, S. & Orford, J. (2005). Women's experiences of workplace bullying: changes in social relationships. *Journal of Community and Applied Social Psychology*, **15**, 29–47.

Liker, J. & Elder, G. (1983). Economic hardship and marital relations in the 1930s. *American Sociological Review*, **48**, 343–59.

Lin, N. (2001). *Social Capital: A Theory of Social Structure and Action.* Cambridge, UK: Cambridge University Press.

Lindström, M. (2004). Social capital, the miniaturisation of community and self-reported global and psychological health. *Social Science and Medicine*, **59**, 595–607.

Lindström, M., and the Malmö Shoulder-Neck Study Group (2006). Psychosocial work conditions, social participation and social capital: a causal pathway investigated in a longitudinal study. *Social Science and Medicine*, **62**, 280–91.

Lindström, M., Merlo, J. & Östergren, P. (2003b). Social capital and sense of insecurity in the neighbourhood: a population-based multilevel analysis in Malmö, Sweden, *Social Science and Medicine*, **56**, 1111–20.

Lindström, M., Moghaddassi, M. & Merlo, J. (2003a). Social capital and leisure time physical activity: a population based multilevel analysis in Malmö, Sweden. *Journal of Epidemiology and Community Health*, **57**, 23–8.

Lira, E. & Weinstein, E. (2000). La tortura: conceptualización psicológica y proceso terapéutico. In I. Martín-Baró (ed.), *Psicología Social de la Guerra* (3rd edn). San Salvador: UCA Editores (cited by Burton & Kagan, 2005).

Little, A. (2002). *The Politics of Community: Theory and Practice.* Edinburgh: Edinburgh University Press.

Lochner, K.A., Kawachi, I., Brennan, R.T. & Buka, S.L. (2003). Social capital and neighborhood mortality rates in Chicago. *Social Science and Medicine*, **56**, 1797–805.

Lock, A. (1996). Psychology in the Maori context. In K.J. Gergen, A. Gulerce, A. Lock & G. Misra (eds), Psychological science in cultural context. *American Psychologist*, **51**, 496–503.

Long, D.A. & Perkins, D.D. (2003). Confirmatory factor analysis of the sense of community index and development of a brief SCI. *Journal of Community Psychology*, **31**, 279–96.

Loomis, C., Dockett, K.H. & Brodsky, A.E. (2004). Change in sense of community: an empirical finding. *Journal of Community Psychology*, **32**, 1–8.

Lopes Cardozo, B., Vergara, A., Agani, F. *et al.* (2000). Mental health, social functioning, and attitudes of Kosovar Albanians following the war in Kosovo. *JAMA*, **284**, 577 (cited by Turner *et al.*, 2003).

López-Sánchez, G. and Serrano-García, I. (1995). Intervenciones de comunidad en Puerto Rico: el impacto de la psicología social comunitaria [Community interventions in Puerto Rico: the impact of community social psychology]. In. E. Wiesenfeld & E. Sánchez (eds), *Psicología social comunitaria. Contribuciones Latinoamericanas* [Community social psychology – Latin American contributions] (pp. 219–48). Caracas, Venezuela: Tropykos-Universidad Central de Venezuela, (cited by Wiesenfeld, 1998).

Lorant, V., Kunst, A.E., Huisman, M., Costa, G. & Mackenbach, J. (2005). Socio-economic inequalities in suicide: a European comparative study. *British Journal of Psychiatry*, **187**, 49–54.

Lorien, R.P. (1987). Applied community psychology: good news for the field from the field. *Journal of Community Psychology*, **15**, 3–6.

Ludema, J.D., Cooperrider, D.L. & Barrett, F.J. (2001). Appreciative inquiry: the power of the unconditional positive question. In P. Reason & H. Bradbury (eds), *Handbook of Action Research: Participative Inquiry and Practice* (pp. 189–99). London: Sage.

Luke, D.A. (2005). Getting the big picture in community science: methods that capture context. *American Journal of Community Psychology*, **35**, 185–200.

Lunt, I. & Poortinga, Y.H. (1996). Internationalizing psychology: the case of Europe. *American Psychologist*, **51**, 504–8.

Lykes, M.B. (2000). Possible contributions of a psychology of liberation: whither health and human rights? *Journal of Health Psychology*, **5**, 383–97.

Lykes, M.B., Blanche, M.T. & Hamber, B. (2003). Narrating survival and change in Guatemala and South Africa: the politics of representation and a liberatory community psychology. *American Journal of Community Psychology*, **31**, 79–90.

Lynch, J. (2000). Income inequality and health: expanding the debate. *Social Science and Medicine*, **51**, 1001–5.

Lynch, J., Davey Smith, G., Kaplan, G.A. *et al.* (2000). Income inequality and mortality: Importance to health of individual income, psychosocial environment, or material conditions. *British Medical Journal*, **320**, 1200–4.

Lynch, J., Davey Smith, G. Hillemeier, M. *et al.* (2001). Income inequality, the psychosocial environment, and health: comparison of wealthy nations. *The Lancet*, **358**, 194–200.

Lyons, A.C. (2000). Examining media representations: benefits for health psychology. *Journal of Health Psychology*, **5**, 349–58 (cited by Prilleltensky & Prilleltensky, 2003a).

Macinko, J. & Starfield, B. (2001). The utility of social capital in research on health determinants. *The Milbank Quarterly*, **79**, 387–427.

Macintyre, S. (1997). The Black report and beyond: what are the issues? *Social Science and Medicine*, **44**, 723–45.

Macintyre, S. & Ellaway, A. (2000). Ecological approaches: rediscovering the role of the physical and social environment. In L. Berkman & I. Kawachi (eds), *Social Epidemiology* (pp. 332–48). New York: Oxford University Press (cited by Baum & Ziersch, 2003).

Macintyre, S., Ellaway, A. & Cummins, S. (2002). Place effects on health: how can we conceptualise, operationalise and measure them? *Social Science and Medicine*, **55**, 125–39.

Macintyre, S., Ellaway, A., Der, G., Ford, G. & Hunt, K. (1998). Do housing tenure and car access predict health because they are simply markers of income or self esteem? A Scottish study. *Journal of Epidemiology and Community Health*, **52**, 657–64.

Macintyre, S., Hiscock, R., Kearns, A. & Ellaway, A. (2001). Housing tenure and car access: further exploration of the nature of their relations with health in a UK setting. *Journal of Epidemiology and Community Health*, **55**, 330–31.

Macintyre, S., McKay, L. & Ellaway, A. (2005). Are rich people or poor people more likely to be ill? Lay perceptions, by social class and neighbourhood, of inequalities in health. *Social Science and Medicine*, **60**, 313–17.

Mackenbach, J.P. & Kunst, A.E. (1997). Measuring the magnitude of socio-economic inequalities in health: an overview of available measures illustrated with two examples from Europe. *Social Science and Medicine*, **44**, 757–71.

Macloed, J. & Davey Smith, G. (2003). Authors' reply to commentary by Singh-Manoux, A. Psychosocial factors and public health. *Journal of Epidemiology and Community Health*, **57**, 553–4.

Macleod, J., Davey Smith, G., Metcalfe, C. & Hart, C. (2005). Is subjective social status a more important determinant of health than objective social status? Evidence from a prospective observational study of Scottish men. *Social Science and Medicine*, **61**, 1916–29.

McCloskey, L.A., Southwick, K., Fernández-Esquer, M.E. & Locke, C. (1995). The psychological effects of political and domestic violence on Central American and Mexican immigrant mothers and children. *Journal of Community Psychology*, **23**, 95–116.

McCulloch, A. (2001a). Social environments and health: cross sectional national survey. *British Medical Journal*, **323**, 208–9.

McCulloch, A. (2001b). Teenage childbearing in Great Britain and the spatial concentration of poverty households. *Journal of Epidemiology and Community Health*, **55**, 16–23.

McCulloch, A. (2003). An examination of social capital and social disorganisation in neighbourhoods in the British household panel study. *Social Science and Medicine*, **56**, 1425–38.

McDougall, W. (1939). *The Group Mind* (2nd edn). Cambridge, UK: Cambridge University Press (cited by Bar-Tal, 2000).

McGhee, J. & Fryer, D. (1989). Unemployment, income and the family: an action research approach. *Social Behaviour*, **4**, 237–52 (cited by Fryer, 1990).

McGuire, J.B. (1997). The reliability and validity of a questionnaire describing neighborhood characteristics relevant to families and young children living in urban areas. *Journal of Community Psychology*, **25**, 551–66.

McKenna, S. (2002). Book review of: *Self-Esteem, the Costs and Causes of Low Self-Worth*, N. Emler, 2001, London: Joseph Rowntree Foundation. *Journal of Community and Applied Social Psychology*, **12**, 307–8.

McKenzie, K., Whitley, R. & Weich, S. (2002). Social capital and mental health. *British Journal of Psychiatry*, **181**, 280–3.

Mclean, C., Campbell, C. & Cornish, F. (2003). African-Caribbean interactions with mental health services in the UK: experiences and expectations of exclusion as (re)productive of health inequalities. *Social Science and Medicine*, **56**, 657–69.

McLoyd, V.C. (1998). Socioeconomic disadvantage and child development. *American Psychologist*, **53**, 185–204.

McMillan, D.W. & Chavis, D.M. (1986). Sense of community: a definition and theory. *Journal of Community Psychology*, **14**, 6–23.

McMunn, A.M., Nazroo, J.Y., Marmot, M.G., Boreham, R. & Goodman, R. (2001). Children's emotional and behavioural well-being and the family environment: findings from the health survey for England. *Social Science and Medicine*, **53**, 423–40.

Mahan, B.B., Garrard, W.M., Lewis, S.E. & Newbrough, J.R. (2002). Sense of community in a university setting: campus as workplace. In A.T. Fisher, C.C. Sonn & B.J. Bishop (eds), *Psychological Sense of Community* (pp. 123–40). New York: Kluwer/Plenum.

Malgady, R.G., Rogler, L.H. & Costantino, G. (1990). Hero/heroine-modeling for Puerto Rican adolescents: a preventive mental health intervention. *Journal of Consulting and Clinical Psychology*, **58**, 469–74 (cited by Durlak & Wells, 1998).

Malson, H. & Swann, C. (1999). Prepared for consumption: (Dis)orders of eating and embodiment. *Journal of Community and Applied Social Psychology*, **9**, 397–405.

Manor, O., Matthews, S. & Power, C. (1997). Comparing measures of health inequality. *Social Science and Medicine*, **45**, 761–71.

Marang-van de Mheen, P.J., Davey Smith, G., Hart, C.L. & Gunning-Schepers, L.J. (1998). Socioeconomic differentials in mortality among men within Great Britain: time trends and contributory causes. *Journal of Epidemiology and Community Health*, **52**, 214–18.

Marinacci, C., Spadea, T., Biggeria, A., Demaria, M., Caiazzo, A. & Costa, G. (2004). The role of individual and contextual socioeconomic circumstances on mortality: analysis of time variations in a city of north west Italy. *Journal of Epidemiology and Community Health*, **58**, 199–207.

Marková, I. (1997). The individual and the community: a post-communist perspective. *Journal of Community and Applied Social Psychology*, **7**, 3–17.

Marková, I. (2003). Book review of Deux, K. and Philogène, G. *Representations of the Social: Bridging Theoretical Traditions*. Oxford, UK: Blackwell. *Journal of Community and Applied Social Psychology*, **13**, 413–16.

Markowe, L.A. (2002). Coming out as lesbian. In A. Coyle & C. Kitzinger (eds), *Lesbian and Gay Psychology: New Perspectives* (pp. 63–80). Oxford: Blackwell.

Marks, D.F. (1996). Health psychology in context. *Journal of Health Psychology*, **1**, 7–21.

Marks, D.F. (2002). Editorial essay. Freedom, responsibility and power: contrasting approaches to health psychology. *Journal of Health Psychology*, **7**, 5–19.

Marmot, M., Adelstein, A.M., Bulusu, L. & OPCS (1984). *Immigrant Mortality in England and Wales 1970–78: Causes of Death by Country of Birth*. London: HMSO (cited by Williams et al., 1998).

Marmot, M., Bosman, H., Hemingway, H., Brunner, E. & Stansfield, S. (1997). Contribution of job control and other risk factors to social variations in coronary heart disease incidence. *The Lancet*, **350**, 235–9.

Marmot, M., Shipley, M., Brunner, E. & Hemingway, H. (2001). Relative contribution of early life and adult socioeconomic factors to adult morbidity in the Whitehall II study. *Journal of Epidemiology and Community Health*, **55**, 301–7.

Marmot, M. & Siegrist, J. (2004). Health inequalities and the psychosocial environment. *Social Science and Medicine*, **58**, 1461.

Martijn, C. & Sharpe, L. (2006). Pathways to youth homelessness. *Social Science and Medicine*, **62**, 1–12.

Martikainen, P., Adda, J., Ferrie, J.E., Davey Smith, G. & Marmot, M. (2002). Effects of income and wealth on GHQ depression and poor self rated health in white collar women and men in the Whitehall II study. *Journal of Epidemiology and Community Health*, **57**, 718–23.

Martikainen, P., Kauppinen, T.M. & Valkonen, T. (2003). Effects of the characteristics of neighbourhoods and the characteristics of people on cause specific mortality: a register based follow up study of 252,000 men. *Journal of Epidemiology and Community Health*, **57**, 210–17.

Martikainen, P., Valkonen, T. & Martelin, T. (2001). Change in male and female life expectancy by social class: decomposition by age and cause of death in Finland 1971–95. *Journal of Epidemiology and Community Health*, **55**, 494–9.

Martinez, M.L., Black, M. & Starr, R.H. (2002). Factorial structure of the perceived neighbourhood scale (PNS): a test of longitudinal invariance. *Journal of Community Psychology*, **30**, 23–43.

Marshall, H. & Yazdani, A. (1999). Locating culture in accounting for self-harm amongst Asian young women. *Journal of Community and Applied Social Psychology*, **9**, 413–33.

Martín-Baró, I. (1994). *Writings for a Liberation Psychology*, edited by A. Aron and S. Corne. Cambridge, MA: Harvard University Press.

Marx, C.M. (2000). *Exploring women's psychological sense of community in two relational communities.*Unpublished senior honors thesis, University of Maryland Baltimore County, Baltimore, Maryland, USA (cited by Brodsky *et al.*, 2002).

Massey, D.S. & Shibuya, K. (1995). Unraveling the tangle of pathology: the effect of spatially concentrated joblessness on the well-being of African Americans. *Social Science Research*, **24**, 352–66.

Masson, J. (1989). *Against Therapy*. London: Harper Collins.

Mathers, C.D., Salomon, J.A. & Murray, C.J.L. (2003). Infant mortality is not an adequate summary measure of population health. *Journal of Epidemiology and Community Health*, **57**, 319.

Maton, K.I. & Salem, D.A. (1995). Organizational characteristics of empowering community settings: a multiple case study approach. *American Journal of Community Psychology*, **23**, 631–56.

Maton, K.I., Perkins, D.D. & Saegert, S. (2006). Community psychology at the crossroads: prospects for interdisciplinary research. *American Journal of Community Psychology*, **38**, 9–21.

Matthews, S., Hertzman, C., Ostry, A. & Power, C. (1998). Gender, work roles and psychosocial work characteristics as determinants of health. *Social Science and Medicine*, **46**, 1417–24.

Matthews, S., Manor, O. & Power, C. (1999). Social inequalities in health: are there gender differences? *Social Science and Medicine*, **48**, 49–60.

Matthews, W.J. (1998). Let's get real: the fallacy of postmodernism. *Journal of Theoretical and Philosophical Psychology*, **18**, 16–32 (cited by Krippner, 2001).

Maughan, B. & Lindelow, M. (1997). Secular change in psychosocial risks: the case of teenage motherhood. *Psychological Medicine*, **27**, 1129–44.

May, R. (1967). *Psychology and the Human Dilemma*. New York: Norton (cited by Krippner, 2001).

Melluish, S. & Bulmer, D. (1999). Rebuilding solidarity: an account of a men's health action project. *Journal of Community and Applied Social Psychology*, **9**, 93–100.

Meltzer, H., Gill, B., Petticrew, M. and Hinds, K. (1995). *Survey of Psychiatric Morbidity, Report 1: The Prevalence of Psychiatric Morbidity Among Adults Aged 16–64 Living in Private Households in Great Britain*, London: HMSO.

Melzer, D., McWilliams, B., Brayne, C., Johnson, T. and Bond, J. (2000). Socioeconomic status and the expectation of disability in old age: estimates for England. *Journal of Epidemiology and Community Health*, **54**, 286–92.

Memmi, A. (1996). *Retrato del Colonizado*. Buenos Aires, Argentina: Ediciones La Flor (cited by Varas-Díaz and Serrano-García, 2003).

Merlo, J. (2003). Multilevel analytical approaches in social epidemiology: measures of health variation compared with traditional measures of association. *Journal of Epidemiology and Community Health*, **57**, 550–2.

Middleton, S. (2002). Transitions from youth to adulthood. In M. Barnes, C. Heady, C. S. Middleton, J. Millar, F. Papadopoulos, G. Room, G. & P. Tsakloglou (eds), *Poverty and Social Exclusion in Europe* (pp. 53–78). Cheltenham, UK: Edward Elgar.

Middleton, S. (2002). Transition into retirement. In M. Barnes, C. Heady, C. S. Middleton *et al.* (eds), *Poverty and Social Exclusion in Europe* (pp. 123–145). Cheltenham, UK: Edward Elgar.

Middleton, S., Barnes, M. & Millar, J. (2003). Introduction: the dynamic analysis of poverty and social exclusion. In E. Apospori & J. Millar (eds), *The Dynamics of Social Exclusion in Europe: Comparing Austria, Germany, Greece, Portugal and the UK* (pp. 1–15). Cheltenham, UK: Edward Elgar.

Millar, J. (2002). Lone parenthood. In M. Barnes, C. Heady, C. S. Middleton *et al.* (eds), *Poverty and Social Exclusion in Europe* (pp. 79–100). Cheltenham, UK: Edward Elgar.

Millar, J. & Middleton, S. (2002). Introduction. In M. Barnes, C. Heady, C.S. Middleton *et al.* (eds), *Poverty and Social Exclusion in Europe* (pp. xi–xiii). Cheltenham, UK: Edward Elgar.

Miller, J.B. (1988). Women and power. In M. Braude (ed.), *Women Power and Therapy*. New York: Harrington Park Press (cited by Friedman & Todd, 1994).

Miller, K. (1996). The effects of state terrorism and exile on indigenous Guatemalan refugee children: a mental health assessment and an analysis of children's narratives. *Child Development*, **67**, 89–106 (cited by Banyard & Miller, 1998).

Miller, K. (2004). Beyond the frontstage: trust, access, and the relational context in research with refugee communities. *American Journal of Community Psychology*, **33**, 217–27.

Miller, R.L. & Shinn, M. (2005). Learning from communities: overcoming difficulties in dissemination of prevention and promotion efforts. *American Journal of Community Psychology*, **35**, 169–83.

Mishler, E.G. (1994). Foreword. In I. Martín-Baró, A. Aron & S. Corne (eds), *Writings for a Liberation Psychology*. Cambridge, MA: Harvard University Press.

Moane, G. (2003). Bridging the personal and the political: practices for a liberation psychology. *American Journal of Community Psychology*, **31**, 91–101.

Mollica, R.F., Poole, C. & Tor, S. (1998). Symptoms, functioning, and health problems in a massively traumatized population: the legacy of the Cambodian tragedy. In B.P. Dohrenwend (ed.), *Adversity, Stress, and Psychopathology* (pp. 34–51). Oxford, UK: Oxford University Press.

Molinari, C., Ahern, M. & Hendryx, M. (1998). The relationship of community quality to the health of women and men. *Social Science and Medicine*, **47**, 1113–20.

Monden, C.W.S., van Lenthe, F., De Graaf, N.D. & Kraaykamp, G. (2003). Partner's and own education: does who you live with matter for self-assessed health, smoking and excessive alcohol consumption? *Social Science and Medicine*, **57**, 1901–12.

Montenegro, M. (2002). Ideology and community social psychology: theoretical considerations and practical implications. *American Journal of Community Psychology*, **30**, 511–27.

Montero, M. (1996). Parallel lives: community psychology in Latin America and the United States. *American Journal of Community Psychology*, **24**, 589–605.

Montero, M. (1998a). Psychosocial community work as an alternative mode of political action (the construction and critical transformation of society). *Community, Work and Family*, **1**, 65–78 (cited by Burton & Kagan, 2005).

Montero, M. (1998b). Introduction: the Latin American approach to community psychology. *Journal of Community Psychology*, **26**, 199–203.

Montero, M. (1998c). Dialetic between active minorities and majorities: a study of social influence in the community. *Journal of Community Psychology*, **26**, 281–9.

Montero, M. (2000). Participation in participatory action research. *Annual Review of Critical Psychology*, **2**, 131–44 (cited by Burton & Kagan, 2005).

Montero, M. (2002). On the construction of reality and truth: towards an epistemology of community social psychology. *American Journal of Community Psychology*, **30**, 571–84 (cited by Burton & Kagan, 2005).

Montero, M. (2004). *Introducción a la Psicología Comunitaria: Desarrollo, Conceptos y Procesos*. Buenos Aires: Paidós (cited by Kagan *et al.*, 2005).

Moodie, E., Marková, I., Farr, R. & Plichtová, J. (1997). The meanings of the community and of the individual in Slovakia and in Scotland. *Journal of Community and Applied Social Psychology*, **7**, 19–37.

Moore, S., Haines, V., Hawe, P. & Shiell, A. (2006). Lost in translation: a genealogy of the 'social capital' concept in public health. *Journal of Epidemiology and Community Health*, **60**, 729–34.

Moos, R.H. (1974). *Evaluating Treatment Environments: a Social Ecological Approach*. New York: John Wiley & Sons, Inc.

Moos, R.H. (1996). Understanding environments: the key to improving social processes and program outcomes. *American Journal of Community Psychology*, **24**, 193–201 (cited by Solomon *et al.*, 2001).

Moos, R.H. (2003). Social contexts: transcending their power and their fragility. *American Journal of Community Psychology*, **31**, 1–13.

Moos, R.H. & Lenke, S. (1983). Assessing and improving social and ecological settings. In E. Seidman (ed.), *Handbook of Social Intervention* (pp. 143–62). Beverly Hills, CA: Sage (cited by Chesir-Teran, 2003).

Morgan, H., Pocock, H. & Pottle, S. (1975). The urban distribution of non-fatal deliberate self-harm. *British Journal of Psychiatry*, **126**, 319–28.

Morgan, M. & O'Neill, D. (2001). Pragmatic post-structuralism (II): an outcomes evaluation of a stopping violence programme. *Journal of Community and Applied Social Psychology*, **11**, 277–89.

Moscovici, S. (1972). Society and theory in social psychology. In J. Israel & H. Tajfel (eds.), *The Context of Social Psychology* (pp. 17–68). London: Academic Press (cited by Hepburn, 2003).

Moscovici, S. (1984). The phenomenon of social representations. In R.M. Farr & S. Moscovici (eds.), *Social Representations* (pp. 3–69). Cambridge, UK: Cambridge University Press (cited by Bar-Tal, 2000).

Moser, K., Li, L. & Power, C. (2003). Social inequalities in low birth weight in England and Wales: trends and implications for future population health. *Journal of Epidemiology and Community Health*, **57**, 687–91.

Mulvey, A. (1988). Community psychology and feminism: tensions and commonalities. *Journal of Community Psychology*, **16**, 70–83.

Mulvey, A., Terenzio, M., Hill, J., Bond, M.A., Huygens, I., Hamerton, H.R. & Cahill, S. (2000). Stores of relative privilege: power and social change in feminist community psychology. *American Journal of Community Psychology*, **28**, 883–911.

Munczek, D. & Tuber, S. (1998). Political repression and its psychological effects on Honduran children. *Social Science and Medicine*, **47**, 1699–713.

Muñoz, M., Panadero, S., Santos, E.P. & Quiroga, M.A. (2005). Role of stressful life events in homelessness: an intragroup analysis. *American Journal of Community Psychology*, **35**, 35–47.

Muñoz, M., Vázquez, C., Bermejo, M. & Vázquez, J.J. (1999). Stressful life events among homeless people: quantity, types, timing, and perceived causality. *Journal of Community Psychology*, **27**, 73–87.

Muntaner, C., Eaton, W.W., Diala, C., Kessler, R.C. & Sorlie, P.D. (1998). Social class, assets, organizational control and the prevalence of common groups of psychiatric disorders. *Social Science and Medicine*, **47**, 2043–53.

Muntaner, C. & Lynch, J. (1999). Income inequality, social cohesion, and class relations: a critique of Wilkinson's neo-Durkheimian research program. *International Journal of Health Services*, **29**, 59–81.

Muntaner, C., Lynch, J. & Davey Smith G. (2000). Social capital and the third way in public health. *Critical Public Health*, **10**, 107–24.

Muntaner, C., Lynch, J. & Davey Smith G. (2001). Social capital, disorganized communities, and the third way: understanding the retreat from structural inequalities in epidemiology and public health. *International Journal of Health Services*, **31**, 213–37.

Murphy, S. & Bennett, P. (2004). Health psychology and public health: theoretical possibilities. *Journal of Health Psychology*, **9**, 13–27.

Murray, M. & Campbell, C. (2003). Living in a material world: reflecting on some assumptions of health psychology. *Journal of Health Psychology*, **8**, 231–6.

Murray, M., Nelson, G., Poland, B., Maticka-Tyndale, E. & Ferris, L. (2004). Assumptions and values of community health psychology. *Journal of Health Psychology*, **9**, 323–33.

Mustard, C.A., Vermeulen, M. & Lavis, J.N. (2003). Is position in the occupational hierarchy a determinant of decline in perceived health status? *Social Science and Medicine*, **57**, 2291–303.

Næss, O., Claussen, B. & Davey Smith, G. (2004a). Relative impact of childhood and adulthood socioeconomic conditions on cause specific mortality in men. *Journal of Epidemiology and Community Health*, **58**, 597–8.

Næss, O., Claussen, B., Thelle, D.S. & Davey Smith, G. (2004b). Cumulative deprivation and cause specific mortality. A census based study of life course influences over three decades. *Journal of Epidemiology and Community Health*, **58**, 599–603.

Nagel, T. (1986). *The View from Nowhere*. New York: Oxford University Press (cited by Fondacaro & Weinberg, 2002).

Najman, J.M., Aird, R., Bor, W., O'Callaghan, M., Williams, G.M. & Shuttlewood, G.J. (2004). The generational transmission of socioeconomic inequalities in child cognitive development and emotional health. *Social Science and Medicine*, **58**, 1147–58.

Nama, N. & Swartz, L. (2002). Ethical and social dilemmas in community-based controlled trials in situations of poverty: a view from a South African project. *Journal of Community and Applied Social Psychology*, **12**, 286–97.

Narayan, D. R., Patel, K., Schafft, A. & Koch-Schulte, S. (2000). *Voices of the Poor: Can Anyone Hear Us?* New York: Oxford University Press, for the World Bank.

Nasser, M. (1999). The new veiling phenomenon – is it an anorexic equivalent? A polemic. *Journal of Community and Applied Social Psychology*, **9**, 407–12.

Nazroo, J.Y. (2001). *Ethnicity, Class and Health*. London: Policy Studies Institute.

Nelson, G. & Prilleltensky, I. (eds.) (2005). *Community Psychology: In Pursuit of Liberation and Well-being*, Basingstoke: Palgrave-Macmillan.

Nelson, G., Ochocka, J., Griffin, K. & Lord, J. (1998). 'Nothing about me, without me': participatory action research with self-help/mutual aid organizations for psychiatric consumer/survivors. *American Journal of Community Psychology*, **26**, 881–912.

Nelson, G., Ochocka, J., Trainor, J. & Janzen, R. (2006). A longitudinal study of mental health consumer/survivor initiatives: part 1 – literature review and overview of the study. *Journal of Community Psychology*, **34**, 247–60.

Nelson, G., Pancer, S.M., Hayward, K. & Kelly, R. (2004). Partnerships and participation of community residents in health promotion and prevention: experiences of the Highfield community enrichment project (better beginnings, better futures). *Journal of Health Psychology*, **9**, 213–27.

Nesdale, D. & Mak, A.S. (2000). Immigrant acculturation attitudes and host country identification. *Journal of Community and Applied Social Psychology*, **10**, 483–95.

Newbrough, J.R. (1995). Toward community: a third position. *American Journal of Community Psychology*, **23**, 9–37.

Ng, S. (1980). *The Social Psychology of Power*. London: Academic Press.

Ngonyama ka Sigogo, T., Hooper, M., Long, C., Brinton Lykes, M., Wilson, K. & Zietkiewicz, E. (2004). Chasing rainbow notions: enacting community psychology in the classroom and beyond in post-1994 South Africa. *American Journal of Community Psychology*, **33**, 77–89.

Ngonyama ka Sigogo, T. & Modipa, O.T. (2004). Critical reflections on community and psychology in South Africa. In D. Hook (ed.), *Critical Psychology*, (pp. 316–34). Cape Town: University of Cape Town.

Nicholson, A., Bobak, M., Murphy, M., Rose, R. & Marmot, M. (2005). Socio-economic influences on self-rated health in Russian men and women – a life course approach. *Social Science and Medicine*, **61**, 2345–54.

Niedhammer, I., Tek, M., Starke, D. & Siegrist, J. (2004). Effort-reward imbalance model and self-reported health: cross-sectional and prospective findings from the GAZEL cohort. *Social Science and Medicine*, **58**, 1531–41.

Nolte, E. (2000). The health impact of German unification: still much to learn. *Journal of Epidemiology and Community Health*, **54**, 565.

Noor, N.M. (1997). The relationship between wives' estimates of time spent doing housework, support and wives' well-being. *Journal of Community and Applied Social Psychology*, **7**, 413–23.

Novo, M., Hammarström & Janlert, U. (2001). Do high levels of unemployment influence the health of those who are not unemployed? A gendered comparison of young men and women during boom and recession. *Social Science and Medicine*, **53**, 293–303.

Nystrom, N.M. & Jones, T.C. (2003). Community building with aging and old lesbians. *American Journal of Community Psychology*, **31**, 293–300.

Oakes, J.M. (2004a). The (mis)estimation of neighborhood effects: causal inference for a practicable social epidemiology. *Social Science and Medicine*, **58**, 1929–52.

Oakes, J.M. (2004b). Causal inference and the relevance of social epidemiology. *Social Science and Medicine*, **58**, 1969–71.

Oakes, J.M. & Rossi, P.H. (2003). The measurement of SES in health research: current practice and steps towards a new approach. *Social Science and Medicine*, **56**, 769–84.

Obst, P., Zinkiewicz, L. & Smith, S.G. (2002). An exploration of sense of community, part 3: dimensions and predictors of psychological sense of community in geographical communities. *Journal of Community Psychology*, **30**, 119–33.

Obst, P. & White, K.M. (2004). Revisiting the sense of community index: a confirmatory factor analysis. *Journal of Community Psychology*, **32**, 691–705.

O'Campo, P., Burke, J., Peak, G.L., McDonnell, K.A. & Gielen, A.C. (2005). Uncovering neighbourhood influences on intimate partner violence using concept mapping. *Journal of Epidemiology and Community Health*, **59**, 603–8.

O'Campo, P., Gielen, A., Faden, R. *et al.* (1995). Violence by male partners against women during the childbearing year: a contextual analysis. *American Journal of Public Health*, **85**, 1092–7.

Office for National Statistics (2002). *The National Statistics Socio-economic Classification User Manual 2002*. London: HMSO.

O'Neill, D. & Morgan, M. (2001). Pragmatic post-structuralism (I): participant observation and discourse in evaluating violence intervention. *Journal of Community and Applied Social Psychology*, **11**, 263–75.

Onishi, A. & Murphy-Shigematsu, S. (2003). Identity narratives of Muslim foreign workers in Japan. *Journal of Community and Applied Social Psychology*, **13**, 224–39.

Onyx, J. & Bullen, P. (2000). Measuring social capital in five communities. *Journal of Applied Behavioral Science*, **36**, 23–42.

Onyx, J. & Bullen, P. (2001). The different faces of social capital in NSW Australia. In P. Dekker & E. M. Uslaner (eds.), *Social Capital and Participation in Everyday Life* (pp. 45–58). London: Routledge/ECPR Studies in European Political Science.

O'Reilly, D. & Stevenson, M. (2003). Selective migration from deprived areas in Northern Ireland and the spatial distribution of inequalities: implications for monitoring health and inequalities in health. *Social Science and Medicine*, **57**, 1455–62.

O'Reilly, D. & Stevenson, M. (2003). Mental health in Northern Ireland: have 'the troubles' made it worse? *Journal of Epidemiology and Community Health*, **57**, 488–92.

Orford, J. (ed.) (1987). *Coping with Disorder in the Family*. London: Croom Helm.

Orford, J. (1992). *Community Psychology: Theory and Practice*, Chichester, UK: John Wiley & Sons, Ltd.

Orford, J., Natera, G., Copello, A., Atkinson, C., Mora, J., Velleman, R., Crundall, I., Tiburcio, M., Templeton, L. & Walley, G. (2005). *Coping with Alcohol and Drug Problems: The Experiences of Family Members in Three Contrasting Cultures*. London: Brunner-Routledge.

Osterkamp, U. (1999). On psychology, ideology and individuals' societal nature. *Theory and Psychology*, **3**, 379–92.

Ostler, K., Thompson, C., Kinmonth, A.L.K., Peveler, R.C., Stevens, L. & Stevens, A. (2001). Influence of socio-economic deprivation on the prevalence and outcome of depression in primary care. *British Journal of Psychiatry*, **178**, 12–17.

Ostrom, E. & Ahn, T.K. (2003). Introduction. In E. Ostrom & T.K. Ahn (eds), *Foundations of Social Capital* (pp. xi–xxxix). Cheltenham, UK: Edward Elgar.

Ostrove, J.M., Feldman, P. & Adler, N.E. (1999). Relations among socioeconomic status indicators and health for African-Americans and Whites. *Journal of Health Psychology*, **4**, 451–63.

O'Sullivan, E. (2000). Critical psychology as critical vision. In T. Sloan (ed.), *Critical Psychology: Voices for Change* (pp.136–46). New York: St Martin's Press.

Otten, F.W.J. & Bosman, H.H.A. (1997). The socio-economic distribution of heart diseases: changing gradients in the Netherlands. *Social Science and Medicine*, **44**, 1349–56.

Otto, S. & Orford, J. (1978). *Not Quite Like Home: Small Hostels for Alcoholics and Others*. Chichester, UK: John Wiley & Sons, Ltd.

Panelli, R., Gallagher, L. & Kearns, R. (2006). Access to rural health services: research as community action and policy critique. *Social Science and Medicine*, **62**, 1103–14.

Papworth, M.A., Milne, D.L. & Taylor, K. (2001). Primary prevention of psychological difficulties in vulnerable mothers: pilot programme evaluation. *Journal of Community and Applied Social Psychology*, **11**, 51–6.

Parker, I. (1997). *Psychoanalytic Culture: Psychoanalytic Discourse in Western Society*. London: Sage (cited by Hepburn, 2003).

Parkes, K.R. (1989). Personal control in an occupational context. In A. Steptoe & A. Appels (eds), *Stress, Personal Control and Health* (pp. 21–48). Chichester, UK: John Wiley & Sons, Ltd.

Parra, G.R., DuBois, D.L., Neville, H.A. & Pugh-Lilly, A.O. (2002). Mentoring relationships for youth: investigation of a process-oriented model. *Journal of Community Psychology*, **30**, 367–88.

Parry, J.M., Orford, J., Laburn-Peart, K. & Dalton, S. (2005). Mechanisms by which area-based regeneration programmes might impact on community health: a case study of the New Deal for Communities initiative. *Journal of the Royal Institute of Public Health*, **118**, 497–505.

Parry, J.M., Mathers, J.M., Laburn-Peart, C., Orford, J.F. & Dalton, S. (2007). Improving health in deprived communities: what can residents teach us? *Critical Public Health*, **17**, 123–36.

Pattenden, S., Dolk, H. & Vrijheid, M. (1999). Inequalities in low birth weight: parental social class, area deprivation, and 'lone mother' status. *Journal of Epidemiology and Community Health*, **53**, 355–8.

Patton, W. & Donohue. R. (1998). Coping with long-term unemployment. *Journal of Community and Applied Social Psychology*, **8**, 331–43.

Pearce, J., Witten, K. & Bartie, P. (2006). Neighbourhoods and health: a GIS approach to measuring community resource accessibility. *Journal of Epidemiology and Community Health*, **60**, 389–95.

Pedersen, A., Beven, J., Walker, I. and Griffiths, B. (2004). Attitudes toward indigenous Australians: the role of empathy and guilt. *Journal of Community and Applied Social Psychology*, **14**, 233–49.

Pensola, T. & Martikainen, P. (2004). Life-course experiences and mortality by adult social class among young men. *Social Science and Medicine*, **58**, 2149–70.

Pepper, S.C. (1942). *World Hypotheses*. Berkeley: University of California Press (cited by Tebes, 2005).

Perilla, J.L. (1999). Domestic violence as a human rights issue: the case of immigrant Latinos. *Hispanic Journal of Behavioral Sciences*, **21**, 107–33.

Perkins, D.D., Brown, B.B. & Taylor, R.B. (1996). The ecology of empowerment: predicting participating in community organizations. *Journal of Social Issues*, **52**, 85–110.

Perkins, D.D., Florin, P., Rich, R.C., Wandersman, A. & Chavis, D.M. (1990). Participation and the social and physical environment of residential blocks: crime and community context. *American Journal of Community Psychology*, **18**, 83–115 (cited by Wandersman & Florin, 2000).

Perkins, D.D. & Long, D.A. (2002). Neighborhood sense of community and social capital: a multi-level analysis. In A.T. Fisher, C.C. Sonn & B.J. Bishop (eds), *Psychological Sense of Community: Research, Applications, and Implications* (pp. 291–318). New York: Kluwer/Plenum.

Perkins, D.D., Meeks, J.W. & Taylor, R.B. (1992). The physical environment of street blocks and resident perceptions of crime and disorder: implications for theory and measurement. *Journal of Environmental Psychology*, **12**, 21–34 (cited by Perkins & Taylor, 1996).

Perkins, D.D. & Taylor, R.B. (1996). Ecological assessments of community disorder: their relationship to fear of crime and theoretical implications. *American Journal of Community Psychology*, **24**, 63–107.

Perkins, D.D. and Zimmerman, M.A. (1995). Empowerment theory, research, and application: an introduction to a special issue. *American Journal of Community Psychology*, **23**, 569–79 (cited by Peterson *et al.*, 2005).

Peters, K. & Richards, P. (1998). Fighting with open eyes: youth combatants talking about war in Sierra Leone. In P.J. Bracken & C. Petty (eds), *Rethinking the Trauma of War* (pp. 76–111). London: Free Association Books.

Peterson, N.A. & Hughey, J. (2004). Social cohesion and intrapersonal empowerment: gender as moderator. *Health Education Research*, **19**, 533–42. (cited by Peterson *et al.*, 2005).

Peterson, N.A., Lower, J.B., Aquilino, M.L. & Schneider, J.E. (2005). Linking social cohesion and gender to intrapersonal and interactional empowerment: support and new implications for theory. *Journal of Community Psychology*, **33**, 233–44.

Peterson, N. & Zimmerman, M.A. (2004). Beyond the individual: toward a nomological network of organizational empowerment. *American Journal of Community Psychology*, **34**, 129–45.

Petrelli, A., Gnavi, R., Marinacci, C. & Costa, G. (2006). Socioeconomic inequalities in coronary heart disease in Italy: a multilevel population-based study. *Social Science and Medicine*, **62**, 1–11.

Pettigrew, T.F. & Meertens, R.W. (1995). Subtle and blatant prejudice in western Europe. *European Journal of Social Psychology*, **25**, 57–75 (cited by Vrij & Smith, 1999).

Philip, K. & Hendry, L.B. (2000). Making sense of mentoring or mentoring making sense: reflections on the mentoring process by adult mentors with young people. *Journal of Community and Applied Social Psychology*, **10**, 221–3.

Pickett, K.E. & Pearl, M. (2001). Multilevel analyses of neighbourhood socioeconomic context and health outcomes: a critical review. *Journal of Epidemiology and Community Health*, **55**, 111–22.

Pikhart, H., Bobak, M., Pajak, A., Malyutina, S., Kubinova, R., Topor, R., Sebakova, H., Nikitin, Y. & Marmot, M. (2004). Psychosocial factors at work and depression in three countries in Central and Eastern Europe. *Social Science and Medicine*, **58**, 1475–82.

Piko, B.F. (2004). Interplay between self and community: a role for health psychology in eastern Europe's public health. *Journal of Health Psychology*, **9**, 111–20.

Pilgrim, D. (1991). Psychotherapy and social blinkers. *The Psychologist*, **4**, 52–55.

Pilgrim, D. (1997). *Psychotherapy and Society*. London: Sage.

Pilisuk, M., McAllister, J. & Rothman, J. (1996). Coming together for action: the challenge of contemporary grassroots community organizing. *Journal of Social Issues*, **52**, 15–37.

Piirainen, T. (1997). *Towards a New Social Order in Russia. Transforming Structures and Everyday Life*. Aldershot: Dartmouth Company (cited by Carlson, 2000).

Pistrang, N. & Barker, C. (1992). Disclosure of concerns in breast cancer. *Psycho-Oncology*, **1**, 183–92.

Pistrang, N., Solomons, W. & Barker, C. (1999). Peer support for women with breast cancer: the role of empathy and self-disclosure. *Journal of Community and Applied Social Psychology*, **9**, 217–29.

Plant, M. & Harrison, L. (2001). Prevention and harm minimisation in the UK. Draft briefing paper for the Alcohol Concern Alcohol Research Forum, London.

Plas, J.M. & Lewis, S.E. (1996). Environmental factors and sense of community in a planned town. *American Journal of Community Psychology*, **24**, 109–43.

Plitchtová, J. and Erös, F. (1997). The significance of political and economic change in two generations of Slovaks and Hungarians. *Journal of Community and Applied Social Psychology*, **7**, 89–101.

Polanyi, M. (1964). *Personal Knowledge: Towards a Post-Critical Philosophy*. New York: Harper and Row (cited by Hess, 2005).

Pooley, J.A., Pike, L.T., Drew, N.M. & Breen, L. (2002). Inferring Australian children's sense of community: a critical exploration. *Community, Work and Family*, **5**, 5–22.

Poortinga, W. (2006a). Social relations or social capital? Individual and community health effects or bonding social capital. *Social Science and Medicine*, **63**, 255–70.

Poortinga, W. (2006b). Social capital: an individual or collective resource for health? *Social Science and Medicine*, **62**, 292–302.

Popay, J., Thomas, C., Williams, G., Bennett, S., Gatrell, A. & Bostock, L. (2003). A proper place to live: health inequalities, agency and the normative dimensions of space. *Social Science and Medicine*, **57**, 55–69.

Popay, J., Williams, G., Thomas, C. & Gatrell, A. (1998). Theorising inequalities in health: the place of lay knowledge. *Sociology of Health and Illness*, **20**, 619–44.

Popper, K. (1959). *The Logic of Scientific Discovery*. New York: Basic Books (cited by Tebes, 2005) (first published in 1935 in German).

Porkorny, S.B., Baptiste, D.R., Tolan, P., Hirsch, B.J., Talbot, B.J.P., Paikoff, R.L. & Madison-Boyd, S. (2004). Prevention science: participatory approaches and community case studies. In L.A. Jason, C.B. Keys, Y. Suarez-Balcazar, R.R. Taylor & M.I. Davis (eds), *Participatory Community Research: Theories and Methods in Action* (pp. 87–104). Washington, DC: American Psychological Association.

Porter, R. (1997). *The Greatest Benefit to Mankind: a Medical History of Humanity from Antiquity to the Present*. London: Harper-Collins (reviewed by Mitchell, A. *Journal of Community and Applied Social Psychology*, 1998, **8**, 377–80).

Portes, A. (1995). Economic sociology and the sociology of immigration: a conceptual overview. In A. Portes (ed.), *Essays on Networks, Ethnicity and Entrepreneurship*. New York: Russell Sage Foundation (cited by Colic-Peisker and Walker, 2003).

Portes, A. (1998). Social capital: its origins and applications in modern sociology. *Annual Review of Sociology*, **24**, 1–24 (cited by Grootaert, 2001).

Potter, J. (1996). *Representing Reality: Discourse, Rhetoric and Social Construction*. London: Sage (cited by Hepburn, 2003).

Potts, R.G. (2003). Emancipatory education versus school-based prevention in African American communities. *American Journal of Community Psychology*, **31**, 173–83.

Power, K.G., Dyson, G.P. & Wozniak, E. (1997). Bullying among Scottish young offenders: inmates' self-reported attitudes and behaviour. *Journal of Community and Applied Social Psychology*, **7**, 209–18.

Prandy, K. (1990). The revised Cambridge scale of occupations. *Sociology*, **24**, 629–55 (cited by Bartley, 1999).

Pratto, F., Liu, J.H., Levin, S., Sidanius, J., Shih, M., Bachrach, H. & Hegarty, P. (2000). Social dominance orientation and the legitimization of inequality across cultures. *Journal of Cross-Cultural Psychology*, **31**, 369–409.

Preti, A. (2003). Unemployment and suicide. *Journal of Epidemiology and Community Health*, **57**, 557–8.

Pretty, G.M.H. (2002). Young people's development of the community-minded self: considering community identity, community attachment and sense of community. In A.T. Fisher, C.C. Sonn & B.J. Bishop (eds), *Psychological Sense of Community* (pp. 183–203). New York: Kluwer/Plenum.

Prezza, M. & Costantini, S. (1998). Sense of community and life satisfaction: investigation in three different territorial contexts. *Journal of Community and Applied Social Psychology*, **8**, 181–94.

Prezza, M. Costantini, S., Chiarolanza, V. & Di Marco, S. (1999). La scala Italianao del senso di communita (The Italian scale of sense of community). *Psicologia della Salute*, **3–4**, 135–59 (cited by Zani *et al.*, 2001).

Prezza, M., Pilloni, S., Morabito, C., Sersante, C., Alparone, F.R. & Giuliani, M.V. (2001). The influence of psychosocial and environmental factors on children's independent mobility and relationship to peer frequentation. *Journal of Community and Applied Social Psychology*, **11**, 435–50.

Price, R.H. & Behrens, T. (2003). Working Pasteur's quadrant: harnessing science and action for community change. *American Journal of Community Psychology*, **31**, 219–23.

Prilleltensky, I. (1994). *The Morals and Politics of Psychology: Psychological Discourse and the Status Quo*. New York: State University of New York Press.

Prilleltensky, I. (2003). Understanding, resisting, and overcoming oppression: toward psychopolitical validity. *American Journal of Community Psychology*, **31**, 195–201.

Prilleltensky, I. & Nelson, G. (1997). Community psychology: reclaiming social Justice. In D. Fox & I. Prilleltensky (eds), *Critical Psychology: An Introduction* (pp. 166–84). Thousand Oaks, CA: Sage.

Prilleltensky, I. & Nelson, G. (2000). Promoting child and family wellness: priorities for psychological and social interventions. *Journal of Community and Applied Social Psychology*, **10**, 85–105.

Prilleltensky, I., Nelson, G. & Peirson, L. (2001). The role of power and control in children's lives: an ecological analysis of pathways toward wellness, resilience and problems. *Journal of Community and Applied Social Psychology*, **11**, 143–58.

Prilleltensky, I. & Prilleltensky O. (2003a). Towards a critical health psychology practice. *Journal of Health Psychology*, **8**, 197–210.

Prilleltensky, I. & Prilleltensky O. (2003b). Reconciling the roles of professional helper and critical agent in health psychology. *Journal of Health Psychology*, **8**, 243–6.

Puddifoot, J. (1995). Dimensions of community identity. *Journal of Community and Applied Social Psychology*, **5**, 1–14.

Putnam, R.D., with Leonardi, R. & Nanetti, R.Y. (1993). *Making Democracy Work: Civic Traditions in Modern Italy*. Princeton, NJ: Princeton University Press.

Putnam, R. (1995). Bowling alone: America's declining social capital. *Journal of Democracy*, **6**, 65–79.

Putnam, R. (2000). *Bowling Alone, the Collapse and Revival of American Community*. New York: Simon and Schuster.

Quaghebeur, I., Masschelein, J. & Nguyen, H.H. (2004). Paradox of participation: giving or taking part? *Journal of Community and Applied Social Psychology*, **14**, 154–65.

Quinton, D., Rutter, M. & Liddle, C. (1984). Institutional rearing, parenting difficulties and marital support. *Psychological Medicine*, **14**, 107–24 (cited by Blair, 1992).

Quirk, G. (1992). Symptoms that do not disappear. *Links Health and Development Report*, **9**, 4–5 (cited by Munczek & Tuber, 1998).

Quirk, G. & Casco, L. (1994). Stress disorders of families of the disappeared: a controlled study in Honduras. *Social Science and Medicine*, **39**, 1675–9.

Raeburn, J.M. & Thomas, D.R. (2000). New Zealand. In J. Rappaport & E. Seidman (eds), *Handbook of Community Psychology* (p. 798). New York: Kluwer/Plenum.

Ragan, P. & Wales, J. (1980). Age stratification and life course. In J. Birren & R. Sloane (eds), *Handbook of Mental Health and Aging*. Englewood Cliffs, NJ: Prentice-Hall.

Rahkonen, O., Arber, S. & Lahelma, E. (1995). Health inequalities in early adulthood: a comparison of young men and women in Britain and Finland. *Social Science and Medicine*, **41**, 163–71.

Raleigh, V.S. & Kiri, V.A. (1997). Life expectancy in England: variations and trends by gender, health authority, and level of deprivation. *Journal of Epidemiology and Community Health*, **51**, 649–58.

Ramella, M. & de la Cruz, R. (2000). Taking part in adolescent sexual health promotion in Peru: community participation from a social psychological perspective. *Journal of Community and Applied Social Psychology*, **10**, 271–84.

Rankin, B.H. & Quane, J.M. (2002). Social contexts and urban adolescent outcomes: the interrelated effects of neighborhoods, families, and peers on African-American youth. *Social Problems*, **49**, 79–100.

Raphael, D., Renwick, R., Brown, I., Steinmetz, B., Sehdev, H. & Phillips, S. (2001). Making the links between community structure and individual well-being: community quality of life in Riverdale, Toronto, Canada. *Health and Place*, **7**, 179–96.

Rapley, M., McHoul, A. & Hanse, S. (2003). I want, therefore I am: tribute to David Smail. *Clinical Psychology*, **24**, 13–19.

Rappaport, J. (1987). Terms of empowerment/exemplars of prevention: toward a theory for community psychology. *American Journal of Community Psychology*, **15**, 121–43 (cited by Zimmerman, 1995).

Rappaport, J. (1990). Research methods and the empowerment social agenda. In P. Tolan, C. Keys, F. Chertok & L. Jason (eds), *Researching Community Psychology: Issues of Theory and Methods* (pp.51–63). Washington, DC: American Psychological Association.

Rappaport, J. (1992). The dilemma of primary prevention in mental health services: rationalize the status quo or bite the hand that feeds you (Commentary on: the role of primary prevention in mental health services: a review and critique by Alan Blair). *Journal of Community and Applied Social Psychology*, **2**, 95–9.

Rappaport, J. (2000a). Commentary on Prilleltensky and Nelson, Social responsibility and psychological language: is anyone else up there? *Journal of Community and Applied Social Psychology*, **10**, 107–22.

Rappaport, J. (2000b). Community narratives: tales of terror and joy. *American Journal of Community Psychology*, **28**, 1–24.

Rappaport, J. (2005). Community psychology is (thank God) more than science. *American Journal of Community Psychology*, **35**, 231–8.

Raven, B.H. (1993). The bases of power: origins and recent developments. *Journal of Social Issues*, **49**, 227–51.

Rawls, J. (1971). *A Theory of Justice*. Cambridge, Massachusetts: Harvard University Press (cited by Sen, 1999).

Reason, P. & Bradbury, H. (eds) (2001). *Handbook of Action Research: Participative Inquiry and Practice*. London: Sage.

Regidor, E., Calle, M.E., Navarro, P. & Dominguez, V. (2003). Trends in the association between average income, poverty and income inequality and life expectancy in Spain. *Social Science and Medicine*, **56**, 961–71.

Reid, J. & Trompf, P. (eds) (1991). *The Health of Aboriginal Australia*. Sydney: Harcourt Brace Jovanovich.

Reid, P.T. (1993). Poor women in psychological research: shut up and shut out. *Psychology of Women Quarterly*, **17**, 133–50.

Reidpath, D.D. & Allotey, P. (2003). Infant mortality rate as an indicator of population health. *Journal of Epidemiology and Community Health*, **57**, 344–6.

Reijneveld, S.A., Verheij, R.A. & de Bakker, D.H. (2000). The impact of area deprivation on differences in health: does the choice of the geographical classification matter? *Journal of Epidemiology and Community Health*, **54**, 306–13.

Reine, I., Novo, M. & Hammarström, A. (2004). Does the association between ill health and unemployment differ between young people and adults? Results from a 14-year follow-up study with a focus on psychological health and smoking. *Public Health*, **118**, 337–45.

Reynolds, W.M. & Coats, K.I. (1986). A comparison of cognitive behavioral therapy and relaxation training for the treatment of depression in adolescents. *Journal of Consulting and Clinical Psychology*, **54**, 653–60 (cited by Durlak & Wells, 1998).

Rhodes, J.E., Bogat, G.A., Roffman, J., Edelman, P. & Galasso, L. (2002). Youth mentoring in perspective: introduction to the special issue. *American Journal of Community Psychology*, **30**, 149–55.

Rich, R.C., Edelstein, M., Hallman, W.K. & Wandersman, A.H. (1995). Citizen participation and empowerment: the case of local environmental hazards. *American Journal of Community Psychology*, **23**, 657–76.

Riger, S. (1993). What's wrong with empowerment? *American Journal of Community Psychology*, **21**, 279–92.

Riger, S. (2001). Transforming community psychology. *American Journal of Community Psychology*, **29**, 69–81.

Rivers, I. (2002). Developmental issues for lesbian and gay youth. In A. Coyle & C. Kitzinger (eds), *Lesbian and Gay Psychology: New Perspectives* (pp. 30–46). Oxford: Blackwell.

Roberts, D. (1998). Self-determination and the struggle for Aboriginal equality. In C. Bourke, E. Bourke & B. Edwards (eds), *Aboriginal Australia* (pp. 259–88). Queensland: University of Queensland Press.

Roberts, I. & Coggan, C. (1994). Blaming children for child pedestrian injuries. *Social Science and Medicine*, **38**, 749–53.

Roberts, L., Smith, L. & Pollock, C. (2002). MOOing till the cows come home: the search for sense of community in virtual environments. In A.T. Fisher, C.C. Sonn & B.J. Bishop (eds), *Psychological Sense of Community* (pp. 223–45). New York: Kluwer/Plenum.

Robertson, R. (1992). *Globalization: Social Theory and Global Culture*. London: Sage (cited by Beck, 1999).

Rodriguez, E. (2002). Marginal employment and health in Britain and Germany: does unstable employment predict health? *Social Science and Medicine*, **55**, 963–79.

Rogers, E.M. (1995). *Diffusion of Innovations* (4th edn). New York: Free Press (cited by Hays et al., 2003).

Romito, P., DeMarchi, M., Turan, J.M., Bottaretto, R.C. & Tavi, M. (2004). Identifying violence among women patients attending family practices: the role of research in community change. *Journal of Community and Applied Social Psychology*, **14**, 250–65.

Romme. A.G.L. (2004). Commentary: action research, emancipation and design thinking. *Journal of Community and Applied Social Psychology*, **14**, 495–9.

Roos, L.L., Magoon, J., Gupta, S., Chateau, D. & Veugelers, P.J. (2004). Socioeconomic determinants of mortality in two Canadian provinces: multilevel modelling and neighborhood context. *Social Science and Medicine*, **59**, 1435–47.

Rose, R. (1995). Russia as an hour-glass society: a constitution without citizens. *East European Constitutional Review*, **4**, 34–42 (cited by Hertzman & Siddiqi, 2000).

Rose, R. (2000). How much does social capital add to individual health? A survey study of Russians. *Social Science and Medicine*, **51**, 1421–35.

Rose, R. & De Bie, M. (2003). From participative research to participative practice – a study in youth care. *Journal of Community and Applied Social Psychology*, **13**, 475–85.

Rosenfeld, S. (1989). The effects of women's employment: personal control and sex differences in mental health. *Journal of Health and Social Behavior*, **30**, 77–91.

Ross, C.E. (2000). Neighborhood disadvantage and adult depression. *Journal of Health and Social Behavior*, **41**, 177–87.

Ross, C.E., Reynolds, J.R. & Geis, K.J. (2000). The contingent meaning of neighborhood stability for residents' psychological well-being. *American Sociological Review*, **65**, 581–97.

Rotter, J. (1966). Generalized expectancies for internal versus external control of reinforcement. *Psychological Monographs*, **80**, No. 609.

Rumbaut, R.G. (1999). Assimilation and its discontents: ironies and paradoxes. In P. Kasinitz & J. DeWind (eds), *The Handbook of International Migration: The American Experience* (pp. 172–95). New York: Russell Sage Foundation (cited by Deaux, 2000).

Russell, G.M. & Richards, J.A. (2003). Stressor and resilience factors for lesbians, gay men, and bisexuals confronting antigay politics. *American Journal of Community Psychology*, **31**, 313–28.

Rutter, D., Manley, C., Weaver, T., Crawford, M.J. & Fulop, N. (2004). Patients or partners? Case studies of user involvement in the planning and delivery of adult mental health services in London. *Social Science and Medicine*, **58**, 1973–84.

Rutter, M. (1985). Resistance in the face of adversity: protective factors and resistance to psychiatric disorder. *British Journal of Psychiatry*, **147**, 598–611.

Rutter, M. (ed.), (1988). *Studies of Psychosocial Risk: The Power of Longitudinal Data*. Cambridge, UK: Cambridge University Press.

Ryan, W. (1971). *Blaming the Victim*. New York: Vintage Books.

Sacker, A., Clarke, P., Wiggins, R.D. & Bartley, M. (2005). Social dynamics of health inequalities: a growth curve analysis of aging and self assessed health in the British household panel survey 1991–2001. *Journal of Epidemiology and Community Health*, **59**, 495–501.

Sacker, A. & Wiggins, R.D. (2002). Age-period-cohort effects on inequalities in psychological distress, 1981–2000. *Psychological Medicine*, **32**, 977–90.

Saegert, S. & Winkel, G. (1996). Paths to community empowerment: organizing at home. *American Journal of Community Psychology*, **24**, 517–50.

Saegert, S. & Winkel, G. (2004). Crime, social capital, and community participation. *American Journal of Community Psychology*, **34**, 219–33.

Sagarin, E. (1969). *Odd Man In: Societies of Deviants in America*. Chicago: Quadrangle.

Saggers, S. & Gray, D. (1998). *Dealing with Alcohol: Indigenous Usage in Australia, New Zealand and Canada*. Cambridge, UK: Cambridge University Press.

Salmond, C. & Crampton, P. (2002). Heterogeneity of deprivation within very small areas. *Journal of Epidemiology and Community Health*, **56**, 669–70.

Salzer, M.S. (1998). Narrative approach to assessing interactions between society, community, and person. *Journal of Community Psychology*, **26**, 569–80.

Salzer, M.S., Rappaport, J. & Segre, L. (2001). Mental health professionals' support of self-help groups. *Journal of Community and Applied Social Psychology*, **11**, 1–10.

Sampson, E. (2000). Of rainbows and differences. In T. Sloan (ed.), *Critical Psychology: Voices for Change* (pp. 1–5). New York: St Martin's Press.

Sampson, R., Morenoff, J.D. & Gannon-Rowley, T. (2002). Assessing 'neighborhood effects': social processes and new directions in research. *Annual Review of Sociology*, **28**, 443–78.

Sampson, R., Raudenbush, S. & Earls, F. (1997). Neighborhoods and violent crime: a multilevel study of collective efficacy, *Science*, **277**, 918–24.

Sánchez-Vidal, A. (1988). Intervención comunitaria: Introducción conceptual, proceso y panorámica [Community intervention: Conceptual introduction, process and overview]. In A. Martin Gonálex, F. Chacón Fuertes and M. Martínez García (eds), *Psicología Comunitaira* [Community Psychology] (pp. 169–86). Madrid, Spain: Visor (cited by Krause, 2002).

Sánchez-Vidal, A. (2003). Report on the Fourth European Congress of Community Psychology, Barcelona, Spain.

Sánchez-Vidal, A. & Musitu, G. (eds) (1996). *Intervención Communitaria: Aspectos Cientifcos, Técnicos y Valorativos*. Barcelona: Editorial Universdad Barcelona (reviewed in *Journal of Community and Applied Social Psychology*, 2000, **10**, 166–7).

Sánchez, E., Wiesenfeld, E. & Cronick, K. (1991). Community social psychology in Venezuela. *Applied Psychology: an International Review*, **40**, 219–36.

Sanmartin, C., Ross, N.A., Tremblay, S., Wolfson, M., Dunn, J.R. & Lynch, J. (2003). Labour market income inequality and mortality in North American metropolitan areas. *Journal of Epidemiology and Community Health*, **57**, 792–7.

Santana, P. (2002). Poverty, social exclusion and health in Portugal. *Social Science and Medicine*, **55**, 33–45.

Santiago-Rivera, A.L., Morse, G.S., Hunt, A. & Lickers, H. (1998). Building a community-based research partnership: lessons from the Mohawk nation of Akwesasne. *Journal of Community Psychology*, **26**, 163–74.

Sarason, B.R., Sarason, I.G. & Pierce, G.R. (eds.) (1990). *Social Support: an Interactional View*. New York: John Wiley & Sons, Inc.

Sarason, S.B. (1974). *The Psychological Sense of Community: Perspectives for Community*. San Francisco: Jossey-Bass.

Sass, L.A. (1988). The self in contemporary psychoanalysis: commentary on Charles Taylor. In S.B. Messer, L.A. Sass & R.L. Woolfolk (eds), *Hermeneutics and Psychological Theory: Interpretive Perspectives on Personality, Psychotherapy, and Psychopathology* (pp. 321–7). New Brunswick, NJ: Rutgers University Press (cited by Krippner, 2001).

Sato, L., Lacaz, F.A. & Bernardo, M.H. (2004). Psychology and the workers' health movement in the State of São Paulo (Brazil). *Journal of Health Psychology*, **9**, 121–30.

Schneiders, J., Drukker, M., van der Ende, J., Verhulst, F.C., van Os, J. & Nicolson, N.A. (2003). Neighbourhood socioeconomic disadvantage and behavioural problems from late childhood into early adolescence. *Journal of Epidemiology and Community Health,* **57**, 699–703.

Schön, D.A. (1987). *Educating the Reflective Practitioner.* San Francisco, CA: Jossey-Bass (cited by Friedman, 2001).

Schuller, T., Baron, S. & Field, J. (2000). Social capital: a review and critique. In S. Baron, J. Field & T. Schuller (eds.), *Social Capital: Critical Perspectives* (pp. 1–38). Oxford, UK: Oxford University Press.

Schulz, A.J., Israel, B.A., Becker, A.B. and Hollis, R.M. (1997). 'It's a 24-hour thing...a living-for-each-other concept': identity, networks, and community in an urban village health worker project. *Health Education and Behavior,* **24**, 465–80.

Schwartz, S.H. (1994). Beyond individualism/collectivism: new cultural dimensions of values. In U. Kim, H. Triandis, C. Kağitçibaşi, S. Choi & G. Yoon (eds), *Individualism and Collectivisim* (pp. 85–119). Thousand Oaks, CA: Sage.

Scott, J. (2000). *Social Network Analysis: a Handbook* (2nd edn). London: Sage.

Seale, C., Ziebland, S. & Charteris-Black, J. (2006). Gender, cancer, experience and internet use: a comparative keyword analysis of interviews and online cancer support groups. *Social Science and Medicine,* **62**, 2577–90.

Seedat, M. (1997). The quest for liberatory psychology. *South African Journal of Psychology,* **27**, 261–70 (cited by Ngonyama ka Sigogo *et al.,* 2004).

Seedat, M., Duncan, N. & Lazarus, S. (eds) (2001). *Community Psychology: Theory, Method and Practice. South African and other Perspectives.* Cape Town: Oxford University Press.

Seidman, E. (1988). Back to the future, community psychology: unfolding a theory of social intervention. *American Journal of Community Psychology,* **16**, 3–24 (cited by Tseng *et al.,* 2002).

Seidman, E. (1990). Pursuing the meaning and utility of social regularities for community psychology. In P. Tolan, C. Keys, F. Chertok & L. Jason (eds), *Researching Community Psychology: Issues of Theory and Methods* (pp. 91–100). Washington DC: American Psychological Association.

Seidman, E. (2003). Fairweather and ESID: contemporary impact and a legacy for the twenty-first century. *American Journal of Community Psychology,* **32**, 371–5.

Sen, A. (1999). *Development as Freedom.* Oxford, UK: Oxford University Press.

Serrano-García, I., López, M.M. & Rivera-Medina, E. (1987). Toward a social-community psychology. *Journal of Community Psychology,* **15**, 431–46 (cited by Newbrough, 1995).

Seymour, F.W. & Davies, E. (2002). Using action research to facilitate change in child protection services. *Journal of Community Psychology,* **30**, 585–90.

Shadish, W.R., Cook, T.D. & Campbell, D.T. (2002). *Experimental and Quasi-Experimental Designs for Generalized Causal Inference.* Boston: Houghton Mifflin.

Sharma, A., Suarez-Balcazar, Y. & Baetke, M. (2003). Empowerment evaluation of a youth leadership training program. In Y. Suarez-Balcazar & G.W. Harper (eds), *Empowerment and Participatory Evaluation of Community Interventions: Multiple Benefits* (pp. 89–104). New York: Haworth Press.

Shevlin, M. & McGuigan, K. (2003). The long-term psychological impact of Bloody Sunday on families of the victims as measured by The Revised Impact of Event Scale. *British Journal of Clinical Psychology,* **42**, 427–32.

Shinn, M. (1990). Mixing and matching: levels of conceptualization, measurement, and statistical analysis in community research. In P. Tolan, C. Keys, F. Chertok & L. Jason (eds), *Researching Community Psychology: Issues of Theory and Methods* (pp. 111–26). Washington DC: American Psychological Association.

Shinn, M. (1992). Homelessness: what is a psychologist to do? *American Journal of Community Psychology,* **20**, 1–24.

Shohaimi, S., Luben, R., Wareham, N., Day, N., Bingham, S., Welch, A., Oakes, S. & Khaw, K-T. (2003). Residential area deprivation predicts smoking habit independently of individual educational level and occupational social class. A cross sectional study in the Norfolk cohort of the European investigation into cancer (EPIC-Norfolk). *Journal of Epidemiology and Community Health,* **57**, 270–6.

Shouls, S., Congdon, P. & Curtis, S. (1996). Modelling inequality in reported long term illness in the UK: combining individual and area characteristics. *Journal of Epidemiology and Community Health*, **50**, 366–76 (cited by Macintyre *et al.*, 2002).

Sidanius, J. & Pratto, F. (1999). *Social Dominance: An Intergroup Theory of Social Hierarchy and Oppression*. Cambridge, UK: Cambridge University Press.

Sideris, T. (2003). War, gender and culture: Mozambican women refugees. *Social Science and Medicine*, **56**, 713–24.

Siegrist, J. & Marmot, M. (2004). Health inequalities and the psychosocial environment – two scientific challenges. *Social Science and Medicine*, **58**, 1463–73.

Siegrist, J., Starke, D., Chandola, T., Godin, I., Marmot, M., Niedhammer, I. & Peter, R. (2004). The measurement of effort-reward imbalance at work: European comparisons. *Social Science and Medicine*, **58**, 1483–99.

Silver, E.J., Ireys, H.T., Bauman, L.J. & Stein, R.E.K. (1997). Psychological outcomes of a support intervention in mothers of children with ongoing health conditions: the parent-to-parent network. *Journal of Community Psychology*, **25**, 249–64.

Simons, R.L., Johnson, C., Beaman, J., Conger, R.D. & Whitbeck. L.B. (1996). Parents and peer group as mediators of the effect of community structure on adolescent problem behavior. *American Journal of Community Psychology*, **24**, 145–71.

Singh-Manoux, A. (2003). Psychosocial factors and public health. *Journal of Epidemiology and Community Health*, **57**, 553–4.

Singh-Manoux, A., Adler, N.E. & Marmot, M.G. (2003). Subjective social status: its determinants and its association with measures of ill-health in the Whitehall II study. *Social Science and Medicine*, **56**, 1321–33.

Skjæveland, O., Gärling, T. & Mæland, J.G. (1996). A multidimensional measure of neighboring. *American Journal of Community Psychology*, **24**, 413–35.

Skrabski, A., Kopp, M. & Kawachi, I. (2003). Social capital in a changing society: cross sectional associations with middle aged female and male mortality rates. *Journal of Epidemiology and Community Health*, **57**, 114–19.

Sloan, T. (ed.) (2000). *Critical Psychology: Voices for Change*. New York: St Martin's Press.

Sloggett, A. & Joshi, H. (1994). Higher mortality in deprived areas: community or personal disadvantage? *British Medical Journal*, **309**, 1470–4.

Sloggett, A. & Joshi, H. (1998). Deprivation indicators as predictors of life events 1981–1992 based on the UK ONS longitudinal study. *Journal of Epidemiology and Community Health*, **52**, 228–33.

Smail, D. (1987). *Taking Care: An Alternative to Therapy*. London: Dent.

Smail, D. (1991). Towards a radical environmentalist psychology of help. *The Psychologist*, **4**, 61–5.

Smail, D. (1994). Community psychology and politics. *Journal of Community and Applied Social Psychology*, **4**, 3–10.

Smail, D. (1995). Power and the origins of unhappiness: working with individuals. *Journal of Community and Applied Social Psychology*, **5**, 347–56.

Smail, D. (2001). Commentary: de-psychologizing community psychology. *Journal of Community and Applied Social Psychology*, **11**, 159–65.

Smail, D. (2003). Therapeutic psychology and the ideology of privilege. Paper presented at the UK Community and Critical Psychology conference, Birmingham, England, 11 September.

Smail, D. (2005). *Power, Interest and Psychology: Elements of a Social Materialist Understanding of Distress*. Ross-on-Wye: PCCS Books.

Smaje, C. & Le Grand, J. (1997). Ethnicity, equity and the use of health services in the British NHS. *Social Science and Medicine*, **45**, 485–96.

Smith, S.J. (1984). Crime in the news. *British Journal of Criminology*, **24**, 289–95 (cited by Perkins & Taylor, 1996).

Social Trends (1994). London: HMSO (cited by Wadsworth, 1997).

Solomon, M., Pistrang, N. & Barker, C. (2001). The benefits of mutual support groups for parents of children with disabilities. *American Journal of Community Psychology*, **29**, 113–32.

Sonn, C.C. (2002). Immigrant adaptation: understanding the process through sense of community. In A.T. Fisher, C.C. Sonn & B.J. Bishop (eds), *Psychological Sense of Community* (pp. 205–22). New York: Kluwer/Plenum.

Sonn, C.C. (2004). Praxis: reflecting on practice: negotiating challenges to ways of working. *Journal of Community and Applied Social Psychology*, **14**, 305–13.

Sonn, C.C. & Fisher, A.T. (2003). Identity and oppression: differential responses to an in-between status. *American Journal of Community Psychology*, **31**, 117–28.

Sooman, A. & Macintyre, S. (1995). Health and perceptions of the local environment in socially contrasting neighbourhoods in Glasgow. *Health and Place*, **1**, 15–26.

Sosin, M.R. (2003). Explaining adult homelessness in the US by stratification or situation. *Journal of Community and Applied Social Psychology*, **13**, 91–104.

Speer, P.W. & Hughey, J. (1995). Community organizing: an ecological route to empowerment and power. *American Journal of Community Psychology*, **23**, 729–48.

Speer, P.W., Hughey, J., Gensheimer, L.K. & Adams-Leavitt, W. (1995). Organizing for power: a comparative case study. *Journal of Community Psychology*, **23**, 57–73.

Speer, P.W., Ontkush, M., Schmitt, B. & Raman, P. (2003). Praxis: the intentional exercise of power: community organizing in Camden, New Jersey. *Journal of Community and Applied Social Psychology*, **13**, 399–408.

Spencer, N. (2001). The social patterning of teenage pregnancy. *Journal of Epidemiology and Community Health*, **55**, 5.

Spencer, N. (2005). Does material disadvantage explain the increased risk of adverse health, educational, and behavioural outcomes among children in lone parent households in Britain? A cross sectional study. *Journal of Epidemiology and Community Health*, **59**, 152–7.

Stanley, J.L. (2003). An applied collaborative training program for graduate students in community psychology: a case study of a community project working with lesbian, gay, bisexual, transgender and questioning youth. *American Journal of Community Psychology*, **31**, 253–65.

Stansfeld, S.A., Bosma, H. Hemingway, H. *et al.* (1998). Psychosocial work characteristics and social support as predictors of SF-36 health functioning: the Whitehall II study. *Psychosomatic Medicine*, **60**, 247–55.

Stansfeld, S.A., Head, J., Fuhrer, R., Wardle, J. & Cattell, V. (2003). Social inequalities in depressive symptoms and physical functioning in the Whitehall II study: exploring a common cause explanation. *Journal of Epidemiology and Community Health*, **57**, 361–7.

Starfield, B., Riley, A.W., Witt, W.P. & Robertson, J. (2002). Social class gradients in health during adolescence. *Journal of Epidemiology and Community Health*, **56**, 354–61.

Staub, E. (1989). *The Roots of Evil: The Psychological and Cultural Origins of Genocide.* New York: Cambridge University Press.

Steel, Z., Silove, D., Brooks, R., Momartin, S., Alzuhairi, B. & Susljik, I. (2006). Impact of immigration detention and temporary protection on the mental health of refugees. *British Journal of Psychiatry*, **188**, 58–64.

Steginga, S.K. & Dunn, J. (2001). The young women's network: a case study in community development. *Journal of Community and Applied Social Psychology*, **11**, 381–8.

Stein, C.H. & Mankowski, E.S. (2004). Asking, witnessing, interpreting, knowing: conducting qualitative research in community psychology. *American Journal of Community Psychology*, **33**, 21–35.

Stein, L. & Test, M.A. (1980). Alternative to mental hospital treatment: conceptual model, treatment program, and clinical evaluation. *Archives of General Psychiatry*, **37**, 392–7.

Steptoe, A. & Marmot, M. (2002). The role of psychobiological pathways in socio-economic inequalities in cardiovascular disease risk. *European Heart Journal*, **23**, 13–25.

Stimpson, N.J., Thomas, H.V., Weightman, A.L., Dunstan, F. & Lewis, G. (2003). Psychiatric disorder in veterans of the Persian Gulf War of 1991. *British Journal of Psychiatry*, **182**, 391–403.

Stronks, K., Dike van de Mheen, H. & Mackenbach, J.P. (1998). A higher prevalence of health problems in low income groups: does it reflect relative deprivation? *Journal of Epidemiology and Community Health*, **52**, 548–57.

Suarez-Balcazar, Y., Orellana-Damacel, L., Portillo, N., Sharma, A. & Lanum, M. (2003). Implementing an outcome model in the participatory evaluation of community initiatives. In Y. Suarez-Balcazar & G.W. Harper (eds), *Empowerment and Participatory Evaluation of Community Interventions: Multiple Benefits* (pp. 5–20). New York: Haworth Press.

Suarez-Balcazar, Y. & Harper, G.W. (eds) (2003). *Empowerment and Participatory Evaluation of Community Interventions: Multiple Benefits*, New York: Haworth Press.

Subramanian, S.V. (2004). The relevance of multilevel statistical methods for identifying causal neighborhood effects. *Social Science and Medicine*, **58**, 1961–7.

Subramanian, S.V., Delgado, I., Jadue, L., Vega, J. & Kawachi, I. (2003). Income inequality and health: multilevel analysis of Chilean communities. *Journal of Epidemiology and Community Health*, **57**, 844–8.

Sue, S. (1999). Science, ethnicity, and bias: where have we gone wrong? *American Psychologist*, **54**, 1070–7.

Sullivan, C.M. (2003). Using the ESID model to reduce intimate male violence against women. *American Journal of Community Psychology*, **32**, 295–303.

Sullivan, C.M., Campbell, R., Angelique, H., Eby, K.K. & Davidson, W.S. (1994). An advocacy intervention program for women with abusive partners: six-month follow-up. *American Journal of Community Psychology*, **22**, 101–22.

Sundquist, J. (1995). Ethnicity, social class and health. A population-based study on the influence of social factors on self-reported illness in 223 Latin American refugees, 333 Finnish and 126 South European labour migrants and 841 Swedish controls. *Social Science and Medicine*, **40**, 777–87.

Sundquist, J., Johansson, S.E., Yang, M. & Sundquist, K. (2006). Low linking social capital as a predictor of coronary heart disease in Sweden: a cohort study of 2.8 million people. *Social Science and Medicine*, **62**, 954–63.

Sundquist, K., Theobald, H., Yang, M., Li, X., Johansson, S.E. & Sundquist, J. (2006). Neighborhood violent crime and unemployment increase the risk of coronary heart disease: a multilevel study in an urban setting. *Social Science and Medicine*, **62**, 2061–71.

Sveaass, N. (2000). Psychological work in a post-war context: experiences from Nicaragua. *Community, Work and Family*, **3**, 37–64.

Swann, K. & Morgan, A. (2002). In, *Social Capital for Health: Insights from Qualitative Research*. London: Health Development Agency (cited by Altschuler *et al.*, 2004).

Swantz, M., Ndedya, E. & Masaiganah, M.S. (2001). Participatory action research in Southern Tanzania, with special reference to women. In P. Reason & H. Bradbury (eds), *Handbook of Action Research: Participative Inquiry and Practice* (pp. 386–95). London: Sage.

Sykes, C.M., Willig, C. & Marks, D.F. (2004). Discourses in the European Commission's 1996–2000 health promotion programme. *Journal of Health Psychology*, **9**, 131–41.

Szendre, E.N. & Jose, P.E. (1996). Telephone support by elderly volunteers to inner-city children. *Journal of Community Psychology*, **24**, 87–96.

Szreter, S. & Woolcock, M. (2004). Health by association? Social capital, social theory, and the political economy of public health. *International Journal of Epidemiology*, **33**, 650–67 (cited by Sundquist *et al.*, 2006).

Tajfel, H. (1981). *Human Groups and Social Categories*. Cambridge, UK: Cambridge University Press (cited by Colic-Peisker & Walker, 2003).

Tandon, S.D., Azelton, L.S., Kelley, J.G. & Strickland D.A. (1998). Constructing a tree for community leaders: contexts and processes in collaborative inquiry. *American Journal of Community Psychology*, **26**, 669–96.

Tay, J.B., Kelleher, C.C., Hope, A., Barry, M., Gabhainn, S.N. & Sixsmith, J. (2004). Influence of sociodemographic and neighbourhood factors on self rated health and quality of life in rural communities: findings from the Agriproject in the Republic of Ireland. *Journal of Epidemiology and Community Health*, **58**, 904–11.

Taylor, G. (2002). Psychopathology and the social and historical construction of gay male identities. In A. Coyle & C. Kitzinger (eds), *Lesbian and Gay Psychology: New Perspectives* (pp. 154–74). Oxford, UK: Blackwell.

Taylor, S.E. & Repetti, R.L. (1997). Health psychology: what is an unhealthy environment and how does it get under the skin? *Annual Review of Psychology*, **48**, 411–47.

Tebes, J.K. (2005). Community science, philosophy of science, and the practice of research. *American Journal of Community Psychology*, **35**, 213–30.

Thomas, D.R. & Robertson, N.R. (1990). A conceptual framework for the analysis of social policies. *Journal of Community Psychology*, **18**, 194–209.

Thompsett, C.J., Toro, P.A., Guzicki, M., Schlienz, N., Blume, M. & Lombardo, S. (2003). Homelessness in the US and Germany: a cross-national analysis. *Journal of Community and Applied Social Psychology*, **13**, 240–57.

Thomson, B. (1990). *Single Mothers' Survival Guide: Resources for Low-Income Single Moms*. Halifax NS: Pandora (cited by Travers, 1997).

Thomson, H., Atkinson, R., Petticrew, M. & Kearns, A. (2006). Do urban regeneration programmes improve public health and reduce health inequalities? A synthesis of the evidence from UK policy and practice (1980–2004). *Journal of Epidemiology and Community Health*, **60**, 108–15.

Thomson, H., Kearns, A. & Petticrew, M. (2003). Assessing the health impact of local amenities: a qualitative study of contrasting experiences of local swimming pool and leisure provision in two areas of Glasgow. *Journal of Epidemiology and Community Health*, **57**, 663–7.

Timotijevic, L. & Breakwell, G.M. (2000). Migration and threat to identity. *Journal of Community and Applied Social Psychology*, **10**, 355–72.

Titmuss, R.M. (1943). *Birth, Poverty and Wealth*, London: Hamish Hamilton Medical Books (cited by Macintyre, 1997).

Tolan, P., Keys, C., Chertok, F. & Jason, L. (eds), *Researching Community Psychology: Issues of Theory and Methods*. Washington, DC: American Psychological Association.

Tolman, C.W. (1994). *Psychology, Society and Subjectivity: An Introduction to German Critical Psychology*. London: Routledge.

Toohey, S.M., Shinn, M. & Weitzman, B.C. (2004). Social networks and homelessness among women heads of household. *American Journal of Community Psychology*, **33**, 7–20.

Topalova, V. (1997). Individualism/collectivism and social identity. *Journal of Community and Applied Social Psychology*, **7**, 53–64.

Toro, P.A. (2005). Community psychology: where do we go from here? *American Journal of Community Psychology*, **35**, 9–16.

Townsend, P., Whitehead, M. & Davidson, N. (1992). *Inequalities in Health*. London: Penguin.

Træn, B. (2003). Effect of an intervention to prevent unwanted pregnancy in adolescents. A randomized, prospective study from Nordland county, Norway, 1999–2001. *Journal of Community and Applied Social Psychology*, **13**, 207–23.

Travers, K.D. (1997). Reducing inequities through participatory research and community empowerment. *Health Education and Behavior*, **24**, 344–56.

Traylen, H. (1994). Confronting hidden agendas: co-operative inquiry with health visitors. In P. Reason (ed.), *Participation in Human Inquiry* (pp.59–81). London: Sage.

Triandis, H.C. (1977). Subjective culture and interpersonal relations across cultures. *Annals of the New York Academy of Science*, **285**, 418–34.

Triandis, H.C. (1994). Theoretical and methodological approaches to the study of collectivism and individualism. In U. Kim, H.C. Triandis, C. Kağitçibaşi, S. Choi & G. Yoon (eds), *Individualism and Collectivisim: Theory, Method, and Applications* (pp. 41–51). Thousand Oaks, CA: Sage.

Triandis, H.C. & Gelfand, M.J. (1998). Converging measurement of horizontal and vertical individualism and collectivism. *Journal of Personality and Social Psychology*, **74**, 118–28.

Trickett, E.J. (1996). A future for community psychology: the contexts of diversity and the diversity of contexts. *American Journal of Community Psychology*, **24**, 209–34.

Trickett, E.J., Watts, R. & Birman, D. (1993). Human diversity and community psychology: still hazy after all these years. *Journal of Community Psychology*, **21**, 264–79 (cited by Banyard & Miller, 1998).

Trout, J., Dokecki, P.R., O'Gorman, R.T. & Newbrough, J.R. (2003). Action research on leadership for community development in West Africa and North America: a joining of liberation theology and community psychology. *Journal of Community Psychology*, **31**, 129–48.

Tsemberis, S.J., Moran, L., Shinn, M., Asmussen, S.M. & Shern, D.L. (2003). Consumer preference programs for individuals who are homeless and have psychiatric disabilities: a drop-in center and a supported housing program. *American Journal of Community Psychology*, **32**, 305–17.

Tseng, V., Chesir-Teran, D., Becker-Klein, R., Duran, V., Roberts, A., Bardoliwalla, N. & Chan, M.L. (2002). Promotion of social change: a conceptual framework. *American Journal of Community Psychology*, **30**, 401–27.

Tuhiwai-Smith, L. (1999). *Decolonizing Methodologies: Research and Indigenous Peoples*. London: University of Otago Press.

Turner, J.C. (2005). Explaining the nature of power: a three-process theory. *European Journal of Social Psychology*, **35**, 1–22.

Turner, S.W., Bowie, C., Dunn, G., Shapo, L. & Yule, W. (2003). Mental health of Kosovan Albanian refugees in the UK. *British Journal of Psychiatry*, **182**, 444–8.

Tyler, T. (1994). Psychological models of the justice motive: antecedents of procedural and distributive justice. *Journal of Personality and Social Psychology*, **67**, 850–64 (cited by Drew et al., 2002).

Ussher, J.M. (1991). Clinical psychology and sexual equality: a contradiction in terms? *Feminism and Psychology*, **1**, 63–8.

Ussher, J.M. (2000). Critical psychology in the mainstream: a struggle for survival. In T. Sloan (ed.), *Critical Psychology: Voices for Change* (pp. 6–20). New York: St Martin's Press.

Ussher, J.M., Kirsten, L., Butown, P. & Sandoval, M. (2006). What do cancer support groups provide which other supportive relationships do not? The experience of peer support groups for people with cancer. *Social Science and Medicine*, **62**, 2565–76.

Valkonen, T., Mfartlein, T., Rimpelia, A., Notkola, V. & Savela, S. (1993). *Socio-economic Mortality Differences in Finland 1981–90*. Statistics Finland Helsinki (cited by Mackenbach & Kunst, 1997).

Van Oort, F.V.A., van Lenthe, F.J. & Mackenbach, J.P. (2005). Material, psychosocial, and behavioural factors in the explanation of educational inequalities in mortality in the Netherlands. *Journal of Epidemiology and Community Health*, **59**, 214–20.

Varas-Díaz, N. & Serrano-García, I. (2003). The challenge of a positive self-image in a colonial context: a psychology of liberation for the Puerto Rican experience. *American Journal of Community Psychology*, **31**, 103–15.

Veno, A. (2000). Australia. In J. Rappaport & E. Seidman (eds), *Handbook of Community Psychology* (p. 797). New York: Kluwer/Plenum.

Veno, A. & Thomas, D. (1992a). Psychology and the process of social change. In D. Thomas & A. Veno (eds), *Psychology and Social Change: Creating an International Agenda* (pp. 15–36). Palmerston North, New Zealand: Dunmore Press.

Veno, A. & Thomas, D. (1992b). Setting agendas for social change: an international perspective. In D. Thomas & A. Veno (eds), *Psychology and Social Change: Creating an International Agenda* (pp. 317–27). Palmerston North, New Zealand: Dunmore Press.

Verhoeven, C., Maes, S., Kraaij, V. & Joekes, K. (2003). The job demand-control-social support model and wellness/health outcomes: a European study. *Psychology and Health*, **18**, 421–40.

Vinck, J., Oldenburg, B. & Von Lengerke, T. (2004). Editorial: health psychology and public health – bridging the gap. *Journal of Health Psychology*, **9**, 5–12.

Visser, M.J. (2004). Implementing peer support in schools: using a theoretical framework in action research. *Journal of Community and Applied Social Psychology*, **14**, 436–54.

Visser, M.J., Makin, J.D. & Lehobye, K. (2006). Stigmatizing attitudes of the community towards people living with HIV/AIDS. *Journal of Community and Applied Social Psychology*, **16**, 42–58.

Visser, M.J., Schoeman, J.B. & Perold, J.J. (2004). Evaluation of HIV/AIDS prevention in South African schools. *Journal of Health Psychology*, **9**, 263–80.

Vrij, A. & Smith, V.J. (1999). Reducing ethnic prejudice by public campaigns: an evaluation of a present and a new campaign. *Journal of Community and Applied Social Psychology*, **9**, 195–215.

Wacker, A. (2001). Review of B. Vogel. (1999) Ohne Arbeit in den Kapitalismns. Hamburg: USA-Verlag. *Journal of Community and Applied Social Psychology*, **11**, 321.

Wadsworth, M.E.J. (1997). Health inequalities in the life course perspective. *Social Science and Medicine*, **44**, 859–69.

Waitzman, N. & Smith, K. (1998). Phantom of the area: poverty-area residence and mortality in the United States. *American Journal of Public Health*, **88**, 973–6 (cited by Macintyre *et al.*, 2002).

Walsh-Bowers, R. (1993). The resident researcher in social ethical perspective. *American Journal of Community Psychology*, **21**, 495–500.

Walters, V. & Charles, N. (1997). 'I just cope from day to day': unpredictability and anxiety in the lives of women. *Social Science and Medicine*, **45**, 1729–39.

Wandersman, A. (2003). Community science: bridging the gap between science and practice with community-centered models. *American Journal of Community Psychology*, **31**, 227–42.

Wandersman, A. & Florin, P. (2000). Citizen participation and community organizations. In J. Rappaport & E. Seidman (eds), *Handbook of Community Psychology* (pp. 247–72). New York: Kluwer/Plenum.

Wandersman, A., Keener, D., Snell-Johns, J., Miller, R., Flaspohler, P., Livet-Dye, M., Mendez, J., Behrens, T., Bolson, B. & Robinson, L. (2004). In L. Jason, K. Keys, Y. Suarez-Balcazar, M. Davis, J. Durlak & D. Isenberg (eds), *Participatory Community Research: Theories and Methods in Action*. Washington, DC: American Psychological Association (cited by Sharma *et al.*, 2003).

Wandersman, A., Kloos, B., Linney, J.A. & Shinn, M. (2005). Science and community psychology: enhancing the vitality of community research and action. *American Journal of Community Psychology*, **35**, 105–6.

Wandersman, A. & Nation, M. (1998). Urban neighborhoods and mental health: psychological contributions to understanding toxicity, resilience, and interventions. *American Psychologist*, **53**, 647–56.

Wardle, J., Robb, K.A., Johnson, F., Brunner, E., Griffith, J., Power, C. & Tovée, M. (2004). Socioeconomic variation in attitudes to eating and weight in female adolescents. *Health Psychology*, **23**, 275–82.

Wardle, J. & Steptoe, A. (2003). Socioeconomic differences in attitudes and beliefs about healthy lifestyles. *Journal of Epidemiology and Community Health*, **57**, 440–3.

Warr, P. (1987). *Work, Unemployment and Mental Health*. Oxford: Clarendon.

Warr, P., Jackson, P. & Banks, M. (1988). Unemployment and mental health: some British studies. *Journal of Social Issues*, **44**, 47–68.

Watts, R.J. (1993a). Community action through manhood development: a look at concepts and concerns from the frontline. *American Journal of Community Psychology*, **21**, 333–59.

Watts, R.J. (1993b). 'Resident research' and community psychology. *American Journal of Community Psychology*, **21**, 483–6.

Watts. R.J., Griffith, D.M. & Abdul-Adil, J. (1999). Sociopolitical development as an antidote for oppression – theory and action. *American Journal of Community Psychology*, **27**, 255–71.

Watts, R.J. & Serrano-García, I. (2003). The quest for a liberating community psychology: an overview. *American Journal of Community Psychology*, **31**, 73–8.

Watts, R.J., Williams, N.C. & Jagers, R.J. (2003). Sociopolitical development. *American Journal of Community Psychology*, **31**, 185–94.

Watzlawick, P., Weakland, J. & Fisch, R. (1974). *Change: Principles of Problem Formation and Problem Resolution* New York: Norton (cited by Tseng *et al.*, 2002).

Webb, Sidney & Beatrice (1901). *The State and the Doctor*. London: Longman (cited by Lewis, 1991).

Weich, S. (1997). Editorial: prevention of the common mental disorders: a public health perspective. *Psychological Medicine*, **27**, 757–64.

Weich, S. (2005). Absence of spatial variation in rates of the common mental disorders. *Journal of Epidemiology and Community Health*, **59**, 254–7.

Weich, S. & Lewis, G. (1998). Poverty, unemployment, and common mental disorders: population based cohort study. *British Medical Journal*, **317**, 115–19.

Weich, S., Lewis, G., Churchill, R. & Mann, A. (1997). Strategies for the prevention of psychiatric disorder in primary care in south London. *Journal of Epidemiology and Community Health*, **51**, 304–9.

Weich, S., Lewis, G. & Jenkinson, S.P. (2002). Income inequality and self rated health in Britain. *Journal of Epidemiology and Community Health*, **56**, 436–41.

Weich, S., Twigg, L., Holt, G., Lewis, G. & Jones, K. (2003). Contextual risk factors for the common mental disorders in Britain: a multilevel investigation of the effects of place. *Journal of Epidemiology and Community Health*, **57**, 616–21.

Wertz, F.J. (2001). Humanistic psychology and the qualitative research tradition. In K.J. Schneider, J.F.T. Bugental & J. Fraser Pierson (eds), *The Handbook of Humanistic Psychology: Leading Edges in Theory, Research and Practice* (pp. 231–45). London: Sage.

West, C. (1982). *Prophesy Deliverance! An Afro-American Revolutionary Christianity*. Philadelphia: Westminster Press (cited by Potts, 2003).

West, P. (1997). Health inequalities in the early years: is there equalisation in youth? *Social Science and Medicine*, **44**, 833–58.

Wetherell, M. & Potter, J. (1992). *Mapping the Language of Racism: Discourse and the Legitimation of Exploitation*. New York: Columbia University Press (cited by Hepburn, 2003).

Whitbeck, L.B., Adams, G.W., Hoyt, D.R. & Chen, X. (2004). Conceptualizing and measuring historical trauma among American Indian people. *American Journal of Community Psychology*, **33**, 119–30.

Whitehead, M. (1988). *The Health Divide*. London: Penguin.

Whitmore, E. & McKee, C. (2001). Six street youth who could... In P. Reason & H. Bradbury (eds), *Handbook of Action Research: Participative Inquiry and Practice* (pp. 396–402). London: Sage.

Wicker, A.W. & Sommer, R. (1993). The resident researcher: an alternative career model centered on community. *American Journal of Community Psychology*, **21**, 469–82.

Widgery, D. (1993). *Some Lives: a GP's East End*. London: Simon and Schuster.

Wiesenfeld, E. (1996). The concept of 'we': a community social psychology myth? *Journal of Community Psychology*, **24**, 337–45.

Wiesenfeld, E. (1998). Paradigms of community social psychology in six Latin American nations. *Journal of Community Psychology*, **26**, 229–42.

Wiggins, R.D., Schofield, P., Sackers, A., Head, J. & Bartley, M. (2004). Social position and minor psychiatric morbidity over time in the British household panel survey 1991–1998. *Journal of Epidemiology and Community Health*, **58**, 779–87.

Wight, D. (1993). *Workers Not Wasters: Masculine Respectability, Consumption and Unemployment in Central Scotland: A Community Study*. Edinburgh: Edinburgh University Press.

Wiking, E., Johansson, S. & Sundquist, J. (2004). Ethnicity, acculturation, and self reported health. A population based study among immigrants from Poland, Turkey, and Iran in Sweden. *Journal of Epidemiology and Community Health*, **58**, 574–82.

Wilkinson, R.G. (1996). *Unhealthy Societies. The Afflictions of Inequality*. London: Routledge.

Wilkinson, R.G. (1998). *Unhealthy Societies*: replies to reviewers. *Journal of Community and Applied Social Psychology*, **8**, 233–7.

Wilkinson, R.G. (1999). Income inequality, social cohesion and health. *International Journal of Health Services*, **29**, 525–43 (cited by Harpham *et al.*, 2004).

Wilkinson, R.G. (2000). Symposium on David Coburn, income inequality social cohesion and the health status of populations and the role of neo-liberalism. *Social Science and Medicine*, **50**, 997–1000 (cited by Forbes & Wainwright, 2001).

Wilkinson, R.G. & Pickett, K.E. (2006). Income inequality and population health: a review and explanation of the evidence. *Social Science and Medicine*, **62**, 1768–84.

Williams, J.M., Currie, C.E., Wright, P., Elton, R.A. & Beattie, T.F. (1997). Socioeconomic status and adolescent injuries. *Social Science and Medicine*, **44**, 1881–91.

Williams, J. & Lindley, P. (1996). Working with mental health service users to change mental health services. *Journal of Community and Applied Social Psychology*, **6**, 1–14.

Williams, J. & Watson, G. (1991). Sexual inequality and clinical psychology training in Britain: workshop report. *Feminism and Psychology*, **1**, 101–9.

Williams, R., Wright, W. & Hunt, K. (1998). Social class and health: the puzzling counter-example of British South Asians. *Social Science and Medicine*, **47**, 1277–88.

Willig, C. (2001). *Introducing Qualitative Research in Psychology: Adventures in Theory and Method*. Buckingham, UK: Open University Press.

Willott, S. & Griffin, C. (1996). Men, masculinity and the challenge of long-term unemployment. In Mac an Ghaill (eds), *Understanding Masculinities* (pp. 77–92). Buckingham: Open University Press.

Wilps, R.F. (1990). Male bulimia nervosa: an autobiographical case study. In A.E. Andersen (ed.), *Males with Eating Disorders*. New York: Brunner/Mazel.

Wilson, K., Elliott, S., Law, M., Eyles, J., Jerrett, M. & Keller-Olaman, S. (2004). Linking perceptions of neighbourhood to health in Hamilton, Canada. *Journal of Epidemiology and Community Health*, **58**, 192–8.

Wingenfeld, S. & Newbrough, J.R. (2000). Community psychology in international perspective. In J. Rappaport & E. Seidman (eds), *Handbook of Community Psychology* (pp. 779–810). New York: Kluwer/Plenum.

Wituk, S.A., Shepherd, M.D., Warren, M. & Meissen, G. (2002). Factors contributing to the survival of self-help groups. *American Journal of Community Psychology*, **30**, 349–66.

Wohlfarth, T. (1997). Socioeconomic inequality and psychopathology: are socioeconomic status and social class interchangeable? *Social Science and Medicine*, **45**, 399–410.

Wohlfarth, T. & van den Brink, W. (1998). Social class and substance use disorders: the value of social class as distinct from socioeconomic status. *Social Science and Medicine*, **47**, 51–8.

Wolff, T. (2001). Community coalition building – contemporary practice and research: introduction. *American Journal of Community Psychology*, **29**, 165–72.

Wong, Y.I. & Piliavin, I. (2001). Stressors, resources, and distress among homeless persons: a longitudinal analysis., *Social Science and Medicine*, **52**, 1029–42.

Woods, L.M., Rachet, B., Riga, M., Stone, N., Shah, A. & Coleman, M.P. (2005). Geographical variation in life expectancy at birth in England and Wales is largely explained by deprivation. *Journal of Epidemiology and Community Health*, **59**, 115–20.

World Health Organization (1999). Poverty and health: report by the Director-General. Executive Board, RB105/5 (cited by Murray & Campbell, 2003).

Wright, E.O. (2000). *Class Counts*. Cambridge, UK: Cambridge University Press (cited by Macleod *et al.*, 2005).

Wright, E.O., Hachen, D., Costello, C. & Sprague, J. (1982). The American class structure. *American Sociological Review*, **47**, 709–26 (cited by Wohlfarth, 1997).

Wrong, D. (1979). *Power: Its Forms, Bases and Uses*. Oxford, UK: Basil Blackwell.

Wundt, W. (1916). *Elements of Folk Psychology*. London: Allen and Unwin (cited by Bar-Tal, 2000).

Yeich, S. (1996). Grassroots organizing with homeless people: a participatory research approach. *Journal of Social Issues*, **52**, 111–21.

Young, A.F., Russell, A. & Powers, J.R. (2004). The sense of belonging to a neighbourhood: can it be measured and is it related to health and well being in older women? *Social Science and Medicine*, **59**, 2627–37.

Zani, B., Cicognani, E. & Albanes, C. (2001). Adolescents' sense of community and feeling of unsafety in the urban environment. *Journal of Community and Applied Social Psychology*, **11**, 475–89.

Zapert, K., Snow, D.L. & Tebes, J.K. (2003). Patterns of substance use in early through late adolescence. *American Journal of Community Psychology*, **30**, 835–52 (cited by Luke, 2005).

Zeichner, K. (2001). Educational action research. In P. Reason & H. Bradbury (eds), *Handbook of Action Research: Participative Inquiry and Practice* (pp. 273–83). London: Sage.

Zeldin, S. & Topitzes, D. (2002). Neighborhood experiences, community connection, and positive beliefs about adolescents among urban adults and youth. *Journal of Community Psychology*, **30**, 647–69.

Zhou, M. (1999). Segmented assimilation: issues, controversies, and recent research on the new second generation. In C. Hirschman, P. Kasinitz & J. DeWind (eds), *The Handbook of International Migration: The American Experience* (pp. 196–211). New York: Russell Sage Foundation (cited by Deaux, 2000).

Ziersch, A.M. (2005). Health implications of access to social capital: findings from an Australian study. *Social Science and Medicine*, **61**, 2119–31.

Ziersch, A.M. & Baum, F.E. (2004). Involvement in civil society groups: is it good for your health? *Journal of Epidemiology and Community Health*, **58**, 493–500.

Zimmerman, M.A. (1995). Psychological empowerment: issues and illustrations. *American Journal of Community Psychology*, **23**, 581–99 (cited by Dalton *et al.*, 2001).

Zimmerman, M.A (2000). Empowerment theory: psychological, organizational and community levels of analysis. In J. Rappaport & E. Seidman (eds), *Handbook of Community Psychology*. New York: Plenum.

Zimmerman, M.A., Bingenheimer, J.B. & Notaro, P.C. (2002). Natural mentors and adolescent resiliency: a study with urban youth. *American Journal of Community Psychology*, **30**, 221–43.

Zimmerman, M.A., Ramírez-Valles, J. & Maton, K.I. (1999). Resilience among urban African American male adolescents: a study of the protective effects of socio-political control on their mental health. *American Journal of Community Psychology*, **27**, 733–51.

Zolik, E. (2000). Poland. In J. Rappaport & E. Seidman (eds.), *Handbook of Community Psychology* (p. 799). New York: Kluwer/Plenum.

Zugazaga, C. (2004). Stressful life event experiences of homeless adults: a comparison of single men, single women, and women with children. *Journal of Community Psychology*, **32**, 643–54.

AUTHOR INDEX

SUBJECT INDEX

Lightning Source UK Ltd.
Milton Keynes UK
UKHW031848040220
358156UK00005B/190